AF361610

Parleying with the Devil

Parleying with the Devil

Prisoner Exchange in Yugoslavia, 1941–1945

Gaj Trifković

Foreword by Klaus Schmider

andarta books
an imprint of the University Press of Kentucky

Brécourt
Academic

Published by Andarta Books
An imprint of The University Press of Kentucky

Scholarly publisher for the Commonwealth,
serving Bellarmine University, Berea College, Centre
College of Kentucky, Eastern Kentucky University,
The Filson Historical Society, Georgetown College,
Kentucky Historical Society, Kentucky State University,
Morehead State University, Murray State University,
Northern Kentucky University, Transylvania University,
University of Kentucky, University of Louisville,
and Western Kentucky University.

Editorial and Sales Offices: The University Press of Kentucky
663 South Limestone Street, Lexington, Kentucky 40508-4008
www.kentuckypress.com

Cataloging-in-Publication data available from the Library of Congress

ISBN 978-1-94-966808-7 (hardcover)
ISBN 978-1-94-966810-0 (pdf)
ISBN 978-1-94-966811-7 (epub)

This book is printed on acid-free paper meeting
the requirements of the American National Standard
for Permanence in Paper for Printed Library Materials.

Manufactured in the United States of America.

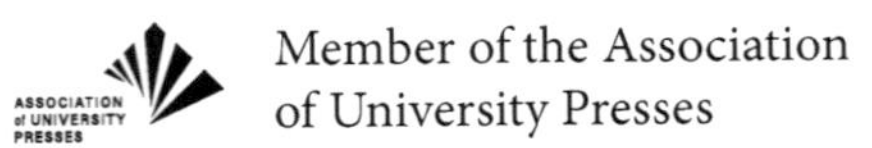

Member of the Association
of University Presses

To my "nuclear family"

Contents

Foreword

Researching the events of the 1940s in war-torn Yugoslavia comes with multi-layered challenges. The most important primary and secondary sources are available in more than half a dozen languages. The antagonisms of the era rose from the grave half a century later and still linger on to this day, thus placing obstacles in the way of unimpeded research and discussion. Available primary sources often reflect the type of bias that can be traced back to the writer's rank, service, or nationality, and also the position he took with respect to the three-cornered Yugoslav civil war and/or relations with other occupation powers. The same dynamic is applicable to protagonists on the side of the resistance.

To navigate these shoals with success is enough of a challenge at the best of times. With *Parleying with the Devil,* Gaj Trifković has set the bar even higher by analyzing the phenomenon of prisoner exchanges in World War II Yugoslavia. The very existence of such arrangements in the midst of a conflict where the most important occupying power was dead set against the idea of negotiating with irregulars and a parallel civil war was fought with the utmost savagery by all contenders appears downright counterintuitive. The best known instance involved the so-called March Negotiations in 1943. Here, a prisoner exchange went hand-in-hand with negotiations regarding the possible recognition of the People's Liberation Army by the Germans as a legitimate belligerent. Hitler quickly eliminated this possibility and what appeared to be a fleeting opportunity to de-escalate the conflict died a quick death.

Thanks to Trifković's groundbreaking research, we now know that the story of prisoner exchanges in wartime Yugoslavia is far more complex than anyone had suspected. The March Negotiations were preceded by incidents that were more important than previously thought; the same goes for the more institutionalized prisoner swaps that were carried out in the last two years of the war. Neither side was too keen to advertise this practice, and this undoubtedly contributed to the scarcity of references in extant sources. The author deserves to be commended for his detailed, in-depth research and for ferreting out any available information.

The story that emerges is of an arrangement that reflects the military realities on the ground (the Germans became more keen as the war turned against them; the Partisans less so), but whose protagonists were well aware of the fact that they were operating on ice so thin that it could collapse at any moment under the weight of the ideological incompatibility of both sides. Hence, it was not uncommon for German and Partisan negotiators to connive in order to pull the proverbial wool over their respective superior's eyes.

World War II was the most global and total conflict in history, and within the European/Middle Eastern theater of war, Yugoslavia certainly had a unique blend of civil war and war of national liberation that brought about an intense level of savagery. That this setting witnessed such a continuous attempt at de-escalation flies in the face of just about everything we thought we knew about the dynamics of escalation. *Parleying with the Devil* will have scholars arguing for a generation.

Klaus Schmider
Royal Military Academy Sandhurst
Camberley, United Kingdom

Abbreviations

AVNOJ—*Antifašističko vijeće narodnog oslobođenja Jugoslavije* (Anti-fascist Council of People's Liberation of Yugoslavia)

ICRC—International Committee of the Red Cross

KIA; WIA; MIA—Killed in Action; Wounded in Action; Missing in Action

KPH—*Komunistička partija Hrvatske* (Communist Party of Croatia)

KPJ—*Komunistička partija Jugoslavije* (Communist Party of Yugoslavia)

NDH—*Nezavisna država Hrvatska* (Independent State of Croatia)

NOP—*Narodnooslobodilački pokret* (People's Liberation Movement)

NOVJ—*Narodnooslobodilačka vojska Jugoslavije* (People's Liberation Army of Yugoslavia)

OKH—*Oberkommando des Heeres* (Army High Command)

OKW—*Oberkommando der Wehrmacht* (Armed Forces High Command)

OSS—Office of Strategic Services

OZAK—*Operationszone Adriatisches Küstenland* (Operational Zone Adriatic Littoral)

OZNA—*Odjeljenje za zaštitu naroda* (Department for the Protection of the People)

POW—Prisoner of War

RSHA—*Reichssicherheitshauptamt* (Reich Main Security Office)

SA—*Sturmabteilung* (Storm Detachment)

SD—*Sicherheitsdienst* (Security Service)

SKOJ—*Savez komunističke omladine Jugoslavije* (Union of the Communist Youth of Yugoslavia)

SS—*Schutzstaffel* (Protection Squad)

Supersloda—*Comando Superiore Forze Armate di Slovenia e Dalmazia* (High Command of the Armed Forces in Slovenia and Dalmatia, alternative designation of the Italian 2nd Army)

UNS—*Ustaška nadzorna služba* (Ustashe Surveillance Service)

ZAVNOBiH—*Zemaljsko antifašističko vijeće narodnog oslobođenja Bosne i Hercegovine* (State Anti-fascist Council of People's Liberation of Bosnia and Herzegovina)

ZAVNOH—*Zemaljsko antifašističko vijeće narodnog oslobođenja Hrvatske* (State Anti-fascist Council of People's Liberation of Croatia)

Note on the use of the terms *Jäger* and *Wehrmacht: Jäger* (literally, hunter) divisions employed by the German Army in Yugoslavia were a cross between infantry and mountain divisions. As the translation "light infantry," which is sometimes used in English-language works, does not seem appropriate to this author, it was decided to leave the original German designation. *Wehrmacht* was the name of the armed forces of the Third Reich and consisted of *Heer* (army, or ground forces), *Luftwaffe* (air force), and *Kriegsmarine* (navy). In the present work, the term will be used to denote the German armed forces in general. However, as the *Luftwaffe* and the *Kriegsmarine* had a relatively small role in the exchanges, *Wehrmacht* will sometimes be used for the ground forces alone.

Spelling and Pronunciation Guide

All names are given in the original spelling, except geographic names with standard Anglicizations, like Belgrade (instead of Beograd), Syrmia (instead of Srem/Srijem), or Munich (instead of München).

Pronunciation Guide for Nonstandard Letters

Letter	Pronounced as
C; c	tz in blitz
Č/Ć; č/ć	ch in chocolate
Dž/Đ; dž/đ	G in George
J; j	y in yes
LJ; lj	ly in will you
NJ; nj	ny in canyon
Š; š	sh in ship
Ž; ž	J in Jacques

Introduction

Prisoner exchange is as old as warfare itself. Along with ransom, it was one of the few hopes for prisoners of war until the advent of modern international law. By the beginning of the 17th century, prisoner exchange had become a recognized institute of rules and customs of war, with European states agreeing on exchange arrangements (so-called "cartels") whenever they fought. The prime motive behind the exchange was the need to get one's own trained soldiers back as soon as possible, but also to minimize the cost of keeping enemy prisoners. Only full-fledged "civilized" nations could form a cartel; native tribes and rebels were not seen as subjects of law. It is therefore not surprising that the British did their utmost to avoid entering a general cartel during the Revolutionary War (1775–83), for by doing so they would recognize the legitimacy of the nascent United States and their Continental Army. Approximately ninety years later, the Federal government in Washington faced the same problem and kept refusing an all-encompassing cartel with the Southern "rebels" for over a year after the beginning of hostilities in April of 1861. The deal was eventually reached in July of 1862 and would be in place until May of 1863. Although the official text read that the Union representatives signed the agreement with the people who had been "commissioned by the authorities they respectively represent," the signing was a *de facto* recognition of the Confederacy as a lawful belligerent.[1] Both episodes from North America serve as a good example of how the question of prisoners was always inextricably connected to politics.

The importance of the cartel began to fade with the beginning of the French Revolutionary Wars in 1792, which ushered in many fundamental changes in the practices of war. The last known prisoner exchange arrangement between European states was signed during the Crimean War in 1854. Further developments in international law regarding the granting of unconditional protection to captives, and the fact that states were now able to support large numbers of them, made prisoner exchanges obsolete by the early 1870s; the Hague Convention of 1907 did not even mention them.[2] All these changes notwithstanding, the practice of prisoner

---

[1] Paul Joseph Springer, "American Prisoner of War Policy and Practice from Revolutionary War to the War on Terror," PhD dissertation, Texas A&M University, 2006, pp. 18, 112.

[2] Peter H. Wilson, "Prisoners in Early-Modern European Warfare," in Sibylle Scheipers, ed., *Prisoners in War* (Oxford: Oxford University Press, 2010), p. 52; Stephen C. Neff, "Prisoners of War in International Law: The Nineteen Century," in ibid., pp. 59–60.

exchange continued whenever belligerents feared that their enemies would not be able or willing to honor international law. In World War II, major powers like Great Britain and Germany made exchange deals through third parties, such as the International Committee of the Red Cross or neutral countries.[3] However, only wounded and non-combat personnel were eligible for exchange and repatriation.[4]

Whereas the prisoners on all sides in the West (including North Africa and the Mediterranean) had a good chance of being taken alive and treated according to the Geneva Convention, the situation in the East and in the occupied territories was altogether different. The Nazi authorities had no intention of honoring the provisions of international law in what they saw as an ideologically motivated, life-or-death struggle with communism. In addition, members of the irregular forces were basically unprotected by contemporary law. The German armed forces knew only one way to counter guerrillas: unrestrained violence.[5] Since the Germans could not be counted upon to spare their captives on humanitarian grounds, they had to be incited to do so by other means. Revenge killing of German prisoners was likely to do more harm than good; any such action would immediately provoke an even more savage response against the civilian population. The only option left to a guerrilla army, whether in France, Greece, or Italy, was prisoner exchange. From late 1943, the Italian Partisans discovered that keeping Germans for exchange also had propaganda and political value.[6] By this time, however, their Yugoslav counterparts were already veteran negotiators.

Swapping prisoners had always been a part of warfare in the Balkans. The near-perpetual, low-intensity conflict that went on in the region for centuries weighed heavily on the comparatively small population, with every loss keenly felt. Therefore, local communities went to war with their neighbors primarily on their

---

[3] For the first successful British-German exchange in October 1943, see Neville Wylie, *Barbed Wire Diplomacy: Britain, Germany, and the Politics of Prisoners of War, 1939–1945* (Oxford: Oxford University Press, 2010), pp. 162–71.

[4] The Germans and the Allies exchanged able-bodied prisoners at least once, in Lorient, France, in the fall of 1944. See Peter Lieb, *Konventioneller Krieg oder NS-Weltan-schauungskrieg?: Kriegführung und Partisanenbekämpfung in Frankreich 1943/44* (München: Oldenbourg Wissenschaftsverlag, 2007), p. 491.

[5] Ben Shepherd, *War in the Wild East: The German Army and Soviet Partisans* (Cambridge, MA: Harvard University Press, 2004), pp. 41–56.

[6] For instance, the infamous massacres at Kalavryta in Greece and Oradour-sur-Glane in France were preceded by unsuccessful attempts at prisoner exchange. Hermann Frank Meyer, *Von Wien nach Kalavryta: die blutige Spur der 117. Jäger-Division durch Serbien und Griechenland* (Möhnesee: Bibliopolis, 2002), p. 218; Robert Aitken and Marilyn Aitken, *Law Makers, Law Breakers and Uncommon Trials* (Chicago: American Bar Association, 2007), p. 252. For more on the Italian Partisans' views on prisoner exchange and other related issues, see Claudio Pavone, *A Civil War: A History of Italian Resistance* (London: Verso Books, 2013), pp. 256, 325, 329, 331, 559–60, 585.

own terms with little regard for how this fit the conceptions of central authorities. Frequent prisoner exchanges have been recorded between the Croatian nobles fighting for the Habsburgs and their Bosnian-Ottoman counterparts along the so-called "Military Border" (*Militärgrenze,* or *Vojna Krajina*) that separated the two empires for approximately three centuries. This was done in spite of the fact that no formal cartel existed between the two states.[7] It is also known that, at the beginning of the 19th century, the Ottomans acquiesced to trading captives with Serbian insurgents whom they considered outlaws.[8] The birth of nation-states in the latter half of that century introduced Western conceptions of law, but those ideas failed to take root due to internal weaknesses and the unstable political situation in the region. To make matters worse, the great powers did not help the process when they bent or even completely disregarded the rules of international law when it suited them. In 1914–15, the Austro-Hungarian Army committed numerous war crimes against Serbian civilians and captured soldiers under the pretext of fighting unlawful belligerents who had broken the universally recognized rules and customs of warfare.[9] In this atmosphere of legal uncertainty, Serbia and Austria-Hungary agreed in late 1916 to exchange sick and incapacitated soldiers through Switzerland. The success of the exchange prompted both sides to discuss exchanging able-bodied prisoners as well. Serbia was especially keen to do so, as her manpower was severely reduced by three years of fighting. The plan foundered on the opposition of senior Allied powers, who saw no point in strengthening the Dual Monarchy with thousands of exchangees.[10] The same pattern would be repeated three decades later when Axis powers invaded Yugoslavia and instituted a brutal occupation with utter disregard for international law. Those perceived as a threat, real or imagined, could hope for little mercy. Under these circumstances, prisoner exchange would again come into play as the only viable method of restraining the captors from taking extreme measures against their captives.[11] Self-interest would once again prove

---

[7] Radoslav Lopašić, *Bihać i bihaćka krajina: mjestopisne i poviestne crtice* (Zagreb: Matica hrvatska, 1890), p. 103; Suraiya Faroqhi, *The Ottoman Empire and the World Around It* (London: I. B. Tauris, 2006), p. 125.

[8] Milivoje Stanković, *Prvi šumadijski partizanski odred* (Belgrade: Narodna Knjiga, 1983), pp. 26–27.

[9] Jonathan E. Gumz, *The Resurrection and Collapse of Empire in Habsburg Serbia, 1914–1918* (Cambridge: Cambridge University Press, 2009), pp. 34–61.

[10] Isidor Đuković, *Austrougarski ratni zarobljenici u Srbiji 1914–1915* (Belgrade: IP Signature, 2008), pp. 175–80.

[11] Sadly, international law remained a dead issue in the former Yugoslavia for the remainder of the 20th century, and the Balkan Wars of the 1990s consequently saw numerous prisoner exchanges between all sides. Two successor-states, the Republic of Croatia and the Federal Republic of Yugoslavia, reached a prisoner exchange agreement in late July 1992 with the help of the International Committee of the Red Cross.

a far more potent incentive than humanitarian considerations. What started as isolated cases, motivated by a spontaneous desire to save captured compatriots, soon evolved into a complex affair involving propaganda and intelligence issues, as well as political talks between two ideological arch-enemies.[12] The last point is particularly controversial, and is taken as proof by some authors that the Communist-led Partisans were not above collaborating with the Germans if doing so could further their political aims.

The main source of the German documents on prisoner exchange with the Partisans that was referenced for this study is found in the holdings of the U.S. National Archives and Records Administration (NARA). These records were captured in 1945, microfilmed, and subsequently returned to archives in the Federal Republic of Germany. I was fortunate to begin my research for this book at the time when the documents had been digitized and were becoming widely available through online exchange. My mentor once asked me how many German documents on prisoner exchange were to be found, on average, on a roll of microfilm (approximately 1,000 frames each). When I answered that I considered myself lucky if I found five pages with at least one sentence on the topic, my mentor's comment was that I was looking for the proverbial "needle in a haystack." Indeed, German primary sources on prisoner exchange with Yugoslav Partisans are fragmentary at best. This is largely due to the fact that the German Army archives in Potsdam were severely damaged in a bombing raid in early 1945. Worst of all, it seems that the documents of the "Special command for prisoner exchange" in Zagreb were completely lost. For this reason, most details pertaining to the functioning of the neutral zone at Pisarovina come from Yugoslav sources. As far as the surviving army records are concerned, it seems as though the commands exercised a degree of self-censorship, especially in the early years of the war—negotiating with Communist guerrillas, for whatever reason, was not something to brag about. The records of the German embassy in Zagreb provide a fair number of documents about the early exchanges. After the German Army took over the responsibility for the matter in early 1943, however, there is only an occasional reference. The reason for this is that comparatively few documents for the period from late 1943 until the end of the war are still extant. As this particularly applies to formations from corps level down, it is difficult to reconstruct many locally negotiated prisoner exchanges from the German perspective.

Croatian State Archives proved to be a true treasure trove. In addition to the microfilmed records of military commands of all sides, this institution holds a valuable collection of documents which were transferred from the archives of the Yugoslav secret police in the mid-1990s. The collection includes the personal estate of Boris Bakrač (one of the main Partisan negotiators) and various documents

---

[12] Gaj Trifković, "Making Deals with the Enemy: Partisan-German Contacts and Prisoner Exchanges in Yugoslavia, 1941–1945," *Global War Studies* 10:2 (2013), pp. 6–37.

pertaining to prisoner exchange, such as after-action reports, lists with names of exchanged persons, etc. The Archive of Hans Helm, named after the German police attaché in Zagreb, contains post-war interrogations of practically all German personnel who were involved with prisoner exchange in Croatia. I am aware of the shortcomings of eyewitness reports, especially if they were given under pressure. As we shall see, some of these statements were indeed intended for use in political power struggles at the top of the Yugoslav Communist hierarchy. Due to the lack of official documents, however, they proved to be critical in reconstructing the inner-workings of exchange arrangements. Needless to say, I compared every detail from these documents with other sources whenever possible.

I also consulted the holdings of several other institutions. At the Military Archive in Belgrade, which holds most of the Yugoslav wartime documents, of special interest were the logbooks of telegrams received and sent between the Partisan Main HQ for Croatia and the Supreme HQ under Tito. The archive also holds the nearly complete correspondence between Partisan and German commands in Eastern Herzegovina from the summer of 1944, which is an important source for understanding the generic functioning of local prisoner exchanges. At the Military Archive in Vienna is found the personal estate of General Edmund Glaise-Horstenau and extensive materials belonging to Dr. Peter Broucek, who edited the general's diary. The UK National Archives houses documents on British-Yugoslav relations, while the German Military Archive in Freiburg im Breisgau contains rare German documents not included in the copies made for NARA. At the Archive of the Museum of Bosnia and Herzegovina is found one important contemporary *Ustasha* document on the early German-Partisan negotiations. Rounding out this list of sources, the Archive of the Institute for Contemporary History in Munich houses post-war interrogations of German personnel by the U.S. Army, and the Central Archives of the Ministry of Defense of the Russian Federation holds rare documents of the ethnic German organization in Croatia.

Of the collections of published documents, *Zbornik dokumenata i podataka o narodnooslobodilačkom ratu naroda Jugoslavije* (Collection of Documents and Data on the People's Liberation War of Yugoslav Peoples, hereinafter *Zbornik*) deserves a special mention. The *Zbornik* is a gigantic, 174-part official collection of documents from Yugoslav archives pertaining to World War II in Yugoslavia. It is divided along both thematic (e.g. Vol. XII: *Documents of the German Reich;* Vol. VIII: *Activities in the Adriatic*) and geographic lines (e.g. Vol. I: *Fighting in Serbia;* Vol. V: *Fighting in Croatia,* etc.). Beginning publication in 1949, the last volume came out in 1986. Because of the highly sensitive nature of non-violent contacts with the Germans, the editors of the *Zbornik* left out many of the most crucial documents. Since it was impossible to avoid all mention of them, the editors chose to either give false explanations or none at all. For instance, when mentioning negotiations about a possible truce, the *Zbornik* states that these were "of a tactical nature" and that the truce was rejected out of hand by the Partisans. A reader hoping to learn more from an accompanying footnote is often frustrated by a line stating that "the complete correspondence pertaining to this matter was not found," or something similar.[13] Self-censorship on the part of the editors is also evident in the case of local prisoner exchanges made for exclusively humanitarian reasons; only one full document pertaining to one such case being published in the whole compendium. Interestingly, negotiations with the Italians over the same issue were apparently thought to be far less incriminating, and the *Zbornik* contains a relatively large number of references to them. Despite its shortcomings, however, the *Zbornik* is an invaluable asset to any researcher of wartime events in Yugoslavia and will be consulted extensively throughout this book.

For several reasons, the phenomenon of prisoner exchanges was, to the best of my knowledge, never dealt with in its entirety in any monograph published in socialist Yugoslavia. There are two principal reasons for why this was so. First, any deeper analysis of the subject could not have been presented without mentioning the political talks with the Germans. Political negotiations with the "fascist enemy" were a taboo topic until the mid-1980s, and even then they were presented to the public only partially and with ideological coloring. Second, it was thought that the lionized portrayal of the Partisans, so intensively built up over decades, would suffer from a lengthy presentation of their non-violent contacts with the invader, no matter how insignificant those interactions were in the context of the overall course of the war. Local prisoner exchanges that were aimed solely at saving comrades and conducted without ulterior motives, on the other hand, were not perceived as dishonorable. As such, they were often mentioned in unit histories and reminiscences of Partisan veterans, the descriptions ranging in size from a single line to a book chapter.[14]

Studies related to the general question of prisoners in wartime Yugoslavia are also few and far between. The topic was a step-child of the historiography of the socialist era; it appears that only one doctoral dissertation was written on the subject, and it remains unpublished.[15] That this would be so should come as no

---

[13] Ibid., p. 14.

[14] Ibid., p. 7. Local prisoner exchanges have also found their way into the popular culture of socialist Yugoslavia. Prisoner exchange with the Germans was part of the plot of the 1969 war movie *Kad čuješ zvona;* one episode of the popular television series *Kapelski kresovi* revolved around a prisoner exchange with the Italians in northwest Croatia (1975); 1976 saw the release of a full-length movie, *Devojački most,* which follows a group of Partisans tasked with escorting a number of Germans to the place of exchange. On the way, they have to fight both enemy patrols and their own mixed feelings about the mission. TV Titograd produced a documentary titled *Za pregovaračkim stolom* in 1973 about prisoner exchange with the Italians in Montenegro during the first two years of the war.

[15] Đoko Ivanović, "Položaj ratnih zarobljenika u međunarodnom pravu," PhD dissertation, Belgrade, Pravni fakultet, 1958. Unfortunately, I was not able to obtain a copy of this work from the National Library of Serbia.

surprise given the previously mentioned issue of censorship and self-censorship. For the same reasons, any historian coming from outside the country with the intention of providing an objective study of the matter would have faced immense difficulties in conducting research in Yugoslavia. Research on the topic by Western scholars consequently remained dependent on the available Axis documents and reminiscences of Axis participants, both of which were heavily biased and, at least in some cases, influenced by the atmosphere of the Cold War; the work of Karl W. Böhme on German prisoners in Yugoslavia comes to mind in this respect. The previously restricted documents became available to researchers after the collapse of the socialist system in the early 1990s. The problem that then presented itself was that the scholarly communities in the successor states had in the meantime lost interest in the topic, preferring to concentrate on other lesser-known aspects of the war.

This book represents a much-revised and updated version of my PhD thesis accepted by the Karl-Franzens University in Graz in 2013 (Mentors: Professor Dr. Siegfried Beer and Professor Dr. Florian Bieber). It represents an attempt to plug a hole in the historiography, and to provide a detailed analysis of the prisoner exchange phenomenon and the accompanying contacts between the German occupation authorities and the Yugoslav Partisans. It will also be a contribution to the research on prisoners during the Second World War in Yugoslavia, a topic which has been long neglected in both former-Yugoslav and Western historiography. More specifically, I will try to answer two major questions: first, whether the contacts between the Partisans and German occupation authorities exhibited elements of collaboration; and second, whether prisoner exchange influenced policies concerning prisoners on both sides and in some way helped reduce the levels of violence for which this theater of war became infamous. It should be by no means taken as the definitive work on the subject, but rather as a solid starting point for future research. Owing to the fragmentary nature of the sources, this will include a fair amount of guesswork; I have done my best to make such guesses as educated as possible. Needless to say, I bear full responsibility for all errors and shortcomings of this work.

The book is divided into six chapters, with the first five covering events which took place in a certain geographical region within a certain time frame. Instances of prisoner exchange and negotiations are described in chronological order. The descriptions vary in size, depending on the availability of sources, with both Yugoslav and German sources on the same event being cited when possible. The reader will notice that I rely heavily on eyewitness reports and recollections of veterans, from generals down to privates, in order to depict the events as vividly as possible. This not only makes the text a more enjoyable read, but, more importantly, it helps us understand one individual's perceptions of his enemy, of captivity, and of prisoner exchange. In addition, I have also tried to provide as much background information as possible (such as details on military operations, short biographies of less important personalities, etc.) so that the reader can better understand "the big picture" and place a particular episode in the proper context. Most descriptions are immediately followed by a short analysis and presentation of relevant findings; particularly controversial events are analyzed in separate sections. Approximately ten percent of each chapter is devoted to conclusions, where the results are summed up and commented on at some length.

Chapter one deals with the events in Serbia from 1941 to 1944. Chapter two describes the events that took place on the territory of the NDH from 1941 to the beginning of 1943. Chapter three analyzes the German-Partisan negotiations from the first half of 1943. Chapter four, the centerpiece of the entire work, concentrates on the creation and functioning of the prisoner exchange cartel and the neutral zone at Pisarovina from 1943 to 1945. Chapter five provides an overview of local prisoner exchanges in Yugoslavia in the last two years of the war. Chapter six contains a short overview of the issues connected with the topic and the most important findings of this study. There are also appendices to provide additional information. As a complete version of the bibliography would comprise many dozens of pages, only a Selected Bibliography is provided herein. Please consult the footnotes for more detail.

Chapter 1

Brutal Until the End

Serbia, 1941–1944

Prologue: March–April 1941

Serbia, with its large population and rich mineral and agricultural resources, was the Kingdom of Yugoslavia's spiritual and economic heartland. It also hosted the Yugoslav capital, Belgrade, and linked Central Europe with Greece and Turkey via strategically important lines of communication. These facts escaped neither the Germans nor the guerrilla movements which came into life after the war had begun. Therefore, Serbia enjoyed a special position in Yugoslavia in terms of the occupation system and how the occupiers dealt with the resistance they encountered. The necessities of war would force the opposing sides in other parts of the country to agree to a limited de-escalation of violence when prisoners were involved. Serbia, apart from the first months of the war, would remain excluded from these arrangements. Consequently, it seems appropriate to deal with the events in Serbia from 1941–44 in a separate chapter.

By the early spring of 1941, the Kingdom of Yugoslavia had managed to stay out of the war which had enveloped Europe for a year and a half. However, diplomatic pressure from the Third Reich to join the Tripartite Pact became unbearable; consequently, Yugoslavia reluctantly signed the accession agreement on 25 March 1941 at Belvedere Palace in Vienna, thus joining the Axis alliance. The news sent shockwaves through the country, stirring dissent among the population as well as the Allied sympathizers in the officer corps. Two days later, the country was in chaos. A group of Anglophile officers, led by Air Force General Dušan Simović, carried out a *coup d'état,* deposed the Prince Regent, Pavle, and made the young King Petar II the new head of state. The new government under Simović had no concrete plan for the future; although the abrogation of the Tripartite Treaty was extremely popular (especially amongst the Serbs), the government publicly assured the Axis powers that it would respect the obligations made in Vienna.[1]

This dubious guarantee was not taken seriously in Germany, and on 27 March 1941, Hitler ordered the *Wehrmacht* to destroy Yugoslavia militarily and as a

---

[1] Jozo Tomasevich, *War and Revolution in Yugoslavia, 1941–1945: The Chetniks* (Stanford: Stanford University Press, 1975), pp. 22–53.

nation "without waiting for possible declarations of loyalty from the new government."[2] The plan for the attack, *Weisung Nr. 25* (Directive No. 25), called for the invasion of the country by the German Army and its Italian, Bulgarian, and Hungarian allies. On 6 April 1941, the *Wehrmacht's* armored spearheads crossed the Yugoslav border at several locations, while the *Luftwaffe* simultaneously carried out massive air raids on Belgrade and other cities. The Royal Yugoslav Army was utterly unprepared for the onslaught. On paper, it looked like a formidable force, with 1,200,000 men in thirty-one divisions for frontline service and an additional 500,000 in reserve.[3] In reality, however, it lacked modern equipment and, more importantly, the morale and cohesion necessary for victory on the battlefield were nonexistent.[4] Consequently, its defenses crumbled amidst the chaos caused by the invasion. Skopje fell on the 8th, Zagreb on the 10th, and Belgrade on the 12th, the latter being captured by a German motorcycle detachment. On 15 April 1941, the nascent King and his ministers fled the country by airplane, leaving the rest of the nation to fend for itself. A day later, the German 16th Motorized Division captured the Yugoslav High Command near Sarajevo. On 17 April, Yugoslav Foreign Minister Aleksandar Cincar-Marković, and the representative of the High Command, General Radivoje Janković, met with a delegation of the 2nd German Army in the "White Palace" (*Beli dvor*) in Belgrade to sign the armistice document. Although the Yugoslav government-in-exile repudiated the terms of the agreement, thereby keeping the country in the war on the Allied side, the fighting was effectively over. In one of the most successful examples of *Blitzkrieg* doctrine, the German Army managed to crush Yugoslavia in only eleven days, and according to official statistics, suffered less than 600 casualties with only 151 killed, 392 wounded, and fifteen missing in action.[5]

---

[2] *Zbornik dokumenata i podataka o narodnooslobodilačkom ratu naroda Jugoslavije* (Belgrade: Vojnoistorijski institut, 1949–86), Vol. II, Book 2, p. 466, Conference with the *Führer* on the situation in Yugoslavia (27 March 1941). Hereinafter abbreviated to: *Zbornik/* volume/book/page.

[3] Velimir Terzić, *Slom Kraljevine Jugoslavije 1941* (Belgrade: Partizanska knjiga, 1984), Vol. II, pp. 106, 108.

[4] Croatian nationalists in the 108th Regiment rebelled near Bjelovar during the night of 7–8 April 1941 and proclaimed Croatia "a sovereign and independent state" the day after. Zdravko Dizdar, "Bjelovarski ustanak od 7. do 10. travnja 1941," *Časopis za suvremenu povijest* 39:3 (2008), p. 595. The Germans were concerned primarily with the fighting skills of the individual Serbian soldier, and the units were instructed to prepare for close combat. See U.S. National Archives and Records Administration (hereinafter NARA), Record Group (hereinafter RG) 242, microfilm publication T-315, Roll 1063, Intelligence summary (4 April 1941).

[5] J. B. Hoptner, *Yugoslavia in Crisis, 1934–1941* (New York: Columbia University Press, 1962), p. 286. Killed, wounded, and missing in action will hereinafter be abbreviated to KIA, WIA, and MIA.

Even if Hitler originally had no intention of breaking up the Yugoslav Kingdom, his attitude changed quickly as a result of the Belgrade coup. He immediately offered his allies territorial gains in Yugoslavia in exchange for their participation in the campaign. Italy, Hungary, and Bulgaria all had claims resulting from unfavorable peace treaties made in the aftermath of the First World War. Italy acquired a portion of Slovenia and almost all of the Croatian Littoral, occupying at the same time Montenegro and a large part of the Kosovo region. Hungary annexed the Bačka province and small parts of Croatia and Slovenia, while Bulgaria received Macedonia and parts of Southern Serbia. The Croatian mainland and Bosnia-Herzegovina were combined to form the puppet "Independent State of Croatia" (*Nezavisna država Hrvatska,* abbreviated to NDH). Germany *de facto* annexed those parts of Slovenia which were deemed historically "German" regions (Upper Carniola and Lower Carinthia and Styria).

The Third Reich was much more interested in economic rather than territorial gains in the Western Balkans. Starting from 1935, Germany gradually brought Yugoslavia within its sphere of economic influence. By 1941, the former had practically obtained a monopoly on Yugoslav exports of agricultural products, as well as ores and nonferrous metals vital to the German war industry.[6] Never losing sight of these considerations, Hitler made sure the region would continue to supply the needed raw materials irrespective of the new borders. In exchange for territorial expansion, Italy and all of the minor Axis states had to relinquish control or grant large concessions over the resources important to Germany. Thus, the mines in Italian-occupied Kosovo and the NDH region of Herzegovina, as well as Bulgarian-occupied Macedonia, were run by German firms, while Hungary acquiesced to deliver the surplus of agricultural products from the Bačka.[7] The lines of communication in the region were of equal importance to Berlin. Substantial parts of both the main railway line to Greece and the River Danube (used for transportation of products from Romanian oil fields) ran through Serbia proper. This fact, combined with Serbia's large and supposedly unruly population, as well as rich farmlands and mines, convinced the Germans to place that territory under their direct military control.

In the course of the April campaign, some 360,000 Yugoslav soldiers were taken prisoner.[8] Since the war was a regular one, these men were entitled to the protections afforded by the Geneva Convention which the Kingdom of Yugoslavia

---

[6] For a brief overview of German-Yugoslav economic relations on the eve of the Second World War, see Branko Petranović, *Istorija Jugoslavije 1918–1988* (Belgrade: Nolit, 1989), Vol. II, pp. 321–33.

[7] For more details on these arrangements, see Jozo Tomasevich, *War and Revolution in Yugoslavia, 1941–1945: Occupation and Collaboration* (Stanford: Stanford University Press, 2001), pp. 620–23.

[8] Terzić, *Slom,* Vol. II, pp. 472, 498.

had ratified in June 1931.[9] The Germans, however, bent the rules according to their own will. While the prisoners belonging to certain nationalities, like Croats or Macedonians, were released shortly after the end of the campaign, German units had an order to treat the captured Serbian officers "in the worst possible manner." This was in reaction to the perceived treachery of the Serbs, and also a tool of the divide-and-conquer policy the Third Reich was utilizing in the former Kingdom of Yugoslavia.[10]

As irregular warfare was considered synonymous with the Balkans, the Germans were certain that it would play a prominent role during the invasion of the country. Intelligence reports suggested that two days before the attack, the Yugoslavs had called for a guerrilla war (*Kleinkrieg*) against the enemy. The German units were therefore ordered to prepare themselves for sudden attacks and ambushes on individual vehicles.[11] Furthermore, it was assumed that not only the Army but also militia-like civilian organizations (*Wehrverbände*) such as armed wings of some political parties, or the *Sokol* association, would function as guerrilla units in the event of war.[12] Contrary to the German belief, the royal army did not place much importance on irregular warfare. Actions of special forces both at the front and rear were theoretically envisaged in the so-called "Plan S," developed by the High Command in late 1939, as well as in similar documents known as R-40 and R-41 composed in early 1940. The first concrete steps in this direction were taken only in the summer of that year, when six Chetnik (later assault) battalions were formed.[13] These units received special training and were charged with a variety of tasks, including serving as a core for future guerrilla forces; carrying out raids on the enemy's flanks and rear; and fighting against airborne landings, enemy spies, and saboteurs.[14] Although representing a part of the regular army and fulfilling all the provisions of the Geneva Convention (wearing recognizable insignia, obeying a clear chain of command, etc.), their legal status was questioned by their

---

[9] Dominik Vuletić, "Kaznenopravni i povijesni aspekti bleiburškog zločina," *Pravnik* 41 (2007), p. 130.

[10] *War Journal of Franz Halder* (Washington, DC: Office of Chief of Counsel for War Crimes, 1950), Vol. VI, p. 61, Entry for 9 April 1941.

[11] NARA, T-315, Roll 1063, Intelligence summary (4 April 1941). Interestingly, the chapter "Fighting Methods of the Enemy" in the document mentions only irregular tactics.

[12] NARA, T-312, Roll 424, Yugoslav armed forces (10 January 1941). *Sokol* was a youth gymnast society founded in Prague in 1863 from where it spread to all Slav-populated countries. In time, it acquired a strong Pan-Slavic character.

[13] The word "četnik" is derived from "četa," meaning "company." The term was coined at the beginning of the 20th century as guerrilla units ("čete") were formed to fight the Ottoman rule in present-day Macedonia.

[14] Aleksandar Životić, "Četničke jedinice Vojske kraljevine Jugoslavije u Aprilskom ratu," *Istorija 20. veka* 1 (2011), pp. 41–42.

enemies. According to the German intelligence services, the Chetnik units would perform their tasks using either civilian clothes or German uniforms, which, in turn, would put them outside the protection of international law. The following remark was made at a command conference of the German 73rd Infantry Division held at the beginning of April 1941: "Whenever the troops meet the men of the assault battalions, they are to be shot without mercy."[15]

Neither the war diary of the 73rd Division, nor the post-war Yugoslav/Serbian sources, can confirm that the quoted remark was the official policy toward the members of the assault units during the April war. There had been several clashes with the advancing German troops before the assault units were taken captive with the rest of the army.[16] There was, however, at least one instance when the Germans used the existence of Chetniks/irregulars as a pretext for committing a war crime. The incident occurred on 11 April 1941 in the village of Alibunar in Vojvodina. On that day, the spearheads of the *Wehrmacht's* 41st Panzer Corps encountered unusually strong resistance from the Yugoslav units on the outskirts of the afore-mentioned town. Worse still, a German major was shot by a sharpshooter as he entered the village.[17] The SS motorized division *Das Reich* exacted vengeance by rounding up Yugoslav prisoners and civilians from Alibunar and adjoining villages and executing them as "Chetniks," that is, as unlawful belligerents.[18] The killings lasted for eight days and claimed an estimated 200 victims.[19] This episode illus-trates the arbitrary way in which the Germans interpreted international law and bent its provisions in a manner that suited them. Although the massacre at Alibu-nar can be seen as an exception in the Balkans Campaign in the spring of 1941, such behavior would become synonymous with the occupation forces during the following months and years.

---

[15] NARA, T-315, Roll 1063, Points for command conference (undated).

[16] Životić, "Četničke jedinice," pp. 42–46.

[17] The incident is mentioned in Hoptner, *Yugoslavia in Crisis,* p. 286, although the author erroneously mentions 56th instead of 41st Panzer Corps.

[18] Lajco Klajn, *The Past in Present Times: The Yugoslav Saga* (Lanham, MD: University Press of America, 2007), p. 82. See also the interview with Serbian historian Čedomir Popov in the television documentary, *Jugoslavija u ratu 1941–1945* (Belgrade: Radio-televizija Srbije, Televizija Beograd, 1991–92), Episode 4.

[19] For a more detailed description of these events and a list of names of those who were ex-ecuted, see Srđan Božović, *Nemački zločin u Alibunaru 1941* (Pančevo: Zavičajni muzej Pančevo, 2004). Reference to the number of victims is on p. 84. I would like to extend my thanks to the Museum of Pančevo for kindly providing me with a copy of this book.

Interregnum, April–June 1941

The Germans spent the period from late April to the beginning of July organizing their administration of rump Serbia.[20] At the head of the occupation apparatus was the Military Commander in Serbia (*Militärbefehlshaber in Serbien*), an officer holding the rank of general, responsible for all military and civilian aspects of running the country. The country was divided into four area (*Feldkommandantur*) and nine district commands (*Ortskommandantur*) to which existing Serbian civilian and police structures were subordinated. In order to ensure complete and prompt fulfillment of the duties imposed on the country, on 30 April 1941 the Germans formed the Serbian Commissary Council under Milan Aćimović. It was comprised of fifteen commissars responsible for various areas, including internal affairs. The backbone of the council was the ever-expanding Serbian *gendarmerie*, which enforced law and order in the country.[21] One German police battalion (the 64th) was tasked with similar duties.

The operational control over German forces in Serbia was in the hands of the 65th Higher Command for Special Purposes (*Höheres Kommando zur besonderen Verwendung 65*). This was a corps-sized formation with three infantry divisions and other, smaller units attached to it. The 704th, 714th, and 717th Infantry Divisions were all formed in April 1941 as a part of the 15th Mobilization Wave of the *Wehrmacht*. As they were envisaged as occupation units, their organization was different from the units raised for combat duties. Most importantly, their strength on paper was set at 6,152, which amounted to roughly half the strength of a front line division. The men serving in these units were well past their prime with the average age of a soldier being above thirty. The divisions were short of artillery, engineering and radio equipment, and were not motorized.[22] The smaller units included the 562nd, 592nd, and 920th Territorial Defense (*Landesschützen*) Battalions whose personnel were comprised mostly of those deemed unfit for front line duty. Their task was primarily to guard strategic points and lines of communication. All in all, the 65th Higher Command could muster some

---

[20] After the division of spoils between the Axis powers, Serbia was practically reduced to its pre-1912 borders. Consequently, this chapter will deal mainly with the events which took place in this region, with an occasional reference to the episodes that occurred in Vojvodina.

[21] In mid-May 1941, 1,932 *gendarmes* returned to duty. When the *gendarmerie* was renamed the Serbian State Guard (*Srpska državna straža*) in March 1942, its strength was estimated at 15,000 men. Milan Borković, *Kvislinška uprava u Srbiji 1941–1944* (Belgrade: Sloboda, 1979), Vol. I, pp. 42, 292.

[22] NARA, T-315, Roll 2262, 000067, Message to 11th Corps (27 May 1941); NARA, T-315, Roll 2236, 000708, Forming of the 704th and parts of 718th Infantry Division (4 April 1941); Georg Tessin, *Verbände und Truppen der deutschen Wehrmacht und der Waffen-SS im Zweiten Weltkrieg 1939–1945* (Osnabrück: Biblio Verlag, 1978), Vol. I, p. 57.

22,500 mostly over-aged and under-equipped men with which to counter potential trouble.[23]

The occupation regime was harsh—a wide range of subversive acts including hiding arms, sabotage, or attacks on German personnel were punishable by death. Serbia had to pay for the costs of the occupation and deliver a large portion of its agricultural and mining output to Germany or other German-occupied areas. Striking was prohibited, as well as the hoarding of goods, holding demonstrations, illegally distributing leaflets, and listening to non-Axis radio stations. The slightest insult to the occupying forces, such as impoliteness toward a soldier in a streetcar or not making room for an officer on a sidewalk, was threatened with harsh penalties.[24] All these measures were employed to one end—to instill fear in the population and make any notion of armed resistance appear futile. While the threat of violence had the desired effect on the urban population "still under shock of the recent events," trouble was already brewing in the province. Small groups of former Yugoslav soldiers roamed the countryside, each group following its own path and agenda, but all armed and refusing to surrender. There are numerous reports of Chetniks who allegedly looted villages and attempted to scare the people out of obeying the invader. The Germans carefully monitored the security situation in the country, reacting promptly to those events which even remotely suggested guerrilla activity. The reports by the local authorities concerning the latter have often proven to be exaggerated. For example, there was an alleged bomb attack in Prijepolje, which turned out to be the result of incompetent handling of explosives. In many cases, the problems were caused by bands of ordinary criminals, who were "nothing new in the Balkans" and were a problem in peacetime as well.[25]

Ordinary bandits, renegade soldiers, or guerrillas were all treated in the same way if captured. Four days after the Yugoslav Army had surrendered, a German patrol came to the village of Dobrić (near Loznica) in search of hidden arms. A firefight broke out in which one German soldier was killed, two were wounded, and the village was subsequently torched. Seven days later, the German 2nd Army issued the first guidelines for reprisals in the occupied country. The instructions read that any person caught with arms in Serbia fell outside the protection of international law and was to be executed immediately. In the event of attack on German personnel, all men capable of bearing arms in the vicinity of the incident should be treated in the same way, and their corpses hanged for added psychological impact. The taking of hostages after an attack was deemed "wrong" (probably for reasons of expediency), and troops were advised to carry on in the manner mentioned previously. On 29 April 1941, the 11th Army Corps issued an instruction specifying

---

[23] Estimate for the end of August 1941. Klaus Schmider, *Partisanenkrieg in Jugoslawien 1941–1944* (Hamburg: Mittler-Verlag, 2002), p. 586.

[24] Tomasevich, *Occupation and Collaboration*, p. 175.

[25] NARA, T-315, Roll 2236, 000507–8, Report of the 60th Motorized Division (17 May 1941).

which reprisals could normally be ordered by battalion commanders and above. If, however, circumstances rendered this impracticable, then they could be ordered by the most senior officer present.[26] In mid-May, Field Marshal Maximilian von Weichs, the commander of the 2nd Army, let it be known that for each German soldier killed, one hundred Serbs would be shot in reprisal. Although there is no evidence that the order was ever carried out, it proved that the Germans were (at least theoretically) envisaging such draconian measures even before there existed any real possibility of a massive uprising which could endanger their position in Serbia.[27]

In May and June, reports of alleged guerrilla groups and their activities became more and more numerous. Some incidents reported concerned the laying of mines in a tunnel, and the cutting of telephone and telegraph wires. Serbian *gendarmes* were usually deemed capable of dealing with these incidents. However, the Germans did intervene once on 3–4 May in Tara Planina (approximately 40km west of Užice) when members of the 2nd Battalion of the 116th Regiment engaged in a firefight with some 100 irregulars. They were dispersed without any casualties on either side.[28] One report, dated 23 June 1941, concerning in all likelihood the same guerrilla group, deserves to be mentioned at some length. A lieutenant of Croatian birth was returning home from Bulgarian captivity when he was captured on 16 May by Chetniks between Valjevo and Čačak.

> The leader of [this] Chetnik group is Colonel of the General Staff, Draža Mihailović. He has with him, among others, Major Palošević, cavalry Captain Reljić, Gendarmerie Captain Uzelac, and 1st lieutenants Ilić and Ratko Martinović, as well as non-commissioned officers [NCOs] and men of various branches of the armed forces. Their liaison officer is the Reserve Cavalry Major Aleksandar Mišić, the son of the late Vojvoda Mišić. He now lives in Struganik (southeast of Valjevo) and supplies the group with money, arms, ammunition, and food. The presence of this group is known to all teachers, communal leaders, and gendarmerie stations in the vicinity . . . as well as to the gendarmerie commander in Gornji Milanovac. . . .[29]

This is one of the first mentions of Dragoljub Draža Mihailović, a man whose guerrilla organization would be of much concern to the Germans, more by its

---

[26] NARA, T-315, Roll 2236, 000487–8, Order of the 2nd Army (28 April 1941).

[27] Venceslav Glišić, *Teror i zločini nacističke Nemačke u Srbiji 1941–1944.* (Belgrade: Izdavačko preduzeće "Rad," 1970), p. 35. The order was posted around Serbia on 19 May 1941.

[28] NARA, T-501, Roll 245, 000119, 122, 127, War diary for April 1941 (Entry Nos. 10, 17, 24).

[29] NARA, T-501, Roll 245, 000129–30, War diary for April 1941 (Entry No. 30).

existence than by its actions.[30] Mihailović developed his strategy after establishing himself on Ravna Gora Mountain between Valjevo and Čačak in mid-May 1941. Understanding the overwhelming power of the *Wehrmacht,* but also confident of ultimate Allied victory, Mihailović was opposed to rash actions against the invader. Rather than engaging the Germans openly, he planned to build up his organization, gather arms and equipment, and actively fight the Germans only occasionally. When the Allied armies arrived at the borders, he would issue a call for a general uprising, help force the Germans out of the country, and restore the monarchy. His movement was nominally all-Yugoslav, but in fact almost exclusively Serbian with a strong chauvinistic streak.

The above-mentioned 1st Lieutenant, Ratko Martinović, had many difficulties with Mihailović because he disregarded the rule of not engaging Germans "until the right time has come" (as the contemporary phrase went). The particular event which caused him trouble almost ended with a prisoner exchange. Just before rejoining Mihailović on the slopes of the Suvobor Mountain, Martinović and two of his companions ran into a lone German soldier repairing a car near the village of Svračkovac. "Such fear on our part, and there was this one German standing carelessly in the heart of Serbia, so to speak. This was too much for me. I lost my temper and told Živić, 'Cover me, I'll take him prisoner.'" The German, a certain "Hans from Leipzig," was quickly overpowered and disarmed. Recovering from the initial shock, he regained his self-confidence and even tried to explain to Martinović and his comrades that it is they who should be his prisoners, given the fact that Yugoslavia had capitulated. The captors deliberated what to do with him. Besides killing him, there was talk of exchanging him for some Serbian officers who were in prison in nearby Gornji Milanovac. In the end, Hans was released without his sidearm and with a letter for the local German command, threatening it with retaliation if the villagers were molested because of this incident.[31]

Martinović kept silent about the event when he rejoined Mihailović. When the latter heard of what had transpired, he was furious and sternly reprimanded the lieutenant. It was the last straw for Martinović, whose desire to fight the invader could not be fulfilled by sitting idly on Ravna Gora. Consequently, he left and eventually joined another group which was the opposite of Mihailović's Chetniks in both ideology and action (or inaction) toward the invader.

---

[30] Mihailović (1893–1946) had a distinguished military career up to 1941, spanning thirty years and three wars. However, his implacable anti-communist beliefs, political ineptitude, poor choice of subordinates, and inability to assert his authority contributed to his organization, the Yugoslav Army in the Homeland (better known as the Chetniks of Draža Mihailović), finishing the war fighting on the losing side. Additional information on his Chetniks will be given at appropriate places in the text.

[31] Ratko Martinović, *Od Ravne Gore do Vrhovnog Štaba* (Belgrade: Rad, 1979), pp. 102–07.

The Communist Party of Yugoslavia (*Komunistička partija Jugoslavije*, KPJ) was founded in 1919, and immediately acquired a large following. In the general elections of November 1920, it received nearly thirteen percent of the popular vote. Fearing its growing influence and radicalization, the ruling circles issued a proclamation (*Obznana*) in December that banned the Party from participating in the dealings of the Constitutional Assembly. When two young Communists assassinated the interior minister, Milorad Drašković, in July 1921, the Party was banned altogether. The KPJ went underground, rapidly losing members to both voluntary resignations and harsh police measures. By the mid-1930s the Party was small, internally divided, and had little influence either at home or in the Communist International (Comintern). In early 1937, the KPJ received a new leader, the metal worker and professional revolutionary, Josip Broz, better known under his *nom de guerre*, Tito. Tito rescued the Party from near-disbandment (seriously contemplated in Moscow at the time), made it financially self-sufficient, and enforced strict discipline. As a result, by the summer of 1941, the KPJ had a membership of nearly 12,000 dedicated men and women who were experienced in underground work. To this number, one should add another 30,000 or so members of the Communist Youth organization (*Savez komunističke omladine Jugsolavije*, SKOJ).[32]

The KPJ was, as were all other communist parties, put in a difficult position by the signing of the Molotov-Ribbentrop Agreement in August 1939. Although undeniably anti-fascist, the Party had to make necessary changes in its propaganda per instructions from Moscow. Consequently, the war raging between Germany on one side, and France and Britain on the other, was portrayed as a typical "imperialist" one, whereby all sides were considered to be equally bad.[33] At the same time, the Party began to prepare for a possible conflict with the Axis powers by forming the Military Committee responsible for training the membership and gathering arms and ammunition. Communists were taken aback by the coup of 27 March and the massive anti-German demonstrations all over the country. Swept by popular enthusiasm, numerous KPJ members took to the streets. This, however, went against the directives, which stipulated restraint and conservation of manpower for a final showdown with the "class enemy."[34]

The same gap between patriotic sentiment and the need to follow the official line from Moscow caused the Montenegrin Communists to agitate against serving in the royal army in May 1940. This provided the foundation for the myth that the Communists sabotaged the Yugoslav armed forces during the April War. In fact,

---

[32] Jovan Vujošević, "1941—Prve oružane akcije protiv okupatora," in A. H. Pape and Nikola Anić, eds., *Drugi svjetski rat* (Belgrade: Narodna knjiga, 1980), Vol. I, p. 269.

[33] Branko Petranović and Momčilo Zečević, eds., *Jugoslavija 1918–1988: Tematska zbirka dokumenata* (Belgrade: Rad, 1988), pp. 416–17, 443.

[34] Aleksej J. Timofejev, *Rusi i Drugi svetski rat u Jugoslaviji: uticaj SSSR-a i ruskih emigranata na događaje u Jugoslaviji 1941–1945* (Belgrade: Institut za noviju istoriju Srbije, 2010), p. 216.

the KPJ welcomed the opportunity to present itself as the only true patriotic force, and its members took part in the war both as conscripts and volunteers. The speed and totality of defeat only seemed to confirm the accuracy of the Party's repeated claims that "pro-fascist" and "defeatist" policies of the ruling circles around the Karađorđević dynasty were leading the country to its doom. The April War benefited the KPJ in another, important way—since the bourgeois parties had ceased to exist, the Communist Party was the only organized political force left in the country. All this, combined with utter disillusionment caused by the spring catastrophe, made the KPJ acceptable to large portions of society.[35]

The Uprising: July–October 1941

The relative peace in occupied Yugoslavia was irreversibly shattered as news of the German invasion of the Soviet Union was published on the morning of 22 June 1941. The uncomfortable cease-fire between the Nazis and the Communists on the basis of the Molotov-Ribbentrop agreement was thus over. Knowing from where the danger would now be coming, German security services prepared to seize all known Communists and veterans of the Spanish Civil War (known as "Spanish Fighters" or "Spaniards") on 22 June. Although dozens of suspects were taken into custody in Serbia in this opening round of the conflict, most managed to evade capture.[36]

The leadership of the KPJ was not surprised by the news of Operation Barbarossa. It immediately prepared a proclamation for the people of Yugoslavia, calling them to arms against the occupier. Five days later, the *Politburo* met in Belgrade and created the Main Headquarters of the People's Liberation Partisan Detachments of Yugoslavia with Tito at the helm, who then ordered the Party cadres to hasten the preparations for the uprising. A week later, on 4 July 1941, these groups were ordered into action specifically to sabotage lines of communication, to ambush smaller enemy units, and to generally make life as miserable as possible for the invader.

As July progressed, the security situation in Serbia deteriorated. There was a steady rise in incidents of sabotage, arson, disarmament, and assassination of collaborationist officials.[37] Originally comprised mostly of KPJ and SKOJ members,

---

[35] Tomasevich, *The Chetniks*, pp. 79–84.

[36] NARA, T-501, Roll 245, 000424–5, War diary entries for 22 and 23 June 1941. By the beginning of August, the Germans reported 412 communist "functionaries" had been shot. NARA, T-501, Roll 249, 000756, Report to intelligence section of the Wehrmacht Commander Southeast/12th Army (2 August 1941).

[37] On 7 July, two *gendarmes* were killed by Communist guerrillas in the village of Bela Crkva (near Krupanj). The date was celebrated as the "Day of the Uprising" in socialist Yugoslavia. For the German report on the incident, see NARA, T-501, Roll 245, 000159, Report by FK 816 (10 July 1941).

these guerrilla groups were beginning to acquire non-Party volunteers in ever growing numbers. The idea of a general uprising was made all the more appealing by several factors. First, the swift German victory in April had come with a price. Due to the impending invasion of the Soviet Union, front line divisions had to be withdrawn from Yugoslavia starting in May, which gave them little time to secure prisoners[38] and equipment. As a result, huge numbers of light weapons remained unaccounted for—mostly hidden by peasants across the country. Second, the number and quality of the replacement troops (divisions of the 15th Mobilization Wave) were substantially lower than the original occupation force. Adding to the difficulties, the recently reconstituted Serbian *gendarmerie* remained numerically weak. Third, by August 1941, occupied Serbia was flooded with an estimated 100,000 refugees[39] from other parts of Yugoslavia. Some of these desperate people, mostly Serbs from Bosnia and Croatia, sought to redress their grievances by joining the guerrillas. Last, but certainly not least, there was a strong psychological motive, namely the deeply-rooted belief in the might of Russia based on pan-Slavic sentiment as opposed to communist ideology—even the royalist officers believed that the Germans would lose the war in a matter of months.[40]

German armed forces and the various security units were rarely targeted by the guerrillas during the first weeks of the uprising. The latter felt too weak to attack the Germans, and concentrated their efforts on *gendarmerie* and municipality offices instead, where they burned archives and appropriated (or in the parlance of their enemy, "plundered") local funds. The German personnel rarely ventured outside their garrisons located in urban areas. On one such occasion, on 12 July 1941, a woodcutting party comprised of eight German privates went to work near

---

[38] Koča Popović, a veteran of the Spanish Civil War and a reserve lieutenant in the royal army, related his experiences from the April War which illustrated the cavalier attitude displayed by the Germans while handling the Yugoslav prisoners. Popović and his transport unit were marching in the vicinity of Ivanjica, Serbia, when their column was overtaken by a German motorcycle. A German NCO, "stern in voice, but relaxed and polite," approached Popović and ordered him to head with his unit to nearby Arilje and surrender. When the German requested that Popović surrender his sidearm, the latter protested, saying he needed the gun to maintain discipline. The NCO seemed convinced by this argument and left. As soon as the Germans were out of sight, Popović "disbanded" his unit and every soldier returned home fully equipped. Aleksandar Nenadović, *Razgovori s Kočom* (Zagreb: Globus, 1989), pp. 34–36.

[39] Borković, *Kvislinška uprava*, Vol. I, p. 199.

[40] Veselin Đuretić, *Saveznici i jugoslovenska ratna drama* (Belgrade: Veselin Đuretić, 1988), Vol. I, p. 48. Milovan Đilas stated in an interview that he had estimated that the war would last no more than two to three months. His opinion was shared by the majority of his colleagues from the *Politburo*. Tito was more cautious; his estimate was six months. Television documentary *Jugoslavija u ratu 1941–1945* (Belgrade: Radiotelevizija Beograd, 1991–92), Episode 5.

the village of Jautina, outside of Valjevo. Just as they were beginning their job, they were surrounded by approximately thirty guerrillas. Two soldiers preparing a meal in a nearby house were warned by the homeowners, Mladen Mitrović and his wife, and escaped. The six remaining men were probably the first German prisoners taken by the Yugoslav Partisans.[41] What ensued highlights the initial confusion regarding what to do with German captives. It also lays bare the delusions about the true nature of this war, no doubt the result of the propaganda agenda of the KPJ prior to 22 June 1941. As evident from proclamations to Axis soldiers, such as the one from mid-May 1941, the Party stressed the class dimension of the conflict, calling upon the German soldiers not to fight for the "small clique of big capitalists, like Krupp, Siemens, Göring, and others."[42] Consequently, the reactionary officer class, and not the ordinary soldiers, was perceived as the real enemy. For this reason, the six soldiers in Jautina were let go after being made aware that the guerrillas were after their superiors—not them.[43]

As July was nearing its end, and as guerrilla actions inflicted the first casualties upon the German occupation forces, the various high commands attempted to formulate a strategy for combating the insurgents. The reports from the field indicated a "downright communist uprising" in the country carried out by an estimated 30,000 insurgents. Surprisingly, the heads of various German services were not overly anxious. It was noted that the majority of the Serbian population "were not swept up by the Communist wave," implying that the guerrillas lacked popular support.[44] As the German occupation forces stationed in Serbia were not trained for this type of warfare, their actions and reactions were bound to fail. This, in turn, only served the Communists, who were quick to exploit the propaganda value of any German blunder regardless of how small. Therefore, it was decided that the police (both German and Serbian) should be responsible for quelling the rebellion.[45] Pursuant to this, the Military Commander in Serbia communicated to the

---

[41] The Valjevo Partisan Detachment carried out this action. *Hronologija Narodnooslobodilačkog rata 1941–1945* (Belgrade: Vojno-istorijski institut, 1964), p. 64.

[42] Glišić, *Teror,* p. 321.

[43] NARA, T-315, Roll 2236, 000942–3, Report by Mladen Mitrović (12 July 1941) and Report on the capture of the wood-cutting party (17 July 1941). For two similar incidents in August, see Aleksandar Vitorović, *Srbija u Narodnooslobodilačkoj borbi: Centralna Srbija* (Belgrade: Nolit, 1967), pp. 78, 105.

[44] This conclusion was probably made on the basis of the numerical strength of the KPJ and its branches. The Party's influence on the population was, however, disproportionate to its size. Throughout the war, Communists would remain a minority in the ranks of the Partisans, and yet would wield absolute control. Despite the intelligence gathered and experience in the country, many high-ranking German officials would inexplicably use this erroneous reasoning for the entirety of the war.

[45] NARA, T-501, Roll 245, 000598–9, Political situation in Serbia (23 July 1941).

Ground Forces High Command (*Oberkommando des Heeres,* OKH) that additional reinforcements were not necessary.[46] The events of the following weeks were to prove this sentiment entirely wrong.

On the morning of 27 July 1941, two German police motorcycles were ambushed outside of Valjevo. One policeman was killed and an NCO was captured. The NCO, Corporal (*Rottwachtmeister*) Wilhelm Schmidt, was brought to the camp of the Valjevo Detachment. The members of the detachment's headquarters debated how to handle him and the decision was made to exchange him. The wife and daughter of the deputy commander of the detachment, Dragojlo Dudić, were in the Valjevo prison, as was the jurist and member of the KPJ's district committee for Valjevo, Stavatije Stanišić, whose wife was with the guerrillas and pleaded for his exchange. According to Rodoljub Čolaković, a high-ranking Communist official with the detachment, Dudić insisted that Stanišić, who was "more important to the cause," should be spared instead of his own spouse and daughter.[47] Schmidt was therefore ordered to write a letter to the *Feldkommandantur* stating he was well-treated and to plead to be exchanged for Stanišić.[48] Before the answer arrived, Schmidt and two other captured Germans escaped on the night of 16–17 August by exploiting the confusion caused by a sudden attack on the column with which they were marching.

Both sides had interesting experiences during their brief encounter. One noteworthy item in the report made by Schmidt after his escape pertains to the details of his treatment in captivity. In his own words, he was "not treated badly from the beginning," received the same food as "the bandits," and occasionally, even a few cigarettes. As the guerrillas were constantly on the march, he could not be isolated from the rest of the group. According to the detailed description he provided later on, it is evident that he had interacted daily with his captors, and that they made few attempts to conceal their activities from him. "That Sergeant [*sic*] Schmidt . . . has become tame lately. . . . He now tries to ingratiate himself with our supply officer [*ekonom*] Ratko, he bows humbly to every Partisan, and tries to pose as our friend," wrote Rudoljub Čolaković. It seems that Schmidt had tried to convince the

---

[46] NARA, T-314, Roll 1531, 000244, Commanding General in Serbia to Army High Command (3 August 1941).

[47] According to Dojčilo Mitrović, the author of *Srbija u Narodnooslobodilačkoj borbi: Zapadna Srbija* (Belgrade: Nolit, 1975), p. 97, guerrilla fighters of the Kolubara Company went on a prisoner hunt as soon as they learned Stanišić was captured. Stanišić died in a firefight on 20 August while still a German prisoner. Dudić's wife and daughter were incarcerated in various camps and prisons during the war and, miraculously, survived. Rade Poznanović et al., *Tragom izdaje: svedočenja o izdaji četnika i streljanju na Krušiku, u Valjevu 1941* (Valjevo: Lazar Ninković, 1987), p. 291.

[48] The letter is not to be found in the otherwise extensive documentation of the 704th Infantry Division preserved in the U.S. National Archives.

latter that he was a private, and not a corporal, thinking this would save his life. He added that his officers did not care about enlisted men and would not agree to the proposed exchange. He further pleaded with the guerrillas to let him go, and in return he would help them capture an officer whom they could then exchange for Stanišić. Once free, he promised that he would assist Stanišić while he was in prison and even help him to escape. By clumsily playing the "class card," Schmidt provided impetus to an unwanted reaction. Čolaković, who did not hide his contempt for these captured Germans in his memoirs, wrote: "That's the first time I realized that these people in field grey uniforms, who conquered the whole of Europe, do not have a shred of pride or ordinary human decency in them."[49]

This was the first attempted prisoner exchange between the two opposing forces in Serbia. Apart from minor details, the account is corroborated by contemporary documents, participants' memoirs, and the official Yugoslav historiography. However, such congruence in the records is an exception, rather than the rule, since the majority of local prisoner exchanges are clouded in varying degrees of controversy.

On 8 August 1941, in the village of Nevade just outside of Gornji Milanovac, elements of the Čačak Partisan Detachment ambushed a German vehicle, killing one occupant and capturing another, while a third managed to escape. A few days later, Gambert (the captured NCO) returned from his captivity. German and Yugoslav sources differ as to what happened between the 8th and Gambert's return. According to one contemporary report of the Čačak Partisan Detachment, the guerrillas offered to exchange the NCO for six of their comrades who were imprisoned in Gornji Milanovac, to which the Germans acquiesced.[50] The official monograph on the Čačak Detachment offers a slightly different story, indicating that the Germans reacted to the ambush by arresting forty people, including a KPJ member, Milutin Todorović Žica. They then began a series of reprisals, torching several houses, shooting a peasant, and capturing two Partisans. "Still, they were forced to negotiate and then to release the hostages in exchange for their NCO."[51] Čolaković recalled later that a village teacher had told him about the exchange in Gornji Milanovac, adding that the released NCO spoke publicly of his good treatment during captivity and was therefore transferred from the town.[52] Another version of

<hr>

[49] NARA, T-315, Roll 2237, 000371–4, Questioning of Wilhelm Schmidt and Heinrich Faßbender (19 August 1941); Rodoljub Čolaković, *Zapisi iz oslobodilačkog rata* (Sarajevo: Oslobođenje, 1985–86), Vol. I, pp. 78, 92–93.

[50] *Zbornik*/I/2/51–52, Čačak Partisan Detachment to Partisan Main HQ for Serbia (25 August 1941). The report gives "Maks Premel" as the name of the captive.

[51] Milojica Pantelić et al., *Čačanski narodno-oslobodilački partizanski odred "Dr. Dragiša Mišović"* (Čačak: Čačanski glas, 1982), p. 99.

[52] Čolaković, *Zapisi*, Vol. I, p. 137. The war diary of the Commanding General in Serbia noted that Gambert was "treated decently." NARA, T-501, Roll 246, War diary entry for 9 August 1941.

the events claims that the exchange took place, but that the Germans nevertheless burned several houses and killed a man who was hiding a cache of weapons in his home. The author adds that the mere fact that the Germans agreed to negotiate signaled that they acknowledged the Partisans as a regular army.[53] The available German sources do not make mention of an exchange. The daily report for 11 August 1941 merely states that the missing NCO was "released."[54] According to Franz Egger, a soldier stationed in Gornji Milanovac at the time, the release of the NCO was a consequence of the decision by his commander to shoot four captured "Communists."[55]

As previously mentioned, captured German soldiers were, on the whole, treated relatively well during the first month or so of the uprising. The same could not always be said about those *Volksdeutschen,* or ethnic Germans, living in Yugoslavia who were unfortunate enough to be taken captive.[56] They profited most from the occupation of the country and were integrated into the occupation system by serving as auxiliary policemen, interpreters, etc. For that reason, and due to the fact that only a small number of them joined the uprising, they were perceived as traitors and thus not protected by international law. On 8 August, the local branch of the KPJ lost three of its leading members in the town of Ćuprija. Two of them were recognized and shot on the street by the local ethnic Germans. The war diary of the Commanding General in Serbia for the same day notes that the bandits stopped a train near the town and shot several ethnic Germans. A day later, "the Communists issued an ultimatum (to whom and from whom is unknown) that if their captured comrades (who captured them and the location in which they were captured is unknown) were not released, they would shoot more ethnic Germans."[57] The attack on the train was carried out by a non-communist group led by Ilija Uzelac, who later became a Chetnik and fought the Partisans. It is unlikely that he would have issued an ultimatum in order to save the captured Communists. According to the Serbian *gendarmerie,* the Communist guerrillas did raid the mines in Sisevac and Senj on 9 and 11 August, and shot six people. According to the post-war Yugoslav historiography, the raids took place between 10–12 August, whereby at least nine ethnic Germans were captured and two were

---

[53] Mitrović, *Zapadna Srbija,* p. 110.

[54] NARA, T-501, Roll 246, Daily report for 11 August 1941.

[55] NARA, T-501, Roll 246, Interrogation of Franz Egger (22 October 1941).

[56] Ethnic Germans were the largest minority in the Kingdom of Yugoslavia, totaling nearly half a million people according to the census of 1931. By the beginning of the April War, the vast majority of them were members of the *Kulturbund,* a pro-Nazi organization with strong ties to Berlin. Tomasevich, *Occupation and Collaboration,* pp. 201–02.

[57] NARA, T-501, Roll 245, 000226, 228, War diary for August 1941 (Entry Nos. 168 and 175). The Germans, unaware of the rank of the three Serbs killed in Ćuprija, paid little attention to this incident.

executed, allegedly by mistake. There is, however, no mention of an ultimatum.[58] The Germans from Ćuprija retaliated the following day and executed several captured "bandits and their ringleaders" by hanging, the same method that the guerrillas had allegedly used on the captured ethnic Germans.[59]

In the interim, the Valjevo Detachment had captured another potentially valuable prisoner. Marko Babić, the mayor of Valjevo, along with his wife and a municipal cashier, were caught by the Partisans during an ambush on 20 August 1941. Not discouraged by the failed attempt to exchange Corporal Schmidt, the detachment decided to try to attempt an exchange again. Contemptuous of the Serbian collaborationist administration and knowing it had no real power, the guerrillas wanted to deal directly with the German town command (*Standortkommandantur*). The cashier, Vasilije Nožica, was released the same day with the message: "The communists want to offer the German *Wehrmacht* an exchange." The Partisans would release the mayor if the Germans would do the same for Milica Mešterović, mother-in-law of Dr. Pantić.[60] He added that the guerrillas were also looking for other prisoners to exchange for their comrades in the Valjevo prison. The town command immediately informed the intelligence section of the 704th Infantry Division, which in turn forwarded the matter to the Security Service (*Sicherheitsdienst,* or SD) in Belgrade, the agency responsible for the arrest of Mešterović.[61] Mayor Babić was not released immediately after capture, as suggested by some post-war publications.[62] The Germans in Valjevo were informed at the beginning of September that Babić had been seen in the town of Ub with Dr. Pantić. The

---

[58] *Zbornik*/I/21/31, 34, Overview of Partisan activities in August 1941 (Entries for 9 and 10 August 1941). Mitrović, *Zapadna Srbija,* p. 89; Boško Živanović et al., *Pomoravlje u Narodnooslobodilačkoj borbi 1941–1945* (Svetozarevo: Sreski odbor saveza boraca NOR-a, 1961), pp. 207–08.

[59] NARA, T-501, Roll 245, 000230, War diary for August 1941 (Entry No. 181). The Partisans in Vojvodina, home to the majority of the Yugoslav ethnic Germans, showed more prudence in dealing with captured ethnic Germans. In late August 1941, they captured a local German official outside Kikinda and had him exchanged for a relative of one of their comrades on 22 August. Đorđe Momčilović, *Kako do brigade: Trinaesta vojvođanska udarna brigada* (Kikinda: Odbor za negovanje tradicija Trinaeste vojvođanske udarne brigade, 1979), p. 120.

[60] Dr. Miša Pantić, the chief medical officer of the Valjevo Detachment, was killed in early 1942.

[61] NARA, T-315, Roll 2237, 000316–18, 321, Specific occurrences (22 August 1941); Intelligence section report (23 August 1941); Additional statement by municipal cashier, Vasilije Nožica (24 August 1941); Report by Vasilije Nožica and Milan Milošević (22 August 1941).

[62] Milosav Bojić, *Posavski partizanski odred: Posavina i Tamnava u oružanom ustanku* (Belgrade: Vojnoizdavački i novinski centar, 1987), pp. 123–24.

planned exchange never materialized and on the night of 6–7 September, he was released by his captors.[63]

By mid-August, the situation in Serbia had deteriorated to a point that required a fundamental revision of the previous directives pertaining to counter-insurgency efforts. The order concerning the exclusive use of police for fighting the guerrillas was thus rescinded only three weeks after it had been issued. Each of the three divisions were now given operational areas, and each of their battalions was ordered to undertake anti-guerrilla operations whenever necessary, using platoon/company-sized "hunting groups" (*Jagdkommandos*). Other measures included the withdrawal of Serbian *gendarmerie* from the countryside into the regional centers and the introduction of a convoy system;[64] however, these efforts resulted in no discernable improvement in the security situation, as evident in the letter written on 28 August by General Paul Bader, commander of the 65th Higher Command, to the *Wehrmacht* Commander Southeast (*Wehrmachtsbefehlshaber Südost*). After listing the tremendous difficulties three under-equipped occupation divisions had in trying to stamp out the fires of resistance, the general requested reinforcements of men, tanks, and motorized vehicles.[65]

At the same time, the German occupation forces suffered a series of defeats in Serbia which exposed the fragile nature of the occupation system. On 31 August 1941, the Chetnik detachment of Lieutenant Colonel Veselin Misita stormed the town of Loznica on the Drina River and took ninety-three German prisoners. Other German outposts in Western Serbia, such as Banja Koviljača, Stolice, and Bogatić, were also raided. On 1 September, a large insurgent force, including elements of the Valjevo Detachment, encircled the town of Krupanj, which was secured by two companies of the 724th Infantry Regiment. The next day, a courier brought the following ultimatum to the Germans who had barricaded themselves in the hospital building: "I summon the commander to surrender the garrison by 21.00. . . . If you do not accept, all the Germans will be massacred. . . . Terms: lay down your arms, in which case I vouch for the lives of German soldiers until the end of the war."[66] It was signed by 1st Lieutenant Ratko Martinović who,

---

[63] NARA, T-315, Roll 2237, 001016, 1058, Intelligence section report (6 September 1941), Special leader [*Sonderführer*] Baumann (10 September 1941). According to an eyewitness report, Mešterović was still in the Valjevo prison in early December 1941. Poznanović et al., *Tragom izdaje*, p. 292.

[64] NARA, T-501, Roll 246, Combat against communist bands (13 August 1941); Transcript of 65th Higher Command, Operations section, No. 406/41 (14 August 1941); Operations section, No. 384/41 (17 August 1941).

[65] NARA, T-314, Roll 1531, 000244, Cable to 12th Army/Wehrmacht Commander Southeast (28 August 1941).

[66] NARA, T-315, Roll 2237, 001338, Translation of the ultimatum to Krupanj (6 September 1941).

in conjunction with an orthodox priest from Krupanj, Vlado Zečević, led the "independent" Chetnik units in the siege of the town.[67] The offer was turned down and on 4 September, the Germans attempted to break out with the support of Stuka aircraft, but they did not get far—the column was forced to stop and surrender just outside the town.[68]

No less than 173 German soldiers were captured with their equipment at Krupanj. Altogether, the German forces suffered a total of 414 KIAs, WIAs, and MIAs in the first week of September.[69] The news of the events in Western Serbia hit Berlin like a bombshell and finally drew Hitler's attention to the brewing unrest in the Balkans. On 16 September 1941, the infamous Directive 31a was issued. The 342nd Infantry Division, a front line unit, was made ready for transfer to Serbia, as were other, smaller units. All counter-insurgency efforts were to be directed by General Franz Böhme, the commander of the 18th Mountain Corps. Field Marshal Wilhelm Keitel issued a separate order which expounded upon the *Führer's* instruction that the uprising must be quelled with the harshest means available. Consequently, fifty to 100 hostages were to be executed for each German soldier killed.[70]

In the interim, the insurgents had to consider how to manage the large number of German prisoners. There were rumors that the guerrillas wanted to exchange them at the rate of one German for 100 Serbs.[71] On 21 September, the Partisans tasked one of the captives, Private Schaarschmidt, to compile a list of all prisoners in order to "commence exchange negotiations." The captured Germans believed it was composed for the sole purpose of deceiving them since the alleged exchange never materialized. Some Partisan veterans recalled attempts to contact the

---

[67] There were three types of Chetniks in Serbia at that time. Besides Mihailović Chetniks, there were also Chetniks led by Kosta Pećanac, the head of the pre-war "Chetnik Organization" and the leader of the so-called "Toplica Uprising" against the Bulgarians in 1917. On 27 August 1941, he called upon the population to obey the occupiers and put his men at the disposal of the Germans. Additionally, there were armed groups which called themselves Chetniks without clear affiliation with either of the two leaders. While Lieutenant Colonel Misita was Mihailović's man, Martinović and Zečević belonged to the third group and co-operated closely with the Partisans. Ostracized by the nationalists, they eventually went over to the former, both ending the war as high-level officials of the "Second Yugoslavia."

[68] For a detailed description of the events from the German perspective, see NARA, T-315, Roll 2237, 001101–4, Report on the breakout from Krupanj on 4 September 1941 (6 September 1941). For the Yugoslav view, see Martinović, *Od Ravne Gore*, pp. 277–89.

[69] NARA, T-501, Roll 246, Daily report for 9 September 1941.

[70] For the wording of the so-called "Keitel Order," see NARA, T-314, Roll 1531, 000097–8, Communist uprising in the conquered territories (16 September 1941).

[71] NARA, T-314, Roll 1531, 001053, Dr. Keidel: Report on the fighting in Krupanj, his time in captivity, and his escape to Bjeljina, Croatia (undated).

German garrison in Valjevo on this matter, but that these efforts failed because the soldiers did not want to talk to "bandits."[72] There is no mention of this offer in the available German documents; however, at about this same time, the Germans noted that the Partisans wanted to capture all of the Valjevo defenders in order to exchange them later.[73]

The Partisans were aware of the propaganda value of the prisoners they used to clear away the rubble in Krupanj and forced to attend Communist rallies, thereby showing the population that the Germans were not invincible. On the whole, the prisoners were treated well, apart from the cramped living conditions at the outset of their captivity. One of the prisoners made a request to a political commissar that they be treated according to international law. The fact that the Partisans granted his request was intended to show that they treated their prisoners in the same manner as would a lawful belligerent power in order to gain reciprocal recognition as such by their enemies.[74]

The Partisans were not alone in attempting to use prisoners to further their political aims. Mihailović's Chetniks, who together with the Partisans were besieging the town of Šabac, used prisoners as a pretext for establishing contact with the German occupation forces. In a series of conciliatory letters, they offered to return some of the wounded prisoners, simultaneously underscoring the fact that they were not the same as the Communists and that they desired an armistice. Indeed, the Chetniks released eight German wounded to the Šabac garrison on 20 September 1941.[75] These were some of the earliest ominous signs of a rift

---

[72] NARA, T-315, Roll 2239, 000642, Report by the members of the former 10th Company, 724th Infantry Regiment on time spent in captivity (undated); Vojin Đurašinović Kostja, "Partizanska država," in *Užička republika: Zbornik sećanja* (Užice: Narodni muzej-Muzej ustanka 1941, 1981), Vol. I, p. 223.

[73] NARA, T-315, Roll 2237, 000856, Testimony of the student Dragoljub Žarić (22 September 1941).

[74] NARA, T-315, Roll 2239, 000637, Testimony of NCO Pfüler (undated). The Germans, of course, refused to recognize the Partisans as lawful belligerents. The United States Military Tribunal V in Nuremberg, which tried a number of high-ranking German commanders from the Balkans in the so-called "Hostage Case" in 1947, found that the Yugoslav Partisans, on the whole, did not meet the requirements of the Geneva Convention. In 1959, a paper prepared by the United States Army Judge Advocate General's School pointed to flaws in court procedures, such as a lack of Yugoslav witnesses and documentary materials. The paper did not question the tribunal's verdict, but questioned instead its value as a possible precedent. *A Treatise on the Juridical Basis of the Distinction Between Lawful Combatant and Unprivileged Belligerent* (Charlottesville, VA: Judge Advocate General's School, 1959), pp. 61–63, 78–81.

[75] NARA, T-312, Roll 460, Daily report for 20 September 1941. For more on Chetnik-German correspondence around Šabac, see Dragoslav Parmaković, *Mačvanski partizanski odred* (Šabac: Fond narodnooslobodilačke borbe Podrinja, 1973), pp. 425–28. The Germans

between the two resistance movements—a rift which would develop into an open confrontation some six weeks later.[76]

Keeping prisoners of war was a characteristic of a regular army, which the Partisans strove to be. The original plan of action drawn up in July called for the creation of small units whose main activities would be small-scale in nature, such as sabotage and assassination. Tito was wary of enemy strength and did not want to begin the general uprising before the circumstances became favorable, i.e. before the Red Army was within striking distance of Yugoslavia.[77] The course of events over the next few weeks made him revise this strategy. The weak collaborationist apparatus was brought to the verge of collapse by repeated attacks and the liberation of vast tracts of territory, while the Germans barricaded themselves in the towns, a sign of weakness which did not go unnoticed by the population. Inspired by these signs of success, Tito decided to accelerate the intensity of the actions against the occupier and broaden the base of the resistance. On 10 August 1941, *Bulletin* No. 1 of the Main Partisan Headquarters announced the guidelines for the armed struggle which unequivocally stated that the Partisan detachments were open to all patriots and not just Communists.[78] Although cautioned by the Comintern to concentrate solely on the anti-occupation struggle and leave the revolution

---

toyed with the idea of retrieving their captured men from the Chetniks via unofficial contacts. A document dated 10 September states that the "Chetnik leaders should be advised to release these men." A handwritten note was added: "Captain Račić [Chetnik commander at Šabac] allegedly has 160 German prisoners from Loznica . . . General Nedić [was] already contacted, [and] he said he had already tried to achieve their release." NARA, T-501, Roll 246, Operations section (10 September 1941). Milan Nedić (1877–1946) was made Serbian Prime Minister on 29 August and was tasked with forming a government to replace the Commissary Council. The first contacts between him and Mihailović's emissaries took place in Belgrade between 29 August and 6 September 1941. Miodrag Zečević, *Dokumenti sa suđenja Ravnogorskom pokretu 10. juni–15. juli 1946* (Belgrade: SUBNOR Jugoslavije, 2001), pp. 178–79. The correspondence between the Cer Chetniks under Račić and German commands continued for at least two more weeks. The Commanding General in Serbia cabled to the 342nd Infantry Division on 4 October: "Answer to Chetnik leader: return the German prisoners; name the date and place; surrender your weapons, in which case, full amnesty." NARA, T-501, Roll 250, Cable to 342nd Infantry Division (4 October 1941).

[76] Mihailović and his Chetniks began to play an active part in the uprising in September. The string of Partisan successes and the growing public support they enjoyed as a result forced Mihailović into action. He stated this was his main motive to German officers in November 1941. Tomasevich, *The Chetniks*, p. 145; Jovan Marjanović, *Draža Mihailović između Nemaca i Britanaca* (Zagreb: Globus, 1979), p. 156.

[77] Milovan Djilas, *Wartime* (New York: Harcourt Brace Jovanovich, 1977), p. 8.

[78] For the full text of the *Bulletin,* see *Zbornik*/II/1/11–18, Bulletin No. 1 of the Main Headquarters of People's Liberation Partisan Detachments (10 August 1941).

for the post-war period,[79] the KPJ pursued the revolutionary agenda from the beginning of the uprising. The People's Liberation Councils were originally formed in the Partisan-held regions as bodies tasked with supplying the Partisan units. Soon, however, they took over administration of the civilian population on the whole, replacing the old municipality system which had already been shattered by guerrilla attacks. Just as these bodies were considered legitimate expressions of the popular desire to break with the previous system of government, the Partisan detachments represented the army of the new Yugoslavia.

On 26 September 1941, Tito held a meeting with the *Politburo* and Partisan commanders from across the country in the West Serbian village of Stolice. The decisions taken here went a step further in the process of regularization within the Partisan forces. The Main Headquarters of the People's Liberation Partisan Detachments of Yugoslavia was renamed Supreme Headquarters, with each province in turn receiving its own Main Headquarters. The units were to be commanded by a trio consisting of a commander, his deputy, and a political commissar. The time had arrived for a wholesale popular uprising and the recruitment base was ordered to be widened as much as possible. The detachment remained the basic unit of the Partisan army, although two or more of these could be grouped for large-scale actions. Detachments were to be divided into battalions, companies, and platoons, and a further strengthening of discipline was ordered. The Partisan salute with the clenched fist was officially introduced, as was the official insignia consisting of a red star and an appropriate national tricolor (Serbian/Croatian, etc.).[80] Efforts to build up a regular army and to be recognized as such by both friend and foe would continue to play a very important role in the overall strategy of the KPJ. Similarly to what the Partisans strove to achieve in Serbia, keeping prisoners and treating them according to international law was aimed at earning recognition as a lawful belligerent.

The fall of Krupanj and the majority of the surrounding area was just the beginning of a massive surge of guerrilla activity in the whole of Serbia, save the Banat. All German district commands sent frantic reports throughout September regarding the wave of sabotage aimed at cutting off garrisons and the supply of raw materials, or about the attacks on German units and the Serbian *gendarmerie*.[81] Arilje and Ivanjica were evacuated on the 18th and Čajetina on 20 September, which made the German hold on Užice and Požega untenable—both towns were evacuated a day later. Gornji Milanovac fell on 29 September, followed by Čačak on 1 October; Kruševac was attacked on 23 September, and Šabac on 22–24 September; Valjevo was blockaded throughout the first half of September; and

---

[79] Petranović, *Istorija Jugoslavije,* Vol. II, p. 153.

[80] *Vojna enciklopedija* (Belgrade: Vojnoizdavački zavod, 1973), Vol. V, p. 773.

[81] See NARA, T-501, Roll 246, Situation reports by FK 809 Niš and FK 816 Užice, and, to a lesser extent, FK 610 Pančevo and FK 509 Belgrade (8 and 18 September 1941).

Kraljevo was under siege from 10 October to 1 November. The insurgents had thereby gained control of two-thirds of occupied Serbia with the exception of the urban centers. It is estimated that at this point the Partisans had around 14,000 fighters divided into twenty-three detachments.[82]

There are several events during this period which deserve to be examined in greater detail. The first two episodes took place at the beginning of September around Jagodina. On 1 September, a train was stopped between Ćuprija and Paraćin and three German soldiers were captured. Along with a fifth columnist from the same train, they were shot on 5 September. The Yugoslav historiography does not give an explanation as to why the captives were executed. It is noteworthy that the Partisan unit that carried out the attack (Paraćin-Ćuprija Company of the Pomoravlje Detachment) lost its commander on 29 August after a trial, which accused him of dereliction of duty—among other charges, he had freed some captured *gendarmes*. It is therefore possible that the new commander wanted to avoid his predecessor's grim fate (execution by firing squad) by demonstrating toughness in dealing with captured enemies.[83] Three days after the execution of the Axis prisoners, another company of the same detachment ambushed a convoy on the Kragujevac–Ćuprija road, killing three and capturing seven Germans, including a doctor. They dispatched a letter to the *Feldkommandantur* in Niš requesting a similar number of their own in exchange for the captives. As no answer was forthcoming, six prisoners were shot. "The doctor was given the choice of joining us or staying with his compatriots," reads the official monograph of the Pomoravlje region, and admits candidly: "Since he chose to stay, and remained in solidarity with the others, he was shot as well."[84]

---

[82] The taking of strategically located towns was devised at a meeting of Partisan detachment commanders on 16 September in order to link-up the "liberated territories" of Central and Western Serbia. *Oslobodilački rat naroda Jugoslavije* (Belgrade: Vojnoistorijski institut JNA, 1957–1965), Vol. I, pp. 57–58. The strength of Mihailović's Chetniks in September is hard to ascertain, but the Germans estimated it at several thousand men. NARA, T-315, Roll 2238, 000251–2, Estimate of insurgents' strength in Serbia (22 September 1941).

[83] NARA, T-501, Roll 246, Daily report for 2 September 1941; Živanović et al., *Pomoravlje*, p. 214–15. One German managed to escape, which induced both the executioner and the company commissar to do the same, fearing possible punishment.

[84] The German sources reported eleven, rather than ten, KIAs and MIAs resulting from this incident. NARA, T-501, Roll 246, Daily report for 11 September 1941; Živanović et al., *Pomoravlje*, p. 178. Such candidness was rare in the official historiography, even for the books appearing at the end of the socialist period. Even more remarkably, the monograph in question was published in 1961. The 714th Division found the bodies of seven men, "including a doctor belonging to the OT," near Ćuprija in early December. NARA, T-315, Roll 2258, 000076, Intelligence Summary for the period 20 November–4 December 1941 (5 December 1941). "OT" is an abbreviation of *Organisation Todt*, an organization tasked with military engineering both in Germany and in the occupied territories.

The German reports from that period do not mention the exchange offer. Either the letter never made it to the city or the *Feldkommandantur* chose to disregard the offer. The latter, indeed, may have been the case as several days earlier, on 5 September 1941, Field Marshal Wilhelm List, *Wehrmacht* Commander Southeast, had issued an order which strictly prohibited both surrendering and negotiating with the insurgents.[85] The *Feldkommandantur* in Niš did contact its superiors in Belgrade in connection with captive guerrillas on 8 September. It informed the Commanding General in Serbia that it did not carry out the shooting of fifteen to twenty Communists for fear of reprisals. Ten German soldiers were known to have been captured in the area in the first week of September and the local military authorities feared for their lives if the captive Partisans were shot. The district command added that it would send all Partisan prisoners from Jagodina that it had in its custody to the regiment in Ćuprija so that they could carry out reprisals for the "murder of the German soldiers at Jagodina."[86] The quote is probably referring to the Germans killed in the ambush on 8 September since, according to a Yugoslav document dated 12 September, the Partisans were still waiting for an answer to their exchange offer.[87]

On the whole, the tone of the report from Niš was unusual for the German commands in Serbia in 1941, which reflected the (relatively) civilized character of the local district commander, Colonel Karl *Freiherr* von Bothmer.[88] The German occupation forces did not generally react to threats made against their captured personnel. The September double issue of the official *Bulletin* of the Supreme Partisan HQ (published on 1 October) carried the proclamation that the German and collaborationist authorities were arresting, torturing, and murdering Serbs in

---

[85] NARA, T-501, Roll 246, Quelling the Serbian insurgency (5 September 1941). The main purpose of the order was to prevent further mass surrenders, such as that in Krupanj, from occuring again.

[86] NARA, T-501, Roll 249, 000735, Shooting of Hostages (8 September 1941).

[87] See the report by Petar Stambolić which mentions the exchange request and the intention to execute the captives if the exchange does not take place. *Zbornik*/I/1/120, Report by KPJ Instructor for Pomoravlje region (12 September 1941).

[88] Karl *Freiherr* von Bothmer (1880–1947) became known for his letter from early August to the Commanding General in Serbia in which he voiced his protest against the randomness of reprisals in general and stated his refusal to pass a death sentence without a proper investigation. NARA, T-501, Roll 249, 000740, Hand grenade attack on the Park Hotel in Niš on 3 August 1941 (6 August 1941). Bothmer was extradited in 1947 to Yugoslavia to stand trial for crimes committed by the occupation forces in the Niš area. As he was the district commander there until 1943, he was pronounced guilty for numerous executions which took place in that period and sentenced to death by firing squad. Đorđe N. Lopičić, ed., *Nemački ratni zločini 1941–1945* (Belgrade: Muzej žrtava genocida, 2009), p. 57, Verdict of Harald Turner and others (7 March 1947).

Belgrade and other locations in the country on a daily basis. "Herewith, we declare that from now on we shall consider as hostages countless spies, fifth columnists, and hundreds of German prisoners in our custody. Ten of these will be shot for each killed Partisan or arrested anti-fascist."[89] The *Bulletin* added that eight "German fascists" had already been shot for the torching of some villages in the vicinity of Valjevo, without providing further details. This proclamation was meant as a threat rather than the genesis of a new policy toward the captured Germans. There is no evidence that the Partisans ever carried out reprisals along the lines proclaimed in the aforementioned *Bulletin*. The execution of the eight Germans might have been carried out as an example or was meant for propaganda purposes. As evident from the quoted sources, the manner in which prisoners were handled depended more on individual commanders and circumstances on the ground than on a prescribed set of policies.

The "no negotiations" order issued by List was far more likely to be obeyed in the second largest city in Serbia than in the interior of the country. Battalions, sometimes fifty or more kilometers distant from each other, had a nearly impossible task of securing every strategic point and line of communication in their operational areas. They rarely fought as a cohesive unit, and were divided into several small garrisons, usually of company strength, always encircled in one form or another. In such an atmosphere of isolation, these units had to learn to fend for themselves and, in the process, sometimes interpret orders on their own.

The town of Veliko Gradište on the Danube was attacked by the Partisans and the Chetniks on 20 September 1941. Its garrison consisted of only twelve German customs officials and members of the Water Protection Police (*Wasserschutzpolizei*), assisted by sixty-five Serbian customs officials and *gendarmes*. The Germans barricaded themselves in their headquarters, holding out for five hours after the attack began. Once it became apparent that their situation was hopeless, they agreed to the Partisans' offer to leave the town unmolested in exchange for their weapons. One policeman was allowed to cross the Danube in a row boat to acquire a larger vessel that could hold his comrades; however, before he returned, the Partisans changed their minds—they took the remaining Germans prisoner, loaded them onto two trucks, and shipped them to their base at Rabrovo, some twenty-two kilometers distant.

The Germans were soon joined by their colleague who had returned with a boat to collect them and who was captured again. They were treated well and subjected to only a brief interrogation—the Partisans were keen to find out if there were officers among them. Around 10.00 on 21 September, one of the captives, Peter Strüder, was chosen to accompany a Partisan envoy to nearby Požarevac in order to negotiate with the Germans. Instead of going to Požarevac, they

---

[89] *Zbornik*/II/2/83, Bulletin Nos. 7 and 8 of the Main Headquarters of People's Liberation Partisan Detachments (1 October 1941).

returned to Veliko Gradište, which had been reoccupied by German units. They met with Lieutenant Buschmann of the Water Protection Police and informed him of the Partisan terms: reprisals against the population of Veliko Gradište, Rabrovo, Kučevo, and Golubac must not be undertaken; twenty to thirty recently arrested political prisoners in Požarevac must be freed; and prisoners must not be harmed. Buschmann agreed to the first point, but declined the other two. He instead offered the exchange of prisoners on a ratio of one-to-one, adding that aircraft would bomb Veliko Gradište if the German prisoners were not released by 16.00.

The envoys returned to Rabrovo with the news. The Partisan command demanded that the terms be put in writing, which was conveyed to Buschmann when the negotiators returned to Veliko Gradište for the second time that day. He agreed, but before the negotiators could travel to Rabrovo once more, a *Wehrmacht* officer intervened, saying the terms were unacceptable. As a result, further negotiations were canceled; Strüder was taken across the Danube to Rumania; and the Partisan envoy was shot. The Germans pulled out of the town, which was bombed soon afterwards.[90]

The willingness of Lieutenant Buschmann to defy his standing orders and accept negotiations in order to free his fellow officers of the Water Protection Police came to naught. The authority in this matter was in the hands of the unnamed *Wehrmacht* officer who, obviously, saw no reason to disregard the order prohibiting negotiations with the guerrillas. In the grand scheme of things, he should not be the only one blamed for short-sightedness and rigidity. The Communist Party's local branch assured its superiors that "the negotiations were initiated without our approval and we have criticized it sternly." In the same report, the authors wrote that the negotiations broke down because the two sides could not agree on the extent of territory for which the Germans would "guarantee security."[91] This detail was not mentioned in Buschmann's report but would nonetheless explain the decision of the army officer to cut the talks short. If indeed this was the case, and if the Party insisted that the prisoner exchange was dependent upon agreement to these conditions, then the words of Moma Marković, written almost half a century after the events, make sense: "The detachment's HQ agreed to negotiate, but I objected to it. When I later heard of secret negotiations . . . between our [command] and [the] German high [command], I remembered my own narrow

---

[90] NARA, T-501, Roll 246, Report on the Attack on Veliko Gradište by Peter Strüder (23 September 1941). In addition to the slain envoy, the German relief force shot another twenty-four "bandits" captured along the way. NARA, T-501, Roll 246, Activity report of the Water Protection Police for the period 15 August–24 September 1941 (Entry for 20–23 September 1941).

[91] *Zbornik*/I/1/129–30, Report by the KPJ district committee for Požarevac (21 September 1941).

view of negotiating with the enemy, and the lost opportunity to save at least some of the arrested comrades in this way."[92]

Although the negotiations were unsuccessful, the mere fact that the Germans agreed to talk to the Partisans on an equal footing was perceived as potentially valuable propaganda. Consequently, Tito had no qualms about publishing the news about the events in Veliko Gradište in the *Bulletin* of the Supreme Headquarters, adding that German offers were rejected out of hand.[93]

On 28 September 1941, the German column coming from Kraljevo to Čačak was ambushed at the town's outskirts. Apart from one captured truck, the German occupation forces also lost three men to the local Partisans. A letter was sent to the German command in Čačak proposing an exchange of the three captured soldiers for a number of hostages held in the town's prison. The local command responded immediately: "Since the German armed forces are leading an uncompromising struggle against communism, the offer is refused." Two days later, the captured Germans were brought before a tribunal, and consequently shot. This was done in response to the execution of a wounded Partisan, Damjan Matović, several days earlier.[94]

The 6th Company of the 920th *Landesschützen* Battalion had been garrisoned in the town of Gornji Milanovac since the beginning of July. As it turned out, the unit found itself in the heart of the guerrilla-infested region of Central Serbia. The town was effectively cut off from the rest of the country by frequent sabotage on the rails and roads leading to it; therefore, at the end of September it was decided that the company should evacuate Gornji Milanovac and join the garrison in Kraljevo. On 26 September 1941, a peasant warned the company about an impending attack, which came three days later when elements of the Takovo Chetnik and Čačak Partisan detachments entered the town. The *Landesschützen* maintained a resolute defense, turning down a surrender ultimatum issued to them after two hours of fighting. Realizing that their position was not likely to improve, they were more willing to listen to the second Chetnik envoy, which appeared half an hour

---

[92] Slavko Odić and Slavko Komarica, *Partizanska obavještajna služba 1941–1942: šta se stvarno događalo* (Zagreb: Centar za informacije i publicitet, 1988), Vol. III, p. 147. Momčilo-Moma Marković (1912–1992) was an instructor of the Central Committee of the KPJ for the Požarevac district, making him the highest Party authority there. Almost exactly half a year later, a German informant, Franz Ketčeg, denounced a Chetnik named Boško Šarunac for taking part in the capture of "nine Water Protection policemen in Veliko Gradište" who were later shot. The report does not mention when the execution took place. NARA, T-315, Roll 2243, 00618, Intelligence section, Report by Franz Ketčeg (25 March 1942).

[93] *Zbornik*/II/2/97, Bulletin Nos. 10 and 11 of the Main Headquarters of People's Liberation Partisan Detachments (1 October 1941).

[94] NARA, T-315, Roll 2262, 000187, 205, War diary entries for 28 September and 1 October 1941; Pantelić et al., *Čačanski NOPO*, pp. 133–34. According to Pantelić, the ambush took place on the 27th.

later. He guaranteed safe conduct to Čačak if the company would leave the town on the same day. "920th *Landesschützen* Battalion has evacuated Gornji Milanovac with honor," reported the company commander, Captain Zerlacher. Furthermore, he requested that the town and its inhabitants be spared from any possible reprisals for they had behaved loyally throughout the fighting.[95] The guerrilla offer, however, turned out to be a ruse. Knowing the Germans were far more likely to talk with the Nationalists than with the Communists, the Partisans allowed the Chetniks to conduct the negotiating in order to lure the garrison out of the town.[96] Three kilometers from Gornji Milanovac, the 6th Company was surrounded by the guerrillas who demanded its immediate surrender—the Germans had little choice but to comply. The material spoils were divided in half between the two guerrilla movements, while the sixty-two prisoners went to the Chetniks. After clearing rubble in Čačak over the following days, the prisoners were sent first to Ravna Gora, and then to Požega.[97]

By 17.35 on 29 September, the Commanding General in Serbia was getting anxious regarding the whereabouts of the 6th Company, cabling to Kraljevo: "Report immediately if the *Landesschützen* from Gornji Milanovac arrived."[98] As the company continued to be missing, a reconnaissance flight was authorized but failed to spot any movement in the town. On 1 October, 3rd Battalion of the 749th Infantry Regiment from Kraljevo was tasked with breaking through to Gornji Milanovac. If the 6th Company was not encountered there, the population should be taken hostage and the town razed.[99] The battalion started its advance on 5 October, fighting its way along the 40km road to Gornji Milanovac and taking casualties in the process. Once the battalion arrived, it gathered all of the male inhabitants it could hunt down, approximately 120–70 men. Among these hostages was a Chetnik commander who was scheduled to meet his superiors the next day. Captain Fiedler, the commanding officer, hoped to use this man to contact the Chetnik command to "exchange the hostages for the captured *Landesschützen* . . . because he thought this was the ultimate objective of the whole action." Fiedler also did not torch the town for fear this would diminish the chances of a positive response to the exchange offer. In the meantime, an SOS call was raised from nearby Rudnik

---

[95] NARA, T-501, Roll 250, 000983–4, Report by Franz Egger (22 October 1941) and 001003, Message from Gornji Milanovac (29 September 1941).

[96] Pantelić et al., *Čačanski NOPO*, pp. 131–32.

[97] Ibid., p. 158; NARA, T-501, Roll 246, Daily report for 3 October 1941. Both Egger and Franz Kleinod (who had been captured on 4 October in Stragari and thereafter joined the prisoners from Gornji Milanovac) confirmed that they were treated well during their captivity. NARA, T-501, Roll 250, 000986–7, Report by Franz Kleinod (22 October 1941).

[98] NARA, T-501, Roll 250, 001011, Message to "Leichtsinn" (29 September 1941).

[99] NARA, T-501, Roll 246, War diary entry for 1 October 1941.

where another German unit was embroiled in heavy fighting with the guerrillas. Fiedler decided to direct his battalion there to relieve the hard-pressed unit. Assuming he would have to go through Gornji Milanovac on his way back, he decided to postpone the taking of hostages and the burning of the town until his return from Rudnik. Contrary to Fiedler's expectations, the battalion was ordered to Kragujevac immediately thereafter, which meant that its original mission could not be fulfilled. After a brief pause in Kragujevac (10–14 October),[100] the battalion was ordered to Gornji Milanovac again and tasked with rounding up hostages. It reached the town on 15 October, but now only forty people could be arrested—the people who "held out" waiting for the Germans to return. Gornji Milanovac was then razed to the ground.[101] This time, attempts to exchange the hostages were not made as they were needed for a much more sinister purpose elsewhere.

Quelling the Uprising: September–December 1941

Hitler's order of 16 September marked the beginning of a massive German effort to crush the rebellion in Serbia. Even before the order was issued, the reinforced 125th Infantry Regiment arrived from Greece and began operating in Western Serbia in the vicinity of Valjevo. The main push began on 23 September when three regiments of the 342nd Infantry Division started crossing the Sava River in order to raise the siege of Šabac and eliminate the insurgents from the Mačva region. This operation was marked by acts of extreme brutality toward the civilian population. The division issued a proclamation ordering the deportation of every male between sixteen and sixty-five years of age to the detention camp at Šabac. Those who did not respond to the call, or those who were caught wandering in the open, were shot; the mere suspicion of an affiliation with the guerrillas was enough to warrant execution. By 20 October, the division had shot some 4,000 people and deported another 21,500, the vast majority of whom were innocent civilians.[102]

---

[100] NARA, T-315, Roll 2262, 000213–4, 218, War diary entries for 5–6 and 10 October 1941; NARA, T-315, Roll 2238, 000086–8, To Commanding General in Serbia (10 October 1941). Chief of the General Staff of the 65th Higher Command, Colonel Erich Kewisch, commended Captain Fiedler in his report for his overall conduct. This implies that the higher authorities did not always insist on a strict interpretation of Field Marshal List's order of 5 September, which forbade any negotiating with the guerrillas.

[101] NARA, T-501, Roll 246, To FK 610 Pančevo (20 October 1941). One other report says the number of hostages was 133, but this may include people captured from the villages situated along the road to Kragujevac. NARA, T-314, Roll 1531, 000173, Report for the period 10–19 October 1941 (20 October 1941).

[102] Schmider, *Partisanenkrieg,* p. 71. The majority of these executions were carried out before the infamous rule of 1:100 became official policy. Schmider concludes that this rule, ironically, brought some moderation to the indiscriminate terror practiced by the 342nd Infantry Division in Mačva.

The reason the 3rd Battalion of the 749th Infantry Regiment did not seek a prisoner exchange when it arrived in Gornji Milanovac for the second time was probably due to the order issued by General Franz Böhme on 8 October. This order was very similar to the one signed by Field Marshal List on 5 September, and it was issued with the same intent. Just as the surrender of Krupanj had provided the stimulus for List's order, the capture of the *Landesschützen* outside of Gornji Milanovac caused Böhme to issue his order in October stating that all units of the *Wehrmacht* were prohibited from negotiating with the insurgents. Furthermore, it stipulated that guerrilla envoys did not warrant the protection of international law, and were to be shot (or shot at) whenever encountered.[103] Though similar in content to List's order, Böhme's order was actually followed more closely because he had the necessary means of ensuring that his instructions were carried out—one extra division already in the field and a second scheduled to arrive in the near future. Furthermore, he intended to "intensify" the already bloody counter-insurgency, making it a total war against the guerrillas and the Serbian population. The war would be fought with unprecedented brutality until one of the opponents was utterly defeated—surrender would not be an option for either side.

Even before the "Keitel Order," which called for the execution of up to 100 Serbs for every German killed and fifty for each German wounded, was officially issued to the divisions on 10 October 1941, Böhme put his plan into operation. On 2 October, a convoy belonging to the 521st Army Communications Regiment (*Armee-Nachrichten-Regiment*) was ambushed by the 1st Šumadija Partisan Detachment not far from the town of Topola: "Bandits have arranged the attack in such a way that the column received fire from three sides at once. Before the convoy came to a halt, it had already suffered casualties. In the following firefight, a coordinated defense was not possible since the bandits were firing from well-built positions. The convoy was destroyed. . . ."[104]

One officer, 1st Lieutenant Lehr, was among the Germans who were captured. Fearing the worst, he approached the guerrilla commander and offered to organize an exchange of his men for captured Communists in Belgrade. The commander simply replied "No!" Lehr tried again, offering safe conduct to Belgrade for the Partisan commander so that he could organize the exchange himself. Lehr added that the Partisans could get ten Serbs for one German. The new propositions were turned down "brusquely."[105] At that moment, a Partisan courier arrived with the message that a second German convoy was approaching. Upon hearing this, the

---

[103] NARA, T-501, Roll 250, 001296, Negotiating with insurgents (8 October 1941). In pursuance of this order, the Germans shot two Partisan envoys who demanded the surrender of the garrison in Ub. NARA, T-315, Roll 2236, 000304, War diary entry for 27 October 1941.

[104] NARA, T-315, Roll 2258, 000109–11, Intelligence section, Activity report for October 1941.

[105] For a full report by one of the survivors, see ibid.

Partisans executed fourteen prisoners, including two seriously wounded, with machine gun fire. They took the remaining six prisoners with them as porters and hurried away.[106]

All in all, the Germans lost twenty-two KIAs, three WIAs, and ten MIAs during the attack. It appears that the execution of prisoners was a matter of expediency, rather than a premeditated act. "The only way for the Partisans to escape to safety before the [other] *Wehrmacht* unit arrived was to have the prisoners either shot or freed," remembered one German survivor. "To take the wounded with them would have cost too much time,"[107] he added. It is doubtful that such a large group of prisoners would have been freed even in August when releasing captives was not unusual.[108] In light of the steadily escalating terror, especially in Mačva, this would have hardly been an option at the beginning of October. Likewise, the proposed exchange would have had little chance of being approved by the new military authorities in Belgrade.[109]

According to the initial reports, the executed soldiers were terribly mutilated, implying that they had been tortured before being shot, and the corpses were therefore sent to Belgrade to be examined by a special commission. Their report concluded that "there were no traceable signs of mutilation or torture." Böhme, however, disseminated the initial unsubstantiated claims for propaganda purposes.[110] It was

---

[106] One Partisan document states there were seven prisoners who were brought to the prisoner camp in Gornji Milanovac. *Zbornik*/I/20/105, Activity report of the 1st Šumadija Detachment for the period 26 September–14 October 1941 (14 October 1941). The Partisan losses were three wounded men.

[107] Walter Manoschek, *Serbien ist Judenfrei: Militärische Besatzungspolitik und Vernichtung der Juden in Serbien* (Munich: Oldenbourg Verlag, 1995), p. 82.

[108] German prisoners continued to be sporadically released until late August/early September. *Zbornik*/I/20/67, Activity report of the 1st Šumadija Detachment for the period September (24 September 1941); NARA, T-315, Roll 2237, 000065–6, Interrogation of Private Müller (1 September 1941).

[109] According to the official monograph of the 1st Šumadija Detachment, the commander of the 714th Infantry Division, General Friedrich Stahl, tried to defuse the situation in his operational zone with negotiations. Immediately after the Topola ambush, he sent a civilian courier to the 1st Šumadija Detachment who offered the Partisans a deal: the Germans would refrain from conducting reprisals if the guerrillas would be willing to abstain from further attacks on the lines of communication. The local Partisan commander dismissed the offer without consulting the detachment's HQ. Stanković, *Prvi šumadijski partizanski odred*, p. 276.

[110] Manoschek, *Serbien ist Judenfrei*, p. 83. Both primary and secondary German sources pertaining to the war in Yugoslavia contain numerous references to alleged mutilation of the bodies of dead German soldiers by the Partisans. Contemporary reports, German veterans, and some early post-war researchers usually attributed this practice to a particular propensity for brutality that the peoples from the Balkans had developed over centuries of

in line with his efforts to raise the fighting spirit of his men and make the escalation of violence all the more acceptable.[111] On 3 October 1941, he ordered that for each of the twenty-one soldiers who had been killed (one was still in hospital, gravely wounded), one hundred hostages should be shot. The executions, targeting mainly Jews and Gypsies, took place over the next week on the outskirts of Belgrade. This event ushered in the beginning of "Bloody October" as the application of the 1:100 rule came into full swing. It was applied again in Kraljevo in a series of executions which took place between 15 and 24 October when the 717th Infantry Division shot some 2,000 people in reprisal for German casualties incurred while fighting around the town. The worst atrocity took place in Kraguevac on 20–21 October when 2,300 hostages were shot in response to the attack launched on the

---

uninterrupted warfare. Sweeping generalizations like this are misleading for several reasons. First of all, they serve to dehumanize the enemy and make one's own war crimes appear to pale in comparison, or even make them seem justified. The Partisans usually stripped the bodies of enemy soldiers of valuables, including the uniform and the footgear, and left them unburied. Both the weather or wild animals could produce effects similar to mutilation, which is confirmed in one early German report from Serbia. The document reads that the body of one soldier was found mutilated and stated that the injuries were caused by a dog. NARA, T-315, Roll 2237, 000428, After-action report Bela Crkva, 16 August 1941. It should be noted that this report was written before Böhme came to Serbia and launched the campaign of unrestrained violence (I have not found similar reports in German documents after September 1941). Second, it is based on a stereotype that the Balkans was a half-civilized "dark corner of Europe" where warfare was still conducted according to tribal traditions. The Partisan army was comprised of hundreds of thousands of people who came from different ethnic and cultural backgrounds. Ritual mutilation of enemy dead was known to have been practiced by Montenegrins as late as the Balkan Wars in 1912–13 as a way of proving bravery in battle. Richard C. Hall, *The Balkan Wars 1912–1913: Prelude to the First World War* (New York: Routledge, 2002), p. 136. Whether or not this tradition survived the interwar period and the strong presence of Communist ideology in the country is difficult to gauge, but it is unlikely that such customs were being followed in the regions where tribal society was long gone and where Central European cultural influences had been present for decades or even centuries (such as Slovenia, Croatia, and Bosnia and Herzegovina under Habsburg rule), or in the newly-independent states that experienced rapid modernization, such as Serbia. There can, of course, be no doubt that the Partisan army had its fair share of sadists. For instance, Đilas recalled how a Slavonian Partisan once decapitated a captured *Ustasha* with a sabre (Djilas, *Wartime*, pp. 326–27); Jovo Kapičić, a high-ranking Partisan functionary, told an interviewer in 2010 about an incident in Montenegro in 1941 in which he and his comrades had doused the corpses of Italian Blackshirts with gasoline and set them alight. Tamara Nikičević, *Goli Otoci Jova Kapičića* (Podgorica: n.p., 2010), p. 37. In any case, until this topic has been sufficiently researched, wartime reports and veteran memoirs should be taken with the proverbial grain of salt.

[111] See Böhme's proclamation of 25 September 1941 in which he called upon his soldiers to avenge the losses that the Austro-Hungarian Army suffered in the ill-fated campaign against Serbia in 1914. Manoschek, *Serbien ist Judenfrei*, p. 60.

3rd Battalion during its second raid on Gornji Milanovac, when the unit suffered nine dead and twenty-seven wounded.[112] "The situation in Serbia is somewhat better," concluded the staff of the 65th Higher Commando on 20 October, "foremost because of the application of reprisal measures."[113]

"Deathly horror . . . had gripped Serbia," wrote Milovan Đilas in his memoirs.[114] The guerrillas were taken aback by the cold, calculated mass terror. Partisan commands and Party bodies reported about the "great fear" amongst the population, which occasionally spread to guerrilla units. Confusion was widespread with some units avoiding combat in order not to provoke German reprisals.[115] The Jovan Kursula Detachment that was besieging Kraljevo at the time wanted to forestall reprisals that would inevitably result from the planned attack on the town; therefore, the Partisans threatened the local enemy command with the shooting of eight Germans if their demands were not met: the cessation of mass arrests; the release of captives; the cessation of the burning of Serbian property; and a 1,800,000 dinar indemnity. The last request was that the Germans "recognize [the Partisans] as a lawful belligerent." The ultimatum remained unanswered.[116] Other detachments, like the one operating around Požarevac, tried to fight terror with terror. After the renewed bombing of Rabrovo village on 8 October, which caused numerous civilian casualties, the unit's command decided to shoot all German prisoners at hand.[117] Although such a course of action was not part of the official policy, it seems that it was adopted by the majority of those units which chose to respond to the reprisals in kind. "The enemy changed his attitude toward German prisoners. They are [now] usually being maltreated and shot," reported Lieutenant Colonel Gravenhorst to the Commanding General in Serbia.[118]

---

[112] Ibid., pp. 155–68.

[113] NARA, T-314, Roll 1531, 000173, Situation report for the period 10–19 October 1941 (20 October 1941).

[114] Djilas, *Wartime,* p. 94.

[115] *Zbornik*/I/20/111, Activity report of the 1st Šumadija Detachment for the period 26 September–14 October 1941 (14 October 1941); *Zbornik*/I/20/123, Letter from KPJ District Committee for Southern Banat (14 November 1941).

[116] *Zbornik*/I/1/633–34, Supplement to the war diary of the 18th Mountain Corps for the period 18 September–6 December 1941 (Entry for 21 October 1941); Gojko Nikoliš, *Korijen, stablo, Pavetina* (Zagreb: Liber, 1981), p. 319.

[117] Mitrović, *Centralna Srbija,* p. 247. On 21 November, a peasant informed the German command in Negotin that Privates Marx and Chigotin, who had been captured on 4 October, were executed in Rabrovo. NARA, T-315, Roll 2237, 001179, 704th Infantry Division, Intelligence section, Telephone request (21 November 1941).

[118] NARA, T-501, Roll 246, Ten-day report (29 October 1941). Tito's often quoted order of 8 November 1941, which prohibited the murder or maltreatment of enemy prisoners, was

According to German reports, that is exactly what happened with Major Renner, the area commander at Leskovac. He was taking part in a local anti-partisan sweep around Lebane on 11 November when he was caught with one of his escorts by the Partisans. The next day they were both reported killed.[119] One Yugoslav source claims the Germans reacted to his capture by threatening to lay waste to the entire area if the major was not promptly returned. The Partisans made an offer to exchange him instead. The Germans declined, and in their written answer addressed the guerrillas as "Partisans" and not as "bandits." Although this small detail was taken by the Partisans as a sign of recognition, it was a bad omen for the captives— the major and his escort were executed, the former as a war criminal. Mistaken identity may have contributed to this turn of events since the Partisans were convinced the man they captured was Major Paul König, the infamous perpetrator of the Kragujevac massacre.[120] The other version of events claims that Major Renner was killed in the battle and his escort captured. The Serbian collaborationists sent a delegation from Leskovac to arrange for the release of Renner's escort, as well as some of their own men in guerrilla captivity. These efforts were doomed to failure since the local German command would not free the three Partisans who were demanded in return.[121]

How did the Supreme Headquarters of the Partisans react to the October events? The *Bulletin* published on 20 October vowed revenge upon "the fascist invaders" for the crimes they committed, but it appears to have been written for propaganda purposes only.[122] There was a large group of German prisoners at hand which could have been used for reprisals, but there were two reasons why these reprisals did not take place. First, the Partisan leadership feared that the execution

---

referring to the Chetniks, rather than the Germans, as was made apparent in the order's preamble. *Zbornik*/I/1/223. For the beginnings of the open confrontation between the Partisans and the Chetniks in Serbia, see below.

[119] NARA, T-501, Roll 246, Daily reports for 12 and 13 November 1941.

[120] Milivoje Perović, *Južna Srbija* (Belgrade: Nolit, 1961), pp. 122–23. The belief that it was actually König who was killed that day at Lebane held for almost half a century. Some attribute it to the rumor that König gave a cigarette case engraved with his name to Renner, which the Partisans subsequently found. In 1952, a plaque was erected at that location and a song was written about the incident. Once it was proven beyond a doubt in the 1980s that the executed major was not König, a new plaque was set in 1990. It is still something of a local legend with the inhabitants periodically arguing about who exactly shot "König" that day, allegedly in a firefight which resembled a western duel. See: http://www.politika.rs/sr/clanak/7235/

[121] Vujadin Blečić, "Oko Leskovca 1941. godine," in *Ustanak naroda Jugoslavije 1941: Zbornik sjećanja* (Belgrade: Vojno delo, 1964), Vol. V, p. 821.

[122] *Zbornik*/II/2/95–96, Bulletin Nos. 10 and 11 of the Main Headquarters of People's Liberation Partisan Detachments (1 October 1941).

of prisoners would provoke even more drastic countermeasures by the Germans. The events in October showed that they were willing to continue to apply the 1:100 ratio as long as there were any hostages left in the country. Aleksandar Ranković, the second-highest ranking functionary in the Partisan leadership, the man who was tasked with internal security, was of the opinion that the German prisoners represented a burden and should be eliminated, but "Tito forbade it because he wanted us to adhere to the provisions of international law."[123] By doing this, the Partisans would acquire a degree of legitimacy, which they sorely lacked at this point in time. The Germans considered them to be bandits, and the British threw their support behind Mihailović as the sole legitimate representative of the Yugoslav resistance. The worst insult for the Partisans was that even the Soviet Union would not support them publicly, sacrificing "international solidarity" to the strengthening of the alliance with Great Britain.[124] Lastly, there was still a faint hope that the German occupation forces would reciprocate Partisan goodwill and begin treating captured guerrillas with a modicum of decency.

Although not condoned by Moscow, the KPJ continued with its revolutionary agenda, adding further trappings of a belligerent power in both a military and political sense. The center of these activities had been the town of Užice ever since the Partisans entered it in late September. They now controlled a relatively large urban center with accompanying infrastructure, along with roughly fifty-five million dinars found in the local branch of the state bank to finance their war efforts. More importantly, they captured a weapons factory which had been left untouched. By November, the output from the factory helped equip some of the estimated 10,000 fighters concentrated in and around Užice.[125] On the political side, the compact territory of about 19,000 square kilometers was administered by a network of People's Liberation Councils, all answerable to the Central Council formed on 17 November 1941. This was, in fact, an attempt to create a provisional Serbian government, a political body with which to counter not only the Nedić cabinet, but also the Yugoslav government-in-exile in London. Behind the scenes, the state-building process in Užice was accompanied with what might be styled as "revolutionary terror," carried out by the forerunner of the future secret police. On the surface, the connection to the Soviet Union could best be seen on 7 November 1941 when selected Partisan units marched pass the *Politburo* who were standing on an elevated platform, an imitation of the famous parades held in Red Square, Moscow. The combination of all of these factors led to the Partisan-controlled

---

[123] Venceslav Glišić, "Razgovori s Rankovićem," retrieved from http://www.pecat.co.rs/2010/01/razgovori-sa-rankovicem/

[124] Branko Petranović, *Srbija u Drugom svjetskom ratu* (Belgrade: Vojnoizdavački i novinski centar, 1992), p. 274.

[125] *Zbornik*/XII/1/718, Report to the Wehrmacht Commander Southeast (5 December 1941).

territory being labeled "The Red Republic of Užice." As is often the case, the name not only stuck, but was embraced by the Partisans, and thus found its way into official historiography.[126]

There were some 330 German prisoners in guerrilla custody by the end of September. The majority of them were transferred from Krupanj to Pecka at the beginning of October. From there approximately 200 of them were marched to Užice, arriving on or about 25 October, the rest (mostly wounded) having been left behind and subsequently recovered by advancing German forces in the towns of Loznica and Krupanj, and the Tronoša Monastery.[127] Upon their arrival, the prisoners were led through the town center, a propaganda stunt that produced the desired result, as indicated by a statement from Đorđe Popović: "The German soldiers had to march barefooted in the worst possible weather all the way from Krupanj to Užice. They were without clothes, dressed only in underwear, and wrapped in rags. . . . They were starved and sickly. Everyone in the town was saying the same: who would have thought we would see the Germans again so soon, and in such a condition."[128]

Although some of the bystanders demanded revenge for the massacres of Kragujevac and Kraljevo, the townspeople were generally well-disposed toward the German prisoners. According to the pro-Axis sources, the reason for this lay within the strong anti-communist sentiments of the local populace, which found its expression in providing food and other commodities to the captives. Yugoslav sources claim it was due to the inborn humanity of the Serbian people and the belief that the kind treatment of the German prisoners would be reciprocated

---

[126] Milovan Đilas mentioned in his memoirs the methods used in fighting the fifth column in Užice: "Torture was applied selectively, in special cases, and executions were carried out secretly at night." Djilas, *Wartime*, p. 101. According to statistics compiled in 2002, Partisans executed seventy-eight people in Užice and its surroundings in 1941. Gojko Škoro, *Istina je u imenima: Stradali u užičkom okrugu u Drugom svetskom ratu* (Užice: Spomen-obeležje Kadinjača, 2002), p. 255. Rumors circulated about the nature of the Užice Republic. One witness, an industrialist who escaped from the town, told the Germans that the Communists opened an "Institute for free love," which was run by a Jewish girl, Vita Gutman, who strolled the town streets dressed in men's clothes and carried a machine-gun (needless to say, rumors like these were untrue). NARA, T-315, Roll 2239, 001119, Statement by Đorđe Popović (30 November 1941).

[127] Of the original 330 men, fifty-six were killed in an air raid on 10 September 1941, and another eight were executed by the guerrillas. The Germans recovered an additional fifty-nine, mostly seriously wounded, when they recaptured Loznica, Krupanj, and the Tronoša Monastery in the first three weeks of October. NARA, T-501, Roll 249, 000819, Cable to 18th Mountain Corps (25 September 1941); NARA, T-315, Roll 2239, 000735, Statement by Kurt Steinert (15 December 1941); NARA, T-312, Roll 460, Daily reports for 13 and 17 October 1941; NARA, T-312, Roll 460, Daily report for 21 October 1941.

[128] NARA, T-315, Roll 2239, 001117–8, Statement by Đorđe Popović (30 November 1941).

toward their kinsmen held in captivity in Germany.[129] While both arguments may have played a part in the formation of the public sentiment, there was also a third factor, one which probably played an overriding role in this matter. Up to this point, Užice was largely spared the horrors which befell the rest of the country, partly attributed to the comparatively mild occupation of the town which had undertaken relatively few reprisals. As a result, the population bore the Germans no ill will, or at least, it was not as strong as in other parts of Serbia.[130]

The prisoners were quartered in the high school building in the center of the town. There was no overcrowding and they received regular, albeit monotonous, rations. Both conditions apparently contributed to the fact that not a single documented death among the prisoners was attributed to malnutrition or disease. Prisoners were divided into sections which would leave the camp in the morning and return at dusk after performing physical labor in the town, such as clearing rubble after air raids, woodcutting, or helping at the local hospital. The only dangerous work they were forced to perform came in the aftermath of the massive explosion which shook the munitions factory in the vaults of the National Bank on 22 November. An estimated 130 people were killed in the accident. The prisoners were rushed to the scene and ordered to enter the vaults, search for survivors, and retrieve the bodies. They were issued gas masks because of the dangerous fumes which had filled the underground galleries. Miraculously, no prisoners were injured, although the ammunition and explosives continued to explode for the next several days.[131]

As explained earlier, the Yugoslav Communists were influenced by their own propaganda which viewed the ongoing European war through Marxist-Leninist lenses. These beliefs were maintained despite the strain placed upon them by the alliance between the "first land of socialism," the Soviet Union, and the arch-imperialist power, Great Britain. As late as September 1941, the *Bulletin* of the Partisan supreme command was reporting on alleged widespread riots in Germany caused by a popular desire for peace and an alliance "with the brotherly Russian working people."[132] Although reports on contacts with ordinary German soldiers

---

[129] Vojin Brašanac, "Kroz Užičku republiku od Kragujevca do Prijepolja," in *Užička republika: Zbornik sećanja*, Vol. I, pp. 399–400; Branka Savić, "Sa radio stanicom," in ibid., Vol. II, p. 505; NARA, T-315, Roll 2239, 001119, Statement of Đorđe Popović (30 November 1941).

[130] See the report by Major König (who later conducted the Kragujevac Massacre) in which he accused the *Feldkommandantur* in Užice of being "utterly soft" on the town's populace. NARA, T-315, Roll 2238, 000676, Situation report on Užice and Požega (20 September 1941).

[131] NARA, T-315, Roll 2239, 000646, Report by the members of the former 10th Company, 724th Infantry Regiment on time spent in captivity (undated).

[132] *Zbornik*/II/2/62, Bulletin No. 6 of the Main Headquarters of People's Liberation Partisan Detachments (18 September 1941). To be equitable to the Yugoslav Communists, it should be stated that they were not the only ones who displayed remarkable naïveté regarding this

provided a disappointing picture of their class consciousness, the Partisans were not yet ready to abandon their dogmatic approach. The relative security of their Užice stronghold gave them both time and the ability to mount an organized attempt to "reeducate" their German prisoners. Only privates and low-ranking NCOs were deemed suitable for reeducation. Officers, Nazi Party members, or those thought to be connected to the infamous Gestapo, were usually sorted out and sentenced to death. Eight prisoners were executed on these grounds in Krupanj. The Partisans were quick to add that ordinary soldiers would be treated as prisoners of war, but "incendiaries and murderers" would be tried and punished as war criminals.[133]

Various methods of persuasion were used with the prisoners. The Communists first tried proclaiming that "one's comrades" received better treatment than mere "prisoners of war," thereby hoping to cause a rift among the Germans. Apparently, all the camp inmates were content to remain as prisoners. To apply added pressure, an interrogation room for fifth columnists was placed directly above the prisoners' dormitory. In the morning, the captors apologized to the Germans for the unpleasant sounds which they may have heard during the night. The Partisans also tried pro-Soviet propaganda techniques by holding a lecture called "The tactics of the Red Army." As Yugoslav lecturers could not make the desired impression on the listeners, the prisoners were ordered to choose the "teachers" from amongst themselves; however, the explosion in the munitions factory, and then the rapidly changing situation at the front, prevented this plan from being realized.[134]

On one occasion, prisoners were made to paint Communist slogans. To their captors' astonishment, they wrote the Cyrillic letters perfectly, but were completely oblivious to the message. "Robots," "sheep," and "apathetic" were the terms most frequently used to describe the Germans by the Partisans who engaged in "political work" with them. What the latter could not understand was that amongst the German prisoners, eighty percent were workers and peasants yet they proved completely impervious to Communist ideology and did not even know who Ernst

---

question. As late as January 1942, Sir Hugh Dalton, the head of the British SOE, also entertained the idea of fomenting proletarian unrest in the hopes of inciting a revolution in the Third Reich. Neville Wylie, "Ungentlemanly Warriors or Unreliable Diplomats? Special Operations Executive and 'Irregular Political Activities' in Europe," in Neville Wylie, ed., *The Politics and Strategy of Clandestine War: Special Operations Executive, 1940–1946* (London: Routledge, 2007), p. 111.

[133] NARA, T-315, Roll 2239, 000642, Report by the members of the former 10th Company, 724th Infantry Regiment on time spent in captivity (undated). Rodoljub Čolaković mentions five, instead of eight, executions. Čolaković, *Zapisi*, p. 273. In Gornji Milanovac in late September, three Germans were discovered to be members of the Nazi Party and were shot. Živka Đurić, "Takovski bataljon u borbama oko Gornjeg Milanovca," in *Užička republika: Zbornik sećanja*, Vol. I, p. 434.

[134] NARA, T-315, Roll 2239, 000645, Report by the members of the former 10th Company, 724th Infantry Regiment on time spent in captivity (undated).

Thälmann and Karl Liebknecht were.[135] The guerrillas, who prided themselves on being an all-volunteer army who understood well the underlying cause for which they fought, were equally bewildered by the frequently encountered "orders are orders" attitude (*Befehl ist Befehl*) of their captives. The Germans appeared meek and sometimes servile toward their captors, which stood in stark contrast to their behavior on the battlefield. This only served to deepen the scorn most of the Partisans felt for them.[136]

In the interim, the Serbian insurgency began showing the first signs of internal strife. Mihailović, whose participation in the uprising was never a matter of conviction but rather of necessity, began to reconsider the usefulness of his uneasy alliance with the Partisans. He reasoned that the Communist attacks were merely bringing suffering to the Serbian population without causing much damage to the Germans. His main concern was that the Partisans were gaining strength and could become a serious competitor in the power struggle after the war. He continued his contacts with the Partisans by meeting with Tito on 26 September and again on 7 October 1941, attempting to resolve differences and to facilitate smooth cooperation between the two movements. Simultaneously, he secretly contacted the Serbian collaborationists and the German authorities in Belgrade seeking arms and ammunition for use against the Communists while he designed a plan for an all-out attack on Užice.[137] The attack came on 1 November but the Chetniks were beaten back in the heavy fighting which raged in the area over the next few days. The Partisans subsequently went on the offensive and had Mihailović's base at Ravna Gora surrounded. In consideration of the Kremlin, which was striving to build an alliance with Great Britain as well as the protecting powers of the Yugoslav government-in-exile and Mihailović at this time, Tito ordered restraint and agreed to a cease-fire.[138]

The Partisans believed they knew who was responsible for the opening of hostilities. Captain Duane T. Hudson, an agent of the Special Operations Executive (SOE), arrived at Ravna Gora in late October as the official British representative to the Yugoslav resistance. Having for years heard Soviet propaganda about the scheming Secret Intelligence Service, the long arm of all imperialist powers and

---

[135] Karl Liebknecht (1871–1919) and Ernst Thälmann (1866–1944) were the most prominent representatives of German communism. The Yugoslav Partisans named a unit comprised of German volunteers after the latter in 1943.

[136] Mitra Mitrović, "Crno-Belo," in *Užička republika: Zbornik sećanja*, Vol. I, p. 353; Borka Demić-Pihler, "Poslednji čaj za ranjenike," in ibid., p. 613; Branka Savić, "Sa radio stanicom," in ibid., Vol. II, p. 505.

[137] The meeting between Mihailović and the German delegation took place in the village of Divci, outside Valjevo on 11 November 1941. German minutes of the conference can be found in NARA, T-314, Roll 1457, 001314–1329; also printed in *Zbornik*/XIV/1/871–78.

[138] Tomasevich, *The Chetniks*, pp. 146–51.

reactionary forces, the Partisans were convinced it was Hudson who had brought the order to attack from London. Additional evidence of this alleged conspiracy came on 9 November when a British transport plane made the first airdrop of supplies to the Chetniks. Although relatively small, this shipment reaffirmed the conviction of Mihailović's men that they were regarded as the sole legitimate resistance movement in Yugoslavia. To the Partisans, it was proof of British double dealing, who on the one hand pursued an alliance with the Soviet Union, and on the other, actively fought Communists.[139]

The Partisan-Chetnik split could not have come at a better time for the Germans. Another front line division, the 113th, had just arrived from the Eastern Front and took up positions to the east of the guerrilla-held territories around Užice and Suvobor Mountain. On 25 November 1941, the 113th and 342nd Infantry Divisions, aided by elements of another four divisions and Serbian collaborationist forces, began Operation Užice, designed to destroy the guerrillas in Western Serbia. The speed and ferocity of the German onslaught astonished the Partisans and their units withdrew quickly, taking heavy casualties in the process. The main base in Užice was hastily prepared for evacuation. On 28 November, a column of 115 German prisoners found during the course of fighting the Chetniks, entered the town. These soldiers had been captured in Gornji Milanovac and Struganik in late September/early October and had previously been Mihailović's prisoners. The Partisans had them transported first to Čačak and then to Užice.[140] In the afternoon, a security detail was ordered to evacuate all of the prisoners, now numbering more than 300, from the town. The long column's first stop was the railway station, where it boarded a west-bound train around 20.00. It reached the station of Kremna, some thirty-five kilometers west of Užice after a three-hour ride. From there, the column marched due south to the village of Gornja Jablanica, where it halted. Most prisoners had wooden shoes or sheets wrapped around their feet and could walk only with great difficulty. The sound of gunfire was growing louder, which meant that the German Army was not far away. The Partisans locked the prisoners in the local school and held a council of war to determine their fate. Some suggested that the Germans be executed. Others disagreed, partly because carrying out such a move in the village would put its inhabitants at risk. The

---

[139] The theory that Hudson brought the order to attack the Partisans from London persisted for many years in Yugoslav historiography. See *Oslobodilački rat,* Vol. I, p. 115. See also a quote from the post-war memoirs of a high-ranking Partisan leader and the adjoining discussion in Venceslav Glišić, *Užička republika* (Belgrade: Nolit, 1989), pp. 226–28.

[140] The Germans kept tabs on the missing soldiers. One report dated 24 October 1941 puts them in Mionica, near Valjevo. A soldier who was released by the Chetniks reported three weeks later that his comrades were still alive, but that the prisoner camp had been moved from Ravna Gora. On 15 November, these prisoners were reported in Čačak. NARA, T-315, Roll 2239, 000414, Report by Chetnik leader Matić (24 October 1941); NARA, T-501, Roll 246, Daily reports for 14 and 15 November 1941.

council lasted until dawn when it was decided to leave the prisoners where they were and continue the retreat without them. On their way south, the security detail met a group of several hundred Partisans, among them Slobodan Penezić Krcun, the second-highest ranking security officer with the Supreme HQ. He was enraged by the decision to release the prisoners and had the commander of the security detail tied to a tree. The officer's life was spared only because his fellow fighters pleaded on his behalf.[141]

The prisoners in the school could hardly believe their good fortune when on the morning of 1 December 1941, they realized that their guards had disappeared. A peasant was dispatched to summon the nearest German unit he could find. German units in the area had been searching for any trace of the prisoners. Upon learning that they were in the vicinity, the Germans promptly rounded up hostages in adjoining villages in case anything happened to the captives.[142] Soon afterwards, a motorized column of the 342nd Infantry Division entered Jablanica and freed 315 soldiers and one officer. The prisoners were first sent to Užice, to the same high school building which was used as a prisoner camp. After recuperating, they were then sent to Belgrade on 6 December and eventually returned to their respective units.[143]

In conjunction with evacuating prisoners, the Partisans were also evacuating their wounded from Užice. By the evening of 28 November, some 700 wounded were concentrated around the hamlet of Kraljeve Vode on Zlatibor Mountain, about twenty-three kilometers south of the town. It was there that they heard the news that Užice had been taken by the Germans. The next day, everyone capable of being moved was sent farther south, toward the Uvac River. About 130 seriously wounded Partisans remained in Kraljeve Vode because there was neither time nor the means to transport them to safety, and it was hoped that the Germans would show them clemency upon arrival. On 30 November, elements of the 342nd Infantry Division entered the village and found the wounded Partisans. The villagers were rounded up to be interrogated or to be used as porters. Twenty-eight of them had a much more gruesome task—carrying the wounded to a nearby ravine where they were all executed by firing squad.[144]

---

141 Miloš Gordić, "Čuvao sam nemačke zarobljenike," in *Užička republika: Zbornik sećanja,* Vol. II, pp. 486–89; Milan Penezić, "Puštanje na slobodu nemačkih zarobljenika u Jablanici," in ibid., pp. 632–33.

142 Gojko Škoro, "Izbeglice u Kremnima," in *Užička republika: Zbornik sećanja,* Vol. II, p. 668. Once the prisoners were found unharmed, the hostages were set free.

143 NARA, T-315, Roll 2239, 000923, 724th Infantry Regiment to 704th Infantry Division (7 December 1941).

144 Miladin Marjanović-Ujko, "Nemci su ranjenike streljali dum-dum mecima," in *Užička republika: Zbornik sećanja,* Vol. II, pp. 655–58. The daily report for 1 December to Armed Forces High Command states that the 342nd Infantry Division has, among other activities,

The news about the fate of their comrades quickly reached the Partisans. Although accustomed to the occupier's brutality, many had hoped that even the Germans would not dare commit such an atrocity against helpless wounded.[145] Unfortunately, it soon became clear that the worst had happened and rumors about the massacre spread like wildfire. It was widely believed that the Germans used tanks and crushed the wounded under their tracks. Some said that the Germans who had received care in Partisan hospitals were especially zealous in killing the victims on Zlatibor Mountain. Likewise, it turned out that those meek and even servile prisoners who had been treated well in Užice were now denouncing all the Partisans they knew from the days of their captivity.[146] Consequently, rage replaced disbelief. Milovan Đilas wrote: "The massacre of the wounded was a decisive turning point in our dealings with the Germans. Thereafter, the Partisans gave the Germans measure for measure and killed their prisoners, except in special cases; nor would we in the leadership come up with any reason to oppose this."[147]

This event also signaled the bloody end of the Užice Republic. There was no doubt that the Communist-led guerrillas suffered a heavy blow. Most of their army melted away, as did most of their supplies and heavy weapons. An estimated 2,000 fighters managed to cross the Uvac River into the Italian occupation zone and thus save themselves from the pursuing Germans. Serbia was lost for the time being.[148]

---

reached Ribnica, some three kilometers southeast of Kraljeve Vode. It reported 106 Partisans killed and another seventy-two captured with a loss of only one wounded. It is obvious that the executed Partisans were simply counted as killed, a common practice in *Wehrmacht* counter-insurgency reports. NARA, T-312, Roll 425, Daily Report for 1 December 1941.

[145] Nikoliš, *Korijen,* p. 340.

[146] Glišić, *Zločini,* p. 77; Čolaković, *Zapisi,* Vol. II, pp. 206–07; Bojić, *Posavski odred,* p. 474. Some former prisoners were indeed sent back to Užice where they helped identify their "tormentors" who were executed shortly thereafter. NARA, T-315, Roll 2239, 000647, Report by the members of the former 10th Company, 724th Infantry Regiment on time spent in captivity (undated). Not all of the Germans behaved this way, however. Two Partisans, Pavle Radovanović and Dragoslav Jovanović, were released from prison thanks to the intervention of a German soldier. In August 1941, he had been found wounded by Radovanović and Jovanović, who dressed his wounds and helped him reach the German garrison at Topola. He met them again in prison by coincidence, recognized them, and paid his debt in kind. Stanković, *Prvi šumadijski partizanski odred,* p. 483.

[147] Djilas, *Wartime,* p. 113. Ranković confirmed Đilas' statement in one of his post-war interviews. Glišić, "Razgovori s Rankovićem."

[148] For an estimate of the Partisan strength, see Schmider, *Partisanenkrieg,* p. 103. The Germans reported 707 Partisans killed in combat, ninety-three executed, and 312 captured by 4 December 1941. They also captured 2,723 rifles, twenty-eight MGs, one mortar, and four cannons, as well as large quantities of war matériel. NARA, T-501, Roll 250, 001102, Report on casualties and war booty in Operation Užice (10 December 1941).

The bitterness of defeat, a growing sense of isolation, and wishful thinking on the part of Tito and the rest of the *Politburo,* had far-reaching consequences for the strategy of the Partisan movement over the next six months and beyond. Their reasoning was as follows: first, the "Chetnik treason," as it was called, was in large measure blamed for the collapse of the Užice Republic and the diminishing guerrilla activity in Serbia in general.[149] The existence of the common enemy—the Axis powers—did nothing to temper the deep antagonism which existed between the reactionary circles and the Communists. Anti-communism, rather than anti-fascism, remained their prime conviction. Draža Mihailović and his entourage promulgated this position by abstaining from fighting at first, and then joining it only half-heartedly for fear of losing public support altogether. He was known to have contacts with Nedić and Dimitrije Ljotić,[150] both of whom were working openly with the Germans. Some of his commanders came from Pećanac's organization and were known for maintaining connections to it. This quiet collaboration with the occupier was not only condoned by the British government, but also openly acknowledged by dispatching Hudson as well as arms shipments to them. Worst of all, the Soviet Union accepted the version of events presented by the British and did little to help the Partisans, either militarily or via propaganda.[151]

The feeling of desperation within the Partisans' ranks was alleviated to a certain extent by the news emanating from the Eastern Front. Beginning on 5 December 1941, the Red Army began their long-awaited counter-offensive and managed to push the *Wehrmacht* from the gates of Moscow. The old belief in a quick victory over Germany was revived. The Red Army was expected to be on the Danube

---

[149] The treason was "symbolically sealed" when one of the Chetnik commanders (only loosely connected to Mihailović) delivered 365 captured Partisans to the Germans in Valjevo. They were shot on 27 November 1941. Tomasevich, *The Chetniks,* p. 150.

[150] Dimitrije Ljotić (1891–1945) was the leader of the *Zbor* Movement, the Serbian political party combining elements of fascism and Nazism with Orthodox mystique and Serbian nationalism. His armed followers, organized in Serbian Volunteer Detachments, were the only native formation in which the Germans had full confidence.

[151] It should be noted that Mihailović was hardly a friend of the Germans at the time. Right after the completion of Operation Užice, the Germans launched Operation Mihailović. His headquarters was overrun, two of his closest lieutenants were tried and shot, and Mihailović himself barely escaped, thereafter a wanted man with a 200,000 dinar bounty on his head. Knowing, however, that most of his men had fought the Communists, the Germans granted them POW status according to the Geneva Convention. Additional reasons for granting them POW status were the desire to deepen the rift between the two guerrilla movements and to weaken Mihailović's own ability to launch future aggressive actions. *Zbornik*/XII/2/1037–39, Fighting against the uprising in the Southeast from June 1941 to August 1942. NARA, T-315, Roll 2258, 000074, Intelligence summary for the period 10–19 November 1941 (19 November 1941).

within the next several months,[152] which meant that the war would be over soon and the question of who would hold power in Yugoslavia thereafter gained importance. Given that the reactionary circles sided with the Axis, the class enemy and the collaborator became one and the same. A series of messages from the *Politburo* to the regional party leadership commands reaffirmed the importance of the class struggle and ushered in the beginning of the so-called "Second Phase of the Revolution," i.e. open struggle for power.[153] These directives resulted in the purging from Partisan ranks of those individuals who were not adhering to the Party line. In some areas, like Eastern Herzegovina and Montenegro, this soon evolved into wholesale terror against all those perceived as "Kulaks" or "counter-revolutionaries." By the spring of 1942, this policy led to diminishing popular support for the Partisans and the strengthening of the Chetnik movement. A change in the Party line came only after Tito managed to attain a direct radio link with Moscow. In March, the Comintern criticized the Yugoslav party for narrowing the base of the resistance movement and for sectarian errors. It also confirmed the validity of the Popular Front policy aimed at uniting all patriotic forces irrespective of political affiliation in the struggle against the Axis powers. Revolution would have to wait for the time being.[154]

In the aftermath of Užice, it was obvious that the upcoming struggle could not be carried out by the old Partisan detachments. These were local units, tied to their regional recruitment bases, with only a small number of dedicated Communists within their ranks. They lacked mobility and cohesiveness, clearly evident during the retreat from Serbia. What was needed was a Partisan type of a "New Model Army." On 21 December 1941 in Rudo, Eastern Bosnia, the 1st Proletarian Shock Brigade was formed. It had some 1,200 fighters well-equipped with automatic weapons, 650 of whom were either members of the KPJ or SKOJ. Although not obvious at that moment, the formation of this unit would turn out to be one of the war-winning decisions. By replacing the stationary detachment with a fully mobile brigade with substantial firepower and motivated members, the Yugoslav Partisans would soon be able to gain the upper hand in fighting against their numerous domestic enemies. The Proletarian brigades, so their statute read, were "the striking fist of the Yugoslav peoples under the leadership of the Communist Party . . . [and a] guarantee against the continuation of both national and social oppression." Apart from being at the forefront of both the liberation war and the revolution, the Proletarian brigades were also "a cradle of the future People's Army"—the first

---

[152] Stalin's comments during the November Day Parade in Moscow that the war would be over in 1942 were taken as gospel by Tito and the rest of the *Politburo.* Petranović, *Srbija,* p. 321.

[153] See, for instance, *Politburo* instructions to the Sandžak and Slovene branches of the KPJ from early January in *Zbornik*/II/2/141–42, 154–57.

[154] Petranović, *Istorija Jugoslavije,* Vol. II, pp. 184–85.

quasi-regular units of the Partisan movement. Their creation represented a milestone in the process of regularization already begun within the guerrilla ranks.[155]

Events in Serbia, 1942–1944

The scale and the brutality of the German counter-insurgency effort in Serbia in late 1941 sent shock waves throughout the country. The downfall of both resistance movements in just a matter of days cost them materials, but also damaged them propagandistically. The exhausted population was beginning to realize that the relative stability offered by the Nedić administration under the slogan "Peace, Work, and Order" was preferable to vague notions of national liberation or patriotic duty. It was obvious to all that the Germans were far too strong to be pushed out of the country without outside assistance. Mere survival became the prime concern for the majority of the population.

The Germans were content, but not overconfident, as a result of their autumn operations: "The uprising will probably flare-up again in the spring," concluded one German report.[156] Still, the expulsion of Partisans from Western Serbia and the heavy blows dealt to Mihailović had won the Germans some precious breathing space. The two front line divisions which had carried the main brunt of the fighting, the 113th and 342nd, were scheduled to leave Serbia—the 113th in January and the 342nd as soon as the planned operations in Eastern Bosnia were concluded.[157] That would leave the strength of the occupation forces at its pre-September 1941 levels, with three garrison divisions and some additional smaller units. A solution was found in strengthening the Serbian collaborationist administration and its armed formations. One way of doing this was to allow a large number of Mihailović's former men to become "legalized," i.e. incorporated into the occupation apparatus. Though the Germans fully understood that most of these units clandestinely remained loyal to Mihailović, their legalization was regarded as the means of bringing these potential guerrillas under control by making them fully dependent on the Germans for arms and ammunition. By mid-1942, the strength of Serbian collaborationist formations, i.e. Ljotić's Volunteers, the Pećanacs, and the legalized Chetniks, rose to 16,401.[158]

---

[155] Jovan Vujošević, "Od Stolica do Rudog: Prva neprijateljska ofanziva," in Pape and Anić, eds., *Drugi svjetski rat,* Vol. I, p. 276; Jovan Vujošević, "Fočanski period: rezultati okupatorsko-kvislinške ofenzive u Istočnoj Bosni," in ibid., Vol. II, p. 102.

[156] NARA, T-501, Roll 246, Ten-day report (10 December 1941).

[157] *Oslobodilački rat,* Vol. I, p. 171.

[158] NARA, T-501, Roll 249, Strength of Volunteer and Chetnik detachments in Serbia (15 May 1942). The Serbian State Guard (*gendarmerie*) had an additional 15,000 men. The Russian Protective Corps (*Russisches Schutzkorps*), comprised of White Russian *emigres* in Serbia, was formed in September 1941 to provide protection to important military and

Mass reprisals were regarded as the centerpiece of the pacification effort in Serbia.[159] Even so, the quota of 1:100 proved impractical as there were always difficulties finding a sufficient number of hostages. Additionally, the much improved security situation after the completion of the autumn operations allowed for a relaxation of the reprisal policy. On 22 December 1941, General Paul Bader, Commanding General in Serbia, signed an order which halved the reprisal quota: fifty hostages for each German killed, and twenty-five for each wounded.[160] The implementation of reprisals would become the main task of the newly-appointed Higher SS and Police Leader in Serbia (*Höhere SS-und Polizeiführer Serbien*), SS General August Meyszner, who arrived in Belgrade in early February 1942. Until his removal two years later, Meyszner would remain the chief opponent amongst the senior German officials in Belgrade of any further relaxation of the reprisal policy.

The People's Liberation Movement (*Narodnooslobodilački pokret*, NOP) in Serbia was thoroughly shattered by the downfall of the Užice Republic. The units dissolved as morale dropped due to the relentless German onslaught and punitive expeditions. The Supreme HQ never lost sight of Serbia, or of its importance, and efforts were made over the next years to light the fires of resistance again. In December 1941, Tito ordered that Partisan groups which remained in Serbia after the fall of Užice were to be reinforced by fighters who had escaped to Sandžak, but the enterprise ended in a total fiasco. The units, some 2,000 in all, had to march through the worst imaginable weather in the rugged mountainous terrain of Western Serbia. The region, depopulated and barren, could not offer shelter or supplies. Additionally, Serbian collaborationist forces were ready and waiting for the weary Partisans. The campaign devolved into a fighting retreat with the number of Partisans constantly declining due to exhaustion and casualties. The last group of some seventy men held a council of war and decided to cross the Drina River and rejoin the Supreme HQ in Eastern Bosnia.[161]

The situation in the urban centers was not noticeably any better. The Germans, in addition to their own *Sicherheitsdienst* personnel, had an experienced group of Serbian agents at their disposal, mostly pre-war members of the IV Directorate of the Special Police who specialized in dealing with Communists. In several well-planned actions beginning in October 1941, they managed to shatter the KPJ's

---

economic installations. It had a strength of nearly 1,500 by late 1941. *Zbornik*/XII/1/753, Report to Wehrmacht commander Southeast (5 December 1941).

[159] According to one German document from early spring 1942, the number of executed hostages since 1 September 1941 was 21,889. NARA, T-311, Roll 175, 000247, Activity report for April 1942 (Entry for 9 April 1942).

[160] NARA, T-315, Roll 2258, 000009, Activity report for December 1941 (undated); Schmider, *Partisanenkrieg*, p. 83.

[161] Petranović, *Srbija*, pp. 322–25.

underground network in all major cities in Serbia. For instance, by the autumn of 1942, Belgrade's organization was penetrated no less than three times, resulting in heavy losses to the Party cadre. Arrested Communists and their sympathizers were usually sent to concentration camps at Sajmište and Banjica, which served as gathering points for hostages in the event that reprisals were necessary.[162]

In the face of the unrelenting terror practiced in the cities by the Germans and in the countryside by the Serbian collaborationist forces, the Partisans understandably found it very difficult to get reorganized. The only part of the country in which they were regularly active during 1942–1944 was Southern Serbia, in the original Bulgarian occupation zone.[163] In other regions, their activity was sporadic at best, aimed more at survival than at actions against the occupier. One factor which greatly contributed to this state of affairs was the rise of the Chetnik movement of Draža Mihailović, now officially named the Yugoslav Army in the Homeland (*Jugoslovenska vojska u otadžbini*). As mentioned, a large number of Mihailović's followers were legalized in early 1942, but he remained underground with a small number of active fighters. After sustaining heavy casualties during the German autumn operations, he reverted back to biding his time. Accordingly, his movement spent time organizing, gathering armaments and supplies, and preparing for the expected Allied invasion of Yugoslavia. In order not to provoke German reprisals, actions against the occupier were reduced to an absolute minimum. The frightened population supported his approach and was wary of providing volunteers to the Partisan movement.[164] Mihailović also made use of this respite to engage the Partisans and win complete control over the Serbian countryside. The Partisans, too weak to attack the Germans, concentrated on their domestic enemies instead. The resistance against the occupier thus became secondary to an all-out civil war.

The whole of 1942 in Serbia was thus marked by reduced, though constant, guerrilla activity. The Germans countered the threat by the application of reprisals. As both guerrilla movements changed their priorities and now avoided attacking the Germans, concentrating on lines of communications and collaborationist forces instead, the reprisal rules had to be changed as well. They were gradually expanded in order to cover both acts of sabotage as well as attacks on auxiliary

---

[162] It is estimated that the KPJ lost four members of the Regional Committee for Serbia, eighty members of district, area, and local committees, as well as more than a thousand other members in urban centers during the war. Ibid., pp. 333–34.

[163] The Bulgarian occupation zone was expanded gradually as the Germans shuffled more of their own troops to the neighboring NDH. By mid-1943, the Bulgarian zone included nearly all of occupied Serbia, excluding Belgrade and its environs.

[164] See, for instance, *Zbornik*/I/20/168, 241, 290, Reports by Požarevac Detachment on 29 June, 16 October, and 31 December 1942.

troops and local administrations.[165] In comparison with 1941, the German troops rarely engaged the Partisans, and when encounters did occur, they were very small in size and the casualties negligible. From April to December 1942, according to incomplete statistics, the Germans incurred some thirty-seven KIAs, forty-four WIAs, and twenty-two MIAs in Serbia due to guerrilla actions.[166] Judging by the absence of any further information on the fate of the missing soldiers, it is safe to assume that most were killed or executed by their captors. The Germans suspected that the guerrillas hid the bodies in order to avoid reprisals. On 10 October 1942, the Commanding General in Serbia issued an order calling for the execution of hostages if missing soldiers did not return within a certain period of time after their disappearance. Judging by the available documents, the reprisal quota was the same as for a soldier killed in action (fifty hostages). The hostages were shot in groups of ten every several days. If the missing were released in the meantime, the executions stopped; if not, the Germans continued until all fifty hostages were executed.[167] These measures were not very effective in ensuring that the captives were retrieved unharmed. Two *Luftwaffe* meteorologists were captured by the Partisans in the vicinity of Donji Milanovac on 19 October 1942. The search for them went on for the next several months. Only on 12 February 1943 were the culprits caught and admitted that both men were killed four days after capture. Because of the allegedly gruesome way in which the prisoners were executed, the local German command requested that in addition to the fifty hostages which had already been shot, a further 200 be executed as well.[168]

In light of the negative experiences from earlier negotiations and the brutality with which the Germans continued to treat their captives, it seems surprising

---

[165] See Bader's order of 22 November 1942 prescribing quotas of 1:10 for each killed and 1:5 for each wounded employee of the collaborationist administration. The same order made any sabotage on land communications punishable by the shooting of up to 100 hostages. NARA, T-501, Roll 352, 000591–3, Letter to Premier Nedić (22 November 1942).

[166] These figures were compiled using the ten-day reports of the Commanding General in Serbia including: Ten-day reports from 10, 20, 30 April 1942 in NARA, T-501, Roll 247; 10 and 22 May; 1, 10, and 20 June; 1, 11, 21, and 31 August in NARA, T-501, Roll 248; 1 and 20 July 1942 in NARA, T-501, Roll 351 (Casualty figures for 10 July not available); 11, 20 September; 1, 11, and 31 October (Casualty figures for 20 October not available); 11 and 20 November; 1, 12, 20, and 31 December 1942 in NARA, T-501, Roll 352. Most of the figures for August, September, and October are expressly denoted as "Losses in Croatia" and have not been included in the total. The vast majority of the eigthy-seven KIAs, 237 WIAs, and fifteen MIAs from the first three months of 1942 were lost during the winter operations in Bosnia, with only a small number lost in Serbia. See ten-day reports from 10, 20, and 30 January, 10 and 20 February, and 1, 10, 20, and 31 March in NARA, T-501, Roll 247.

[167] NARA, T-501, Roll 352, 000301, Precautionary measures against enemy attacks (10 October 1942).

[168] NARA, T-315, Roll 2245, 001233, War diary entry for 23 February 1943.

that Partisan commands in Serbia still entertained the idea of exchange as late as spring 1942. On 7 April, Blagoje Nešković, the head of the entire Party organization in the country, sent a letter to the Party leadership in Požarevac containing instructions on the treatment of captured members of various hostile formations. He divided them into two categories: the first were the Germans and Ljotić's Volunteers, and the second were Mihailović's followers and the Chetniks of Kosta Pećanac. Taking into account the heterogeneous character of both Chetnik groups, Nešković ordered their members to be treated on a case-by-case basis according to the level of hostility that local commanders exhibited toward the Partisans. The primary purpose of these instructions was to separate the Chetnik commanders from their men—ordinary peasants, many of whom were forcibly conscripted—and to counter the enemy propaganda which was accusing the Partisans of inciting a fratricidal war between the Serbs. No such niceties were to be observed when dealing with ideological foes, be they Germans or Serbian fascists, who were to be "liquidated without mercy." Nešković, however, added that these prisoners could be spared and exchanged at any time, but only "if they request [it]."[169] Despite the memories of 1941, the Partisan leadership did not lose sight of the potential dividends of sparing captives, but wished to avoid appearing weak by offering negotiations. In other words, if the Germans wanted their prisoners returned alive, they would have to initiate the request.

The Germans showed no such intention throughout 1942, but rather continued with a widespread application of terror which seriously constrained the growth of the Partisan units in Serbia at the time.[170] The Partisan leadership recognized the adverse effect of the reprisals on the fighting spirit of their units, but nonetheless attempted to spur them on to new ventures.[171] The Supreme HQ's proclamation of 10 February 1943 ordering all guerrilla units in Yugoslavia to step up their attacks on the occupier would not have remained unanswered by the

---

[169] *Zbornik*/I/3/174–75, Regional Committee of KPJ to Party Delegate for Požarevac (7 April 1942). It is interesting that the Partisans had no qualms about taking the initiative when facing the other occupying army in Serbia, the Bulgarians. In the first week of February 1942, one Partisan unit in Southern Serbia offered several soldiers for exchange despite the fact that the Bulgarian command threatened to execute civilians and burn villages if the captives were not returned. Ibid., p. 63, Babički Partisan Detachment to KPJ's Regional Committee, 6 February 1942. The difference in approach to negotiating with the Bulgarian commands might have had to do with the fact that Bulgarian soldiers, much like the Italian soldiers, were largely perceived as unwilling conscripts manipulated by their reactionary officers.

[170] The number of Partisans in early 1943 was estimated at approximately 1,200 fighters. Petranović, *Srbija*, p. 339.

[171] See *Zbornik*/I/5/10, Proclamation of the Partisan Main HQ for Serbia to all subordinated units (1 January 1943).

Serbian Partisans. They needed a victory, no matter how small, to serve as a reminder to the population and to their own weary fighters that they were still in the fight. Consequently, they were quite prepared to accept the large-scale reprisals which were sure to follow in the wake of any successful action. On 15 February, they ambushed a *Kübelwagen* (a German light military vehicle) just outside Požarevac. Its occupants, wounded in the firefight, were executed on the spot.[172] The fact that one of them was Colonel Hensel, commander of the 734th Grenadier Regiment, who might have been a valuable asset for an exchange, did nothing to influence the Partisans' attitude. They were not looking for prisoners, but rather to deal a violent blow against the occupier which would show both friend and foe that they were far from being defeated.

The "no quarter-no negotiations" policy continued to be practiced by the Serbian Partisans throughout the remaining period of the occupation, with few exceptions.[173] Sometimes, the Partisans tried to differentiate between the "innocent" and "guilty" prisoners. As all of their detachments in Serbia were static, regional units, the Partisans had a chance to observe the patterns of behavior of certain members of the occupation forces within their operational areas. For instance, during the skirmish which took place on 24 April 1943 south of Smederevo, the Partisans killed four Germans. At least one of them, a certain "Hans" known for his brutality, was executed after surrendering. Four wounded soldiers, captured in the same fight, claimed they were forced to fight and were left alone.[174] Still, the release of captured Germans was rare by the second half of 1943—prisoners were usually shot immediately after capture.[175] The application of reprisals does not seem

---

[172] *Zbornik*/I/5/73–77, Report by Morava Company to Požarevac Detachment (16 February 1943); NARA, T-315, Roll 2245, 001211, War diary entry for 15 February 1943.

[173] According to Yugoslav authors Đurica Labović and Milan Basta, the representatives of the Main HQ for Vojvodina made a verbal agreement with the commander of a German artillery regiment in the town of Belegiš (forty-five kilometers north of Belgrade) in mid-July 1944, according to which the Germans would refrain from plunder and maltreatment of the civilian population in exchange for the cessation of guerrilla attacks on the regiment. Đurica Labović and Milan Basta, *Partizani za pregovaračkim stolom 1941.–1945.* (Zagreb: Naprijed, 1986), pp. 261–64. One member of the American Office of Strategic Services (OSS) observed that both sides "adopted a 'live-and-let-live' policy toward one another" in the region in 1944. Kirk Ford, Jr., *OSS and the Yugoslav Resistance, 1943–1945* (College Station: Texas A&M University Press, 1992), p. 152.

[174] *Zbornik*/I/5/141, Report by the KPJ's district committee for Mladenovac (1 May 1943). The German sources mention five wounded, without saying whether they were captured or not. NARA, T-501, Roll 249, 000339, Daily report for 25 April 1943.

[175] See the daily reports of Military Commander Southeast for 7 and 15 January 1944 for additional instances of the execution of German prisoners. NARA, T-501, Roll 352, 000857, 895.

to have affected the Partisans' policies in this respect, as was the case with the Chetniks.[176]

The German policy regarding captured Partisans changed little from 1942–1944. In mid-March 1942, General Bader issued an order designating which members of both guerrilla movements could be spared and used for forced labor. In reality, this order merely replaced the firing squad with death through exhaustion, exposure, and disease in the work camps in northern Norway.[177] This order notwithstanding, the Partisans continued to face the prospect of summary execution after capture, and those suspected of aiding them were sent to prisons and camps and used as hostages. Hostages were normally taken and reprisals exacted according to the 1:50 or 1:25 quotas whenever a guerrilla attack caused a loss of German life.[178] Slight changes in the reprisal rules came in late July 1943 when it was decided that those casualties caused by German actions (i.e. when the guerrillas were forced into direct confrontation) would be exempted from the application of reprisal rules. The casualties resulting from guerrilla actions (like ambushes or acts of sabotage) were still to be avenged as per existing directives.[179] On 6 August 1943,

---

[176] Nine German workers were captured in mid-September 1943 on the Draglica–Kokin Brod road. After the Germans threatened retaliation, these men were set free. The author of the daily report for 16 September concluded that this incident "proves again the sensitivity of the DM [Draža Mihailović] movement to reprisals." NARA, T-313, Roll 483, 000163, Daily report of Military Commander Southeast for 16 September 1943. I have never encountered a similar comment in the German reports pertaining to the Partisans. The Chetniks, although they usually released German prisoners, sometimes treated them in the same manner as the Partisans. On 27 September 1943, seven German customs officials and some thirty Bulgarians near Užice were captured. The latter were released, but the Chetniks retained the German prisoners despite threats of reprisals from German authorities if they were not released. After their bodies had been found on 14 October, the Germans executed 250 hostages. NARA, T-501, Roll 266, 000940, 930, 900, 892, Daily reports of Military Commander Southeast for 27 September, 3, 14, and 17 October 1943.

[177] Out of 4,200 prisoners shipped to Norway, only some 2,400 returned to the country after the war. Glišić, *Teror*, pp. 122–23.

[178] Both the attack on Colonel Hensel's car and the one south of Smederevo were avenged by the execution of 550 hostages over the ensuing days. One should note that in the first case, the German authorities executed 100, rather than fifty, hostages for each of the four killed. Glišić, *Teror*, p. 71; *Zbornik/I/5/456*, War diary of the 104th Jäger Division for the period 25 April–14 May 1943 (Entry for 24 April 1943). Only rarely was the application of repressive measures canceled. The destruction of the village of Dubac was ordered on 19 March 1943 because a harvest-collecting party in its vicinity was attacked. Because the local *Feldkommandantur* failed to do so in the three ensuing weeks, the Commanding General in Serbia rescinded the order, adding that reprisal measures must be carried out without delay in the future. NARA, T-501, Roll 249, 000237, Message to FK 610 (8 April 1943).

[179] NARA, T-501, Roll 252, Reprisal order of the Commanding General in Serbia (31 July 1943).

Bader ordered that captured Partisans should be shot or hanged "only in exceptional cases" due to shortages of forced labor, and from that point on, were to be treated as prisoners of war.[180] The final changes in reprisal policies came in late December of the same year, the most important of which was the abolition of fixed reprisal quotas: the number of hostages to be executed in reprisal for a guerrilla attack would henceforth be decided on a case-by-case basis. Furthermore, combat casualties, regardless of whether they occurred as the result of guerrilla activity or German offensive actions, were "in principle" not to be avenged by the execution of hostages.[181] Clauses such as "exceptional cases" and "in principle" were vague enough to allow the occupation authorities to circumvent the new orders whenever they saw fit. Although the overall number of hostage executions dropped sharply in the last year of the war in Serbia, the Germans continued to execute captured Partisans until the end of the war.[182]

The first part of 1943 was marked by momentous events on the battlefields of Europe and Africa. In May, Army Group Africa capitulated in Tunisia. On 12 July, the first phase of the Battle of Kursk ended in a German failure to penetrate Soviet defenses. Two days earlier, the much awaited Second Front was opened as the Western Allies invaded Sicily. The fall of Italy was expected to occur in the

---

[180] Glišić, *Teror*, pp. 170–71. This last measure was the result of Hitler's new order that nominally recognized the rights of captured guerrillas. For more information on this decision, see Chapter 4.

[181] The appointment of Hermann Neubacher as Hitler's representative for the Balkans in late August 1943 helped usher in an end to the mass terror that had been practiced since 1941. Although it took him several months to outmaneuver the hardliners like Meyszner, he managed to bring about the relaxation of reprisal rules in Serbia. Neubacher, a practical politician, sought to unite all nationalist elements with the Third Reich in a joint front against communism. Reducing the size and scope of reprisals was one means of facilitating future collaboration with the Nedić government. Hermann Neubacher, *Sonderauftrag Südost 1940–1945: Bericht eines fliegenden Diplomaten* (Götingen: Musterschmidt Verlag, 1956), p. 137. For the full text of the new order, see NARA, T-501, Roll 267, 000033–6, Reprisal measures (22 December 1943).

[182] For instance, the Germans shot fifty Partisans for the death of a police captain in late January 1944 (NARA, T-501, Roll 352, 000927, Daily report for 22 January 1944); thirty "Communists" were shot in Serbia in the week prior to 3 April 1944 (NARA, T-78, Roll 331, 6288550, Daily report for 3 April 1944); in mid-May, twenty-five hostages were shot in Sandžak after the Partisans failed to release some captured German soldiers (Ibid., 6288817, Daily report for 14 May 1944); the Commander-in-Chief Southeast reported that altogether 110 Partisans were executed in reprisals in Serbia in June 1944 (NARA, T-311, Roll 190, 000802, War diary entry for 10 July 1944); and on 11 July 1944, forty Partisans were executed for an attack on an ethnic German refugee convoy in the Banat (Ibid., 000808, Daily report for 11 July 1944). According to an incomplete survey, 148 inmates of the Banjica concentration camp were shot from August to October 1944. Glišić, *Teror*, p. 140.

following months. This, combined with the successes the Partisans enjoyed in the rest of Yugoslavia and the general discontent caused by two years of harsh occupation, made the Partisan cause all the more attractive to the Serbian population. During the latter half of 1943, the communist-led guerrillas managed to both strengthen their positions in the country and to even form brigades. On 28 August 1943, Tito ordered the Main HQ for Serbia to limit the size of operations against the occupier and concentrate on organizing, recruiting, and fighting collaborationist formations and the Chetniks of Draža Mihailović instead.[183] However, the German grip on the country was still too strong for these large units to operate freely, causing some units to be disbanded while others were either evacuated to Bosnia or sought refuge in the unruly southern part of the country.

Tito and the Supreme HQ were always conscious of the great importance Serbia held for the region as a whole—whoever held it, held Yugoslavia. These considerations were primarily political in nature, and Serbia, the bastion of Draža Mihailović and his royalist movement, was seen as a potential Yugoslav *Vendée*, which could endanger the ongoing revolution. Therefore, in September 1943, Tito ordered Bosnian and Proletarian units to start concentrating along the left bank of the Drina River. From there, these units were to invade Serbia as soon as circumstances permitted. After this concentration had been dispersed by German operations in late autumn and early winter, Tito decided to try again, this time approaching from the south, from Sandžak. The plan was to secure a foothold in the southwestern part of Serbia, and use it both for strengthening the local Partisans and as a springboard for future operations. Starting in mid-March 1944, two Partisan divisions (the 2nd Proletarian and 5th Krajina) crossed the Lim River and reached positions south of Kraljevo. The Germans parried by using the only reserves they had in the country, one police regiment and one regiment of the Brandenburg Division. These served as the backbone of a large, heterogeneous force which included Bulgarians, White Russians, Serbian State Guards, Volunteers and, most importantly, Mihailović's Chetniks.[184] With them, and with the help of the signals intelligence which allowed them to read all the communication between the Partisan divisions and the Supreme HQ,[185] the Germans managed to push back

---

[183] *Oslobodilački rat,* Vol. I, pp. 611–12, 615–16, 619–20.

[184] Beginning in late November 1943, several of Mihailović's senior commanders signed written agreements with the *Wehrmacht,* stipulating a cease-fire and collaboration in the struggle against the Partisans. Tomasevich, *Occupation and Collaboration,* p. 224. Although the Chetniks cooperated with the Germans and received ammunition shipments in the above-mentioned battles, the Germans did not trust them and still viewed them as potential enemies. *Zbornik*/XII/4/250–51, Instructions for dealing with Chetniks (16 May 1944).

[185] Petar Višnjić, *Prodor II. i V. divizije NOVJ u Srbiju 1944* (Belgrade: Vojnoizdavački zavod, 1968), pp. 379–81. Thanks to imperfect ciphers and the lack of discipline amongst Partisan radio operators, the Germans managed to read 91% of all enemy messages prior to April

the Partisan force first to the west and then across the Lim. By mid-May, Western Serbia was again fully under German control.

The second invasion attempt came in the summer of the same year. This time, the Partisans amassed much larger forces which could now depend on being resupplied by Allied air drops. After successfully avoiding annihilation during German operations in June and July, this group managed to cross the Ibar River in early August 1944 and gain a permanent foothold in Serbia. At the same time, the Germans attempted to eliminate the traditional Partisan stronghold in Southern Serbia in a series of operations lasting from June until August. The guerrilla bastion became even more dangerous as the recruitment drive in the spring yielded enough manpower to allow the Partisans to form five purely Serbian divisions. The fighting there managed to steal the initiative from the Partisans for a brief period, but the breakthrough of two additional Partisan corps across the Ibar River in late August and the quickly approaching Soviet forces changed the situation in Serbia completely. When the Partisans and the Soviets began their advance on Belgrade, the Germans attempted to escape.[186]

The fighting in Serbia in the second half of 1944 was marked by great brutality against prisoners, particularly Germans, as "payback" was exacted. After almost three years, the Partisans returned to Serbia in force. The headiness of victory and the burning desire to avenge the crimes committed by the occupier and his collaborators were the main factors behind the harsh treatment of captives, especially if they were known for any brutality during the occupation.[187] While Đilas admits

---

1944. NARA, T-311, Roll 194, 000457, Notice from intelligence section (14 October 1944). For additional information, see Gaj Trifković, "The German 'Ultra': Signals Intelligence in Yugoslavia 1943–1944," *Journal of Intelligence History* 17:2 (2018), pp. 104–20.

[186] Due to the deteriorating situation on the southern flank of the Eastern Front which, by the beginning of September, reached Bulgaria and Romania, Hitler ordered the 350,000-strong Army Group E to begin evacuating from Greece. Army Group F, deployed in Yugoslavia, was tasked with keeping the communications in its operational area open. Due to Soviet and Partisan pressure, large numbers of Army Group F found themselves in danger of being surrounded and had to fight their way out of Serbia. For more information on operations in Serbia from March to October 1944, see Gaj Trifković, "The Key to the Balkans: The Battle for Serbia 1944," *The Journal of Slavic Military Studies* 28:3 (2015), pp. 524–55, and Gaj Trifković, "Damned Good Amateurs: Yugoslav Partisans in the Belgrade Operation," *The Journal of Slavic Military Studies* 29:2 (2016), pp. 253–78.

[187] The level of hatred against Germans in general was witnessed by two German defectors who arrived with the Red Army in Kragujevac, the scene of massive reprisals in the fall of 1941. The moment the Partisans and the townsfolk saw them wearing *Wehrmacht* uniforms, they demanded that the Soviets immediately hand over the two Germans for execution. The Red Army soldiers had great difficulty in preventing a lynching and persuading the Yugoslavs that the Germans in question were anti-fascists. Heinz Kühnrich and Franz-Karl Hitze, *Deutsche bei Titos Partisanen 1941–1945: Kriegsschicksale auf dem Balkan in*

that summary executions were fairly common in this period, he maintains that the mass shooting of German Army prisoners was not practiced in Serbia.[188] In light of the available evidence, his statement cannot be validated. Given that the operations in Serbia were to a large degree carried out by joint forces of the Yugoslav Partisans and the Red Army, it is sometimes impossible to discern who bore the greater responsibility for the war crimes which were committed. The published Yugoslav documents indicate that the Soviets often insisted that the Partisans deliver captured Germans to them, or sometimes even took them by force.[189] There was a great deal of arbitrariness in the way prisoners were treated afterwards, and one group assuredly had no hope for mercy—Soviet citizens fighting in German uniform.[190] On the other hand, a Soviet officer, Boris Sluistky, remembered there were orders not to deliver prisoners to the Partisans because they routinely shot them, so the high command advised the units to send them to provisional POW camps instead. This statement is corroborated by German eyewitnesses who confirmed that on more than one occasion, it was the Soviets who put an end to the mass executions of prisoners by the Partisans.[191] Such incidents seem to have been especially frequent during the Belgrade Operation in the second half of October 1944. Colonel Charles Thayer, an American officer who witnessed the fighting, remembered how General Peko Dapčević, commander of the 1st Proletarian Corps, proudly announced the opening of the Partisans' first true POW camp while the battle for the capital was still raging,[192] but by then, it was too

---

Augenzeugenberichten und Dokumenten (Schkeuditz: GNN Verlag, 1997), pp. 75–76; Branimir Tomić, "Kako smo uhvatili Hansa Tilera," in *Sedma srpska udarna brigada: zbornik sećanja* (Belgrade: Stručna knjiga, 1988), Vol. I, pp. 208–09.

[188] Djilas, *Wartime*, p. 424.

[189] See *Zbornik*/I/14/210, 229, reports by 12th Proletarian Corps (19 October 1944) and 17th Slavonian Brigade (22 October 1944), respectively.

[190] The 4th Krajina brigade reported to its commander on 14 October 1944 that the Soviets pressed them to shoot all Turkestanians captured as members of German formations. Instead, these prisoners were sent to the divisional HQ with the comment that they "should sort it out with the Russians and act accordingly." *Zbornik*/I/13/350. Fitzroy Maclean remembers a conversation he had with a Red Army soldier in Serbia at that time who recalled how the Soviets dealt with prisoners. Large groups were sent to the rear, the soldier said, "'but if,' he added, 'there are only a few of them, we do not bother,' and he winked. I wondered how many prisoners it took to constitute a large group." Fitzroy Maclean, *Eastern Approaches* (London: Jonathan Cape, 1949), p. 508.

[191] Timofejev, *Rusi*, p. 380. See the eyewitness reports in Karl W. Böhme, *Die deutschen Kriegsgefangenen in Jugoslawien* (München: Verlag Ernst und Werner Gieseking, 1962), Vol. I/1, pp. 89–90.

[192] Charles Thayer, *Hands Across the Caviar* (London: Michael Joseph, 1953), pp. 38–40.

late for hundreds of Germans captured in the city.[193] Although orders prohibiting the arbitrary execution of prisoners were released several times during September and October, most of the units did not observe them.[194] Since there is no evidence that the Partisan commands ever used disciplinary measures to curb such behavior, one can safely assume they wanted to appease the public outcry for revenge by denying the German prisoners the privileged status guaranteed by international law.

Both post-war testimonies and contemporary accounts confirm that the German prisoners from the Yugoslav capital were at one point transferred to the Soviets. The Partisans first tried to win them over to their cause and thereafter sent them east, to the Soviet Union.[195] The fact that the majority of prisoners were delivered to the Soviets made the exchange of these men impossible. In early November 1944, the International Committee of the Red Cross (ICRC) offered to broker an exchange arrangement with the Yugoslav government through its delegate to Serbia, Dr. Rudolf Voegeli. The Armed Forces High Command agreed, but added that the approval must under no circumstances be mistaken as a recognition of "Tito's bandit government."[196]

With the fall of Belgrade, the battle for Serbia was essentially over. The Germans held a strip of land in the west of the country around the so-called "Kraljevo Bridgehead" (*Brückenkopf Kraljevo*) until early 1945 when all units of Army Group E reached the relative safety of Bosnia. With control of Serbia, Montenegro, and Macedonia, Tito's position as the new ruler of Yugoslavia was undisputed.[197] Militarily speaking, for the first time, the Partisans controlled large swaths of territory

---

[193] For example, one after-action report of the 1st Proletarian Brigade dated 18 October 1944 reads in part: "Captured enemy officers, NCOs, and soldiers: 300 (most of who [*sic*] were executed);" 3rd Krajina Brigade reported that it had "killed or shot" 1,011 enemy personnel during the battle. Milan Radanović, *Oslobođenje. Beograd, 20. oktobar 1944.* (Belgrade: Rosa Luxemburg Stiftung, 2014), pp. 234, 347.

[194] See the orders of the 1st Proletarian Division (11 September 1944) and the 13th Proletarian Brigade (1 October 1944) in *Zbornik/I/12/9–10* and *Zbornik/I/13/38*, respectively. German intelligence picked up a similar order by the 1st Proletarian Division which strictly forbade the shooting of prisoners and ordered that they be sent to the camp at Banjica. NARA, T-311, Roll 189, 001101, Signals intelligence summary (17 October 1944).

[195] Böhme, *Die deutschen Kriegsgefangenen,* Vol. I/1, pp. 90–91; NARA, T-311, Roll 189, 000707, Appendix to interrogation of Vosdine Illitsch (19 November 1944).

[196] NARA, T-77, Roll 1419, 001099–1100, Subject: ICRC's care for German prisoners held in captivity by Tito's bandits (9 November 1944). I found no further reference to the ICRC's initiative in the available sources.

[197] For additional information, see Gaj Trifković, "'The German Anabasis': The Breakthrough of Army Group E from Eastern Yugoslavia 1944," *The Journal of Slavic Military Studies* 30:4 (2017), pp. 602–29.

that were not cut off from the outside world, enabling them to harness all agricultural, industrial, and manpower resources available therein and put them to martial use. The process of regularization within the Partisan army could now be completed with Serbia furnishing the soldiers and the Soviet Union providing the military hardware for the units now taking the field in Syrmia and Eastern Bosnia.

Analysis of Prisoner Exchange in Serbia, 1941–1944

As described above, Serbia enjoyed a unique position in the strategic considerations of the main protagonists of the war in Yugoslavia due to the region's particular combination of geographic, economic, and historical contexts as the heartland of Yugoslavia. Consequently, both the German occupation regime and the Communist-led resistance movement treated Serbia differently than the rest of Yugoslavia. Naturally, such a state of affairs also influenced the way in which the enemies interacted, including the treatment of prisoners and prisoner exchanges.

The Yugoslav Partisans were faced with the perpetual dilemma of all guerrilla movements: what to do with the prisoners? At first they did not have the facilities to accommodate prisoners and bringing them along carried huge security risks. The most expedient option would have been to take no prisoners at all, but in the first few months of fighting, the Partisans rarely opted for this solution, instead electing to release enemy prisoners, knowing full well it would invalidate the main dividend of prisoner-taking, i.e. causing the enemy an irrecoverable loss. The only profit which could be drawn from such conduct was of a psychological and propagandistic nature. It won the captors the moral high ground and deepened their self-confidence, while shattering that of the enemy. The idea of sparing a surrendering enemy—important in international law, but vitually unknown as far as the war in Eastern Europe was concerned—fit well within the credo of the Communist-led guerrillas. It was modeled after the system of principles of the Communist Party and further developed in the first months of the uprising. In short, it aimed to create a new, all-volunteer army which would uphold the noblest virtues of the people it represented. Consequently, the main emphases were placed on winning over the population by orderly conduct and harshly punishing those who disobeyed the rules. The ideal of a truly righteous army would be incomplete if it did not include chivalrous treatment of the captured enemy.

Aside from these universal ideals, there was also a strong, ideological element underlying the policy pertaining to Germans based upon the dogmatic Marxist-Leninist worldview frequently taught at Party meetings and repeated incessantly in Communist propaganda—the conviction that class differences lay at the core of historical processes. Invariably, the worker-peasant class, represented by the rank-and-file of the armies of capitalist countries, was oppressed by the *bourgeoisie,* or the officer class. While this may have been true of the Tsarist army Lenin sought to subvert during the First World War, the advent of fascism and Nazism made such considerations obsolete by the early 1940s. Nevertheless, the notion of class solidarity prevailed in the first phase of the insurgency in Serbia. The ordinary German soldiers, eighty percent of whom were workers and peasants, were still seen as "oppressed" and were released when captured. Those few officers who were captured were usually executed on the spot. The Yugoslav Communists accepted these views as late as November 1941, a lasting monument to dogmatic blindness. Although prisoners were not just simply released at that time, these considerations were largely responsible for the good treatment of the captives in Užice.

Tito also had more practical reasons for keeping German prisoners. He overruled the pragmatic, but short-sighted, solution to the prisoner question as proposed by Ranković, who reasoned that since German authorities could not be compelled to treat Partisan prisoners well through threats of mass reprisals against their countrymen in Užice, there were no moral obstacles to executing the captives and certainly no practical reasons for keeping them alive. Tito's opposition to this course of action was based on his long-term political considerations. The fight the Communists took up in early summer was not only for the liberation of the country, but also for the revolution. On the ground, this fight was reflected in incessant attacks on the pillars of the *ancien régime,* the administration, and the *gendarmerie,* which were now serving the occupier. They were replaced by Communist-controlled bodies, the People's Liberation Councils, which were nominally provisional but were, in fact, conceived as the foundations of the post-war administration of the country. In the same vein, the Central Council formed in Užice in early November was meant to represent an interim Serbian government. These developments were considered illegitimate not only by the British and the Yugoslav government-in-exile, but also by the Soviets, who expressly cautioned against any attempts at seizing power by revolutionary means while the war still raged.

Parallel to the attempts to create a civilian administration and provide it with an air of legitimacy, the KPJ strove to organize the Partisan detachments in such a way that they would resemble a regular army. If they were able induce the Germans to recognize it as such, the Allies and the Soviets would then have to follow suit. The regularization process began with the decision to broaden the base of the resistance by welcoming everyone willing to fight against the occupier to join them. Internally, the process was marked by the formation of platoons, companies, and battalions, and by the introduction of a tight chain of command and strict discipline. *Esprit de corps* was strengthened by the introduction of an oath, insignia, and the clenched-fist salute. Outwardly, recognition of their status as legitimate belligerents could only come through adherance to the rules and customs of warfare, particularly with respect to the treatment of enemy captives. The existence of POW camps was the most visible manisfestation of their adherence to international law and to the increasing strength of the People's Liberation Movement. Although the mass atrocities perpetrated by the Germans in October 1941 forced the Supreme HQ to consider reprisals against German POWs, they never took such actions to avoid subjecting the civilian population to additional suffering and squandering any chances of recognition as a belligerent force.

Regardless of the generally good treatment accorded German prisoners both before and during the Užice period, the occupying forces routinely executed captured Partisans, so clearly their release had to be achieved by other means. The *quid pro quo* of captive for captive presented itself as a logical solution. This matter, however, was not officially regulated and depended greatly on a commander's personality, the importance of a specific captive to his fellow combatants, and the particular set of circumstances on the ground. Whether or not an exchange was offered was deferred to the commander's (and political commissar's) discretion. The chances for exchange improved if the individual involved was important to the cause, for example, if he or she was a member of the Communist Party. The next group of individuals most likely to be requested for exchange were the relatives of Partisan leaders. Their captivity posed a security risk for the whole Partisan organization in a particular region due to their intimate knowledge of the underground activities of their relatives. In all instances, the choice had to be made carefully since the number of prisoners and hostages far exceeded the number of captured Germans. Offering an exchange also resolved an unpleasant moral dilemma—the assurance of having tried every means possible to dispense with the prisoners peacefully before resorting to extreme measures. A prisoner exchange solved the problem of feeding and guarding prisoners as well.

Offering a prisoner exchange could be interpreted as a sign of weakness—whoever made the first overture automatically appeared weaker regardless of the reason behind the offer. It also clearly identified the individuals of special interest to the opposing side, an especially dangerous situation for the Partisans. Still, as there was apparently no other avenue to get their people returned unharmed, the Partisans usually assumed the risk. Had the Partisans been under the protection of international law, they would certainly have been less inclined to contact the enemy.

Through the offer of an exchange, the Communist-led guerrillas endeavored to force the *Wehrmacht* to officially acknowledge them. By delegating the responsibility for the fate of the captured men to the enemy, the Partisans were pressing them for an affirmative response. When the Germans did reply, which did not always transpire, it was widely regarded as a sign of recognition. Even the choice of words could have a positive impact on the self-esteem of the guerrillas, such as at Lebane in November 1941 when the German command addressed them as "Partisans" and not as "bandits." In this respect, the Partisan message to the Kraljevo garrison in early October is worthy of special mention. It was not an exchange offer *per se*, but rather an ultimatum threatening reprisals against prisoners if the demands were not met. The most important and far-reaching demand was for the recognition of the Partisans as a legitimate belligerent force. It was the first instance that a Partisan command openly asked for such status and linked it to the treatment of German captives. Although made at the local level for immediate purposes, the last point reflects the desire of the People's Liberation Movement as a whole to be accepted as an equal adversary. The demand for this recognition would play a prominent part in the future prisoner-related negotiations between the two sides.

The episode in late September in the town of Veliko Gradište on the Danube deserves additional discussion. On this occasion, the Partisans conditioned the prisoner exchange on receiving written assurance from the Germans that they would not attack the guerrilla-held territory. This was the first offer of its kind, and as will be shown in subsequent chapters, comparable terms would often surface in later negotiations. It is unsurprising that the German Army officer present at the time refused to accept such terms even though it meant probable death for the seven captured Germans. This highlights a fine example of how factors such as a commander's personality and the *esprit de corps* of a particular unit could influence the outcome of an exchange attempt. The officer of the Water Protection Police immediately agreed to listen to the Partisan offer in order to save the lives of the men from the same service branch. He was even prepared to sign a written agreement on the matter, regardless of the fact that it would represent a flagrant breach of the no-negotiations order of 5 September; however, his counterpart from the Army, who was not acquainted with the captured men, was not disposed to continue negotiations with the insurgents.

For their part, the self-confident Germans were much less inclined to take the inititive with respect to offering a prisoner exchange in light of their strength on the ground and the string of victories they had hitherto enjoyed over the course of the war. In the summer of 1941, they saw no reason to compromise with the enemy in general, much less with one they considered illegitimate. As time progressed, the situation became more complicated. Small units, spread across vast areas in a multitude of isolated outposts, were now facing a strong enemy who had both intimate knowledge of the terrain and the support of the population. In such conditions, conceit was slowly beginning to give ground to practicality. The willingness of the company-sized detachments in Krupanj and other places in Western and Central Serbia to negotiate with the guerrillas can be explained along these lines. Further examples of this changing attitude are the successful exchange of prisoners around Gornji Milanovac and the preliminary acceptance of the Partisan offer to exchange the mayor of Valjevo. The same practical thinking was behind the decision to try to exchange the captive members of the *Landesschützen* Company for hostages from Gornji Milanovac in late September. Incidentally, this was the only instance where the Germans were prepared to take the first step. Surprisingly, the initiative was condoned by the higher authorities in Belgrade despite the existence of orders prohibiting any negotiating with the insurgents. The affair illustrates the proverbial gap between the expectations of a distant high command (Field Marshal List in Thessaloniki) and the grim realities on the ground. In this case, a manpower shortage in Serbia at that time compelled the Germans to try to get their men released via an exchange.

No analysis of the phenomenon of prisoner exchange would be complete without a brief overview of the historiographical difficulties connected with it. The available Yugoslav sources, both primary and secondary, are surprisingly abundant with information concerning the various attempts at prisoner exchange made in Serbia in 1941 principally due to the fact that these attempts had humanitarian objectives, and as such, could be freely addressed in post-war literature. These events, unlike some later exchanges which had ulterior agendas, were not perceived as a danger to the idealized portrayal of the "People's Liberation War." Unlike Yugoslav sources, the German sources are more problematic. None of the exchange attempts in Serbia are mentioned in the war diaries, daily reports, or ten-day reports of the highest German commands in the country. These events were probably considered too insignificant to be included in the overview of the most important daily activities. In addition, it is obvious that the authors of these reports did not find it necessary to expose the fact that their units occasionally negotiated with the enemy. Therefore, words like "freed" or "let go" were sometimes used when a German soldier was released in a prisoner exchange (see the daily report from Gornji Milanovac from mid-August). The exchange offers were generally not mentioned in daily reports at all (see, for instance, the events around Ćuprija in mid-September or Leskovac in mid-November). Judging by the case of Veliko Gradište, such occurrences were dealt with in special reports, most of which have not survived the war. Furthermore, historians are fortunate to have both Partisan and German documents from this early period of the war concerning this episode, and for that of the prisoner exchanges in general, still available today. The negotiations in Veliko Gradište are characteristic in another respect—when comparing the contemporary reports of both sides, it is impossible to ascertain who took that first step since all concerned parties were clearly afraid of being accused of contacting the enemy first. Also, the German report does not mention the issue of security of the Partisan territory and the commitments made in this respect by the officer on the ground, while the Partisan report depicts this as the central issue. As will be shown in later chapters, these inconsistencies are repeatedly encountered when researching the prisoner exchanges in Yugoslavia.

In the period from the fall of Užice until the end of the war in Serbia, there is no record of any prisoner exchanges, or even attempts. This fact seems implausible in the face of the numerous prisoner exchanges in other parts of Yugoslavia beginning in the second half of 1942. It is clear that Serbia held a special position within wartime Yugoslavia in this respect as well, and the explanations for the absence of prisoner exchanges are manifold. The Germans were especially keen to ensure that Serbia remained stable because of its extraordinary importance to the overall German position in southeastern Europe. The general uprising from late summer 1941 came dangerously close to overthrowing the occupation apparatus. In order to forestall a reoccurrence of this phenomenon, from 1942 onwards the Germans based their occupation on two pillars: the strong collaborationist forces and the consistent use of mass reprisals. The intent was clear—eliminate any and all guerrilla activity. The need to keep such a tight grip on both the population and the guerrillas was imperative since Serbia was constantly drained of German forces which were increasingly needed in the neighboring NDH. Negotiating with the Partisans, even about a possible prisoner exchange, would be incompatible with this policy, and would be perceived merely as a sign of weakness, a quality the Germans could not allow in Serbia.

The population opted either for the Nedić administration simply because it offered peace, or for Mihailović's Chetniks because of their doctrine of not provoking the enemy out of fear of reprisals. This made it very difficult for the Partisans to gain wider support, which in turn, made it impossible to form larger units and carry out more brazen actions against the occupier. Although they never departed from the policy of open confrontation with the occupier, at times they had to take into account the effect of the ruthless retaliations against the civilians. The result was that actions taken against the Germans were few and far between, and consequently, German prisoners were a rare commodity. Even when captives were taken, they were not exchanged for myriad reasons. First, by making an exchange offer, the Partisan unit in question would draw attention to itself and increase the certainty that swift countermeasures by a numerically superior enemy would follow. Second, in Bosnia and Croatia, the propensity for violence against the captured enemy had been partially curbed through repeated exchanges. The consistent refusal on the part of the local German occupation authorities to engage in any kind of non-violent contact with the guerrillas precluded the same from happening in Serbia; therefore, the Partisans would shoot their prisoners, or in exceptional cases, release them, but would not put forth an exchange offer knowing it would be flatly refused.

Once changes in the tides of war during the summer of 1944 propelled the Partisans to successes in Serbia, the roles reversed. Supported by the Soviets, it was the Partisans who now enjoyed the position of strength and saw no reason to negotiate with the enemy. The treatment of enemy prisoners was decidedly influenced by the thirst for revenge and the headiness of victory which gave them license to deal with the Germans however they pleased. Furthermore, they could now put the prisoners in camps or deliver them to the Soviets. The presence of their Russian allies also influenced the Partisans' decision not to pursue prisoner exchanges as it would have been difficult to explain negotiating with the Germans to the Red Army, irrespective of the humanitarian reasons involved.

Chapter 2

Political Discussions, Round 1

1942

Introduction: April 1941–June 1941

The April War had raged for only four days when German spearheads reached the Croatian capital of Zagreb. On 10 April 1941, a group of Croatian nationalists proclaimed the Independent State of Croatia (*Nezavisna država Hrvatska*, NDH). The new state was born of Hitler's plans for the geopolitical rearrangement of Southeastern Europe. Formed as an Italian-German condominium, it would soon become a thorn in the relations between the two countries. Moreover, due to its internal policies, it would become a hotbed of insurgency which would decisively influence the course of the war in the Western Balkans as a whole.

The Croatian nationalists who proclaimed the NDH were members of the underground organization known as *Ustaša* (literally, the insurgent).[1] It was established in early 1929 by the Zagreb attorney and parliamentary representative, Dr. Ante Pavelić. The *Ustashe* Movement was formed as a result of the political turmoil in the Kingdom of Yugoslavia. In June 1928 during a parliamentary session, a Serbian nationalist shot Stjepan Radić, the leader of the Croatian Peasant Party (*Hrvatska seljačka stranka*, HSS), the strongest Croatian political party, and a number of his colleagues. In January 1929, King Aleksandar I Karađorđević abolished the parliament and all political parties and inaugurated a dictatorship with himself at the helm. This was seen by many in Croatia as the last straw in what was perceived to be a continuous campaign by the Serbs to divest the Croats of their political and civil rights. Pavelić and his followers were already under suspicion for their nationalism, so they were forced to leave the country and live in exile in neighboring Italy. Mussolini welcomed them with open arms since he could make use of them for his own plans aimed at destabilizing the South Slav Kingdom. The *Ustashe* found refuge in Hungary as well, which also had territorial designs on Yugoslavia.

The aim of the *Ustashe* Movement was to achieve Croatian independence from Yugoslavia by any means necessary, including violence. In 1932, the organization attempted to incite a general uprising in the Dalmatian hinterland. The attempt

---

[1] For additional information about the NDH, *Ustashe,* etc., see Tomasevich, *Occupation and Collabortion,* pp. 233–398.

failed when the Yugoslav *gendarmerie* and Army intervened quickly and ruthlessly. In 1934, the *Ustashe* and Macedonian revolutionaries organized and successfully carried out the assassination of King Aleksandar in Marseilles. This act of terrorism was condemned internationally and Mussolini was forced to cut all aid to the Croatian exiles and detain most of them, including Pavelić. Thanks to the rapprochement between Yugoslavia and Italy beginning in 1937, the *Ustashe* were pushed further into the periphery. Some of them were allowed to return to Yugoslavia where they continued with their clandestine work. By 1941, the future of the organization looked bleak: it had only several hundred full-time members and little influence in Croatia. Yet the events of March–April 1941 would propel them to the forefront of the political situation in the Balkans.

In the lead-up to their Balkans campaign, the Germans relied primarily on Vladko Maček, Stjepan Radić's successor at the helm of the Croatian Peasant Party, to form a new, Axis-friendly government after the defeat of Yugoslavia. Maček, a pro-Allied proponent of a peaceful resolution of the Croatian problem within Yugoslavia, refused to take up the offer. Out of necessity, the Axis turned to Pavelić. He and several hundred of the so-called "*Ustashe* Returnees" (*ustaški povratnici* or simply *povratnici*, i.e. "returnees") entered Zagreb during the night of 15–16 April, where he was officially inaugurated as the *Poglavnik* (leader) of the new state, which included all of present-day Croatia, Bosnia and Herzegovina, as well as Syrmia and the town of Zemun, just across the Sava River from Belgrade. The *Ustashe* ideology was known as the "Seventeen Principles," a mixture of fascism, Croatian ultra-nationalism, and clericalism. It envisaged the creation of an ethnically pure Croatian state, where all power would be wielded by a single political party, the *Ustashe,* with the *Poglavnik* as its absolute ruler.

As far as the foreign relations of the NDH were concerned, it could hardly be described as "independent." Its genesis was a direct result of the Axis invasion of Yugoslavia, and was maintained by the strength of German, and to a lesser extent, Italian military power. This support carried a heavy price. In order to secure the *Ustashe* hold on power, Pavelić had to make huge territorial concessions to his neighbors. In May 1941, he and Mussolini signed what were commonly referred to as the "Rome Agreements," whereby the new state ceded a large part of Dalmatia to Italy. Likewise, the region known as Međimurje in the northwest of the country was ceded to Miklós Horthy's Hungary. Furthermore, the NDH was divided into two occupation zones, the demarcation line splitting the country in half. The Italian sphere of influence was to the southwest and the German sphere of influence was to the northeast. The Italian sphere was further divided into three zones. The First Zone was the coastal territory which was ceded to Mussolini as a result of the May Treaty and was therefore considered a part of Italy. Farther inland, in the Second Zone, the NDH agreed to refrain from establishing military installations of any kind (this territory was therefore known as the "Demilitarized Zone"). The Third Zone was a strip of land adjacent to the demarcation line. The Germans were not interested in territory, but were very much interested in the country's economic wealth. The aim of the German presence in the country was to more or less ensure that the export of important war materials continued unhindered and that communications remained intact. In a series of trade agreements, the NDH became a *de facto* economic colony of the Third Reich. It had to bear the full cost of the presence of German troops, provide the necessary manual labor, and deliver the largest portion of its mineral wealth and agricultural products at low prices to Germany.

The creation of the new Croatian state, independent from Belgrade, was initially viewed favorably by the majority of Croatians. Soon, however, popular support for the *Ustashe* began to dwindle. The first blow came with the ceding of Dalmatia, the historical heartland of the state, to Italy, which was perceived as the traditional enemy of Croatia. Worse still, the internal policies of the new state did not provide for the protection of everyone. Because of Nazi influence, Jews and Gypsies found themselves outside the rule of law. They became the target of a series of discriminatory directives; their property was confiscated and divided as spoils amongst the adherents of the new order. Furthermore, the *Ustashe* enacted laws which allowed them to dispose of anyone who was perceived as hostile. An atmosphere of lawlessness and fear enveloped the urban areas, worsened by the rumors of what was taking place in the countryside.

Serbs, numbering some 1,820,000 by April 1941, comprised roughly a third of the population of the newly created NDH. The *Ustashe* movement, built on the hatred of Serbian-dominated Yugoslavia, saw them as the main obstacle to the creation of a Croatian nation-state. Beginning immediately upon coming to power, the *Ustashe* enacted anti-Serbian laws. Serbs lost their jobs and were pushed out of public life; those who had come as "colonists" after the unification with Serbia in 1918 lost their land and were forced to leave the country altogether. The last measure was a part of the plan to expel a large number of prominent people, including priests, intellectuals, and other undesirables, thereby depriving the remainder of the Serbs of their elite. Spurred on by hate speech often heard at public gatherings and printed in official newspapers, the anti-Serb measures became increasingly drastic, with people being arrested, robbed, and even murdered. Pogroms took place starting in April, in which entire villages were burned and their occupants brutally murdered. These became common occurrences over the following months, but were especially frequent in those regions with mixed Croat-Serb-Muslim populations, such as Lika, Eastern and Western Bosnia, and Eastern Herzegovina.

The Serb population, faced with extermination, increasingly took to the woods and the mountains. Initially, acts of spontaneous resistance occurred in Eastern Herzegovina in late June 1941, when insurgents effectively closed off Serb-populated areas to the security organs of the NDH.[2] Across the country, Serb

---

[2] For more on this event, see Davor Marijan, "Lipanjski ustanak u istočnoj Hercegovini 1941. godine," *ČSP* 35:2 (2003), pp. 545–76. "The June Uprising" was the first of its kind in the

villagers took up arms (left over from the April War) and formed militias. This mass of armed men had no ideological denomination; they were simply trying to protect themselves and their villages. Their leaders were usually prominent men from their respective regions, such as former Army officers, *gendarmes,* and even priests. Beginning in early July, they were joined in ever-increasing numbers by Communists, who were leaving the urban centers in order to organize guerrilla units.

German strength in the NDH consisted of only one weak division, the 718th, and some auxiliary units, an estimated 8,600 men.[3] Most of these units were deployed in Bosnia, where they were tasked with protecting the major urban centers (Sarajevo and Banja Luka), the main lines of communication, and industrial sites of special interest to the Reich. Woefully underequipped and undermanned, these units found themselves fighting a kind of war they knew nothing about. However, since the Croatian regular forces (*Domobranstvo,* or Home Guard) could not cope with the insurgency on their own, the Germans had to assist them. On 27 July 1941, the 718th Infantry Division reported that unrest had broken out in the town of Drvar in Western Bosnia, and from there it spread to nearby areas. The German units from Banja Luka were already engaged in fighting and suffered their first casualties at this time.[4] The Germans noted that they were involved in a typical guerrilla war, during which prisoners were routinely shot, "even the seriously wounded ones."[5] The second observation made by the German troops on the ground was that the *Ustashe* were the main culprits responsible for the worsening situation in the country. Edmund Glaise-Horstenau, the acting German General in Zagreb, summarized this sentiment in a report to the Armed Forces High Command in early August: "Contrary to the official communiques from Zagreb which lay the blame [for the unrest] squarely on the hostile Serbian influence, all German commands and upright Croatians are unanimous in the opinion that it was the *Ustashe,* and their blind and bloody rampages, which carry the lion's share of responsibility for this state of affairs."[6]

---

territory of the NDH, but was never officially recognized as such in socialist Yugoslavia. The reason for this decision was that the uprising was spontaneous, and not planned by the KPJ.

[3] NARA, T-501, Roll 251, Memorandum on the visit to the 718th Infantry Division in Zagreb. This report is undated, but was probably written either in June or July 1941.

[4] NARA, T-315, Roll 2265, 000065, War diary entry for 27 July 1941. Drvar, being an industrial town, had a sizable KPJ presence. They organized the resistance against the *Ustashe* and thus placed themselves at the forefront of the local insurgents. Thereafter, 27 July 1941 was celebrated as the beginning of the People's Liberation War in the Socialist Republic of Bosnia and Herzegovina.

[5] NARA, T-315, Roll 2265, 000632, Situation report by medical NCO Hinrichs (31 July 1941).

[6] NARA, T-312, Roll 460, Daily report for 9 August 1941. The post of "German General in Zagreb" (*Deutscher General in Agram,* later changed to *Deutscher Bevollmächtigter General in Kroatien,* or German Plenipotentiary General in Croatia) was created on 14 April 1941

First Prisoner Exchanges in the NDH, August 1941–June 1942

The Independent State of Croatia was in total chaos by the early summer of 1941. Pogroms against Serbs caused the majority of them to flee their villages and to arm themselves. Fighting began in earnest in August, as the KPJ raised Partisan detachments from amongst these desperate men, and started an organized campaign against the garrisons, industrial installations, and lines of communication in the NDH. The Home Guard and the *gendarmerie* were utterly incapable of quelling the uprising, and thus the *Wehrmacht* had to become increasingly embroiled in combating the guerrillas. As the vast majority of German assets were concentrated in what would become present-day Bosnia and Herzegovina, most of the casualties were incurred in these two provinces.

On 7 August 1941, near the town of Sokolac located some twenty kilometers east of Sarajevo, two (empty) German ambulances were fired on by the Partisans. Although both vehicles were destroyed, their occupants managed to escape unharmed. It was the proverbial final straw for the German garrison in Sarajevo and they moved to take action against the guerrillas on Romanija Mountain. This took place on 9 August, when a task force consisting of a battalion of infantry plus a battery of artillery left Sarajevo in motorized transport and headed east. The next days were spent in sporadic skirmishes with light casualties. However, on 19 August, one Partisan company ambushed a bus laden with German soldiers near the hamlet of Mokro. The Germans suffered six killed, four wounded, and one missing. The missing man was taken prisoner by the Partisans: "We took the wounded German and treated his wounds. We were thinking of keeping him until he recovered completely, but his wounds were too serious. He was therefore sent to the hospital with the help of a peasant girl. Before he departed we told him who we are and what we do."[7] The German sources do not expressly confirm that the guerrillas returned the wounded man. However, in the after-action report on the fighting on Romanija, there are two references to a soldier who spent time in guerrilla captivity. He obviously managed to rejoin his compatriots by the time the report was compiled (22 August) as he provided both the estimate of the enemy strength at Mokro and the number of casualties sustained.[8]

---

for the purpose of military liaison with the new Croatian government. Glaise-Horstenau was initially well disposed to the *Ustashe,* but began to turn against them in the summer of 1941. He was both genuinely shocked by the atrocities and worried that these would make the German position in the country untenable.

[7] *Zbornik*/IV/1/75, Report by the headquarters of Sarajevo area to KPJ's regional committee for Bosnia-Herzegovina (22 August 1941). The hospital in question was located in German-occupied Mokro; Momir Koprivnica, "Prva akcija u Mokrom i borba sa Nijemcima na Romaniji," in *Sarajevo u revoluciji* (Sarajevo: Svjetlost, 1977), Vol. II, p. 412.

[8] NARA, T-315, Roll 2265, 000759, 761, After-action report by 2nd Battalion, 738th Infantry Regiment (22 August 1941).

The treatment of the wounded Germans on Romanija is not surprising; the Partisans conducted themselves in the same fashion during this period in Serbia. Two orders issued by the Partisan headquarters in the Sarajevo area in early September also dealt with the question of prisoners. Enemy soldiers, as long as they did not commit crimes, were to be lectured on the aims of the Partisan movement and then released. If an enemy unit did commit war crimes, its officers, NCOs, and identifiable culprits were to be punished by death.[9] While these instructions were primarily concerned with the Home Guard soldiers, the treatment of the wounded soldier at Mokro shows that they could be applied to members of the German occupation forces as well. As the war progressed and the enemy showed no inclination to reciprocate in kind, it became clear that the plight of captured insurgents had to be alleviated by other means. In December 1941, the 2nd Krajina Detachment reported on two occasions that it released some captured Home Guard soldiers, but retained their officers for exchange.[10] A successful exchange of several Home Guard officers for imprisoned Communists on the outskirts of Sarajevo in the late autumn of that same year shows that the exchange of prisoners was perceived by Partisan commands throughout Bosnia as a legitimate way of protecting their fighters from reprisals.[11]

The initial disposition of the insurgents toward the Germans was influenced by several factors. The power of the Third Reich's war machine was obvious to all, and no one was keen to provoke it unnecessarily. In addition, the German anti-guerrilla sweeps lagged far behind those of the *Ustashe* in terms of brutality. At this point, the insurgents still had no quarrel with them, only with the *Ustashe*. This mindset was dominant during the early days of the uprising when it had no ideological background and Communists were only beginning to gain influence among the insurgents. For instance, one German Army report from mid-August 1941 claimed the armed Serbs in the area around Bosanska Dubica in northwestern Bosnia refused to deliver their prisoners to the NDH, but that they were willing to

---

[9] *Zbornik*/IV/1/197, 216, Instructions by HQ of Sarajevo District (4 September 1941) and Order of Bosnian-Herzegovinian Partisan Brigade (6 September 1941), respectively. The orders also stipulated that the members of the *Ustashe* organization, regardless of their conduct, could not expect mercy if captured.

[10] *Zbornik*/IV/1/209, 211, Activity report by 2nd Krajina Detachment for the period 10–20 December 1941.

[11] For details on the exchange from the perspective of one of the Communists, see Vjera Kušec, "Razmjenom do slobode," in *Sarajevo u Revoluciji* (Sarajevo: Svjetlost, 1979), Vol. III, pp. 305–10. This is most likely the same exchange that Dedijer mentioned in November 1941. Vladimir Dedijer, *Dnevnik* (Belgrade: Prosveta, 1946), p. 421, Entry for 17 April 1942. For similar negotiations by the Croatian Partisans from Kordun, see Dušan Korać, *Kordun i Banija u Narodnooslobodilačkoj borbi i socijalističkoj revoluciji* (Zagreb: Školska knjiga, 1986), pp. 234, 245.

do so to the German occupation forces. They also asked for German protection if they laid down their weapons.[12]

The fact that the German Army was prepared to accept the request of a group of insurgents in this case should not be mistaken for clemency toward the guerrillas in general. Once a unit suffered casualties, retaliation was swift and ruthless. Just as in Serbia, all those suspected of hostile action (including women) were to be executed on the spot and their dwellings razed.[13] The humane treatment of the wounded German at Mokro did not elicit reciprocity as upon reaching the battlefield, his commanding officer ordered a man suspected of being an insurgent shot.[14] There was, however, one major difference between the NDH and occupied Serbia. Since the former was a nominally independent country, its security organs, rather than the German occupation forces, were responsible for carrying out the reprisals. The Germans could collaborate and give advice, but the meting out of punishment was a matter handled by the local authorities.[15] The indiscriminate *Ustashe* terror, however, had undone any impact which calculated terror might have had on the insurgents. Unlike in Serbia, the Orthodox population would always remain armed because their existence was permanently threatened by the *Ustashe*. The guerrillas could thus count on a certain level of popular support. This, in turn, made them strong and less likely to back down under threat of force.

---

[12] NARA, T-315, Roll 2265, 000711, Report No. 3 by 1st Battalion, 750th Infantry Regiment (12 August 1941). This report, however, might also have dealt with the negotiations held at the same time for the release of six children captured in the ethnic German settlements on the outskirts of Bosanska Dubica. The insurgents were holding the children as hostages to prevent any repetition of *Ustashe* atrocities, and offered them in exchange for all Serbs held in the town's prison. The insurgents' "committee" also offered the Axis representatives the possibility to evacuate the aforementioned settlements. In this case, all villagers would be allowed to leave in peace, taking no more than 50 kilograms of baggage and 500 dinars per person, the same conditions imposed by the NDH upon the Serbs who were forced to emigrate to Serbia. Dragutin Ćurgut, Milorad Vignjević, *Drugi krajiški narodnooslobodilački (Kozarski) partizanski odred "Mladen Stojanović": izdano povodom 40-godišnjice kozarske epopeje* (Prijedor: Nacionalni park Kozara, 1982), pp. 334–35; Marica Karakaš Obradov, "Migracije njemačkog stanovništva na hrvatskom području tijekom Drugog svjetskog rata i poraća," *Scrinia Slavonica* 12 (2012), p. 272. The negotiations with the insurgents outside Bosanska Dubica were conducted by members of the ethnic German organization. Thanks to their knowledge of the language, terrain, and contacts with their Slavic neighbors, local Germans continued to act as middlemen in future negotiations in the territory of the NDH.

[13] NARA, T-315, Roll 2265, 000788, Operational order No. 20 (20 August 1941).

[14] NARA, T-315, Roll 2265, 000760–1, After-action report by 2nd Battalion, 738th Infantry Regiment (22 August 1941).

[15] The quota was not fixed until October 1941 and was much lower than in Serbia: ten hostages were to be executed for each German killed. NARA, T-501, Roll 266, 000263–5, Reprisals for German losses in Croatia (16 October 1941).

Captured Germans could not always expect humane treatment, especially if they did not belong to the armed forces. In mid-August, on the border between Western Bosnia and Croatia at Ripač, the insurgents captured two German engineers from *Organisation Todt*. The embassy in Zagreb requested the help of Italian military authorities in obtaining the release of the captives. Preliminary reports were promising that some kind of arrangement with the insurgents could be achieved. The German authorities in Zagreb dispatched SS Major Wilhelm Beissner of the SD to Knin with the task of overseeing the talks. On 26 August 1941, he returned to Zagreb and reported that he had made contact with the guerrillas, but could not proceed with negotiations because of the ongoing operations of the NDH armed forces in the area. Embassy officials traveled to Knin three more times in September in order to spur the Italians into action, but to no avail. In the end, all these efforts proved to be in vain—the insurgents concluded that the prisoners were spies and had them executed in Drvar.[16]

The Serbs in Eastern Bosnia particularly suffered at the hands of the *Ustashe* in the months following the creation of the NDH. By early September 1941, the region had devolved into a chaotic and bloody struggle between hastily organized Serb militias who fought both the *Ustashe* and the local Muslim population.[17] The uprising had already pushed the NDH authority out of large parts of territory along the Drina River. This was especially worrying to the Germans, as they feared a possible link-up with the insurgents in Serbia. After Loznica and Banja Koviljača fell in early September, the focus of the fighting was transferred to the town of Zvornik, which possessed a strategic crossing over the Drina. Bosnian insurgents laid siege, but the German-NDH garrison managed to hold out. Inspired by the successful actions of their Serbian counterparts at Krupanj, the Bosnians sent a captured German officer, Lieutenant Lorenz, to Zvornik with an offer for the garrison to surrender with honor. The ultimatum was turned down, and the envoy, contrary to the customs of war, did not return with the answer to his captors; he remained instead in Zvornik.[18]

---

[16] Hrvatski državni arhiv (Croatian State Archives), Fond HR HDA 1450, microfilm roll D-280, frame H312635, Missing OT-people (20 August 1941); ibid., H312630, For Mr. Ambassador (26 August 1941); ibid., H312631–4, Report on OT-people (28 September 1941); ibid., H312628, Note (28 September 1941); (hereinafter abbreviated to: HR HDA, fonds, designation of microfilm roll or sub-fond, frame or document number); Ervin Šinko, *Drvarski dnevnik* (Belgrade: BIGZ, 1987), p. 227.

[17] The Bosnian Muslims, numbering some 700,000 in 1941, were designated "Croats of Muslim faith" by the *Ustashe*, who spared no effort in trying to win them over for the new state. In revenge for the crimes committed by the Muslim members of the *Ustashe* organization, the Serb insurgents began to indiscriminately target Muslims in general, committing numerous atrocities in the process.

[18] NARA, T-315, Roll 2265, 001012, Captain Strecker to Major Fröhlich (8 September 1941).

The insurgents still lacked political orientation, but as in Serbia, monarchists and Communists were competing for control. The leader of the former, *Gendarmerie* Major Jezdimir Dangić, was overtly committed to a united front with the Partisans, but was at the same time covertly seeking contact with the Germans and the Nedić Government. One German report, compiled in early 1942 by General Bader, stated that three captured German soldiers and their weapons were returned by Dangić.[19] The same information is found in both post-war Yugoslav historiography and in the memoirs of the Chetnik leader, Pero Đukanović, published in the nineties.[20] On the other hand, Stevo Voinović, a *gendarmerie* officer, claimed in his memoirs that these men were not simply released, but exchanged for thirty Serbs from the Zvornik prison with the consent of Communist representatives.[21] Both

---

[19] *Zbornik*/XII/2/114, Report by plenipotentiary general on the negotiations with Major Dangić in Belgrade (5 February 1942).

[20] Dr. Zdravko Antonić, ed., *Zapisi Pere Đukanovića: Ustanak na Drini* (Belgrade: SANU, 1994), pp. 106, 115–16.

[21] Stevo Voinović, *Na službi kod Dangića* (Kragujevac: Pogledi, 2001), p. 69. In spring 1942, the Chetniks in Bosnia and Herzegovina began taking a neutral stance toward the Germans. By the summer, individual groups across the country, especially in Western Bosnia, were in tactical cooperation with the NDH and German troops. They served mostly as auxiliaries and scouts in Axis anti-Partisan sweeps. The alliance was an uneasy one and punctuated with incidents; the Germans had to launch a regiment-sized expedition in order to bring to heel Chetnik groups in Northern Bosnia in spring of 1943. However, as soon as the Partisans appeared in one region or another, differences were forgotten and a united front presented. There were several instances of prisoner exchange between the Chetniks and the Germans. In October 1943, the Chetniks found a German colonel who was trying to escape from Partisans who had just captured the Bosnian town of Tuzla. The Chetniks returned the officer to the 369th Infantry Division in exchange for a shipment of ammunition meant to be used against the Partisans. Franz Schraml, *Kriegsschauplatz Kroatien: die deutsch-kroatischen Legions-Divisionen: 369., 373., 392. Inf.-Div. (kroat.) ihre Ausbildungs- und Ersatzformationen* (Neckargemünd: Kurt Vowinckel Verlag, 1962), p. 72. In late summer and early fall of 1944, some Chetnik units in Herzegovina turned their arms against the Germans in anticipation of Allied landings in Dalmatia. One Chetnik commander offered to release ten German soldiers if the other side would provide medical treatment for ten of his men and provide some additional medical supplies. The exchange occurred and at least one of the wounded Chetniks was released from the hospital afterwards. Kurt Hildebrandt, "Gefangenenaustausch in Kroatien," *Deutscher Soldatenkalender* 22 (1976), pp. 286–88. In late September, the Germans negotiated the release of more than 300 of their men from Chetnik captivity in Serbia (NARA, T-311, Roll 193, 000887, Daily report for 22 September 1944). By early November 1944, it was clear that the Allies would not land, and Draža Mihailović sought to improve his relations with the Germans who were the only ones who could provide him with ammunition and supplies. As a token of goodwill, the Chetniks promised to release some 320 German officers and men who had been captured in earlier battles (NARA, T-311, Roll 184, Conversation with Draza Mihailovic's Chief of Staff, Major Jevdjenijevic,

Đukanović and Voinović wrote that the prisoners were returned or exchanged in the second half of September. The German primary sources do not mention any MIAs in this period; however, they do mention that three men went missing on 2 October just outside of Zvornik. While the contemporary documents of the 718th Infantry Division are silent regarding a possible exchange, one of these men returned as "an envoy of the insurgents" on 9 October.[22] Had he brought yet another call for surrender to the Zvornik garrison,[23] it would have been mentioned in German reports. One of the members of the 718th Infantry Division remembered that this "envoy" returned because of the "prisoner exchange with the Partisans."[24]

Eastern Bosnia remained a troublesome spot for the Axis over the following months despite the defeat of the guerrillas in Serbia and the ever-widening gap between the Partisans and the Chetniks. Insurgent activity in the region was now concentrated on Ozren Mountain. The local Partisan detachment, several thousand strong, was causing trouble for the Germans by frequently raiding the important railway line between Doboj and Tuzla. In late March 1942, the commander of the detachment, Todor Vujasinović, learned that the *Ustashe* authorities in Tuzla were preparing to try three captured Partisans from his unit. Knowing that the *Ustashe* would not accept Home Guards, not even their officers, in exchange, Vujasinović ordered his unit to capture some Germans from the trains operating on the above-mentioned rail line. In two ambushes on 29 March and 4 April, the Ozren Partisans managed to capture several Germans, *gendarmes,* and Muslim militiamen. While the militiamen were exchanged for sacks of salt (a rare commodity in large parts of the country), the Germans were kept in captivity. The letter of offer to the local Home Guard command failed to elicit a response and the Partisans suspected that the *Ustashe* did not want to inform the Germans. Vujasinović thereupon ordered his technicians to tap into the telephone lines used by the authorities and repeat the offer several times. This had the desired effect and several days later, Čedo Popović, "who had come to us once already over a similar matter,"[25] appeared in the Partisan camp. He had written authorization to conduct

---

3 November 1944). At least one group of thirty-two soldiers was released by the Chetniks in Sandžak in early December 1944 (NARA, T-314, Roll 1630, 000051, War diary entry for 11 December 1944).

[22] NARA, T-315, Roll 2265, 001297, Report by 3rd Battalion, 738th Infantry Regiment (9 October 1941).

[23] After Lieutenant Lorenz, the insurgents sent envoys with the same proposal again on 28 September 1941; the Germans declined. NARA, T-315, Roll 2265, 001171, Cable No. 73/304 (28 September 1941).

[24] A. Strecker, "An der Drina," in Otto Weingartner, ed., *Erinnerungen an die 118. Jäger-Division (frühere 718. Infanterie Division)* (Klagenfurt: Eigenverlag, 1982), p. 21.

[25] Popović first came to the Partisans in late August 1941 to arrange the exchange of several captured *Ustashe* from Tuzla. However, they were shot before any agreement could be reached. Odić and Komarica, *Partizanska obavještajna služba,* Vol. III, pp. 144–45.

the negotiations on behalf of the German command. The Partisans wanted three of their captured men, plus two of their sympathizers. After hearing their names, as well as the proposed place and time of the exchange, Popović left. Several days later, a Home Guard unit delivered an answer from the Germans which was very forthcoming: since the requested sympathizers could not be found, they offered two other captives in their stead. The Germans also promised they would deliver the former as soon as they were found.

The exchange took place around 10 April 1942 not far from the railway station at Boljanić. Twenty Partisans, specially dressed and equipped for the occasion, lined up near the railway tracks with German prisoners in front of them. An armored train appeared and stopped, and while the guards were unloading the Partisan prisoners, a German major and Čedo Popović approached Todor Panić, the guerrilla envoy. "The major was very polite and spoke to me in Serbian," recalled the latter. The German wanted to speak to him privately. Panić refused, but the major was adamant. He showed Panić a signed photograph of a round-faced man with a fur hat. "It is a gift from Jezdimir Dangić," the major said and added that "he's a fine gentleman." "Maybe to you, to us he's a traitor!" responded the Partisan envoy. The major clearly wanted to check the pulse of the local Partisans and to establish whether the split between the Communists and Nationalists was complete.[26] He suggested that they meet again and talk for "this would be beneficial to both sides." Panić declined and urged the major to complete the exchange. The German thereupon signaled his men to release the captives. The Partisans reciprocated and the two sides parted.[27]

There is some controversy as to how many Germans were exchanged on this occasion. Vujasinović claims there were a total of five captives, four from the first and one from the second train. In his book, Vujasinović quotes official NDH reports regarding these events which state that the Axis forces managed to free two Germans in the aftermath of the attack on the first train. This would leave the Partisans with two Germans. Both Partisan and NDH sources state there was only one additional prisoner from the second train. The German reports on the matter

---

[26] At about that time, the episode known as the "Dangić Affair" was nearing its end. It began in earnest in late January 1942 when Dangić traveled to Belgrade and had a series of meetings with high-ranking German officials. They had reached an agreement that Eastern Bosnia would be administered by Dangić and his Chetniks, who in turn would answer directly to the office of the Commanding General in Serbia. The Germans in Belgrade were content with the agreement as it would mean pacification of that troublesome corner of the country. Zagreb, however, got wind of these talks and protested vigorously to Berlin, which subsequently ordered General Bader to cut off all contacts with the Chetnik leader. Dangić, fighting the Partisans since January, continued efforts to reach a deal with the Germans and Italians for the next two months. Nevertheless, he was arrested on 13 April in Serbia and sent to a prisoner camp four days later. He was extradited to Yugoslavia after the war, tried, and executed in 1947 in Sarajevo. See Schmider, *Partisanenkrieg,* pp. 114–17, 124–25.

[27] Todor Vujasinović, *Ozrenski partizanski odred* (Sarajevo: Svjetlost, 1978), pp. 332–36.

mention three MIAs on 28 March and one on 4 April.[28] Again, German primary sources provide no information as to what happened next. Neither the papers of the 718th Infantry Division nor the archival sources pertaining to the Commanding General in Serbia mention the exchange. However, there is one document which might contain a hint regarding the meeting between the Partisans and the Germans at Boljanić. The daily report for 11 April 1942, prepared by Bader's staff at Belgrade for the Armed Forces Commander Southeast in Salonika, contains the following: "718th Infantry Division: [. . .] one light machine gun, three rifles, and twenty-two hand grenades captured during mopping-up at Bratunac; eleven enemy dead. Three missing German soldiers liberated [. . .]."[29] There are several reasons to assume that the last sentence referred to the exchange. First, it took place in the area of responsibility of the aforementioned division, or to be more precise, its 750th Infantry Regiment stationed in Tuzla. Second, the date corresponds to the time frame Vujasinović mentioned in his memoirs. Third, the usage of terms such as "liberated" or "returned" to denote a prisoner exchange was a fairly common practice in German reports. At first glance, it appears as though the three men were rescued in the Bratunac area. However, there is no mention whatsoever of German prisoners in that area in any of the available German documents. It would therefore be safe to assume that the daily report indeed refers to the men captured around Ozren. The real question is why it mentions only three prisoners instead of four.[30]

The situation in the Italian occupation zone in the first months of the uprising was scarcely better than in the rest of the NDH. The elements of the Italian 2nd Army had already begun to withdraw from the second and third occupation zones in May of 1941. This gradual drawback was reversed two months later as the entire area exploded in violence sparked by *Ustashe* atrocities. Rome saw this as a chance to destabilize the new state which had been steadily drifting into the German sphere of influence since the day of its inception. Consequently, the returning Italians suspended the NDH administration and disarmed both the *Ustashe* militias and Home Guard units in the Dalmatian hinterland, Herzegovina, and southwestern Bosnia. Furthermore, the Italians advanced under the pretext of protecting the Serbs, causing a substantial number of insurgents to adopt a neutral stance toward them. By September, this led to an open alliance between the Italians and Serbian nationalists. The advantage of this alliance to Rome was twofold. First, the insurgency was split and the Communists isolated. Also, the 2nd Army now had a potent native auxiliary force to fight against the Communists. Second, the regime in Zagreb was permanently weakened by the loss of authority over large swaths of

---

[28] NARA, T-315, Roll 2266, 000669, War diary entry for 28 March 1942; NARA, T-501, Roll 247, Daily report for 9 April 1942.

[29] NARA, T-501, Roll 247, Daily report for 11 April 1942.

[30] I have been unable to discover what happened to the fourth man.

its territory. The Germans could do little more than defend the interests of the NDH in official meetings with their allies, and complain about the latter's conduct in internal correspondence. They had very few of their own troops and the Italian decision to take a more active role in stamping down the insurgency could only be welcomed from a strategic point of view.[31]

As previously indicated, the Germans had economic interests in the Italian zone, especially the bauxite reserves in Western Herzegovina. The exploitation of this resource was undertaken by a German company and controlled by the bureau of the Military Economy Officer (*Wehrwirtschaftsoffizier*) in Zagreb. One German motorized unit was stationed in Mostar and tasked with transporting the bauxite ore to the port of Ploče on the Adriatic. In early March 1942, the local German officers decided on their own to use the unit to transport tobacco from the factory at Ljubinje to Čapljina. The column, consisting of nine NCOs, 119 men (armed with light machine guns, submachine guns, and rifles), twenty-seven trucks, and four motorcycles made two deliveries on 9 March.[32] A day later, just as it began its journey back from Ljubinje for the third time, the column was fired upon from point-blank range, first from the right and then from the left flank. The front section of the column sustained casualties but managed to make its way through the ambush. The remaining Germans, caught in a deadly crossfire, found what cover they could and fought back. The firefight lasted for five hours. By then the Partisans had also suffered casualties and were close to breaking off the engagement when someone suggested they call upon the Germans to surrender. The problem now was how to convey the message as apparently none of the Partisans spoke German. Fortunately, one of the them was a veteran of the Austro-Hungarian Army and knew some basic phrases. The Partisans ceased firing but the Germans continued shooting for some time before finally stopping. The eerie silence that covered the battlefield was eventually interrupted by calls in broken German offering surrender as the only way out for the survivors. Shortly afterwards, the soldiers of the transport column came forward and dropped their weapons.[33]

It was the first clash between the Partisans and the Germans in Herzegovina and a resounding victory for the Partisans. The immediate German losses were twenty-seven killed, seven wounded, and no less than forty-five captured; additionally, large quantities of small arms, five trucks, and some of the precious tobacco were captured as well. Caring for such a large number of prisoners (some of them wounded) presented an additional strain on the already acute supply

---

[31] Schmider, *Partisanenkrieg,* pp. 91–93, 98.

[32] NARA, T-77, Roll 895, 5646560, Plenipotentiary General in Zagreb for Armed Forces High Command (17 March 1942).

[33] Simo A. Radić, "Neprijatelj o porazu na Badrljačama," in *Hercegovina u NOB-u* (Mostar: Istorijski arhiv Hercegovine, 1986), Vol. IV, p. 143; Petar Milidragović, "Pobjeda na Badrljačama," in ibid., p. 136.

problem of the guerrillas. Furthermore, they feared that the Axis would seek to avenge their defeat by taking reprisals against the nearby villages. Consequently, the Partisan command decided to contact its nearest German counterpart via a letter in which they threatened to shoot the prisoners should reprisals against civilians occur. The guerrillas asked for medical supplies for the wounded, as well as coffee, tea, sugar, and tobacco for other captives. The letter was given to one of the Germans, Johann Schmidt, who was chosen to act as courier (apparently because of his working-class background). The next day, against all expectations, Schmidt returned with some of the materials the Partisans had requested. The answer he brought from the Germans inquired whether they could collect their dead, have their wounded returned for proper hospital treatment, and if there was any possibility of a prisoner exchange. Whereas the Partisans readily agreed to the first point, they conditioned the return of the wounded on a delivery of 7.9 milli-meter ammunition, gasoline, and medical supplies. As for the proposed prisoner exchange, the Partisans replied that they had no authority on this issue, but that they would inform their higher command of the German proposal. Schmidt delivered the German reply the same day. Captain Heyss, the representative of the Military Economy Officer in Mostar, refused to give ammunition or gasoline, but agreed to exchange medical supplies for the wounded. At 11.00 on 12 March, a German-Italian motorized column, adorned with a large white flag, approached the Partisan lines and left shortly thereafter, laden with corpses. Some of the trucks returned late in the afternoon to pick up some bodies which were overlooked during the first visit. They also brought the medical supplies in exchange for two seriously wounded soldiers "who probably died before reaching Mostar."[34]

The 10th of March 1942 was the costliest day for the German occupation forces in terms of personnel losses since the uprising in Serbia in the early fall of 1941. As the attack took place in the Italian occupation zone, the Germans could not react militarily. What they could do was attempt to retrieve their missing men as their number was too large to be ignored. A German official tasked with investigating the ambush inquired of an Italian officer as to what would transpire regarding the German prisoners. The latter answered that the guerrillas usually requested their people, ammunition, or supplies in exchange. The German then asked if negotiations on these matters bore fruit. "Occasionally, they do," replied the Italian.[35] Indeed, in two costly engagements in December 1941 and January

---

[34] Ibid., pp. 137–38.

[35] Radić, "Neprijatelj o porazu na Badrljačama," p. 141. The Italians nominally had a policy against exchanging prisoners. Like the Germans, they feared that the Partisans would acquire a degree of legitimacy through repeated negotiations. However, in the field, Italian commands had accepted prisoner exchanges since July 1941 and were overall much more flexible on this issue than their German counterparts. For a detailed study of prisoner exchanges between the Partisans and the Italians in Montenegro, see Zoran Lakić, "Razmjena

1942, nearly one hundred Italian prisoners had been taken by the local Partisans. The Italians had been attempting to exchange these men ever since, and the commander of the Italian garrison in Stolac was tasked with negotiating the exchange of both Italian and German prisoners. Both the German embassy and the office of the German General in Zagreb were aware of the need to have their representative present. On 17 March, they asked for permission to send one officer to Herzegovina "to guard the German interests in this matter."[36] The Commander-in-Chief Southeast gave his approval, but stressed that the envoy would not be authorized to accept enemy terms on his own. He would merely convey them to the higher commands to decide whether to accept them or not. Captain Julius Vassary, who was chosen as the representative, received further instructions from General Glaise-Horstenau: the Italian command was responsible for leading the negotiations; Vassary was to engage personally only if German interests dictated it. While this was done primarily to avoid insulting the Italians (it was their occupation zone), there was certainly an additional reason—the Germans did not want the appearance of personally negotiating with the guerrillas. Vassary, equipped with a wireless set, arrived at Mostar on 23 March and immediately contacted the Italian command. Two days later, he was informed that the first round of talks with the Partisans had been led by an Italian major and that the prospects for the release of prisoners looked good.[37]

This information was not entirely correct, for the Italian major could have been killed during the negotiations. The first meeting between the Partisans and the Italians was the result of a letter from the "Operational Headquarters for Herzegovina" sent on 21 March 1942 in answer to Captain Heyss' proposition made on 10 March. In the letter, the Partisan command proposed a meeting on either 25 or 26 March, in an area some six kilometers outside of Stolac. Both sides could bring altogether six armed men; the Partisans would carry a red flag and the Axis envoys a white flag (the intended slight is obvious).[38] On 25 March, Major Bartelleo, the

---

ratnih zarobljenika u Crnoj Gori u toku Narodnooslobodilačkog rata," *Vojnoistorijski glasnik* 18:1 (1967), pp. 69–117. In late March 1943, the Italian High Command officially sanctioned the pursuit of prisoner exchange with the Partisans; see the documents titled "Scambio prigionieri" [Exchange of Prisoners] (23 March 1943) and "Trattamento ribelli catturati in combattimento" [Treatment of Rebels Captured in Combat] (27 May 1943), retrieved from http://www.criminidiguerra.it/DocumRob.shtml#segre

[36] NARA, T-501, Roll 266, 000146, German General in Zagreb to Armed Forces High Command (17 March 1942).

[37] *Zbornik*/XII/2/238–39, Abwehr in Zagreb to Abwehr directorate with the Armed Forces High Command (26 March 1942). This is the only German document pertaining exclusively to prisoner exchanges which was printed in the "Zbornik" edition.

[38] NARA, T-77, Roll 884, 5633868–9, Bauxite column to German Plenipotentiary General (22 March 1942).

commander of the Stolac garrison, arrived at the designated location with a small escort. As soon as he stepped out of his car, he was arrested. He and his translator were taken away while the rest of his entourage was set free.[39] The reason for such a flagrant breach of the customs of war by the Partisans was due to the fact that the Italians had rounded up between twenty and thirty people from a nearby village in the aftermath of the Ljubinje ambush. Before negotiating the exchange of the captured soldiers, the Partisans wanted to trade Bartelleo for these people. The major wrote a letter asking for the release of these hostages and gave it to a Partisan commissar who volunteered to take it to Stolac. The guerrillas underestimated the Italians—their envoy was seized as soon as he showed the letter. His release, as well as that of the other hostages, now depended upon the safe return of the major. This infuriated the Partisans and they threatened to shoot Bartelleo and all other prisoners if their compatriots were not released within forty-eight hours. The Italians finally backed down and freed thirteen female hostages and the commissar; the major and his translator were released on the same occasion.[40]

The negotiations at Stolac produced no agreement regarding the exchange of the remainder of the Axis soldiers. In early April, the Germans and Italians agreed to jointly handle future negotiations and decided to exchange prisoners on a one-to-one ratio. Another important provision was that Germans and Italians would be exchanged in equal numbers. The German general in Zagreb reported that "the exchange can commence as soon as the Partisans furnish the names of the individuals they want. This has not happened yet. Not clear when it will happen. Once the names arrive it could take another two weeks. Negotiations rest for the time being. Captain Vassary is back in Sarajevo."[41] This report is undated, but it was probably compiled before 18 April. On that day, the NDH authorities in Dubrovnik sent a message to the Ministry of the Interior in Zagreb, informing it of another letter from the local Partisan command addressed to Major Bartelleo. In addition to the reaffirmation of their wish to exchange prisoners, the letter included the names of 131 people the Partisans wanted released. They claimed they now had

---

[39] *Zbornik*/XII/2/311, Entry for Stolac area, 25 March 1942.

[40] Ibid., p. 317, Entry for Stolac area, 26 March 1942. The Italian document does not mention the commissar. The Yugoslav sources claim the Italians released him along with eighteen other men and women. The other ten hostages had already been taken away, but the Italians promised they would retrieve them as soon as possible. The Yugoslav sources also differ as to the circumstances that led to Bartelleo's capture: while some claim he was arrested because of his uncompromising stance on the exchange issues, others say the arrest was premeditated. I am inclined to believe the second version. See Radić, "Neprijatelj o porazu na Badrljačama," pp. 145–46, and *Sjećanja boraca stolačkog kraja* (Stolac: Opštinski odbor SUBNOR-a, 1984), pp. 593–95.

[41] NARA, T-501, Roll 266, 000120, German General in Zagreb to Armed Forces Commander Southeast (undated).

forty-three German prisoners, and had executed ten Italian soldiers and one officer for the crimes they had allegedly committed. As there were now an estimated 116 Axis prisoners held by the Partisans, the figures seem to confirm that the Partisans essentially agreed to the one-to-one ratio proposed by the Germans and Italians.[42]

Contact was broken off after this letter due to the intensification of fighting in this part of Herzegovina in late April/early May. The local Partisan units were ordered to step up their attacks on enemy communications and troops in order to alleviate the pressure on the main Partisan force under Tito in Eastern Bosnia. During this period, the Partisans reached the Neretva River and jeopardized the Mostar–Dubrovnik rail line. The Italians reacted by shuffling additional troops to the area and by launching Operation Stolac in mid-May.[43] The fighting continued throughout June as the Italians, reinforced by the Chetniks, launched an all-out offensive against the Herzegovinian Partisans. Demoralization set in amongst the guerrilla ranks, as whole units deserted to the Monarchists. In the end, only some six hundred Partisans joined the main Partisan force coming from Montenegro.

In late May, the advancing Italian and NDH units liberated fifty Italian prisoners whose exchange had been negotiated during the preceding months. The German prisoners from Ljubinje, however, were "taken away to an undisclosed location" by the Partisans.[44] A partial explanation came several months later when a German envoy inquired after the prisoners' fate from one of his Partisan counterparts. The answer was that—along with some wounded Partisans—they were shot and thrown into a ravine by the Chetniks. According to the same source, the Chetniks found the Italian prisoners at the same time and led them behind their lines. The Partisan commander added that he personally tried three times to contact the Germans in Mostar in order to have the prisoners exchanged. The Italians thwarted all these efforts and even threatened him with death if he tried to contact the Germans again.[45]

---

[42] Radić, "Neprijatelj o porazu na Badrljačama," p. 146. In the *Abwehr* cable of 26 March, the Italians reckoned there were eighty-four of their men in captivity. Without the eleven men who were shot, the number is reduced to seventy-three. The original number of Germans (forty-five) was reduced by two, for unknown reasons. The total is thus 116. The difference of fifteen persons between the figures the Partisans wanted and the number they were offered may be accounted for by an unknown number of officers or specialists who would have been exchanged at a higher ratio.

[43] *Oslobodilački rat,* Vol. I, pp. 203, 208; *Zbornik*/XIII/2/363–64, Operational bulletin of the 2nd Army (3 May 1942).

[44] NARA, T-501, Roll 265, 000912, Document pertaining to Partisan attack on bauxite column (30 September 1942).

[45] NARA, T-501, Roll 265, 001034, Report by German citizen Hans Ott from Livno (26 September 1942). The fate of these German prisoners was never sufficiently explained in the

This information, obtained in September, seems to confirm the unpleasant experiences alleged by Germans in the area in March and April. The NDH authorities requested that the Germans in Mostar make their motorized unit available for the transportation of tobacco because the Italians refused to provide protection for civilian vehicles. The Italians had not been informed in advance of the columns' itinerary, a move justified by the Germans who claimed that "[since] the Italian troops were covertly in contact with the Serbs, Freemasons, and Jews, they . . . would not take kindly to . . . the cooperation between [the German motorized unit] and the Croatian [state tobacco] monopoly." Even worse, it appears as though the Italians in Stolac had known about the ambush, and had failed to either warn or protect the column.[46] The earlier complaints from German officials in Zagreb about the sustained Italian efforts to undermine the NDH and the German position there were additionally confirmed by eyewitness reports from Herzegovina.

While the talks in Herzegovina dragged on, the Germans were able to gather important information about their enemies. The courier, Johann Schmidt, traveled frequently between the Partisan headquarters and Mostar and reported his observations to his superiors. The Partisans were full-time soldiers, he said, well-armed and well-disciplined; orders were obeyed immediately. Schmidt also related some political statements made by the guerrillas. They considered the Chetniks to be their main enemies, then all fascists, but also "the capitalist Churchill." The last remark was illustrative of the Partisans' deep antagonism toward the British which was rooted in ideological differences and exacerbated by Britian's support of the Monarchists.[47] As the latter were openly acting as Italian allies,

---

Yugoslav historiography. The depictions of this episode rarely venture beyond the exchange of Major Bartelleo. The 2nd part of *Zbornik* Vol. XIII, using a selection of Italian documents for 1942, does not include any detailed reports from the area from late May. I assume that the Partisans held on to the German prisoners as long as possible. Constantly pursued by the Italians and the Chetniks, their ability to guard and feed them grew more and more tenuous. Once the Partisans were faced with the choice of either releasing the prisoners or killing them, they chose the latter. Blaming the Chetniks can be regarded as propaganda aimed at deepening the Germans' mistrust toward the Chetniks and their Italian mentors.

[46] Radić, "Neprijatelj o porazu na Badrljačama," pp. 142–43.

[47] While many Partisans shared this feeling, the British were rarely overtly criticized by Communist propaganda. The Herzegovinian Partisans were counted among the most radical in the whole country. This fact accounted for the extraordinarily bloody "Red Terror" in the eastern part of the province in late 1941 and early 1942. It also meant that the local Partisans were more zealous than others in explaining the war in terms of class struggle. The British, "the kulaks," and the Orthodox Church were therefore publicly named as the main enemies of the revolution. A popular song in Herzegovina at the time contained the lines "Partisans, prepare your guns to meet the king and the Englishmen." Rasim Hurem, *Kriza NOP-a u Bosni i Hercegovini krajem 1941. i početkom 1942.* (Sarajevo: Svjetlost, 1972), p. 148; see also ibid., pp. 144–60.

the Partisans must have assumed that they were doing so if not on direct orders from London, then certainly with its tacit approval. The Germans must have also noted that they were not explicitly mentioned as the enemy. The Partisans said that their column had been attacked "because it was robbing the poor Herzegovinian people of their tobacco."[48] Judging by this statement, the motives behind the attack were of a social, not an ideological, nature—the column was not attacked simply because it was German. All this, combined with the decent treatment of their prisoners, provided evidence that not all the Partisan groups operating in the NDH were as hostile to the Third Reich as had been generally thought.

Political Talks, Round 1: August–September 1942

After the defeats of November and December 1941, Tito attempted to find a base from which the Partisans would be able to return to Serbia in the shortest time possible. Having left Sandžak in December, Tito moved to Eastern Bosnia. After being driven from the Sarajevo area during the Axis winter offensive in January 1942 (Operation *Ostbosnien*), the Partisans captured the town of Foča and made it their capital for more than three months. This much-needed respite was used to continue the regularization process within the army and further develop the concept of provisional administration in the liberated territories. The military reforms included the publication of the Statute of Proletarian Brigades, detailing the inner organization and tasks for this new type of Partisan unit. As the organization of large, mobile units comprised of dedicated fighters had produced benefits during the fighting against the Bosnian Chetniks, Tito formed another Proletarian brigade in early March 1942.[49]

Although the radical revolutionary line introduced in early winter was replaced in April by the more moderate "popular front" line, serious damage had been done. Owing to what were known as "leftist deviations," large numbers of the population in Eastern Bosnia, Eastern Herzegovina, and Montenegro were turning to the Chetniks. When the Germans, Italians, and the armed formations of the NDH launched a new offensive in late April, the majority of the Partisan forces in Eastern Bosnia melted away. Many units were taken over by pro-Chetnik elements in a series of coups, but others simply buckled under pressure and deserted. This was especially true of the so-called "Volunteer Army" formed by Tito in January 1942 in order to attract those Serbian insurgents who still wanted to fight against the *Ustashe* (and, theoretically, the occupiers), but did not want to take sides in

---

[48] Radić, "Neprijatelj o porazu na Badrljačama," p. 144.

[49] Jovan Vujošević, "Fočanski period: rezultati okupatorsko-kvislinške ofenzive u Istočnoj Bosni," in Pape and Anić, eds., *Drugi svjetski rat,* Vol. II, pp. 102–03.

the conflict between the Communists and the Nationalists.[50] The influence of the KPJ in the Volunteer Detachments was limited, the discipline was lax, and the Partisan *esprit de corps* non-existent. After the spectacular failure of this concept in April–May, the Party would never again experiment with creating units whose political or military reliability could not be absolutely assured.

In early May 1942, the Partisans had to leave Foča because of the new Axis offensive, Trio. The escape of the main force under Tito coincided with the rapid disintegration of the liberated territories in Herzegovina and Montenegro. The local Partisans in the area were ordered to break through to the Supreme HQ which had retreated to northern Montenegro. When these forces met in mid-June, their situation was desperate. Only about 4,000 fighters remained from the once numerous Partisan units. The choice for the new base was strategically convenient (close to Serbia), but was unfavorable from any other point of view: its terrain was among the most rugged in the whole of Yugoslavia, with barren mountain peaks above 2,000 meters; it was under-populated; and it had a food shortage. Tito convened the *Politburo* on 19 June to decide the next course of action. A return to Serbia was considered, but ultimately rejected because the local Partisans were too weak and the population too fearful of German reprisals. The second option was Eastern Bosnia, but this was also rejected. In the end, Tito's proposition to move to Western Bosnia was adopted.[51] On 24 June 1942, the small Partisan Army, now made up of five Proletarian brigades, left its mountain hideout and commenced its long march to the west.

The move to Western Bosnia could not have come at a better time for the Partisans. In mid-May, the Italian High Command decided to reduce its troop contingent in the Western Balkans. This would require the 2nd Army to withdraw from some of the territory in Croatia and concentrate the rest of its units closer to the coast. This decision was made for a number of reasons. The High Command needed more troops for its main theaters of operation. It also enabled Rome to respond favorably to repeated requests from Zagreb calling for the reduction in the costs of occupation borne by the Croatian taxpayers. In the official agreement reached in Zagreb on 19 June, the Italians pledged to complete the first stage of the withdrawal by 10 July. They also promised to inform the Croatians about these moves in advance, allowing for the replacement of the Italian garrisons in a timely

---

[50] For this reason, the Partisans decided not to introduce the red star insignia in the Volunteer units. Rudolf Primorac, *Operativno-taktička iskustva iz prve polovine narodnooslobodilačkog rata* (Belgrade: Vojnoizdavački i novinski centar, 1986), p. 19.

[51] Mišo Leković, *Ofanziva proleterskih brigada u leto 1942* (Belgrade: Vojnoistorijski institut, 1965), pp. 23–25, 40. The additional reason for not returning to Serbia was that the Soviet defeat at Kharkov in May had finally convinced Tito that the war would last for a long time. Consequently, the takeover of power in Serbia would have to be postponed until the Red Army appeared on the Yugoslav borders. Petranović, *Srbija*, p. 604.

fashion if necessary. The Italians, however, did not honor the last condition. The withdrawal from the Third Zone was so precipitous that it was largely completed by the beginning of July, nearly ten days before the agreed deadline. The NDH authorities asked repeatedly for a more gradual drawdown so that they could muster enough troops to secure a proper takeover. These entreaties went largely unheeded, and in some cases, the Italians even relinquished control of the evacuated areas to their Chetnik auxiliaries. This intensified the mistrust held by the Germans, who had suspected the withdrawal of being another Italian scheme to weaken the NDH.[52] On the ground, the main consequence of the speedy Italian withdrawal was that a large area of Herzegovina and Western Bosnia was left without any military presence. The brigades under Tito began arriving from the east just in time to exploit the vacuum.

The town of Livno was the center of the region known as the "Bauxite Area," which extended to Mostar. A German company, Hansa Leichtmetall, held the concession for the exploitation of the valuable ore; therefore, a number of its engineers had been present in the region since the late summer of 1941. On 5 August 1942, there were seven German technicians remaining in Livno as the Partisan brigades began to encircle the town. In the next two days of fighting, the guerrillas managed to capture the whole town except for a villa which served as the German administrative center. The defenders (Germans and a company of *Ustashe* soldiers) repelled several attacks. After a call for surrender went unheeded, the Partisans brought forward a field piece and began firing at the villa. After a few rounds, a white flag was raised; one after another, all hundred or so defenders came out with their hands raised.[53]

As soon as the garrison surrendered, the Partisans requisitioned all the supplies, began a recruitment drive, and held political rallies explaining their aims to the population. They also meted out their own form of justice. Because of the division amongst the ethnic and religious groups living in Bosnia, the Partisans had to tread carefully in order not to appear to be favoring one group over another. The process lasted a little over a week. The prisoners were treated as follows: the Home Guards and the younger, recently drafted members of the *Ustashe* militia were released immediately; suspicious civilians were locked up and interrogated, with most of them eventually being released. Ranković, who was in charge of these matters, questioned 500 people from Livno and the surrounding area. Based on their testimonies and interrogations, he separated a number of civilians who were actively hostile to the Partisans or who had been accused of committing crimes. They, along with the captured *Ustashe* soldiers, were sentenced to death and shot (120 in all). "Eight Germans and five civilians [. . .] are still

---

[52] NARA, T-501, Roll 268, 000302, German general in Zagreb to Armed Forces High Command (18 June 1942).

[53] Leković, *Ofanziva proleterskih brigada*, pp. 376–86.

in custody and waiting to be exchanged," Ranković stated in his report dated 15 August 1942.[54]

Only seven days earlier, the captured Germans were condemned men. "It was taken for granted that they would be shot," wrote Đilas in his reminiscences.[55] As this large a number of Germans had not been captured by the Partisans in the vicinity of the Supreme HQ since the fighting in Serbia, they were naturally keen to interrogate them. This task was entrusted to Vladmir Velebit, the Chief of the Military-Judicial Department of Tito's staff, who spoke excellent German. During the interrogations, he was approached by an engineer, Hans Ott, who said: "I know you are going to shoot us. This will not bring you any advantage, and it will not be a great loss to Germany, either. Why not let me go to the nearest German command so that I can arrange an exchange?" Velebit immediately informed Tito and Ranković of the German's proposal. Tito's first reaction was that "he just wants to save his own skin." Velebit, on the contrary, was convinced that the proposal was made in good faith and lobbied for its approval. In the end, the Partisan supreme commander agreed. Ott was provided a list of requested individuals, a car, and an escort to the Axis lines. He was also given an ultimatum to return within several days.[56]

Ott hurried to Mostar where he made contact with the local OT office. The office, in turn, provided for Ott's transportation to Sarajevo and then to Zagreb. The news he brought with him on 14 August 1942 caused a sensation in Zagreb. Both Ambassador Kasche and General Glaise-Horstenau agreed to facilitate the exchange. Their main problem was that all eleven individuals named on the list had been arrested and detained by the NDH authorities. The next three days were spent in frantic efforts to find and secure the release of those prisoners. All appeared to have been in vain as the *Ustashe* said they could not find any of the individuals in their prisons and concentration camps. However, this was not true. For instance, Andrija Hebrang, the head of the Central Committee for Croatia whose name was at the top of the list, was still alive.[57] Zagreb most likely did not want to lose such a valuable hostage in exchange for some German civilians. None-theless, with the deadline for the envoy's return approaching, the Germans had to

---

[54] *Zbornik*/II/5/307–10, Ranković to Tito: situation report for Livno area (15 August 1942). This document also contains candid details on the lack of discipline in some Partisan units, including plundering of goods, "sectarianism," and the settling of old scores.

[55] Djilas, *Wartime,* p. 198.

[56] Vladimir Velebit, *Tajne i zamke Drugog svjetskog rata* (Zagreb: Prometej, 2002), pp. 197–98.

[57] Andrija Hebrang (1899–1949) had been a member of the KPJ since the mid-1920s. The fact that Tito was his close collaborator and personal friend helped facilitate his rise to the head of the Communist Party of Croatia in November 1941. From 1945 to 1948 he held a number of high state functions. His downfall came in 1948 as a result of his popularity and personal ambitions, both of which alarmed Tito. He committed suicide in 1949 in his prison cell under ambiguous circumstances.

accept their answer. On 17 August, Ott returned to Livno with the message that although the German authorities agreed to the exchange, none of the people from the list could be found. He therefore proposed that the Partisans compile another list.[58]

In the interim, Kasche and Glaise-Horstenau were hard at work trying to secure any hostages the Partisans were likely to accept. Under their pressure, Pavelić's police had managed to "find" six of those named on the original list. Together with eleven prisoners, they were sent to Mostar, where they would be kept until the deal was negotiated. An additional twenty-two people being held in Mostar, arrested in Livno as Communist sympathizers, could also be used in the exchange, either for the Germans or for the captured NDH government officials. There were some complications concerning these prisoners as the *Ustashe* were reluctant to exchange them for the Hansa Leichtmetall employees; they wanted to use them to exchange for their own people in Partisan captivity. The Germans, on the other hand, desired first to secure their own citizens. Kasche arranged with Zagreb that the exchange of the Croats would not take place before the exchange of the Germans.[59] The Italian military and diplomatic authorities in Mostar, Zagreb, and Sušak (the HQ of the 2nd Army) were also requested to place a number of Partisan suspects at the disposal of the Germans for the planned exchange.[60]

Tito was still hoping that Hebrang and a few others would be found, so he included their names on the second list. As for the rest, the Partisans had to choose from whomever the enemy was prepared to offer. It was clear that the search for suitable candidates would take too much time if it was left to the Germans. It had to be done by someone experienced and who knew the Party cadres well. On 22 August, Marijan Stilinović, a veteran Communist from Croatia, was called to Supreme HQ in Glamoč and asked whether he would be willing to do the job. Furthermore, he had to find out what the "other questions" were that the Germans wanted to discuss. Stilinović had not been to Zagreb for nine years and it was questionable if anybody would recognize him. Nonetheless, he was furnished with a complete set of false documents identifying him as Srećko Šunjevarić, a Serb from Eastern Bosnia and a pre-war businessman. He was introduced as such to Ott on the evening before their departure.[61]

---

[58] Slavko Odić, *Neostvareni planovi* (Zagreb: Naprijed, 1961), p. 72.

[59] NARA, T-120, Roll 5799, H311311, Cable to War Economy Officer Zagreb (22 August 1942); NARA, T-120, Roll 5796, H308811–2, Memorandum for police attaché (27 August 1942).

[60] NARA, T-120, Roll 5796, H308824, Cable to German liaison staff with the 2nd Army (13 August 1942); ibid., H308819–20, Dear comrade Casertano (14 August 1942). Kasche also urged the German foreign ministry to intervene with Rome. Ibid., H308821, Cable to Foreign Ministry (13 August 1942).

[61] Labović and Basta, *Partizani za pregovaračkim stolom 1941–1945*, p. 103. Marijan Stilinović, *Bune i otpori* (Zagreb: Zora, 1969), p. 217, Entry for 22 August 1942.

On 23 August, the two left Glamoč in a car accompanied by a civilian from Livno and headed southeast. On the advice of the commander of the Herzegovinian Brigade, Stilinović remained at Posušje, while Ott went ahead to Mostar to obtain clearance for the arrival of the Partisan envoy. The next day, a car arrived for Stilinović. His escort was Captain Heyss of the Mostar branch of the Military Economy Office in Zagreb. The two did not converse much during the first leg of their journey, but the proverbial ice was broken when an *Ustashe* patrol near Široki Brijeg stopped the car and asked Heyss if he knew where the Partisans could be found. He angrily replied that he did not and slammed the door shut.[62]

Stilinović and Heyss arrived in Mostar that evening and went to dinner. Heyss' initial arrogance had all but dissipated and he engaged Stilinović in a lengthy and seemingly honest discussion. Heyss spoke of his great admiration for Hitler and predicted a favorable outcome of the war for Germany; otherwise, he added, the German people would perish. He admitted that the German occupation policies in Yugoslavia were sometimes quite harsh, but he blamed it on Prussians who did not understand the local mentality. He also openly admired the Serbs and the Partisans for their unrelenting struggle for freedom. For the Croats, on the other hand, he could not find any good words: "A Croat would murder his own brother over a bare bone." Furthermore, he spoke with contempt for the Italians "who lost every war they fought in the last century and only got what they have through political scheming." He went on to ask Stilinović if the Partisans had some sort of an agreement with the Italians given the lack of vigor with which the latter carried out their anti-guerrilla operations in Herzegovina.[63]

In the early morning on 25 August 1942, Stilinović and Heyss left by car to Sarajevo where a transport plane was standing by, ready to take them to Zagreb. There was some confusion when police tried to confiscate two hand grenades the Partisan envoy was carrying around his waist. Stilinović saw this as an infringement of his rights as an envoy and refused the police demand. Heyss diffused the situation by proposing that he take possession of the grenades during the flight and return them to Stilinović once they landed in the Croatian capital. When all parties agreed, the plane took off and Stilinović and Heyss arrived safely at their destination in a little over an hour. Two cars retrieved them at the airfield and drove them to an office building where several German officers awaited them. Stilinović was told he would be quartered in the building of the local *Feldkommandantur* and was warned not to leave unaccompanied. The meeting with a German delegation was set for the next day at 18.00. When the Partisan envoy reached his new quarters, he was unpleasantly surprised: the room was dirty and full of old, barely usable furniture. It appeared as though the choice of dwelling had been consciously made with the express purpose of reducing the status of the guerrilla

---

[62] Stilinović, *Bune,* pp. 217–18, Entries for 23 and 24 August 1942.

[63] Ibid., pp. 218–19, Entry for 24 August 1942.

negotiator; however, it was probably just an oversight on the part of the German personnel. Captain Heyss was visibly angry as he confronted the soldiers responsible for setting up the "guest room." Stilinović, a professional revolutionary since 1920, was less interested in his accommodations than in possible escape routes from the building. After having found one, he went to sleep with a pistol under his pillow.[64]

On the morning of 26 August, the Partisan envoy was awakened by soldiers bringing in new furniture. "In a matter of minutes, they transformed that filthy chamber into quite a pleasant drawing room," remembered Stilinović. He also mentioned a strange event, one he never managed to explain completely. One German officer entered his room two times that morning and left messages scribbled on a piece of paper which said "Jastrebarsko is burning" and "5000 Italians broke into Samobor."[65] In the afternoon, Stilinović was accompanied by Ott and Heyss to a villa in the Zagreb neighborhood of Tuškanac, an upper-class residential area where high level *Ustashe* and Axis officials lived. Stilinović was met by a delegation consisting of one colonel, two lieutenant colonels, a major, and a representative of the German embassy.[66] "We drank Turkish coffee and brandy . . . and made small talk. Schäffer, who speaks some of our language [i.e. Croatian/Serbian], is constantly prodding Kreiner to get on with it. Kreiner does not know how to begin. Finally, the talks on the exchange start and end quickly. They agree to all our demands, although they cannot guarantee they will get everyone we want because Croatia is 'independent' and they cannot interfere with its internal matters."[67]

Having agreed to the details about the exchange, Stilinović and Ott returned to Glamoč. On 4 September, the Axis prisoners were led to Duvno and then farther southeast to the vicinity of Posušje. On the following day, at a place called Studeno Vrelo, the Partisan and German delegations met. According to Vladimir Velebit, the exchange went smoothly, without formalities or complications; prisoner lists were read aloud by Velebit and his German counterpart, after which the prisoners of both sides rejoined their compatriots. The available sources differ on the exact number of Partisans exchanged on this occasion: the estimates vary between thirty-eight and forty-nine. They were exchanged for ten German citizens and

---

[64] Ibid., pp. 219–20, Entry for 25 August 1942.

[65] On 26 August 1942, a Partisan brigade attacked Jastrebarsko (southern outskirts of Zagreb), disarmed the Home Guards, and destroyed the rolling stock it found in the town. *Hronologija*, p. 326. The Italians reported sending motorized units to the scene. *Zbornik/* XIII/2/707, 5th Corps to 2nd Army, Entry for 27 August 1942.

[66] These men were Colonel Albrecht von Funck, Glaise-Horstenau's Chief of Staff; Lieutenant Colonels Schäffer (*Abwehr*) and Schardt (Military Economy Officer); Major Eugen von Pott (of Glaise-Horstenau's staff); and Dr. Emmerich Kreiner of the German embassy's economic department.

[67] Stilinović, *Bune*, pp. 220–21, Entry for 26 August 1942.

twenty-two Home Guard officers and government officials from Livno.[68] One of the Partisans who provided the security at Studeno Vrelo recalled the psychological impact of the proceedings: "The exchange was not big, but it was very important in political terms and for [our] morale. In September 1942 there were still no visible signs of Hitler's weakness on any front [. . .] [and yet] the Germans arrived under a white flag [to make an exchange]."[69]

The German authorities in Zagreb had every reason to be content with the release of their compatriots; they regarded it as a diplomatic and humanitarian success.[70] The exchanged employees of Hansa Leichtmetall were celebrated as heroes when they returned to Zagreb. In April 1943, they received decorations for their gallantry at Livno: Ott received a clasp for the Iron Cross he had won in the First World War, while the others were awarded the War Merit Cross.[71] The Partisans, on the other hand, were less than happy with the people they got from the Germans: "Apart from Beba [Bosiljka Krajačić], Zoga [Olga Kovačić-Kreačić], and one member of the SKOJ [Ivan Kranželić], we received only some treacherous and anti-Party elements."[72] Following the exchange, the returnees were interrogated in order to establish the circumstances of their capture, with particular attention being paid to their conduct whilst in police custody. Depending on the results, they were either retained by the Supreme HQ or sent to various units and Party organizations.[73]

---

[68] In addition to the eight German citizens captured at Livno, there were two ethnic Germans, Fritz and Emma Szedressy, who were captured in Prozor in late August 1942. Due to Mrs. Szedressy's acquaintance with Dr. Alfred Heinrich, the chief of the SD in Sarajevo, she and her husband were included in the arrangement (Odić and Komarica, *Partizanska obavještajna služba*, Vol. III, pp. 225–30). For a detailed analysis of the controversy on the number of prisoners, see ibid., Vol. III, pp. 209–11.

[69] Sveto Kovačević, "Od Une do Neretve," in *Neretva: proleterske i udarne divizije u bici na Neretvi* (Belgrade: Vojnoizdavački zavod, 1965), Vol. III, pp. 312–13.

[70] Kasche sent a telegram to the Foreign Ministry on 8 September: "Thanks to the energetic efforts of the embassy and the Military Economy Officer, eight German employees of the Hansa Leichtmetall company, who had been captured by the Partisans in Livno, were liberated through a prisoner exchange. They are now in Mostar." NARA, T-120, Roll 5796, H308806, Kache to Foreign Ministry (8 September 1942).

[71] Odić, *Neostvareni planovi*, pp. 76, 254; NARA, T-120, Roll 5787, H301616, Cable to ambassador Kasche (18 May 1943).

[72] *Zbornik*/II/6/183, Vladimir Popović to Edvard Kardelj (28 September 1942).

[73] Here is one example: "Nikola Cvitaš, a worker from Garešnica, thirty years old, joined the Party in May 1940 in Zagreb. He was brought into the Party by Ivan Burija, currently in a [concentration] camp. He was arrested on 27 July 1942 in his brother's house, where one of our printing presses was preparing materials for the local and Central committees. He came to that post as a district technician. Before being identified by Cincipinka, he had confessed

The first prisoner exchange negotiated by the high commands of the Yugoslav Partisans and the German occupation authorities had been completed successfully. Initially, both sides were motivated primarily by humanitarian reasons. These were soon overshadowed as both sides recognized that there were other benefits to be gained by maintaining contact. The most important was the chance to discern the political views of the enemy and to gain insight into his organization. The political aspect of the talks was, by far, the most controversial.

As mentioned earlier, Stilinović recalled that the Germans wanted to talk about "some other questions" apart from the prisoner exchange. Judging by the tone of his diary, the prisoner exchange itself was of secondary importance to the Germans when he met them on 26 August 1942. Indeed, their accommodating stance on this issue may have been the result of their wish to "soften" the Partisan envoy for what they had to say next:

> Kreiner then began talking in a prevaricating manner about the senselessness of killing, the need to bring order to the NDH, and that the whole of Europe would soon be brought to order. I expressed doubt that we could find a negotiating partner in this matter in the NDH. Kreiner and the other Germans answered that their side would be willing to negotiate. After a while I agreed to hear their views in order to find out what they actually wanted to achieve through such negotiations. They said they wanted to secure the exploitation and transportation of Bosnian ore, especially bauxite. If we would be willing to refrain from interfering with it, they would welcome our recommendations for the reorganization of the NDH, as well as for the solution of the Serbian question therein. Schäffer then said, "For God's sake, we are not occupiers," adding they had absolutely no political or military interests in the Balkans, especially not in Yugoslavia, but only a limited economic one. I replied I had no authorization for negotiating on these matters. With that, our talks were brought to an end.[74]

The war between Nazism and Communism had been raging for fourteen months and had already claimed millions of lives. It was fought with great brutality and marked by an uncompromising win-or-die mindset on both sides. Bearing

---

to being a Party member and also identified Daskijević, Dolinčić, and Anton Rihtner (previously expelled from the Party, now in a camp). By decision of the Central Committee of the KPJ, he was expelled from the Party because of his treacherous behavior during his police interrogation. He will be sent to you for further deployment." *Josip Broz Tito: Sabrana djela* (Belgrade: Izdavački centar "Komunist," 1982), Vol. XII, pp. 33–35, To the comradely Central Committee of Communist Party of Croatia (10 September 1942).

[74] Stilinović, *Bune,* pp. 221–22, Entry for 26 August 1942.

this in mind, the passage from Stilinović's diary quoted above reads almost incredibly. However, if we examine the specific circumstances in Yugoslavia and especially in the Croatian puppet state at the time, the passage begins to make sense.

By the summer of 1942, the German military authorities in the region were unanimous in the opinion that the genocidal policies of the *Ustashe* regime were directly responsible for the present difficult situation. Unlike their own calculated reprisals, they regarded the wanton atrocities of the Croatian fascists as senseless and counter-productive.[75] In order to curb the activities of *Ustashe* militias in the areas targeted for pacification, the German occupation forces had been declaring various parts of the NDH as "Operational Areas" since January 1942, with reluctant approval from Zagreb. In these areas, the civil administration was suspended and taken over by the German Army. German units also intervened locally on several occasions, disarming undisciplined *Ustashe* units and arresting their members suspected of committing crimes.[76]

The agreement which was almost signed in February 1942 in Belgrade between the Commanding General in Serbia and Chetnik Major Dangić essentially denuded the NDH of Eastern Bosnia. The deal was canceled owing to strong opposition on the part of German political authorities, and led to the Armed Forces High Command reprimanding General Bader for making arrangements on his own.[77] Although the outright removal of the *Ustashe* would have undoubtedly been preferred by the higher commands in the Balkans, no one had the temerity to propose it.[78] As the Third Reich's policy toward the NDH and its rulers was not likely to change fundamentally in the near future, the military began to push for at least a more active German approach to the country's internal affairs. The Home Guard was seen as utterly incapable of defeating the insurgency. The Germans therefore lobbied for the *Wehrmacht* to have more oversight over the NDH

---

[75] For more details, see Jonathan E. Gumz, "Wehrmacht perceptions of mass violence in Croatia, 1941–1942," *The Historical Journal* 44:4 (2001), pp. 1015–38. When a German company executed 257 civilians in Grgurevci, Syrmia in early June 1942 as revenge for the death of some its comrades, Ambassador Kasche wrote a letter to General Bader. Judging by the latter's response, Kasche equated this incident with similar acts perpetrated by the *Ustashe*. Bader responded that the shooting brought an end to guerrilla activity in the area around the village, and added: "I find the comparison between the conduct of this German company and *Ustashe* atrocities insulting to the German troops." NARA, T-501, Roll 248, Letter to the German ambassador in Zagreb (18 June 1942).

[76] See NARA, T-501, Roll 250, 001072, Commanding General in Serbia to Armed Forces High Command (9 June 1942); NARA, T-501, Roll 352, 001253, Situation report for the period 30 October–8 November 1942 (9 November 1942).

[77] Schmider, *Partisanenkrieg*, p. 115.

[78] Glaise-Horstenau mentioned this radical measure in February 1942, but was quick to add that he thought it would do more harm than good. Schmider, *Partisanenkrieg*, p. 161.

military establishment and to play a role in its thorough reorganization. Furthermore, the German Army argued that the lack of the rule of law, the uncontrollable behavior of the *Ustashe,* and the total failure of the civil administration were responsible for the rapidly deteriorating security situation in the early summer of that year.[79] Even Ambassador Kasche, the staunchest supporter of Pavelić and the *Ustashe,*[80] lobbied for some kind of internal reform. On 24 June 1942, he delivered a memorandum to Pavelić proposing a number of measures for the pacification of the country. The emphasis was now on winning over the hearts and minds of the population by fair treatment and by establishing an efficient administration and judicial system.[81] Military solutions were not mentioned—it was obvious that the insurgency could not be put down by sheer force alone.

When Ott returned to Zagreb the first time, he had lengthy talks with both Glaise-Horstenau and Kasche. There is no documentary evidence for it, but he was probably instructed at that point to convey the message that the German authorities would like to talk about the "other things" Stilinović mentioned in his diary. However, his primary task was to gather intelligence about the strongest guerrilla formation (i.e. the group of Proletarian brigades around Tito) in the country. The Germans had no knowledge of its intentions, neither politically nor militarily, as they had very few contacts with it since Operation Trio. The situation had changed drastically in the meantime. In mid-May, the Partisans around Tito appeared spent after they were compelled to evacuate Eastern Bosnia; by mid-August they were deep in the territory of the NDH, threatening to shatter its foundations. Furthermore, their movements shadowed German intentions to bring about some kind of internal reform in the *Ustashe* state. The arrival of the envoy of the Partisan leadership to Zagreb in late August gave the German authorities an opportunity to sound out the opinion of their main enemy on pressing issues through informal, nonbinding talks.

In the conversation with Stilinović on 26 August, there was no mention of the removal of the *Ustashe,* only of a "reorganization" of the NDH. This was partly because such a move was not officially contemplated, and partly because the Germans did not want to disclose just how troubled their relations with Pavelić were at that moment.[82] As the Partisan movement was still very much recognized as a

---

[79] NARA, T-501, Roll 351, Situation report for the period 21–30 June 1942 (1 July 1942) and ibid., Report of battle group "Western Bosnia" for the period 5 June–4 July 1942 (5 July 1942).

[80] Kasche was mockingly nicknamed "bigger Croat than Pavelić" and "the envoy of the Poglavnik to the Reich." Odić, *Neostvareni planovi,* p. 61.

[81] NARA, T-501, Roll 268, 000262-7, German general in Zagreb to Armed Forces High Command (27 June 1942).

[82] Although the talks were meant to be strictly informal, the size and composition of the German delegation meant that it acted in a semi-official manner. The *Wehrmacht* representatives could not openly criticize the *Ustashe* due to the presence of Kasche's envoy, Kreiner.

purely Serbian cause, the offer for them to be part of the solution of the Serbian question in the Croatian state was thought to be attractive. The problems the Germans had with the regime in Zagreb, however, were not as acute as the danger to their own economic interests from Partisan operations around Livno. The output of bauxite in Herzegovina filled approximately ten percent of the Third Reich's overall needs,[83] and any prolonged Partisan presence in the region could lead to serious disruptions in war production. Furthermore, the Germans were very worried about the recent surge in sabotage on the all-important Zagreb–Belgrade railway line which occurred despite the *Wehrmacht's* growing presence north of the Sava River.[84] They made no secret that they wanted an end to the sabotage campaign against this vital line of communication. The fact that Stilinović agreed to listen to their proposals and to convey them to his superiors was perceived as a sign that the Partisans were open to further discussion on these matters.

Stilinović and Ott brought a concrete offer from Glaise-Horstenau when they returned to Glamoč in the first days of September. It stated that if the Partisans would cease their attacks on the German economic interests in the country, then the German occupation forces would be willing to recognize a certain region as "Partisan territory" against which no offensive actions would be undertaken.[85] On

---

Privately, the Germans usually did not hide their contempt for the *Ustashe*. Ott told his Partisan captors "that we [the Germans] would send them to hell and hang the whole bunch if only we could find suitable replacements. These fools and their bloodthirsty policies have caused the present discontent and have driven the people to arms." *Sabrana djela,* Vol. XII, pp. 115–16, Tito to Comintern (14 October 1942).

[83] The estimate is for February 1943. NARA, T-77, Roll 780, 5507223, War Diary of Armed Forces High Command, Entry for 13 February 1943.

[84] The Germans had three *Landesschützen* battalions deployed along the main railway line. They, along with a German armored train and all NDH security forces adjacent to the line, were commanded by a special German staff. NARA, T-501, Roll 351, Order for continuation of operations in Western Bosnia and for the securing of the railway line Zagreb–Belgrade (17 July 1942). A month later, the German general in Zagreb reported: "One could safely ride on a train from Zagreb to Belgrade until three weeks ago. Since then, however, the acts of sabotage have increased not only in number, but also in intensity." NARA, T-501, Roll 264, 000982, Cable to Armed Forces High Command (21 August 1942). In order to counter the guerrilla threat, the 714th Infantry Division had to shift one of its two regiments to the north of the Sava River. Five days later, General Glaise-Horstenau requested that the area around Zagreb be included in the division's operational zone as attacks were already taking place on the city's outskirts. NARA, T-501, Roll 248, War diary entry for 26 August 1942.

[85] Arhiv muzeja Bosne i Hercegovine (hereinafter AMBiH), Fond UNS, 509–3, Report of county commissioner Marko Šakić on the negotiations between the Partisans and the Germans. The document is erroneously dated 14 October 1943 even though it is clear from the content that it was written in 1942. Šakić was exchanged at Studeno Vrelo with the rest of

3 September, Ott had a lengthy conversation with Tito over this and other political issues. Based on these discussions, and the contacts he had with other Partisans, Ott reported that the Communist-led insurgents maintained a great deal of hostility toward the nationalist Chetniks, whom they considered their main enemies. The Partisans were no less bitter regarding the mentors of Mihailović, the British, and to a lesser extent, the Italians. Tito remarked that the Soviet-German war had to end in a compromise otherwise Great Britain and the United States would be victorious, which would in turn mean the continuation of the oppression of the working class. As for the Germans, their achievements (presumably of a military nature) were "uniquely praised" by the Partisans. On the other hand, the German racial theory was "especially condemned," as was the subjugation of the Slavs. When the Germans protested against the execution of the *Ustashe* commander in Livno saying he was merely doing his duty, they were repudiated as not everyone shared their concept of doing one's duty (ie. blindly following orders). Tito also mentioned the atrocities committed by the Germans in Belgrade, which included the use of poison gas: "He knew the Germans well and was astonished that they were actually capable of committing such crimes." Ott replied that was propaganda similar to what the English had used during the First World War.[86] While Tito did not make any comments which would lead Ott to question his Communist credentials, the other Partisan commanders did not hide the fact that they had been drawn into the war mainly by the *Ustashe,* and less out of international solidarity with the USSR. "They are only against the current Croatian regime," Ott said, "and are even seeking German support to a certain extent [. . .]. They remarked that if the Italians were negotiating with the Chetniks, why could the Germans not negotiate with the Partisans?" The excellent treatment the Germans received in

---

the prisoners. While in hospital in Livno, he had a chance to talk with many Partisans who did not mask the fact that they were negotiating with the Germans. Rather, they boasted that "Sunjarević" had a conversation with the German general who was flown from Germany to Zagreb just for this occasion (Glaise-Horstenau was not present at the talks with Stilinović). That openness can sometimes be a double-edged sword is confirmed by the following anecdote. The political commissar of the 2nd Krajina Brigade was informed about a rumor that claimed that a representative of the Communist Party traveled to Zagreb unhindered and met Pavelić. The commissar, who was unaware of the talks, immediately suspected a plot and proposed punishing the rumormongers with the utmost severity for it was well known "that our Party had never in its history negotiated with the enemies of the people." Kosta Nađ and Jovo Popović, *Ratne uspomene Koste Nađa—Bihaćka republika* (Zagreb: Spektar, 1982), pp. 205–06.

[86] The mass murder of Belgrade Jews and other "undesirables" using a gas van was hardly a secret by early August 1942, as corroborated by a letter from Ivo-Lola Ribar in which he informed Tito that his (Ivo-Lola Ribar) wife and her whole family were killed in this way. *Zbornik*/II/5/205, Letter to Tito (3 August 1942).

captivity, which included a lavish dinner on one occasion, seemed to confirm this sentiment.[87]

While the conversation with Tito was only informational, and no agreement was made on any of the issues, there was no doubt that the Partisan leader was interested in continuing the contacts. The first concrete proof came only three days after the prisoner exchange. On 8 September 1942, Koča Popović, the commander of the 1st Proletarian Brigade, signed a letter addressed to the German General in Zagreb, Glaise-Horstenau, concerning the future exchange of prisoners. The letter proposed establishing preliminary contact between the representatives of both sides in order to agree to the terms for the next round of talks: "We see no objection to holding the talks right away if your envoy would come with the proper authorization."[88] More proof of Tito's intentions came on 12 September 1942 when the Central Committee of the KPJ announced the transfer of Marijan Stilinović from Supreme HQ to the Main HQ for Croatia. Geographically closer, he would presumably be in a much better position to maintain contact with Zagreb rather than with Supreme HQ, which was constantly on the move. Officially, Stilinović was sent to the Croatian Central Committee as an experienced Party functionary suited for both administrative matters and for political work in general; no mention was made of him being involved in contacts with the Germans.[89]

The news Ott and others brought seemed to offer new possibilities for some kind of political solution to the problems in Croatia. The fact that the Partisan leadership expressed the same views as those of the local Partisan command at Stolac several months earlier led to the conclusion that these views were not an isolated sentiment, but the official line of the Communist-led guerrillas. Theoretically speaking, the Partisans could be included in any future pacification process as their interests seemed to converge with that of the Germans' on several points. In addition to disaffection with the current state of affairs in Croatia, there was the mutual opposition to the Italian-Chetnik and Anglo-Chetnik alliances. The Chetniks, with their Greater-Serbian agenda, were regarded by the Germans as a permanent threat to the "new order" in southeastern Europe, which was based, in part, on keeping Serbia as weak as possible. Although the Chetniks had in many places found a *modus vivendi* with the Germans (and even with the NDH) based on the mutual fear of the Partisans, there could be no doubt that they would turn their guns

---

[87] NARA, T-120, Roll 5787, H301696–7, Situation in Livno (15 August 1942); NARA, T-120, Roll 5799, H311302–3, 310, Partisan attack on Livno (21 September 1942); ibid., H311312–13, Negotiations over a united front: Chetniks and Partisans in Italian occupation zone (24 September 1942).

[88] Petranović and Zečević, eds., *Jugoslavija 1918–1988*, p. 605.

[89] *Sabrana djela*, Vol. XII, p. 42, To the comradely Central Committee of Communist Party of Croatia (12 September 1942).

against the Axis as soon as the Allied forces landed in the Adriatic.[90] This possibility notwithstanding, the Italian 2nd Army had formed them into a 30,000-strong auxiliary force (Volunteer Anti-Communist Militia or *Milizia volontaria anticomunista*, the MVAC) and supplied them lavishly with light weaponry and ammunition. Italophobe German officials in Yugoslavia (especially Kasche and Glaise-Horstenau) suspected that such a close collaboration with the Chetniks had other purposes aside from the struggle against the Partisans. The first one of these, as already mentioned, was the Italian desire to destabilize the NDH and to penetrate deeper into the Balkan Peninsula. To the Third Reich, the second and much more dangerous facet of this was the suspicion that the Italian Army was Anglophile and that it was maintaining a link with the Allies through the Chetniks. The Germans suspected the link would help facilitate the Italian Army's smooth transfer into the Allied camp as soon as the latter landed in the Balkans.[91]

The talks concerning political topics, although informative, did not lead to concrete results. The real value of the contacts established in Livno and Zagreb lay in the sphere of intelligence, and this was especially true for the Germans. Since the fall of Užice in late November 1941, very few of them, if indeed any, had the chance to report what they saw while in Partisan captivity. The trickle of information extracted from the few defectors or captured guerrillas prior to their execution had only limited value. The employees of Hansa Leichtmetall spent almost a month with the main Partisan force and had the good luck to survive and share their experiences. The results of their debriefing, conducted by the SD branch in

---

[90] Beginning in late April 1942, most of the Chetniks in Bosnia had concluded non-aggression and cooperation agreements with the NDH authorities. The main motive for both sides was fear of the Partisans. A truce with Serbian nationalists was a part of the new policy of the Pavelić regime aimed at pacification of the country. It included the reduction of terror against the Serbs and the creation of the Croatian Orthodox Church. For more details, see Tomasevich, *Occupation and Collaboration*, pp. 256–57, 544–45. The Germans not only condoned the truce between the NDH and the Chetniks, but began cooperating with some Royalist groups in Western Bosnia in the summer of 1942. This directly contradicted the official policy from Berlin, but the situation facing the *Wehrmacht* on the ground forced Hitler to turn a blind eye. In November 1942, Glaise-Horstenau summed up the German motives for tolerating the Chetniks in the NDH: "We cannot [. . .] afford ourselves the luxury of attacking the now-tamed Bosnian Chetniks at the same time [as the Partisans], for it would mean the complete loss of what little security is left in our rear." NARA, T-501, Roll 268, 000102, Letter to Alexander Löhr (16 November 1942).

[91] For Glaise-Hortsenau's opinion on this issue, see NARA, T-501, Roll 268, 000206, General survey of situation in Croatia (19 August 1942). Ott revealed the same suspicions to his Partisan captors. *Sabrana djela*, Vol. XII, pp. 115–16, Tito to Comintern (14 October 1942). Roughly a week before the fall of Livno, Tito informed Moscow of the rumors that the Slovenian reactionaries were maintaining a link to London "through Rome." *Zbornik*/II/5/166, Tito to Edvard Kardelj (1 August 1942).

Sarajevo, were used for preparing a special report for the 718th Infantry Division. This document gave a detailed description of the Partisan forces operating in the Livno–Glamoč area.[92] The overall strength of the Communist-led guerrillas was estimated at 25,000 well-equipped men. The mainstay of their army was five brigades named after the regions where they were formed. Their battle complement was thought to be 2,500 fighters, with every tenth man equipped with a light machine gun; infantry weapons were almost exclusively of Yugoslav or Italian origin.[93] Additionally, they had fifteen field pieces of various caliber, as well as fourteen motor vehicles. The prisoners also noticed that Tito's headquarters at Glamoč had good telephone communications with the rest of the Partisan-controlled territory. It also had a very active propaganda section tasked with disseminating news over radio and through leaflets, and organizing rallies and speeches. Furthermore, there was a judicial branch "led by a court official from Zagreb" who was aided by a Yugoslav military judge and several lawyers. "English and Yugoslav general staff officers" were also reported being present in the headquarters.[94] The discipline was generally good and insubordination was punished with the utmost severity. The 1st Proletarian Brigade was considered to be the best disciplined unit as "over seventy percent of its fighters were intellectuals [. . .] led by a university professor from Belgrade, Koča Popović."[95] The 5th Montenegrin Brigade, on the contrary, was "made up exclusively of criminals [. . .]. Their commander, who was of the same sort, made a comment that all of the Germans should be slaughtered and thrown to the pigs [. . .], which prompted the guards to keep him away from the prisoners." The report went on to mention that all Partisans wore the red star insignia as well as rank markings modeled on the Soviet pattern.[96]

---

[92] NARA, T-120, Roll 5799, H311306–9, Partisan attack on Livno (21 September 1942).

[93] Unlike this one, Ott's report of 15 August correctly estimated the strength of a brigade at 1,500. Likewise, Ott (again correctly) estimated the strength of the Partisan army at 7–8,000 men. The discrepancies may have arisen out of the fact that the September report, prepared for 718th Infantry Division but also for the head of the SS, Heinrich Himmler, included the new estimates of Partisan strength adjusted to reflect their latest successes. For the figures from Ott's original report, see NARA, T-120, Roll 5787, H301693, Situation in Livno (15 August 1942).

[94] There were no British officers with the Partisans in the summer of 1942. The Yugoslav staff officers that the report mentions are probably Arso Jovanović and Velimir Terzić, former captains of the royal army, who were serving as the chief of Tito's staff and his aide, respectively.

[95] Koča Popović (1908–1992) never worked as a university professor; however, given his education at the Sorbonne, flawless French, and cultured manners, it is not surprising he was mistaken for one.

[96] Rank markings were introduced in Foča in March 1942 and their design was finalized by the beginning of October. *Zbornik*/II/1/172, Bulletin of the Supreme Staff No. 17–18–19

Since the beginning of the Communist-led insurgency, the Germans had attempted to find out who was at its helm. It was a daunting task, however, since the leader's identity was unknown even to most Party members. This should come as no surprise as the KPJ had been operating underground practically since its inception: frequent police raids made secrecy an absolute must if the Party was to survive. Therefore, captured Communists could give no reliable information about the identity of the man at the top of their organization. In late November 1941, the intelligence section of the German 113th Infantry Division identified "a person hiding behind the name 'Tito'" as one of the leaders of the guerrilla movement in Užice, but not as its commander.[97] In January 1942, "Tito" was named as one of the two Partisan commanders in Eastern Bosnia. His real name was still unknown, and the rest of the intelligence about him was only partially true; while he was indeed short and Croat by ethnicity, he was not from Dalmatia, nor a high school teacher from Belgrade, nor a worker from a factory in Slavonski Brod.[98] In April, one *Ustashe* source named "a certain Tito Popović" as the commander of the Montenegrin Proletarian Brigade operating around Vlasenica, Eastern Bosnia.[99] Another report, compiled exactly one month before the fall of Livno, claimed that "Tito" was a pseudonym of either "Marko Curovic or Mrso Pijada." While the first name does not correspond to any of the guerrilla leaders, the second probably refers to Moša Pijade, a close colleague of Tito.[100] After almost one year of fighting, the Germans evidently had not made any progress in identifying the elusive Partisan commander.

The employees of Hansa Leichtmetall captured in Livno were probably the first Germans who were able to not only take a closer look at the Partisan supreme commander, but also have a conversation with him. There are details about Tito in two reports made after the exchange. The first is essentially a compilation of rumors the captives had heard while spending time in Livno and Glamoč. According to the report, Tito was the chief Communist representative in Yugoslavia after the Party

---

(July–August–September 1942). The introduction of rank insignia was yet another step toward the creation of the "regular" Partisan Army.

[97] NARA, T-312, Roll 460, Daily report of the intelligence section (24 November 1941). Dragiša Vasić, the chief political advisor of Draža Mihailović, recognized Tito during one of their meetings in the autumn of the same year. Mihailović, curiously, did not relate this information to the Germans at the meeting in Divci on 11 November. He told them instead that the Communists were led by a group of non-Serbs and gave the Germans their names, all but one of which were false. Marjanović, *Draža*, p. 155.

[98] NARA, T-315, Roll 2266, 000985, Intelligence summary No. 4/42 (10 January 1942).

[99] NARA, T-315, Roll 2268, 000666, Cable from Lieutenant Colonel Francetić (4 April 1942). The source had obviously combined the names of Tito and Koča Popović.

[100] NARA, T-315, Roll 2268, 000891, Situation report for the period 1–8 July 1942 (7 July 1942).

had been dissolved. He was also supposed to have commanded a unit larger than a brigade in the Spanish Civil War. After the war, he left for Moscow and returned to the country in a British submarine in the autumn of 1941. Along with one British and one Yugoslav general staff officer, he brought a wireless set with him in order to be able to communicate with the outside world.[101] As nothing in this report was true save for the fact that Tito went to the Soviet Union for several months after the Spanish Civil War, it most likely did more harm than good to the German intelligence effort.[102] The second report, containing the physical description of Tito among other things, was much more valuable. The information came from Ott who had a lengthy discussion with Tito on 3 September. The Partisan leader was "between 42 and 45 years of age with energetic features and a slightly protruding chin; one half of the fingernail on his right index finger is missing," reported Ott. In addition, Ott and Tito talked about the organization of the Austro-Hungarian Army. Judging by his deep knowledge of the subject, as well as the fact that Tito spoke "impeccable German," Ott assumed that he must have served as an Austrian officer during the First World War. Furthermore, the Partisan leader also displayed a sense of humor; after asking Ott where he intended to go after his release, Tito advised him not to stay south of the Sava River for too long or the two of them might soon "celebrate a happy reunion."[103]

Throughout this period, the Germans in Zagreb informed their superiors about the negotiations concerning prisoner exchange with the Partisans. Despite the standing orders prohibiting any contact with the insurgents, the higher commands did not intervene. The reason for this was that the dispatches sent from either Glaise-Horstenau or Kasche prior to Ott's final return to Zagreb failed to

---

[101] NARA, T-120, Roll 5799, H311303, Partisan attack on Livno (21 September 1942).

[102] Tito went to Paris in 1936 to facilitate the transfer of Yugoslav volunteers from France to Republican Spain without ever visiting the latter. The story about the submarine was probably based on the landing of British Captain Terrence Atherton, along with a Yugoslav officer from Cairo, on the Montenegrin coast in April 1942.

[103] NARA, T-120, Roll 5799, H311309–10, Partisan attack on Livno (21 September 1942). Ott's description notwithstanding, Tito's true identity continued to elude the Germans until the end of the year. Only after they managed to obtain his photograph in December did the mystery begin to unravel. On 11 January 1943, German intelligence issued a biographical sketch of the guerrilla leader named "Ivan Brozović" (NARA, T-315, Roll 2271, 000048, War diary entry for 23 December 1942; ibid., 001270, [no subject], 11 January 1943). Tito's personal dossier, compiled by the Zagreb *Abwehr*, reads that Brozović and Josip Broz showed such "striking similarity that it is possible that they are one and the same. The issue is to be investigated and the results will be made known in a short while." HR HDA 1521, Box 32, Communist and Partisan leaders in word and picture—prepared by Captain von Golinek of Abwehr Station Croatia (undated).

mention any details that went beyond the simple exchange of prisoners.[104] Behind the scenes, Glaise-Horstenau was seeking the approval of the higher military authorities for future contact with the Partisans. He had the good fortune that the new Commander-in-Chief Southeast was his old friend and colleague from the Austrian Army, Colonel General Alexander Löhr. During his first visit to Zagreb in late August, Löhr was decidedly against any negotiations with the guerrillas.[105] Glaise-Horstenau, however, managed to convince him otherwise within a month. The two met in Sofia on 17 September 1942 to discuss the situation in the Balkans prior to their trip to Hitler's field headquarters in Vinnytsia, Ukraine. Apart from agreeing to present the situation in the NDH without the slightest embellishment and to request greater German participation in Croatia's internal affairs, they also discussed further contact with the Partisans: "The Partisan envoys […] expressed the wish to arrange a meeting between the representative of the German General [in Zagreb] and the Partisan leader in Bosnia known as 'Tito.' Such a meeting could not possibly lead to an agreement, but it could offer an inside view of the enemy's intentions and the conditions under which he would be ready to cease his resistance."[106] "Request further instructions," which concludes the paragraph, referred in all probability to the upcoming conference in Ukraine. A document dated 22 September, compiled by either Glaise-Horstenau or his chief of staff one day before the scheduled meeting with Hitler, contained a list of topics and requests to be brought to the *Führer's* attention, such as the personnel changes in the top circles of the *Ustashe* regime; the inclusion of the Croatian Peasant Party into the government; and the proposed reform of the Home Guard. Another point reads simply "Tito-Popović-Livno," referring almost certainly to the recently concluded talks with the Partisans.[107] Neither the minutes of the conferences held in Vinnytsia 17–23 September 1942, nor any other document pertaining to it, hold explicit evidence that the topic was mentioned in Hitler's presence.

There are, however, indications that the *Führer* was informed about the subject. During the talks at Vinnytsia, Hitler emphasized the need for brutal suppression of the insurgents and complained that there were still "too few [guerrilla] suspects shot while trying to escape." His tirade was so ferocious that even Kasche feared Pavelić would use it as a pretext for stepping up the persecution of the Serbs. One can therefore safely assume that Hitler was signaling his displeasure with the fact that the German authorities were communicating with the Partisans. This was confirmed in the "*Führer's* opinion" (which had the authority of an order),

---

[104] See, for instance, Glaise-Horstenau's report in NARA, T-501, Roll 268, 000205, Estimate of current situation in Croatia (19 August 1942).

[105] Schmider, *Partisanenkrieg,* p. 162.

[106] NARA, T-501, Roll 264, 000623, Meeting with the C-in-C Colonel-General Löhr in Sofia (17 September 1942).

[107] Ibid., 000618, Points for discussion (22 September 1942).

expressed on 4 September and noted by the Commanding General in Serbia, that all "negotiations with the bandits are forbidden." Judging by the timing of its release, it is obvious that this order referred to the prisoner exchange which was then being negotiated in Zagreb and Glamoč.[108] Hitler was displeased, but was not decidedly against Glaise-Horstenau's actions. Indeed, there is evidence that the latter obtained tacit approval for the continuation of talks with the Communist-led guerrillas. Hans Ott recalled that Glaise-Horstenau told him that he had had a conversation with Field Marshal Keitel, the Chief of the Armed Forces High Command, and convinced him of the advantages of keeping this "back channel" open. Keitel's only condition was that Ott, a civilian, should continue serving as the middle man. In that way, the German Army would "save face" and at least appear to be uninvolved.[109] That this was the semi-official attitude of the *Wehrmacht* is confirmed in Löhr's statement to Glaise-Horstenau in mid-December 1942, in which the former declared he had nothing against the continuation of contacts with Tito for "informational reasons only and through intermediaries," adding that German participation "should not be overt."[110]

We do not know what arguments Glaise-Horstenau used to sway Keitel. The general most likely stressed that maintaining contact with the Partisans could facilitate the gathering of intelligence. From a military point of view, this seemed perfectly legitimate and therefore acceptable to Keitel. It is unlikely that Glaise-Horstenau accentuated the possible political dividends that negotiations with the guerrillas could yield; Keitel would most certainly have refused to give his blessing without Hitler's approval in such a case. An additional reason for not mentioning this subject was that Glaise-Horstenau himself was still not convinced that any serious benefits were to be gained. As much a politician as a soldier, Glaise-Horstenau was cautious enough not to draw any hasty conclusions. At the same time, he wanted to keep his options open and, as the document from Sofia confirms, desired for the contacts to continue. Ironically, it was the staunch National Socialist, Kasche, who was absolutely certain that some kind of accommodation with the Communist-led Partisans was possible. The cable to the foreign ministry which he sent on 21 September is bristling with optimism and stands in stark contrast to the cautious tone of both Glaise-Horstenau's and Löhr's memorandum written four days prior: "Tito wants Greater Yugoslavia, refuses [cooperation with] Mihailović and the English, and has his doubts about Moscow. He informed us recently of his wish for pacification."[111] Interestingly, some of this optimism found its way into the

---

[108] Schmider, *Partisanenkrieg*, pp. 165–66. For Hitler's opinion, see NARA, T-501, Roll 352, 000049, Securing of Croatia (4 September 1942).

[109] Odić, *Neostvareni planovi*, p. 87.

[110] NARA, T-501, Roll 267, 000437, Meeting between the Plenipotentiary General and Colonel-General Löhr on 15 December 1942 (18 December 1942).

[111] NARA, T-501, Roll 265, 001024, Kasche to Foreign Ministry (21 September 1942).

higher echelons of the German Army in Yugoslavia despite the misgivings of the *Wehrmacht's* Commander-in-Chief Southeast. More than a month after Kasche sent his telegram to Berlin, the intelligence section of the Commanding General in Serbia compiled a report on the Partisan movement in Yugoslavia, which read in part, "Tito considers economic cooperation with Germany as her equal partner by all means possible."[112]

In order to ascertain whether it was Glaise-Horstenau or Kasche who correctly gauged the situation, one must take a look at the contemporary atmosphere amongst the staff of the Partisan's Supreme Headquarters and their intentions. First of all, there can be no doubt that the Partisan political and military leadership, from top to bottom, was comprised either of Communists or those who were aspiring to join the Party. The impression that these men were somehow less Communist by treating their German captives in a correct manner can be attributed to stereotypes built up over years of incessant anti-communist propaganda. Simply put, the Germans were convinced they could not expect humane treatment from a foe who was represented as the embodiment of evil. Furthermore, the previously described events took place in a period when the Partisan movement was trying to reform its image as an ideological force, or a "political party army." This image arose as the result of the hard line the KPJ maintained from the early winter of 1941 through the late spring of 1942. When the Partisan army reached Western Bosnia in August, it was accompanied by a revised propaganda program. It was still decidedly pro-Soviet in outlook, but the notions of class struggle and revolution gave way to patriotic slogans calling for a struggle against the Axis powers as a part of the international anti-fascist effort. The fact that Great Britain was one of the pillars of the anti-fascist coalition and that Anglo-Soviet relations were improving had to be taken into account as well. In the early summer, the *Politburo* began dispatching instructions to its regional leaders on how to interpret these new trends in inter-allied relations, and how to depict them in their propaganda: "The Anglo-Soviet pact,"[113] read one letter of 5 July to the Serbian leadership, "represents a great victory for the Soviet foreign policy devised by Stalin [. . .] The British agreed to it because they have begun to feel that not only their imperialistic but also national interests are at stake in this war." Almost two months later, the *Politburo* chastised the Syrmian Communists for failing to grasp the essence of the Soviet-British-American relations and their continued insistence that Great Britain was responsible for the hostile policy toward the USSR and Communists in general: "The main issue today is not the struggle between the *bourgeoisie* and the

---

[112] NARA, T-315, Roll 2258, 001258, Communist insurgency in former Yugoslavia (31 October 1942).

[113] The Treaty of Alliance between the Soviet Union and Great Britain was signed in London on 26 May 1942 by the two foreign ministers, Molotov and Eden. Winston S. Churchill, *The Second World War* (Boston: Houghton Mifflin, 1985), Vol. IV, p. 300.

proletariat, but that of Hitlerism and the freedom-loving peoples, i.e. the people's liberation struggle [. . .]. It is high time that we root out the sectarian and naïve suspicions that the English want to trick us, and so on [. . .]. It should be understood that not only the Soviet Union, but also England and America are conducting a righteous war of liberation."[114]

The last document also carried the warning that there was still a substantial number of "reactionary circles centered on big capital" in the USA and Great Britain who sympathized with Germany and her war against the Soviet Union. It was thought that these circles, although on the fringes, had a degree of influence in the formation of official policies of the Western governments. The Yugoslav Communists could best see their influence in the support Whitehall (and to a lesser degree, the White House) was extending to the Yugoslav *émigré* government in London and its Minister of War, Draža Mihailović. Whereas they could understand the motives of the Western powers, the Partisans were perplexed and increasingly frustrated by the *realpolitik* the Soviets had been practicing on this issue ever since the war began. By August 1942, however, Moscow finally agreed to lend the Partisans moral support by establishing a pro-Partisan broadcasting station (Free Yugoslavia) and presenting the issue of Chetnik collaboration before the *émigré* government. Besides this, little else changed.[115] The Kremlin's policy toward Yugoslavia was still based on a wish to maintain good relations with Great Britain. Consequently, the Soviet government agreed with its Royal Yugoslav counterpart to elevate their respective diplomatic missions to the rank of embassy. Tito reacted by sending an almost desperate message to the Comintern on 18 September 1942. In it, he reiterated that the armed formations of the Yugoslav government-in-exile (the Chetniks) were collaborating with the occupier and that the last Soviet move would make the "people's liberation struggle much more difficult":

[. . .] Can nothing more be done to ensure that the Soviet government be better informed of the treacherous role of the government-in-exile and the unparalleled sacrifice of our peoples in their struggle against the invader, the Chetniks, the *Ustashe,* and the others? Do you not believe in what we are reporting to you daily? The questions [about this] come from every direction and we do not know what to say. Apathy has already set in

---

[114] *Zbornik*/II/5/26, Politburo instructions to Serbian (5 July 1942) and Syrmian (25 August 1942) regional committees, respectively; Churchill, *The Second World War,* Vol. IV, pp. 382–83.

[115] Petranović, *Istorija Jugoslavije,* Vol. II, p. 190. Free Yugoslavia was formed in November 1941 around a core of Yugoslav Communists who were at the time living in the USSR. The station broadcasted daily news in Serbo-Croatian, Slovene, and Macedonian languages, and also transmitted Tito's instructions to units with which the Supreme HQ could not communicate directly. The station ceased to exist in January 1945 and its personnel returned to Yugoslavia. *Vojna enciklopedija,* Vol. VIII, p. 676.

amongst the ranks of our fighters. This could have disastrous consequences for our struggle. We repeat: the government-in-exile collaborates
overtly with the Italians and covertly with the Germans. Its policy is
treacherous to both our peoples and to the Soviet Union. We suspect that
the [British] Intelligence Service is among the supporters of this course.[116]

The tone of the telegram corresponds roughly to what Kasche reported to the
German foreign ministry. It shows that Great Britain was still treated with great
suspicion by the highest Partisan leadership, despite the recently introduced
change in the official line. The change itself was more a result of the obligations the
KPJ had to Moscow than a matter of conviction; the widespread bitterness toward
the British among the rank-and-file of the Communist-led resistance movement
was hard to eradicate. Therefore, it should not have come as a surprise that the
German captives in Livno and Glamoč felt it while communicating daily with their
captors. The alleged "doubt" regarding the Soviet Union would be much harder to
perceive as the Partisan propaganda glorified the "First Land of Socialism" and its
leader; no rally or proclamation ended without slogans like "Long live the glorious
Red Army" and "Long live comrade Stalin."[117] It is highly unlikely that any of the
Partisans expressed their doubts in private, not only because of the watchful eye of
political commissars, but also because of the very nature of the army around the
Supreme Headquarters in the summer of 1942. The brigades were composed of
those who chose to remain with the flag despite all the setbacks which befell the
Partisan movement in the first half of the year. This meant that the majority of
them were volunteers who strongly believed in the cause for which they were
fighting. Apart from patriotism, the cause was based on "internationalist duty" (the
KPJ launched the uprising after the Soviet Union had been attacked on 22 June
1941). The members of the Supreme Headquarters or *Politburo* were even less
likely to show they had any doubts in the Soviet Union when in the presence of the
Germans. They were depressed, sometimes even exasperated, over the lack of
Soviet support, but they always kept it to themselves. There is no evidence that
these feelings ever translated into disloyalty.[118]

If Kasche did not receive the information about the alleged doubt in Moscow
from the Partisans, then from where or from whom did it come? The most likely

---

[116] Petranović and Zečević, eds., *Jugoslavija 1918–1988*, p. 576–77, Tito to Comintern
(18 September 1942).

[117] The Stalin cult was built up in Partisan-controlled areas similar to the way it was in the
Soviet Union. One of the best examples found in Dedijer's diary was a popular song from
Lika which included the following verses: "Oh, Stalin, you're the people's god/life without
you is impossible." Dedijer, *Dnevnik*, p. 246, Entry for 30 October 1942. Interestingly, Tito is
not mentioned in the song at all.

[118] Djilas, *Wartime*, pp. 143–44, 188.

explanation is that Kasche reached such a conclusion himself on the basis of the intelligence he was privy to and his own wishful thinking. The factors which must have played a prominent part in his reasoning were the previously mentioned correct treatment of the prisoners and the relatively low number of card-carrying Communists in the Partisan ranks. Another important fact was that neither Soviet officers nor weapons were observed in Tito's headquarters. Furthermore, there was no evidence that any regular courier or radio link between the Partisans and Moscow existed.[119] All of this led Kasche to conclude that the Yugoslav Partisans were only loosely connected to the Kremlin. Admittedly, their leaders were Communists, but the great majority of common fighters joined the uprising not for ideological reasons, but for reasons of survival and discontent with the present situation in the country. Without a firm ideological base, the guerrilla movement would be much easier to split from within without relying exclusively on military means.[120]

Tito was in fact communicating news to the Comintern whenever practicable, sometimes several times a day. The events from August and September, including details of the prisoner exchange, were reported as well. Fearing a backlash, however, Tito omitted those details which could be incriminating. On 14 October 1942, he informed Moscow about the content of his conversations with Ott in Glamoč. The event was portrayed as an interrogation, rather than a conversation, with a list of questions on political issues put to Ott along with his answers. In this way, contact with the Germans appeared to be purely an intelligence operation which could produce valuable insights into the enemy's thinking. Apart from the issues pertaining exclusively to Yugoslavia, such as the relations between the Germans and the *Ustashe* and the German strategic interests in the country, a substantial part of the "questioning" was directed at the Third Reich's situation in general. The relations with Italy were reported as especially troubled owing to the strong Anglophile sentiment of the royal house of Savoy and the officer corps. Furthermore, Ott mentioned the existence of German resistance, such as the group

---

[119] During the conference at Vinnica on 17 September 1942, Löhr reported to Hitler that the order had been intercepted (not mentioned was whether it was a radio message or a courier) which revealed "that the guerrilla bands are directed by a central agency of the Comintern." *Foreign Military Studies #C-065a: Greiner Diary Notes, 12 Aug 1942–17 Mar 1943* (n.p.: Historical Division, Headquarters, United States Army Europe, 1946), p. 66. The report by the intelligence section of Bader's staff in Belgrade about the Communist insurgency in the country stated that the regular communication between Tito and Moscow could not be confirmed. NARA, T-315, Roll 2258, 001258, Communist insurgency in former Yugoslavia (31 October 1942).

[120] The other possible explanation for Kasche's optimism would be that the Partisan negotiators intentionally made derogatory remarks about the Soviet Union in order to trick the Germans into continuing the contacts. I have not been able to find any evidence to support this possibility.

of officers under Field Marshal von Rundstedt, "the Catholic center of Beuning [*sic*],"[121] and the German Communists. The situation within Germany was presented as being very bad, the discontent with Nazi rule widespread amongst the population.

The fourth "question" Tito posed to Ott was, "Do the Germans believe they will achieve victory over the Soviet Union?" Ott's alleged response was especially interesting: "We believe that the war against the Soviet Union will soon end in a compromise, because Germany needs to finish off England." The answer appears very similar to the one Tito allegedly gave Ott in Glamoč on 3 September, according to the latter's report to his superiors. More importantly, one finds a similar style of reporting in the all-important question of which side actually initiated the talks. On two occasions, 30 September and 14 October, Tito reported to Moscow that it was the Germans who had taken the first step. For instance, the second cable reads: "[Ott] brought a proposition for negotiations between one of the envoys from our headquarters and the German plenipotentiary general." The wording is almost identical to the one Glaise-Horstenau used in his Sofia memorandum of 17 September, only with reversed roles. And whereas Glaise-Horstenau lobbied for approval from his superiors for the continuation of the contacts, Tito finished his cable with an outright lie: "They repeated the proposition several times, but we declined any notion of negotiations." He wrote this because he suspected how negatively the Soviets might react to any talks with the Germans while the battle for Stalingrad was raging. Still, Tito did ask for Moscow's opinion on the matter and requested that they not disclose the source of the information provided in the telegram in case they wanted to use it.[122]

What were Tito's motives for maintaining contact with the German authorities in Zagreb? The only way to save valuable Party cadres from the almost certain death which awaited them in *Ustashe* custody could come through prisoner exchange. The success of the first such exchange showed that one could "do business" with the Germans, and that they were as interested in saving their men as were the Partisans. As it turned out, the Germans were open to discussions on subjects which went beyond the simple exchange of captives, and Tito immediately engaged in such talks with them. Like Glaise-Horstenau, however, he did not make any hasty agreements, but agreed to "play the game" in order to learn more about the true intentions of the enemy. Prisoner exchange opened a back channel to the highest German authorities in this part of Yugoslavia and Tito was intent on maximizing that benefit. This was especially important given the fact that the Partisans admittedly had an extensive network of agents and sympathizers within the

---

[121] Most likely a reference to Heinrich Brüning, Chancellor of Germany from 1930–1932.

[122] For the full text of the two cables, see *Sabrana djela,* Vol. XII, p. 90 (Tito to Comintern, 30 September 1942) and ibid., pp. 115–16 (Tito to Comintern, 14 October 1942).

military and administrative apparatus of the NDH,[123] but none within the *Wehrmacht* or other German services. There was another important reason to engage in the talks with the Germans. In the summer of 1942, the Partisan movement was considered illegitimate both inside and outside of the country. No Allied power, including the Soviet Union, saw fit to send representatives to Tito's headquarters; ironically, only the Germans seemed willing to do so. If they could be made to recognize the Partisans as a major factor in Yugoslav affairs either openly or tacitly, then the Allies would be compelled to do so as well.

Irrespective of what both sides were reporting (or failing to report) to their superiors, there can be no doubt that there was a strong mutual desire to continue with the contacts established during the first large-scale prisoner exchange in September 1942. The course of events in the NDH during the last quarter of the year would give them ample opportunity to do precisely that.

The Failed Exchange and Talks in Livno: September 1942–January 1943

The first prisoner exchange and the establishment of contact between the Partisan Supreme HQ and the German authorities in Zagreb were not followed by a reduction in combat activities. On the contrary, the fighting in Western Bosnia and adjoining parts of Croatia was becoming more ferocious by the day. In August and September, the Partisans managed to liberate numerous towns and villages in the area, and inflicted heavy casualties on the NDH forces. As a result, their units not only captured large quantities of arms and ammunition, but also won new recruits and gained experience and much needed self-confidence. It was during this period that the Partisan brigades directly confronted German battalion-sized formations for the first time, managing to push them back on several occasions.[124] The crowning achievement of the Partisan offensive up to that point came on 25 September 1942 with the fall of Jajce, a regional administrative center with well-developed communications and industries. Among the estimated 200 enemy prisoners were four German civilians. Three of them, Othmar Siegelhuber, Franz Leinschütz, and Otto Bayer were employees of the Elektrobosna company tasked with operating

---

[123] For instance, Popović once quoted Pavelić and members of his inner circle in front of Ott, which led the latter to suspect the presence of a Partisan spy at the very top of the *Ustashe* state. NARA, T-120, Roll 5787, H301695–6, Situation in Livno (15 August 1942).

[124] *Oslobodilački rat,* Vol. I, p. 275. The Germans did not fail to spot the metamorphosis their enemy was experiencing: "Enemy forces, organized along military lines, and coming across the demarcation line from the south, were exerting strong pressure on Western Bosnia. These forces were comprised of well-organized units which were well-led and well-armed; their operations were impaired only by the lack of food." NARA, T-315, Roll 2258, 000888, Activity report of the operations section for September 1942.

the local chlorine factory, and the fourth captive was Theresa Mehr, the secretary of the local ethnic German organization. The four were taken to Glamoč and placed into custody.[125]

Due to the success of the exchange at Studeno Vrelo, the Partisan leadership decided to attempt another one, again using captured German civilians as bargaining chips. The preliminary list of requested prisoners included Hebrang and the others which the Germans had failed to deliver at Posušje. However, just as the names were being agreed upon, the news reached Tito that Hebrang had been exchanged in Slavonia on 23 September 1942.[126] It was therefore decided to ask for the commander, the deputy political commissar, and one battalion commander from the 3rd Sandžak Proletarian Brigade who went missing in early October. In addition, the Partisans were interested in Momir Tomić, a Communist functionary from Serbia who was captured during the April War and was now a prisoner of war in Germany.[127] Several individuals from Zagreb, known to be in the custody of the NDH police, were on the list as well. Once the list had been finalized, it was sent to the headquarters of the 1st Proletarian Brigade which was again tasked with establishing contact with the Axis authorities; one of the captured Germans, Franz Leinschütz, was chosen as courier. On 31 October 1942, he reached Banja Luka and delivered the offer to the headquarters of the 714th Infantry Division. The Partisan command proposed an exchange of four civilians from Jajce for altogether twelve Partisans. The recipients were also reminded of their obligation to deliver Vanda Novosel, whose release had been agreed as part of the first exchange but had not yet taken place. Setting the time and place of the exchange was left to the Germans; the letter, however, stipulated that the envoy must return within ten days with an answer.[128]

---

[125] NARA, T-120, Roll 5800, H311695–6, Letter to German General in Zagreb (31 October 1942).

[126] On 10 September 1942, the Partisans sent an offer directly to the NDH authorities to exchange Hebrang for some Home Guard officers, but the offer was not answered. Hebrang and some other individuals on the original list assembled in Livno and Glamoč were exchanged for two *Ustashe* police officials in Slavonia on 23 September 1942. When Hebrang was arrested in 1948, allegedly because he had supported Stalin during the Soviet-Yugoslav split, he was accused of being recruited by the *Ustashe* during his captivity in 1942. The exchange served to infiltrate him into the Partisan ranks. Thereafter, he allegedly worked as an agent for the *Ustashe* regime in Zagreb for the duration of the war. This official version of events, devised to discredit Hebrang, was maintained throughout the duration of socialist Yugoslavia. There is, however, no conclusive evidence that Hebrang was ever a *Ustashe* agent.

[127] *Zbornik*/II/6/201, 210, Ranković to Tito (9 October 1942) and Tito to Ranković (dated "October '42").

[128] Odić and Komarica, *Partizanska obavještajna služba*, Vol. III, pp. 275–76.

Leinschütz went from Banja Luka to Sarajevo, where he was debriefed by the intelligence officer of the 718th Infantry Division. The courier brought new information about the location of the Partisan Supreme HQ and the existence of Partisan agents in the NDH's military and political structures. Concerning the exchange, Leinschütz was told by "Vlado" (Vladimir Velebit) that the Partisans asked specifically for those people whom they knew were still alive; no mention was made as to what was to be done in case some of them had died in the meantime.[129] On 5 November 1942, the courier reached Zagreb and contacted both the embassy and the office of the German plenipotentiary general,[130] who were already scouring Croatia for the individuals in question. Dr. Kreiner of the embassy in Zagreb (who was present at the talks with Stilinović in August) summed up the results of the search thus far: of the twelve individuals wanted, only the four female Partisans were found (they were in the custody of the 714th Infantry Division); three leaders of the Sandžak Brigade were captured and killed by the Chetniks;[131] and four were supposed to be either in the Jasenovac concentration camp or in some other *Ustashe* prison. Momir Tomić, according to the Partisan letter of offer, was captured in April 1941 under a pseudonym. Given that his false name was unknown, the representatives of the German Army decided to strike him from the list as there was no time for a comprehensive search of the prison camps—the courier had to return to the Partisans by 8 November at the latest.[132] Leinschütz brought disappointing news to his captors in regard to their demands. The Germans were able to secure less than half of the desired individuals. Most likely fearful of a complete loss of credibility, the Germans decided to act in the case of Vanda Novosel. She was known to be in the Zagreb clinic for infectious diseases under police guard. The NDH security organs had postponed her extradition to the Germans

---

[129] NARA, T-120, Roll 5800, H311680, Interrogation Protocol (31 October 1942).

[130] Until the early fall of 1942, operational command of German troops in the NDH was in the hands of General Bader, who was also the Commanding General in Serbia. Pavelić opposed the idea of a unified command structure for the Serbo-Croatian areas for reasons of prestige. Hitler agreed to form separate military posts for these two countries partly because it was becoming increasingly difficult to lead the operations in the NDH from Belgrade. Therefore, on 1 November 1942, General Rudolf Lüters was made Commanding General of German Troops in Croatia (*Befehlshaber der deutschen Truppen in Kroatien*). While his area of responsibility was to the south of the River Sava, General Glaise-Horstenau was tasked with securing the territory to the north of the river. His title was changed to German Plenipotentiary General in Croatia, and his authority and responsibilities now equaled those of a head of a military district (*Wehrkreis*).

[131] Žarko Vidović, *Treća proleterska sandžačka brigada* (Belgrade: Vojnoizdavački zavod, 1972), p. 94.

[132] NARA, T-120, Roll 5800, H311688–90, Memorandum on conversation with Mr. Leinschütz (4 November 1942).

ever since it had been requested through official channels in August. Without waiting any further, the *Feldkommandant* of Zagreb, Major Knehe, dispatched two military policemen to fetch her. Novosel was taken from the hospital directly to the railway station and sent to Sarajevo that same day.[133] This action, it was hoped, would help prove to the Partisans that the Germans intended to keep their promises and were able to enforce their will on the *Ustashe*.

In the meantime (4 November), Bihać, the regional center with some 15,000 inhabitants, fell after two days of fighting in a coordinated attack by eight Partisan brigades. From a military point of view, it was the biggest victory yet for the Communist-led guerrillas: a large amount of material and over 800 Home Guard prisoners fell into their hands. The strategic and political dividends were even greater. The fall of Bihać made other garrisons in the area untenable and they either fell shortly thereafter or were evacuated. This in turn allowed the strike force under the direct command of the Supreme HQ to link up with the numerous Croatian Partisans in Lika, Kordun, Banija, and Dalmatia. Tito was now in command of a compact territory of almost 25,000 square kilometers in size, located in the midst of the Croatian puppet state. Her weakness was now becoming obvious even to ethnic Croatians and Muslims who had participated only sporadically in the Partisan movement until then. With a steady influx of new fighters who could now be armed and supplied thanks to the newly-created rear areas, the guerrilla army grew by the day.[134]

The recent fighting in Western Bosnia was far more complex than that of previous campaigns as it included frontal battles, maneuver operations, and the storming of fortified urban centers, all involving several brigades simultaneously. The brigade had shown its worth as the mainstay of the army, yet changing circumstances required the forming of larger commands which could handle the growing number of fighters and more complicated operational tasks. Therefore, on 1 November 1942, Tito created the 1st and the 2nd Proletarian Divisions, followed by the 3rd Assault Division eight days later. On the same day, the 1st Bosnian Assault Corps, made up of the newly-created 4th and 5th Krajina Divisions, was formed as well. Each division had three to four brigades; depending on the size of the latter, an average division had a strength of between 2,800 and 4,000 fighters. The corps were devised as stationary commands, while the divisions were meant to execute mobile operations. The detachment was retained, both as a territorial unit and as a source of future brigades, but its secondary role was cemented. In a way, brigades, divisions, and corps represented the regular forces of the Communist-led resistance movement, while detachments continued to serve as purely irregular units. The distinction between "regular" and "irregular" units was fluid. Brigades and divisions did not abandon guerrilla tactics but were expected to fight frontally

---

[133] Odić and Komarica, *Partizanska obavještajna služba*, Vol. III, p. 280.

[134] *Oslobodilački rat*, Vol. I, pp. 281–85; Schmider, *Partisanenkrieg*, p 178.

if necessary and solve more complicated battlefield tasks. There were no practical differences in the status of a common fighter serving in a brigade and one serving in a detachment. To serve in a brigade was regarded as an honor (especially in the elite Proletarian units), and its members could expect stricter discipline, but no improvement in food or clothing.[135]

The reforms applied to more than just combat units. A number of directives issued in November regulated the functioning of the supply system, expanded technical and medical services, and created an officer school and rear area commands. The intelligence service was reorganized into two branches: "territorial service," with a number of so-called "Intelligence Centers" spread out across the occupied territory; and "troop service," attached to combat units. Apart from gathering information on the enemy, the service was also responsible for counter-espionage. In December, the Supreme HQ was expanded to eight sections and its Escort Company into a full battalion. The growth of the Partisan movement in Dalmatia warranted the creation of the Partisan Navy tasked with maintaining the link between the coast and the islands, and interdicting Italian coastal shipping.[136]

The new name of the Partisan forces (People's Liberation Army and Partisan Detachments of Yugoslavia; *Narodnooslobodilačka vojska i partizanski odredi Jugoslavije,* or NOVJ) reflected the growing self-confidence of the Partisan movement and its wish to be recognized as a legitimate belligerent. Since only states have regular armies, the military reforms had to be followed by steps aimed at gaining political legitimacy as well. Therefore, on 26–27 November 1942, at a meeting held in Bihać, some seventy delegates from across the country proclaimed the Anti-Fascist Council of the People's Liberation of Yugoslavia (*Antifašističko vijeće narodnog oslobođenja Jugoslavije,* or AVNOJ). The AVNOJ was formed as the political body of the People's Liberation Movement as a whole. Non-Communists were not only allowed, but even invited to join it since their presence would help widen the popular basis of the movement. The AVNOJ's Executive Council was envisaged as a transitional Yugoslav government, and a rival to the royal government-in-exile. However, on Moscow's intervention, Tito (who was the chief architect of the AVNOJ) had to scale down the envisaged scope of the AVNOJ's activities. The Council had neither a portfolio for defense, nor for foreign affairs; the planned proclamation forbidding the king to return to the country before the war had ended was not issued.[137]

---

[135] Primorac, *Operativno-taktička iskustva,* pp. 103–06.

[136] Ibid., pp. 107–11.

[137] Anonymous Yugoslav authors, "Parlament nove Jugoslavije: formiranje Narodnooslobodilačke vojske u Jugoslaviji i prvo zasjedanje AVNOJ-a," in Pape and Anić, eds., *Drugi svjetski rat,* Vol. II, pp. 120–21. In the spring of 1942, Tito had toyed with the idea of forming a provisional government. He asked the Comintern for its opinion on the matter on 7 April 1942, but the cable remained unanswered. Petranović and Zečević, eds.,

The military reforms within the Partisan Army were in full swing as the German and Partisan delegations met on the guerrilla-controlled territory just outside Livno on 17 November 1942. The German side was represented by the veteran negotiators, Ott and Heyss, and an Army officer who introduced himself as Captain Kulich. Velebit's partner this time was Mihovil Tartaglia, a Partisan commander from Dalmatia. The first topic of discussion was the exchange of prisoners. The Partisan delegates proposed including four NDH airmen, nineteen Home Guard officers, and 860 men captured in Bihać, as well as a number of *Ustashe* functionaries. The latter came from Bihać and included the local deputy-governor, the head of the *Ustashe* organization, the chief of police, and his aide. Given the high positions of the first three prisoners, the Partisans wanted them exchanged at a higher ratio: ten hostages for each of the first two, and five for the chief of police. The Home Guard officers (excluding four or five who chose to join the Partisans) and NCOs were to be exchanged on a ratio of 1:1. If the Axis side would agree to this arrangement, the Partisans declared they would release the common soldiers without any conditions. Captain Heyss proposed that they discuss only the exchange of the German prisoners and the NDH airmen.[138] In this regard, Heyss said that the Partisans' demand for an exchange of the captured Germans at a ratio of 1:3 could not be accepted for they were civilians and not soldiers. Velebit saw no point in arguing and agreed, but insisted that the Germans deliver precisely the individuals whom the Partisans desired. For the airmen, the Partisans requested a number of female hostages, some of whom allegedly went voluntarily to Germany as workers. "The opposing [Partisan] side led the negotiations in a most forthcoming manner and the written protocol was ready within half an hour," wrote Captain Kulich. The business-like atmosphere notwithstanding, Velebit used the opportunity to demonstrate the effectiveness of the Partisan intelligence service by providing original NDH documents concerning the current whereabouts of certain persons. He also hinted at the deceitful manner in which the *Ustashe* had treated the Germans: "Eight days ago I spoke with a person that you had told me during our last meeting was dead. The *Ustashe* themselves offered him for exchange several weeks ago."[139] The Partisan delegate concluded this part of the talks with the desire that the prisoner exchange take place somewhere near Zagreb since the guerrillas would soon be operating extensively in that direction.

Jugoslavija 1918–1988, p. 571. For Tito's telegram of 12 November 1942 pertaining to the forming of the AVNOJ and Moscow's response, see Petranović and Zečević, eds., *Jugoslavija 1918–1988,* pp. 579–81.

[138] The four airmen were the crew of an NDH bomber shot down over Kupres in late August 1942. The 718th Infantry Division insisted on their exchange because they were experienced airmen who were flying ground support missions for the division. Odić, *Neostvareni planovi,* p. 77.

[139] Velebit was in all probability referring to Andrija Hebrang.

The delegations then moved on to the second point of discussion, which revolved around the Partisans' request that the NOVJ be acknowledged by the German occupation forces as a regular army. The Partisans' wish for recognition was as old as the insurgency itself and was expressed on numerous occasions at the local level, at times indirectly (in their propaganda directed at German prisoners), or directly (in an ultimatum to the German garrison in Kraljevo in October 1941). Since Velebit was acting as the official representative of the Supreme HQ, the wish was now a formal request from the top level of commmand during this round of negotiations.[140] As expected, the German envoys said that they had no authority on this matter but that they would pass on the request as a part of the written protocol to their superiors.

Once the formal part of the negotiations was concluded, Velebit engaged his German counterparts in a lengthy conversation on political issues. According to Kulich, "Dr. Petrović [Velebit's false name] speaks perfect German and gives the impression of being anything but a fanatical Communist [. . .] His views concerning the current state of affairs in Croatia, the country's leadership, and lesser authorities are completely correct." Velebit then went on to explain the political program of the Partisan movement. It was centered on uniting all ethnic groups in the country and creating a new Yugoslavia (abolition of the monarchy was not mentioned). Velebit added that the Partisans would not repeat the mistake of having one ethnic group dominating the others, as was the case in the Kingdom of Yugoslavia and especially in the NDH. The conversation then moved to the war situation in general. The Partisan envoy said that Germany faced a well-equipped and brave enemy in Soviet Russia, and that failing to capture the oil reserves in the Caucasus would have grave consequences for the *Wehrmacht's* ability to wage war in the future. The American intervention in North Africa would eventually lead to the Axis withdrawal from the continent, which would in turn expose their positions in the Mediterranean. Once Italy was invaded by the Anglo-Americans, the Axis downfall would soon follow. Germany would simply have no available reserves to hold all of her positions, whether in the East, in Italy, or the Balkans. Velebit added that there were vast differences between the Italian fascists and the Italian Army. Furthermore, Italy was cooperating with the Chetniks of Draža Mihailović, who was at the same time Minister of War in the government-in-exile in London; Velebit asked how Germany could tolerate this.

As the conversation reverted to the Yugoslav matters, Ott said that at his last meeting with "Šunjevarić" (Marijan Stilinović), the latter "offered [Partisan] cooperation with the German troops similar to that which the Italians enjoyed with the so-called 'Anti-Communists' [Chetniks] in Herzegovina." Velebit replied that, in general, cooperation was possible on certain questions, but that he would have to consult his superiors before giving any definitive answers. "One way or the other,"

---

[140] Velebit, *Tajne i zamke,* p. 199.

the Partisan envoy said, "[the Partisans] were and are still the enemies of the Chetniks and the Anglo-American plutocrats." Ott then mentioned the "neutral zone," General Glaise-Horstenau's idea of granting the Partisans a certain territory from where they could carry out the civil war against the Chetniks unmolested by the German occupation forces, and in which the Partisans would abstain from attacking German interests. Velebit countered with a question of whether the Germans would be willing to furnish weapons to the Partisans as the Italians were doing with the Chetniks. Ott and Kulich rejected this possibility, pointing out that by withdrawing from other areas, the Partisans would be able to achieve numerical superiority in the neutral zone and supply themselves with arms on the spot, ostensibly by taking them away from the Chetniks. Velebit replied that if the proposition was to be accepted, the Partisans would have to be granted a sizable piece of territory. He added that he would convey the details of the conversation to his superiors to obtain their opinion on the matter, and would bring their response to the Germans at their next meeting.[141]

While these talks were being held, the German military and civilian authorities were trying to obtain the release of those individuals on the Partisan list from their Croatian allies. Once again, this proved to be an uphill struggle as the *Ustashe* did everything they could to avoid relinquishing the captured Partisans. SS Sergeant Stüwe, the liaison officer of the German police attaché to the *Ustashe* Surveillance Service (*Ustaška nadzorna služba*, UNS), had to wait for four days before being admitted to the chief of the UNS, Drago Jilek, on 9 November. Two days later, the UNS reported its findings about the four captives the Germans wanted: Ozren Novosel and Stjepan Kokot had been transferred from Jasenovac and were now in the UNS prison in Zagreb; Zvonko Bilan was in the same camp and his transfer to Zagreb had already been approved; Jelka Šutić was not to be found in any of the camps or prisons. If the good news had raised the Germans' spirits, they were sorely disappointed on the following day. Dr. Aleksander Benak, one of Jilek's close associates, called Stüwe and told him that Bilan had actually died in Jasenovac on 26 October. This meant that only two of the four individuals from the Partisan list were secured. Benak offered three other Jasenovac inmates instead who would be prepared for the exchange and sent to Zagreb as soon as possible. On the same day, the SS liaison officer went to the UNS prison to collect Novosel and Kokot. To his dismay, he was told that Novosel was never transferred out of Jasenovac and that Kokot had been released and had returned to his native village on parole; UNS officials whom he met there even showed him a written order to release all four of

---

[141] Odić and Komarica, Partizanska obavještajna služba, Vol. III, pp. 294–300. Four days later in the same area, the Ustashe and Partisans conducted a prisoner exchange: twenty-seven citizens of Livno were exchanged for an unknown number of captured Partisans. AMBiH, Fond UNS, 615–3, Subject: exchange of Partisans for our people (20 December 1942). There is no evidence that this exchange was a subject of the talks between Velebit and Ott—it was strictly a local affair.

the prisoners from the original list as soon as they came into their custody. Stüwe immediately tried to reach Jilek and Benak, but to no avail. He tried again on the 13th with the same result, and he was told that neither of them were available as they had been summoned to see Pavelić. Benak left Stüwe a message that he had issued an order for Kokot's arrest. Resigned, Stüwe reported the state of affairs to Kasche and SS Lieutenant Colonel Hans Helm (the German police attaché in Zagreb), implying that without applying further pressure, the *Ustashe* would not cooperate. The ambassador said he would intervene with the chief of Zagreb police when he met him on Saturday, 14 November.[142]

On Monday, 16 November 1942, Stüwe went to another meeting with Jilek and Benak and protested the handling of the case of Novosel and Kokot. The UNS officials assured him of their goodwill by making a telephone call to Jasenovac camp in his presence, ordering the immediate transfer of Novosel to Zagreb. Furthermore, Jilek officially made Benak responsible for the matters of prisoner exchange. The situation appeared to finally be moving in the right direction that Monday as the news came in the early evening that Kokot had been arrested and put into the *Feldkommandantur's* prison. The next two days proved to be bitterly disappointing to the Germans, however. On the 17th, Benak informed Stüwe that Novosel had been killed while trying to escape. The following day, it came to light that two of the three "replacement" hostages from Jasenovac originally promised on 11 November had died the previous week. Benak candidly added that since one could assume that the third had died as well, the UNS had identified three new Partisan suspects for the exchange. The Germans had no choice but to accept this news, and on 20 November all four hostages were finally in German custody in Zagreb. Their departure for Sarajevo could take place as soon as the date and place of the exchange was negotiated.[143]

The Germans were enraged over the obvious attempts by the *Ustashe* to hamper the exchange. Stüwe was told by NDH officials that they took a dim view of the exchanges, especially of high-ranking Communists whose capture came only as a result of months, sometimes even years, of painstaking detective efforts. One police official said that the agents were at one point on the verge of mutiny when they heard that these precious captives were to be exchanged. Stüwe wrote that this attitude was understandable given the current situation in the country, but that the

---

[142] NARA, T-120, Roll 5800, H311674–8, Memorandum (12–13 November 1942).

[143] NARA, T-120, Roll 5800, H311661–4, Sequel to memorandum of 12 November (25 November 1942); ibid., H311665, Transfer of prisoner Stefan Kokot (17 November 1942); ibid., H311666, Death of Ozren Novosel (17 November 1942). The other four exchange prisoners (female Partisans of the 3rd Sandžak Brigade) arrived in Sarajevo from Banja Luka several days earlier. NARA, T-315, Roll 2271, 000036, War diary of the intelligence section (Entry for 16 November 1942).

conduct of the NDH police was nevertheless "shameful."[144] The plenipotentiary general had by then received Ott's report from Livno that included Velebit's statement concerning *Ustashe* double-dealing. Glaise-Horstenau intended to broach the topic in his meeting with Pavelić scheduled for 12 December 1942. The subject, however, was not discussed for unknown reasons.[145] On the same day, the NDH Ministry of Foreign Affairs delivered a note to the German embassy protesting the way the Germans had snatched Vanda Novosel from police custody. The note also stated that "the arrangement between the German military and the Croatian authorities must be honored at all times," and requested that the embassy intervene at "appropriate places" to this effect. Kasche's response was mild (as usual when he dealt with complaints from the officials in Zagreb), merely stating that the release of Novosel had been negotiated with the police authorities beforehand, and that the Germans had no intention of acting without the knowledge of the NDH government. The only hint of the ambassador's displeasure with the tone of Zagreb's note was the fact that he waited almost a month and a half before delivering his answer.[146]

It was clear to all that the success of future exchanges would be jeopardized if the NDH authorities remained solely responsible for furnishing the needed prisoners. On 1 December 1942, the embassy councilor, Herbert von Troll-Obergfell, wrote a letter to Glaise-Horstenau suggesting that the German Army keep some of the prisoners captured during anti-guerrilla operations for purposes of prisoner exchange. As concessions, the NDH police would be given the opportunity to question them, and the release of any higher ranking KPJ functionaries would require approval of the German police attaché.[147] The idea that the occupation forces should have their own pool of exchange prisoners was taken up by the German military authorities. On 16 January 1943, representatives of Glaise-Horstenau's and Lüters' staff met to discuss the handling of prisoners in the upcoming winter operations. The plan was to set up special commissions, partially staffed with SD personnel, within each German division. Their task would be to sort

---

[144] NARA, T-120, Roll 5800, H311664, Sequel to memorandum of 12 November (25 November 1942). On 13 November, the German Consul in Sarajevo, Erich Gördes, reported to Kasche that on 23 October, the 718th Infantry Division issued a written request to UNS in Sarajevo not to move Bilan without the division's explicit approval, but the *Ustashe* transferred him to Jasenovac on the very same day. Ibid., H311672, Cable to embassy in Zagreb (13 November 1942).

[145] NARA, T-501, Roll 267, 000352, Notice for conference with Poglavnik on 12 December 1942 (undated); ibid., 000349, Conclusions of conference with Poglavnik on 12 December 1942.

[146] Odić and Komarica, *Partizanska obavještajna služba*, Vol. III, p. 281.

[147] NARA, T-120, Roll 5800, H311659–60, Letter to Plenipotentiary General (1 December 1942).

captives into different categories. Whereas Lüters opposed the involvement of NDH officials in the selection process, Glaise-Horstenau lobbied for it to ensure that the troops unfamiliar with circumstances in their operating areas would not act "radically" in friendly villages. Those suspected of helping the guerrillas would be sent to the camp at Zemun, then shipped to Norway; those not suspected of helping the guerrillas were to be kept at the transit camp at Osijek prior to being sent to Germany as laborers; those who needed further observation were destined for the Special Camp I at Sisak. The fourth group (actually, the first one on the list), comprised the "exchange prisoners, including some 150 prominent figures and 300 reprisal hostages who are to be kept at the disposal of the Commanding General."[148]

One important aspect of the negotiations in Livno and the concurrent events in Zagreb should be mentioned here, namely the involvement of the SS and the German police authorities. The "*Wehrmacht* captain," Kulich, who took part in the talks in Livno, was in fact none other than SS Major Dr. Alfred Heinrich, the chief of the SD station in Sarajevo. His presence at the talks concerning prisoner exchange surprised his superior in Belgrade, SS Colonel Emanuel Schäffer, who added the word "impossible" with red pencil on the margin of Heinrich's report.[149] Schäffer's reaction was due more to the fact that his subordinate was acting independently rather than to the news that the Germans in the NDH were negotiating with the Communists over a prisoner exchange. The SD in Belgrade was informed of the exchange proceedings in August 1942, and the German authorities in Zagreb requested that it secure at least one of its hostages for that exchange, which it did.[150] Heinrich's involvement in the negotiations was reported to the Reich's Main Security Office (*Reichssicherheitshauptamt*, RSHA) at the beginning of December. The reply came on 25 January 1943: "[. . .] The Chief of the IV Directorate [Gestapo] considers [Heinrich's involvement] inappropriate. The police attaché in Zagreb has also been instructed not to take part in these negotiations unless requested by the German Embassy."[151]

In his reply, which was sent the next day, Schäffer stated that Heinrich's presence during the talks was expressly requested by the 718th Infantry Division in Sarajevo. Furthermore, he added that he had prohibited Heinrich from taking further actions of this kind the moment he received his report. The SS clearly did not want to get involved in a delicate issue such as negotiating with Communist

---

[148] NARA, T-501, Roll 267, 000428–30, Memorandum for conference on treatment of expected prisoners (16 January 1943).

[149] Odić, *Neostvareni planovi*, p. 81.

[150] Vladimir Dedijer's wife, Olga, was arrested in Belgrade in early 1942. Ranković included her name on the list of persons wanted in exchange for the Germans from Livno. She was transferred from Belgrade to the NDH and subsequently rejoined her husband on 5 September. Dedijer, *Dnevnik*, pp. 206–07, Entries for 2 and 7 September 1942.

[151] Facsimile of the telegram reproduced in Odić, *Neostvareni planovi*, p. 85.

guerrillas, and wanted the Army to take the blame in case Berlin intervened decisively against it. The military and diplomatic authorities in Zagreb had already divided responsibilities pertaining to prisoner exchange. Kasche's letter to Glaise-Horstenau on 20 January 1943 reaffirmed that the treatment and exchange of prisoners was under the aegis of the Army. "Because of the political repercussions," the task of the German embassy (and consequently of the chief SS representative in the country, Helm) would be merely to secure the needed prisoners from the NDH authorities.[152] As a consequence of this arrangement, and due to the unwillingness of the upper echelons of the SS to get directly involved with the prisoner exchanges, Helm kept himself out of the negotiations for the duration of the war. This did not mean that the police and security apparatus were not informed of prisoner exchanges and contacts with the Partisans. Apart from the intelligence received through official channels from Kasche and Glaise-Horstenau and his own network of agents, Helm could count on Ott to provide him with first-hand details about the proceedings.[153]

Heinrich's report about the talks in Livno is important in one additional aspect. As he had created an internal document written exclusively for his superior in Belgrade, Heinrich saw nothing problematic in openly explaining the negotiating tactics employed by the Germans: "The German ambassador suggested that Mr. Ott broach the following possibility in his private conversations with Partisan negotiators: to avoid conflict that was in neither party's interest, the Partisans should approach the Germans about establishing a neutral zone."[154] This is one of the rare pieces of written evidence which illustrates just how keen the German authorities were to make the Partisans appear to be the party which initiatived talks on sensitive issues. Consequently, the reader should treat with caution those reports made to Berlin.[155]

Did the contacts between the two sides in the second half of 1942 have a mitigating effect on the brutal guerrilla war raging in Yugoslavia? In order to answer this question we must briefly analyze the conduct of the warring parties pertaining to prisoners at the time. On 22 October 1942, shortly before Bader's intelligence officer gave an optimistic view of Tito as Germany's future trading partner, the 718th Infantry Division released a set of instructions concerning the treatment of captives. The provisions in the document were not any milder than those which had been valid since March—actually, their wording was even more harsh. Anyone

---

[152] NARA, T-120, Roll 5800, H311656, Subject: Jajce prisoner-exchange (20 January 1943).

[153] *Nemačka obaveštajna služba* (Belgrade: Savezni sekretarijat unutrašnjih poslova, 1959), Vol. VI, p. 481; Odić, *Neostvareni planovi*, p. 253.

[154] Odić and Komarica, *Partizanska obavještajna služba*, Vol. III, p. 301.

[155] In his post-war interrogation, Hans Ott confirmed that he introduced the sensitive subject on orders from General Glaise-Horstenau. HR HDA 1521, Box 31, File 561 Tartaglia, Statement of Hans Ott.

caught with a weapon, including "invalids, sick, pregnant women, and persons over 60 years of age," was to be shot after a short interrogation. Enemy non-combatants (medical personnel, rear area personnel), and all those caught without weapons but suspected of helping the enemy, were to be taken to the division's prison in the Alexander Barracks in Sarajevo.[156] Judging by the casualty returns, the order remained a mere formality and the war continued to be conducted without any restraints. In the period from 16 to 25 October 1942, the German occupation forces reported 2,156 guerrilla casualties in the NDH, capturing at the same time only 383 rifles, fourteen machine guns, forty-eight pistols, and one cannon.[157] The next report, for the period from 26 October to 5 November, contained even greater discrepancies: 1,895 guerrilla losses compared to 158 rifles and twenty-nine machine guns captured.[158] These returns hardly differed from the ones from late August and early September when the negotiations for the first prisoner exchange were being successfully concluded.[159] In short, these had next to no impact on the German counter-insurgency doctrine, which remained centered on the indiscriminate application of violence.

The conduct of the German fighting units remained very much the same partly due to the lack of opportunity to exchange their own members—they had so far acted merely as intermediaries for the exchange of German civilians. By late December, even such limited participation in contacts with the guerrillas was beginning to soften their previously uncompromising attitude regarding the enemy. For instance, the 714th Infantry Division received at least two letters from the Partisans in late October and late November concerning the planned exchange of the Germans from Jajce. The intelligence on the increasing regularization within the guerrilla army, which included the formation of divisions and corps and the adoption of regular battlefield tactics, was confirmed in the second letter which was signed "1st Assault Corps."[160] The Germans decided to utilize these "regularization" efforts by the Partisans to request a courtesy related to the disposition of the dead and wounded which was commonplace among regular armies. The second week of December 1942 was marked by intense fighting in the Sanski Most–Prijedor area, which cost the German occupation forces several dozen dead and over a hundred wounded.[161] Several days after the fighting had subsided, the request came from the German garrison in Prijedor asking the 1st Krajina Brigade

---

[156] NARA, T-315, Roll 2271, 000126, Subject: prisoners (22 October 1942).

[157] NARA, T-501, Roll 352, 000431, Situation report for the period 16–25 October 1942 (26 October 1942).

[158] Ibid., 000525, Situation report for the period 1–10 November 1942 (11 November 1942).

[159] Ibid., 000097, Situation report for the period 1–10 September 1942 (11 September 1942).

[160] NARA, T-315, Roll 2258, 001181, Situation report (26 November 1942).

[161] NARA, T-314, Roll 554, 000287, Situation estimate for the period 7–16 December 1942; ibid., 000292, Situation estimate for the period 17–26 December 1942.

to deliver the bodies of the German soldiers which remained on their side of the front line. The HQ of the garrison also asked for the release of any wounded soldiers in order to provide them with medical care. The Yugoslav sources differ as to whether the Germans extended their request to include six of their missing soldiers. It is highly unlikely that the Germans would ask for the prisoners without offering something (or somebody) in return; the offer of prisoner exchange is, however, not mentioned in any of the sources. Regardless, the Partisan commander replied sternly that his battalion had no enemy wounded in their custody and that the Germans would have to look for the corpses of their men in the Sana River. Although unsuccessful, this was the first time a *Wehrmacht* unit in the field showed initiative and approached the Partisans with such a request. To be sure, the Germans who made the request took great pains to make it look as informal as possible—it was delivered verbally by two civilians from Prijedor.[162] Despite the fact that the highest commands were communicating through letters and authorized envoys, the situation was not yet conducive to direct, official communication with the guerrillas on a local level.

The attitude of the Partisans regarding the taking of German prisoners continued to vary throughout this period. Here one must differentiate between the units around the Supreme HQ and Partisan units in other parts of the NDH. The former were being instructed to spare enemy prisoners in order to exchange them, as corroborated by a written order drafted during the attack on Bihać dated 1 November 1942.[163] As with similar orders which had previously been seen in Bosnia, this one does not specify if this provision was applicable to the Germans as well as to the Home Guards. Evidence to support its applicability was the fact that by early 1943, the main body of the NOVJ held some twenty German prisoners from battles around Sitnica and Prijedor in November and December 1942.[164] At that same time, the exchange of prisoners became an officially recognized proceeding amongst the units around the Supreme HQ. Whether or not a prisoner was deemed worthy of exchanging determined if he lived or died. The order for the 1st Krajina Brigade to attack Bosanski Novi on 26 November 1942 read "all prisoners who deserve a death sentence or cannot be exchanged are to be executed on the spot."[165]

---

[162] Borko Arsenić, "Bitka završena u virovima Sane," in *Prva krajiška udarna proleterska brigada—sjećanja boraca* (Prijedor: Skupština opštine, 1981), p. 398; Ljubomir Zastavniković, "Mrtvački sanduci ostali su na obali Sane," in ibid., pp. 404–05.

[163] *Zbornik*/V/9/9, Order of 8th Croatian Brigade for attack on Bihać (1 November 1942). Even more important than the shift in the official line was the realization by low-ranking Partisan officers that prisoners were now worth more alive than dead. Gajo Vojvodić, *Priča jednog proletera* (Cetinje: Obod, 1987), p. 301.

[164] NARA, T-315, Roll 2271, 001461, Group interrogation (23 March 1943). There were no Germans in Bihać at the time of its capture.

[165] *Zbornik*/IV/35/359, Order of the 1st Krajina Brigade for attack on Bosanski Novi (26 November 1942).

Other units facing the Germans in this period included those in Slavonia. They were isolated from the main body of the Partisan army in Western Bosnia and adjoining parts of Croatia by large swaths of enemy-held territory. Communication with headquarters was sporadic at best and was maintained exclusively through couriers. As a consequence, the local guerrillas more or less had a free hand in deciding how to treat their captives. On 6 September 1942, Croatian Partisans attacked the oil wells at Gojilo which were defended by a Home Guard garrison and a detachment of Germans. While most of the latter were killed during the attack, the Communist-led guerrillas managed to capture at least three of them.[166] The Germans discovered later that all of their captured compatriots were shot immediately.[167] Four days later, the same units involved in that attack stormed the village of Velika Mlinska, which was defended by some thirty ethnic Germans. Four of them were captured and released, a move "that had a tremendous [propaganda] effect."[168] These two actions illustrate how the treatment of enemy prisoners varied even on a daily basis with Germans being both executed and released (the latter course of action is especially worth mentioning given the advanced phase of the war and the hatred toward the ethnic Germans). There is no evidence that the local Partisans in Northern and northeastern Croatia attempted to exchange prisoners with the Germans in 1942. The absence of such an initiative can be partly attributed to the fact that the two sides had been facing each other in Croatia for only a short while, so had little time, opportunity, or need to change their methods. Therefore, the capture of a small number of German soldiers usually resulted in their immediate execution.[169] Still, there are indications that by the late fall of 1942, the local Partisan commands began taking measures aimed at curbing arbitrary violence toward the enemy prisoners, such as an order from the 1st Slavonian Assault Brigade dated 21 November which explicitly forbade its fighters from meting out justice on their own as that was the exclusive prerogative of the brigade's HQ. Although the order was primarily aimed at improving discipline and the execution of prisoners was not abolished *per se*, it can still be viewed as a small step toward the improvement of the prisoners' lot.[170]

---

[166] *Zbornik*/V/7/69, Report of 1st Slavonian Detachment on attack on Gojilo (6 September 1942).

[167] NARA, T-315, Roll 2258, 001386, Enemy intelligence report No. 3 (7 December 1942).

[168] *Zbornik*/V/7/211, Report to Main Partisan HQ for Banija (22 September 1942).

[169] *Zbornik*/V/6/277, Activity report of 3rd Operational Zone for the period March–August 1942 (Entry for 27 July 1942); ibid., p. 370, Report of police district Nova Gradiška (27 August 1942).

[170] *Zbornik*/V/9/282, Order of 1st Slavonian Assault Brigade for attack on Velika (21 November 1942).

As far as the Partisans in Croatia were concerned, ideological reasons do not seem to have posed a major obstacle in seeking a prisoner exchange. As long as an agreement over the release of their fighters could be worked out, the Partisans had no qualms about negotiating with their foes, be they Italians[171] or even *Ustashe*.[172] As they had positive experiences with both, the Partisans took pains to secure as many prisoners as could be exchanged. They had no similar experiences with the German occupation forces and were consequently less inclined to spare Germans.

The treatment of exchange prisoners varied, but their lot was on the whole much better than of those destined for the firing squad, concentration camp, or forced labor. Vanda Novosel, held by the *Ustashe* in a Zagreb hospital, was "kidnapped" by the Germans, transferred to Sarajevo at the beginning of November, and placed in the local German prison. She spent two weeks there until her release could be arranged. Novosel related her experiences while in captivity as follows: "The Germans told me I would be treated very correctly and receive food from the officers' mess. And whether you believe it or not, I had butter for breakfast every morning! I reckoned that before going to the Partisans, I'd better check my teeth. Therefore, I requested to be allowed to visit the dentist. [The request was granted] and I went to the dentist several times accompanied by a guard."[173] Novosel, together with Franz Leinschütz (the Elektrobosna employee serving as a courier between the two sides), left Sarajevo on or about 20 November, and after several days journey by train and on foot, reached the Partisan lines around Bosanski Petrovac.[174] With her arrival, the exchange at Studeno Vrelo was finally concluded.

After roughly two months of absence, Leinschütz appeared again in the headquarters of the 718th Infantry Division in Sarajevo on 25 January 1943. He was sent by the Partisans to hasten the long-overdue exchange of the Elektrobosna

---

[171] According to the documents published in *Zbornik*, the Croatian Partisans were swapping prisoners with the Italians throughout 1942. See *Zbornik/V/3/101–02*, 129, 221–22; *Zbornik/V/4/70–71,176*; *Zbornik/V/5/115*, 137; *Zbornik/V/6/13–14*, 316.

[172] The success of the so-called "Slavonian Exchange," in which the Partisans received Hebrang and thirty-two Partisans for just two high-ranking *Ustashe* policemen, motivated the Slavonian Partisans to offer the exchange of four NDH government officials who had been captured on 22 October 1942 near Nova Gradiška. *Zbornik/V/9/231*, Report of 3rd Operational Zone to Main HQ for Croatia (20 November 1942). There was also a planned attempt to exchange *Ustashe* prisoners in mid-December in Western Croatia. *Zbornik/V/10/207*, Report of 5th Operational Zone to Main HQ for Croatia (18 December 1942). An order of the 6th Division of the 1st Croatian Corps dated 27 December stipulated that captured officers, NCOs, and "prominent *Ustashe*" should be sent immediately to the division's HQ. *Zbornik/V/10/288*.

[173] Interview with Vanda Novosel in the television documentary, *Tito-posljednji svjedoci testamenta* (Zagreb: Hrvatska radiotelevizija, 2011), Episode 6.

[174] Odić and Komarica, *Partizanska obavještajna služba*, Vol. III, pp. 280–81.

employees from Jajce and the German soldiers captured in the meantime.[175] The intelligence section of the aforementioned division immediately proceeded to interrogate the courier about the condition of these people. Whereas there were no lavish dinners this time, the treatment of the prisoners was still "correct according to Partisan standards." They were quartered in a building in Bosanski Petrovac and could move freely between the (heated) rooms. The food was monotonous and consisted of half a loaf of bread, meat, and beans. The biggest problem was hygiene as the prisoners were infested with lice most of the time. Likewise, they could only bathe when the Partisans were not using the facilities of the Hygienic Institute located in the town. Leinschütz also made interesting observations concerning the differences in the treatment of prisoners of various Axis formations. Home Guard officers were left in possession of their money, while initially the Germans were not (this practice changed in the interim).[176] Both the Italians (some twenty Italian prisoners were in Bosanski Petrovac) and the Germans had to swap their clothes for whatever their captors provided, and the Italians could move freely about the town whereas the Germans could not. All were employed as manual laborers, but Leinschütz pointed out the fact that the Germans, and not the Italians, had to do heavy jobs like woodcutting. He also added that the only officer among the Italians was employed in drawing propaganda posters for the guerrillas.[177]

Owing to severe winter weather and heavy fighting across Western Bosnia, Leinschütz's speedy return to his captors was impossible. The Germans from Bosanski Petrovac would have to wait for another two months before they could rejoin their compatriots. The course of events would place them in the midst of one of the most controversial episodes of the Second World War in Yugoslavia.

---

[175] HR HDA 1450, Roll D-2222, Frame 414, Prisoner exchange (undated); ibid., Frame 445, List of prisoners in Partisan captivity (undated). Jajce was retaken by the *Wehrmacht* in late October and then lost to the Partisans once more in late November. On this occasion, the latter captured five Croat chemical engineers and technicians of Elektrobosna. On 14 December 1942, the company made an official request to Glaise-Horstenau to include these men in the exchange proceedings. NARA, T-120, Roll 5800, H311657–8, Exchange of leading personalities in Partisan hands (14 December 1942).

[176] Preferential treatment of the captured Domobrans over Germans was not coincidental. The Germans learned from captured Partisan documents that the Home Guards were to be treated exceptionally well in order to win them over to the Partisan cause. The Germans, on the contrary, were to be treated with "hostility." NARA, T-315, Roll 2258, 001342, Enemy intelligence report No. 4 (15 December 1942).

[177] NARA, T-315, Roll 2271, 001304–5, Interrogation of Franz Leinschütz (25 January 1943).

Conclusion

After the downfall of the Užice Republic in late November 1941, the focus of the war was transferred from occupied Serbia to the neighboring Independent State of Croatia. Unlike in Serbia, there were comparatively few encounters between the Partisans and the Germans west of the Drina River for the better part of 1942. The crisis with the Communist-led guerrillas and their concentration on domestic enemies, as well as the weak German presence in the country, were responsible for a relatively small number of German prisoners taken by the Partisans. Notwithstanding the hostility toward the German prisoners as a consequence of the *Wehrmacht's* brutal counter-insurgency tactics employed in Serbia and, to a lesser extent, in Croatia as well, the Partisans in the NDH made several local attempts to exchange prisoners. After a group of German civilians was captured in Livno in August 1942, the exchange of prisoners was increasingly negotiated between the highest commands of both sides. These talks were perceived by all as a means to sound out the enemy's intentions and political aims. Consequently, both the Partisans and the Germans were keen to continue them into 1943.

During the first phase of the uprising in the NDH (July 1941–May 1942), the insurgents and the Germans negotiated several times over prisoner exchange. As in Serbia, these were purely local affairs, motivated by the guerrillas' wish to save their comrades from *Ustashe* or German captivity. The exchange of prisoners was considered legitimate by the Bosnian Partisans, even if it involved contacts with the hated Croatian puppet state. Since the Ozren Partisan Detachment had some experience in these matters, it is no surprise they went purposefully on a prisoner hunt in early April 1942 in the hope that the Germans would agree to an exchange as well. The Partisans in Eastern Herzegovina may not have entered into such deals themselves prior to March 1942, but they were aware of them because of their close ties with their Montenegrin comrades who frequently exchanged prisoners with the Italians. At first they hoped to receive much needed supplies in exchange for the captured Germans of the bauxite column, but readily accepted the offer to receive their incarcerated fighters instead. Even the Herzegovinian Partisans, who were counted among the most fanatical in the whole country, were willing to sacrifice some of their ideological purity to the pressing needs of the war.

The Germans in the NDH were compelled to make similar compromises. Their forces, consisting of one under-strength division and several security battalions, were thinly spread out across the country and were struggling to both secure the important industrial sites and to quell the ever-growing flames of the uprising. Consequently, they acted just as their comrades in tiny, isolated garrisons in Serbia had done the previous summer by disregarding the orders which strictly prohibited any negotiations with the insurgents in order to save their men, each of whom was hard to replace. Given their own counter-insurgency practices, they could safely assume what fate awaited the prisoners if they were not exchanged. The Germans' concern for the employees of their organizations tasked with the exploitation of natural resources in the NDH was especially great. In August 1941, the Germans intervened on behalf of two members of the *Organisation Todt* who were captured by insurgents in Western Bosnia. The capture of forty-five members of the bauxite column at Stolac in March 1942 set in motion a concerted effort by the German embassy, the *Wehrmacht's* representatives in Zagreb, and the Commander-in-Chief Southeast to try to exchange them via Italian mediators. Notwithstanding the relative flexibility in the matter of prisoner exchange itself, the Germans were wary of involving themselves openly in these matters. Their prime concern was to not grant legitimacy to the guerrillas by sitting at the negotiating table with them—which was exactly what the Partisans were trying to achieve through the exchange of prisoners. Therefore, they always sought to act through intermediaries, be it Croatian authorities, civilian couriers, or Italian commands.

Until August 1942, the attempts at prisoner exchange were local in nature—their only purpose was to save lives. The capture of Hansa Leichtmetall mining experts at Livno and the employees of the Elektrobosna Company in Jajce brought a new dimension to the Partisan-German contacts. For the first time, the highest military and political authorities on both sides were involved in talks about topics far more important than the mere swapping of prisoners. It is also important to note that the Germans did not act through intermediaries this time, but negotiated directly through their military, political, SS, and police representatives. Dissatisfaction with *Ustashe* rule and Italian policy in the Balkans, as well as concern over Germany's economic interests, were the main motives behind German dialogue with the Partisans about the possibility of some kind of political settlement. If the latter agreed to cease attacking lines of communication and allowed the exploitation of ores, then the Germans were willing to grant them a territory from whence the Partisans would be able to wage war against the Chetniks unhindered by the German occupation forces. Furthermore, the Germans considered limiting the *Ustashe* authority, or even removing them from the political scene entirely. For their part, the Communist-led guerrillas sought to gain privileged status for their captured and wounded, which in turn would earn them recognition as a legitimate belligerent in the political sense. Aware that negotiating with the enemy could produce a terrible backlash from Moscow and Berlin, both Tito and the Germans in Zagreb were careful about how they reported the proceedings to their superiors. They all reported that the enemy was the one who initiated the talks and that their primary concern was to retrieve their men safely. Whereas Tito remained silent about the political dimension of the talks in his cables to the Comintern, Glaise-Horstenau did (unofficially) inform his superiors about what was being discussed and managed to receive their reluctant approval for the continuation of the contacts. Hitler, who was known to be adamantly opposed to any sort of political compromise (especially with an enemy whom he considered to be "bandits"), voiced his displeasure at the talks held in Glamoč and Zagreb. Interestingly, however, he did not intervene decidedly against this flagrant breach of discipline on the part of the German Army and the diplomatic representatives in the NDH. This may have been because Glaise-Horstenau managed to persuade the Chief of the Armed Forces High Command, Keitel, to allow him to continue the game with Tito's representatives, ostensibly for reasons of intelligence gathering.

The gathering of intelligence was the prime motive for both sides, as no one (except perhaps Kasche) really believed in a political settlement. The exchange of prisoners and the accompanying talks were a unique opportunity to sound out the enemy's opinions and intentions, and provided the means to spy on him in general. The Germans were in dire need of intelligence on their toughest enemy in the region because they knew very little about the organization and inner workings of the main Partisan force before Ott and the other Germans from Livno made their reports. Especially crucial was the intelligence the returnees provided about Tito, about whom the German authorities knew next to nothing. The contacts were as valuable to the Partisans in this respect as they were to the Germans. Although they had a wide network of agents and sympathizers within the political and military establishment of the *Ustashe* state, they had none within the German occupation apparatus. The negotiations over prisoner exchange unveiled surprising intelligence about the troubled nature of the relations between the Germans and their allies. The Partisans consequently tried to exploit German suspicions regarding the Italians. They fed their negotiating partners with information on the alleged anti-German actions of the Italians, such as them refusing to exchange the personnel of the bauxite column and maintaining a link to the Western Allies through the Chetniks. Better treatment of Italian prisoners by the guerrillas, although not staged for propaganda purposes, also served to deepen German suspicion toward their allies. In short, intelligence and propaganda dividends were great enough to warrant the continued interest of both sides in the continuating their contacts.

The successful exchange of prisoners near Livno in September 1942 helped alter the ruthless nature of guerrilla war on the territory of the NDH to a certain degree. This was especially true for the Partisan forces subordinated directly to Tito. Whereas the German engineers from Livno escaped execution thanks only to Ott's initiative, by early November the Partisan units were officially instructed to spare prisoners so that they could be exchanged. The guerrilla units not directly under the control of the Supreme HQ, on the contrary, still had a mixed record in the matter of prisoner-taking. The fate of the prisoners was decided by conditions on the ground and the decisions of local commanders. As they had no experience in such deals with their German counterparts, they were less likely to spare Germans than Italians, or in some cases, even *Ustashe*. The German occupation forces, for their own part, largely continued applying their earlier policies regarding captured guerrillas, the majority of whom were still executed immediately after capture. Only after it became clear that the *Ustashe* were sabotaging the exchange process by deliberately holding back those individuals the Partisans wanted did the Germans begin to realize the necessity of keeping at least some of the captured guerrillas in their own custody. The treatment of the few chosen individuals who were destined to be exchanged was relatively good on both sides; they were neither tortured nor over-worked, and they were reasonably well fed and well accommodated.

At the beginning of January 1943, the Partisans sent one of the German civilians captured in late September to the Axis-held territory to optimize the exchange which had been negotiated both directly and indirectly. His mission was doomed to failure because of the extraordinarily harsh winter and heavy fighting in Western Bosnia. The two sides found themselves sitting across from each other at the negotiating table again in mid-March. The exchange of prisoners was the means, rather than an end, of this round of talks.

Chapter 3

March Negotiations

1943

Introduction

The aim of this chapter is to examine the most controversial episode of the Partisan-German contacts, namely, the negotiations between the two sides which occurred throughout the early spring of 1943. Few episodes from the war in Yugoslavia have received as much attention from scholars and the general public, primarily because of the alleged cease-fire which was brokered between the Communist-led guerrillas and the German occupation forces. This chapter shall attempt to provide an appraisal of these events using published works as well as new archival materials.

By November 1942, the Third Reich's position was far from satisfactory. The brutal battle which had been raging amongst the ruins of Stalingrad since August took a decisive turn for the worse on 19 November when the revitalized Red Army commenced its winter operations aimed at cutting off the German Sixth Army. Within a week, the worst fears of the German leadership materialized when the Soviets sealed a gigantic ring around the doomed army. The beginning of the month also brought a conclusion to the Battle of El Alamein, which had been contested for almost two weeks. Its results were disastrous for Rommel's *Afrika Korps,* the remnants of which had to relinquish their foothold in Egypt and undertake a long retreat westwards to Libya. On 8 November, the Anglo-Americans landed in Morocco and Algeria, hoping to trap the Italian-German forces between themselves and Montgomery's armies approaching from the east. This turn of events cast a spotlight on the Mediterranean, making it an object of concern for Berlin. Should the Axis positions in Africa fall, the Allies were sure to continue their offensive by attempting a landing somewhere in the Mediterranean. Aside from Italy, the Balkans were considered a possible target.

Yugoslavia suddenly gained strategic significance due to its long coastline along the Adriatic and because it was the location of the main German lines of communication to Greece. In any event, reinforcements and supplies that needed to be rushed to Dalmatia or southern Greece would likely suffer casualties or face delays owing to the widespread insurgency in the NDH. The main threat to the Axis was the approximately 25,000 square kilometers of territory controlled by the Yugoslav Partisans, comprised of parts of Western Bosnia and Herzegovina and the adjacent Croatian regions of Lika, Kordun, and Banija. The Germans estimated the number of Partisans there at 63,000, a force to be reckoned with in the event of an Allied invasion.[1] The second flashpoint in the NDH was Slavonia, where numerous Partisan units constituted a serious threat to the all-important Zagreb–Belgrade railway. The Germans were no less worried about the existence of Chetniks in the Italian occupation zone. At a series of meetings in Berlin from 18–20 December 1942, Hitler managed to secure Italian support for a joint operation in Yugoslavia against "bandits of all kinds," which also nominally entailed the disarming of the Chetniks serving in the Italian auxiliary militia, the *Milizia Volontaria Anti Comunista* (MVAC). On 28 December 1942, Hitler released "Instruction No. 47" (*Weisung Nr. 47*), which officially gave the green light for offensive operations in the Balkans.[2]

Colonel General Löhr traveled to Rome and held a series of meetings with his Italian counterparts from 3–4 January 1943. After considering a large-scale winter campaign against the Slavonian Partisans, the Axis high command opted for an operation against the "Tito State" to the south of the Sava River. The operation, codenamed *Weiss,* was originally intended to consist of three phases: *Weiss I* was aimed at the encirclement and destruction of the Partisans in the Bihać-Petrovac area; *Weiss II* would then be launched against the Communist guerrillas in the Petrovac-Livno sector and adjoining parts of Dalmatia; and *Weiss III* would target the Chetniks in Eastern Herzegovina once they had dealt with the Partisans. Before the former were eliminated, however, the Italians insisted that there could be no disarmament of the Chetniks; the Germans had to grudgingly accept that the Serbian Royalists would be their allies in the upcoming battle. The *Wehrmacht* amassed three full divisions, as well as elements of two additional divisions, and 100 aircraft for the first phase of Operation *Weiss.* Supplementing this force were three Italian divisions and various NDH units; the grand total of Axis troops was an estimated 90,000 men.[3]

Although the German commands were aware of major shortcomings in the operational plan, there was no time to make modifications and operations commenced on schedule on 20 January 1943. The main body of the NOVJ, informed well in advance of the Axis preparations, began pulling out of the Bihać area and retreated to the southeast.[4] Harsh winter weather, skillful rear guard actions of the

---

[1] NARA, T-315, Roll 2271, 000165, Situation report for the period 17–25 December 1942 (26 December 1942). Because of its size and the internal organization of the Partisan-controlled territory, the Germans called it "Tito's State" (*Titostaat*). The Partisan name for it was the "Bihać Republic" (*Bihaćka republika*).

[2] Gaj Trifković, "Schwarz auf Weiss: 1943-Das Jahr der deutschen Großoperationen in Jugoslawien," unpublished master's thesis, Karl-Franzens University Graz, 2010, pp. 49–50.

[3] Schmider, *Partisanenkrieg,* pp. 210–11; Nikola Anić, "Operacija 'Weiss': Četvrta neprijateljska ofenziva," in Pape and Anić, eds., *Drugi svjetski rat,* Vol. II, p. 244.

[4] Supreme HQ had planned to launch a strategic operation in Serbia, Montenegro, and Kosovo from the Bihać Republic as soon as units were rested and refitted. The preliminary

guerrillas, and the wholesale demolition of roads slowed the pace of the Axis advance to a crawl. When the two German pincers met to the south of Bihać on 9 February, the cauldron was largely empty. "Our own casualties small," concluded the operations section of Army Group E, "and those of the enemy not as high as hoped. Still, OKW [*Oberkommando der Wehrmacht*] pleased with results."[5]

The Axis plans for the continuation of the offensive[6] were seriously disrupted by the operations of the Main Operational Group of the NOVJ whose strike force consisted of five divisions under Tito's personal command. While the Germans and the Italians were discussing their plans in Rome, the guerrilla leader issued directives for the next phase of withdrawal. In short, the Partisans were to continue their movement to the southeast, smash through the line of Italian garrisons along the Neretva between Mostar and Konjic, and cross the river into Eastern Herzegovina. The advance of the Main Operational Group through Western Herzegovina, the location of the bauxite mines, alarmed Berlin. Overnight, the German commands in the NDH were forced to change their plans; the two strongest divisions, the 7th SS Volunteer Mountain Division *Prinz Eugen* and the 369th Infantry, were ordered to secure this strategic area at the cost of allowing the guerrillas to slip away. It was hoped that they could be stopped on the Neretva by the Italians and destroyed by the operations of two weaker German divisions, the 717th and the 718th. The plan appeared to have gone awry by the third week of February; all Italian garrisons in the river valley north of Mostar had successfully been stormed by the Partisans. The only exception was the strategically important Konjic, whose garrison was reinforced by a mixed German-NDH column at the last moment. Despite the arrival of these reinforcements, the fall of the town seemed imminent; once this happened, the road to Eastern Herzegovina would be open to the NOVJ.

At this point, Tito made a serious error in judgment; believing that Konjic would soon be taken, he ordered all bridges across the Neretva destroyed in order to protect his flank against a large force of Chetniks arriving from the east. Much to his dismay, however, the tenacious resistance of the town's garrison could not be broken. By the beginning of March, the Partisans found themselves in a desperate situation: their only line of retreat was blocked at Konjic; they could not cross the river elsewhere as all bridges were blown and the Chetniks held the eastern bank;

---

moves had already been made with two Proletarian and one assault division moved to outside of the Bihać area. Nikola Anić, "Operacija 'Weiss': Četvrta neprijateljska ofenziva," in Pape and Anić, eds., *Drugi svjetski rat,* Vol. II, pp. 245–46.

[5] NARA, T-311, Roll 175, 000428–31, Activity report of the operations section for the period 1–28 February 1943 (1 March 1943).

[6] The continuation of the operation was discussed at a conference in Rome in the first week of February. The Italians insisted that *Weiss III* and the disarmament of the Chetniks be canceled. The Germans saw no alternative but to comply. NARA, T-77, Roll 780, 5507192, War Diary of Armed Forces High Command, Entry for 7 February 1943.

the Italians and Chetniks were advancing along the Neretva from Mostar; and the Germans were pressing from the west. The Main Operational Group, the flower of the People's Liberation Movement, appeared to be facing imminent destruction.[7]

Judging by the evidence, it would be safe to assume that a large part, if not all, of the stranded Partisan army would indeed be physically destroyed if it surrendered to the German occupation forces. Operation *Weiss* had hitherto been conducted with great brutality toward both the captured Partisans and the civilian population in the area of operations. It was not merely the result of spontaneous violence undertaken by brutalized soldiers on the heels of counter-insurgency operations, but rather actions that were premeditated and ordered by the highest echelons of the Third Reich. On 16 December 1942, Hitler issued his notorious "Order for the suppression of bandits," which stipulated that women and children were legitimate targets in anti-partisan operations, and that no German soldier would be held accountable for his actions in the struggle against the guerrillas.[8] Even though the shooting of women and children was rejected at the meeting of top German military commanders in Belgrade on 30 December, all unarmed male civilians between the ages of 15 and 60 caught in the territory of "Tito's State" were destined for deportation.[9] For those caught with arms or aiding the guerrillas in any way, punishment was to be swift—either with a bullet or the rope. The order stated that "no one may be punished for taking drastic measures," and soldiers and officers who "act energetically and assert themselves" could count on the full support of their superiors. The wording of the order meant that the troops were essentially given *carte blanche* with respect to their conduct toward the guerrilla suspects.[10] Given this and similar previous orders, it should come as no surprise that the Germans executed prisoners without delay. "Defectors who come over to us with our passes are shot after interrogation," concluded an exasperated Lüters at a conference held on 16 February 1943, "sometimes only because they cannot be transported to the rear immediately. This attitude is impossible!"[11] This also meant that one of the provisions of the "Combat instructions for Croatia," which called

---

[7] Trifković, "Schwarz auf Weiss," pp. 59–67.

[8] Kerstin Freudiger, *Die juristische Aufarbeitung von NS-Verbrechen* (Tübingen: Mohr Siebeck, 2002), p. 127.

[9] According to Glaise-Horstenau's diary, he was the one who protested against the ill treatment of women and children; thereupon the other generals agreed to employ less drastic measures. Vasa Kazimirović, *Nemački general u Zagrebu* (Kragujevac: Prizma, 1996), pp. 128–30.

[10] NARA, T-315, Roll 2271, 000407–9, Combat instructions for Croatia (12 January 1943). See also the 718th Infantry Division's version released six days later in ibid., 000411, [no subject] (18 January 1943).

[11] NARA, T-315, Roll 2271, 000770, Minutes of conference of divisional commanders held in Sanski Most (16 February 1943).

for sparing any guerrilla leaders for exchange, was not satisfied. Statistics confirm that Operation *Weiss* was carried out in the spirit of Hitler's orders; over a period of two months, only fifty-seven defectors were reported taken and all 616 prisoners who survived immediate capture were executed thereafter. On the other hand, the German occupation forces claimed 11,915 enemy killed, but little evidence about captured weapons exists to support such a high figure.[12]

The actions of the main Partisan force throughout this period were influenced to a considerable degree by the presence of a large number of wounded: 3,800 severely wounded cases were being cared for at the so-called Central Hospital, with an additional 700 lightly wounded fighters in divisional hospitals.[13] During the zenith of Operation *Weiss* (late February–early March), the fate of the Main Operational Group was tied to the fate of the wounded. The Partisan leadership's plans were centered on saving both; leaving the wounded, which would allow for increased mobility and open new possibilities for the remainder of the army, was out of the question. Remembering how their enemies had treated the Partisan wounded in the past, Tito was not going to chance leaving the Central Hospital at the mercy of the advancing Axis troops.[14]

After realizing his error in demolishing the bridges over the Neretva, Tito concocted a bold plan to extricate his army, along with the wounded, from the trap. The German 717th Infantry Division, advancing from the west, was perceived as the greatest danger to the Main Operational Group; its advance guard was already dangerously close to the hospital column in the Rama River Valley. The Partisans would first subdue this threat and use the breathing space to make a 180-degree turn, ford the Neretva, and confront the Chetniks. Utilizing interior lines, within three days the Partisans concentrated seven brigades on the sector opposite the German division. On 2 March, the attack began south of Gornji Vakuf with a massive artillery barrage, the bulk of which was ordnance captured from the Italian garrisons. The Germans, already weakened by constant fighting, buckled and started to give ground. By 7 March, they were pushed some fifteen kilometers to the northwest. On the same day, special assault details crossed the Neretva by improvised means and managed to form a bridgehead on the eastern bank.

---

[12] NARA, T-314, Roll 554, 000377–8, Appendix to letter to Minister of Armed Forces Begić (31 March 1943); NARA, T-78, Roll 332, 6290065, Situation estimate for March 1943 (1 April 1943).

[13] *Sabrana djela,* Vol. XIV, p. 331.

[14] On 2 March, Tito inquired frantically about the possibility of evacuating the Central Hospital either to Lika (*Sabrana djela,* Vol. XIV, p. 102, Tito to Bosnian Corps) or to the Biokovo mountain range in Dalmatia (ibid., p. 103, Tito to 9th Dalmatian Division). One day later, he agreed to the second option (ibid., p. 112, Tito to Bosnian Corps), but changed his mind on 5 March when it was decided that the wounded would go with the Main Operational Group into Eastern Herzegovina (ibid., p. 122, Tito to 1st Proletarian Division).

Partisan engineers quickly constructed a pontoon bridge at Jablanica and the first units crossed that very day.[15]

Negotiations in Gornji Vakuf, 11–14 March 1943

"Just as my runner and I wanted to leave the small, undergrowth-covered valley in the vicinity of Hill 952, we were suddenly showered with a hail of bullets, some coming from as close as fifteen to twenty meters distant. We heard calls in Serbian and realized we were surrounded. We immediately tried to make a fighting retreat through the thick undergrowth. This proved to be impossible, since the depression [where we were] was surrounded by forty to fifty Partisans. Therefore, we had to surrender."[16]

The quote above is how Major Arthur Strecker, commander of the 3rd Battalion, 738th Grenadier Regiment of the 718th Infantry Division, described the circumstances of his capture not far from Gornji Vakuf on 4 March 1943. By that time, the Partisan counterattack was proceeding well, and the greatest threat to the wounded was removed. Overall, however, the situation was far from satisfactory; the Neretva had not yet been forded and the Chetniks were known to be concentrating in strength on the eastern bank. Even if the Partisans crossed the river successfully, there was no guarantee that the Germans would not pursue them as their reinforcements were already arriving from the rear. In short, the fate of the wounded still hung in the balance.

As soon as the news about Strecker's capture reached Supreme HQ, Tito summoned Đilas, Ranković, and Moša Pijade to a small watermill in the Rama Valley. Upon their arrival, Tito suggested they contact the Germans, ostensibly in order to exchange Strecker and other Germans. The prime motive behind the offer, however, was the revival of talks and the recognition of the NOVJ as a legitimate belligerent force. If the Germans agreed, then the patients of the Central Hospital could hope for at least a modicum of protection in the event they were captured. In order to make sure the Germans would not reject the request out of hand, the Partisan leadership decided to make it more attractive by including the withdrawal of guerrilla forces to a mutually agreed upon territory as a provision. This had already been the topic of talks in Zagreb in August 1942 and in Livno in November of the same year. Tito's overriding wish was to achieve a cease-fire, at least during the talks, in order to gain a free hand for the upcoming battle against the Chetniks. The offer was "worded in a way . . . that left room for negotiations" and was signed by Velimir Terzić, Tito's acting Chief of Staff.[17]

---

[15] *Oslobodilački rat,* Vol. I, pp. 383–92.

[16] NARA, T-315, Roll 2271, 001448, Report on my capture on 4 March 1943 (21 March 1943).

[17] Djilas, *Wartime,* p. 229. Đilas stated that the meeting was held "the day after the Chetniks were defeated on the Neretva," which would correspond to 8 March; Leković established

In order to lend credence to the offer, high-ranking Partisan officers engaged Strecker in conversation on the evening of his capture. They openly advocated the Communist cause and expressed belief in a swift victory for the Soviet Union over German and Italian capitalists led by Hitler and Mussolini, but added that world peace could only be achieved by the defeat of British and American capitalism as well. They said that once the Soviets crossed the Polish border, the Western Allies would open the Second Front (ostensibly in order to stem the Soviet advance, and not to hasten victory over the Axis powers). At the same time, they expressed regret over having to fight the German people, and asked Strecker why the *Wehrmacht* fought against the Partisans at all. Furthermore, they made it clear that they regarded the Chetniks as their main enemies and wanted to know how the Germans felt about the Royalists. As the initiation of contact with the German command was also a topic, Strecker was asked to draft a letter for his superiors to plead for a round of talks between the opposing commanders at their earliest convenience, and for an "allocation of a territory" (per Tito's proposal). The letter was carried across the lines by a captured German soldier the following day.[18] As the German answer to Strecker's letter was not forthcoming over the next two days, the NOVJ leadership prepared a similar offer on 8 March. This time it was addressed to Captain Heyss in Mostar, an experienced negotiator from the talks in August and November. There is no evidence that this letter was ever sent, but the fact that it was written at all underlines the sense of urgency on the part of the Partisan leadership to begin the negotiations.[19]

Immediately after the arrival of the courier to the positions of the 717th Infantry Division on 5 March, Strecker's message was dispatched to the HQ of the Commanding General of German Troops in Croatia. It took several days to inform all relevant commands about the Partisan offer and to decide on a reply. On 9 March, Lüters instructed the 717th Infantry Division to inform the guerrillas that the German command would be willing to receive a plenipotentiary envoy in the town of Bugojno in three days' time and that "the safety of the envoy is guaranteed."[20] Once the German answer reached the Partisan lines the following day, Tito summoned Đilas and Ranković in order to discuss the details. First, the Partisans would send more than one delegate in order to lend weight to the negotiations. As the matter

---

that the conference took place on the 4th. Mišo Leković, *Martovski pregovori 1943* (Belgrade: Narodna knjiga, 1985), p. 50. For Tito's motives, see ibid., pp. 50–51.

[18] NARA, T-315, Roll 2271, 001449–51, Report on my capture on 4 March 1943 (21 March 1943). It is not known whether the original offer was attached to Strecker's letter. Leković, *Martovski pregovori*, p. 54.

[19] Ibid., p. 67.

[20] NARA, T-315, Roll 2264, 000731, Lüters to 717th Infantry Division (9 March 1943). The official letter to the Partisans allowed for up to three envoys. NARA, T-315, Roll 2263, 000036, To a higher command of NOVJ (10 March 1943).

was extremely delicate, Đilas, a member of the *Politburo,* would lead the delegation. Koča Popović, known to the Germans from earlier talks, would go as well. Velebit, likewise a veteran Partisan "diplomat," was chosen for this mission mostly because of his linguistic skills. The delegates were provided with only general guidelines and the details were left to their discretion. The aim of the Main Operational Group—the advance into southern Serbia and Kosovo—was not to be disclosed as the Germans were known to be sensitive about Serbian security. The province of Sandžak would be designated as the territory to which the Partisans would be willing to withdraw. From that territory, the delegates were to inform the Germans, the Communist-led guerrillas would wage their war against the Chetniks who were to be unequivocally designated as the Partisans' main enemies. Đilas remembered that the cease-fire was not mentioned during the meeting, but "this, too, was understood." The pseudonyms of the delegates were also discussed: Velebit was already known to the Germans as Vladimir Petrović, a lawyer from Zagreb; Đilas assumed the name of Miloš Marković, "a common name—one borne by a Montenegrin hero of long ago." Only Popović used his real name.[21]

During the conversation, Đilas raised a sensitive issue: how will Moscow react to the negotiations? "Well, they also think first of their own people and the army!," replied the Partisan commander in an angry voice. Đilas was astonished: "It was the first time that a *Politburo* member, let alone Tito, so vehemently expressed any difference with the Soviets." This reaction can be attributed to mounting frustration over the complete lack of Soviet aid. As the situation of the Main Operational Group grew ever more precarious, Tito sent increasingly desperate cables to Moscow. The one from 31 January contained, in part, the following: "I have to ask you again: is it truly not possible to send us any help? Hundreds of thousands of refugees are in danger of starving to death. Can there not be a way of providing us help after twenty months of our heroic, almost superhuman struggle? For twenty months we have been fighting without even the slightest help from the outside. . . ."

On 25 and 27 February, Tito informed the Comintern that the Chetniks had rushed to the Italians' aid around Mostar and accused the Yugoslav government-in-exile of sponsoring this move. As evidence, Tito provided Mihailović's order for the upcoming attack on the Partisans. He requested that Stalin be informed of this so that Moscow could intercede with London and demand a clarification. "This is urgent, for we are in a critical situation," added Tito. On 4 March, at the height of the counterattack at Gornji Vakuf, Tito sent yet another plea: "Can we hope for any help from our allies? Please respond because it is uncertain for how much longer we can endure such pressure. Our casualties are immense and the wounded are limiting our operational freedom to the extreme."

---

[21] Djilas, *Wartime*, pp. 230–31, 234. Velebit remembered that he was told at a meeting with Tito, Đilas, and Popović that a possible cease-fire was to be one of the topics of the negotiations. Velebit, *Tajne i zamke*, p. 216.

The Comintern replied only to the January telegram—with ten days' delay. Apart from conveying the admiration and "deep brotherly sympathies" which the Soviet people and their leadership had for the "People's Liberation Struggle," the telegram failed to deliver any good news. It quoted insurmountable technical difficulties as the main reason for the lack of Soviet help and advised the Partisans to use their own devices to weather the current storm.[22]

On 11 March, Đilas, Popović, and Velebit ventured alone by foot on the main road toward Prozor. The countryside was peaceful and not a living soul was seen along the way. The scattered hulks of military equipment were the only testament to the fact that this ground had been the scene of heavy fighting in the preceding days. The eerie atmosphere only added to the tension the delegates must have felt. The prospect of running into *Ustashe* instead of Germans was particularly worrying. Đilas and Popović quipped that Velebit, being junior in rank to both, should carry the white flag which would make him the target of choice for the enemy. The three men reached the outskirts of Prozor without encountering patrols or being fired upon. Just as they arrived amongst the first houses, a dozen Germans appeared before them. When asked if they had come to surrender, Velebit explained that they were envoys from Partisan headquarters, expected by the German command. The delegates were disarmed and kept under guard until transportation was available. One hour later, they were blindfolded and taken to a car which left immediately.[23]

After a short drive, the car stopped and the envoys' blindfolds were removed— they were in Gornji Vakuf, just as expected. They were taken to the headquarters of the 717th Infantry Division where General Benignus Dippold awaited them. After courteously greeting the delegation, the general offered them a seat at a small table. The envoys then went on to expound on the three proposals listed in their letters of authorization:

1. Exchange of prisoners, including the employees of Elektrobosna, Major Strecker and twenty-five other German soldiers, as well as

---

[22] See Tito's cables to Comintern in *Sabrana djela*, Vol. XIV, p. 28 (7 January 1943), pp. 95–96 (25 and 27 February 1943), and p. 121 (4 March 1943). The Comintern's response of 11 February can be found in ibid., p. 298. For a short discussion on the lack of Soviet help in the first phase of the war, see Othmar Nikola Haberl, *Die Emanzipation der KP Jugoslawiens von der Kontrolle der Komintern/KPdSU, 1941–1945* (Munich: Oldenbourg Verlag, 1974), pp. 38–40.

[23] Djilas, *Wartime*, pp. 232–33. The delegates' worst fears were realized when they happened upon a group of *Ustashe* on a street in Prozor. As the delegates were under German protection, they let them pass. Interestingly, both Đilas and Popović remembered one of the *Ustashe* commenting loudly about the envoys' good boots. Miloš Vuksanović, ed., *Koča Popović: Beleške uz ratovanje-dnevnik, beleške, dokumenti* (Belgrade: BIGZ, 1988), p. 90, Entry for 27 March 1943.

some 120 Home Guards and over 600 Italians. Professor Ivo Marinković from Karlovac was demanded in exchange for Strecker. As Marinković was in *Ustashe* custody, the NOVJ delegates pointed out that NDH authorities would often kill those prisoners wanted by the Partisans, and then tell the Germans they could not be located.

2. Recognition of the NOVJ as a legitimate belligerent force. The envoys explained that the Partisans were not "bandits," but an organized and disciplined force which had always obeyed the rules and customs of warfare. In this respect, they reminded their counterparts about the humane treatment of the German prisoners in Užice in late 1941. Consequently, the wounded and captured members of the NOVJ should be accorded the same protection of international law. For their part, the envoys pledged that their side would reciprocate.

3. "Political questions . . . touched on in the letter of 17 November 1942 which was addressed to Glaise-Horstenau."[24] In short, the envoys stated that the Chetnicks were their primary enemy and that they fought against the *Wehrmacht* only because they had to defend themselves. They were a completely independent resistance movement; their propaganda leaned on Moscow only because they wanted to have nothing to do with London. The Chetniks, agents of the Yugoslav government-in-exile, received weapons from the Italians, who also did not protest the presence of British officers among the Royalists. "The NOVJ would fight the English as well if they tried to make a landing; the Chetniks would not."

The delegation warned that "this is not an offer of capitulation . . . ; they only want to carry out their main thrust against the Chetniks and would therefore suggest that the two sides mutually agree on a neutral zone [i.e. Sandžak]. The delegation requests that the third point remain confidential."[25]

---

[24] There is some confusion in the historiography concerning a letter which was allegedly sent to Glaise-Horstenau during the negotiations in Livno on 17 November 1942. Tomasevich (*The Chetniks,* p. 244) and Leković (*Martovski pregovori,* p. 83), to name two sources, claim that this letter could not be found in the archives. Odić and Komarica offered a simple, yet plausible answer to this mystery: Glaise-Horstenau was not sent a special letter, but a memorandum of the meeting held on the 17th which we know existed thanks to Dr. Heinrich's report. See Odić and Komarica, *Partizanska obavještajna služba,* pp. 294–99.

[25] NARA, T-1119, Roll 16, 0068–70, Memorandum from a meeting at Gornji Vakuf (11 March 1943). The signature of this and other German documents from the same source about this particular round of talks is sometimes cited as "NOKW-1088." A copy of this document is also available in NARA, T-315, Roll 2263, 000031–4.

Dippold listened attentively to the envoys, repeating "I do not know much about politics, but..." several times during the process. He made it very clear, however, that he had daily objectives to achieve and he intended to do so, negotiations notwithstanding.[26] He also confessed that he had no authorization to either accept or decline the guerrillas' terms—his task was merely to relate them to higher commands. After the meeting concluded, the envoys were taken to a room where they waited for the preliminary German answer. They were joined by a German officer who worked with Velebit to draft an official document containing the list of Partisan demands.[27]

This document, signed by all three envoys, had a total of five points. The first two concerned the exchange of prisoners and the mutual recognition of the rights of prisoners and wounded, respectively. The third point read, in part, "that there was no reason for the German *Wehrmacht* to continue its combat operations against the NOVJ given the situation, enemies, and the interests of both sides." If the Germans agreed to this, then the two sides should determine a zone to which the Partisans could retreat, taking into consideration economic and other interests. In the same context, the third point explicitly named the Chetniks as the main enemies of the Partisans. The fourth point formally requested a truce "for as long as negotiations on all these matters last." The fifth point read that the Partisan delegation is authorized to lead the preliminary talks, but that any final agreement would have to be confirmed by their higher commands. At the conclusion, the delegation re-emphasized its wish to conclude these negotiations at the earliest opportunity and requested the appointment of authorized representatives from the Germans. It is important to note that the envoys' statement concerning a potential Allied landing was not included in this official document.[28]

The HQ of the Commander of German Troops in Croatia was immediately informed of these proceedings. Lüters' Chief of Staff, Colonel Werner Pfafferott, placed a telephone call later that day to Glaise-Horstenau's office and also informed Löhr, who was in Vienna at the time. The colonel reported that three Partisan envoys came to Gornji Vakuf that day to propose a prisoner exchange, demanding Professor Ivan "Uminković" [*sic*] from Karlovac for Major Strecker. The call had been placed earlier to the *Ustashe* police authorities who, unsurprisingly, answered

---

[26] Velebit wrote: "I remember well that, after hearing this, I said to myself, we failed in our main intention; we cannot count on a respite needed for the crossing over the Neretva." Velebit, *Tajne i zamke,* p. 224.

[27] Leković, *Martovski pregovori,* pp. 82–89. Velebit made the statement that the German citizen, Hans Ott, was well acquainted with the matter, and that his presence at the negotiations would be desirable. This had already been requested in the letter to Captain Heyss dated 8 March. Ibid., p. 67.

[28] NARA, T-1119, Roll 16, 0071, Gornji Vakuf, 11 March 1943.

that they could not find the person in question.[29] The guerrillas also hoped to achieve an agreement on "humane treatment" of prisoners on both sides. Additionally, they requested a truce and recognition of their army as a legitimate belligerent force. The first request was refused by Lüters out of hand. As an officer of the old school, he distanced himself from the second request, the one "which could have sweeping political consequences," and requested Glaise-Horstenau's involvement. The fourth point of the stenograph of the conversation deserves to be quoted here: "They [the Partisan envoys] also stated that their struggle is not aimed against the Croatian state, and especially not against the Germans, but exclusively against the Chetniks. They would be willing to oppose with weapons any enemy we identify, including the disembarking English. The envoys did not have the Soviet star on their caps, but the letter 'M,' which purportedly stands for 'Maček.'"[30]

The only explanation for the discrepancies between this passage and what was actually said and written down in Gornji Vakuf is that Pfafferott's knowledge was based on verbal reports, rather than on the two official documents prepared during the negotiations. First, Marinković's name was evidently misspelled. Second, there was no mention of the NDH during the first round of talks. Third, the stenograph offers an exaggerated version of the Partisan envoys' statement about the possible British landing; while the delegates indeed said the NOVJ would oppose the British landing with arms, there was no mention of their doing so as German auxiliaries. Fourth, and most bizarre of all, is the notion that the guerrilla representatives were somehow connected to Vladko Maček, head of the pre-war Croatian Peasant Party. Even if Maček, a known Anglophile, had any armed formations under his command (which he did not), it is a mystery why his followers would have stated that they wanted to fight against the British.[31] The stenograph is a good example of how easily facts could get distorted or exaggerated. While not implying that Pfafferott, or any of his high-ranking colleagues, unreservedly believed all the information contained in the stenograph, there were those who would have readily acted upon such information as it corresponded to their beliefs or convictions.

Given the fact that the inquiry about Marinković was made on the very same day the exchange offer arrived, it is evident the Germans were willing to talk to the Partisans. Indeed, interest for the exchange of the military economic experts from Jajce and the soldiers captured in Bosnia was not waning despite Operation *Weiss*.[32]

---

[29] Information regarding Ivo Marinković's ultimate fate would continue to elude the Germans for months after the March talks (see next chapter).

[30] NARA, T-501, Roll 267, 000528–9, Stenograph of telephone call from Colonel Pfafferott on 11 March 1943.

[31] For an overview of the wartime activities of Maček and his party, see Tomasevich, *Occupation and Collaboration*, pp. 356–68.

[32] HR HDA 1450, Roll D-2222, 419, Report of Lieutenant Colonel Severović on prisoner exchange (undated, probably from the second half of February 1943). The document reads

On 3 March, two days before Strecker's letter reached its destination, Glaise-Horstenau had a meeting with Pavelić. One of the points of discussion was the long-overdue exchange of these individuals. The general had a list of eleven names the Partisans wanted exchanged for their prisoners, which included a Partisan commander and several public figures, mostly intellectuals arrested for their leftist leanings or for participating in underground activities.[33] Some of them were currently in custody in Zagreb, and Pavelić's approval had to be obtained for their exchange. Judging by remarks added in pencil, the latter gave his permission and informed Glaise-Horstenau that one of the candidates was already deceased.[34]

In the interim, the Partisan envoys remained in Gornji Vakuf as guests of the German garrison and were treated correctly for the duration of their stay. After the meeting with Dippold, they were given food and cigarettes, and their pistol clips, which had been taken away in Prozor, were returned to them. Given the circumstances, their lodgings were good ("not even the general's was much better," Đilas wrote later), and one German soldier (of Croatian origin) was seconded as the delegates' orderly. While waiting for the Germans' response, the Partisans had a unique opportunity to gain a different perspective of their enemy, free of propaganda clichés. They were surprised by the attitude shown by native Austrians and Croatians serving with the *Wehrmacht*. Some of the former greeted them with the clenched-fist salute, while one of the latter provided a valuable glimpse into the troubled relations between the 369th Infantry Division's rank-and-file and its officers: "Those [expletive]! They treat us incredibly harsh. We are forced to fight in their uniform. . . . They ordered us to tell everyone that we have been to the Eastern

---

that the Military Economy Officer was especially interested in the exchange of the engineers so that production in Jajce could be resumed as soon as possible. Severović also added that the talks were on hold owing to the ongoing operations south of the Sava.

[33] The Partisan commander was Riko Žnidarić, whom his comrades wanted to exchange for some *Ustashe* in December 1942. Veljko Kovačević, *Ratna sjećanja* (Belgrade: Vojnoizdavački i novinski centar, 1989), p. 221. Interesting is the case of Dr. Vuk Vernić, a professor at the University of Zagreb's Faculty of Law. He was arrested in January 1942 and sent to Jasenovac concentration camp in June. Glaise-Horstenau interceded with Pavelić on his behalf on 5 September 1942, saying that Vernić had a family to support, that two of his cousins were officers (presumably in the Home Guard), and that the rumors of his communist leanings were "totally false." NARA, T-501, Roll 267, 000367, Notice for a conversation with Poglavnik (5 September 1942). Pavelić obviously knew better. Vernić was, in fact, a candidate for full-time membership in the KPJ. Leković, *Martovski pregovori*, p. 133.

[34] NARA, T-501, Roll 267, 000320, Reception of German Plenipotentiary General by Poglavnik (3 March 1943). The words "prisoner exchange" were underlined and "P[oglavnik]: yes" added on the margin. The prisoner who died (marked with a cross) was Mihovil Pavlek Miškina, a Croatian poet and member of the Croatian Peasant Party. He died in Jasenovac in June 1942. *Tko je tko u NDH: Hrvatska 1941.–1945.* (Zagreb: Minerva, 1997), pp. 313–14.

Front. That is a lie. I was captured by the Partisans at Livno and was punished for it by being sent to a legionnaire outfit."[35]

Ðilas was also surprised to learn that the usual stereotypes applied to the German Army had little basis in reality: there was no mention of Nazi ideology; officers and soldiers were often informal with each other and even ate the same food. In short, they resembled any other front line unit comprised of men who had no wish to be in the war, but since fate had brought them there, were determined to prevail.[36]

The Germans used every opportunity to size up their adversaries by engaging the envoys in conversation. According to the accounts of the Partisan negotiators, the questions posed to them were never phrased in an interrogatory manner. All Germans, from general to private, seemed genuinely curious about their strange guests, and especially about the guerrillas' relations to the Soviet Union. Two intelligence officers, the most frequent visitors to the NOVJ delegates, also shared their own experiences and thoughts on the war. They defended the Third Reich's cause and spoke of ultimate victory, but without ideological overtones; they gave the impression that they "simply hoped for an outcome which would not bring ruin to Germany." As far as Yugoslavia was concerned, the officers shared the attitudes of all of their colleagues whom the Partisans had met in the past; they spoke of the *Ustashe* with a mix of contempt and horror and quipped about the incompetence of the Italians. The conciliatory tone of the discussion up to that point changed dramatically as soon as the parties touched upon the German-Partisan conflict. The officers questioned the purpose of the insurgency, claiming it only brought immeasurable suffering to the country and its population. The Partisans retorted by saying that living had been hard but manageable before the war, and that they had no intention of laying down their arms. Furthermore, it was the Germans who should question the rationale behind combating the insurgency since the guerrillas could not be destroyed—if one group was defeated, another would take its place. Although they acknowledged the bravery and skill of the Partisans, the German officers remained contemptuous of guerrilla warfare. When Popović commented that he could slip his whole division through the German lines whenever he liked, one of the officers remarked: "Yes, it is easy to make war that way—a piece of bread and some bullets in a bag, and off you go into the mountains." The Partisan commander, known for his sharp wit, retorted by offering the Germans an exchange—they could have the bread and the bullets, and the Partisans would get tanks and other vehicles. "You'll never get your hands on that. Never!," shouted the officer. Curiously, words—not guns—were the weapons of the moment.[37]

---

[35] Vladimir Dedijer, *Novi prilozi za biografiju Josipa Broza Tita*, Vol. II (Rijeka: Liburnia, 1981), p. 671.

[36] Djilas, *Wartime*, p. 234.

[37] The German officers sought to retaliate during their next visit to the delegates on 14 March. Upon entering the room, they wished Popović a happy birthday with ironic

The First Round of Talks in Sarajevo

The delegates had been in Gornji Vakuf for two days waiting for an answer from the Germans. On 13 March, the commander of the 369th Infantry Division, which had replaced the 717th as the envoys' host, sent an inquiry to Lüters' staff as to how they should be handled. The answer was that the plenipotentiary general would send a negotiator (presumably Ott) as soon as possible. If the Partisan negotiators could be "induced" to wait a while longer, then the German emissary could be flown to Gornji Vakuf in a courier plane. If not, then the date for a new meeting should be set. Probably as a sign of goodwill, Lüters ordered that "due to the ongoing negotiations, all executions of prisoners are to be stopped."[38] This proved to be one of the few concrete results of the whole episode; Đilas remembered that the Germans began sparing captured Partisans, even providing first aid to the wounded on several occasions, and giving them chocolate and cigarettes.[39]

Deciding he would be more useful back with his division, Koča Popović prepared to return to the Partisan lines the next day. He was provided with a letter of safe conduct and a car to take him to the German lines on the outskirts of Jablanica. He covered the rest of the way by foot, joining Supreme HQ on the banks of Boračko Lake on the evening of the same day. He reported the lack of progress to Tito, and added that if the German reply was not forthcoming, Velebit and Đilas would rejoin them in two days' time.[40] Several hours after Popović left, good news finally reached the NOVJ delegates—Hans Ott had arrived and a car would take them all to Sarajevo that night. The trip was uneventful and they reached their destination on schedule. They were billeted in a spacious flat in a building overlooking the Miljacka River that had been transformed into a hotel for OT functionaries. Their hostess was a woman of Slovenian origin, Ines Rakuša, whose husband was purportedly a Yugoslav officer, now a prisoner in Germany. She was very hospitable to her strange guests—so hospitable, in fact, that it aroused their suspicion.[41]

---

cordiality: "Koča wasn't at all taken aback," remembered Đilas. "He thanked them and added that this was 'easy enough for you to find out [as] the Belgrade police have had a file on me for a long time.'" Djilas, *Wartime*, pp. 235–36; Vuksanović, ed., *Popović-Beleške*, p. 91, Entry for 27 March 1943.

[38] NARA, T-315, Roll 2154, 000408–9, War diary entry for 13 March 1943 (15.00; 16.00; 17.20 hours).

[39] Djilas, *Wartime*, p. 240.

[40] Leković, *Martovski pregovori*, pp. 97–98.

[41] NARA, RG 226, Entry 108a, Box 276, p. 2, SAINT Salzburg to SAINT Washington, Re: Ing. Hans Ott intermediary between Tito and the Germans (13 March 1946); Velebit, *Tajne i zamke*, p. 217. Velebit wrote that he received a letter in 1947 or 1948 from Rakuša, who had returned to her country of origin where she ran a hotel. In his "Geneva Statement" of 1967 about the March Negotiations (written on specific order of the Central Committee), Velebit

After spending the night in what seemed to be unimaginable luxury, Velebit and Ðilas were taken to the German command.[42] They were met there by at least one intelligence officer and Ott. The Germans expressed a desire to exchange prisoners as soon as possible, but declined making any commitments on political questions. They also informed their counterparts that the pre-condition for the continuation of talks was the immediate cessation of sabotage on the Zagreb-Belgrade railway line. The Partisan envoys tied this issue to the recognition of the NOVJ as a legitimate belligerent force. As neither side was ready (or authorized) to give in, the talks ended in a stalemate. Under these circumstances, Ðilas saw no alternative but to return to Supreme HQ to receive new instructions and to gather the exchange prisoners. Velebit would stay behind and await word of whether or not the negotiations would be continued.[43]

The next day, 16 March 1943, Ðilas left Sarajevo in a truck accompanied by a German sergeant. As the battle around Konjic was still raging, crossing over to the Partisan lines proved more difficult than expected. One obstinate Partisan machine gunner would not heed Ðilas' calls and kept him and his German companion pinned down the whole day. Only when dusk set in were the two able to safely cross the lines. There was some bewilderment amongst the Partisans upon learning that one of their top commanders was negotiating with the Germans while they were doing their best to kill them. Savo Kovačević, the veteran Montenegrin brigade commander, half-jokingly remarked to the high-ranking envoy: "Do not go making peace between us and the Germans." Ðilas was dumbfounded and could not think of a better answer except to reprimand the commander for his lack of faith in the higher command. "I do trust them!," Kovačević replied, "But the army has just barely gotten started against the Germans. They are our worst enemies."[44]

The higher commands were eagerly awaiting news about the course of the negotiations. Thus, after Ðilas joined the Supreme HQ, he spent considerable time relating his experiences from within enemy territory. "Ha, I knew that is where it hurts them," was Tito's comment on the German demand for a halt to sabotage on the Zagreb-Belgrade railway line. He added that the Germans would have to first cease their own attacks before he sent corresponding orders to Slavonian units.

---

suggested Rakuša should be sought out and asked for her version of events. Unfortunately, it seems that his advice was not followed. Djilas, on the other hand, remembered that she was a Serb, and that she did not hide her hatred toward the *Ustashe;* "And like all Serbian women, she was an excellent cook." Djilas, *Wartime,* p. 236.

[42] While walking down a corridor, Ðilas had a close encounter with a deserter from the 1st Proletarian Division, who, for unknown reasons, failed to disclose Ðilas' real identity. Leković, *Martovski pregovori,* p. 107.

[43] Ibid., pp. 107–08.

[44] Djilas, *Wartime,* pp. 237–39.

Although the last Partisan had crossed over from the west bank of the Neretva on 15 March, the fighting had not yet been concluded. The German offensive in the vicinity of Konjic indicated that they were still pursuing the Main Operational Group as it withdrew deeper into Eastern Herzegovina. It was therefore decided not to refuse the enemy conditions out of hand, but to keep negotiating in order to buy more time. As a gesture of goodwill, Tito ordered that the German captives be sent to their compatriots as soon as they could be assembled without waiting for a formal prisoner exchange. Đilas would accompany them to the village of Bijela (south of Konjic), where he would also wait for news from Velebit. As for the individuals the Partisans wanted in return, Tito repeatedly mentioned the name of Herta Haas, a KPJ member and his common law wife. She was known to have been arrested in Zagreb, but her fate was uncertain.[45]

Velebit's Trip to Zagreb and the Release of German Prisoners

On the same day Đilas went back to the Partisans, Velebit was invited to visit the German High Command in Zagreb. As there was no time to request instructions from Supreme HQ, he decided on his own to accept the invitation. Accompanied by Ott, he boarded a transport plane to Zagreb and was received by Glaise-Horstenau that day. No notes were taken, but according to Velebit's post-war memoirs, it was merely another informal conversation pertaining to the topics listed in the memorandum from Gornji Vakuf. Velebit inquired again about the possibility of a cease-fire, while Glaise-Horstenau was interested in how the Partisans would react to an Allied landing in the Balkans. The Partisan envoy replied that "in the spirit of the received directives," the NOVJ would oppose any foreign operation which had not been sanctioned by the AVNOJ, with force if necessary. "There was never any mention of us doing this together with the Germans," commented Velebit.[46]

The following day, the Partisan envoy held a meeting with the Italian military attaché in Zagreb, Brigadier General Giancarlo Re. They discussed a possible exchange of more than 600 officers and men of the Italian Army who had been captured during the fighting in the Neretva Valley for a similar number of Partisans and their sympathizers in Italian captivity. Both sides agreed to exchange accurate lists of these individuals as soon as possible. The Italian brigadier general requested that *Comando Superiore Forze Armate di Slovenia e Dalmazia,* or Supersloda (High Command in Slovenia and Dalmatia, an alternative designation of the Italian 2nd Army), send a special envoy to Zagreb with the names of available prisoners and an authorization to further negotiate the exchange. The next opportunity to do so was not long in coming. On 18 March, Velebit and Ott left for Sarajevo

---

[45] Ibid., p. 240.

[46] Velebit, *Tajne i zamke,* pp. 219–20.

by plane with the expectation that the guerrilla envoy would return to Zagreb in four to five days with new instructions from his superiors.[47]

The German authorities used the respite to gather instructions from their own superiors. Kasche sent a lengthy cable to von Ribbentrop on the evening of 17 March which summarized the results of the talks thus far and offered his personal views and suggestions on the matter. The information was provided by the engineer, Ott, "who had already worked" for the ambassador as a liaison with the guerrillas:

> There is a possibility that Tito and his followers might cease hostilities toward Germany, Italy, and Croatia, and withdraw to Sandžak in order to settle the score with Mihailović's Chetniks. It is, under the circumstances, possible that he will make a demonstrative renouncement of Moscow and London which have abandoned him. The Partisans request the following: to fight it out with the Chetniks in Sandžak and to return to their villages thereafter, thereby bringing about the pacification of Croatian and Serbian territories; the return of their followers to their villages after surrendering arms; a pledge from our side that there will be no executions of leading personalities. My opinion is that we must exploit this opportunity since the defection of this group—which is respected internationally—from the camp of our enemies, would be very important.[48]

To further strengthen his case, Kasche added that only a minority of Partisans were Communists, and that their movement did not commit "excessive" crimes

---

[47] Leković, *Martovski pregovori*, pp. 265–66. The Italians lost altogether 2,300 men during the battles in the Neretva Valley. *Zbornik*/IV/11/368–72, Supersloda to 6th Corps, 5 March 1943. The Prozor garrison (some 640 men) suffered an especially grim fate. After declining a surrender ultimatum and repulsing the first two Partisan attacks, its defenses finally crumbled on 17 February. The Partisans took their revenge by executing most of the prisoners after the battle. Djilas, *Wartime,* p. 220; Schmider, *Partisanenkrieg,* p. 229; NARA, T-315, Roll 2271, 001395, Interrogation of Fortunato Zavaglia, 4 March 1943. The rest of the Italians captured in Jablanica and other strongpoints in the Neretva Valley were spared; the Partisans demanded and received food for these prisoners from the Italian command in Mostar. A prisoner exchange was also discussed, but it did not materialize. Labović and Basta, *Partizani za pregovaračkim stolom 1941–1945,* pp. 129–34. The prisoners were subsequently used as porters and specialists (truck and tank drivers, etc.). A large (though unspecified) number of them died of typhus, hunger, and exposure during the following months.

[48] *Akten zur deutschen auswärtigen Politik 1918–1945* (Göttingen: Musterschmidt Verlag, 1978–79), Series E, Vol. V, pp. 416–17 (hereinafter: ADAP/series/volume/page), Kasche to Foreign Ministry (17 March 1943).

against prisoners or the local population. The ambassador concluded the cable by pointing to the fact that Germany's partners (Minister Mladen Lorković of the NDH and Ambassador Raffaele Casertano of Italy) also shared his opinion on Tito's offer.

On what basis Kasche concluded that the Partisans were, in effect, offering to capitulate, is difficult to determine. One possible answer is that his main source, Hans Ott, was either a victim of a misunderstanding or had exaggerated what he had heard from his Partisan counterparts.[49] Ott, according to the Yugoslav historiography, was not a person likely to do either; his "objective and realistic" reports about the NOVJ, as well as the good contacts he maintained with the insurgents' representatives, would eventually earn him the nickname *Partisanenhecht* (roughly, "Partisan Daredevil").[50] Even if Ott misunderstood what Velebit, in particular, had been telling him, the memorandum from the preliminary talks in Gornji Vakuf unequivocally quoted the Partisan envoys stating that their offers should not be mistaken for offers of capitulation. Naturally, they would not have flaunted this sentiment too often if they wanted to appear flexible and open-minded to their German counterparts; after all, they had taken the initiative for the talks and hoped to obtain concessions. The need for flexibility notwithstanding, the envoys would not have strayed too far from their written statement, even in private conversations. Furthermore, Pfafferott's telephone call demonstrated just how quickly rumors spread and found their way into official documents. It is not surprising that Kasche chose to believe some of them, especially given his well-known habit to adapt facts to his own wishes. His latest cable to the foreign ministry was similar to the one sent on 21 September 1942 in the aftermath of the first exchange, only more exaggerated.

As the period from late September 1942 to early March 1943 was—contrary to Kasche's estimate of Tito's intentions—marked by ever-increasing Partisan activity, it was understandable that Berlin was skeptical of his latest report. Von Ribbentrop's answer arrived on 19 March. First, the Reich's foreign minister thought that any contact between the ambassador and the Partisans would be "inappropriate." More importantly, he did not seem to share Kasche's enthusiasm about the negotiations. It was feared that the Partisans, once allowed to rest and replenish in Sandžak, would simply recommence hostilities against the Axis powers at a later date; even worse, they could do this in alliance with the Chetniks. In light of this possibility, von Ribbentrop wanted to know the opinion of the generals on the ground. He also wanted to know what guarantees Tito's envoys offered that they would honor their part of the agreement.[51]

---

[49] Schmider, *Partisanenkrieg,* p. 245.

[50] In addition, Odić wrote that Ott was "an intelligence operative of high caliber . . . almost without equal in the German intelligence service." Odić, *Neostvareni planovi,* pp. 249, 253.

[51] Leković, *Martovski pregovori,* p. 115.

After he landed safely in Sarajevo, Velebit dispatched a message for Đilas through German couriers, inviting him back to continue the talks. On the same night (18 March 1943), the high-ranking *Politburo* member proceeded to Konjic and then to Sarajevo. There he was briefed by Velebit about his activities in Zagreb, as well as the details of the upcoming journey. The decision was made to delay the trip to the NDH capital until the German prisoners arrived safely from the Partisan territory. On 19 March 1943, the six Elektrobosna engineers who had been captured months prior in Jajce were finally returned to the Germans. A day later, Major Strecker and twenty soldiers arrived at Konjic around 07.00.[52]

All former prisoners were brought to Sarajevo where they were questioned about their experiences while in Partisan captivity by the intelligence section of the 718th Infantry Division. As expected, most answers pertained to various aspects of the guerrilla army. The returnees reported on multiple topics: the Partisan order of battle; the identity of several high-ranking commanders; the food; the clothing; and the weapons of the units. Their strength after crossing the Neretva was estimated at 35,000.[53] In addition, the guerrillas managed to bring a substantial number of Italian mountain guns and heavy mortars with them, while the rest of their heavy equipment was destroyed on the west bank of the river. All agreed that discipline was strict—cases of desertion or drunkenness were punished by firing squad. German propaganda had little to no effect; the airborne leaflets encouraging surrender were openly ridiculed. Air strikes, on the contrary, had a far greater psychological impact as the Partisans had no means of defending themselves. However, casualties were low; the guerrillas marched only in the dark and were adept at the arts of dispersion and camouflage. Unsurprisingly, the returnees were also questioned about the appearance and whereabouts of the Partisan supreme commander. They confirmed that the photograph of Tito obtained in late 1942 was authentic, adding that he "did not look like a Jew at all." The civilians from Jajce concluded their statements with the following: "The growth of the Communist movement is generally underestimated. They cling to their ideals so firmly that they would never cease their subversive activi-

---

[52] NARA, T-315, Roll 2271, 000840, After-action report on operation "Konjic" (Entry for 19 March 1943). Between December 1942 and March 1943, four German soldiers died in captivity from exhaustion, exposure, or untreated wounds. Three soldiers, sick and wounded, remained in Livno. Ibid., 001461–2, Group interrogation of German soldiers released from Partisan captivity (23 March 1943). Theresa Mehr, one of the original prisoners from Jajce, was not among the returnees. I have not been able to determine her ultimate fate.

[53] This figure was highly inflated. On 7 March, Tito reported to the Comintern that he had some 20,000 able-bodied men and 5,000 sick and wounded. As heavy weapons could not be taken across the Neretva, they were destroyed. The Main Operational group retained eighty mortars and twenty mountain guns. Leković, *Martovski pregovori,* p. 64.

ties, not even if they were scattered into small groups, or even if they had to continue as individuals."[54]

In addition to the report written immediately after his release, Strecker attended a number of high-level meetings in Sarajevo from 23–25 March. Participants at the meetings included the new commander of the 718th Infantry Division, General Josef Kübler; German consul, Erich Gördes; SA Colonel Willi Requard of the embassy staff; NDH Plenipotentiary-Minister, Pavao Canki; and General Mihajlo Lukić, commander of the 2nd Corps of the Home Guard. Strecker repeated his observations made while in captivity, emphasizing the organization of the Partisan army and the fact that they left none of their wounded behind. The major also pointed out that their strength was still considerable; the column with which he had marched had an estimated 10,000 fighters alone. After the meetings, SA Colonel Requard concluded that the "informal talks with the Partisans should be continued in order to achieve not a lasting agreement, but rather a temporary pacification."[55]

Judging by these first-hand accounts, the main guerrilla force had successfully weathered the last storm. The Partisans took heavy casualties, but inner cohesion remained intact. This fact was reluctantly acknowledged by the higher German commands. In his after-action report on Operation *Weiss*, which was officially concluded on 17 March 1943, General Lüters wrote merely that it was a "nice success." Reinhard Gehlen, head of the Ground Forces High Command's "Foreign Armies East" intelligence section, concluded that *Weiss* was only partially successful, shifting a portion of the blame to the poor performance of the Italian Army. General Dippold was much more honest, saying that the enemy in Operations *Weiss I* and *Weiss II* could be described as "poorly-equipped troops, but not as bandits."[56] This particular wording with which he described the increasing professionalism of the NOVJ undoubtedly had its origins in the "regular" nature of the Partisans' counterattack south of Gornji Vakuf. Consequently, this may have also been a way for Dippold to express his personal opinion regarding the Partisans' request to be recognized as an equal adversary.

One other event should be mentioned here. While waiting at a local inn in Konjic for a truck which would take him to Sarajevo, Đilas encountered some Chetniks. Although the event passed without incident, Đilas' presence was duly

---

[54] NARA, T-315, Roll 2271, 001458–60, Group interrogation of Othmar Siegelhuber et al. (21 March 1943); ibid., 001461–5, Group interrogation of German soldiers released from Partisan captivity (23 March 1943).

[55] Leković, *Martovski pregovori,* pp. 129–30.

[56] NARA, T-314, Roll 554, 000375, Letter to Minister of Armed Forces Begić (31 March 1943); NARA, T-78, Roll 332, 6290089, Short summary for Operation Weiss (10 April 1943); NARA, T-315, Roll 1299, 000306, For Commander of German Troops in Croatia (8 April 1943).

noted, and the Germans disclosed to the Royalists his pseudonym, rank, and itinerary, but not the subject of the negotiations. Chetnik commands were aware of the propaganda potential of this information and took steps to inform the government-in-exile and the British. On 22 and 25 March, Mihailović sent two telegrams to London: one through Colonel William Bailey, chief of the British mission at his HQ; the other one directly to Prime Minister Slobodan Jovanović. Mihailović reported on the "continued negotiations between the Communists and the Germans, which the latter use to destroy us separately, primarily by pitting the Communists against us."[57] Bailey's cable was not deciphered for some time, so it was mid-April before London had an inkling of what had transpired. Ultra intercepts may have also provided more evidence of the negotiations. This information, combined with the success achieved by the Partisans against the Chetniks, led some SOE officials to suspect that the Germans were arming both groups so that they could fight each other more effectively. Even so, the news did not warrant the cancellation of sending military missions to the Partisans, which were under discussion at that time. On the contrary, the rumors only served to hasten the dispatch of observers in the hopes that they would be able to shed more light on the true aims of the Communist-led guerrillas.[58]

Velebit and Đilas Visit Zagreb

The NOVJ delegates, accompanied by the ubiquitous Ott, left Sarajevo on the same day Major Strecker and his men were released (20 March 1943). They traveled by car to Slavonski Brod on the first leg of their trip, then caught a train to Zagreb. During their journey, representatives of the two sides discussed the current war situation. While Velebit made an effort to refrain from insulting Ott, Đilas admitted that he was "quite tactless" in accusing the Germans of being brainwashed by Nazi propaganda and believing that the war could still be won. The German engineer denied the accusation, but apparently without much vigor, even calling Hitler "a maniac" at one point. On the whole, Ott seemed to be speaking for those circles in Germany which held an increasingly dim view of the war's possible outcome. When not discussing high politics, the delegates spoke about the prisoner exchange. The name of Herta Haas was mentioned so often that at one point Ott asked openly why she was so important. "She is the girlfriend of one of our commanders," admitted Đilas, and the answer seemed to have satisfied Ott's curiosity.[59]

After arriving in Zagreb, Đilas and Velebit were billeted in a hotel-like room in the headquarters building of the local *Feldkommandantur.* Two meetings occurred

---

⁵⁷ Leković, *Martovski pregovori,* p. 122.

⁵⁸ Mark C. Wheeler, *Britain and the War for Yugoslavia, 1940–1943* (Boulder: East European Monographs, 1980), pp. 227–29.

⁵⁹ Djilas, *Wartime,* pp. 241–42.

over the next few days—one held in the aforementioned building and the second in the German embassy. Đilas was disappointed by the fact that the other side still had not appointed an authorized delegation and that the talks were being held in a semi-official environment. Glaise-Horstenau, who had been expected, did not attend. The German representatives were officers of mid-rank, probably from the Army's intelligence branch. As the German prisoners had already been released, it remained only to choose those Yugoslav prisoners who would accompany the NOVJ envoys on their return trip to Supreme HQ. In addition to the four Partisans the Germans managed to secure from NDH authorities in mid-November 1942, eight other names were added to the list. Herta Haas was not amongst them—the Germans assured their opposite numbers that they had done everything to find her, but to no avail. They pledged to continue the search and to keep their adversaries informed of the progress.[60] As for the political questions, the NOVJ delegates repeated their earlier statements: they considered the Chetniks their main enemies and wanted to engage them from a certain territory without German interference; it would be regrettable if the Italians suffered in the process, but it was, as Velebit put it, "the fate of the allies." The Germans seemed to have accepted this explanation and remained silent when the Italians were mentioned. The cessation of hostilities between the *Ustashe* and the Partisans was not discussed; like the Chetniks, they were the Partisans' internal enemies and the latter would deal with them as they saw fit. If the Germans tried to include the *Ustashe* in the deal, the envoys would decline such a proposition on the grounds that the Croatian facists were still determined to eliminate the Serbs. At the same time, the envoys were not to overemphasize the NOP's hostility toward the Croatian puppet state for this could jeopardize the negotiation's main issue. In addition, the Partisan delegates ". . . did not shrink from declarations that [they] would fight the British if they landed. Such declarations did not commit us, since the British had not yet landed, and we really believed that we would have to fight them if—as could still be concluded from their propaganda and official announcements—they subverted our power, that is if they supported the Chetnik establishment."[61]

The Partisan request for a truce remained the main topic of the talks. The NOVJ delegates repeated that there was no real reason for the continuation of fighting and that their side had already shown its goodwill by releasing the German prisoners without waiting for a formal exchange. Their counterparts were

---

[60] On 24 March 1943, Colonel Mičić of the NDH's Ministry of Defense had a conversation with Dr. Aleksandar Benak of the *Ustashe* security service. Benak told him that the whereabouts of Ivo Marinković were not known to the service and added that the Germans still preferred to take the exchange candidates from the NDH prisons and camps, although they had enough prominent Communists in their own custody. HR HDA 1450, Roll D-2222, 469, Report to chief of information section (24 March 1943).

[61] Djilas, *Wartime*, p. 243.

adamant that the sabotage on the Zagreb-Belgrade railway line would have to stop if the Partisan proposals were to be seriously considered. Đilas and Velebit could do nothing but convey the terms to Supreme HQ and await its decision.[62]

It took several days to collect all exchange prisoners and send them to Sarajevo. On 25 March, the envoys and Ott returned by train to the Bosnian capital. Before setting out for the Partisan-controlled territory, they visited a German prison to pick up the four female Partisans from the 3rd Sandžak Brigade who had been waiting since late November 1942 to be exchanged. On 26 March, sixteen prisoners, accompanied by the envoys and several Germans, left in two trucks and headed southeast. That day they successfully crossed into Partisan territory, thereby concluding the prisoner exchange; altogether, twenty-seven Germans were swapped for sixteen Partisans. Officially, the Germans owed the Partisans additional prisoners which they promised to deliver as soon as possible. In the evening, Đilas and Velebit made a report to Tito. Although "not as interested as before" in the progress of the talks, the Partisan leader immediately decided to prolong them by sending Velebit back to Zagreb. Velebit was to inform the Germans that their demand would be fulfilled; the main German transport artery in Yugoslavia, the Zagreb-Belgrade railway line, would be off limits for the time being. The envoy would also inform them that he would have to convey a similar order to the Partisan units in Eastern Bosnia.[63] Whereas the first instruction had no purpose other than to spur the Germans to further negotiations, the order dispatched to those Partisans in Eastern Bosnia was dual-purpose. Velebit's real task was to locate the Bosnian KPJ leadership and deliver a letter which, in part, read:

> Head immediately with your 6th [Eastern Bosnian] Brigade, reinforced either by elements of the Majevica or Fruška Mountain Detachment, to the area between Goražde and Međeđa and cross from there into Sandžak. [Your task] is to clear the territory of Chetniks by moving toward Zaborak and Čajniče. Once there, you will link up with the left flank of our 1st Division and receive new instructions. During your advance, neither engage the Germans nor undertake any sabotage on the railway lines because this would not be advantageous in light of our current operations. Our main task now is to destroy Draža Mihailović's Chetniks and his administrative apparatus which represents the main threat to our People's Liberation Struggle. . . .

---

[62] Ibid., pp. 242–43; NARA, T-315, Roll 2271, 001475–6, Conversation with Dr. Vladimir Petrović from Partisan HQ (31 March 1943); Leković, *Martovski pregovori*, p. 133. This description is based on the memoirs of and one contemporary statement made by the NOVJ envoys. Kasche's account of the talks is somewhat different and will be dealt with separately (see below).

[63] Djilas, *Wartime*, p. 244; Leković, *Martovski pregovori*, p. 152.

The order was signed by three members of the *Politburo,* including Tito. Assuming that the content of the letter would confuse the recipients regardless of the signatures, Ranković added in his own handwriting: "Receive the courier and this letter without reservation." He also mentioned some individuals known to him and Iso Jovanović, the secretary of the Bosnian regional committee, thus hoping to dispel any suspicions about the veracity of the directive.[64] On 30 March 1943, Koča Popović issued a similar order to the 1st Proletarian Brigade, cautioning them to avoid at all costs any clashes with the Germans in the Goražde sector. As the instruction was written for one of his colleagues from the Spanish Republican Army, Popović wrote the closing line in Spanish: "It is very important that there are no [hostile] activities from our side."[65] Interestingly, and probably as an additional gesture of goodwill toward the Germans, Tito extended the truce to central and western parts of Bosnia, and included the local *Ustashe* units in the bargain. In the instructions for the 1st Bosnian Corps written on the same day as Popović's letter, Tito informed the corps commander, Kosta Nađ, that the Supreme HQ managed to "neutralize the Germans by using the negotiations on prisoner exchange, [thereby isolating them] from the Italians and the Chetniks. You must take this into account and concentrate all your [offensive] efforts on the Chetniks. . . . Engage the *Ustashe* defensively if they attack you or support the Chetniks. This is only temporary—until further orders."[66]

Berlin Forbids Further Talks; Moscow Protests

Von Ribbentrop's cable of 19 March remained unanswered for an entire week, mostly owing to the ongoing contacts with the Partisan envoys in Zagreb. Once the results of the talks were known, Kasche prepared a three-page summary for his superior, along with his views and recommendations. In the document, he informed the foreign minister that two envoys from Tito had engaged in talks with "German, Italian, and Croatian representatives."[67] The Germans insisted on the cessation of

---

[64] *Sabrana djela,* Vol. XIV, p. 188, Tito to Iso Jovanović (29 March 1943).

[65] Vuksanović, ed., *Popović-Beleške,* p. 114, Entry for 30 March 1943.

[66] *Sabrana djela,* Vol. XIV, p. 190, Tito to Bosnian Corps (30 March 1943). This order had little impact on the events in the corps' area of responsibility. On 1 April, German and NDH forces launched mop-up operations in Western Bosnia while the Partisans continued storming towns in Central Bosnia. Ibid., p. 226, Tito to Comintern (7 April 1943); NARA, T-314, Roll 554, 000395–6, Situation estimate for the period 1–15 April 1943 (14 April 1943).

[67] Đilas does not mention conducting talks with either the Italians or the NDH authorities; Velebit expressly denies the presence of NDH authorities at the talks. Velebit, *Tajne i zamke,* p. 220. In his post-war statement, Hans Ott mentioned that one military and two political representatives of the NDH took part in the negotiations. HR HDA 1521, Box 31, File

Partisan activities north of the Sava if the talks were to be continued. Tito's envoys were told that their terms could be considered for the long term only if they publicly renounced the alliance with the USSR and Great Britain. The second condition was that the Partisans had to acknowledge the current political landscape of the region, which meant the recognition of the NDH. Kasche pleaded for permission to continue the talks, citing several reasons. First, the proposed renunciation of the Western Allies should not be problematic—the antagonism the Partisans felt toward London seemed to have reached a zenith, and they had no established connections to Washington. Conditions were ripe for defection from the Communist camp as well—the absence of Soviet help had destroyed the Partisans' belief in the USSR. The ambassador continued that since Operation *Weiss* had been successful, the Germans could negotiate from a position of strength. Last but not least, the Italian and NDH officials expressed support for an arrangement along the abovementioned lines, which would enable the Axis to present a united front. Kasche warned that if the Partisans continued their activity, it would take months—or even years—of extensive efforts to quell the uprising which was not fueled by Communist agitation as much as it was by "the combative attitude and political psychosis amongst the frightened population." If Tito broke ties with Moscow and London, then the wholesale pacification of the region could be achieved by political means: "I see here a possibility to spare our resources and blood, and to quickly achieve the success which will have more than just regional importance." Kasche added that the matter was sensitive and should be handled with care: "My confidant [the engineer, Ott] has so far proven himself in this regard."[68]

Three days later, the Reich's foreign minister responded. He demanded unequivocal answers to his inquiries made in the cable of 19 March which Kasche had failed to provide. Von Ribbentrop also proceeded to instruct the ambassador on the official stand of the German government in regard to the negotiations with the Communist-led guerrillas:

> [I would herewith ask you] to refrain from all official or unofficial contacts or negotiations with Tito in the future. . . . This is not only because Tito's promises, or those of his envoys, cannot be trusted, but primarily because of the fear that we would totally compromise ourselves before the Italians in light of the similar negotiations they are conducting with the Chetniks. If we now negotiate or make arrangements with Tito, I fear the Italians will use this as a pretext to renounce the German-Italian agreement made in Rome, which clearly foresaw a decisive action against the Chetniks and Mihailović. . . . If Tito tries to contact you

---

Velebit, Statement of Hans Ott. The statement of Major Eugen von Pott does not contain a similar reference. Ibid., Statement of Eugen von Pott.

[68] NARA, T-501, Roll 265, 001281–3, Kasche to Foreign Ministry (26 March 1943).

through intermediaries again, please make it clear to him that we will only negotiate concerning his surrender. . . . Please, press this point most energetically in your dealings with Lorković and Casertano. There can be no negotiations with Tito under any circumstances.[69]

Kasche perceived von Ribbentrop's cable as a criticism of his diplomatic activities toward the guerrillas in general, and took considerable time to explain himself. First, he emphasized that neither he nor any of the embassy's employees dealt directly with the Partisans, for this was the responsibility of German military authorities. He defended his efforts connected with prisoner exchanges by saying that the industrial experts captured by the guerrillas could not be replaced. Without them, production of important war materials in mines and factories would grind to a halt. As these installations could not be properly protected due to the lack of resources, the embassy had to provide the employees with some level of protection by not refusing the prospect of exchange. The exchange of prisoners also provided an opportunity to gather intelligence on the inner-workings of the insurgent army, its mentality and intentions, as well as its leadership "on a scale previously unimaginable." Kasche also made an effort to answer von Ribbentrop's two questions as clearly as possible. While General Lüters still considered himself "unauthorized to make decisions over political questions," Glaise-Horstenau stated that he "would welcome any solution which brought about a speedy end to the Partisan resistance." As for Tito's guarantees, the ambassador wrote that he had honored all his commitments in the past, and that additional assurance of his future compliance could be provided by "taking his close associates hostage." Kasche concluded the telegram with a remarkably sober situation estimate:

> I believe that the Partisan question is generally misunderstood by our side. Struggle against them failed to produce results everywhere. The root of the problem is political, not military, in nature. Total destruction of the Partisans to the last man through military and police efforts is completely out of the question. Military measures can only succeed in breaking apart compact insurgent territories; police measures can break up insurgents' connections and help kill Partisans and their helpers. The success of either of the two depends on available time and troops. Since both are in short supply, we at least should not reject out of hand all possibilities of a political solution. [Your] cable No. 396 denies me the opportunity to explore these possibilities.[70]

---

[69] ADAP/E/V/501–02, Ribbentrop to Kasche (29 March 1943).

[70] Kriegsarchiv Wien (hereinafter KAW), B/67:141, Kache to Foreign Ministry (30 March 1943). The quoted portion of the cable was published in ADAP/E/V/502.

Kasche's enthusiasm for a deal with Tito can be explained by the fact that he truly believed the Partisans were on the verge of making a *volte-face* in their "foreign policy." This would not only strengthen the position of his beloved NDH, but also improve his own standing within the Nazi hierarchy. If the arrangement was made, it would be a major diplomatic coup reminiscent of the Molotov-Ribbentrop Pact of 1939, and Kasche would be hailed as its chief architect.[71]

Von Ribbentrop's cable of 29 March spelled the end of the March Negotiations. Exasperated, Ott exclaimed that this was "the dumbest move the Germans could possibly make, for such an opportunity will not present itself again."[72] With it, the already limited maneuvering space of the military and diplomatic circles in Zagreb all but disappeared. The talks went far beyond local prisoner exchange, and the reported willingness of the Communist-led guerrillas to discuss wholesale pacification now became a matter of high politics. Under these circumstances, it was not surprising that Berlin declined to play along. The decision was perfectly in line with the Third Reich's foreign policy which "intentionally denied itself all diplomatic options regardless of the hopeless war situation."[73] There is evidence that the outcome of the talks was already decided on 11 March 1943 after the Partisan envoys signed the original offer. After receiving the document, Glaise-Horstenau called his friend at the *Reichssicherheitshauptamt* (RSHA), Wilhelm Höttl, and informed him of the news. The information traveled through the chain of command and found its way to von Ribbentrop, who informed Hitler that very day. His immediate (and much quoted) reaction was: "Rebels are not being negotiated with; rebels are being shot!"[74] This statement, more than any other, sums up Hitler's well-known antagonism toward any notion of a negotiated settlement. Kasche informed Lüters and Glaise-Horstenau of von Ribbentrop's cables when they met in Zagreb on 1 April 1943. Lüters, always the aloof soldier, repeated that the talks with Tito's representatives were not his responsibility. Glaise-Horstenau was still "for any solution which would bring about a quick pacification of the country."[75] Despite

---

[71] Kazimirović, *Nemački general,* pp. 173–74; Schmider, *Partisanenkrieg,* p. 248.

[72] The quote comes from a report made in early 1946 by an unnamed "occasional informer" of the OSS office in Salzburg. The author was of Serbian origin, with obvious Chetnik sympathies, and was a personal acquaintance of Ott. NARA, RG 226, Entry 108a, Box 276, p. 3, SAINT Salzburg to SAINT Washington, Re: Ing. Hans Ott intermediary between Tito and the Germans (13 March 1946). I wish to thank my colleague, Duncan Bare, for providing me with a copy of this document.

[73] Schmider, *Partisanenkrieg,* p. 248.

[74] Kazimirović, *Nemački general,* p. 171.

[75] Leković, *Martovski pregovori,* pp. 149–50; the first page of Kasche's memorandum from this meeting was reproduced in Vasa Kazimirović, *NDH u svetlu nemačkih dokumenata i dnevnika Gleza fon Horstenau 1941.–1944.* (Belgrade: Nova knjiga, 1987), unpaginated.

the orders from above, the Germans would continue to maintain contact with the Partisans, though more informally than before.

The German ambassador in Zagreb was not the only one encountering difficulties with his superiors regarding the negotiations. Tito was experiencing problems with Moscow and in his early dispatches to the Comintern, he omitted all details relating to contact with the Germans, stating only that Major Strecker was captured in the fighting around Gornji Vakuf. The silence lasted until after Đilas and Velebit returned from Zagreb. On 29 March, Tito briefly mentioned the prisoner exchange, adding that his delegates witnessed large troop movements in easterly directions on the Zagreb-Belgrade railway line. They were informed that these transports were part of an upcoming "German invasion of Syria, with a [possible] connection to the Caucasus."[76]

One day later, 30 March 1943, Tito dictated a telegram to Moscow in which he elaborated—for the first time—about the contacts with the Germans. In "various talks," the German officers in Zagreb again presented the NOVJ envoys with a wealth of information which hinted at the double-dealing of the British. The Partisan delegates were told that "authoritative German circles" did not believe that the British would invade Europe. Their lack of aggressiveness was illustrated by the fact that they had 250,000 men in North Africa while the Germans had only 50,000, yet no large offensive operations had been launched. The Germans believed in a victorious conclusion to the war in 1943 (presumably against the Soviets), which would then pave the way for a settlement between Germany and Great Britain. The Germans were less optimistic about their alliance with Italy. They suspected that the Italians, especially the circles around Prince Umberto, were secretly maintaining contact with the British, purportedly with the help of the Vatican; links between Mihailović and the British were maintained partly through Vatican channels as well. The dispatch to the Comintern also read: "German military circles are full of contempt for the Italian Army and do not hide their malicious pleasure over our victories against Italian divisions. . . . The Germans openly told our delegates that they considered our people's Partisan movement as their most dangerous enemy in the Balkans. They know they cannot destroy us, but they hope to break up our army into smaller groups and eradicate our bases. . . . The German ambassador in Zagreb conveyed a message through a major [who was serving as an intermediary] that he wanted to meet me." Tito ended the cable by adding that the hatred toward the British amongst both the population and the Partisans was steadily rising, mainly because of the delay in opening a Second Front in Europe. "[The delay] is perceived as a premeditated act on the part of the English, who want to see the Soviet Union weakened by a prolonged struggle against the Germans."[77]

---

[76] *Sabrana djela,* Vol. XIV, p. 132, Tito to Comintern (7 March 1943) and ibid., p. 189, Tito to Comintern (29 March 1943).

[77] Ibid., pp. 201–02, Tito to Comintern (30 March 1943).

As in the earlier reports concerning prisoner exchanges, great importance was placed on the intelligence gained through such actions. The conciliatory attitude toward the British contained in the German sources could be explained in two ways. First, the Germans had deliberately planted such information in order to play on Moscow's fears about a separate peace between Great Britain and Germany. The second explanation could be that the information came from those Germans who had by then lost faith in Hitler, and were genuinely hoping for an arrangement with the Western Allies. Judging by the reports of the Partisan envoys, such an attitude was not rare among the Germans they encountered. The allegations concerning British inactivity, although far from true,[78] fell on fertile soil. Anglophobia in the Partisan leadership had by then reached an all-time high and such information was readily accepted at face value. The opening of the Second Front would generally be welcomed since it meant the shifting of German reserves from the Soviet Union; however, should Yugoslavia be the stage, the story was quite different. The information concerning Italian peace feelers to the Western Allies through the Vatican was genuine.[79] However, the possibility of a separate peace between Italy and Britain was not seen as a major blow to the Axis, but rather as a step in the formation of a united reactionary front in which the Chetniks would play a prominent role. The *schadenfreude* of the Germans with respect to their Italian comrades-in-arms was also genuine; the unwillingness of the latter to disarm the Chetniks and to engage more actively in military operations, as well as their continuing efforts to undermine the NDH, meant that early 1943 witnessed the nadir in German-Italian relations.[80]

---

[78] On 6 March 1943, Rommel launched his ill-fated assault at Medenine; an assault that he halted within hours. The lull in the fighting lasted for two weeks until Montgomery started his own offensive against the Mareth Line on the 20th. Jan Bank, "Finale u sjevernoj Africi: kraj rata u Pustinji," in Pape and Anić, eds., *Drugi svjetski rat*, Vol. II, p. 225. Theoretically, it would be possible that the envoys were informed of British "inactivity" during the preliminary talks in Gornji Vakuf and their first visits to Sarajevo and Zagreb, all of which took place during this period. The two-week pause between the two rounds of ferocious fighting could hardly give rise to these claims, however. By the time Tito sent this dispatch, it must have been obvious to all that the allegations of inactivity of the 8th Army in North Africa were unfounded. The intelligence on the strength of the German contingent in Africa was also false; by the time it capitulated in May 1943, it had 102–60,000 men. Rick Atkinson, *An Army at Dawn: The War in North Africa, 1942–1943*, Volume One of the Liberation Trilogy (New York: Henry Holt, 2002), p. 537.

[79] Princess Maria José, the wife of Prince Umberto of Italy, was involved in peace initiatives with the assistance of the Vatican in late 1942. For more on this and other attempts at reaching a separate peace, see William S. Linsenmeyer, "Italian Peace Feelers before the Fall of Mussolini," *Journal of Contemporary History* 16:4 (1981), pp. 649–62.

[80] Schmider, *Partisanenkrieg*, p. 248.

Unlike the similar cable from mid-October 1942 which reported the results of Tito's conversation with Ott in Glamoč, the latest dispatch caused a speedy—and very sharp—reaction. Moscow's response came on 1 April, unusually prompt by Comintern standards. Despite the fact that the message was only partially received, that segment which was transcribed left no doubt as to Moscow's reaction to the talks. The full telegram read:

> We are confused by the fact that you are exchanging prisoners with the Germans. Your envoys are leading all kinds of talks with the Germans and the German ambassador wants to meet you [Tito] in person. What is this all about? The people are waging fierce war against the invaders, and all of a sudden [we hear of] these contacts between you and the Germans. Could not all this be part of a German ploy to use our people to incite infighting between the Yugoslavs, and in this way achieve the destruction of the People's Liberation Army? We request clarification. Furthermore, the resentment of the people toward the English is understandable, but do you not think that the interests of the People's Liberation Struggle would now best be served by firing up the hatred of the people toward the occupier, foremost against the Germans, rather than by fostering resentment against the English? Any kind of contact with the German authorities can only weaken the hatred of the people, which is absolutely necessary. I await your answer [Dimitrov's initials].[81]

Tito's telegram from October 1942 was similar to the one from March 1943, yet only the latter provoked such a harsh response. The deteriorating situation on the Eastern Front might have been the reason behind this. In mid-October, the Germans were on the cusp of taking Stalingrad and were nearing the oil fields in the Caucasus; the outcome of the war was hanging in the balance. In these circumstances, the Soviets probably paid scant attention to the first telegram. Even if they did, they probably thought it wiser not to overreact and risk alienating an important ally. The situation on the front changed dramatically between October and March when the Sixth Army was destroyed at Stalingrad, and the German lines were pushed hundreds of kilometers to the west. Having regained its confidence, Moscow could now pay more attention to the activities of the Communist parties abroad and take any action as necessary.

---

[81] German translation is quoted in Bernhard H. Bayerlein, ed., *Georgi Dimitroff: Tagebücher, 1933–1943* (Berlin: Aufbau-Verlag GmbH, 2000), p. 671; Russian original can be found in *Komintern i Vtoraja mirovaja vojna* (Moscow: Pamjatniki istoričeskoi misli, 1998), Vol. II, pp. 341–42, Dimitrov to Tito (1 April 1943). Incomplete Yugoslav version can be found in *Sabrana djela,* Vol. XIV, pp. 349–50, Comintern to Tito (31 March/3 April 1943).

There may have been another reason behind the chastisement of the Yugoslav Communists. Circumstantial evidence shows that Stalin contemplated using the morale and material momentum of the victory at Stalingrad to sound out the possibility of an arrangement with the Third Reich. Around November of 1942, Soviet propaganda aimed at the Germans increasingly began to stress peace. At the same time it ceased mentioning the Allies and their contribution to the war effort. Stalin's speech on 28 February 1943 presented the war as a purely Soviet-German one; the call for the unconditional surrender of Germany, recently formulated at the Casablanca Conference, was not echoed. All of this was sufficient cause for the British ambassador to the USSR, at the behest of his government, to openly ask the Kremlin to explain its actual war aims; the reply he received was "not very friendly."[82]

After the Red Army's westward advance had been stopped by a successful German counter-offensive at Kharkov in mid-March, an unprecedented lull set in on the Eastern Front. This sudden reversal reinforced Stalin's belief that the *Wehrmacht* was far from being a spent force, and that years would pass before the Germans could be expelled from the Soviet Union. If the Kremlin wanted to explore the possibility of a separate peace, establishing contact with Berlin would not be difficult; the Italians and the Japanese in particular were known to be keen on some kind of Soviet-German rapprochement.[83]

It is questionable as to whether Stalin believed that an arrangement with Hitler would be based on a return to the pre-1941 borders; for Stalin, this condition was the absolute minimum for any further peace talks. Even if the outcome of the negotiations was highly dubious, mere rumors about them still served a purpose. By spreading the fear of a Soviet-German separate peace, Stalin hoped to hasten the Western Allies' opening of the Second Front in Europe.[84] It was a risky game, one which required well-calculated moves and careful timing because if Great Britain and the United States learned of the peace feelers,[85] and believed they were leading to an arrangement, they might seek one for themselves. This would leave the Soviet Union facing Germany alone with only a dim possibility of a negotiated

---

[82] Vojtech Mastny, "Stalin and the Prospects of a Separate Peace in World War II," *The American Historical Review* 77:5 (1972), pp. 1369–74.

[83] Gerhard L. Weinberg, *A World at Arms: A Global History of World War II* (Cambridge: Cambridge University Press, 1994), p. 609; Rolf-Dieter Müller and Gerd R. Ueberschär, *Hitler's War in the East, 1941–1945: A Critical Assessment* (New York: Berghahn Books, 2008), p. 39.

[84] Weinberg, *A World at Arms*, p. 610.

[85] For instance, on 26 March 1943, Allen Dulles of the OSS reported from Switzerland on "the danger of a separate Soviet peace with the Axis." Neal H. Petersen and Allen W. Dulles, *From Hitler's Doorstep: The Wartime Intelligence Reports of Allen Dulles, 1942–1945* (University Park: Pennsylvania State University Press, 1996), p. 55.

settlement. Tito's telegram about the recent round of talks with the Germans came at precisely this moment. Prior to that, according to Russian historian Leonid J. Gibiansky, "Moscow had absolutely no knowledge of the [March] negotiations. . . . Moscow was very frightened at the prospect of Allied intelligence services learning about these negotiations. The Allies always thought that the KPJ, as well as all other Communist parties, were mere exponents of Moscow. Consequently, they would think that the negotiations were led at Moscow's behest. It was feared that this, in turn, could cause a rift in the anti-Hitler coalition. . . . This is why the Soviet leadership reacted so sharply to the March Negotiations."[86] Although Gibiansky did not mention the Kremlin's own diplomatic maneuvering (which should come as no surprise given that his statement was recorded in 1991), it is evident that the Soviet reaction was motivated by political, rather than by ideological, concerns. In short, Tito's independent decision to contact the Germans threatened to narrow the options open to the Soviet leadership and disrupt its timetable.[87] In the worst-case scenario, the alliance with the Western powers would be endangered before a viable alternative could be found. At best, the Soviet Union would find itself in an embarrassing situation, forced to explain the actions of its *protégées* to London and Washington. Either way, the incident provided additional reason for reigning in the Communist parties abroad.

After receiving Moscow's cable, Tito promply sent a lengthy response defending his actions with surprising tenacity: "Your dispatch of 3 March [should read: 1 April] affected us deeply. The confusion and doubts caused by the information I sent you speak of a certain amount of distrust and doubts about our actions. The fact that this became evident after two years of superhuman efforts in this struggle is not the least encouraging in our present difficult situation, but quite the opposite." In the rest of the cable, Tito emphasized the fact that the mortality rate under the Party cadres was especially high, and that the Partisans could therefore ill afford to let their activists rot in prisons and concentration camps. Prisoner exchanges were important for reasons of morale, too, for it made it clear to both the fighters and the population that the Partisan leadership looked after its people. The exchange also solved the major problem of feeding and guarding prisoners. Killing them would not be "politically opportune," especially those Home Guard officers whose exchange was "the main issue here." He added, "There were only twenty-seven Germans in our captivity; they were mostly civilians, since our fighters kill almost every German prisoner. These Germans had been with

---

[86] Interview with Dr. Leonid J. Gibiansky in the television documentary, *Jugoslavija u ratu 1941–1945* (Belgrade: Radio-televizija Srbije, Televizija Beograd, 1991–92), Episode 6.

[87] The spring and summer of 1943 saw repeated contacts between the Soviets and the Germans through intermediaries in Stockholm. Given Hitler's disdain for political compromise, it is unsurprising that no progress was made. Mastny, "Stalin and the Prospects of a Separate Peace," pp. 1375–88.

us since the liberation of Jajce, and the negotiations for their exchange began after [the fall of] Livno, when we exchanged eight Germans, who were also civilians."[88]

The Partisans would not set their captives free; they had lost more than "a thousand German and Italian prisoners" since 1941 without getting anything in return. The delegates who traveled to the enemy territory had also brought back much needed vaccines against typhus, which was just beginning to take its toll amongst the army. Given the fact that the Soviet Union could not help the Communist-led guerrillas "because of the technical difficulties," and that the English directed their help to the Chetniks "who collaborated with the occupier," the Partisans were forced to obtain medical supplies in this fashion. As for the contacts with the Germans, Tito repeated that he had turned down their offer of negotiations after the first exchange. "That the German ambassador wants to talk to me despite all the dirt that the German and Croatian newspapers are publishing about me is no one's fault—I have absolutely no intention of meeting him," Tito remarked. The secretary general of the KPJ concluded the telegram by saying that the Partisan struggle against fascism would continue in force, but that they were responsible for the lives of the millions who supported them. Consequently, the Partisans had to do everything to maintain that trust. After repeating that the reproaches from Moscow were groundless and left a bitter taste, Tito indirectly criticized the fact that the Soviet-sponsored radio station Free Yugoslavia had stopped mentioning Mihailović's Chetniks.[89]

Although Tito wanted to appear forthright, this was not true. Just as in previous cables, this one presented a sanitized version of recent events. First, Tito was not informing Moscow about his "diplomatic" maneuvers on a daily basis, primarily out of fear of interference. He preferred to wait until the results of the talks were known and then to present the Comintern with a *fait accompli*. As before, Tito named humanitarian and intelligence reasons as his main motives for sending the NOVJ envoys to enemy territory, and supported his statement with a number of

---

[88] Unlike the rest of the cable, I quote this passage from the collection of documents pertaining to the history of Yugoslavia, published in 1988. Petranović and Zečević, eds., *Jugoslavija 1918–1988*, p. 607, Tito to Comintern (31 March 1943). The version of the same cable printed in the official collection of documents signed or written by Tito (which appeared in the early 1980s) does not contain the excerpt regarding the killing of prisoners. The difference appears, at first, difficult to explain, as both collections used the same original from the Archives of the Central Committee of the League of Communists of Yugoslavia (A-CK SKJ, Fond KPJ-KI, reg.br. 1943/76). The most likely reason for the difference is that the official collection was published immediately after Tito's death and that the incriminating section was simply left out so as not to blemish the image of the deceased Yugoslav president. The "Jugoslavija" collection was published in the last days of Socialism, which enabled the editors to quote the document in full.

[89] *Sabrana djela,* Vol. XIV, pp. 204–05, Tito to Comintern (31 March 1943).

half-truths. For instance, the delegates were not tasked with procuring typhus vaccines on their trips in March; Velebit received such an order just prior to the transmission of the latest dispatch.[90] Half-truths gave way to outright falsehoods whenever contact with the enemy was mentioned. The Home Guard prisoners were not "the main issue" of the latest talks, nor did Tito turn down German offers of negotiations. However, the leader of the Partisans did not miss the opportunity to chastise the Chetniks.

The tone of Tito's answer was unprecedented for his correspondence with the Comintern not only because of how he drafted his defense, but more because of what he failed to write. In short, the Secretary General of the KPJ failed to repent and pledge an immediate cessation of all contacts with the Germans, as per Moscow's wishes. That he decided to take such a bold move can be attributed to his mounting frustration with the combination of neglect and cynicism with which the Kremlin had been treating the Yugoslav Communists since the beginning of the war. Their revolutionary zeal was constantly dampened, and their political aims either thwarted or re-directed, all to best serve the immediate interests of the "First Land of Socialism." Tito's answer was also a product of his newly-won self-confidence. In the first three months of 1943, the Partisans made a fighting retreat of several hundred kilometers in the midst of winter and avoided encirclement on several occasions, tackling no less than four different enemies in the process. Even when they were hemmed in by the enemy in the narrow Neretva Valley and their destruction seemed imminent, they still managed to find enough physical and moral strength to pull off a daring escape. The key was that all this was accomplished without any outside help. This self-sufficiency reinforced the growing sense of independence and the belief that the methods used to wage war in their own country were right. These methods included swapping prisoners with the enemy and even negotiating with him if it served the immediate needs of war. All members of the *Politburo*, as well as non-members who took part in the talks with the Germans—needless to say, all staunch Communists—had no pangs of conscience. "The history of Bolshevism," Đilas wrote, "even without the Brest-Litovsk Treaty and the Hitler-Stalin Pact, offered us an abundance of precedents." The main point here is that Yugoslav Communists felt secure enough to assume the responsibilities of running a fully independent state and to conduct foreign policy accordingly. The March Negotiations were the first time the KPJ placed its own

---

[90] Velebit, *Tajne i zamke,* p. 221. At that time, it was rumored in certain German and *Ustashe* circles that the Germans gave five lorries and "a large amount" of medical supplies in exchange for some of their men. "Hitler allegedly commented that he could replace lorries, but not good officers;" see the report of a Partisan agent from Zagreb titled "Agents of the Gestapo" in HR HDA 1450, Roll D-1083, 63 (6 May 1943). Also printed in *Građa za povijest Narodnooslobodilačke borbe i socijalističke revolucije u sjeverozapadnoj Hrvatskoj 1941.– 1945.* (Zagreb: Institut za historiju radničkog pokreta Hrvatske, 1981–89) (hereinafter *Sjeverozapadna Hrvatska 1941–1945*), Vol. IV, p. 759.

interests ahead of the interests of the Soviet Union, and can therefore rightly be described as the "[first] venture of the KPJ into the domain of *Realpolitik*."[91]

Moscow decided not to press the matter any further, partly due to the resolute tone of Tito's dispatch and the fact that the silent criticism he leveled at the USSR's policies toward the KPJ was not groundless. Even if they wanted to discipline the Yugoslav leadership and its secretary general, this was neither politically opportune nor technically possible at the present juncture. Besides, the discontent of the Yugoslav Communists was not motivated by seditious intentions; they had been fulfilling their "Internationalist Duty" with great ardor and self-sacrifice ever since the beginning of Operation Barbarossa. Nevertheless, despite the March Negotiations never being mentioned in official correspondence again, they cast long shadows. One year later, in March 1944, Đilas was chosen to lead the first Partisan mission to the USSR. Ranković, possibly at Tito's behest, asked Đilas how he would respond should someone in Moscow inquire about the talks. Đilas replied that it was all about the exchange of wounded, which made Ranković laugh. Dimitrov, the head of the Comintern, mentioned the March episode in a meeting with Đilas, but without holding it against him or the Yugoslav leadership in general. "We were afraid for you at the time," said Dimitrov, "but luckily everything turned out well." Đilas did not reply but took this as a warning that old sins were not forgotten.[92] The controversial topic resurfaced during a private conversation between Stalin and Tito in the same year. The Soviet ruler reproached him for the sharp cable of 1 April 1943, to which Tito allegedly responded, "Comrade Stalin, if you had been in my place, you would have written it [with an] even sharper [tone]."[93]

---

[91] Haberl, *Die Emanzipation der KP Jugoslawiens*, pp. 52–53.

[92] Djilas, *Wartime,* pp. 380, 383. Dimitrov, who famously stood trial in Leipzig in 1934, was allegedly exchanged for a number of German engineers arrested in the Soviet Union. Marietta Stankova, *Georgi Dimitrov: A Biography* (New York: I. B. Tauris, 2010), p. 113.

[93] *Josip Broz Tito: autobiografska kazivanja* (Belgrade: IRO Narodna knjiga, 1983), Vol. I, p. 353. This episode seemed to have been forgotten for good in light of the very cordial relations between the Soviets and the Yugoslav Communists in the immediate post-war period. It was not until the Tito-Stalin split of 1948 that the March Negotiations were mentioned publicly for the first time. During the show trial of László Rajk and his group in Budapest in 1949, one of the accused, Lazar Brankov, spoke of the negotiations with the Germans in 1941, 1942, and early 1943. According to his testimony, Tito offered to discontinue the fight "provided that the Germans would consent to him setting up the government in Yugoslavia. . . . In 1943, toward the middle of the year when the Soviet Union was gaining great victories over the German Army, Tito discontinued these negotiations. . . ." The topic was taken up by the propaganda campaign in the Eastern Bloc countries against "Tito's fascist clique." *László Rajk and his accomplices before the people's court* (Budapest: Budapest printing press, 1949), pp. 142–43, retrieved from: http://mek.oszk.hu/10900/10919/10919 .pdf Leković, *Martovski pregovori*, p. 223.

Velebit's Trip to Slavonia and Events in Eastern Bosnia

On 30 March, Velebit headed once more to German-held territory, accompanied by two Germans and a courier, Grujo Soknić, who knew the terrain in Eastern Bosnia. When they arrived in Sarajevo a day later, Velebit had a conversation with intelligence officers of the 718th Infantry Division, and provided them with the details of his itinerary, including stops in Eastern Bosnia and Slavonia. He was to convey orders from the Supreme HQ to the 6th Brigade to "commence the withdrawal to Sandžak," and to the 3rd Operational Zone to cease sabotage on the Zagreb-Belgrade railway line. Velebit also recounted the details of the previous round of talks in Zagreb and repeated the Partisan stand on political issues. He gave a short description of the fighting against the Chetniks in Eastern Herzegovina and offered to provide documentary evidence of the Italian-Chetnik alliance.[94] On 1 April, Soknić, carrying the letter written by Tito and Ranković, traveled on a German motorcycle toward Birač, a Partisan stronghold in Eastern Bosnia, where the Main HQ for Bosnia and its units were thought to be located. As Velebit was preparing for a trip to Zagreb, German officers approached him with the news that their troops had been attacked by a Partisan unit north of Sarajevo. They asked Velebit to contact them and inform them of Tito's orders. It was a test of sincerity regarding Partisan promises, and Velebit readily accepted. Accompanied by a German escort, he immediately headed north.[95]

The Partisan units in question were the 6th East Bosnian and Majevica Brigades. Unknown to the Partisan delegates, they had left Birač on the 29th and headed south in response to Tito's directive aired over the radio station Free Yugoslavia. Therefore, Soknić could deliver Tito's letter only to the local Partisans in Birač. Velebit faced a difficult task; he had no proof of his identity and did not know anyone in the Bosnian regional leadership. Understandably, he was treated with suspicion when a Partisan patrol brought him to the brigade's staff in the late afternoon of 1 April. Velebit had great difficulty convincing the Bosnians that he was indeed an envoy from the Supreme HQ. Even so, the order not to engage the Germans on their way to the main Partisan force around Foča was met with

---

[94] NARA, T-315, Roll 2271, 001475–9, Conversation with Dr. Vladimir Petrović from Partisan HQ (31 March 1943). For their part, the Germans also offered documents on the Chetniks, but not in such a straightforward way. When Velebit and Đilas arrived in Sarajevo on their return trip from the main talks in Zagreb, they had a conversation with a German intelligence officer in his office. The officer excused himself at one point, thus allowing the delegates to catch a glimpse of a document which detailed the Chetnik dispositions and strength in various parts of Bosnia. Velebit, *Tajne i zamke*, p. 220. One should remember that Stilinović obtained intelligence on the Italian movements to the south of Zagreb in late August 1942 in a similar manner. Consequently, there can be no doubt that the Germans chose to disclose specific information to the Partisan envoys in this way.

[95] Leković, *Martovski pregovori*, p. 186.

disbelief. "He told us things which we did not believe at first," Uglješa Danilović, a member of the Main HQ for Bosnia and Herzegovina wrote in his diary, "It is about an important change of tactics."[96] Either the disbelief held, or Tito's orders were not conveyed to all units, but the movement south did not occur without incident. On 8 April, near Goražde, a column of *Feldgendarmerie* belonging to the 717th Infantry Division was ambushed by Partisans from Eastern Bosnia. This resulted in one dead, two wounded, and nine captured Germans.[97] One of the captives, Lieutenant Kühnle, decided to use his knowledge of the negotiations to affect the release of his men. He approached his captors and protested against the attack. He pointed out that Tito had ordered a cease-fire and added that he personally knew "Brigadier Popović" from the talks in Gornji Vakuf. Instead of releasing the prisoners, the Partisans took them along and delivered them to Supreme HQ the following day.[98]

Once they had rejoined the main Partisan force, the Bosnian leaders attended a meeting with Tito. Danilović noted the details of the conversation in his diary:

> He gave us the proper explanation of Vlatko's [Velebit's nickname] words. . . . The whole thing is not about a truce of any kind, but about ceasing an attack on one enemy while we deal with another. The Chetniks are our worst enemies now because of the possible Allied landing in the Balkans which might happen tomorrow. In this case, the Yugoslav government in London will try to take advantage of the situation and reap the rewards of our struggle. We have not used the tactic of playing one enemy against the other until now, but this should be done. . . . He [also] fully approved of our action at Hranjen [the attack on the *Feldgendarmerie* column]. We were especially worried about it and thought we had made a mistake.[99]

The German prisoners were billeted in a separate building in Kalinovik and received better food than the Home Guard and Italian prisoners. On 11 April, Ranković was handed a letter written by Lieutenant Kühnle which requested that his superiors facilitate an exchange. This would, however, prove unnecessary; Tito,

---

[96] In a statement given almost thirty years after the event to Tito's biographer, Vladimir Dedijer, Danilović said that he used the phrase "the important change of tactics" for reasons of secrecy—he feared that his diary might be captured by the enemy. The second reason was that he did not believe Velebit's explanations "which really hinted at the possibility of a truce." Dedijer, *Novi prilozi*, Vol. II, pp. 809–10.

[97] NARA, T-315, Roll 1299, 000248, War diary entry for 8 April 1943.

[98] Leković, *Martovski pregovori*, p. 191; Andrija Blagojević, "Borbe 4. bataljona od formiranja do početka Pete neprijateljske ofanzive," in *Petnaesta majevička brigada: sjećanja i članci* (Belgrade: Vojnoizdavački zavod, 1979), p. 173.

[99] Leković, *Martovski pregovori*, pp. 190–92.

under the impression that German inactivity in Eastern Bosnia was the result of contact with their commands in Sarajevo and Zagreb, ordered the prisoners released.[100]

The apparent lack of German interest in this sector of the NDH must have seemed odd. The first two weeks of April were marked by a series of defeats inflicted by the Partisans on the Italians and their Chetnik allies in what Yugoslav historiography termed "The Battle of the Drina." It began in late March when the 1st and 2nd Proletarian Divisions received orders to ford the Drina in the Foča-Goražde sector. The river had been crossed in strength by 10 April after encountering strong resistance from the Italian *Taurinense* Division supported by Montenegrin Chetniks. The town of Foča was surrounded and its fall appeared imminent. The Italian calls for German intervention increased, and against the advice of the commands in the field, the OKW finally acquiesced to send one German battalion to relieve the garrison. By 19 April, this modest force was augmented by another battalion creating a regimental-sized battle group.[101] Only five days before, Tito had cautioned his commanders not to engage the Germans in Goražde; he feared that they would thereby be forced to take part in the fighting on the side of their hard-pressed allies. The beginning of German intervention in Eastern Bosnia in the last ten days of April made such orders superfluous.[102]

While these events were taking place, Velebit was hard at work trying to fulfill his mission. Immediately after the meeting with the Bosnian leadership, he returned to Sarajevo, then proceeded to Zagreb a day later. This time he was not a guest of the *Feldkommandantur,* but was billeted in the Hotel Central near the railway station. He spent an entire week in the city attempting to arrange the release of Herta Hass and the other Partisans whom the Germans still owed from the last exchange agreement. His German counterparts (Ott and several other officers) repeated that they were doing all they could, but that the NDH police continued to claim that she could not be found. Velebit's main task was to reach the HQ of the

---

[100] *Zbornik*/II/9/85, Report of intelligence section of Supreme HQ to Ranković (11 April 1943); Leković, *Martovski pregovori,* p. 201. The release of the prisoners is not explicitly mentioned in the surviving records of the 717th Division or any other unit operating in the area at the time. However, the casualty return of the 717th Division for April, compiled at the end of the month, does not list any missing men. NARA, T-315, Roll 1299, 000268, Casualty figures for April 1943 (undated).

[101] *Oslobodilački rat,* Vol. I, pp. 409–13; NARA, T-311, Roll 175, 000582, Memorandum from meeting with Chief of Staff (19 April 1943).

[102] *Sabrana djela,* Vol. XIV, p. 270 (Tito to Velimir Terzić, 14 April 1943) and p. 274 (Tito to 1st Proletarian Division, 14 April 1943). On 26 April, the Partisans captured six German soldiers in a skirmish with elements of the 369th Infantry Division south of Goražde. Ibid., Vol. XV, p. 56 (Tito to Comintern, 26 April 1943) and p. 58 (Tito to 1st Proletarian Division, 26 April 1943). Unlike their comrades who were captured at the beginning of April, there is no evidence that these men were either freed or exchanged.

3rd Operational Zone in Slavonia and convey Tito's temporary ban on railway sabotage. On 9 April, Velebit left Zagreb with a German escort for Pakrac. Upon reaching his objective, he was informed that the Axis forces had been engaged by guerrillas not far from the town. Crossing into the Partisan territory proved to be a difficult task. A Home Guard major whose unit had sustained heavy casualties the night before angrily refused to help Velebit in his endeavors. Only after repeated demands from the Germans did the major agree to help; he chose one of the reprisal hostages to act as a courier between Velebit and the nearest Partisan command. However, the letter which the NOVJ envoy wrote failed to produce a response over the ensuing days (for reasons unknown, it was never delivered). As he could not wait in Pakrac indefinitely, Velebit decided to undertake a risky venture—he would go alone and unannounced across the lines. The driver dropped him outside of the town and he then continued on foot, hoping to find some Partisans along the way. In short order, he stumbled onto a pair of fighters who directed him to the 3rd Operational Zone's HQ. Upon arrival, he requested to see Marijan Stilinović, who knew him and could vouch for him. Stilinović, who had recently been wounded, confirmed Velebit's identity, so the envoy from Supreme HQ proceeded to relate the details of his mission.[103]

On the same day, the 3rd Operational Zone informed its subordinate units about Velebit's arrival and the "special directives" from Supreme HQ. On 14 April, the 4th Slavonian Division of the NOVJ issued an order in all capital letters that "all brigades should withdraw their demolition teams and order them to cease their activities against the railway lines, the Zagreb-Belgrade line in particular," and that the units should limit their activities to foraging and training. Furthermore, the Slavonian units were expressly warned not to execute German Army prisoners or the local ethnic Germans because they could now be exchanged.[104] The result was a marked drop in railway sabotage: in January there were 124 incidents; in February, 135; in March, 156; and in April, ninety-nine.[105] Both the 3rd Operational Zone and the KPJ's regional committee reported Velebit's mission to the Main HQ for Croatia. It took some time for the information to reach its destination as the latter was located in Lika, in the opposite part of the country. Although the envoy's identity had been validated by the Slavonian leadership, the

---

[103] Leković, *Martovski pregovori*, pp. 193–94; Velebit, *Tajne i zamke*, pp. 223–24.

[104] For more information on the effect of this instruction, see Chapter 5 in the present volume.

[105] Leković, *Martovski pregovori*, pp. 193–96. The figures pertain to Croatia proper (without Bosnia and Herzegovina), including the Italian occupation zone. One report by the commander of Demolition Group Slavonia-Syrmia from early June is indicative of the decrease in activity in that region; the group did not attack rail lines between 18 April and 25 May 1943. Ljubomir Bošnjak, *Diverzantska dejstva u narodnooslobodilačkom ratu 1941.–1945.* (Belgrade: Vojnoistorijski institut, 1983), pp. 183–84. Unsurprisingly, the author did not explain the reasons for the reduced activity of the Croatian Partisans.

directives he carried continued to raise a considerable amount of suspicion. On 5 and 8 May, the Main HQ for Croatia sent cables to Tito requesting a confirmation of both the delegate's particulars and his mission orders. On the 7th, Supreme HQ responded that it had indeed tasked Velebit with traveling to Slavonia and halting the sabotage of railway communications. Tito added that "full-scale" attacks would eventually be resumed and that an appropriate order would soon be aired by Free Yugoslavia.[106]

Before returning to the Axis-held territory, Velebit visited a Slavonian brigade in order to pick up an ethnic German doctor and bring him across the lines. It was already dark as the two of them ventured into no man's land. The first attempt to reach Pakrac failed; Velebit, who went ahead to scout the terrain, ran into the same hostile Home Guards he had met on his way to the Partisans. Deciding it was better not to take any risks, he and the doctor spent the night in a barn. The next morning, Velebit simply walked into the town without being stopped. As soon as he contacted his German escort, a courier was sent to fetch the doctor from his hiding place.[107]

Velebit returned to Zagreb to complete his final remaining task—to find Herta Haas. After several days of waiting, the Germans brought the long-awaited news that Haas was alive and released to German custody. However, convincing her to go with Velebit took some effort. "I knew that the Fourth Offensive [Operation *Weiss*] had just passed and I thought Velebit had been captured," Haas told an interviewer almost seventy years after the event, "I therefore pretended that I did not know him." She agreed to go along only after Velebit made it clear to her that it was Tito's personal request. "And then I realized why they [the Germans] kept asking me whom did I know in the Supreme HQ," recalled Haas. Accompanied by Ott and a sergeant, the two Partisans took a train to Sarajevo.[108] It was planned that the

---

[106] Leković, *Martovski pregovori*, pp. 197–98; *Sabrana djela*, Vol. XV, p. 84, Tito to Main HQ for Croatia (7 May 1943).

[107] Ironically, Velebit came closer to death while in Partisan territory. Radojica Nenezić, his acquaintance from Supreme HQ and by that point a brigade commander, tasked a patrol with escorting Velebit and the doctor to the front lines. He thereby inadvertently used the word "povesti" ("to conduct") which, in the local Partisan jargon, meant "to execute." Fifteen minutes after Velebit had departed, Nenezić realized what he had said and sent a mounted courier after them. Luckily for Velebit, the courier reached them before the patrol could fulfill its "mission." Velebit, *Tajne i zamke*, pp. 225–26.

[108] Interview with Herta Haas in the television documentary, *Tito: posljednji svjedoci testamenta* (Zagreb: Hrvatska radio televizija, 2011), Episode 6. While traveling, Velebit observed troop movements and asked the German soldiers about their itinerary and unit numeration. Tito reported this to the Comintern, saying the intelligence was obtained by "a reliable comrade who traveled by train from Zagreb to Brod." No further details on Velebit's mission were mentioned, ostensibly because of the recent heated exchange with Moscow. *Sabrana Djela*, Vol. XV, p. 54, Tito to Comintern (25 April 1943).

rest of the exchange prisoners would be waiting for them there; however, it turned out that the other captives were stricken by typhoid and could not travel. Velebit used the three-day stay in Sarajevo to buy a supply of thermometers from a pharmacist he had known since before the war. Early on 23 April, the party left for Trnovo in a truck adorned with a white flag. The flag failed to produce the intended effect; the vehicle was fired upon by the Partisans although miraculously no one was injured. Velebit had to use his diplomatic skills again to explain his mission and convince the attackers to take him and Haas to Supreme HQ. At this point, Velebit and Ott bade each other farewell after spending more than three weeks in close contact as fellow negotiators. Velebit and Haas walked several more hours before they rejoined Tito at his command post in the village of Govza, situated between Foča and Kalinovik.[109]

Ott did not return immediately to Zagreb. Before they parted, it was agreed that as soon as Velebit arrived at Supreme HQ, he would send Ott a letter that would contain details on two open issues: the transfer of Chetnik documents Velebit promised to the 718th Division in late March; and the date and place for a meeting between Ott and Tito. Two days later, on 25 April 1943 (Easter Sunday), the letter came across the lines to Trnovo. It read that Tito agreed to meet Ott on or about 10 May somewhere between Foča and Kalinovik. Furthermore, Velebit requested that the prisoners the Germans still had not delivered be brought over at the same time. There were two letters addressed to Ambassador Kasche and General Glaise-Horstenau attached to the original message which dealt with the long-overdue exchange of 104 Home Guard officers and civilians still being held in Partisan captivity; the guerrillas were anxious to exchange them as it was becoming increasingly difficult to care for them.[110] Ott attempted to make contact with

---

[109] Leković, *Martovski pregovori*, pp. 199–200; Velebit, *Tajne i zamke*, pp. 226–27.

[110] The list of the people whom the Partisans wanted in exchange was updated throughout this period. *Zbornik*/II/9/134, Pijade to Ranković (18 April 1943). On 30 April, Ranković sent Velebit to check on the health of the NDH and Italian prisoners; each day, one or two died due to exhaustion or typhus. Ranković concluded that they should insist upon the exchange not only because of the rapidly deteriorating medical condition of the Axis prisoners, but first and foremost for the sake of the Partisan prisoners languishing in enemy prisons and concentration camps. Ibid., p. 184, Ranković to Tito (30 April 1943). NDH authorities were also very interested in the exchange of the officers and requested Glaise-Horstenau's assistance in this matter. HR HDA 1450, Roll D-2222, 466–7, To German Plenipotentiary General (undated). It was planned to release seventy-three inmates from concentration camps and bring them to Trnovo, where Ott and the 369th Infantry Division stood ready to complete the exchange. Ibid., 520, Cable to Main Directorate for Public Order and Security and to Dr. Vjekoslav Vrančić (undated); ibid., 526, Government to Ministry of Defense, 17 April 1943. The swap probably did not take place due to the intensification of fighting in the area in mid-May.

the Partisans after the receipt of the letter, but this proved to be impossible due to Chetnik bands patrolling in the area.[111]

Contrary to what his cables to Moscow had relayed, Tito was willing to meet a close associate of the German ambassador. Likewise, Kasche acted directly against his superior's (von Ribbentrop) instructions, which had explicitly prohibited him from having any contact with the Partisan leader. A possible meeting had been discussed as early as 1942, but the latest initative had its roots in Velebit's recent stays in Sarajevo and Zagreb. In mid-April, Kasche cautiously began mentioning contacts with the Partisans in official correspondence with Berlin. There are two plausible reasons for this: the renewed tensions with the Italian 2nd Army; and Kasche's firm belief in the possiblity of an accommodation with Tito, which was reinforced by the absence of sabotage against the Zagreb-Belgrade railway line. On 17 April, he sent a cable to the foreign ministry outlining the present military and political situation in the NDH. The root of the problems lay in the decision of the Italian 2nd Army to stage a phased withdrawal from the interior and to concentrate on the Adriatic coastline. The Italians had already begun pulling out of the province of Lika without attempting to coordinate with the Germans and the NDH. This caused a fury in Zagreb as no reserves were available to plug the gap. Due to the duplicitous Italian policy, the sole aim of which was to "foster unrest" in the country, Kasche advised against coming to the aid of the Italians at Foča. Additionally, such a move would be detrimental to German interests. The bloody fighting between the Chetniks and the Partisans was welcomed as it took place in the area targeted by the German occupation forces for large-scale operations in the near future. If the German troops intervened against Tito, he would then promptly make peace and form a united anti-German front with the Chetniks. "As we are continually well informed on the affairs in Tito's HQ," wrote Kasche, "there is no possibility of deceit." Four days later, von Ribbentrop replied that the aim of the German endeavors was not to play the Partisans against the Chetniks, but to destroy them both. The ambassador's proposal was not very different from the old Italian tactic of divide and conquer. Given that *Il Duce* had recently been persuaded that the Chetniks should be destroyed, the application of such methods by the Germans would be inopportune.[112]

Like the German embassy, the office of the plenipotentiary general in Zagreb was interested in cultivating contact with the Partisan high command despite Berlin's discontent. Upon his return from Slavonia, Velebit was invited to meet with General Glaise-Horstenau. The details of this meeting are unknown, but it was apparently yet another informative conversation without spectacular conclusions.

---

[111] The first page of Ott's report was reproduced in Leković, *Martovski pregovori*, p. 299.

[112] ADAP/E/V/616–19, Kasche to Foreign Ministry (17 April 1943); ibid., pp. 668–69, Ribbentrop to Kasche (21 April 1943).

The general did not voice his opinion on the continuation of negotiations in the official correspondence, but confided to his diary that "we could have made politics here which would be agreeable even to Kasche. But what can one hope to achieve when everyone keeps meddling into one's affairs?"[113] Unfortunately, it is not known just how much stock Glaise-Horstenau placed in Tito's promises, nor whether his thinking was influenced by the ban on sabotage and the lack of activity in Eastern Bosnia. On the other hand, Colonel Pfafferott, Lüters' Chief of Staff, was convinced of the veracity of Partisan offers. In a telephone conversation on 21 April with his counterpart from the HQ of General Bader, Pfafferott "was of the opinion that the Communists in Montenegro do not plan to act against us, but only to establish new supply bases there."[114]

The previously quoted lines from Glaise-Horstenau's diary are the only reference to the March Negotiations. He also gives a short description of the Partisan envoy who visited him twice over the past months: "Petrović . . . was 35 years old, in civilian life a lawyer from Zagreb. . . . He was Orthodox, but spoke good Austrian-German and he turned out to be a son, a grandson, and a great-grandson of Austrian officers. . . . He disclosed his real name to me and Metzger [Glaise-Horstenau's adjutant]."[115]

The plenipotentiary general discovered Velebit's identity by accident. While walking through Zagreb, Velebit was greeted several times by pre-war acquaintances whom he pretended not to know. When he visited a pharmacy to purchase a toothbrush, the cashier recognized him and said, "You are here, doctor? I heard that you were with the Partisans!" All this did not escape notice by Velebit's German escort. Therefore, when Velebit met Glaise-Horstenau, the general told him they knew he was Vladimir Velebit, the son of General Ljubomir Velebit. The Partisan envoy, realizing that the game was up, introduced himself with his real name. Thereupon, Velebit was allowed to visit his parents at their house in a Zagreb suburb where he had a chance to bathe and change clothes—an unimaginable luxury for a guerrilla fighter. Interestingly, Glaise-Horstenau did not disclose Petrović's real identity to German intelligence or other authorities in Zagreb for the duration of his stay in the NDH capital. "What made the Germans treat me with such correctness is hard to say," wrote Velebit in 1967, "I believe that General Glaise-Horstenau, as an Austrian, did so out of friendship for my late father. They were both officers in the Austro-Hungarian Army, which had a very distinct *esprit de corps*."[116]

---

[113] Velebit, *Tajne i zamke*, p. 226; Peter Broucek, ed., *Ein General im Zwielicht: Die Erinnerungen Edmund Glaises von Horstenau* (Vienna: Böhlau Verlag, 1988), Vol. III, pp. 220–21, Entry for May 1943.

[114] NARA, T-501, Roll 249, 000179, War diary entry for 21 April 1943.

[115] Broucek, ed., *Ein General im Zwielicht*, Vol. III, p. 220, Entry for May 1943.

[116] Velebit, *Tajne i zamke*, p. 219.

Đilas was treated equally correctly, although he was only the son of a Montenegrin officer. Having no family in Zagreb to visit, he went to the cinema instead, discreetly followed by a German soldier. At the beginning of the contacts, it occurred to Đilas that their hosts might simply hand them over to the Gestapo for torture and execution. The Germans, however, "gave no reason for such misgivings, and eventually the misgivings vanished."[117] During their stays in Sarajevo and Zagreb, and the long trips in the company of the Germans, the stereotypical image of their enemies eroded further. Đilas, for instance, was taken aback by the tenderness with which one officer treated a wounded soldier outside of Konjic; in the Partisans' mindset, care for the wounded was a trait they considered uniquely their own. Velebit remembered that during his last visit to Sarajevo in mid-April, he was not billeted in the comfortable apartment on the Miljacka prospect, but in the local *Feldgendarmerie* barracks. He did not get much rest that night because curious military policemen wanted to talk to him. Velebit was surprised by their pessimism regarding the eventual outcome of the war: while they did not agree with him that the Third Reich had already lost the war, not one of them expressed a firm belief in Germany's ultimate victory.[118]

The Final Act: Operation *Schwarz*

Velebit's return to Supreme HQ and the German incursion into Eastern Bosnia in late April marked the end of the March Negotiations. However, what transpired over the ensuing month and a half is closely related to the events from January through April, and it seems appropriate that it be covered in this chapter.

On 31 March 1943, Hitler approved the sequel to Operation *Weiss*, codenamed *Schwarz*, targeting the Chetniks in the Italian occupation zone, specifically Eastern Bosnia, Eastern Herzegovina, and Montenegro. Preparations began immediately. On 1 April, all four infantry divisions of the 15th Mobilization Wave were redesignated *Jäger* and began receiving young recruits, who replaced the older soldiers. Additionally, mountain warfare training was implemented.[119] The Armed Forces High Command also finally saw fit to transfer one of the German Army's elite units, the 1st Mountain Division, to the region and keep it there for as long as the operation lasted. All in all, by early May 1943, the Commander of German Troops in Croatia had at his disposal approximately 70,000 German troops in

---

[117] Djilas, *Wartime*, p. 244. After hearing of the correct treatment of the envoys, Tito remarked: "Yes, it seems that the German Army has kept something of the spirit of chivalry." Ibid., p. 240.

[118] Djilas, *Wartime*, pp. 240, 242, 244; Velebit, *Tajne i zamke*, pp. 226–27.

[119] The reorganization of the divisions of the 15th Mobilization Wave was primarily motivated by the possibility of an Allied landing in the Balkans. NARA, T-315, Roll 1301, 001154, Subject: training (22 March 1943).

four reinforced divisions. The *Luftwaffe* contingent was also reinforced to 100 air-craft, including a large number of Ju-87 Stuka dive-bombers. This was the largest anti-Partisan force the German occupation forces had mustered in Yugoslavia thus far. The number of Chetniks in Herzegovina and Montenegro was estimated at approximately 20,000. Also facing them was the Main Operational Group of the NOVJ with four divisions, altogether more than 18,000 able-bodied fighters and some 3,500 wounded and sick.[120]

The secrecy of the operation was maintained; the Italians, particularly, were not apprised of the details. Judging by their policy in the past, they were not likely to allow the Germans to disarm their Serbian charges, the Chetniks; therefore, Hitler ordered that they be kept out of the preparations. The German commands in the field were content to have their troublesome allies out of the way. As we have seen, they obeyed the politically motivated orders to advance on Foča with great reluctance. However, as April gave way to May and as the fighting moved into northern Montenegro, their attitude began to change. As their efforts against the NOVJ's main force ended in a series of disasters, the Italians were forced to step up their requests for help.[121] The Germans discovered that they could use their ally's predicament to their advantage. By moving troops deeper into Sandžak, Eastern Bosnia, and Montenegro under the guise of helping their hard-pressed allies, the Germans managed to surprise the main Partisan force and form a wide operational encirclement made up entirely of their own troops. Both friend and foe were equally stunned by the sudden beginning of Operation *Schwarz* on 15 May 1943. Four thousand Chetniks were disarmed while the rest scattered, sometimes with Italian assistance. The Italians protested and even tried to stop the German advance at some points, but eventually buckled under the well-balanced combination of diplomacy and threat of force. By 19 May, the Chetniks were largely eliminated as a potential threat and the Germans could now concentrate solely on the NOVJ. By 22 May, the Italians joined the operation and provided elements of three divisions to support the encirclement, thereby freeing up more German troops for offensive actions against the Communist-led guerrillas.[122]

The Partisans were in the dark concerning enemy intentions until it was too late. The trickle of intelligence at the beginning of May admittedly registered German troop movements into Sandžak, but their strength gave no grounds for concern. Tito could therefore inform the leadership at Central Hospital on 6 May

---

[120] Trifković, "Schwarz auf Weiss," pp. 94, 96–99; NARA, T-314, Roll 566, 000778, Chetnik forces in Croatia, Slovenia, and Montenegro on 1 May 1943 (5 May 1943); Viktor Kučan, *Borci Sutjeske* (Belgrade: Zavod za udžbenike i nastavna sredstva, 1996), p. 12.

[121] The Italians lost two battalions in the fighting around Nikšić (2 May) and Podgorica (14–18 May). Schmider, *Partisanenkrieg*, p. 272.

[122] Gaj Trifković, "A Case of Failed Counter-Insurgency: Anti-Partisan Operations in Yugoslavia 1943," *The Journal of Slavic Military Studies* 24:2 (2011), pp. 319–20.

that "there is no reason to fear an enemy offensive at this moment."[123] Furthermore, the German objectives were reported as largely defensive in nature—securing the Lim valley and building an airstrip around Pljevlja.[124] Interestingly, several accounts mentioned that the Germans praised the Partisans in conversations with the local population and treated captured Partisans with dignity. The Chetniks, on the other hand, were either arrested or shot. The inter-Axis relations were reported as tense—the animosity between the Germans and Italians often resulted in arguments in Prijepolje's taverns.[125] The first intelligence on the upcoming attack came as late as 10 May from a German who defected to the 1st Bosnian Corps.[126] On 14 May, one day before the launching of *Schwarz*, the 2nd Proletarian Division reported that there were "unconfirmed" rumors about three German divisions moving into Montenegro and Eastern Herzegovina. Needless to say, by then it was too late to adjust plans and troop dispositions accordingly.[127]

It remains to be determined whether the lack of Partisan preparedness was caused by Tito's ill-placed belief in the success of his diplomatic maneuvering, or whether there were other, more concrete reasons. "The Germans are lying! We have never been in greater danger!," exclaimed Tito after reports confirmed the massive German presence around the Main Operational Group. "So much for our negotiations," commented Đilas, feeling that the Supreme HQ had been lulled into a false sense of security which now threatened to have disastrous consequences.[128] Tito's ego might have contibuted to the fact that the *Wehrmacht* had achieved full operational surprise. Self-confident and aware of his own charisma, it is possible he believed that his diplomacy, which included the expedient prisoner exchange, the ban on sabotage of the Zagreb-Belgrade railway line, and exclusive concentration of the activities of the Main Operational Group against the Chetniks from late March onwards, could have produced the desired effect. Although he announced an immediate lifting of the ban in his cable to the Croatian leadership on 7 May, he waited for another two weeks before he actually confirmed it. The delay can only be explained by the fact that Tito waited until it became unequivocally clear that the period of German inactivity in this area was over.[129]

---

[123] *Sabrana djela,* Vol. XV, p. 83, Tito to Commissar of Central Hospital (6 May 1943).

[124] *Zbornik*/IV/13/91–92, Order of 1st Proletarian Division (7 May 1943).

[125] Ibid., pp. 146, 148–49, Intelligence bulletin of the 1st Proletarian Division (13 May 1943); ibid., p. 185, 2nd Proletarian Division to Supreme HQ (15 May 1943).

[126] Ibid., p. 129, 1st Bosnian Corps to Supreme HQ (10 May 1943).

[127] Ibid., p. 154, 2nd Proletarian Division to Supreme HQ (14 May 1943).

[128] Djilas, *Wartime,* p. 248.

[129] On 21 May, in a message aired on Free Yugoslavia, Tito ordered all Partisan units in the country to step up their attacks on Axis garrisons and lines of communication: "This order pertains especially to our units in Slavonia, where the most important railway line is situated." *Sabrana djela,* Vol. XV, p. 141, Tito to radio station Free Yugoslavia (21 May 1943).

Unlike Đilas, Velebit denied that Tito lowered his guard in Montenegro because of the March Negotiations.[130] Tito was a cautious person; he had spent the better part of his life as a professional revolutionary, evading both police raids and Stalin's purges. It is hard to believe that he would have taken the Germans at their word, even if it had been given, that they would not attack him. Instead, there is evidence that Tito's misplaced sense of security was caused mainly by the failure of the Partisan intelligence service. After their main force was chased out of Montenegro and the eastern parts of Bosnia and Herzegovina in the summer of 1942, the Partisan presence there was reduced to a small number of resistance fighters primarily concerned with their own survival. The local intelligence network was therefore essentially non-existent when the Partisans returned in the early spring of 1943. Because of the unprecedented security surrounding the operation, Partisan sympathizers within the Home Guard—otherwise an important source of information—also had no knowledge of the impending attack. Furthermore, the geographic position of the Main Operational Group at the beginning of May additionally obstructed any intelligence gathering. Northern Montenegro and the bordering parts of Bosnia and Herzegovina are extremely rugged, home to Europe's only rain forest (Perućica) with mountain peaks reaching 2,500 meters above sea level. Couriers from outside would have encountered enormous difficulty in this terrain even if there were no heavy concentrations of enemy troops around the perimeter of the area. Needless to say, maintaining a reliable radio link in such conditions entailed immense technical difficulties. It would appear that the surprise the Germans managed to achieve resulted from a combination of Tito's wishful thinking and the failure of Partisan intelligence. Whereas the first factor certainly played a role, it is doubtful that Supreme HQ would not have adjusted its plans and dispositions had the news of enemy movements and preparations arrived earlier.

Some of the spirit of the March Negotiations was noticeable even amongst the troops on the battlefield. On 11 May 1943, the 369th Infantry Division reported one NCO and three men missing during the fighting just south of Foča.[131] Several days later, the deputy commander of the 2nd Proletarian Brigade sent a letter across the lines offering an exchange. The Germans responded affirmatively on the 17th, demanding that two unarmed Partisans bring the captives over the lines. The guerrillas replied they would agree to go only as far as no man's land. This proposition was ultimately accepted, and the Germans used the lull in the fighting the next day to deliver three Partisans in the sector of the Majevica Brigade. However, they did not get their men in return. The three "German" prisoners were in fact Croats from Zagreb and Sarajevo who did not want to be exchanged as they had surrendered of their own free will. Apparently, the Partisans obliged them for there is no

---

[130] Schmider, *Partisanenkrieg*, p. 278.

[131] NARA, T-315, Roll 2154, 000973, War diary entry for 11 May 1943 (23.30 hours).

mention of their release in the surviving records of the German units in the area.[132] On the same day, however, another German soldier of the 369th went missing but "returned from Partisan captivity" on 20 May. It is possible that the Partisans let him go in an attempt to at least partially fulfill their obligations.[133]

This was the last time the NOVJ and the German occupation forces extended such courtesies to one another in the late spring of 1943. Over the next four weeks, some of the bloodiest fighting in the Second World War occurred in Yugoslavia. The Germans had their guerrilla opponents exactly where they wanted them— completely surrounded and with no possibility of a bloodless withdrawal. This would be a battle of annihilation. General Lüters did not mince words in his operational directive released on 6 May 1943—all captured Partisans, with or without weapons, were to be executed. Unlike the order for Operation *Weiss,* no mention was made for the exchange of prisoners.[134] As the battle neared its climax, Lüters released the infamous order of 10 June stipulating that "no able-bodied male must leave the cauldron alive." Statistics show that the German units usually carried out this order: out of a total of 1,022 prisoners reported amongst the 1st Mountain, 118th *Jäger,* and 369th Divisions, 716 were shot.[135] That the March Negotiations failed to exert any long-term influence on German counter-insurgency policies is best demonstrated in the fate of the wounded Partisans; they were routinely shot both during and after the fighting. An especially macabre episode took place in the immediate aftermath of the destruction of the 3rd Assault Division of the NOVJ on the banks of the Sutjeska River. Beginning on 13 June, German units, most notably the 7th SS Mountain Division, carried out mop-up operations in the northernmost part of the cauldron. A substantial part of the Central Hospital, estimated at 1,000 wounded and medical personnel, perished at the hands of their captors.[136]

---

[132] Miodrag Milovanović-Lune, *Dnevnik* (Titovo Užice: Vesti, 1989), pp. 111–12, Entries for 17 and 19 May 1943; *Zbornik*/IV/15/243–45, War diary of the commander of the 2nd Proletarian Brigade, Entries for 17 and 18 May 1943. I was unable to determine the fate of the fourth German prisoner.

[133] NARA, T-315, Roll 2154, 000973, War diary entry for 20 May 1943 (23.40 hours).

[134] The same order stipulated that the Chetniks, unlike the Partisans, were to be treated as prisoners of war. NARA, T-315, Roll 2154, 001415, Operational order for Schwarz (6 May 1943). There were several motives behind this provision: it was in line with preferential treatment of the captured Royalists in general; it served to undermine their will to resist; and it was deemed acceptable to the Italians.

[135] Lüters' directive was not always carried out; some 1,500 captives, both Partisans and civilian suspects, survived the battle. Trifković, "A Case of Failed Counter-Insurgency," pp. 335–36.

[136] According to the testimony of one German soldier, Major Strecker (who was exchanged just in time to command his 3rd Battalion of the 738th *Jäger* Regiment in Operation

The Partisans responded in kind; out of 425 Germans reported as missing during Operation *Schwarz*, only a small number were found alive after the battle.[137] Even if a large number of the missing could be attributed to the fact that the fighting took place in inaccessible terrain, there is enough evidence in post-war literature to assume that German prisoners were shot out of hand.[138] Such treatment was not reserved for all Axis prisoners, however, as the Germans found 371 Italians alive inside the cauldron as of 20 June, increasing to 650 by mid-July.[139] Evidently, there was a vast discrepancy between the number of Germans and Italians who survived captivity, closely linked to the varying attitudes the Partisans held toward

---

Schwarz), personally ordered one of his subordinates to shoot all Partisan wounded who could not walk. Obrad Egić, "Brigada u bici na Sutjesci," in *Druga dalmatinska proleterska brigada* (Split: Institut za historiju radničkog pokreta Dalmacije, 1982), p. 172; Kučan, *Borci Sutjeske*, p. 29. Judging by the available sources, all seriously wounded were executed, while individual units decided whether or not to take the less seriously wounded Partisans prisoner. Dr. Safet Latifić left a remarkable account of the circumstances of his capture in June 1943, and the treatment that he and some wounded Partisans received at the hands of their captors. The doctor was promptly fed and his wounds were dressed; two "young German doctors" also provided him with some bandages for the other wounded Partisans. Dr. Latifić recalled, "Some German soldiers had even furtively thrown us food and cigarettes. We were very surprised at this, because we thought all soldiers of Hitlerite Germany were the same." Two days after their capture, Latifić and the others were ordered to march to nearby Foča. An officer approached him and told him that he must exhort the wounded to make the trip at all costs, "crawling if need be, for another German unit was scheduled to move in, and they would not have much mercy for the prisoners." Dr. Safet Latifić, "Bilo nas je petorica," in *Sutjeska–Zbornik radova* (Belgrade: Vojnoizdavački zavod JNA "Vojno delo," 1959), Vol. III, pp. 259–67.

[137] NARA, T-315, Roll 1302, 000554, Daily report for 25 June 1943; NARA, T-314, Roll 560, 000750, After-action report for Operation Schwarz (20 June 1943).

[138] Zora Ćulibrk, a female fighter in the 3rd Krajina Brigade, remembered how a German captured by her unit "had to be killed, because we could not exchange him." *Treća krajiška proleterska brigada: Zbornik sjećanja* (Belgrade: Odbor sekcije boraca Treće proleterske krajiške brigade u Beogradu, 1985), Vol. III, p. 541. See also Lazar Savičević, "Pokošeno polje," in *Treći kragujevački bataljon Prve proleterske brigade: sećanja boraca* (Kragujevac: Svetlost, 1974), Vol. II, p. 145; Luka Božović, "Omladinci na Balinovcu," in ibid., p. 156.

[139] NARA, T-315, Roll 1302, 000554, Daily report for 25 June 1943; NARA, T-314, Roll 560, 000750, After-action report for Operation Schwarz (20 June 1943). The latter figure comes from an Italian report and represents the grand total of prisoners freed by all Axis formations which took part in the fighting. *Zbornik*/XIII/3/366, Report on offensive operations in Montenegro in spring and summer of 1943 (16 July 1943). Most of the prisoners came from the two battalions destroyed at Nikšić and Podgorica. Just prior to the beginning of Operation *Schwarz*, the Italians received seven officers and 154 men in exchange for a similar number of Partisan sympathizers. Ibid., p. 377. Partisan sources cite a figure of approximately 300 exchanged Italians. Lakić, "Razmjena ratnih zarobljenika u Crnoj Gori," p. 97.

each of them. Italian soldiers were perceived as being conscripted peasants and workers who were unwilling to die for fascism. In general, they were much less ferocious in battle and more willing to serve the Partisans as porters and specialists than were the Germans. Consequently, the guerrillas developed a curious fondness for such captives, one that made them unwilling to dispose of Italians even once they became an unbearable burden.[140] There is no evidence that there was an ulterior motive for the release of the prisoners. If the Partisans had hoped that by sparing them they would make the Italians reciprocate, they were sorely disappointed as the Italian mop-up actions in June 1943 were as brutal as their German counterparts.[141]

The bitter fighting in Montenegro lasted an entire month. Thanks only to the enormous self-sacrifice of the fighters and the initiative of the field commanders did the main force of the NOVJ manage to break out of the encirclement. Its losses were horrendous—out of approximately 22,000 Partisans, some 7,500 lost their lives in the encirclement. Although the Germans included a large number of civilians in their estimate of enemy casualties, the number of captured arms shows that the NOVJ suffered a serious defeat at the operational level.[142] The main guerrilla force was cut by one-third and forced to escape to Eastern Bosnia; the Adriatic hinterland was secured, as was all-important Serbia. On a strategic level, however, no breakthrough had been achieved; one flashpoint was merely succeeded by another. The fact that Tito's group broke through in an organized manner and retained inner cohesion under immense pressure confirmed that the Partisan problem in the NDH could not be solved by military means alone.

The Effects of the March Negotiations on German Operations in Herzegovina and Eastern Bosnia

The March Negotiations remain the single most controversial episode of the Second World War in Yugoslavia, mostly because of the alleged impact they had on

---

[140] Đilas recalled that the Supreme HQ ordered all Italian prisoners killed on or about 10 June; thereupon, fighters of the 3rd Assault Division under his command reluctantly carried out the executions. Djilas, *Wartime,* pp. 268–69. The fact that such a large number of Italians survived captivity demonstrates that either the Supreme HQ never issued such an order, that it was rescinded, or that NOVJ units refused to execute it *en masse.*

[141] For instance, the *Ferrara* Division executed 150 wounded Partisans on 16 June 1943. Schmider, *Partisanenkrieg,* p. 280.

[142] Kučan, *Borci Sutjeske,* p. 30; Axis forces captured six guns, twenty-three mortars, 146 machine guns, and 6388 rifles in Montenegro in May and June 1943. NARA, T-311, Roll 175, 001306, Daily report of Armed Forces Command Southeast (13 June); *Zbornik*/XIII/3/378, Report on offensive operations in Montenegro in spring and summer of 1943 (16 July 1943).

the military and political landscape of the country. The negotiations were held at the same time that the Partisans dealt a decisive blow to the Chetniks, who thereafter ceased to be a major military factor in the country. According to the revisionist version, the Royalist defeat was directly caused by a truce between the Partisans and the Germans; the latter pledged not to advance across the Neretva, which in turn enabled Tito to concentrate all his forces against the Chetniks. The argument that Tito was successful in his endeavors to obtain a cease-fire is found not only in older works written by Serbian authors sympathetic to Draža Mihailović and in post-Yugoslav literature, but also in some works published recently in the West.[143] This part of the chapter will therefore be devoted to a deeper analysis of the German actions in March and April. Apart from the impact the talks had on German operations, this study will also attempt to establish other possible consequences of this episode.

In order to reconstruct the events properly, one must return to the period immediately preceding the beginning of Operation *Weiss*. The arrival of Partisan brigades into the bauxite belt between Livno and Mostar in mid-February 1943 had thrown German operational planning into disarray. In light of the shortages of the precious ore which the Partisan occupation of the area was likely to cause, the encirclement and destruction of Tito's forces now became a matter of secondary importance. As the Italian 6th Corps could not provide the needed protection for the mining facilities (allegedly because of its depleted strength), Hitler was determined to secure them with German troops. The imminent incursion of German divisions into Herzegovina was greeted with considerable suspicion by the Italian 2nd Army for two reasons. First, the Italians feared that what was announced as a temporary measure would lead to a permanent German occupation of these areas. Second, any German move in this direction would certainly bring them into contact with Italian Chetnik auxiliaries. Given Hitler's desire to see them disarmed, violent conflict could not be ruled out. The Italians therefore tried to curb German operational freedom by requesting that all Axis troops in the area be subordinated to the 6th Corps. In order to keep the Germans and the Chetniks apart, on 26 February the *Comando Supremo* further requested that the former limit their actions to the area north of the Prozor–Rama Valley–Neretva Valley–Konjic line. The Germans declined both requests and declared that they would continue their drive toward Mostar on their own terms. In order to avoid confrontation with the Chetniks, the Italians were asked to withdraw their Serbian auxiliaries "from the area north of Mostar to a line running roughly five kilometers east of the Neretva

---

[143] Ivan Avakumović, *Mihailović prema nemačkim dokumentima* (London: Oslobodjenje, 1969), pp. 112–13; Aleksandar Bajt, *Bermanov dosije* (Belgrade: Srpska reč, 2006), pp. 481–82; Heather Williams, *Parachutes, Patriots, and Partisans: The Special Operations Executive and Yugoslavia, 1941–1945* (London: Hurst, 2003), pp. 106–07.

Valley."[144] As the Partisans were still on the right bank of the Neretva in the first days of March, the two German divisions operating against them had no orders to cross the river.[145] On 4 March, the Italian 6th Army Corps requested that the 718th Infantry Division not cross the line running from Konjic to Rama. The division responded that it could not oblige, as its actions were determined solely by instructions from German commands. However, the reply continued that the division was already under orders "not to cross the Neretva to the south in Konjic-Rama sector."[146] On 5 March, Colonel General Löhr reiterated that there were no plans to cross the line over the next several days because of the course of fighting in the area (the Partisan counterattack at Gornji Vakuf), stating that "the objective of the operations is occupation of the bauxite area around Mostar."[147] On that same day, the courier carrying Strecker's letter reached the Germans.

By the time the Germans agreed to receive the NOVJ's envoys, the situation at the front had changed dramatically. After having pushed back the 717th Division, the Partisans turned and began crossing the Neretva on 7 March. Four days later, when Đilas, Popović, and Velebit formally requested a truce, a substantial part of the Partisan army was still on the right bank. Consequently, the Germans saw no reason to alter the plans for their two divisions operating in the area. Regarding the Partisan request, there are corresponding statements from the Partisan negotiators that Dippold refused to stop the advance of his division; the division's war diary provides unambiguous confirmation of their claims.[148] Furthermore, General Lüters explicitly rejected any notion of a truce on the same day, as related in Pfafferott's telephone call to Glaise-Horstenau's staff. The surviving German records show no reduction in German activities on the right bank of the river in the following days. Only after the last Partisan was across the river on the 15th, and the 717th and 718th Divisions joined forces, did Lüters proclaim Operation *Weiss* to be concluded: "The pursuit of the insurgents to the south and east of the Neretva is not possible owing to the political commitments to the Italians."[149]

------

[144] Schmider, *Partisanenkrieg*, pp. 227–31; NARA, T-311, Roll 175, 000444, War diary entry for 1 March 1943.

[145] See operational orders dated 2 March 1943 of the 717th Division (NARA, T-315, Roll 2264, 000622–3) and the 718th Division (NARA, T-315, Roll 2271, 000958–9).

[146] Ibid., 000283, War diary entry for 4 March 1943 and ibid., 000980, Cable from Major Poche on 4 March 1943 (22.30 hours).

[147] NARA, T-311, Roll 175, 000445–6, War diary entry for 5 March 1943.

[148] The war diary for 11 March reads: "Intentions for 12 March: continuation of pursuit [of the Partisans] to the line Majan-Kučani-Studenica," NARA, T-315, Roll 2264, 000543, War diary entry for 11 March 1943.

[149] NARA, T-314, Roll 554, 000368, Situation estimate for the period 1–15 March 1943 (16 March 1943).

The three German divisions were now tasked with mop-up operations on the right bank of the Neretva and with securing communications from Konjic to Mostar. Tactical necessity required them to cross over to the opposite bank in order to fulfill the second task.[150] Once the main operations were over, however, the Italians sought to curb further German encroachment into northern Herzegovina. Consequently, when the 369th Division tried to cross the river south of Jablanica on 17 March, the Italians prevented them from doing so. Still, the division managed to smooth out the problems with its allies and camped on the eastern bank that same day.[151] To the northeast, around Konjic, the Italians were too weak to interfere in German actions. The 718th Infantry Division had crossed the river at several places downstream from the town in order to take possession of the heights overlooking the Konjic-Ostrožac section of the road. The retreating Partisan columns were arriving from the west, perpendicular to the division's front, and were headed for the area south of Konjic. On 17 March, while Velebit was requesting a cease-fire in the name of the Supreme HQ in Zagreb, the division had a fierce battle with guerrilla rear guards west of the town. Despite the use of Stuka aircraft and artillery, the 718th suffered six dead and fourteen wounded.[152] The fighting would continue here for the next several days.

The arrival of the new divisional commander, General Josef Kübler, to Konjic on 18 March only added to the intensity of the fighting in this sector. After learning that the Partisan rear guard elements passing through the hamlet of Bijela (immediately south of the town) were not interdicted with sufficient vigor, Kübler ordered *Kampfgruppe* Annacker to attack "as soon as Major Strecker and twenty-one German soldiers in Partisan captivity were exchanged." Later that day, one German arrived from the Partisan lines and conveyed a message from the guerrillas requesting that the Germans pick up their negotiator, "Professor Marković" (Đilas), and one wounded soldier from Bijela. The division readily obliged and sent one lieutenant and nine men. The officer had the task of memorizing the terrain features for the upcoming attack. The plan was ready by 19 March, but the attack could not be carried out "because of the delayed prisoner exchange."[153] The Germans were given yet another chance to scout the terrain and enemy forward positions when the same group of soldiers returned to the Partisan lines to pick up Major Strecker and the rest of the prisoners. By mid-morning of 20 March, the

---

[150] For an overview of German positions on the left bank of the river on 16 March 1943, see the map in NARA, T-315, Roll 2271, 001074–6.

[151] NARA, T-315, Roll 2154, 000431–2, War diary entry for 17 March (16.40 and 18.20 hours).

[152] NARA, T-315, Roll 2271, 000301, War diary entry for 17 March (13.40 hours).

[153] It should be noted that in other sectors (e.g. northwest of Bijela), the Germans continued with their operations throughout that day. Ibid., 000840, After-action report on operation "Konjic" (Entry for 19 March 1943).

returnees arrived safely in Konjic. At 17.00, *Kampfgruppe* Annacker was ordered to attack that evening. The fighting around Bijela lasted two days. The Partisans mounted a counterattack, killing one lieutenant and destroying one tank before withdrawing to the south.[154] Judging by the available German Army documents from battalion-level upwards, the one-day delay of Kübler's attack on Bijela was the sole instance of the March Negotiations influencing German operations in the field.

Over the course of hundreds of hours of research, this author has only been able to find one relevant, near-contemporary document that supports the truce theory. This document, not quoted by any of the proponents of the aforementioned hypothesis, is an extract from the post-war interrogation of Hans Ott by the Yugoslav secret police. Ott claimed that General Fritz Neidholdt, commander of the 369th Infantry Division, had a meeting with the Partisan envoys in Gornji Vakuf and promised to "keep his troops in peace [*držati u miru*] while the negotiations lasted as per the wish of General Lueders [*sic*]." Thus, "the Partisans' wish for several days of truce to facilitate the extrication of their wounded was fulfilled."[155] First of all, there is no evidence that Neidholdt ever met with Velebit and Đilas in Gornji Vakuf; both primary sources and the memoirs of all three Partisan envoys state that General Dippold of the 717th Infantry Division was the only high-ranking German officer with whom the envoys met in this town. Second, Ott's statement about Lüters' alleged involvement is refuted by contemporary German documents, such as the stenograph of Pfafferott's telephone call on 11 March and the memorandum for the meeting in Zagreb on 1 April 1943. Third, Neidholdt could not have allowed the Partisans to escape even if he had wanted to do so; the 717th and 718th Infantry Divisions were the units that were directly opposing the majority of the retreating Partisans, while the 369th was more or less relegated to a support role. The division could not cross the Neretva around Jablanica due to both Italian opposition and its own operational orders, which called for a halt at the river. The claim that Neidholdt kept his troops "in peace" is most likely a reference to his order from 13 March not to shoot captured Partisans while the talks lasted. It is difficult to explain the discrepancies between Ott's statement and contemporary documents and the reminiscences of other participants. It may have been a memory lapse, or—more likely—an attempt to ingratiate himself with his captors and portray his mediation between the two sides as instrumental in the fulfilment of Partisan aims.

If the German halt on the left bank of the Neretva in the immediate aftermath of Operation *Weiss* is easily explainable, the next event for consideration is not so straightforward. On 22 March, the commander of the Italian 2nd Army, General Vittorio Ambrosio, made a 180-degree turn in his policy toward the Germans. In

---

[154] Ibid., 000840–2, After-action report on operation "Konjic," Entries for 18–23 March 1943.

[155] HR HDA 1521, Box 9, File Neidholdt, Statement of Hans Ott.

light of the heavy blows the advancing Partisans dealt his Chetnik auxiliaries and Italian units around Nevesinje, the general was compelled to request that the Germans intervene in Eastern Herzegovina with five battalions. The latter refused, citing the fatigue of their own units.[156] It is possible that the refusal was in fact based on some kind of secret deal Velebit and Glaise-Horstenau agreed to during their meeting on 17 March. The German answer could have also been based on the positive outcome of the "main talks" in Zagreb, which were taking place precisely at this time. This theory is flawed for several reasons. Even if Glaise-Horstenau had negotiated a truce, it is highly unlikely that this would have had any impact on Lüters, who held actual command over the troops in the field. Second, there is no evidence whatsoever for such a theory in the surviving German documents.[157] Third, proponents of this theory have chosen to disregard the practical reasons behind the refusal which are abundantly supported by the archival sources.

The German decision not to help the Italians in Eastern Herzegovina was motivated by calculated self-interest and operational concerns. In short, the German occupation forces were not yet ready for the continuation of anti-guerrilla operations in this part of the country. Even if the requested five battalions could have been scraped together, the units were still badly in need of rest and refitting. The divisions of the 15th Mobilization Wave were hard-hit during the recent fighting and generally seen as unfit for this particular kind of warfare. Precisely for this reason, the German high command decided to reorganize them to strengthen their readiness for mountain warfare. The reorganization was to be arranged in a manner which, it was hoped, would allow them to remain involved in the continuation of *Weiss* which would target the Chetniks in the area to the east of the Neretva.

This fact leads one to the underlying motive for the refusal to intervene in this area in late March. German intelligence was always on the lookout for signs of rapprochement between the two largely Serbian guerrilla movements. There was widespread fear among the German occupation authorities—in reality, unsubstantiated—that the two might "bury the hatchet" and unite again in a common struggle against the occupier. It is safe to assume that the fear was especially great in the spring of 1943 because both guerrilla movements had their main forces concentrated along the coast. If the Allies landed on the southern Adriatic, they would be in a prime position to broker a truce between the two and thus secure the combined strength of Partisans and Chetniks for their own purposes. "Any advance by our side with stronger forces across the Neretva," it was concluded by the HQ of the Commander-in-Chief Southeast in Thessaloniki, "would be taken as an act of war by Mihailović. Consequently, we would have to start the

---

[156] NARA, T-311, Roll 175, 000563, Memorandum from a conference with the Chief of Staff (22 March 1943).

[157] For similar conclusions, see Schmider, *Partisanenkrieg,* p. 252.

struggle against him before we wanted to."[158] The bloodletting the Chetniks and the Partisans were administering to each other east of the Neretva in late March and throughout April was playing perfectly into German plans: "This development can only be seen as advantageous to us in light of the upcoming Operation *Schwarz*."[159] Much to their dismay, Berlin ordered the relief of Foča in the second half of April and the brief role of the German occupation forces as *"Der lachende Dritte"* was over.

Conclusion

As 1942 came to a close, Berlin could no longer ignore the Partisan problem in the Balkans. With unfavorable developments in North Africa, the threat of an Allied invasion of southern Europe became real. The Axis, therefore, embarked on a series of large-scale anti-guerrilla operations whose objective was to destroy the Communist-led Partisan movement and thus bring about the pacification of the region, as well as secure the lines of communication leading to the Adriatic coast. By late February 1943, the plan seemed to be working; the bulk of the NOVJ, including thousands of wounded, was surrounded in the Neretva River Valley by a heterogeneous coalition of Germans, Italians, NDH forces, and Chetniks. With the choice of possible escape routes rapidly dwindling, Tito decided to use diplomacy. Under the guise of prisoner exchange, Partisan envoys sought to obtain recognition of the NOVJ as a regular army from the Germans, in which case the wounded would be protected from reprisals. This request, although important, was not the main reason for starting negotiations at the top level for the first time since November 1942; Tito actually wanted a cease-fire with the Germans. The Partisans were preparing to cross the Neretva and face the main Chetnik force on the river's eastern bank. Not knowing whether or not the Germans would continue operations in Eastern Herzegovina, Tito wanted to buy some time for the withdrawal of his army across the Neretva. In return, his high-ranking delegation would downplay the importance of the Partisans' struggle against the Germans and emphasize their hatred of the Chetniks. They were also authorized to reveal the Partisans' genuine animosity toward the main sponsors of their Royalist enemies, the British, and to state that their landing would be opposed, with arms if necessary, by the NOVJ.

Although the Germans did not stop their operations in the Neretva Valley after the Partisan delegates arrived in Gornji Vakuf, they did listen to their enemy's proposals. Ambassador Kasche and General Glaise-Horstenau were in favor of maintaining contacts with the Partisans ever since the first two rounds of talks were held in August and November of the previous year. The Partisan envoys traveled

---

[158] NARA, T-311, Roll 175, 000563, Memorandum from a conference with the Chief of Staff (22 March 1943).

[159] Ibid., 000586, Memorandum from a conference with the Chief of Staff (12 April 1943).

several times to Sarajevo and Zagreb under German protection. While they could not complain about the way in which their hosts treated them, the German style of "negotiating" caused much frustration; the latter kept the talks as informal as possible and never appointed an officially authorized delegation. As for the substance of the talks, little was achieved—the Germans rejected both the offer of truce and the request for recognition of the NOVJ as a legitimate belligerent force. Discussion on these points was tied to the cessation of sabotage on the Zagreb-Belgrade railway line. The Germans, however, did halt the executions of captured Partisans during the talks and agreed to a prisoner exchange. Although the NOVJ managed to push deep into Italian-occupied Eastern Bosnia and Herzegovina by late March 1943, Tito still feared a German intervention in this area, therefore he gave the green light for the continuation of the talks in the hope it would buy his troops more time. He was under the impression that his diplomacy was working because the German occupation forces were still showing no intention of pursuing the Partisans into Eastern Bosnia. In order to keep the negotiations going, Tito ordered a temporary ban on sabotage on the Zagreb-Belgrade railway line in mid-April. At the same time, the German Army crossed into the Italian occupation zone in order to help its hard-pressed allies, and the fighting against Tito's force erupted again.

Much has been written about Tito's real motives for entering the talks. His detractors maintain that in order to defeat his domestic enemies, he was quite prepared to arrange a *modus vivendi* with Nazi Germany. As a result of the alleged truce reached through secret negotiations in Zagreb and Sarajevo, the Partisans were able to deal the Chetniks a crushing defeat in Eastern Herzegovina. The declaration by the NOVJ envoys that they would fight the British if they landed in the Adriatic is taken as proof that Tito was far more willing to collaborate with the Germans than his adversary, Mihailović. Judging by the available primary sources, memoirs of key participants (who were not necessarily Tito apologists), and serious detailed research, these claims cannot be verified. Tito's offer was, in all likelihood, derived from the desperate situation in which he and his army found themselves in late February 1943. It was a last-ditch attempt to stave off an imminent military disaster and improve the chances of survival for wounded Partisans should they be captured. Through the talks held in late 1942, the highest German political and military authorities signaled that they were sympathetic to the idea of some sort of political solution to the chaos reigning in the NDH. Tito decided to take advantage of the situation and offered the Germans a truce and a withdrawal of his forces to Sandžak, which would become a neutral zone where the Germans would not intervene militarily. By professing that the NOVJ fought the German occupation forces only while it had no choice, stressing that the Chetniks were his main enemies, and that the British would be opposed by force if they attempted a landing on the coast, Tito attempted to create the impression that his offer could lead to a more permanent pacification. In fact, the offer was tactical in nature, devised to allow the main Partisan force to cross the Neretva and extricate its wounded; it would also enable the Partisans to concentrate squarely on the large Chetnik army waiting for them on the opposite bank.

There is no evidence that the Partisan leadership contemplated a long-term arrangement with the Germans between March–April 1943. The claim that the Royalists were the main enemies of the Partisan movement can be taken at face value. However, to the Yugoslav Communists, the struggles against the domestic reactionaries and against the Axis were inseparable and complementary. Had they not been, there is little doubt that Tito would have sought a *modus vivendi* with the Germans earlier in the war, in the way Mihailović had with the Italians. As for the Partisan's declaration concerning the British, all the major participants in the March Negotiations agreed that the NOVJ would indeed have had to fight them if they had chosen to intervene in the Yugoslav civil war on the Chetnik side. It was the Yugoslav Communists' good fortune that the course of events never forced them to actually fight the British.

The March Negotiations also precipitated the first open rift in the relations between the KPJ and the Soviet Union. Although Tito carefully camouflaged the information about the talks in his cables to the Comintern, the Soviets discerned that more was afoot than a simple prisoner exchange. Perhaps fearing that the independent policy-making of the KPJ would betray their own clandestine diplomatic approaches to Germany to their Western Allies, the Soviets sent a vindictive telegram to Tito. The critique leveled at Tito was made to appear ideological in nature, mentioning nothing of the other, more practical and realistic reasons. Much to Moscow's shock, Tito replied in an equally stern tone, defending his actions and failing to pledge that he would break off the talks. This unusual exchange ended in victory for the Partisan leadership because Moscow decided not to press the issue any further. Tito's decision to defend what has been termed as his first venture into the world of *realpolitik* came after a long period of frustration regarding Soviet foreign policy. The USSR's prime concern was to maintain good relations with Great Britain, who was the main protector of the Yugoslav government-in-exile and its armed formation, the Chetniks. In order to achieve this goal, the Kremlin was willing to disregard its "internationalist" obligation to support the KPJ by all means available. Even if the Partisans were forced to accept the fact that the Soviets could not provide material help because of technical difficulties, they could not understand why their mentor would not openly take sides in the civil war between the Communists and the Royalists. Although the March Negotiations were not mentioned again in official correspondence, the bitter taste remained. And when the final split between Tito and Stalin came in 1948, the memories of the talks that the Yugoslav Communists had with the Germans at the height of the war were revived and exploited in the form of propaganda by the Eastern Bloc countries.

As stated previously, some of the highest-ranking German dignitaries in the NDH were interested in the revival of top-level contacts with the Partisans. The Third Reich's ambassador, Siegfried Kasche (ironically, an ardent Nazi), was undoubtedly the most vociferous proponent of a possible deal with Tito. The original Partisan propositions from March and April left much to be desired, but from Kasche's point of view, they represented a valid starting point for further discussion. If the arrangement could be made, it would strengthen the foundations of the NDH and raise his own standing within the diplomatic and political hierarchy of the Third Reich. The plenipotentiary general in Zagreb, Glaise-Horstenau, was much more cautious regarding the sincerity of the Partisan offers, yet extended his support to the continuation of talks; if nothing else, frequent contact with guerrilla emissaries provided insight into the intentions and mindset of their leadership. Nonetheless, any hopes Glaise-Horstenau and especially Kasche might have had about the offer were shattered following the intervention from Berlin. As he was aware of Hitler's deep-seated aversion to both negotiated solutions and guerrillas in general, von Ribbentrop ordered the ambassador to break off all contacts with the Partisans; fearing backlash, Glaise-Horstenau also backed down. However, like their counterparts in the Partisan camp, the Germans in Zagreb did not always heed their superiors' instructions. Having to tackle the insurgency and troublesome allies, as well as Berlin's lack of understanding and interest in Balkan affairs, they often found ways to circumvent the orders emanating from Berlin. Consequently, although no Partisan delegations were received in Zagreb after von Ribbentrop intervened and expressly cautioned them not to do so, both Glaise-Horstenau and Kasche maintained contact informally with Tito's representative, Velebit, though Kasche preferred to act through a trusted intermediary, Ott. These instances of insubordination were illustrative of the fact that neither the general nor the ambassador considered totally breaking off contacts with Tito's HQ.

The German occupation forces halted on the Neretva not because of Tito's diplomatic maneuvering, but due to other reasons. The attack into Eastern Herzegovina was at first inopportune because of the tense relations with the Italians who were largely unwilling to facilitate the expansion of German authority in their occupation zone. After the Italians requested German help in the final week of March, the latter declined. They would intervene in Herzegovina and Montenegro only after their troops were rested and reorganized—in mid-May at the earliest. In the meantime, fighting between the Chetniks and the Partisans to the east of the river could only be welcomed from the German point of view since there was widespread fear that the two guerrilla movements would make a deal and turn on the Germans. The local commands would not even have intervened at Foča in late April had they not been ordered to do so by their superiors. Tito's illusions about the success of his diplomatic ploy were laid to rest for good with the beginning of Operation *Schwarz* in mid-May.

In the end, the results of the March Negotiations were modest at best. A local German attack south of Konjic was delayed for one day until the exchange of seventeen Partisans for twenty-seven Germans was completed. Tito's ban on sabotage on the Zagreb-Belgrade railway line, which lasted for a little over a month, was lifted in late May. Although the Germans ceased executing Partisan prisoners during the talks, the NOVJ was not recognized as a legitimate belligerent. The fact that the measure was only tactical in nature is confirmed by events during Operation *Schwarz* in which the Germans reverted to their old policies regarding the treatment of guerrilla captives, wounded or otherwise. The NOVJ responded in kind and the brief improvement of the prisoners' lot achieved in March and April would be undone by a period in which the fighting was conducted with customary brutality.

Chapter 4

The Neutral Zone at Pisarovina

1943–1945

Introduction

What transpired in Pisarovina, a small village located on the outskirts of Zagreb, is unique not only to Yugoslavia, but to the Second World War in general. Pisarovina was the location officially agreed by both the German occupation authorities and the Yugoslav Partisans to function as the center of the prisoner exchange cartel at the end of 1943. In order to facilitate this, the village and its immediate surroundings were declared a neutral zone, quite possibly the only such place in war-torn Europe. How surprisingly well the system functioned is attested to by the fact that the last swap was made at the time when the Red Army was mopping-up the last pockets of resistance in Berlin in late April 1945. The system saved hundreds, if not thousands, of prisoners who faced an uncertain fate. Furthermore, the success of the cartel was instrumental in raising the willingness of troop commanders across the country to seek out their nearest counterpart in order to make an exchange. Frequent contacts between the envoys provided both the Germans and the Partisans with a "back-channel" for talks on political issues and trade, as well as the opportunity to spy on each other.

In order to place the events described in this chapter into the proper perspective, it would seem appropriate to outline the main political and military events in the territory of the NDH in the last two years of the war.[1] The second half of 1943 was marked by the Italian capitulation in early September. This event caused all sides to direct their attention to the former Italian occupation zone and the disarming of the once-powerful 2nd Army. Although the NOVJ managed to obtain large quantities of military equipment, it had to evacuate from the coast to both the islands and the interior. The objective of the 2nd Panzer Army was to secure the coastal belt in the anticipation of Allied landings and prevent the NOVJ from mounting the invasion

---

[1] For additional information regarding the events described in this chapter, see Klaus Schmider, "Der jugoslawische Kriegsschauplatz (Januar 1943 bis Mai 1945)," in *Das deutsche Reich und der Zweite Weltkrieg* (Munich: Deutsche Verlags-Anstalt, 2007), Vol. VIII, pp. 1009–88; Tomasevich, *Occupation and Collaboration*, pp. 294–335; Petranović, *Istorija Jugoslavije*, Vol. II, pp. 280–342.

of Serbia. The winter witnessed bitter fighting across southern Croatia, and parts of southern and Eastern Bosnia and Herzegovina, as the Germans launched a series of offensive operations aimed at breaking up those Partisan concentrations. These operations managed to bring only temporary improvement—the guerrillas suffered heavy casualties and lost some important territory (the Dalmatian islands, except Vis), but remained far from destroyed.

Politically, 1943 was marked by the Tehran Conference of "The Big Three" and the official recognition of the People's Liberation Movement as a member of the Allied coalition. The AVNOJ held its second session in late November and created the Communist-sponsored interim Yugoslav government. Among its other decisions, the AVNOJ also laid out the basis for the post-war federalist constitution of the country, barred King Petar II from returning to Yugoslavia, and conferred the rank of marshal on Tito. Across the lines, the hope that the return of Dalmatia to the NDH would strengthen the *Ustashe* regime failed to materialize. Equally fruitless were the German attempts to improve the reliability of the Home Guard. Considering the incompetence (or unwillingness) of the *Ustashe* to improve the administration and economy of the land, high-ranking Army and SS officials in Yugoslavia were in favor of an outright takeover of executive power in the NDH. The foreign ministry and Hitler were against it, arguing this would remove the last vestiges of the country's "sovereignty" and would deal a fatal blow to their *Ustashe protégées*. Faced with the realities on the ground, however, and despite pleas from Pavelić, Hitler gave his reluctant blessing for the Chetnik-friendly policy practiced by the military commanders in the country.

As the troop levels continued to drop due to the needs of other fronts, the German commands had to revert to smaller-scale operations with the limited objective of containing the increasingly stronger NOVJ and maintaining the status quo throughout 1944. A notable exception was the concerted effort to capture or kill Tito in his base at Drvar, Western Bosnia, by using ground and airborne troops in late May 1944 (Operation *Rösselsprung*). By late summer, the situation was beginning to deteriorate rapidly, as reorganized and Allied-equipped NOVJ units began offensive operations in Dalmatia. Even greater danger loomed from the Partisans and Soviets who, after having liberated Belgrade, continued with their offensive to the west. In Bosnia and Herzegovina, the Germans were struggling to keep the lines of communication open for the great mass of soldiers belonging to Army Group E, which had retreated all the way from Greece.

1944 was also the year in which Tito's People's Liberation Movement established itself as the only Allied partner in Yugoslavia after the British cut all ties to Mihailović in mid-spring. Although the Chetnik leader was now out of the picture, the King and the Yugoslav government-in-exile were still supported by Whitehall. In exchange for material help, Tito had to make political concessions to Prime Minister Winston S. Churchill and agree to the merger of the Communist-sponsored "National Committee" with the exiled Royal government (the so-called "Treaty of Vis" from June 1944). Anglo-Partisan relations began experiencing a steep decline in the following months, as Tito kept postponing the merger in order to consolidate the Communist grip on power in the territories liberated from the Axis. His efforts were facilitated to a large degree by the appearance of the Red Army on the Serbian borders and the increasing flow of Soviet material help (the creation of the unified Yugoslav government would occur only in March 1945). The Germans had trouble with their Balkan allies as well. Seeing that the war was lost for the Axis, two high-ranking NDH ministers began exploring the possibility of the NDH changing sides and sought contact with the members of the pro-British Croatian Peasant Party. Pavelić most likely encouraged these actions at the beginning, but changed his mind in the meantime—the plotters were arrested and executed later on. This move secured Hitler's continued support for the regime and also enabled Pavelić to get rid of his long-time adversary, General Glaise-Horstenau. The NDH remained firmly on the side of the Third Reich.

The first months of 1945 were marked by successful local German counter-attacks on the Syrmian front and the Yugoslav offensive in the southern parts of the NDH, which succeeded in pushing the Germans out of Herzegovina. On 20 March, the Yugoslav Army commenced its offensive in Western Bosnia and the northern Croatian Littoral. Axis positions in central Bosnia were becoming increasingly untenable and the German troops had to perform a fighting with-drawal from Bosnia in order to link up with the units in Slavonia. These units were themselves in retreat after the lines in Syrmia had finally been pierced in mid-April 1945. The fighting did not slacken in the remaining weeks of the war as Army Group E and the remainder of the NDH armed forces desperately tried to reach the relative safety of Austria and surrender themselves to the Allies. These hopes failed to materialize—the remaining German troops began surren-dering on 7 May, while the remnants of the NDH forces followed suit one week later.

Setting Up the Neutral Zone: First Contacts, July–November 1943

The late spring and early summer of 1943 were marked by the struggle between the German forces and the core of the NOVJ under Supreme HQ in Bosnia and Montenegro in which quarter was neither asked nor given. In Eastern Croatia, the Partisans continued sabotaging lines of communication and attacking Home Guard units whenever the opportunity presented itself. Unlike with the Germans, they maintained prisoner exchange contacts with NDH authorities throughout this period. The latter proved to be much more practical in this respect than their allies. In mid-January 1943, the NDH Ministry of Defense officially legalized the exchange of especially valuable officers from Partisan captivity and issued guide-lines for such proceedings. Although the instructions emphasized that a general swap of all captured officers was not envisaged "for morale and political reasons," in reality it meant that any officer who did not decide to stay with the Partisans of his own free will was eligible for exchange.[2]

The exchange contacts in Croatia were especially intensified in late May and early June 1943 after the Partisans captured Colonel Vjekoslav Klišanić, Chief of Staff of the 1st Home Guard Corps, Colonel Karlo Lalić, Commander of the 5th Mountain Brigade, and 1st Lieutenant Ivan Lalić just outside of Glina. The first attempt to negotiate their release with the local Partisan unit failed because the NOVJ's Main HQ for Croatia insisted on having the last word in every case of exchange; this was to become a hallmark of the entire exchange business in this part of the country.[3] The exchange of the Home Guard officers was approved shortly afterwards by the Main HQ but then another problem arose—the Partisans would swap these men only for Ivo Marinković, a university professor from Zagreb. He was the same individual whom the Supreme HQ wanted in exchange for German specialists from Jajce in late 1942, and for Major Strecker in March and April 1943. The *Ustashe* security services continued to deny any knowledge of his whereabouts, claiming that Partisan envoys were "misinformed."[4] The guerrillas would continue to demand Marinković over the following months, having more valuable captives to offer in return.

The event that triggered the renewal of contacts between high Partisan commands and the office of General Glaise-Horstenau was the capture of Lieutenant Colonel Pokay on 12 July 1943. He was the head of the commission for the purchasing of horses and was touring the countryside around Zagreb accompanied by a Home Guard officer and a party of German soldiers. In an ambush, the Partisans managed to capture both officers, along with one NCO and one private.[5] Pokay was the highest-ranking German to be taken captive up to that point and it was only a matter of time until his exchange would be requested. In late July, the seasoned Partisan envoy, Marijan Stilinović, sent a letter to Glaise-Horstenau proposing a new round of talks. The general promptly agreed, summoning Hans Ott to Zagreb for this purpose. The latter picked up Stilinović in the guerrilla-held village of Pisarovina from whence they drove to the Croatian capital. There were two rounds of talks in Glaise-Horstenau's HQ, roughly at the beginning and at the end of August, interrupted by a two-week pause used by the Partisan envoy to receive new instructions. In short, Stilinović demanded the recognition of the NOVJ as a lawful belligerent and the establishment of a permanent exchange system; he even floated

---

[2] HR HDA 1450, Roll D-2222, 374–6, Guidelines for exchange of captured officers (16 January 1943). Rolls D-2222 through 2224 contain numerous requests for exchange made by family members of the captured officers as well as by their units.

[3] HR HDA 1450, Roll D-2223, 55, 30th Ustashe Battalion to Ministry of Defense (4 June 1943).

[4] Ibid., 229, Letter to command of Banija district (11 July 1943).

[5] *Zbornik*/V/17/429, Main HQ of Home Guard, Daily report No. 194 (13 July 1943).

the idea of including captured Chetniks and collaborationist troops of Nedić in the deal. The purpose of this suggestion was obvious—not only would it give the Partisans more prisoners to bargain with, but it would also lead to the *de facto* recognition of Chetniks as German auxiliaries. Glaise-Horstenau was generally in favor of accepting the first two points, while he declined the third. He said that he had no authority in Serbia and that any attempt to include members of the aforementioned formations would only be a waste of time.[6]

After Stilinović departed Zagreb for consultations, the first steps were taken to exchange Pokay; on 10 August, the Home Guard's Main HQ instructed the 1st Corps to offer the Partisans a swap. An underlined passage read that the guerrillas would receive "mostly" their fighters in return, which in effect meant that no political prisoners would be exchanged.[7] The 1st Mountain Division of the Home Guard subsequently arranged a meeting with the Moslavina Detachment outside of Kutina for the 22nd. The Partisans put forth their demands: Pokay was worth twenty men; each of his two German companions were worth five.[8] Even more problematic than this extraordinarily high ratio of exchange was the fact that the guerrillas continued demanding prominent Party members instead of common Partisans. It was reported on 31 August that the talks were on hold; fighting around Glina became so heavy that the local command was afraid to send envoys to the Partisans, and likewise, the Germans could not guarantee the safety of guerrilla delegates if they arrived in town. The biggest obstacle was, however, that the latter kept insisting on Marinković and hinged any exchange on his release.[9]

The Germans decided to intervene at the highest level. During a meeting with Pavelić on 1 September, Glaise-Horstenau personally requested the transfer of Marinković—now hiding under the name of Franjo Šulentić[10]—to the *Feldkommandantur* in Zagreb. Eight days later, Pavelić's military office sent a letter to Glaise-Horstenau which repeated that these names were unknown to the NDH authorities. The photograph which the German general had provided at the meeting with Pavelić corresponded to one Franjo Golik, born on 13 December 1905 on

---

[6] HR HDA 1521, Box 31, File 546 Stilinović, Statement of Hans Ott.

[7] HR HDA 1450, Roll D-2223, 328, Main HQ of Home Guard to 1st Corps Area (10 August 1943).

[8] Ibid., 333, Town command in Kutina to 1st Mountain Division of Home Guard (23 August 1943).

[9] Ibid., 352, 1st Mountain Division of Home Guard to Main HQ of Home Guard (31 August 1943).

[10] NDH authorities were provided with Marinković's false name in late August. *Vojni arhiv Srbije* (Serbian Military Archive), Box 82, Folder 5, Document No. 5-4, Cable from Main HQ for Croatia (20 August 1943) (hereinafter abbreviated to: VA, box number, folder number, document number).

the island of Brač, who had been executed as a hostage on 14 April 1943.[11] The general could have easily checked with Stilinović to see if the date of birth in the letter corresponded with the data in the Party's archives. Why he chose not to do so is unclear. Most likely he feared that the news of Marinković's death would cause reprisals, or even worse, disruption of the negotiations in general.[12]

The Marinković episode had an all-too-familiar end; as in the past, the *Ustashe* refused to deliver the prisoners to the Germans and thus received nothing in return. On the whole, they had little interest in the exchange business as the Partisans showed little inclination to spare captured *Ustashe*. An exception was made in the case of Colonel Jure Francetić, one of the most skilled *Ustashe* field officers, who had been seriously wounded and captured in Lika in late 1942. Pavelić wanted to affect his release through Glaise-Horstenau and Ott, and the Germans seemingly complied by broaching the possibility of an exchange with Partisan agents in Zagreb. In the meantime, however, Francetić had succumbed to his wounds, and the contact was broken off.[13] The Home Guard, on the other hand, had its officers captured practically on a daily basis and was very keen to see them exchanged. In order to facilitate this, the NDH's regular army often sought the help of its ally. In June 1943, Glaise-Horstenau had officially been requested to do everything in his power to free Klišanić and Lalić if the Partisans offered their exchange to German units in the area around Bihać.[14] One month later, a similar request was put forth to the 7th SS Mountain Division regarding some officers captured in Eastern Bosnia.[15] There is no evidence that the Germans made any attempts to contact the Partisans during this period, probably because of the fierce fighting they were engaged in at the time. By September, however, German units on the ground began taking a more active role in local exchanges. Toward the end of the month, the *Ustashe* acquiesced to releasing one female Communist from the concentration camp Stara Gradiška in return for 1st Lieutenant Lalić from Kilšanić's group. The swap itself was made in Glina on 27 September 1943 by a special envoy of the NDH's Ministry of Defense who was assisted by members of the newly-arrived SS Division *Nordland*. Two of the division's officers traveled to the guerrilla-held territory

---

[11] NARA, T-501, Roll 267, 000252, Conversation with Poglavnik (1 September) and 000262, Poglavnik's military office to Plenipotentiary General (9 September 1943).

[12] The birth date provided in the letter corresponded to the actual birth date. *Vojna enciklopedija,* Vol. V, pp. 286–87. Although proclaimed "People's Hero" in 1945, the details on Marinković death eluded historians until the mid-1970s, when it was discovered that he died in April 1943. *Narodni heroji Jugoslavije* (Belgrade: Mladost, 1975).

[13] Željko Karaula, "Prilozi za biografiju zapovjednika ustaške Crne legije Jure Francetića (1902.–1942.)," *Prilozi* 42 (2013), p. 107.

[14] HR HDA 1450, Roll D-2222, 608, General Prpić to Plenipotentiary General (undated).

[15] HR HDA 1450, Roll D-2223, 189, General Lukić to Main HQ and 7th SS Division (20 July 1943).

under a white flag to retrieve the Home Guard lieutenant. One Partisan officer accompanied them on the return trip and claimed his comrade from the town's prison.[16] In mid-November, four Partisans were transported to nearby Petrinja "with German consent" so that they could be exchanged for two Home Guard officers; civilian authorities were instructed to make the swap "in the presence of the German representative."[17]

Both the German willingness to discuss the recognition of the NOVJ as a legitmate belligerent and their increasing involvement in the exchange activities on the ground were rooted in Hitler's July 1943 directive concerning the treatment of captured guerrillas. It represented a radical departure from the way the counter-insurgency had been previously conducted. The reasons behind the order were practical in nature. According to the new regulation, all guerrillas aged sixteen to fifty-five captured in the occupied eastern territories and the Balkans, as well as those assisting them, were not to be shot but used as forced labor. It was part of an attempt to acquire an additional 200,000 prisoners in order to increase coal mining output.[18] Additionally, it was hoped that the order would encourage the Partisans to defect and would counter the enemy's propaganda which claimed that the Germans were killing everyone.[19] Glaise-Horstenau wrote in his diary that by issuing this order, Hitler turned the nature of warfare in Yugoslavia "upside down."[20] His dealings with the Partisans, as well as those of other German officials, had now seemingly acquired a degree of legitimacy.

The new regulation caused much confusion on the ground, however, and the High Command of the Armed Forces was compelled to issue a clarification on 18 August 1943. The document confirmed the prisoner of war status for guerrillas captured in battle, suspicious civilians caught in the vicinity of the battlefield, and defectors. The privileged status was explicitly denied to any enemy personnel

---

[16] Oluf Krabbe, *Danske soldater i kamp på Østfronten 1941–1945* (Odense: Odense Universitetsforlag, 1976), p. 148; HR HDA 1450, Roll D-2223, 483, To HQ of 1st Corps area (undated). The Partisan envoy said during the meeting that his side continued to insist on obtaining Marinković in exchange for Klišanić and Colonel Lalić. In the end, the Partisans succeeded in persuading the two to stay with the NOVJ; the former was appointed to staff duties in the Main HQ for Croatia and in the Supreme HQ, while the latter became Chief of Staff of the elite 1st Proletarian Corps.

[17] HR HDA 1450, Roll D-2224, 155, Security directorate to 1st Corps area (undated) and 156, 1st Corps area to district head of Glina (15 November 1943).

[18] NARA, T-77, Roll 787, 5515936–7, Labor force for coal mining (8 July 1943). Fritz Sauckel, "Plenipotentiary for Labor Deployment," wanted to use guerrilla prisoners from the East as laborers since at least early 1943, but the idea was rejected by Himmler. NARA, T-175, Roll 81, 2601707, Himmler to Sauckel (9 February 1943).

[19] NARA, T-315, Roll 2155, 000044, Treatment of bandits (29 July 1943).

[20] Broucek, ed., *Ein General im Zwielicht,* Vol. III, p. 287 (Entry for October 1943).

wearing German or any other Axis uniforms, and, implicitly, to those guerrillas caught outside of open combat (sabotage, espionage, etc.). The clarification also contained one clause which practically granted the right for troops in the field to disregard the new regulation entirely if they chose to do so. Each divisional commander, the clause read, could order that no prisoners were to be taken in cases where the guerrillas acted in a "particularly dastardly way;" in absence of instructions, lower-ranking officers were to "act correspondingly on their own responsibility."[21]

In an area as volatile as occupied Yugoslavia, there was little doubt as to which course of action General Lothar Rendulic, the new commander of the 2nd Panzer Army, would take. Nicknamed "The Bloodhound" by Glaise-Horstenau, Rendulic was of the opinion that the insurgency could only be fought with sheer violence. In order to curb sabotage on the rail lines in the NDH, Rendulic instituted a harsh reprisal system not unlike the one in Serbia. Furthermore, he increased the quota of hostages which were to be executed for each German soldier killed or wounded (fifty and twenty-five, respectively). As a result of these measures, the closing months of 1943 were marked by mass executions and the burning of villages throughout the region.[22] Rendulic also chose to avail himself of the opportunity provided by the clarification of 18 August 1943 to maintain a harsh line toward Partisan prisoners. This is evident from the order of the 369th Infantry Division from 25 October 1943, based on instructions issued by the 2nd Panzer Army in mid-September, that read, in part, that the taking of prisoners could be prohibited by senior officers if it posed a risk for a German unit. If there were no such orders, junior officers were to act at their own discretion. Able-bodied guerrillas could be treated as POWs but could also be used as hostages. However, this only applied to prisoners not caught in German uniform, or in a uniform of any of the German allies—such "bandits" were to be shot after careful interrogation.[23] One month later, the commander of the 369th wrote to the 5th SS Mountain Corps that although these instructions "satisfied the troops' security needs," they were detrimental to the efforts to increase the number of defectors and laborers. He therefore

---

[21] NARA, T-77, Roll 787, OKW, Nr. 03408/43 geh. WFSt/Op. (H) (18 August 1943).

[22] Rendulic had no illusions regarding the conduct of the Germans: "We are terrorists and that's it!," he once exclaimed. On another occasion, he wrote to Glaise-Horstenau: ". . . if only I had twenty divisions at my disposal, I would kill everybody in this country." Kazmirimović, *Nemački general,* pp. 132–35. The second remark is probably more a sign of frustration rather than genocidal intentions.

[23] NARA, T-315, Roll 2155, 000090–1, Combating the bandits, reprisal and evacuation measures (25 October 1943). For the text of Rendulic's order, see NARA, T-314, Roll 1544, 000341–2, Order of commander of 2nd Panzer Army concerning combat against bandits, reprisal and evacuation measures (15 September 1943).

requested that matters be clarified and priorities set.[24] On 2 December 1943, the issue was resolved once and for all: "As of immediately, all bandits who are captured alive . . . are to be treated as prisoners of war. . . . Prisoners or defectors are under no circumstances to be shot."[25] Knowing that the troops on the ground would find it difficult to adjust to such a drastic shift and would likely continue their "old ways," the 187th Reserve Division prepared a special leaflet for its soldiers which in part read: "Naturally, the fight goes on until the enemy is destroyed. But those bandits who are captured during the fighting are POWs and must be treated as POWs like our other enemies on regular fronts are treated."[26]

The episode involving *Luftwaffe* Captain Joachim Kirschner is characteristic of these changes in German counter-insurgency policies. Kirschner was only twenty-three, yet he had already downed 188 enemy planes, making him one of the most successful *Luftwaffe* fighter pilots; for his exploits, he was awarded the Knight's Cross with Oak leaves, one of the Third Reich's highest military decorations.[27] On 17 December, his Messerschmitt was shot down over Herzegovina south of Stolac, but Kirschner parachuted to safety. Once he was on the ground, however, he was taken prisoner by the South Herzegovina Partisan Detachment. When news that Kirschner had gone missing reached the German troops on the ground, they prepared a search and rescue operation. On 20 December, the Partisans routed one search party and captured all twenty-eight of its officers and men. Undeterred, the

---

[24] Ibid., 000129–30, Propaganda directed at enemy treatment of defectors and prisoners (24 November 1943).

[25] Ibid., 000164, Treatment of prisoners (2 December 1943).

[26] NARA, T-315, Roll 1553, 001092, To German soldiers in Croatia (undated, probably the end of December 1943). General Dehner, the commander of the 69th Reserve Corps, continued to complain in a letter dated 19 December 1943 that his units were shooting defectors and even German agents trying to come over. Klaus Schmider, "Auf Umwegen zum Vernichtungskrieg? Der Partisanenkrieg in Jugoslawien, 1941–1944," in Rolf-Dieter Müller and Hans-Erich Volkmann, eds., *Die Wehrmacht: Mythos und Realität* (Munich: Oldenbourg Verlag, 1999), p. 913. It should be noted that the NDH authorities were once again a step ahead of the Germans in clarifying matters. At a conference held on 14 September 1943, representatives of the Ministry of Defense met with envoys of the International Committee of the Red Cross to discuss the establishment of the Bureau of POW affairs. The question of the legal status of captured Partisans was also discussed. Mr. Schmidlin of the ICRC argued that it would be reasonable to treat Croatian citizens belonging to the guerrillas in the same way as foreign nationals (British), especially if the former were forcibly recruited into Partisan ranks. The NDH officials agreed that these people, in line with Hitler's directive, could be granted POW status "on the grounds of expediency" without formally recognizing the NOVJ as a legitimate belligerent. HR HDA 1450, Roll D-2233, 135–7, Preliminary meeting pertaining to establishment of the office of POW affairs (14 September 1943).

[27] See: http://www.lexikon-der-wehrmacht.de/Personenregister/K/KirschnerJ.htm

Germans continued raiding the villages south of Stolac over the period of 22–24 December, killing altogether twenty-three civilians in the process, according to the NDH *gendarmerie* (whether these atrocities occurred before or after it become known that the Partisans had Kirschner and all other German prisoners shot is unclear).[28] By 30 December at the latest, Field Marshal Maximilian von Weichs informed the Supreme Command of the incident. He proposed a massive reprisal which would involve the shooting or hanging of some 220 Partisans captured in the recent fighting on the island of Korčula; Hitler personally approved this proposal.[29]

By the time the order reached the troops, it was altered in one significant way. On 2 January 1944, the 2nd Panzer Army issued instructions for carrying out the reprisal. Instead of executing Partisans from Korčula, who were in no way responsible for Kirschner's death, the Germans decided to punish the 29th Herzegovina Division only.[30] The 5th SS Mountain Corps was ordered to organize an operation in Eastern Herzegovina, the objective of which was to capture around 200 Partisans from the aforementioned division.[31] Although vastly disproportionate, von Weichs' order was a far cry from the indiscriminate policies of the first two-and-a-half years of war for three reasons. First, this reprisal order was meant to deter further executions of German prisoners in this particular area rather than to simply reduce the number of guerrillas. Second, the *Führer's* HQ had to be consulted beforehand as the reprisals were aimed at the enemy which was *de facto,* if not *de jure,* recognized as a legimate belligerent. Third, moderation on the part of Army Group F was a result of the knowledge that Partisan leadership had strived for de-escalation as well; one indiscriminate act of violence could reverse this trend.[32]

---

[28] *Zbornik*/IV/20/475–76, 656, Activity report of the 3rd Brigade for the period 15–31 December 1943 (31 December 1943) and 29th Division to 10th Herzegovina Brigade and to South and North Herzegovina Detachments (26 December 1943).

[29] NARA, T-77, Roll 1426, 000270, War Diary of Armed Forces High Command, Entry for 30 December 1943.

[30] 550 Partisan prisoners from Korčula were transported to the rear area by train in early January 1944. *Narodnooslobodilačka borba u Dalmaciji: zbornik dokumenata* (Split: Institut za historiju radničkog pokreta Dalmacije, 1986) (hereinafter *Dalmacija 1941–1945*), Vol. X, p. 1530, Daily report of gendarmerie command Mostar (5 January 1944).

[31] *Zbornik*/XII/4/18–19, 2nd Panzer Army to 15th Mountain Corps (2 January 1944).

[32] The Germans learned about Kirschner's fate through signals intelligence (one such decrypt can be found in NARA, T-313, Roll 196, 7456774, 2nd Panzer Army/Intelligence section, Appendix to daily report for 28 December 1943). Rendulic remembered being shown an intercepted cable from Tito pertaining to this incident. In it, the Partisan supreme commander demanded an immediate report on "why the captured German pilot was killed contrary to the orders." In their reply, the Herzegovinian Partisans cited transportation difficulties and a misunderstanding, respectively, as the reasons for Kirschner's execution.

The change in the policy toward the Partisan prisoners, in general, is attributable to several factors. First, the events on the ground had proven once more that the guerrillas were insensitive to reprisals (against both civilians and their own comrades) and that sabotage continued on the same level as before.[33] Second, the Germans placed a great deal of faith in their new program aimed at increasing the number of defectors from the Partisan ranks.[34] And third, the negotiations with Tito's representatives concerning a cartel on prisoner exchange were making good progress. Further rounds of talks were held in Zagreb and Pisarovina in late September and late October. On the 26th, the Main HQ for Croatia informed Tito of the proceedings and requested the names of the prisoners worth exchanging. The Partisan leader responded in two telegrams over the next five days, naming several

---

Evidently, the negotiations on the creation of a neutral exchange zone had a positive effect on the Partisan leadership as well: "We did not have the impression that Tito encouraged the brutality of the Partisans. On the contrary, we knew for certain that he preferred to take prisoners in order to have them exchanged for the captured Partisans through negotiations." Lothar Rendulic, *Gekämpft, gesiegt, geschlagen* (Heidelberg: Verlag Welsermühl, 1952), p. 221.

[33] For more information on railway sabotage in Croatia during the second half of 1943, see the ten-day reports submitted by the General of Transportation to Army Group F in NARA, T-311, Roll 285, 000001–000592. The best example of how the threat of death failed to deter sabotage can be found in the daily report of the Inspector of Railway Security for 3 December 1943. The report states that the NDH commissioner for railways contemplated introducing pecuniary fines instead of hanging because the former "would have a much greater effect." NARA, T-313, Roll 486, 000296.

[34] Judging by the available sources, the program moved into full swing in November. In early November, a large-scale action was planned in northern and central Croatia where ten agents ("spiritual leaders of the new movement") were supposed to distribute 10,000 "defector passes" among the guerrillas. Reception camps were prepared in the nearby towns and a permanent camp for 1,000 people in Graz, Styria. NARA, T-313, Roll 484, 001068–9, 3rd SS Panzer Corps to 2nd Panzer Army, 9 November 1943. A steady, methodical approach by the 15th Mountain Corps had more success than this grandiose plan. The corps had established its own camp in Banja Luka by mid-November and tried to increase the number of defectors by providing them shelter, food, and the opportunity to communicate with their families. NARA, T-314, Roll 560, 000395–7, Defectors, 19 November 1943. This approach seemed to be working; whereas there were only 102 defectors in November, there were 994 in December and early January 1944, a ten-fold increase. Ibid., 000488, Intelligence report for the period 1 December 1943–10 January 1944, 12 January 1944. By early April 1944, the 15th Mountain Corps reported a total of 2,589 defectors in its sector in the previous six months. NARA, T-314, Roll 564, 000749, Monthly refugee report—defectors, 4 April 1944. There were a further ninety-nine defectors in May, less than half as many as in April. NARA, T-314, Roll 565, 000946, Monthly refugee report, 2 June 1944. Intelligence reports for the following months are not available, but it would be reasonable to assume that the numbers continued to drop due to the Third Reich's increasingly unfavorable war situation.

prominent Party members, some of whom were in camps in Italy and Slovenia, and others in Sarajevo or Zagreb.[35]

These people would have to wait for the second exchange, however, because the first one had already been made in Pisarovina. On 15 October 1943, Stilinović had a meeting with German envoys there and agreed to make the swap in one week. The exchange had to be postponed for another week, ostensibly in order to include more people into the bargain.[36] On 30 October 1943 at 12.00, sixteen German soldiers and NCOs and eleven Home Guard officers were swapped for sixty members of the People's Liberation Movement.[37] The 3rd SS Panzer Corps reported that "further exchange, on a 1:1 ratio, is being prepared."[38]

The first exchange was somewhat of a "test"—neither side committed its most valuable prisoners yet. Since the swap was conducted successfully and in good will, Stilinović could devote his next visit to Zagreb to discussing their exchange as a part of a wider agreement. By 4 November, he reported on the progress of the talks up to that point. The Germans proposed the establishment of prisoner exchange commissions on both sides and a permanent location for the exchanges. Stilinović was informed of Hitler's latest order concerning the treatment of captured Partisans and was even offered the opportunity to inspect the premises of the newly-created prisoner camps himself.[39] Aware of the Partisans' sensitivity to their

---

[35] *Sabrana djela,* Vol. XVII, pp. 138, 160, Tito to Main HQ for Croatia (27 and 31 October 1943). See also accompanying footnotes on p. 341.

[36] *Sjeverozapadna Hrvatska 1941–1945,* Vol. VI, p. 463, KPH District committee for Pisarovina to KPH County committee for Pokuplje (the document is dated 11 October 1943, but was probably written between 15 and 22 October).

[37] Fifty of these individuals (twenty-two men and twenty-eight women) came from the concentration camp at Stara Gradiška. The camp's Party organization wrote several months later that the majority of female exchangees were "negative," i.e. conducted themselves poorly while in *Ustashe* custody. VA, CK KPH, Roll 42, 340, Letter from the Party organization in Stara Gradiška (April 1944). In order to dispel any fears the inmates might have had about their departure from the camp, Stilinović sent a hand-written note to an acquaintance informing her of the exchange and suggesting she and other exchangees stay out of trouble on the way to Pisarovina. This remarkable document can be found in Antun Miletić, ed., *Koncentracioni logor Jasenovac 1941.–1945.: dokumenta* (Belgrade: Narodna knjiga, 1986–87) (hereinafter *Jasenovac 1941–1945*), Vol. III, pp. 323–24, Note to Terka Gojmerac, Pisarevina [*sic*], 30 October 1943.

[38] HR HDA 1450, Roll D-2224, 96, Statement of Vladimir Novaković (9 November 1943); NARA, T-313, Roll 484, 001097, Daily report of 3rd SS Panzer Corps for 1 November 1943.

[39] On 14 October 1943, the NDH's Ministry of Defense informed the ICRC that the organization of POW camps was being developed. HR HDA 1450, Roll D-2233, 134. One Partisan intelligence report from October confirmed that one such camp had been established on the outskirts of Zagreb. According to the report, the captured Partisans were initially placed under relatively minimal security and could even visit their acquaintances in the town, but

wounded, the Germans pledged to treat them in their military hospitals. In exchange, they demanded that their own men be treated humanely and that officers be freed from manual labor while in guerrilla captivity, as per provisions of the Geneva Convention. Knowing that Partisans could not take care of their prisoners for long, the Germans proposed that they be delivered to the nearest Axis unit; the commission in Zagreb would then make up the difference by delivering exactly the same number of men to their Partisan colleagues in Pisarovina.[40] Concerning individual prisoners, the Germans were especially interested in the exchange of some captured airmen and Lieutenant Colonel Pokay. He was reported to be in a Partisan prisoner camp where he had to perform the same menial tasks as the captured Home Guard officers; the only difference in treatment was that he was not hounded to join the Partisans.[41]

Tito sent his answer to the German proposals on 5 November. He felt that they were not offering enough prisoners for Pokay and also ordered the Main HQ for Croatia to postpone the exchange of the airmen. As for the negotiations on the cartel, Tito agreed they should be continued. He insisted that the members of the People's Liberation Movement who were not members of the armed units be treated in the same fashion as were the Partisans caught on the battlefield. This was an attempt to protect the Party members and sympathizers engaged in underground activities in occupied territories who, in the event of capture, faced deportation to NDH concentration camps or execution as hostages. Additionally, he demanded that the agreement be made in writing and that the Germans pledge they would obey the rules and customs of war "which they had already broken by shooting our wounded in Montenegro."[42] The last request was bound to come up sooner or later, knowing Tito's desire to be recognized as an equal. As for the Germans in Zagreb, the negotiations on the establishment of a full-fledged prisoner exchange cartel could not be carried out "under the table" indefinitely. The ever-cautious Glaise-Horstenau therefore wrote a letter to his old Austrian

---

that changed after some captives used an air raid alarm to escape. The report also confirmed that Partisans were not to be shot, but sent in groups of 200 to Germany. The order was, however, not heeded by some individual commanders: "The order is there as a rule, but exceptions are tolerated." HR HDA 1450, Roll D-1083, Report on conditions in Zagreb, p. 17 (undated, probably October 1943).

[40] *Sabrana djela*, Vol. XVII, p. 352–53; see the contemporary German translation available in NARA, T-313, Roll 196, 7456990, 2nd Panzer Army/Intelligence section, Appendix to daily report for 9 November 1943.

[41] HR HDA 1450, Roll D-2223, 513, Statement of Ivan Lalić (undated, probably early October 1943).

[42] *Zbornik*/II/11/33, Tito to Main HQ for Croatia (5 November 1943); also available in German in NARA, T-313, Roll 196, 7456979, 2nd Panzer Army/Intelligence section, Appendix to daily report for 12 November 1943.

acquaintance, Neubacher: "On this occasion, I would like to ask you for a favor. We have been negotiating with Tito's people concerning prisoner exchange for a long time. Counter-proposals made by the other side are being discussed as we speak and will be submitted for your approval. I would be grateful if you could legalize these contacts by granting me the [needed] authorization as per the latest directives from the *Führer*."[43]

In the meantime, Stilinović made another trip to Zagreb but returned to his base on 16 November. The Main HQ for Croatia informed Tito that very day of the news Stilinović brought back with him: the Germans agreed "in principle" to the proposal by Supreme HQ, but the last word still had to come from Belgrade (i.e. Neubacher/von Weichs). Once it arrived, they would propose a final draft of the agreement. The Partisans were requested not to mention the deal in their propaganda before it was finalized. In addition, the Germans re-affirmed their pledge not to shoot prisoners and stated that they had assumed responsibility for the behavior of all directly subordinated native troops, including Nedić's forces in Serbia. The arrangement was also valid for ordinary *Ustashe* formations, but not for Pavelić's elite bodyguard formation operating from Zagreb. The Main HQ for Croatia concluded its cable with the request to Tito to clarify who, and on whose authority, could agree to the final draft of the agreement. The supreme Partisan leader was also requested to issue orders regarding reciprocal treatment of German prisoners.[44]

On 18 November, Tito replied that the document could be signed by someone from the Main HQ for Croatia in the name of the Supreme HQ. Instead of confirmation that the order on the humane treatment of captured Germans had been issued, however, the cable brought radically different news: "The Germans have been hanging innocent peasants along the railroad lately; inform them that we shall do likewise to them if they do not stop."[45] This was not only an immediate reaction to Rendulic's policy of terror, but also a message that the NOVJ would reciprocate only when Glaise-Horstenau's promises began to be matched with deeds. Although reprisals against German soldiers were not carried out (at least not systematically), no steps aimed at regulating their status were taken, either. The main reason for this lay in the policy of expedience the Partisans practiced concerning prisoners. The Home Guards and Chetnik rank-and-file often put up only token resistance and surrendered in droves knowing that they would receive fair treatment or even be released after capture.[46] The Supreme HQ regulated the

---

[43] NARA, T-501, Roll 264, 000468, Horstenau to Neubacher (9 November 1943).

[44] *Sabrana djela*, Vol. XVII, pp. 362–63.

[45] *Zbornik*/II/11/90, Tito to Main HQ for Croatia (18 November 1943).

[46] This policy was practiced throughout the war, but could be revoked by local commands depending on the specific circumstances. For instance, the capitulation of Italy and the increased possibility of Allied landings in Dalmatia prompted the Main HQ for Croatia to

treatment of Italian prisoners as soon as it realized that this could bring practical advantages to the People's Liberation Movement. On 29 July 1943, five days after Mussolini lost a vote of no confidence at the Fascist Grand Council, the Main HQ of Croatia ordered the immediate release of all Italian enlisted men in anticipation of Italy's change of camp.[47] Fair treatment of Italians played a crucial role in the plan to win them over for a joint struggle against the Germans in Montenegro after 8 September 1943. "Beware of the recurrence of sectarianism in Montenegro and treat the Italians who lay down their weapons and come over to us in the best possible manner. Do not take any vengeance against them or you will bear full responsibility," wrote Tito.[48]

On 9 October, the Partisan supreme commander repeated this order with the addition that the Italian Fascists who committed crimes were to be brought before courts and tried.[49] This in effect meant that the old rules concerning captured Blackshirts were still in force. They, as with all other ideological enemies, could hope for little mercy. A month earlier, on 11 September 1943, Georgi Dimitrov sent a short cable to Tito from Moscow: "We agree with your proposal concerning the captured Russian soldiers of General Andrei Vlasov—death by firing squad."[50]

The fact that Russian emigrants serving in various Army, SS, and police formations in Yugoslavia had the same legal status as their German colleagues[51] did not

---

escalate violence against Chetnik prisoners. An order issued on 16 September 1943 stated that captured Chetniks "are to be shot because of the danger [their movement] represents at this time." VA, 110, 7, 13, Order of the Main HQ for Croatia (16 September 1943).

[47] HR HDA 1450, Roll D-1081, 166, Main HQ for Croatia to Military–judicial branch of the Main HQ for Croatia (29 July 1943). Only two days prior, these prisoners were supposed to be exchanged for some Partisans in Italian prisons. Ibid., 98, Military–judicial branch of the Main HQ for Croatia to Main HQ for Croatia (27 July 1943).

[48] *Zbornik*/II/10/315, Tito to 2nd Corps (22 September 1943). The "sectarianism" Tito was referring to was the "Red Terror" from late 1941 and early 1942.

[49] Ibid., p. 368, Tito to 2nd Corps (9 October 1943).

[50] *Komintern i Vtoraja mirovaja vojna*, Vol. II, p. 339, Dimitrov to Tito (11 September 1943). Soviet General Andrei Vlasov (1901–1946) surrendered to the Germans in July 1942 and then attempted to build an anti-communist army comprised of Russians who were, for various reasons, dissatisfied with Soviet rule. The term "Vlasovite" came to be used to denote all Soviet citizens who collaborated with the Germans.

[51] At the time, White Russian *émigrés* and ex-Soviet POWs were serving in two German formations in Yugoslavia: the Russian Protective Corps (*Wehrmacht*) and the 3rd Auxiliary Battalion of the 2nd Volunteer Police Regiment (*Polizei*). Timofejev, *Rusi*, pp. 46–49. It would therefore be reasonable to assume that Tito's proposal was aimed at the members of these formations. Judging by the number of references to Soviet citizens who had defected to the Partisans from various German units, the order was enforced only haphazardly. In March 1945, the Main HQ for Croatia was ordered to transfer all 420 Soviet citizens from

play any part in these considerations; they were seen not only as ideological foes, but also as traitors to Russia. In addition, their case provided Tito a good opportunity to improve his standing with the Kremlin, which had already suffered as the result of his independent policies on the ground.

Unlike the Home Guard, Chetnik, or Italian prisoners, the Supreme HQ had no use for captured Germans, at least not in the months following Operation *Schwarz*. The hope that the contacts from late 1942 and early 1943 would curb the worst excesses toward wounded Partisans and prisoners disappeared amidst the excessive brutality with which the German occupation forces carried out their late spring offensive. It appeared that sparing Germans would neither weaken their morale, nor cause reciprocity, nor induce their superiors to request their exchange. Attempts to "convert" captive Germans to the Partisan cause were all but completely abandoned.[52] One intelligence report of the 369th Infantry Division from October 1943 claimed that, according to the statements of several prisoners, Tito had ordered "everything in a German uniform killed."[53] Although it is unlikely that such an order had ever been issued in writing, this rumor is illustrative of the attitude of the Supreme HQ on the issue of German prisoners at the time.

The lack of prisoners meant, however, that the Partisans were in the dark as to German dispositions and intentions. Consequently, the Intelligence Branch of the Supreme HQ issued an order in mid-September 1943 that commanders, political officers, and common fighters should strive to take at least one prisoner for the purpose of questioning.[54] The last provision was partly attributable to the arrival of Allied military missions whose primary task was to gather intelligence on the German order of battle in the Balkans. In the words of U.S. Major Richard Weil, the Partisans "up to and including Tito were realists and horse-traders" who would facilitate the acquisition of intelligence in return for material help.[55] Although the need for information and Allied supplies probably saved some prisoners from

---

the ranks of Croatian units to Belgrade, where they would be handed over to the Red Army. VA, 119/4, 2–5/2, Main HQ for Croatia to Supreme HQ (13 March 1945).

[52] For one such attempt from late summer 1943, see NARA, T-313, Roll 488, 001282, Interrogation of Alois Nogly (26 September 1943).

[53] NARA, T-315, Roll 2155, 000063, Enemy intelligence report (15 October 1943).

[54] *Zbornik*/II/10/295, Intelligence branch of Supreme HQ, instructions to 2nd Bosnian Corps (13 September 1943).

[55] Franklin D. Roosevelt Library and Museum, Safe Files, Box 4, OSS April 1944–45, Report of Major Weil on Yugoslavia, p. 20 (undated, probably May 1944). 2nd Assault Corps wrote to the Main HQ for Sandžak on 15 December 1943 (*Zbornik*/I/16/279): "Marshal Tito has demanded that we capture at least one German prisoner. Allied missions request the same. Instruct all units to do so at all costs."

being shot out of hand, there was no guarantee that a local commander would not dispose of them once he got what he wanted.[56]

One of the best examples of how little even important prisoners mattered to the Supreme HQ at the time can be found in the recollections of Captain F. W. D. Deakin, a member of the British mission to Tito. In November 1943, Deakin was in Jajce, the new seat of the Supreme HQ and was visited one day by three senior Partisan officers. While chatting over a glass of brandy, they disclosed that a German officer had been captured and that he would be shot. Upon his request, Deakin was shown the major's *Soldbuch* (identification and service book), which clearly indicated he was serving with the *Abwehr* in Belgrade. Realizing the prisoner's value, the British captain requested that his fate be decided by the Supreme HQ. Heated discussion followed, in which the Partisans pointed out that Deakin's "consistent disapproval of the execution of German prisoners had been causing a rift between the two sides ever since the first British mission arrived." Seeing no point in discussing the matter further with his guests, Deakin appealed to Arso Jovanović, Chief of Staff of the Supreme HQ. The latter sided with his officers and flatly refused the request that the prisoner be released into British custody and flown to Bari for interrogation. In a last-ditch attempt to save the prisoner, Deakin requested a formal audience with Tito. During the conversation, Deakin explained "in a most tactful manner" that the Allied interrogators were much more experienced in handling these things and that the intelligence provided by this German could be of great benefit to both the Allies and the NOVJ. The British captain gave his word that a copy of the interrogation report would be sent to the Supreme HQ. Deakin later commented: "Tito approved my proposal without objections, but with one condition—the German major must be extradited to Yugoslavia after the war in order to stand trial. Perhaps this was only Tito's characteristic sense of humor and his way of teaching me a lesson for my stand on the whole issue of prisoners, which I have taken as my own responsibility."[57]

The wounded prisoner—"Captain Meyr," as Deakin recollected—was handed over to the British and flown to Bari at the beginning of December. His branch of service, and thus his potential value, had been known to the Partisans from the beginning, and it is not clear why they insisted on his execution. Still, he was spared the moment Tito concluded that doing so would further his relations with the Allies.[58]

---

[56] "20 October [1943]: two German NCOs of the 664th Artillery Regiment of the 114th *Jäger* Division captured: one small Škoda automobile, one machine gun, and two pistols. Both prisoners shot after interrogation." *Zbornik*/V/21/72, 20th Dalmatian Division, Activity report for the period 20–31 October 1943 (2 November 1943).

[57] F. W. D. Deakin, *Bojovna planina* (Belgrade: Nolit, 1973), pp. 284-86.

[58] The 20th Dalmatian Division reported that one of its detachments captured "a German captain, a member of the Gestapo and functionary of the German intelligence service in the Balkans" northeast of Trogir. *Zbornik*/V/21/571, 20th Division to 8th Corps (30 November

Drafting the Agreement, November 1943—January 1944

In the interim, the Partisan envoy returned to Zagreb on 19 November 1943 for a new round of talks. It was agreed that prisoner exchanges would be made exclusively in Pisarovina. In order to facilitate them, the village would be declared a "neutral zone," off-limits to Axis troops. General modalities of the cartel were also discussed[59] and the results included into a draft agreement comprised of seven articles. The first three articles dealt with the treatment of prisoners, wounded, and deceased along the lines of the Geneva Convention of 1929. Article 4 stipulated that the preceding rules would also apply to auxiliary services of the *Wehrmacht* (*Organisation Todt,* railway personnel, etc.) and similar elements of the NOVJ. The fifth point contained guidelines on prisoner exchange: the captives were to be swapped on a ratio of one-to-one and that both sides would act "generously," i.e. deliver prisoners as soon as they captured them, without waiting for immediate compensation. The sixth point dealt with two categories of prisoners for whom the rules would not apply: deserters from the German Army and Partisans caught in Axis uniform, but without proper NOVJ markings. The seventh point read that "upon signing," the agreement would become valid for the whole territory of the

---

1943). On at least two occasions in January 1944, the German envoys in Pisarovina inquired about the fate of a certain "pilot, Captain Brandelmeyr . . . captured near Trogir and taken to the Supreme HQ where he lies sick at the moment. . . . The Germans are willing to do anything [to exchange him]." HR HDA 1450, Roll D-1090, 515, Main Intelligence Center Croatia to Main HQ for Croatia (8 January 1944) and ibid., 667, Report on state of prisoner exchange (30 January 1944). Both "Meyr" and "Brandelmeyr" refer to the same person. German envoys, fearful of disclosing Brandelmeyr's real duties, claimed he was a pilot. In this way, they hoped to avoid drawing unnecessary attention as *Luftwaffe* aircrews always topped German exchange requests. In March 1944, German envoys told their Partisan counterpart that they discovered that Brandelmeyr had been shipped to the United States. *Jasenovac 1941–1945*, Vol. II, p. 727, Report on prisoner exchange (15 March 1944). Captain Otto Emil Friedrich Mayer was actually taken to the so-called "Camp 020," an interrogation center for captured German agents located in southern London. "Courageous enough to be indifferent to his fate," Mayer remained silent under interrogation. Retrieved from: http://discovery .nationalarchives.gov.uk/details/r/C11090194 John Bryden, *Fighting to Lose: How the German Secret Intelligence Service Helped the Allies Win the Second World War* (Toronto: Dundurn, 2014), EPUB file, Prologue. The same caution was exercised in the case of one Branko Bolić (alias "Herzeg," alias "Horvat"), one of the *Abwehr's* chief agents in Western Bosnia, who had been captured by the Partisans in early February 1944. The 15th Mountain Corps instructed the 373rd Infantry Division to bargain for Bolić's release if the Partisans offered him, but not to appear too eager in doing so. Herzeg was never offered for exchange, but was interrogated and executed after his capture. NARA, T-314, Roll 566, 000473, 15th Mountain Corps to 373rd Infantry Division (20 February 1944); *Nemačka obavještajna služba*, Vol. V, pp. 194, 246.

59 HR HDA 1521, Box 31, File 546 Stilinović, Statement of Hans Ott.

Independent State of Croatia, but that it should be widened "as much as possible to other parts of southeastern Europe, especially the whole Adriatic region and Serbian territory." On 29 November, Glaise-Horstenau sent a copy of the document to the NDH Ministry of Defense with the recommendation that it be used as a template for the ministry's own separate agreement with the NOVJ. He also requested that the prisoners taken by the NDH's armed formations be sent to German POW camps and that all exchange business be conducted centrally through the office of the plenipotentiary general. On 1 December 1943, the Croatian draft was submitted after it had been approved by the minister of defense.[60] One day later, the Main HQ for Croatia reported that Stilinović was back with the draft and that the signing of the agreement should take place in two weeks' time.[61]

Further prisoner exchanges were made parallel to the talks concerning the cartel. One report read that "the exchange of captured Germans is being conducted in an organized manner through the office of the plenipotentiary general, which maintains regular contacts with the insurgents." The 15th Mountain Corps therefore ordered its units to report German soldiers who were known to be in captivity and to spare "appropriate exchange prisoners (active Communists)."[62] Units on the ground were discouraged from leading direct exchange negotiations themselves or through the NDH civilian or military authorities. For instance, in early November, a locally exchanged Croatian lieutenant smuggled a note from three Germans in captivity who pleaded to be swapped. The request went up the chain of command and was ultimately granted by the 2nd Panzer Army, and at the same time, relayed to Glaise-Horstenau's staff.[63] The exchange of Home Guard officers was increasingly handled through this office as well, with Stilinović providing up-to-date lists during his frequent visits.[64]

The success of the first prisoner exchange and contacts in Zagreb and Pisarovina slowly began to influence the attitudes of Croatian Partisans. On the eve of the first attack on Virovitica in early November, the 12th Slavonian Division ordered that all captured Germans, *Ustashe,* and *gendarmes* "who seemed important

---

[60] HR HDA 1450, Roll D-2223, 102–4, Plenipotentiary General to Ministry of Defense (29 November 1943); For Croatian text, see ibid., 117–18.

[61] VA, 119/1, 1, 1, 89, Main HQ for Croatia to Supreme HQ (2 December 1943).

[62] NARA, T-314, Roll 560, 000303, Activity report of intelligence section for November 1943 (December 1944).

[63] NARA, T-313, Roll 488, 000443, German training battalion with the 4th Croatian Mountain Brigade to 187th Reserve Division (1 November 1943); ibid., 000442, 187th Reserve Division to 69th Reserve Corps (12 November 1943); ibid., 000441, 69th Reserve Corps to 2nd Panzer Army (17 November 1943); ibid., 000440, 2nd Panzer Army to Plenipotentiary General (24 November 1943).

[64] HR HDA 1450, Roll D-2222, 147, Plenipotentiary General to Ministry of Armed Forces (12 November 1943).

enough to be exchanged" had to be brought to the divisional HQ.[65] It turned out that the majority of the *Ustashe* and "Gestapo people" (referring most likely to German-Croatian police) who were taken prisoner during the fighting in the area over the next twelve days were not deemed important enough to be spared; "most" of the fifty-five captured were executed.[66] On 18 November, the Main HQ for Croatia ordered that "captured Germans are, in principle, not to be shot": information concerning their number and personal data should be sent to the aforementioned command which would use it for compiling the exchange lists. The same was to be done for captured Home Guards and *Ustashe,* as well as for all missing Partisans or individuals connected to the People's Liberation Movement. Furthermore, the units were forbidden from conducting exchanges on their own;[67] all prisoners were to be brought to the Main HQ for Croatia which would then swap them in Pisarovina.[68]

Two exchanges were completed during this period: one in late November and one on 12 December 1943. The Partisans received altogether seventy-nine of their sympathizers and Party members from NDH prisons and concentration camps (forty-seven on the first, and thirty-two on the second occasion).[69] Ivo Marinković was not among them, though Stilinović had reported a rumor on 16 November that he was alive and would probably be exchanged for Pokay. Realizing it was

---

[65] *Zbornik*/V/21/138, Order of 12th Slavonian Division for attack on Virovitica (4 November 1943). Capturing enough prisoners for exchange was a high-priority task of the division's 18th Brigade. Its intelligence officer had a list of important persons in the town and was ordered to round them up with the help of a special detachment.

[66] Ibid., 330, Activity report of 12th Slavonian Division for the period 1–15 November 1943 (16 November 1943). The German 69th Reserve Corps reported thirty-nine missing *Ustashe* and twenty Germans from Virovitica. NARA, T-313, Roll 485, 000317, Daily Report of 69th Reserve Corps for 16 November (17 November 1943). It is noteworthy that there were no *Wehrmacht* units in the town during the fighting.

[67] HR HDA 1450, Roll D-1154, 177, Order concerning the proper conducting of prisoner exchanges (18 November 1943).

[68] See, for instance, HR HDA 1450, Roll D-1082, 201–2, 1st Croatian Corps to Main HQ for Croatia (25 October 1943); ibid., 594, 2nd Assault Brigade of 8th Division to Main HQ for Croatia (9 December 1943).

[69] HR HDA 1491, Series/sub-series 2.41, p. 203, Summary of prisoner exchanges made hitherto (5 January 1945). (Note: due to the fact that most documents from this record group have multiple paginations, I have chosen to use the numbers under which these files are stored in the archive's digital repository. If, for whatever reason, original pagination is used, page numbers will appear in brackets.) The second group was comprised almost entirely of female inmates from Stara Gradiška (twenty-five out of thirty-two). Some of them were apparently not keen on being exchanged; one even begged the chief *Ustashe* overseer not to let her go. VA, CK KPH, Roll 42, 340, Letter from the Party organization in Stara Gradiška (April 1944).

futile to continue insisting on his release, the Partisans acquiesced to swap their long-time, high-ranking captive for other prisoners. The number and composition of the Axis prisoners from these two swaps is unknown, but it is certain that Pokay was among them.[70]

As the year drew to a close, so too did the negotiations. Stilinović arrived in Zagreb on 22 December 1943 and did not leave before 7 January 1944. Although some Germans remembered that this prolonged visit was "private in nature"[71] (i.e. not connected to the talks), it is clear that the Partisan delegate spent most of his time preparing for the next prisoner exchange and the signing of the agreement. On 26 December, Stilinović was issued a pass signed by Glaise-Horstenau himself, probably after a meeting they had in the general's HQ.[72] One day later, they met with the representative of the NDH Ministry of Defense, Colonel Žarko Verić. On this occasion, Stilinović stated that the Supreme HQ accepted the text of the draft from 29 November "in full," whereupon "the German side expressed the wish that the agreement be signed and its implementation begin as soon as possible." Verić then submitted the Croatian version to Pavelić for approval.[73]

While waiting for the next move from the Axis side, Stilinović worked out the details for the coming swap. He was given the names of several missing men whom the Germans were interested in for exchange, and was also requested to intervene with the Kalnik Detachment which had still not delivered some soldiers the Partisan side owed from the previous swap. On the last day of 1943, he visited twenty-four Partisan wounded, who in marked contrast to the standard German practice, had been taken prisoner several days before and brought to one of Zagreb's hospitals. It was agreed that they would be exchanged as soon as their wounds were healed.[74]

According to the German envoys, their wounded in Banja Luka were not as lucky; it was brought to Stilinović's attention that the Partisan units massacred inmates of a military hospital during the attack on that city on New Year's Day

---

[70] HR HDA 1450, Roll D-1090, 666, Report on state of prisoner exchange (30 January 1944).

[71] HR HDA 1521, Box 31, File 546 Stilinović, Statement of Willibald Nemetschek. Ott recalled that Stilinović stayed in Zagreb even longer, from 20 December to 15 January. Ibid., Statement of Hans Ott.

[72] HR HDA 1521, Box 31, File 546 Stilinović, Statement of Eugen von Pott.

[73] NDH Ministry of Defense to Military office of Poglavnik (28 December 1943); facsimile reproduced in Odić, *Neostvareni planovi,* p. 192.

[74] HR HDA 1450, Roll D-1090, 515, Main Intelligence Center Croatia to Main HQ for Croatia (8 January 1944); HR HDA 1521, Box 31, File 546 Stilinović, Statement of Willibald Nemetschek. These wounded were captured by the 371st Infantry Division which had been stationed in France and Italy prior to its transfer to Croatia in early December 1943; therefore, the division's troops were not as jaded as the units which had been serving in Yugoslavia for a longer period.

1944.[75] Upon receiving this protest, the Main HQ for Croatia requested a clarification from the Supreme HQ. On 16 January, Tito sent a cable in which he denied the massacre and pledged that the NOVJ would abide by international law. He also threatened reprisals for the killing of Partisan wounded be it by the Germans, *Ustashe*, or any other Axis formation: "We therefore demand that they fulfill their obligations in this respect." The Secretary General of the Croatian Communist Party, Andrija Hebrang, deemed it wiser to drop the threat of reprisals; he instructed the Partisan envoys to simply deny the accusations and convey assurances that the Partisan units were under orders to obey the rules and customs of war.[76] The Germans did not press this issue any further; however, they did insist on acquiring passes of safe conduct similar to the one issued to Stilinović. On 10 January 1944, their wish was granted and four German envoys received appropriate documents which read that they were authorized to approach the Partisan forward lines "regardless of their location" in order to conduct prisoner exchange. They were to be brought to the nearest command which would validate their passes and provide them with an escort: "All units of the People's Liberation Army are herewith ordered to assist the bearer of this document in all matters pertaining to the exchange."[77]

The final prisoner exchange made before the cartel officially came into effect was made in Pisarovina on 18 January 1944. According to the detailed six-page report to the Main HQ for Croatia, forty-four Germans, including two officers and eighteen NCOs, were swapped for the same number of Partisans from the German prisoner camps. Among the exchanged Partisans were two lieutenants and one political commissar of a battalion, and seven NCOs or junior political officers. In addition, sixteen *Ustashe* officials, policemen, and Home Guard officers were exchanged for sixteen inmates of the concentration camps at Jasenovac and Stara Gradiška. All in all, the Germans owed the Partisans one wounded man and one functionary who still had not been flown from Sarajevo as planned. There were at

---

[75] Banja Luka was the second largest city in Bosnia and the seat of several state ministries. The attack by the NOVJ's 5th Corps commenced on 31 December 1943 and was broken off on 1 January 1944. Most of the city was overrun, but the Germans managed to hold out in the old Ottoman fortress and in several other strongpoints. According to the report made by Dr. Byloff, there were nine patients in the hospital when the Partisans captured it and of these, two were killed, one was wounded, and one went missing. NARA, T-314, Roll 558, 000954, Losses according to the inquiries made so far (1 January 1944).

[76] *Sabrana djela*, Vol. XVIII, p. 192, Tito to Hebrang (16 January 1944). See also accompanying footnote on pp. 329–30.

[77] HR HDA, Roll D-1090, 149, Main HQ for Croatia to German Plenipotentiary General (8 January 1944); HR HDA 1521, Box 31, File 546 Stilinović, Statement of Willibald Nemetschek. The text is quoted from the pass issued to Hans Ott in October 1944 (HR HDA, Roll D-1090, 162, 14 October 1944), and there is no evidence to suggest that the one from January was any different.

least thirty-four German soldiers (some of them captured in Dalmatia)[78] who were available for the next swap. This did not represent the grand total of prisoners since many units in the field were slow in conveying exact figures. The envoys from Glaise-Horstenau's staff inquired about the fate of seventeen people who went missing between May and December 1943. The Partisan delegates could not provide any information, "and for most of them we have not even tried, as the chances are slight." The author of the report therefore proposed regulating this matter by concentrating all prisoners in several designated spots. For their part, the Partisans demanded a complete list of their people in German custody and also protested against the alleged poor conditions in German prisoner camps. There were also eleven individuals to be offered to the NDH authorities on the next occasion. The Partisans intended to organize their exchange in such a way as to receive fifteen to twenty of their own: "We can count on the support of the German officers in charge of the exchange, who could make this offer acceptable [to the *Ustashe*]." On the whole, the *Ustashe* were interested in swapping only those persons known to have friendly relations with, or family ties to, Pavelić and his entourage. The Germans on the contrary, showed great interest in the exchange, whether of officers or common soldiers. To this effect, they promised to include the following provision in the arrangement: if a Partisan patrol escorting the prisoners destined for exchange was ambushed by a German unit, the escorts would be freed, prisoners retained, and the Partisan side compensated with the same number of their fighters who would be delivered to Pisarovina.[79]

According to the same report, the Germans stated again that they would accept all prisoners delivered by local Partisan units outside of Pisarovina. Knowing that prisoners became a liability to the Partisans once they were surrounded or hard-pressed, the Germans devised a method which would preclude the worst from occurring. This modality was known as "delivering prisoners on receipt" or "exchange on receipt." The idea was that a Partisan unit, if in danger, could deliver its prisoners to the nearest German unit, and receive a receipt in return. With this receipt, the Partisans could claim the same number of prisoners from the Germans in Pisarovina. The proposal must have sounded practical to the Main HQ for Croatia for it had ordered all units under its command to undertake this course of action starting in mid-November 1943.[80] However, the Supreme HQ was not consulted beforehand, and once Tito learned of it in late January 1944, he immediately countermanded the order, most likely due to his apprehension about the lack of a guarantee that the Germans would honor their promises about the recently agreed

---

[78] See next chapter.

[79] HR HDA 1450, Roll D-1090, 664–70, Report on state of prisoner exchange (30 January 1944).

[80] HR HDA 1450, Roll D-1082, 386, Order concerning the proper handling of prisoner exchange (18 November 1943).

upon neutral zone. The Main HQ for Croatia responded that this modality was not a part of the agreement, and that the NOVJ had the right to deliver prisoners on receipt, but was not obliged to do so; it was the Germans who were actually obliged to even the balance in the event they received any of their men in this way.[81] Despite Tito's objections to this concept in general, the Main HQ of the Croatian Partisans managed to find a compromise. On 6 February 1944, it released an order according to which prisoners could be delivered with receipt to the enemy provided the unit in question had the express permission to do so. Such an arrangement admittedly still did not allow units to act independently and with the needed speed, but it did spare them the trouble of having to send prisoners on a long and arduous journey to Pisarovina.[82] In time, delivering captives on receipt would prove to be very practical and would become an integral aspect of the prisoner exchange cartel.

The first such exchange occurred in January 1944 and involved some 120 ethnic Germans from Slavonia. Before being drafted into village militias, police, the *Wehrmacht*, or the *Waffen-SS*, able-bodied ethnic Germans were required to serve in the Labor Service (*Reichsarbeitsdienst*) for a certain period of time. One of the labor camps was located at the village of Josipovac, outside of Osijek. In the last week of October 1943, the Partisans attacked the site and captured 184 workers who were then taken to guerrilla-held territory. On 4 November, the German police and security service command in Osijek rounded up 664 hostages from two villages and offered them in exchange for the captured laborers.[83] The Partisans would not accept civilians and demanded the same number of their fighters instead. A deal was reached: the ethnic Germans would be released in Slavonia as soon as possible, and the same number of men would be delivered to the NOVJ envoys in Pisarovina as they became available. Pursuant to the agreement, the 6th Corps appointed a plenipotentiary and contacted its nearest German counterpart in the second half of January 1944 in order to arrange the handover.[84] The first group of thirty Partisans was received on 21 January, and the remaining ninety arrived over the following months;[85] the last

---

[81] *Sabrana djela,* Vol. XVIII, p. 228, Tito to Main HQ for Croatia (29 January 1944); VA, 119/1, 2, 4, 51, Main HQ for Croatia to Supreme HQ (30 January 1944).

[82] *Zbornik*/V/24/503, Main HQ for Croatia to 6th and 10th Corps (6 February 1944).

[83] NARA, T-311, Roll 484, 001186, Daily report of 69th Reserve Corps (5 November 1943).

[84] *Građa za historiju narodnooslobodilačkog pokreta u Slavoniji* (Slavonski Brod: Historijski institut Slavonije, 1962–1984) (hereinafter *Slavonija 1941–1945*), Vol. X, p. 321, Letter of authorization for Mirko Habdija, 24 January 1944, and p. 227, 6th Corps intelligence section to the command of German troops, 17 January 1944.

[85] HR HDA 1450, Roll D-1090, 664, Report on the state of prisoner exchange (30 January 1944). According to a police report from the same month, the Partisans freed a total of 147 of their prisoners. Twenty-three ethnic Germans ("mostly those from mixed marriages or coming from culturally and linguistically de-Germanized settlements") chose to stay with

group of laborers, plus eight other prisoners, were released by the 6th Corps several days later.[86]

The previously quoted six-page report, dated 30 January 1944, also contained the following request to the Main HQ for Croatia: "The exact copy of the agreement, as made by Comrade Marijan [Stilinović], should be demanded from the Germans. The draft we possess has so many corrections and additions that it is not completely readable. . . . The agreement was sent for approval to the Germans in Belgrade and it should be returned any day now." Only a day earlier, Tito also requested a copy of the agreement.[87] The Croatian leadership responded that the document would be sent through courier and added: "The text of the agreement which is based on your instructions has been handed over to the Germans. . . . The text does not contain any commitments which would be detrimental to us. . . . We have informed you of this in our cables from 16 November and 2 December and asked for your opinion, but received no answer. The negotiations on prisoner exchange with the Germans were conducted by the Central Committee with our help and cooperation."[88]

These cables were exchanged exactly forty-five days after the date which had originally been set for the signing of the agreement (15 December). As described earlier, Stilinović came to Zagreb on the 22nd and had a productive two-week stay in the city, during which the draft was accepted by both sides and safe conduct passes issued to the envoys. We can assume that the commencement of the agreement was delayed over the issue of signing. It is unknown why the drafts included the provision regarding signing as this possibility had already been rejected by Neubacher on 19 November 1943: "Please inform the German plenipotentiary general . . . that there are no objections to these negotiations from a political standpoint, but all demands that German authorities commit themselves in writing to abide by international law in their conduct with prisoners and wounded must be refused, for this would represent the recognition of Tito as a [legitimate] belligerent power."[89]

---

the guerrillas, five of whom eventually came to the NOVJ's Thälmann Company. Redžić, *Telmanovci*, p. 15; Thomas Casagrande, *Die Volksdeutsche SS-Division "Prinz Eugen": die Banater Schwaben und die nazionalsozialistichen Kriegsverbrechen* (Frankfurt: Campus Verlag, 2003), pp. 283–84.

[86] VA, 119/1, 2, 4, 52–3, Main HQ for Croatia to 6th Corps (30 January 1944) and VA, 119/1, 2, 1, 75, 6th Corps to Main HQ for Croatia (31 January 1944).

[87] VA, 119/1, 2, 1, 71, Supreme HQ to Main HQ for Croatia.

[88] VA, 119/1, 2, 4, 51, Main HQ for Croatia to Supreme HQ (30 January 1944). Tito's silence during the last phase of negotiations caused frustration in the Croatian leadership. On 31 January, they sent a cable which read that they could not steer the war effort properly without clear and timely instructions from the top. Ibid., 53, Main HQ for Croatia to Supreme HQ (31 January 1944).

[89] Quoted in Odić, *Neostvareni planovi*, p. 193.

At the Tehran Conference, "The Big Three" decided to officially embrace the Partisan Movement as a member of the anti-Hitler coalition.[90] According to a post-war statement of General Hermann Förtsch, Chief of Staff of Army Group F, the *Wehrmacht* commanders began discussing whether they should do the same shortly after the news had reached occupied Yugoslavia. On behalf of Colonel General Löhr and Field Marshal von Weichs, Förtsch suggested to the Armed Forces High Command that the NOVJ be recognized as a legitimate belligerent. The request, the general added, was based on expediency rather than on the conviction that the Partisans fulfilled all the requirements prescribed by international law. The recognition should serve two purposes: first and foremost, it should make the Partisans conduct themselves like regular armed forces where the treatment of prisoners was concerned; second, the German commands in the country hoped that Berlin would be more inclined to grant them extra resources and medals (which, in the Balkans, were awarded sparingly compared to the main fronts) if they fought a regular opponent. The request was denied.[91] In the first days of 1944, the Commander-in-Chief Southeast officially requested that the Armed Forces High Command approve the organization of the exchange cartel. On 9 January, the answer from Berlin arrived: "Prisoner exchange with Tito is allowed, whereby it must be made clear that this in no way represents the recognition of Tito's bandits as a [legitimate] belligerent power."[92] Seeing that Glaise-Horstenau's hands were tied and that the insistence on signing would only endanger the whole project, the Partisans backed down. Instead, both sides verbally pledged to honor the treaty without actually signing it.[93]

The final text of the treaty had a total of twelve articles, and the Partisans received a copy in the first days of February 1944. Technical details were agreed upon as follows: the village of Pisarovina and its environs in a five-kilometer radius was declared a neutral zone; Axis troops would not attempt to occupy the village

---

[90] *Foreign Relations of the United States* [hereinafter FRUS]: *Diplomatic Papers, The Conferences at Cairo and Tehran, 1943* (Washington, DC: GPO, 1961), p. 652, Military conclusions of the Tehran Conference (1 December 1943).

[91] Böhme, *Die deutschen Kriegsgefangenen,* Vol. I/1, pp. 82–83. I could not find any evidence of the alleged request in primary sources. Förtsch's statement, given before the U.S. military tribunal in 1947, is somewhat dubious considering that German witnesses often portrayed the army in the best possible light.

[92] Quoted in NARA, T-77, Roll 1419, 001100, ICRC's care for German prisoners in Tito's bandits captivity (9 November 1944).

[93] HR HDA 1521, Box 31, File 546 Stilinović, Statements of Hans Ott and Eugen von Pott. Yugoslav historiography confirms that the deal was not signed. Odić, *Neostvareni planovi,* p. 193; *Sabrana djela,* Vol. XVII, p. 355. By January 1944, the Partisans might also have had a good reason not to sign the agreement (see below).

and the Partisans were obliged to hold it with no more than fifteen to twenty men;[94] in case Axis troops had to move through the zone, no harm would be wrought upon either civilians or the Partisan guard detail; the NOVJ agreed to refrain from using the zone for staging offensive actions; the *Luftwaffe* and the NDH Air Force would not undertake reconnaissance flights over the zone or bomb the village; and the Partisans would not interdict traffic on the Zagreb–Klinča Sela–Pisarovina road which would be used for prisoner transport.[95]

These provisions were not yet final and were discussed by the envoys in the following months. In late February 1944, the word came through that the Germans allegedly demanded the right to post their own guard detail in Pisarovina. The Main HQ for Croatia replied on 3 March with the following: "The county of Pisarovina is our liberated territory. In order to facilitate the prisoner exchange, we have chosen to refrain from undertaking operations in one of its areas and convert it into a neutral zone. [Consequently] the presence of a foreign army there is out of the question."[96]

Approximately two weeks later, the Partisan representative informed his superiors that this information was incorrect and that the enemy had no interest in keeping its troops in the village. At the same time, both sides agreed to retain the zone in Pisarovina, although there were suggestions to the contrary. The Germans said that they were interested not in the size of the zone as much as its inner workings; for instance, they proposed the establishment of two sub-zones within the area. The outer one would include the terrain within a five-kilometer radius from the village church which should be spared from aerial bombing. The inner ring would be two kilometers in diameter and the Partisans would not keep troops there. The space in between the two rings could "theoretically" be used by the latter for troop movements, but the Axis ground forces would have the right to attack them.[97]

On the same occasion, the delegates also discussed one core provision of the treaty. German sources claimed that Partisans shot sixty-four captured policemen

---

[94] One Partisan order from early March 1944 reads: "No unit is allowed to remain at Pisarovina [for a longer period of time]." *Zbornik*/V/25/53, Daily order of 2nd Brigade of 8th Division for 3 March 1944.

[95] HR HDA 1521, Box 31, File 546 Stilinović, Statement of Willibald Nemetschek. Dragutin Kabalini, a Partisan intelligence operative from Zagreb, reported on the terms in a report written shortly after 5 February 1944. Boris Bakrač, "Razmjena ratnih zarobljenika i uhapšenika na području Pisarovine," in *Treća godina narodno-oslobodilačkog rata na području Karlovca, Korduna, Like, Pokuplja i Žumberka* (Karlovac: Historijski arhiv u Karlovcu, 1977), p. 846.

[96] Ibid.

[97] *Jasenovac 1941–1945*, Vol. II, p. 725, Report on prisoner exchange (15 March 1944). One German document reads that Glaise-Horstenau had simply "reduced" the size of the perimeter to two kilometers on an unspecified date. NARA, T-314, Roll 1546, 000484, 1st Cossack Division to 69th Reserve Corps (12 May 1944).

near the town of Čazma in late November 1943. Spurred by this information, the Germans inquired after the possibility of including the members of the police and the SS into the exchange arrangement, which should also entitle them to protected status. Their side would in turn agree to treat members of the People's Liberation Councils and underground workers as "military personnel on a special mission." The Germans also protested against the execution of one Muhamed Hadžiefendić who held the rank of a German major. It was alleged that his only guilt was that he, as a Muslim, had joined a foreign army.[98] Lastly, it was also demanded that the relatives of those who served in German formations not be persecuted in any way by the Partisans. The NOVJ's representative denied that the massacre at Čazma took place ("of course I refused to confirm it") and said that the family members of German servicemen were expelled, presumably from the Partisan-held territory, only if they engaged in hostile activities such as espionage. It seems that the conversation was merely informative in nature and that the Germans did not insist on firm commitments from the other side on any of the issues.[99]

During the same meeting, the German plenipotentiaries also requested a list of all officers and men captured by the Partisans in Bosnia and Herzegovina. This point leads us to the question of how these provinces, which continued to bear the brunt of the fighting, were incorporated into the cartel. The preamble of the draft from late November 1943 stated that the agreement was valid for the whole of the NDH; in reality, this was never the case. The exchange cartel was basically valid only for the area of responsibility of the Main HQ of Croatia (4th, 6th, 8th, 10th, and 11th Corps of the NOVJ) which approximated the borders of present-day Croatia. Of the two original Bosnian Corps, the 3rd and 5th, only the latter was included into the cartel by means of participating in exchanges "on receipt." The sources are silent as to why the 3rd Corps did not take part in the arrangement, but one possible answer lies in geography. The 5th Corps was responsible for the area to the west of the River Bosna and the 3rd for the area east of it. This meant that the former was in closer proximity to the Croatian Partisans (Pisarovina is only sixty kilometers by road from the Bosnian border) and could communicate more easily with the Main HQ of Croatia. Although the 3rd Corps also covered a large

---

[98] The matter was not as simple as that because Hadžiefendić served as an officer in three different armies prior to 1943. The Muslim militia he created in northeastern Bosnia in late 1941 was held responsible for plundering and committing atrocities against the Serbs. In early 1943, this formation served as a cadre for the *Waffen*-SS Mountain Division *Handschar*. When the Partisan units entered Tuzla in early October 1943, they captured Hadžiefendić and sentenced him to death. *Tko je tko*, pp. 148–49.

[99] *Jasenovac 1941–1945*, Vol. II, pp. 725–26, Report on prisoner exchange (15 March 1944). Members of police formations, especially of the mixed German-Croatian units, remained outside the protection of the agreement. For example, according to German sources, Slavonian units shot most of the 150 policemen captured in Podgorač in June 1944. HR HDA 1451, 2.41, 156–7, (untitled) (4 August 1944).

part of Central Bosnia, its main task was to maintain the Partisan presence in Eastern Bosnia and use it as a springboard for any offensive operations into Serbia. For example, the air distance between Majevica Mountain (where 3rd Corps' HQ was located in early February 1944) and Pisarovina was some 270 kilometers. The distance to the Partisan stronghold in Eastern Herzegovina (held by the 29th Division, which was at first independent and later subordinated to the 2nd Assault Corps based in Montenegro) was even greater. Transporting prisoners over such a large swath of terrain, a good part of which was in the hands of various hostile formations, was out of the question. As will be shown in the next chapter, the warring sides in Eastern Bosnia and Herzegovina tried at least twice during 1944 to duplicate the Pisarovina cartel and exchange their prisoners on a more regular basis, but these attempts were only partially successful.

The other possibility is that the Partisan leadership refused to enter into any agreements which would make it recognize, directly or indirectly, the Croatian puppet state. As we know, Stilinović accepted the clause concerning the validity of the agreement for the "whole of the NDH" in late November 1943. The Partisan movement, of course, never recognized the regime in Zagreb, but the move was considered a formality. After all, it was a small sacrifice compared to the immense practical dividends of a permanent exchange agreement. Things may have changed as a result of Tito's intervention at some point in January 1944, after which the Main HQ for Croatia replied that his "instructions" were followed and that the agreement contained no provisions "detrimental" to the Partisan cause. The intervention possibly came as the result of the second session of the AVNOJ and the creation of the Communist-sponsored interim Yugoslav government. In light of these developments, Tito had to avoid any concession, however informal, which could compromise the new government and make it appear as though it accepted the German rearrangement of the Western Balkans from 1941. Consequently, it was possible that the cartel was formally downgraded to include only the units under the command of the Main HQ which was responsible for Croatia, but not Bosnia and Herzegovina. In this case, the 5th Corps was involved with the cartel only because it could provide more German prisoners for exchange and had the means of coordinating its actions with the Croatian Partisans.[100]

After almost seven months of talks (July 1943–January 1944), the delegates of the Main Partisan HQ for Croatia and the office of the German plenipotentiary general in Croatia had finally reached an agreement on the permanent exchange of prisoners. It was hoped that the cartel would provide a modicum of protection to

---

[100] The first hypothesis about the exclusion of eastern parts of Bosnia and Herzegovina from the cartel is based on the fact that I have never encountered any mention of the Pisarovina arrangement in any of the primary or secondary sources pertaining to the war in this country. The second is purely speculative; the final text of the agreement would probably solve the mystery, but, unfortunately, I have not been able to obtain a copy.

prisoners of both sides and facilitate their speedy exchange. It remained to be seen whether the system would continue to work in practice, and if the German occupation forces and the NOVJ would be willing to honor their commitments from the treaty which, from a legal perspective, amounted merely to a "gentlemen's agreement."

The Functioning of the Neutral Zone, February–December 1944

Before examining the inner-workings of the cartel, some detail should be provided pertaining to the people on both sides who negotiated the deal and made the first exchanges in Pisarovina. Stilinović was originally chosen to lead the talks since he had already proven his diplomatic skills in the summer of 1942 and was on good terms with his German counterparts. The treatment of the Partisan envoy during his visits in Zagreb was always correct. He could move freely around the city (albeit escorted by a German NCO) and visit friends and relatives. During one of his early stays in Zagreb, Stilinović was accommodated in the city's best hotel, the Esplanade. Soon, however, he moved into the flat where his mother and sister were living. Although Ott remembered that he, unlike Velebit, never requested special protection for his family, Stilinović did ask for and obtain special passes which placed his closest relatives under German protection and enabled them to visit the Partisan territory outside of Zagreb.[101] The Partisan-German "friendship" reached its height when Stilinović invited two of his German colleagues to a family dinner at his home on Christmas 1943.[102]

It turned out that his long visit to Zagreb at that time was to be the last in his capacity as chief delegate for the prisoner exchange. With the agreement reached, the Main HQ for Croatia decided that Stilinović should return to other duties. While he would continue to appear at the meetings in Pisarovina to discuss delicate issues, running the day-to-day business of exchange was entrusted to someone else. In December, Stilinović presented his successor to the Germans. On 8 January 1944, the Main HQ issued a letter of authorization to "Stanko Perović," the new Partisan envoy. Two days later, Glaise-Horstenau's office issued him with a German safe-conduct pass. Perović was in fact the pseudonym of Josip Brnčić, a high Communist official from Zagreb and an officer of the Main Intelligence Center of the Main HQ of Croatia.[103] As will become clear later, he had strong personal reasons for participating in the exchange process.

---

[101] HR HDA 1521, Box 31, File 546 Stilinović, Statements of Hans Ott and Willibald Nemetschek.

[102] HR HDA 1521, Box 31, File 546 Stilinović, Statement of Willibald Nemetschek.

[103] HR HDA 1450, Roll D-1090, 148, Authorization for Stanko Perović (8 January 1944); HR HDA 1521, Box 31, File 65 Brnčić, Statement of Eugen von Pott; HR HDA 1450, Roll D-1083, 48, Composition of Main Intelligence Center (undated, probably late 1943).

All the German envoys were either members of Glaise-Horstenau's staff or his confidants. The most important among them remained Hans Ott. After his contract with the Hansa Leichtmetall Company expired in March of 1943, Glaise-Horstenau found him a job as an associate of the *Abwehr's* branch in Zagreb. When the Partisans in Croatia signaled their willingness to negotiate, Ott was in Herzegovina, helping to establish an *Abwehr* network there.[104] Thanks to his extensive involvement in the contacts with the Partisans, Ott's main task in the summer of 1943 was to "break the ice" and facilitate the conduct of the talks—for instance, he was the one who introduced new members of the German team to the Partisan envoys. In autumn of that year, Glaise-Horstenau deemed that Ott, as a civilian, should not be involved with the exchange of the Army personnel. Consequently, he took an active part in the exchange talks only if they involved captured members of *Organisation Todt.*[105] The second reason for this decision was that Glaise-Horstenau felt that Ott should not waste his time and energy on technicalities of the everyday exchange business. He, just as his veteran counterpart Stilinović, would continue to return to Pisarovina only when there were more important matters to discuss.

The man in charge of the German commission (*Deutsches Sonderkommando für den Gefangenenaustausch,* or German Special Commando for Prisoner Exchange) was Major Eugen von Pott, who acted as Glaise-Horstenau's first intelligence officer as well as his first operational officer. He and Stilinović had negotiated the details of the cartel agreement in Zagreb and had, over time, developed very good relations.[106] The rest of the German team consisted of several officers and clerks whose main tasks were to put the exchange agreement into practice, including searching for prisoners, updating the exchange lists, and making trips to Pisarovina to make the swaps. Lieutenant Model, an O3 (second intelligence officer) in the office of the plenipotentiary general, took an active part in the dialogue from the second half of 1943, playing "the leading role on the German side" during the rounds of talks held in Pisarovina. At the end of the year, he was transferred to the 1st Cossack Division and met his tragic end shortly thereafter. Model was shot dead by a German sentry on New Year's Eve 1943 after failing to respond to calls to halt.[107]

---

[104] Odić, *Neostvareni planovi,* pp. 249–50. Odić claims Ott received a general's pay on a monthly basis for his services. Kasche, on the contrary, claimed that Ott's job was "honorary" and that he only received funds to cover his expenses. HR HDA 1521, Box 9, File 164 Ott, Statement of Siegfried Kasche. Ott was known in Zagreb for his "jovial" personality, "and obviously had enough money to spend." Ibid., Statement of Albrecht von Brauchitsch.

[105] HR HDA 1521, Box 9, File 164 Ott, Statement of Willibald Nemetschek.

[106] HR HDA 1521, Box 31, File 546 Stilinović, Statements of Eugen von Pott and Willibald Nemetschek.

[107] HR HDA 1521, Box 9, File Model, Statement of Willibald Nemetschek. Model managed to combine business with pleasure during his visits to Pisarovina. He made a number of

Two additional members of the exchange commission who should be mentioned here were ethnic Germans from Croatia. One was Eduard Peternell, an NCO with *Organisation Todt* and an acquaintance of Ott since 1942. He joined Glaise-Horstenau's staff prior to September 1943.[108] Like Ott, Peternell was chiefly responsible for the exchanges of OT members. The other was Willibald Nemetschek, a twenty-seven-year-old native of Zagreb and a *Sonderführer* (Z)[109] with Glaise-Horstenau's staff. He had served as an interpreter until the summer of 1943 when he was transferred to the exchange detail. He was introduced to the Partisans in Pisarovina in September of that year and was soon to become a leading member of the German team.[110]

Othmar Unger, a *Wehrmacht* non-commissioned officer, became Nemetschek's aid in early 1944, just in time to witness the functioning of the exchange system at its height. He described the mechanism in some detail:

> A prisoner exchange was set up in the following way: the Partisans informed us, usually through a courier, that they would like to send envoys to the office [of the plenipotentiary general] for a meeting. They would then be picked up by a German car and brought to Zagreb. The lists of the prisoners wanted [were exchanged] and . . . the next meeting scheduled, usually in one to two weeks' time. A copy of the list would then be sent to various German and Croatian establishments tasked with keeping Partisan prisoners. . . . Getting the prisoners from the *Wehrmacht's* military camp was the easiest. The Commander-in-Chief Southeast would order their release as soon as he received the request from [Glaise-Horstenau's] Chief of Staff. . . . If necessary, Nemetschek would visit camps and prisons in person in order to affect the transfer of those people wanted for exchange. He obtained the prisoners from the camps in Slavonski Brod and Zenica, the *Ustashe* prison at Savska cesta, the SS [prison] at the former Kulin Ban Square, and the SS camp "Jankomir" in Stenjevac.[111] [The prisoners would also come] from Dachau, Buchenwald,

---

female acquaintances there and courted the cousin of a local tavern keeper, whom he subsequently took to Zagreb.

[108] HR HDA 1521, Box 9, File 196 Peternell, Statement of Willibald Nemetschek.

[109] *Sonderführer,* or "special leaders," were individuals drafted into the *Wehrmacht* who possessed special skills but lacked military training, and were considered unsuitable for front-line service. *Sonderführer* (Z) corresponded to the rank of lieutenant.

[110] HR HDA 1521, Box 9, File 289 Nemetschek, Statement of Willibald Nemetschek.

[111] The latter three camps were all situated in Zagreb. The SS camp "Jankomir" was the main collection point for the Partisans captured by the Germans; its capacity was between 200 and 300 people. Slavko Odić and Slavko Komarica, *Noć i magla: Gestapo u Jugoslaviji* (Zagreb: Centar za informacije i publicitet, 1977), pp. 255–56.

and Ravensbrück camps in Germany. According to Nemetschek, particular individuals often could not be found, so other prisoners were simply put in their stead. . . . If the desired prisoners were in the custody of the *Ustashe* or the SS, the former would make the exchange difficult. Glaise-Horstenau himself had to intervene every now and then.[112] . . . In the end, [we] usually succeeded in locating the desired prisoners. Apart from [these problems], it was not always easy to make contact with the Partisans . . . [especially] if Partisan units unfamiliar with the exchange were moving around Rakov Potok, or in cases when we did not know if the higher commissars, Stilinović or Bakrač, were in Pisarovina at that moment. In such a case, Nemetschek would go to the *Wehrmacht's* prisoner camp or the *Ustashe* prison at Savska cesta and find a Partisan who would volunteer to go to Pisarovina and return [with a reply]. . . . As soon as there were ten to thirty Partisans available, trucks would take them to Pisarovina where a similar number of German prisoners would be waiting.[113]

Both the *Sonderkommando* and the Partisan commission had the unenviable job of choosing the candidates for exchange. Requests from up and down the hierarchy had to be carefully considered when compiling the official document. The Germans had an easier task in this respect, as they were basically interested in every one of their missing soldiers and had more than enough prisoners to offer in return. The issue was much more complicated on the NOVJ side. The individuals chosen for exchange by higher commands (i.e. Supreme HQ, regional HQs, and Party committees) were always at the top of every list. Lower commands put forth their proposals through the chain of command in the hopes of influencing the choice. One such request came from the 5th Bosnian Corps to exchange four people from the Muslim-populated Cazin Krajina in Western Bosnia, with the explanation that these individuals "could do more [for us] in Muslim Krajina than all other political workers combined."[114] A second instance occurred in March 1945 when the editorial board of the Party newspaper, *Naprijed*, requested the exchange of one of its members, explaining that he had been in the Partisan ranks for a long time, that several of his family members had died in combat (a brother, a first cousin, and an uncle) or were missing (his mother and a second brother), while the

---

[112] The plenipotentiary general intervened for prisoners of both sides: "[Glaise-]Horstenau helped an incredible number of people. [Archbishop Alojzije] Stepinac also got several of his people out through him." KAW, B/67:145, Interview with Willibald Nemetschek conducted by Peter Broucek (10 September 1981).

[113] HR HDA 1521, Box 9, File 289 Nemetschek, Statement of Othmar Unger.

[114] HR HDA 1450, Roll D-1091, 34, Exchange of our prisoners (10 March 1944). At the time, all warring factions were striving to win over the Muslim population in the region.

third brother was also with the Partisans.[115] However, due to the ever-changing situation (the requested people could not be found or even refused to be exchanged), the envoys often had to make changes on the spot using their own discretion. This fact made them very influential and they were literally bombarded with pleas for exchange of, or information about, friends or family members of various individuals.[116] The universal rule applied here—the more powerful the individual, the more likely his "candidates" were to be accepted for exchange.[117] Personal interventions seemed to have gotten out of hand by mid-1944, as illustrated by a bitter letter from an underground Party organization in Stara Gradiška concentration camp to the Central Committee of the *Komunistička partija Hrvatske* (KPH, or Communist Party of Croatia). According to the letter, the exchange system was seriously abused: inmates of dubious conduct, but with good connections on the outside, were exchanged, whereas worthy Party members were left to rot in the camp.[118]

The end of 1943 and the first weeks of 1944 were marked by several *Ustashe*-related incidents. Pursuant to the negotiations in Zagreb, German troops which entered Pisarovina on 27 December vacated the village and its surroundings only two days later. Just as the Germans left, the *Ustashe* came to the village on 29 and 30 December with the intention of making some arrests. One of the people they caught was fortunate to have the German envoys in the village at that very moment. According to the local *Komunistička partija Jugoslavije* (KPJ, or Communist Party of Yugoslavia) branch, they "ordered the *Ustashe* to release him and leave Pisarovina and Kupčina immediately, and [added] that they do not have the right to come here at all."[119]

On 12 January, Glaise-Horstenau received a letter from his old friend and subordinate, Captain Arthur Haeffner: "I can happily inform you," wrote the Captain, "that the exchange of my nephew, despite the sabotage of some Croatian 'friends of Germany,' succeeded thanks to a lucky coincidence." Haeffner's nephew was supposed to be exchanged for Dr. Dančević, a native of Pisarovina, who was believed to be held in an NDH prison. On 8 January, after nine days of effort and Glaise-Horstenau's personal intervention, the *Ustashe* police finally promised to inform

---

[115] HR HDA 1491, 2.41, 33, Naprijed to comradely 3rd Directorate of OZNA (24 March 1945).

[116] One such request can be found in ibid., 22, Dear Lieutenant Colonel (20 February 1945).

[117] The future head of the Croatian secret police had thus succeeded in exchanging his wife in October 1943. *Jasenovac 1941–1945*, Vol. II, p. 612 (Letter from Ivan Krajačić to Rade Bulat, undated) and p. 678.

[118] Ibid., pp. 755–57, KPH Organization in Stara Gradiška to KPH Central Committee (15 August 1944).

[119] *Sjeverozapadna Hrvatska 1941–1945*, Vol. VIII, p. 30, KPH District committee for Pisarovina to KPH County committee for Pokuplje (3 January 1944).

the plenipotentiary general about the doctor's whereabouts. Two days later, while driving to Pisarovina, Nemetschek encountered Dančević by coincidence, who was on his way home. Nemetschek quickly put him in the car and exchanged him for Haeffner's nephew as planned. "There can be no doubt," the letter concluded, "that Dr. Dančević was simply released so that [we] could be told that he had not been in the custody of the *Ustashe* police in the first place. It is certainly not the last time that the *Ustashe* allow themselves such impudence."[120]

The third incident occurred on the night of 15 January 1944 when a group of *Ustashe* burst into Pisarovina and killed a local Communist Party official, wounded one Partisan, and captured another. Some said that the motive for the incursion was a bet among the perpetrators; others suspected that it was done with the purpose of spoiling the relations between the Partisans and the Germans.[121] Brnčić's aide, Dušan Tepšić, informed Ott about the attack, whereupon the latter immediately telephoned the NDH command and said, "Hopefully, these things will not happen again." After the chief Partisan envoy filed a protest from the Main HQ for Croatia, the Germans promised to do everything they could to reign in the *Ustashe*, at the same time voicing their doubts about the ultimate success of these endeavors. As a sign of goodwill, it was promised that the captured Partisan from Pisarovina would be returned without compensation. The Germans were true to their word, and he was released from prison in Karlovac that same month.[122]

Because of these unfortunate events, it must have been difficult for Brnčić to negotiate with the *Ustashe* directly, but he had little choice—his brother was known to be in the Jasenovac concentration camp. During one of his two or three visits to Zagreb (the sources differ), he met with an official of the NDH's Ministry of Interior, Blažeković. They discussed the terms of the exchange of a number of inmates from Jasenovac, including Brnčić's brother. The rest of the time was spent updating the prisoner lists in conjunction with von Pott and persuading some of the captured Partisans to be exchanged—not an uncommon occurrence, as many prisoners suspected foul play. While off duty, Peternell and Nemetschek hosted dinners for their Partisan guests. It seems that the delegates had developed very friendly relations in the short period they worked together; Brnčić revealed his real name to Nemetschek and promised him protection after the war.[123] An unpleasant episode in the village of Zdenčina (some ten kilometers northwest of Pisarovina) may have served to forge these ties. On one of the trips to Zagreb, the envoys were

---

[120] NARA, T-501, Roll 265, 000026, Haeffner to Horstenau (12 January 1944).

[121] HR HDA 1450, Roll D-1090, 772, Excerpts from various reports (9 February 1944).

[122] Ibid.; HR HDA 1450, Roll D-1090, 668, Report on state of prisoner exchange (30 January 1944); *Sabrana djela*, Vol. XVIII, p. 330.

[123] HR HDA 1521, Box 31, File 65 Brnčić, Statement of Willibald Nemetschek. In 1947, Nemetschek pleaded with Brnčić on behalf of his uncle, who had been arrested. The uncle was released before Brnčić had time to intervene.

forced to spend the night in the village due to heavy snow. Some drunken German officers did not like Brnčić's presence and resolved to kill him despite the fact that he was under General Glaise-Horstenau's protection. Only after Peternell and Nemetschek had drawn their pistols and advised Brnčić to do likewise if need be did the officers back down.[124]

During his tenure as the man in charge of prisoner exchanges, Brnčić organized four swaps in Pisarovina, the first one taking place on 21 January as previously mentioned. There was a pause until 10 March, when the Partisans received fifty-seven people (one of them Brnčić's brother who would be killed only a month later), and then an additional thirty on 15 March 1944.[125] Twelve days later, the fourth and final exchange occurred: five Party members from concentration camps and sixteen common Partisans were exchanged for a similar number of Axis captives.[126] In his letters to the Main HQ for Croatia from this period, Brnčić reported on the current state of affairs, listed the names of the persons wanted by either the Germans or the NDH authorities, and gave recommendations. He concluded the letter dated 27 March 1944 with the request that the Main Intelligence Center inform his successor of all details pertaining to the exchange business.[127] The end of Brnčić's short career as the main Partisan negotiator coincided roughly with the release of his brother. This led many of his German colleagues to conclude that this personal connection was the reason for his appointment to the job.[128] Brnčić, of course, could not choose his job and had to go wherever he was sent; his withdrawal in late March was because the newly-created 10th Zagreb Corps of the NOVJ needed an experienced intelligence officer.[129] Despite his transfer, he would continue to play a role in the contacts with the Germans throughout 1944.

Brnčić "initiated" his successor by taking him along during the last exchange. He was Boris Bakrač, a thirty-two-year-old technical engineer from Zagreb who, unlike Stilinović—a Communist since the early 1920s—became a full Party member only

---

[124] Brnčić told the story to his successor. Bakrač, "Razmjena ratnih zarobljenika," pp. 845–46.

[125] HR HDA 1491, 2.41, 203, Summary of prisoner exchanges made hitherto (5 January 1945). These prisoners included the Partisans owed for the release of the ethnic German laborers.

[126] The 6th Slavonian Corps delivered altogether twenty-seven German prisoners on two occasions near Požega in late March 1944. *Zbornik*/V/25/636, Main HQ for Croatia for 6th Corps (21 March 1944).

[127] HR HDA 1450, Roll D-1091, 59–60, Brnčić to Main HQ for Croatia (dated between 15 and 27 March 1944).

[128] HR HDA 1521, Box 31, File 65 Brnčić, Statements of Willibald Nemetschek and Hans Ott.

[129] *Zbornik*/V/25/661, Monthly organizational report of 10th Corps for March 1944 (31 March 1944).

in 1942. Despite this late appointment, Bakrač's reliability could not be doubted as he had spent two years working underground in Zagreb, leaving the city in September 1943 to become a political worker in the Partisan-held territory. In mid-March 1944, he was summoned to the Main HQ for Croatia and met Ivan Krajačić, the head of what would soon become the Croatian branch of the *Odjeljenje za zaštitu naroda* (OZNA, or Department for the Protection of the People),[130] who told him simply that he would be in charge of prisoner exchange from then on.[131]

According to Bakrač's estimate, he visited Zagreb no less than twenty-five times during his tenure as the chief NOVJ envoy. On several occasions he was billeted in the Palace Hotel, which was turned into a kind of auxiliary barracks for the *Wehrmacht*. Most of the time, however, he stayed at Nemetschek's apartment with whom he had developed good relations (as he did with most of his German colleagues). For instance, Bakrač's family and friends visited him frequently at Nemetschek's apartment, and he was also introduced to his host's next of kin. The German envoy remembered how Bakrač obtained large quantities of cigarettes from one of his friends and some other commodities from Peternell's daughter, which Nemetschek then took to Pisarovina. He also carried private letters across the lines, and on one occasion, a supply of makeup for the famous Croatian actor, August Cilić, who was practicing his trade in the guerrilla army. More importantly, Nemetschek arranged the evacuation of some Partisan families from the occupied territory and the release of a number of Partisan sympathizers, all as a personal favor to Bakrač or other envoys.[132]

The NOVJ envoy's visits to Zagreb did not always pass without incident. Once, while he was staying at the Palace Hotel, a random check conducted by the German military police found his identification card suspicious and he was placed under arrest. Fortunately, Nemetschek immediately found out and arranged his release. The second incident was much more serious. As he was walking down a

---

[130] *Odjeljenje za zaštitu naroda* (OZNA) was formed on 13 May 1944 as an organization responsible for all questions of security and intelligence within the Partisan-held territories. It had four directorates: I (foreign intelligence); II (counter-intelligence); III (internal security); IV (technical branch/statistics).

[131] Bakrač, "Razmjena ratnih zarobljenika," p. 847. Bakrač's authorization bears the date 15 March 1944. HR HDA 1450, Roll D-1090, 152, Letter of authorization for Ivan Žuljević (15 March 1944).

[132] Bakrač, "Razmjena ratnih zarobljenika," pp. 847, 850. HR HDA 1521, Box 31, File 24 Bakrač, Statement of Willibald Nemetschek; HR HDA 1521, Box 9, File 289 Nemetschek, Statement of Willibald Nemetschek; ibid., Entries for "Miletić or Miliković" and "Žganjer," Statement of Willibald Nemetschek. Some Yugoslav sources claim Nemetschek was instructed by his superiors to be friendly to the Partisan envoys. *Nemačka obavještajna služba*, Vol. V, p. 587.

street with Peternell, Bakrač was recognized by a *Ustashe* policeman who threatened to kill them both. In the end, the persuasive prowess of the German envoy saved the day; Peternell managed to convince him to check with the NDH's Ministry of Interior before taking any action. After the ministry "told him not to touch them, he left them in peace."[133]

Bakrač's first month of duty was one of the busiest, with exchanges taking place approximately once every week. On 7 April, the Germans delivered five Partisans (one KPJ member); on 15 April, thirty-two Partisans, including one battalion and one company commander (six members of the KPJ); on 25 April, thirty-two prisoners, including one company commander, one battalion commissar, and one company commissar (eleven Party and two SKOJ members); on 27 April, twenty-three people, including two company commanders (one SKOJ member). In exchange for them, the Partisans freed twenty members of the *Wehrmacht* and forty-one Home Guards. In order to "get out of the red," the Partisans had to deliver another twenty Germans. The unusually large number of exchanged Home Guards was a novelty: "The Germans are in need of every man," Bakrač wrote to his superiors; "they, themselves, offered to take the Home Guards, something they have not done before." The Germans also requested that their prisoners not be stripped as the Partisans now had enough new English uniforms. The *Ustashe* refused to deliver three prisoners as the Partisans still owed them two of their own. Bakrač spent two days in Zagreb in late April negotiating with the NDH authorities and reported that they would probably agree to an exchange at the favorable ratio if the Partisans would settle the debt: "Something should be done about this, otherwise we will not get our comrades from the [concentration] camps."[134] Still, Bakrač hoped the swap could be made the next time he met with his counterparts in Pisarovina on 10 May 1944.[135]

The planned exchange did not occur owing to a "tragic misunderstanding" (Bakrač's words), which threatened to derail the whole cartel. On 2 May 1944,

---

[133] HR HDA 1521, Box 31, File 24 Bakrač, Statement of Willibald Nemetschek.

[134] Two *Ustashe* were among the six prisoners who were sent to the HQ of the Kordun area (responsible for exchanged prisoners) on 11 April 1944. HR HDA 1450, Roll D-1091, 123. The sources do not provide an explanation as to why they were not delivered with the other Axis captives. In March, Brnčić warned that if concentration camp inmates were to be exchanged, at least lower-ranking *Ustashe*, i.e. "those not earmarked for the people's tribunal," should be spared. *Jasenovac 1941–1945*, Vol. II, pp. 725–26, Report on prisoner exchange, 15 March 1944. The necessity of sparing captured *Ustashe* for exchange was also mentioned in contemporary Party documents. *Sjeverozapadna Hrvatska 1941–1945*, Vol. IX, pp. 512, 515. KPH County committee for Bjelovar, Minutes on the conference held on 21 April 1944. In spite of these efforts, captured *Ustashe* continued to be treated in the same harsh manner.

[135] HR HDA 1450, Roll D-1091, 138–42, Reports on prisoner exchange (16 and 27 April 1944).

Peternell, along with his driver, went to Pisarovina in a car belonging to the SD. On their way back, the car was fired upon despite being properly marked by white flags; both men were killed and left on the road. The attack was probably carried out by the Partisan Žumberak Detachment, although documentary evidence to this effect is scarce.[136] According to several German sources, Peternell undertook the trip on his own, without prior announcement to German authorities.[137] Bakrač wrote that Peternell came to Pisarovina in order to deliver "some things" to the Partisans,[138] which confirms that the trip was unofficial, i.e. not connected to prisoner exchange. This fact might have caused the incident, as the Partisans were not to interfere with traffic on the Pisarovina–Klinča Sela–Zagreb road during prisoner swaps.

Glaise-Horstenau was enraged and had all contact with the guerrillas severed. Five days later, and seemingly unconnected to the Peternell incident, units of the 1st Cossack Division and the NDH armed forces violated the neutral zone and entered Pisarovina. Ever since the existence of the neutral zone had been officially sanctioned in late January 1944, German troops were under orders not to occupy the area nor harm the local population.[139] Whereas the first clause was belatedly honored and Pisarovina had already been evacuated on the 8th, the second clause

---

[136] The evidence of the Žumberak Detachment's involvement in the incident is in one of Bakrač's notes from January 1945. HR HDA 1491, 2.41, 204, Summary of prisoner exchanges made hitherto, 5 January 1945. We know that the Žumberak Detachment had one of its battalions astride the road around the village of Galgovo on 30 April. *Sjeverozapdna Hrvatska 1941–1945*, Vol. IX, p. 604, Activity report of 34th Division in the period 15 April–1 May 1944, 1 May 1944. The activity report of the Žumberak Detachment for the period 17 April–12 May 1944 contains no mention of an ambush on the second day of May, only fighting with the enemy coming from Samobor. The report mentions an ambush near the village of Horvati on 17 April (just across the road from Galgovo) in which the detachment killed "one German officer and one NCO" and destroyed their car. *Zbornik/V/27/273*. The daily report of the 1st Cossack Division for 4 May 1944 reads: "An army car (BMW, WH 824 154) containing two mutilated and unrecognizable bodies found 7km south-southeast of Samobor [in the Galgovo–Horvati area]." NARA, T-314, Roll 1547, 000902, Daily report for 4 May 1944.

[137] HR HDA 1521, Box 9, File 289 Nemetschek, Statement of Johann Halbwidl. General Glaise-Horstenau wrote a letter to the chief of the SD in Zagreb, Hermann, in which he informed him that Peternell was killed while traveling to Pisarovina "without the knowledge or protection of our envoy." KAW, B/67:164, Živorad Mihailović-Šilja, *O razmeni zarobljenika,* p. 14.

[138] HR HDA 1491, 2.41, 204, Summary of prisoner exchanges made hitherto (5 January 1945).

[139] NARA, T-314, Roll 563, 001288, 2nd Panzer Army to 15th Mountain Corps (28 January 1944).

was flagrantly breached and many instances of looting and rape were recorded.[140] Glaise-Horstenau's office, fearing that the Partisans might take reprisals against German prisoners, demanded an explanation from the 1st Cossack Division. The latter responded that the perimeter had not been properly secured by a police unit from Samobor, and that its units encountered enemy fire from within the zone.[141] On 20 May, the 69th Reserve Corps issued orders for Operation *Schach,* which was designed to tie down the 4th Corps of the NOVJ in the Kordun region during Axis operations in Western Bosnia. Aware of the possibility that the repeated incursions into Pisarovina and acts of violence against the civilians living there might have long-lasting consequences, the order expressly stipulated that "the neutral zone of Pisarovina must not be violated for any reason."[142]

Relative peace returned to the area in the last days of May and the Germans decided it was time to re-establish contact with the Partisans. It would be safe to assume that the rising number of casualties was the main reason for this decision. Nemetschek's lists of German MIAs reflected the ever-increasing intensity of fighting in western Yugoslavia: in early March, there were 101 names; a month or so later, 258; and in early June, already 306.[143] If the cartel continued to be suspended, these men would face an uncertain fate. The contact with the Partisans was established through the personal driver of one of Zagreb's businessmen who had ties to both the Germans and the Partisans.[144] The Partisans were also very interested in resuming the talks as evidenced by Stilinović being dispatched to Zagreb in late May.[145] On 1 June 1944, the Supreme HQ for Croatia replied to Major von Pott's message regarding the renewal of prisoner exchanges and suggested the delegates meet in Pisarovina on 10 June.[146]

Whether at this meeting or through a courier, von Pott wrote a letter to the Partisan command dated 9 June 1944, and addressed it to a "Dear Doctor" whose name is not mentioned. Given that the letter makes reference to the "personal discussion" the two had in 1943, which in turn served as a basis for the agreement

---

[140] *Zbornik*/V/27/201, Turopolje-Posavina Detachment to 34th Division (9 May 1944) and ibid., p. 277, Rear area of 4th Corps to Corps HQ (14 May 1944).

[141] NARA, T-314, Roll 1546, 000483, German Plenipotentiary General to 69th Reserve Corps (12 May 1944); ibid., 000481, 69th Reserve Corps to 1st Cossack Division (14 May 1944); ibid., 000484, 1st Cossack Division to 69th Reserve Corps (13 May 1944).

[142] *Zbornik*/XII/4/287, 69th Reserve Corps, Orders for Operation *Schach* (20 May 1944).

[143] The lists can be found in HR HDA 1491, 2.41, 113–5, 120–4, 132–37.

[144] HR HDA 1521, Box 31, File 546 Stilinović, Statement of Willibald Nemetschek. The same man served as a courier whenever the envoys could not meet in person.

[145] Ibid., Statement of Hans Ott.

[146] HR HDA 1450, Roll D-1091, 277, Supreme HQ for Croatia to German Plenipotentiary General (1 June 1944).

reached with the help of "Mr. Šunjevarić" (Stilinović), it is obvious that the addressee was in fact Vladimir Velebit, or "Dr. Petrović," as he was known to the Germans. The fact that von Pott was writing to Tito's personal emissary and a member of the Supreme HQ underlined the importance the Germans attached to the issues contained in the letter. In the opening lines, the major briefly recounted how the prisoner exchange had been agreed in order to improve the lot of prisoners on both sides, and that the system had functioned well despite occasional incidents. The "monstrous" murder of Eduard Peternell (and the alleged mutilation of his corpse) now made any further exchanges impossible. In addition, reports of widespread abuse and executions of German prisoners were mounting.[147] This represented a flagrant breach not only of the agreement's provisions, but also of "those principles . . . which you claimed your movement made its own." For "purely humanitarian reasons," von Pott offered the Partisans one last chance to save the agreement before he informed his superiors that the whole matter could be viewed as a failure. His conditions were that Peternell's case be thoroughly investigated and the guilty parties punished. Furthermore, the NOVJ leadership was called upon to issue clear and unequivocal orders concerning the humane treatment of German prisoners. The letter also contained an indirect threat in case of non-compliance: "The troop commanders have informed me that if the shooting of German prisoners continues, they will take the sharpest possible reprisals against the members of those [NOVJ] divisions which perpetrated the shootings." At the end of the letter, von Pott expressed his hope that the Partisans would reject the path of escalation and inform him of their decision either through an envoy or in writing.[148] The Main HQ for Croatia replied on the same day: "We have already been informed of the death of Mr. Paternell [*sic*] and regret this unfortunate incident. Our investigation has shown that none of our units or individual fighters committed this act. The *Ustashe* have attacked the envoys several times already, all with the intention of making the exchange impossible. They must have done it again for the same purpose. We are willing to continue the prisoner exchange and request that you send your plenipotentiary to Pisarovina for consultations. Please inform us of his arrival beforehand so that we can secure a safe trip for him."[149]

The Main HQ for Croatia chose to deny responsibility and blame the *Ustashe* instead. Given their long record of covert or open attempts to sabotage the German-Partisan contacts, the *Ustashe* were perfect scapegoats. Glaise-Horstenau

---

[147] For instance, the 892nd Grenadier Regiment reported that three German sailors were found gruesomely murdered on the island of Šolta. NARA, T-314, Roll 562, 000666, Combat report Šolta (12 May 1944).

[148] HR HDA 1689, Document No. 78, Dear doctor (9 June 1944).

[149] HR HDA 1450, Roll D-1091, 324, Supreme HQ for Croatia to German Plenipotentiary General (9 June 1944).

could do little else but accept the Partisan version and the cartel became functional again.[150]

On 1 June 1944, the Main HQ requested an accounting from its subordinate units on the exact number of prisoners they each held. The corps on the mainland (4th, 6th, and 10th) reported fifteen Germans and sixteen Home Guard men and officers; the 8th Dalmatian Corps reported it had "plenty" of captured Germans and requested further instructions.[151] Due to problems with the British (see below), the prisoners from Dalmatia could not be brought to Pisarovina and the exchange had to be conducted with the captives at hand. After a pause in exchanges that lasted longer than two months, the swap was completed on 6 July 1944, with the Partisans receiving thirty-seven of their men, most of them Party and SKOJ members.[152] Captain Gerhard-Oskar Merrem of the *Abwehr* could therefore report to his superiors in Army Group F that the prisoner exchange negotiations were proceeding "constantly and smoothly."[153]

Colonel Hans Harald von Selchow,[154] Glaise-Horstenau's Chief of Staff, remembered that Nemetschek approached him in the days following the unsuccessful attempt on Hitler's life (20 July 1944) and conveyed a new proposition from the Partisans. They were in dire need of medical supplies and were inquiring about the possibility of receiving them from the Germans. Von Selchow met twice with Bakrač, who reported that Partisan hospitals could not provide aid to captured Germans unless they were supplied with the needed materials. As there was no

---

[150] According to Nemetschek, Stilinović wrote him a letter in which he blamed the incident on the "White" or "Wild" partisans, referring presumably to the militias affiliated with the Croatian Peasant Party. (The KPJ organization at Pisarovina warned of their existence in March 1944. *Sjeverozapdna Hrvatska 1941–1945*, Vol. IX, p. 90, Minutes of the meeting of KPH district committee for Pokuplje, 23 March 1944). Nemetschek wrote that as Glaise-Horstenau "knew that such groups existed," he accepted the explanation. HR HDA 1521, Box 31, File 546 Stilinović, Statement of Willibald Nemetschek. According to family history, Peternell was killed by the Cossacks. Email to author from Ms. Marlisa Fašaić, 3 March 2014.

[151] See *Zbornik/V/28/539*, Main HQ for Croatia to 4th Corps (1 June 1944) and the accompanying footnotes.

[152] HR HDA 1491, 2.41, 204, Summary of prisoner exchanges made hitherto (5 January 1945).

[153] NARA, T-311, Roll 195, 000785, Experiences made on duty travel through Serbia and Croatia from 20 June to 4 July 1944 (5 July 1944).

[154] Colonel von Funck was replaced as Glasie-Horstenau's Chief of Staff in mid-May 1943 by Colonel Eberhard Kaulbach (Broucek, ed., *Ein General im Zwielicht*, Vol. III, p. 230, Entry for June 1943), and he stayed in Zagreb for only a few months before Lieutenant Colonel von Selchow took his place in mid-summer of the same year. Although von Selchow was kept apprised of the running of the cartel, he did not wish to take an active part and left the details to von Pott. HR HDA 1521, Box 31, File 368 von Selchow, Statement of Willibald Nemetschek.

way to guarantee that the supplies would in fact be used for treating the prisoners, von Selchow suggested a direct trade instead. Bakrač agreed and ten German soldiers were exchanged in Pisarovina for several crates of bandages and medication.[155] The deal was shrouded in secrecy; von Selchow did not inform the Armed Forces High Command or Army Group F, fearing they would not give their blessing in the aftermath of the failed assassination attempt in East Prussia. It is possible that he had an unlikely ally in the person of the German ambassador who had just undertaken a new diplomatic initiative directed at the Partisan leadership. It is possible that he procured the needed medical supplies as a gesture of goodwill.[156]

Several days after this unusual swap, on 14 August, the Germans secured the release of another ten Communists, members of the KPJ's Zagreb organization, from an *Ustashe* concentration camp. The exchanges intensified over the next three months. In this period, the Partisan movement received the following:[157] eighty-two prisoners on 30 September; twenty-four Partisans on 12 October; 184 Partisans released in advance on 15 November, as the Germans could not feed them; seventy-nine Partisans on 30 November; thirty-two Partisans, including two SKOJ functionaries, on 4 December; thirty-nine prisoners, including two KPJ and two SKOJ members and one delegate of the *Zemaljsko antifašističko vijeće narodnog oslobođenja Hrvatske* (ZAVNOH, or State Anti-Fascist Council of the People's Liberation of Croatia) on 20 December.[158]

A number of the Partisans and their sympathizers exchanged in the last quarter of 1944 came from German camps in Serbia. German officers would often visit the prisoners at the camp located in the Zvezadara suburb of Belgrade, inquiring about

---

[155] Böhme, *Die deutschen Kriegsgefangenen,* Vol. I/1, p. 84. Bakrač's overview of the exchange activities in 1944 does not mention any swap being made between 6 July and 14 August.

[156] Kasche stated several times to his Yugoslav interrogators that he had supplied the Partisans with a substantial quantity of medications and vaccines through Ott, without specifying the date. See Kasche's statements in HR HDA 1521, Box 9, File 164 Ott, and ibid., Box 31, File 546 Stilinović. Von Selchow's initiative coincided with Kasche's back-channel maneuvering and Ott's return to the negotiating table, both of which occurred in the second half of July 1944 (see below).

[157] HR HDA 1491, 2.41, 204, Summary of prisoner exchanges made hitherto (5 January 1945); ibid., 49–50, List of persons exchanged on 30 September 1944 (undated). In mid-October, Kasche reported that 164 Germans were exchanged "in the recent period," probably referring to the time between July and October. NARA, T-311, Roll 194, 000440, Memorandum on duty travel to Zagreb on 13 October 1944 (14 October 1944).

[158] ZAVNOH was a wartime precursor to the Croatian parliament and the highest legislative and executive body of the Partisan movement in Croatia.

their rank and asking who would like to be exchanged. Many feared for their lives if they agreed, so they refused the offer. In August 1944, a relatively large group of 180 people was herded into freight cars in Belgrade and taken for an eight-day journey across Hungary and Austria to Zagreb. Once they arrived, the prisoners were taken to the *Ustashe* prison at Savska cesta. On several occasions, a German officer came to the prison, selected a group of inmates, and took them to Pisarovina for exchange.[159]

The final months of 1944 also saw several cases of prisoners being delivered on "receipt." These handovers were usually negotiated in Pisarovina and completed between units on the ground. The youngest of the German "legionnaire" divisions, the 392nd, had been deployed in the northern Croatian Littoral since early 1944. The Germans knew from captured documents that the Partisans in this region applied different standards to the treatment of Croatian soldiers and their German officers and NCOs. In 1943, the former were still to be disarmed and sent home; however, in sharp contrast to earlier instructions, the latter were not to be executed, but exchanged. The legionnaire divisions were not comprised exclusively of Croats and Germans, however. By late September 1944, the Partisan reports spoke of "all possible nationalities imaginable" present in the German units in the region. As a consequence, the guerrillas had thirty Polish prisoners from the 392nd by early October.[160] The German command in Ogulin proposed an exchange of these men for the same number of Partisan sympathizers. After having exchanged several letters, both sides agreed to conduct the swap at St. Jacob's church outside Ogulin. Zvonko Barac, an officer of the OZNA and the Partisan representative, was surprised to find two agents of the *Ustashe* Surveillance Service waiting for him instead of the Germans. Barac refused to talk to them and insisted that the Germans send their own envoys. Shortly thereafter, several officers wearing the field gray uniform of the *Heer* appeared in front of the church; the captured Partisans were not with them. The officers explained that all of the individuals wanted by the Partisans were in the Karlovac prison. Barac protested, but was finally persuaded to free the Poles in exchange for a guarantee and an official document securing the immediate transfer of thirty Partisans to Pisarovina, where they would be handed over to the NOVJ's exchange commission. The Germans kept their word and the prisoners were delivered as promised.[161]

---

[159] Radivoje Kovačević, *Sjeveroistočna Bosna 1944–1945: prilog istoriografiji* (Brčko: Savez udruženja boraca NOR-a Brčko Distrikta BiH, 2002), p. 68.

[160] NARA, T-314, Roll 566, 000204, 392nd Infantry Division, Prisoner interrogation No. 136 (14 March 1944); *Zbornik*/V/33/373, Order of 13th Division of the NOVJ (23 September 1944). Poles with German ancestry, or those considered to be likely candidates for Germanization, were registered in the "German People's List" (*Deutsche Volksliste*) and were subjected to conscription; an estimated 250,000 were recruited into the German armed forces. Retrieved from: http://www1.ku-eichstaett.de/ZIMOS/forum/docs/kochan.htm

[161] Labović and Basta, *Partizani za pregovaračkim stolom 1941–1945*, pp. 230–31. One document confirms that the 11th Corps which operated around Ogulin delivered on receipt at

On 21 October 1944, the Moslavina Detachment sent a letter to the nearby German command, offering to deliver on receipt twenty-three Home Guards and one officer in return for the same number of Partisans, which had already been freed in Pisarovina. The proposed date of the handover was 25 October. The detachment's command promised it would not carry out any action in the area on this day if the other side would agree to do the same. The German command responded on the 27th, agreeing to complete the handover on the following day and pledging to strictly abide by the terms laid down in the letter. It also inquired about the exchange of a wounded German soldier known to be held in captivity in the area.[162]

One battalion of the detachment was tasked with providing security to the Partisan delegation in the village of Katoličko Selišče, where the negotiations were to take place. The German delegation, (one of them from the 1st Cossack Division), an NCO, and a young female interpreter, appeared on time in a black Mercedes and were met by the Partisan delegation in a secluded house at the edge of the village. While the negotiations were underway, the Partisans noticed enemy movements in the vicinity of the village, a flagrant violation of the agreed provisions. Their suspicions of foul play were confirmed when a search of the staff car revealed three hidden submachine guns. The security detail, fearing that the Germans wanted to capture the Partisan delegation, burst into the house, interrupting the negotiations. The misunderstanding was soon cleared up, but the incident provided the Germans reason to fear for their safety. Wary of an ambush, they refused to drive back to their lines unescorted. Consequently, the Partisan battalion commander had to ride with the Germans to the "front line" and see them safely through the heavily armed guerrilla pickets.[163]

This episode is particularly interesting as it illustrates the inherently fragmented nature of the war in the country, which made any possibility of a universally binding

---

least one group of "captured legionnaires" prior to October. *Zbornik*/V/31/497, Main HQ for Croatia to 11th Corps (11 August 1944). The 392nd Division was no stranger to non-violent contacts with the Partisans, as witnessed by one of its officers, Major Hübner: "Telephone line from Fužine to Delnice ran parallel to the power line, and we sometimes could not hear each other because of the jamming caused by electric induction. Consequently, we had to shut down the power line every now and then. The Partisans repeatedly complained about this and threatened to cut the supply of electric power to our territory. There was an unofficial agreement that nothing would happen to the power plant which was located in Partisan territory, as it supplied both us and the Partisans with electricity. We, however, had to furnish the oil needed to run it." Schraml, *Kriegsschauplatz*, p. 269.

[162] HR HDA 1491, 4.7.7, 9–10, Command of Moslavina sector to the German command in Popovača (21 October 1944); ibid., 18, German command in Popovača to the command of Moslavina sector of the 10th Zagreb Corps (27 October 1944).

[163] Vukašin Karanović, *Moslavački partizanski odred 1941.–1945.* (Kutina: Skupština općine Kutina i Općinski odbor SUBNOR-Kutina, 1981), pp. 407–09.

agreement regarding prisoner exchange virtually impossible. Katoličko Selišče was only sixty kilometers from Pisarovina, yet judging by the tense atmosphere, it could have been hundreds of miles away. The fear and suspicion which surrounded the October handover in Moslavina stands in stark contrast to the relaxed, even friendly relations between the envoys in the neutral zone.[164]

In one of its letters to the 5th Bosnian Corps, the Main HQ for Croatia wrote that the majority of the exchangees were enlisted men or officers from the Partisan units. Political prisoners from the NDH's prisons and camps could be retrieved only in return for *Ustashe* or prominent German prisoners.[165] The Main HQ therefore advised the corps to spare as many *Ustashe* as possible ("cutthroats excluded") and to submit their names for exchange. The other side, the letter continued, delivered 239 prisoners in advance and the Partisans now owed the same number of German nationals, legionnaires, or Home Guards. The Germans were willing to release prisoners without immediate compensation in the future as well, but the NOVJ had to show goodwill by occasionally releasing captives in groups of no more than fifty: "In this way, the balance will always be at around 200 Germans." The 5th Corps was asked to release its nine prisoners to the nearest German unit and collect the receipt in return, which would then be shown to the German parliamentaries in Pisarovina who would adjust the balance.[166]

---

[164] One officer of the 1st Cossack Division remembered receiving between twenty-six and thirty-six Axis soldiers ("only a few of them Germans") at an undisclosed location not far from the main railway line Zagreb-Belgrade, presumably sometime in late 1944. According to the same account, it was the Partisans who came armed this time, but this did not stop the delegations from sharing a meal and, apparently, a sizable quantity of local brandy. The officer used the opportunity to lobby for an informal cease-fire in his sector, which was allegedly agreed to by the opposite side. As no dates or place names are mentioned, it is impossible to say whether the meeting happened after the events at Katoličko Selišće (repeated contacts usually reduced tensions), and if the truce had really gone into effect as claimed. Friedrich Kübler, *Kosaken mit uns im Kampf gegen Stalin und dem Bolschewismus. Überlebende berichten* (Bad Herrenalb: self-published, 1982), pp. 143–46.

[165] Gabrijel Cvitan, a Croatian writer and functionary of the NDH Ministry of Education, won fame (or notoriety) for writing a poem about Pavelić in 1941. In September 1944, he was captured and recruited into the 2nd Brigade of the 7th NOVJ Division as a war correspondent. According to his OZNA personnel file, he saw combat and proved to be a good fighter. Nevertheless, the Partisan command agreed to exchange him in November and he was turned over to the Germans one month later in Pisarovina. Jere Jareb, "Svjedočanstvo hrvatskog književnika Gabrijela Cvitana iz jeseni 1944," *ČSP* 3 (2003), pp. 973–94. According to the same source, Cvitan was glad to be back in Zagreb where his old job was waiting for him. He was probably one of the rare exceptions (or indeed the only one) offered for exchange by the NOVJ despite being an active-duty Partisan.

[166] HR HDA 1491, 2.41, 17, Main HQ for Croatia to 5th Corps (6 December 1944).

1944 ended with an incident which involved an incursion of German and *Ustashe* forces into the neutral zone. The incursion was a reaction to the attacks carried out by the NOVJ's 34th Division on the Axis strongpoints along the vital Zagreb–Karlovac line, including one on the village of Horvati, where an entire Home Guard battalion was routed.[167] The Axis strike force, consisting of one battalion of the 1st *Jäger* Reserve Regiment and a company of *Ustashe*, gathered at Zdenčina on 12 December and began their advance southeast early the next day. The Žumberak Partisan Brigade was deployed in the village of Bratina and to the east of it, along the edge of the neutral zone. Since the brigade's command had information that a prisoner exchange was set for that day, the forward units were instructed to let the Germans pass without interference. At 11.00, patrols warned that the enemy was approaching from the north, but the brigade took no action, presuming it was the prisoner transport headed for Pisarovina. By the time the Partisans realized the Germans had come with an altogether different agenda, it was too late. Bratina was lost and the "front line" pushed to the south of the village. The Axis strike force continued its attack the next day and by noon it had advanced to within two kilometers of Pisarovina. Shortly thereafter, the Germans turned around and retreated with some haste back to their starting positions of 12 December. The 34th Division lost a total of five dead, ten wounded, and four missing: "The confusion and indecisiveness on the part of our forward units was caused by information that the Germans were coming to negotiate a prisoner exchange; in this way, the enemy could fire first on our unprepared units, killing one fighter and wounding five."[168]

The attack came in the midst of the preparations for the second December exchange (which took place on the 20th), so it is almost certain that the couriers and envoys frequently crossed the lines during this period. Whether the German battalion knew about the scheduled talks and decided to use them as cover to achieve surprise is not known. One must bear in mind, however, that this attack was provoked by the rout of the Home Guard battalion at Horvati. The involvement of, or coordination with, the German prisoner exchange commission therefore seems unlikely. The hasty departure of the battalion on the 14th was in all probability caused by fear that any prolonged presence of the Axis troops in the neutral zone would have adverse consequences for the functioning of the cartel.

The reluctance of the Partisans to open fire on the Germans may have been caused by an incident which occurred during one of the earlier exchanges. Because of a misunderstanding, a Partisan unit guarding the approaches to the neutral zone failed to remove the landmines it had laid on the road leading to Zagreb. As a consequence, a truck carrying the Yugoslav exchangees was severely damaged and

---

[167] *Zbornik*/V/36/671–72, NDH ministry of defense, daily report for 14 December 1944.

[168] Ibid., pp. 331–33, 34th Division of the NOVJ, After-action report concerning fighting around Bratina on 13–14 December 1944 (21 December 1944).

several of the occupants wounded.[169] Nemetschek, who was injured himself, remembered that "the guilty sentry was shot in front of my eyes."[170] The severity and swiftness of the punishment symbolized the Partisan leadership's resolve not to permit any breakdown in the prisoner exchange, as had occurred in the aftermath of Peternell's death, even at the price of a reduced level of initiative on the tactical level.

January 1945 saw two exchanges, one of which was major in size—on the 17th, the Partisans delivered around eighty Germans captured in the recent fighting in the Dalmatian hinterland. The number of fighters and sympathizers they received in return is not mentioned, so it is possible these prisoners were used to reduce the NOVJ's debt. The same was probably true with the next swap in Pisarovina on 26 January, where the Germans, represented by both Nemetschek and Ott, received sixteen of their men. It was agreed that Bakrač would join them for a trip to Zagreb and the convoy left the village around 16.00. Two hours later, as the column was threading slowly through high snow drifts, the lead car was suddenly peppered by machine gun fire. Calls to get out and surrender were intermingled with further shots aimed at the car. Bakrač and the others jumped from the vehicle into the nearby ditch in order to find cover. He tried to explain to the assailants who he was and his mission, but to no effect—the Partisans took the whole group prisoner and drove off. One Partisan lieutenant ordered Bakrač to leave Nemetschek and Ott, who were both wounded, and to follow him. The NOVJ envoy refused, and tried again to identify himself by producing his letter of authorization. The lieutenant had no desire to examine the papers, but insisted that Bakrač follow him. Much to the dismay of the German envoys who pleaded not to be left alone, Bakrač finally acquiesced and was taken to the nearby Partisan command. To his relief, the commander and the political commissar of the unit recognized him immediately and offered to do whatever was necessary to ameliorate the situation. Declining the proposal to send the Germans to Zagreb straight away, Bakrač had them taken to Pisarovina with orders that they be treated in the best possible manner; additional medical assistance was provided and their belongings were returned. "They were well accommodated, excellently cared for, and they were simply delighted! Their only reproach was that the detachment [which carried out the ambush] had not been informed [about the convoy] and that they continued shooting even after we had stopped. [They also commented that] if our people would not heed my explanations and even look at my personal documents, what good were theirs," reported Bakrač.[171]

On 29 January, Nemetschek and Ott were visited by Unger and a German doctor, and they all returned to Zagreb on the same day. On 1 February, the 1st *Jäger* Reserve Regiment repeated its action from mid-December by sallying forth into

---

[169] Bakrač, "Razmjena ratnih zarobljenika," p. 848.

[170] KAW, B/67:145, Interview with Willibald Nemetschek conducted by Peter Broucek (10 September 1981).

[171] HR HDA 1491, 2.41, 209–10, Bakrač to Krajačić (29 January 1945).

the neutral zone; although the available sources do not mention the reason, it is probable that this incursion was linked to the wounding of the German envoys. One battalion of the Žumberak Brigade intervened attempting to save the NCO school of the 34th Division, which was under attack and surrounded. After the commander, commissar, and twelve others had been killed, the remaining 110 men and officers surrendered;[172] sixteen of the latter were subsequently shot. These killings represented the culmination of the terror campaign practiced by the *Ustashe* and the Germans in the final months of the war. On 2 February, the Main HQ for Croatia dispatched the following cable to Supreme HQ: "The Germans are constantly murdering our hostages. They hanged 100 hostages in Zagreb for the dead general. Similar cases occur regularly. We are of the opinion that we should take reprisals. Clarification requested."[173]

Tito responded two days later and ordered the "sharpest reprisals" for the killing of hostages and added that the Germans and the *Ustashe* should be told about these measures.[174] Consequently, Bakrač reported that he "protested vehemently against the shooting of the sixteen officers and informed them that we would shoot 160 of their men." Two weeks later, the NOVJ envoy confirmed that the reprisal had been carried out in the meantime and that he would bring the list of names of the executed on one of his next visits.[175] Surprisingly, the Germans refrained from taking revenge and from continuing the vicious circle of reprisals and counter-reprisals. Bakrač's collocutor, Lieutenant Colonel von Stephani, commented about the incident: "He was extremely upset [by the shooting of sixteen Partisan officers] and by the fact that irresponsible individuals were trying to deepen the hatred between us and the Germans. Judging by his attitude, the whole thing came at a very bad moment."[176]

---

[172] *Zbornik*/V/38/441–42, Main HQ for Croatia to Supreme HQ (4 February 1945).

[173] *Zbornik*/V/38/440, Main HQ for Croatia to Supreme HQ (2 February 1945). SS Brigadier General Willi Brandner, chief of German police for Zagreb, was killed in an ambush on 28 December 1944.

[174] VA, 119/4, 2, 1–19/2, Tito to Main HQ for Croatia (4 February 1945).

[175] HR HDA 1491, 2.41, 216–7, Bakrač's reports from visits to Zagreb from 26 February–1 March and 12–16 March 1945 (undated). Bakrač quoted these reports in his article on prisoner exchanges written in the late 1970s, but added that he invented the shooting of 160 prisoners in order to "terrify" the Germans. Bakrač, "Razmjena ratnih zarobljenika," p. 855. Judging by the original reports, the threat was real and the reprisal was carried out. In early February 1945, the Croatian OZNA instructed the 8th Corps to execute "a number of Germans [više Nijemaca]" and the 11th Corps to shoot or hang sixty German prisoners in reprisal for the execution of thirty Partisans in one of Zagreb's prisons. Vladimir Geiger, Mate Rupić, et al., eds., *Partizanska i komunistička represija i zločini u Hrvatskoj 1944.–1946.—Dokumenti— Knjiga 3: Zagreb i središnja Hrvatska* (Zagreb: Hrvatski institut za povijest, 2006), pp. 196–97.

[176] HR HDA 1491, 2.41, 216–7. The incident came in the midst of the negotiations on a possible German withdrawal from the Western Balkans. For more details, see below.

Despite all the incidents which occurred over the previous twelve months, the existence of the neutral zone centered around Pisarovina never came into question. In late March 1945, however, the Germans put forth a proposal to relocate it beyond the River Kupa, in the village of Lasinja, some 5.5 kilometers south of Pisarovina. The Germans cited several specific repeated violations of the original agreement by the NOVJ as the reason for their demand: the neutral zone was used as a transit area for reinforcements and as a safe haven for retreating Partisans; artillery and mortar fire was reported to be originating from within the zone on several occasions; and Pisarovina was garrisoned with more troops than agreed, and was used as a communications and logistical base. All this made it impossible for the German troops to respect the neutrality of the area. The draft of the proposal included an important instruction—the representatives of the NOVJ were to be informed that the proposal was not aimed at "curtailing . . . the talks on prisoner exchange in any way."[177]

The proposal was delivered on 28 March 1945. Bakrač denied the German accusations and stated that the NOVJ had already agreed to a major concession when it chose to relinquish the right to keep troops on a piece of territory under its control; therefore, the neutral zone could only be relocated closer to Zagreb and not any deeper into Partisan-held areas. He also maintained that only civilian institutions were present within the zone which, of course, was not the case. In support of his argument that the proposal should be turned down, Bakrač wrote that Pisarovina housed "all possible" civilian institutions, military schools, and supply dumps, and that it was an important station for moving troops and material from Slovenia to Kordun and vice versa. The officers of the 34th NOVJ Division proposed moving the neutral zone to a village ten kilometers to the north of Pisarovina, stating that they would be able to hold the latter against any possible attack. Contrary to this opinion, Bakrač thought that Pisarovina could not be defended with the forces available and that if the "bandits" took possession of it, the NOVJ would lose one of the richest counties in this part of the country. The Main HQ for Croatia was asked to make the decision by 11 April[178] and as expected, the proposal was turned down and Pisarovina remained the center of the neutral zone for the duration of war.

The German proposal was in all probability not motivated solely by moral objections to the abuse of the neutral zone by the NOVJ. Had this been the case, the issue would have been raised immediately after any of the incidents which transpired after Peternell's death. Judging by the timing of the proposal, more practical reasons were involved. On 20 March 1945, the Yugoslav 4th Army began its offensive against the German positions in Lika and Western Bosnia. One week later, Yugoslav tanks entered Bihać, thereby threatening to unhinge the entire right

---

[177] Ibid., 219–20, Relocation of neutral zone (undated).

[178] Ibid., 218, Bakrač's report on visit to Zagreb from 26–29 March 1945 (undated).

flank of the German front in the country. Karlovac now became strategically important as it controlled the communication lines leading to the Croatian capital from the southwest.[179] Pisarovina, due to its location, was ideal for launching sabotage actions and attacks on the road and railway connecting the two places. Relocating the neutral zone to the south, beyond the Kupa River, would enable the Germans to deepen their defensive belt in the area without jeopardizing the prisoner exchange cartel.

Despite being wounded, Nemetschek continued working on prisoner exchanges from his hospital bed. He was often visited by Bakrač, and the two would configure each particular swap; implementation of their agreements was entrusted to Unger and Lieutenant Paul Manns, quartermaster in the office of the plenipotentiary general. Some cases were negotiated for months before they could be completed. The case of General Karl von Dewitz genannt von Krebs was by far the most complicated. He was captured during the second battle for Banja Luka in mid-September 1944 by the 5th Corps of the NOVJ. The Germans soon requested an exchange for both the general and SS Major Willi Wolter, chief of the SD in Banja Luka.[180] The 5th Corps had apparently negotiated directly with the German commands in Bosnia in November, but to no avail.[181] Despite the fact that the Partisans received in advance thirty prisoners for the former and nineteen for the latter,[182] the release of the high-ranking captives was postponed again and again.

---

[179] Erich Schmidt-Richberg, *Der Endkampf auf dem Balkan: Die Operationen der Heeresgruppe E von Griechenland bis zu den Alpen* (Heidelberg: Kurt Vowinckel Verlag, 1955), pp. 109–10; *Oslobodilački rat,* Vol. II, pp. 550–51; NARA, T-77, Roll 1426, 000917–8, War Diary of Armed Forces High Command, Entry for 31 March 1945.

[180] Von Dewitz was the only German general to be taken captive in Yugoslavia prior to May 1945. For more details on his capture, see Milan N. Zorić, *XIII krajiška brigada* (Belgrade: Vojnoizdavački zavod, 1968), p. 234. The Germans also wanted to exchange Lieutenant Colonel Werner Bornhausen, captured in Serbia in late August and for whom the Partisans demanded ten of their men. NARA, T-311, Roll 193, 000016, Daily report for 1 September 1944; ibid., Roll 195, 000662, Supplement to activity report of Abwehr officer with Army Group F for period 1–15 October 1944, 14 November 1944; ibid., Roll 189, 001219, Daily report of 4th Signals Intelligence Regiment for 13 November 1944. Kasche commented that this would not be easy because "Tito's bandits do not have radio communication with [their] Main HQ for Serbia." Ibid., Roll 194, 000440, Memorandum on duty travel to Zagreb on 13 October 1944, 14 October 1944. By late November 1944, Army Group F was still looking for any information concerning the missing officer. The National Archives, London (hereinafter TNA), HW 5/632, CX/MSS/R. 399 E, p. 4, 16 December 1944. I was not able to find any further details on Bornhausen's fate.

[181] VA, 461a, 5, 1/30, 5th Corps for 3rd Directorate of OZNA (8 November 1944).

[182] Bakrač, "Razmjena ratnih zarobljenika," p. 849. One of the thirty captives to be exchanged for von Dewitz was the famous Slovenian poet, Oton Župančič (1878–1949). Knowing that Župančič's presence in Partisan ranks would have great political resonance, the Slovenian

Bakrač reported several times in February and March 1945 that the Germans were becoming nervous about this. In early March, he had a "very sharp exchange" with Lieutenant Heinze of the SD in Zagreb, who threatened reprisals against the captured Partisans unless the general was freed. Bakrač replied that in this case, the NOVJ would respond in kind. In communication with his superiors, he suggested that the 5th Corps set up a meeting with the Germans between 8 and 10 March but postpone the release by another ten days.[183] The handover did not take place as planned, however, and Bakrač wrote that von Dewitz should be released quickly as the pressure in Zagreb was becoming unbearable. Furthermore, the Germans began to stall with other exchanges. The Main HQ for Croatia took his advice and ordered the 5th Corps to make the necessary arrangements. On the last day of March, the corps informed the Croatian Partisan leadership that they could not deliver the general and Wolter to the Germans because of heavy fighting in its area of operations.[184]

Other high-profile prisoners were exchanged during these months. These included two of the NDH's provincial governors and several *Ustashe* officers. The Partisans received up to ten of their own for each one of these men.[185] A higher ratio was also applied for a group of twenty-six German officers for which the NOVJ received 100 prisoners. The Germans also offered to exchange "2,000 wounded Serbs who were in captivity in Germany" (probably referring to soldiers of the former royal army captured in 1941) for the same number of wounded Germans. However, due to the immense logistical difficulties which would be involved in such a massive swap, the plan was never put into motion. According to the available information, the following were brought to Pisarovina in February and March: forty-one Germans on 25 February; sixty camp inmates and thirty-one

---

leadership requested his inclusion into the deal. Tito granted the request and sent appropriate instructions to the Supreme HQ. *Zbornik*/II/14/193, Kardelj to Tito (1 October 1944) and ibid., p. 220, Tito to Supreme HQ (6 October 1944). Whether or not Župančič was actually exchanged is unclear.

[183] HR HDA 1491, 2.41, 216–8, Bakrač's reports on visits to Zagreb from 26 February–1 March, 12–16 and 26–29 March 1945 (undated).

[184] HR HDA 1491, 2.41, 39, 5th Corps of the NOVJ for the Main HQ for Croatia (31 March 1945). Von Dewitz and his group were released sometime in early April. Ironically, the general survived Partisan captivity but not his return to Germany. He was tried for treason and executed by his own side in late April 1945. Norbert Haase, "Aus der Praxis des Reichskriegsgerichts: Neue Dokumente zur Militärgerichtsbarkeit im Zweiten Weltkrieg—Dokumente zur Militärgerichtsbarkeit im Zweiten Weltkrieg," *Vierteljahresheft für Zeitgeschichte* 39:3 (1991), p. 409.

[185] HR HDA 1491, 2.41, 189, To the command of Pisarovina (10 February 1945); ibid., 218, Bakrač's report on visit to Zagreb from 26–29 March 1945 (undated); Bakrač, "Razmjena ratnih zarobljenika," p. 849.

fighters of the Žumberak Brigade on 1 March; forty Partisans and twenty-six Germans on 12 March; forty Partisans and thirty-five Germans on 26 March; and thirty Partisans and seven Germans on 29 March.[186]

According to Bakrač, the NOVJ's debt fluctuated between fifty and 190 prisoners; in late March, the precise number amounted to 129, including two captains, three senior lieutenants, two lieutenants, and one sergeant.[187] The figures for April are sketchy, but it appears that the debt was at least partially settled: fifty-three Germans on 11 April; five Germans delivered on receipt by the Moslavina Area Command circa 13 April; and fifty-four Germans in exchange for sixteen to eighteen camp inmates on 28 April.[188]

Late April saw one of the last attempts to exchange a high-ranking prisoner. Vito Kraigher, one of the chief Partisan intelligence officers in Slovenia, had been captured at the beginning of the month and was taken to a prison in Ljubljana. Aware of the possibility that he might break under torture and yield valuable information, the Slovenian leadership intervened. On 18 April, the head of the Croatian OZNA, Ivan Krajačić, wrote a letter to Bakrač: "Request the exchange of Kraigher, Perc, and Veludček, who were captured eleven days ago. Slovenians have taken captive the commander of the 847th . . . Infantry Regiment [of the 392nd Legionnaire Division], Colonel Reisinger, and another eight officers. Slovenians would give all of them for the aforementioned three. If Germans ask for more, we will give. Arrange the exchange at any price."[189]

Offering German soldiers captured in Slovenia for exchange in Pisarovina was nothing new. In one recorded case, the Partisans captured an officer around Novo Mesto in the spring of 1944. While transporting him to their base, they stated that he would be sent to Kordun and swapped for captured Partisans.[190] Kraigher's exchange, however, could not be organized in time—he was executed on either

---

[186] HR HDA 1491, 5.13.10, 78, German prisoners (undated); ibid., 50, List of exchangees (29 March 1945); ibid., 2.41, 207–8, 216, Bakrač's reports on visits to Zagreb from 12–16 March and 26 February–1 March 1945 (undated).

[187] Bakrač, "Razmjena ratnih zarobljenika," p. 849.

[188] HR HDA 1491, 4.7.7, 31, Moslavina Area Command to *Feldkommandantur* in Kutina (8 April 1945); ibid., 5.13.10, 78, German prisoners (undated); ibid., 2.41, 63, Following comrades were exchanged (29 April 1945). At least two of these people had been in the Jasenovac concentration camp since 1941 and had the incredible good fortune to survive. *Jasenovac 1941–1945*, Vol. III, p. 328, footnote 2.

[189] HR HDA 1491, 5.13.10, 61, Krajačić to Bakrač (19 April 1945). According to a German witness, the Partisans were sometimes required to give up fifty Germans for one of their "heroes." Böhme, *Die deutschen Kriegsgefangenen*, Vol. I/1, p. 84. Although this figure seems excessive, Krajačić's letter confirms that the Partisans were generally willing to "pay" more for prominent members of their movement.

[190] Ivo Pirkovič, "Pozabljena diplomacija v gozdu," *Delo* 3 (July 1980), p. 21.

3 or 4 May 1945.[191] Several days later, the Yugoslav Army marched into Zagreb and the neutral zone at Pisarovina ceased to exist.

Political Talks, 1943–1945

Contact between the representatives of the NOVJ and German authorities from late 1943 to 1945 was not restricted to discussing prisoner exchanges. "The other part of my job, and that of my German counterparts," wrote Bakrač, "was to take the pulse of the other side and react to current events."[192] This, of course, meant talking politics. The German ambassador in Zagreb, Siegfried Kasche, remained a staunch supporter of some sort of accommodation with Tito, and had therefore welcomed Stilinović's return to Zagreb in early August 1943. He did not hide his intention to revive talks with the Communist-led guerrillas along the lines of the March Negotiations. On 27 August, he drafted a memo in which he restated his dim view of the current German approach to the problem of the guerrillas. Quelling the uprising using only martial and constabulary means had failed, as illustrated by the outcome of Operation *Schwarz*. The issue of a 100,000 *Reichsmarks* bounty on Tito in late July was counterproductive—it only served to enhance his reputation and increase his number of followers. Although the ambassador lamented that his earlier attempts to bring about a change in the German attitude toward Tito "were unfortunately turned down," he was nevertheless willing to try again. Thus, in spite of the fact that the chances for political accommodation were slight, Kasche sought "to establish contact" with the Partisan leadership.[193] Several days later, he stated these views directly to Hitler. He mentioned Ott's actions from May of that year and suggested that a political arrangement with Tito would have brought immense advantages. "At this point, the *Führer* made a depreciative remark, but was not decidedly against it," wrote Kasche.[194]

The capitulation of Italy gave new impetus to Kasche's initiative. On 9 September 1943, he dispatched a cable to the foreign ministry in which he requested a reevaluation of the attitude toward Tito and his Partisans. The latest developments

---

[191] Ljuba Dornik Šubelj, "Podatki o dr. Vitu Kraigheru so bili državna tajnost," *Arhivi* 28:1 (2005), p. 77.

[192] Bakrač, "Razmjena ratnih zarobljenika," p. 850.

[193] KAW, B/67:141, Memo from Ambassador Kasche (27 August 1943).

[194] ADAP/E/VI/504, Memo on the meeting with the Führer on 30–31 August 1943 (8 September 1943). Kasche repeated these arguments almost word for word in the cable dated 29 September 1943. The length of his telegrams and his self-righteousness prompted sharp criticism from the foreign ministry which reminded him that the sole task of an ambassador was to implement the policy devised exclusively by the chief of state and the foreign minister. KAW, B/67:141, Kasche to Foreign Ministry (29 September 1943) and ibid., State Secretary to Kasche (21 December 1943).

prompted the Germans and the *Ustashe* to launch a propaganda offensive aimed at salvaging what they could from the debris of the September debacle. As Axis troops entered what was once the occupation zone of their former ally, they presented themselves as liberators from the Italian yoke. At the same time they promised amnesty to all those who had joined the guerrillas because of the Italian terror. German and NDH authorities reasoned that since Dalmatia and other territories were returned to the Croat state, many of the Partisans could be persuaded to break with the Communists and head home. The plan was but a repetition of previous attempts to drive a wedge between the rank-and-file and the leadership of the NOVJ, and thus bring the uprising to its knees. The fact that one of Tito's envoys was a frequent visitor to Zagreb presented a perfect opportunity to gauge the feasibility of this approach. Kasche wrote, "Moreover, I am of the opinion that we should use any possible opportunity for establishing contact with Tito and exploit any possibility which would lead to the cessation of hostilities between us."[195]

Hans Ott continued serving as Kasche's proxy during the summer and early fall of 1943. Judging by the previously quoted documents, he devoted at least a part of his energies to engaging Stilinović on political matters. The details of these talks are, unfortunately, not known—neither Ott nor any of the German witnesses mentioned them in their post-war interrogations. According to Helm, the whole matter was shrouded in secrecy. Kasche kept Ott in close proximity and attempted to reserve his services exclusively for himself. Ott did occasionally share some information about the Partisans with Helm, but received instructions only from Kasche. The monopolization of Ott's services was done out of fear that any outside interference might compromise the link to the Supreme HQ of the NOVJ. For the same reason, Ott never disclosed any details of conversations he had with the ambassador.[196]

Two surviving documents from November 1943 provide a glimpse into the topics that were discussed between Stilinović and Kasche's envoys. Although Tito had explicitly forbidden the Main HQ for Croatia to conduct any talks not pertaining directly to the prisoner exchange,[197] Stilinović was still willing to hear out his counterparts' opinions on political issues. On 4 November, the Main HQ for Croatia dutifully informed Tito of the details; according to Ott, the Germans recognized the fact that the NOVJ was a popular movement and even "approved of the creation of new Yugoslavia." They added that they would be willing to "protect the borders against an American landing" if the Partisans would make "some" economic concessions and allow the Germans to use "some" land communications.[198]

---

[195] ADAP/E/VI/511, Kasche to Foreign Ministry (9 September 1943).

[196] HR HDA 1521, Box 9, File 146 Hans Ott, Statment of Hans Helm.

[197] *Zbornik*/II/10/430, Tito to Main HQ for Croatia (27 October 1943).

[198] NARA, T-313, Roll 196, 7456990–1, 2nd Panzer Army/Intelligence section, Appendix to daily report for 9 November 1943. Vladimir Bakarić noted in his personal diary (Entry for 3 November 1943): ". . . Krauts came to Pisarovina in a tank flying a white flag and asked

The offer was apparently worth discussing, as Stilinović returned to the issue of a truce during his meeting with Ott and others in late November 1943. Ott's impression was that this latest move reflected a general desire for a cessation of hostilities amongst the guerrillas; Stilinović appeared war-weary and apparently longed to return to his native Zagreb. The two agreed that the talks on a truce should be continued in Tito's headquarters in December. The invitation led Kasche to conclude that the Partisan leader sought to reach some sort of long-lasting arrangement with the Germans. He therefore provided Ott with guidelines for future talks on the subject—basically, a repetition of the instructions used previously during the March Negotiations. Ott was to emphasize that the Third Reich had no territorial ambitions in the Balkans. On the contrary, Germany was willing to heed the national aspirations of individual peoples for their own sovereign states, proof of which could be seen in the creation of the NDH. The creation of Yugoslavia was a mistake—anyone attempting to resurrect her should bear in mind that these strong centrifugal tendencies would eventually resurface again. The invasion of the Balkans in 1941 was aimed solely at securing Germany's geostrategic interests which were endangered by British scheming. Economic cooperation still lay at the heart of German policy in the region. The ambassador's envoy was instructed to emphasize that the Germans were not simply plundering the land and that the native population could profit from cooperation if the Partisans would only cease their senseless actions. For example, the road leading from the Reich's border to Zagreb was financed and built by German companies and equipment and was 75% complete. The undertaking could not be finished because the guerrillas destroyed the machines, killed one senior official of *Organisation Todt,* and scared off the others.

Kasche hoped that talks conducted along these lines could fulfill a number of aims. First and foremost, the Partisan leadership should be made aware that the Germans were open to some sort of settlement ("the cheap way out," as the ambassador phrased it). Second, the contacts should pave the way for a mitigation of violence; mass reprisals along the rail lines in Croatia could be stopped in exchange for a halt in sabotage. Third, the above-mentioned offers should provide an incentive for further talks, which could open new possibilities for the Germans. Kasche noted: "Another old guideline is still in force and is therefore to be followed: after each meeting, the Partisans must be the ones to provide the initiative for further talks. Our side must [not approach] but always be approached [with such requests]. The Partisans must never have a justified reason for waiting for us to take the initiative, and we must never be in danger of being late with our answer."[199]

---

where the demarcation line [*granica*] was. [They also said] that they will not make incursions [into Partisan territory] if we leave the Zagreb–Karlovac railroad alone." Dedijer, *Novi prilozi,* Vol. II, p. 1149.

[199] See ADAP/E/VII/208–11, Note for Mr. Ambassador (29 November 1943) and an accompanying memo (28 November 1943).

The Partisans' apparent interest in the possibility of a cease-fire should be viewed in the wider context of the relations between the People's Liberation Movement and the Allied powers, and especially in light of the second session of the AVNOJ and the creation of the Communist-sponsored Yugoslav government. Outwardly, British policy toward the Partisans seemed to have changed dramatically compared to the period March–April 1943. The first military mission to Tito's HQ arrived in late May and its members reported favorably on what they observed. In September, the mission was expanded with the arrival of Brigadier General Fitzroy Maclean. Complementing the arrival of the missions, supply drops from Britian's Royal Air Force to the Partisans across the country also increased. Despite the fact that the People's Liberation Movement was now *de facto,* if not *de jure,* recognized as an ally in the struggle against Nazi Germany, its leadership was still wary of British intentions. In early October, Tito wrote a letter to the Montenegrin command in which he expressed his view that the Western Allies were basically buying their way into the country with empty promises of material help.[200] He repeated his misgivings in a letter to the Macedonian leadership, adding that the British had a secret agenda and that they were still maintaining contact with Mihailović, which was "by all means absurd, but perfectly in line with English policy."[201]

Evidently, Tito was convinced that the change in British attitude was cosmetic in nature, and that the possibility of their intervention in the civil war was still very real. Chetnik propaganda, allegedly based on the statements of British officers, claimed for some time that Allied landings in Dalmatia could be expected soon; these rumors had already convinced some Italian units in Montenegro to desert from the Partisans.[202] On 12 October, Tito dispatched a cable in which he informed Moscow that Maclean had tried to sound out his opinion on the possibility of a coastal landing, even with smaller forces. The leader of the Partisans retorted that such an action would carry immense difficulties and prove strategically useless: "He probably understood this as a sign of our opposition to such a landing. Nevertheless, their activities show that they intend to go ahead with the operation. We shall not allow this landing to take place without our permission and we are ready to oppose it by force. We request your opinion."[203]

In effect, Tito was attempting to obtain Moscow's help in dissuading the British from conducting any unilateral operations in the country. As long as the latter

---

[200] *Zbornik*/II/10/368, Tito to 2nd NOVJ Corps (9 October 1943).

[201] Ibid., p. 362, Tito to Vukmanović (9 October 1943).

[202] Ibid., p. 323, Tito to 2nd NOVJ Corps (26 September 1943); see also accompanying footnotes.

[203] Petranović and Zečević, eds., *Jugoslavija 1918–1988,* p. 635, Tito to Moscow (12 October 1943). Stilinović told the Germans much the same. NARA, T-313, Roll 196, 7456861–2, 2nd Panzer Army, Intelligence section, Appendix to daily report for 10 December 1943.

confined their actions to sending observers and supplies, the Partisans were keen on receiving continued Allied support. On 29 October 1943, an NOVJ mission was established in Bari. On 16 November, the Supreme HQ requested that the Royal Navy intervene in the fighting for the islands in the northern Adriatic; three days later, the Main HQ for Croatia was given the green light to evacuate the seriously wounded, sick, and invalids to Italy in accordance with the agreement reached with Allied authorities.[204] In addition to using transport aircraft, the Allies also delivered some 3,000 tons of supplies by sea in November.[205]

By the time the Partisan envoy in Zagreb brought the topic of a truce to the fore, the position of the People's Liberation Movement was immeasurably better than in the early spring of 1943. The Soviet Union now provided unequivocal diplomatic support and the Western Allies had more or less acknowledged the NOVJ as a partner and had begun to supply it with war material. There was no reason for Tito to abandon the Allied camp now that he had finally secured himself a firm place in it. In light of these facts, it is not surprising that Vladimir Velebit described the November initiative as "a complete puzzle" in an interview given more than half a century after the events. The most likely explanation is that Stilinović merely employed the same tactic Kasche prescribed for Ott—provide incentives in order to keep the interest alive from the other side for future talks.[206]

Another old topic resurfaced during the contacts in November 1943—the possibility of economic cooperation between the two sides. Ott informed Kasche that he and Stilinović discussed three separate deals. The first revolved around the intended purchase of 9–10,000 horses through the same German military commission whose chief, Lieutenant Colonel Pokay, had been captured by the Partisans in July. The other two offers were made by private firms: Elektrobosna wanted to export chlorine to Germany; Slavex wished to secure a large consignment of timber for Switzerland. As the Partisans controlled the countryside and could disrupt the flow of goods on roads and railways, their approval was essential for the success of these business ventures. Stilinović replied that the purchase of horses would be agreeable, and that his side would even encourage peasants to sell the animals as long as 2–2,500 head were reserved for the Partisans. According to Ott, he gave a positive response to the Slavex offer. As far as the Elektrobosna request

---

[204] See cables from Supreme HQ to Main HQ for Croatia on 16 and 19 November 1943 in *Zbornik*/II/11/78 and 99, respectively.

[205] Harris G. Warren, *Special Operations: AAF Aid to European Resistance Movements 1943–1945* (n.p.: AAF Air Historical Office, 1947), p. 82.

[206] Schmider, *Partisanenkrieg,* pp. 333–34. Schmider speculates that the real motive behind the initiative was to confuse the Germans and make them postpone the first phase (Operation *Kugelblitz*) of their winter offensive. This implies that Supreme HQ knew approximately when the offensive was to begin; however, according to the official Yugoslav historiography, the offensive caught the NOVJ completely by surprise. *Oslobodilački rat,* Vol. I, p. 69.

was concerned, Stilinović said that he would have to consult his superiors before giving a definitive answer.[207]

Neither side was honest regarding these propositions. Allowing the German Army to obtain fresh horses and feeding the German industry with war materials was tantamount to collaboration. The published parts of Bakarić's diary contain no mention of these proposals, and neither does the Main HQ for Croatia's cable to Tito on 16 November 1943. However, Bakarić does mention in his diary an interesting offer made by one Ferdinand Preindl, representative of the Slavex timber company from Zagreb. Preindl told Stilinović that his company would like to export some fifty freight cars (*vagona*) of firewood from Pakrac to Zagreb and put them at the disposal of its employees for the upcoming winter. In return, the company would use its connections to facilitate the disbanding of the Pakrac prisoner camp.[208] As the negotiations concerning the prisoner exchange cartel were entering their final phase, the Croatian Partisan leadership thought that the acceptance of the proposition would not compromise the war effort, and would at the same time constitute a gesture of goodwill toward the Germans. Consequently, the Main HQ for Croatia suggested that the export of timber "for the clerks of Slavex be permitted, for [this would have a] positive effect."[209]

The wording of both the cable and Bakarić's diary implies that the Germans did not mention any trade deal with possible international implications. Whether the Slavex proposal was conceived as a preliminary step toward a broader agreement which would ultimately involve exports to Switzerland is not certain. In any case, it seems that the Main HQ for Croatia agreed to Preindl's proposal without waiting for permission from the Supreme HQ.[210] During the meeting in Pisarovina on 16 January, Preindl informed Josip Brnčić that the first fifty "cords" (*hvati*) of firewood had already reached their destination, and that his company would now like to secure the export of fifty more. If the Partisans would allow the woodcutting

---

[207] Kazimirović, *Nemački general*, p. 175. For the facsimile of the ambassador's memo from 27 November 1943 concerning these talks, see Kazimirović, *NDH u svetlu nemačkih dokumenata*, unpaginated.

[208] Diary of Vladimir Bakarić, Entry for 16 November 1943, reproduced in Dedijer, *Novi prilozi*, Vol. II, p. 1150.

[209] VA, 119/1, 1, 1, 55, Main HQ for Croatia to Supreme HQ (16 November 1943). This sentence was omitted from the version included in the *Sabrana djela* collection (Vol. XVII, pp. 362–63).

[210] According to Nemetschek, Preindl once requested "in the autumn of 1943" that von Pott intervene with Stilinović and "renew" the agreement on the export of timber from the Našice area. Von Pott complied "and after two months, the timber arrived at the office of the plenipotentiary general. . . . The interesting fact is that Preindl apparently knew Stilinović's name." HR HDA 1521, Box 9, File Stilinović, Statement of Willibald Nemetschek.

parties to work unhindered in an eight-kilometer radius around Pakrac, the company could arrange the release of captured Partisans from the local prison. Preindl added that some of them had already been released. Brnčić replied that he had no knowledge of this arrangement and that he would pass the offer on to his superiors, adding that the chances of a positive outcome were slight.[211] At first it seemed that Brnčić was wrong. Two days after the meeting, the long-overdue response from the Supreme HQ had arrived: Tito approved the Slavex request. On 20 January, however, the Main HQ for Croatia rescinded the approval on the grounds that the Germans had not released the Partisans from Pakrac.[212]

The Germans continued to hope that the Partisan movement could be split, both internally and from its allies abroad. The belief that the gap between the Communist leadership minority and the majority of ordinary fighters was wide and open to exploitation was seemingly confirmed by a number of sources in early 1944. The large number of defectors in the early winter months indicated that the Party was losing its grip on the army and that the process of decay had irreversibly begun.[213] At the beginning of January, Glaise-Horstenau was

---

[211] HR HDA 1450, Roll D-1090, 669, Report on state of prisoner exchange (30 January 1944). Peternell also requested that the OT's Zagreb office be allowed to import a certain quantity of firewood, offering medical supplies in exchange. I have not found any additional information pertaining to this particular offer.

[212] VA, 119/2, 1, 4–26, Tito to Main HQ for Croatia (18 January 1944); VA, 119/1, 2, 4, 32, Main HQ for Croatia for 6th Corps (20 January 1944). The Jamnica Company from Zagreb had been producing its famous brand of mineral water since 1828. The spring itself was located just outside Pisarovina, in the hamlet of Jamnica. The company's owner, Rottenbucher, reached an agreement with the Partisans that allowed him to export a certain quantity of mineral water to Zagreb. The deal was brokered through the office of the German plenipotentiary general. What the Partisans received in return is not known. Rottenbucher acted as a sort of a middle-man between the two sides; his driver served as a courier during the pause in the contacts following Peternell's death in May 1944. HR HDA 1521, Box 9, File 289 Nemetschek/Rottenbucher, statements of Willibald Nemetschek, Hans Ott, Eugen von Pott, Othmar Unger. As the war neared its end, some businessmen used the Partisan-German contacts to align themselves with the future victors. In April 1945, Ott arranged a meeting between a certain Đuričić of Elektrobosna and Dr. Pfaff of the Wiener Bankverein, and Bakrač. They handed over 850,000 kuna (and a typewriter) to the Partisan envoy and informed him of the bank withdrawals made in preparation for Pavelić's escape. In return, Bakrač assured them that the new rulers of Croatia would require their economic expertise after liberation. HR HDA 1491, 2.41, 223, Report on visit to Zagreb from 16–19 April 1945 (undated). According to a German witness, Nemetschek used his good standing with the Partisans to barter foodstuffs for rare commodities like salt and tobacco, which he then sold in Zagreb. HR HDA 1521, Box 9, File 289 Nemetschek, Statement of Johann Halbwidl.

[213] NARA, T-314, Roll 563, 001077, Situation report of intelligence section for period 1 December 1943–10 January 1944 (12 January 1944).

informed by his confidant, Captain Haeffner, of an opportunity to exploit this state of affairs. One of his informants, "a man who had proven his influence among the nationally-oriented Partisans by deeds," told him that the guerrillas in Western Croatia would be willing to get rid of the Communists and other enemies of the Germans in their midst. In exchange, they demanded a guarantee that their territories would be occupied by the Germans and not by the *Ustashe*. As a token of goodwill, they were prepared to relinquish control over a sizable area along the Croatian-Slovenian border within three weeks. The Captain added that "the willingness of the Partisans to collaborate politically and militarily" is the most striking proof that the guerrillas fought the Germans only because the latter supported Pavelić, and concluded: "Now is the right time to put into motion the suggested plan for action against the Communist faction of the Partisan [movement]. The differences between Tito and the Yugoslav government-in-exile in Cairo caused a split in the Partisan camp, [especially] as it turned out that all hopes which had been set on England and America were betrayed by London and Washington. We must act quickly, however, before Tito succeeds in tricking the majority of the population into believing that his regime is one of nationalist orientation."[214]

The plan Haeffner referred to almost certainly was intertwined with the ongoing dialogue concerning prisoner exchange. The meetings in Pisarovina and Zagreb provided a good opportunity to demonstrate to the Partisans that their struggle was essentially futile and brought only suffering to the population. Josip Brnčić reported in late January that Major von Pott had broached the subject of the Allied bombing campaign against the NDH. The vast majority of casualties during the air raids were civilians; the German occupation forces lost a negligible number of soldiers. The major did not forget to emphasize that the choice of targets rested with the Supreme HQ. The message was clear—the Communist leadership was squandering the lives of innocent people without achieving any tangible military results; the British, for their part, were willingly playing the role of executioner.[215] It may be assumed that this subtle propaganda offensive continued whenever the delegates met from January to April despite scarce reference to it in the surviving documents.[216] Far-reaching political issues do not appear to have been discussed

---

[214] NARA, T-501, Roll 265, 000028, Haeffner to Horstenau (12 January 1944). Additional details on this scheme are not known, but what is certain is that the Partisans did not (peacefully) relinquish any territory in northwestern Croatia.

[215] HR HDA 1450, Roll D-1090, 669, Report on state of prisoner exchange (30 January 1944).

[216] In one of his reports from late April 1944, Bakrač wrote that while en route to Zagreb, he had to spend one hour in the company of some German officers of the 1st Cossack Division in the village of Zdenčina. He stated that "this arrogant bunch of Prussian *Junkers* wanted to talk about the German victory and similar topics. I asked them to change the subject." HR HDA 1450, Roll D-1091, 142, Report on prisoner exchange (27 April 1944).

during this period. Following the death of Peternell, all contacts were broken off with the ensuing pause in talks lasting nearly a month.

As spring turned into summer, the contacts were not only re-established, but significantly intensified. The choice of envoys on both sides signaled that these negotiations were sensitive in nature. Hans Ott, absent from the talks since the beginning of the year, returned to the negotiating table. As his presence in Zagreb was explicitly requested by the German ambassador, the chief intelligence officer of Army Group F recalled him from Bosnia and Herzegovina and put him at Kasche's disposal.[217] Ott and Nemetschek traveled to Pisarovina in the early summer of 1944 where they were met by Bakrač and Stilinović. After they had finished with exchange-related business, the latter invited Ott for a short drive to the nearby village of Lasinja. Upon arrival, they were met by the Secretary General of the Communist Party of Croatia, Andrija Hebrang, and some twenty minutes later, Nemetschek and the two Partisan envoys were asked to leave Hebrang and Ott alone. What they discussed remains unknown—the German engineer later claimed that they only discussed the exchange of some people from Jasenovac.[218] However, it seems improbable that Hebrang would devote his time and energy to doing what was essentially Bakrač's job. Ott went to Pisarovina again in September and mid-October, and Hebrang and the chief Partisan intelligence officer in Croatia, Ivan Krajačić, served as his collocutors. That something was afoot is also confirmed by the fact that Stilinović traveled to Zagreb at least two times during the summer. On at least one of those occasions, he was accompanied by both Bakrač and Dušan Tepšić. According to one source, the delegation was received by Major von Pott at the office of the plenipotentiary general;

---

[217] The sources differ as to the exact date of the meetings during this period; Ott remembered that they took place on 20 June and 10 July. HR HDA 1521, Box 31, File 546 Stilinović, Statement of Hans Ott. Dr. Anton Fest, who was the head of "Action Commando 2" of the SD in Sarajevo remembered that Ott had been in that city "in mid-1944" on intelligence business. Ibid., Box 9, File 164 Ott, Statement of Dr. Anton Fest. His claim seems to be corroborated by a letter from the chief intelligence officer of Army Group F, Lieutenant Colonel Franz von Harling, to Kasche dated 12 July 1944. Von Harling informed the ambassador that Ott would be sent to him from Mostar where he "is currently employed with one of the front reconnaissance troops." NARA, T-120, Roll 5787, 438219.

[218] HR HDA 1521, Box 31, File 546 Stilinović, Statements of Hans Ott and Willibald Nemetschek. Yugoslav interrogators noted that Ott denied that he had asked Nemetschek to leave. Nemetschek, however, stood by his statement given in 1948 that Ott held talks with high-level Partisan functionaries, including Hebrang, but that he did not know the details of the meetings. KAW, B/67:145, Interview with Willibald Nemetschek conducted by Peter Broucek (10 September 1981). Ott was probably referring to dozens of Party members who were arrested in Zagreb in the previous weeks. At least ten of them were requested for exchange. *Sjeverozapadna Hrvatska 1941–1945*, Vol. X, p. 477, KPH Commission for Northern Croatia to KPH Central Committee (10 July 1944).

according to another source, the Partisans were granted a personal audience with Glaise-Horstenau.[219]

Captain Gerhard-Oskar Merrem, an *Abwehr* officer who extensively toured the western parts of Yugoslavia in the late spring and early summer of 1944, used his visit to Zagreb to confer with Nemetschek about his impressions of the enemy's situation. Nemetschek told him that the latest political developments concerning the rapprochement between the government-in-exile and the Communist-dominated National Committee[220] had led to the weakening of the Partisan movement. As an example, the German envoy to Pisarovina cited the fact that the clenched-fist salute had already been abolished.[221] Nemetschek also said that he could detect a certain amount of dejection among the Partisans as a result of these events, and if Tito would agree to serve under the Serbian King, then "the subversive propaganda [*Spaltepropaganda*] could have great effect."[222]

While the envoys continued to observe developments in the enemy camp, Ambassador Kasche continued lobbying for a cessation of hostilities with the Partisans under terms favorable to Germany. A visit to Hitler's headquarters in mid-August 1944 seemed a perfect opportunity to assess the attitude of his superiors on the matter. Kasche wrote: "I mentioned the possibility of a cessation of hostilities against Tito which had presented itself in 1943. The *Führer* remarked that in this case we would have to let Pavelić fall. I denied this and said that we did not need to make any far-reaching political deals with Tito. As I declared that such a

---

[219] KAW, B/67:145, Interview with Willibald Nemetschek conducted by Peter Broucek (10 September 1981); HR HDA 1521, Box 9, File 289 Nemetschek, Statement of Othmar Unger.

[220] Under pressure from Whitehall, King Peter II dismissed his government, which was overwhelmingly Serb and staunchly pro-Mihailović, and tasked Ivan Šubašić, a moderate monarchist and member of the Croatian Peasant Party, with forming a new government. Šubašić, Churchill hoped, would be acceptable to Tito and the two could work together toward creating a unified front against the Germans; the move would also help save the monarchy and give the non-Communists a modicum of influence in the National Committee. In mid-June 1944, the new prime minister of the royal government visited Tito on the island of Vis. After several days of talks, they reached an agreement aimed at paving the way for a unified Yugoslav government in the near future. In exchange for being recognized by the Šubašić administration as the leading force in the country, the Partisan leadership agreed to negotiate with the government-in-exile which had been pronounced illegitimate by the AVNOJ in November 1943; Tito also agreed that the question of the monarchy should be settled after the war by popular referendum. Petranović, *Istorija Jugoslavije*, Vol. II, pp. 318–19.

[221] The clenched-fist salute had been replaced by a common military salute on 25 April 1944. The change applied only to field units and not local detachments. *Hronologija*, p. 722.

[222] NARA, T-311, Roll 195, 000785, Experiences made during duty travel through Serbia and Croatia from 20 June to 4 July 1944 (5 July 1944).

possibility, although not as favorable as in 1943, might still exist and should be exploited, the *Führer* made no objections."[223]

Deteriorating relations between the Partisans and Western Allies seemed to play into Kasche's hands. Tito's hesitation to form a coalition government led Churchill to believe that he had made empty promises at Vis in order to secure continued material support from the Allies. To make matters worse, reports from liaison officers in the field stated that these supplies were used to fight the Chetniks, rather than the Germans. The Partisan leadership, for their part, remained deeply suspicious of British intentions in the country. Numerous military missions and the increasing presence of British forces along the Adriatic coast were seen as harbingers of impending large-scale operations. Tito reasoned that an Allied landing at this point could serve no purpose other than to support the fledgling Chetnik movement whose last stronghold in Serbia was under direct threat from converging NOVJ forces.[224]

Ott had another meeting with Andrija Hebrang, probably during the prisoner exchange in Pisarovina on 12 October 1944. The details were related to Kasche, who then passed them on to the foreign ministry: "Above all, the latter [Hebrang] wanted to know whether Germany would rather come to an understanding with the English or the Russians; he also wanted to hear whether, for this purpose, we had any contact with England. In this connection, the Partisans are not happy about Churchill's visit to Moscow. They are afraid that the Soviets will concede Trieste, Istria, and neighboring territory to the Anglo-Americans. Hebrang explained that nationalist Serbs were now once again leaning more strongly toward the

---

[223] KAW, B/67:142, Memo to Foreign Minister on meeting with the Führer (18 August 1944). For a slightly different version, see ADAP/E/VIII/456, Conversation with the Führer in main headquarters "Wolfschanze" on 14 August 1944 between 17.30 and 18.30 (16 September 1944). Hitler's silent approval of Kasche's plan was at least in part the result of his ongoing frustration with the state of affairs in the NDH. In May 1944, he exclaimed that he would get rid of Pavelić as soon as the war was finished. Only eight days after the conference with Kasche, Hitler told Field Marshal von Weichs that he was thinking about dismantling the Croatian state and annexing her territory to the Third Reich. Schmider, *Partisanenkrieg*, p. 404.

[224] Petranović, *Istorija Jugoslavije*, Vol. II, pp. 322, 326–30; Dušan Biber, "The Yugoslav Partisans and the British in 1944," in William Deakin, Elisabeth Barker, and Jonathan Chadwick, eds., *British Political and Military Strategy in Central, Eastern and Southern Europe in 1944* (London: Macmillan Press, 1988), pp. 117–25. The tensions culminated in mid-September when Tito left Vis aboard a Soviet aircraft headed for Romania without informing the British. The island had a large British garrison and Tito, as he remarked, felt as though he was "in a mouse-trap." The trip to Romania was made in secret allegedly because Tito feared he might meet the same fate as that of Polish General Wladyslaw Sikorski. The latter was under British protection and had a troublesome relationship with Churchill prior to dying under mysterious circumstances in a plane crash in 1943.

Anglo-Americans: this would open up the possibility of landings by the latter, which the Partisans vehemently reject."[225]

Kasche thought he had every reason to be optimistic about his initiative. On 13 October, he held a meeting with Franz von Harling and used the opportunity to explain his views on the matter. The ambassador reminded the lieutenant colonel of his old plan from spring 1943 for "closer collaboration" with Tito's troops, which called for the cessation of hostilities and the withdrawal of the Partisans to a certain territory from whence they could wage the war against the Chetniks undisturbed by the Germans. Kasche told von Harling that he now had "good reason to hope that he could reach an agreement with Tito's bandits, if even a loose one." The chief *Abwehr* officer of Army Group F expressed his doubts by pointing out the close cooperation between the NOVJ and the Red Army in Serbia. Kasche was not concerned and replied that much could still be achieved in this field by sustained effort.[226] He made his intentions known that he would do precisely that in a cable to the foreign ministry that same day. In the list of high priority special tasks he set for himself, one included ". . . maintaining constant contact with Tito's organization with the objective of gathering intelligence on its political and military intentions. [This should also enable us] to spread subversive propaganda with the aim of splitting [the organization] from within [. . . *und Einschaltung unserer Tendenzen zwecks innerer Aufspaltung*]."[227]

Kasche remained convinced until the end that he was doing a good job; Hitler, the Army, and SS authorities in the NDH, however, did not share his conviction.[228] Likewise, Ott was apparently clever enough not to waste his own time, or that of his Partisan colleagues, on talks along the unrealistic lines proposed by the ambassador. Bakrač's reports from the final six months of the war contain no mention whatsoever that Ott discussed the possibility of the Partisans switching sides. Even if he had been willing to implement Kasche's ideas, his prestige and influence were in decline—senior *Wehrmacht* commands were now assuming the lead role in the negotiations with the NOVJ.[229] Now the main focus for the Germans was not on

---

[225] Kasche to Foreign Ministry (15 October 1944), quoted in Biber, "The Yugoslav Partisans," p. 114.

[226] NARA, T-311, Roll 194, 000439–40, Memorandum on duty travel to Zagreb on 13 October 1944 (14 October 1944).

[227] ADAP/E/VIII/499, Kasche to Foreign Ministry (13 October 1944).

[228] Hitler called Kasche "a daydreamer" in early September and let his displeasure with the ambassador be known through official channels of the foreign ministry in late October. Kasche, unsurprisingly, replied with his well-known self-righteous attitude. See ADAP/E/VIII/517, Foreign Ministry to Kasche (30 October 1944) and accompanying footnotes.

[229] In his report on the visit to Zagreb in late February 1945, Bakrač wrote that Ott had become redundant now that high-ranking *Wehrmacht* officers were spearheading the talks: "They had apparently lost the trust they once had in him." HR HDA 1491, 2.41, 216, Bakrač's report on visit to Zagreb from 26 February–1 March (undated).

how to spread discord among their enemies, but on how to get out of the country as soon as possible.

Ott had been serving as both Kasche's confidant and Glaise-Horstenau's top agent simultaneously. Judging by the available sources, Glaise-Horstenau's agenda in the spring and summer of 1944 was markedly different from that of the ambassador. The Third Reich's situation became increasingly bleak and, at least since the Italian capitulation in 1943, Glaise-Horstenau was convinced that the war could not be won. Under these circumstances, the general began to explore the possibility of reaching some sort of accommodation with the Western Allies. He maintained close contacts with highly-placed functionaries of the HSS, as well as with several moderate members of the *Ustashe* leadership who shared his views. Both groups hoped to gain Allied support for an independent Croatia after the war by switching sides at the most opportune moment. The Home Guard was supposed to seize control of the country, thus providing the Allies with a secure bridgehead on the eastern coast of the Adriatic. Beginning in early 1944, the HSS made contact with the Allies through defectors and intermediaries in Italy and Switzerland. By the early spring, they had also begun negotiating with the Croatian Partisans. In exchange for accepting the HSS as an equal partner in the resistance movement, the Croatian branch of the Communist Party would be assured a place in the sharing of post-war power.[230]

According to Major von Pott, Glaise-Horstenau wanted to ascertain the Croatian Communist leadership's opinions through his envoys in Pisarovina and Zagreb. His ultimate aim was to either secure the silent recognition of the new, moderate Croatian government, or to induce the local Partisans to join her. This would bring not only short-term dividends in the form of pacification of the country, but would also represent a major blow to the Yugoslav idea propagated by the KPJ. Furthermore, Tito's prestige as the leader of a unified resistance movement would be ruined.[231] Andrija Hebrang's presence at the talks with Ott was not requested by coincidence—he was known for his moderate stance toward non-Communist organizations such as the HSS and the Catholic Church. Furthermore, he was often at odds with the Central Committee of the KPJ because of his alleged Croatian nationalist leanings.[232] Despite the sustained efforts found in the Yugoslav historiography that seek to defame him as a traitor sympathetic to the plans of the HSS and Glaise-Horstenau, there is no evidence that Hebrang made any commitments, either personally or through the Partisan envoys in Zagreb.[233] He

---

[230] For more details on the Croatian peace feelers, see Tomasevich, *Occupation and Collaboration*, pp. 442–49.

[231] HR HDA 1521, Box 9, File 123 Horstenau, Statement of Eugen von Pott.

[232] See, for instance, Tito's cables to Hebrang on 7 April 1944 (*Zbornik*/II/12/460) and 17 September 1944 (*Zbornik*/II/14/124). See also Djilas, *Wartime*, pp. 315–17.

[233] The Yugoslav secret police exerted a great deal of effort in uncovering evidence of Hebrang's alleged personal contacts with Glaise-Horstenau. Nemetschek later wrote that he

almost certainly informed his superiors of the contacts with Glaise-Horstenau's representatives just as he had done in the past, and requested instructions on negotiating techniques. The decision to receive Ott for a personal audience was a signal to the German commands in the NDH that the Partisan leadership had a lively interest in keeping the back-channel open. Apart from the fact that these contacts would allow for the gathering of information on German intentions at this critical phase of the war, they could also be used for advancing one's own diplomatic proposals when the right time came (see below).

If the NDH joined the Allies, one question that remained to be answered was the fate of the German troops in her territory. This issue was closely connected to the 20 July Plot against Hitler and the political designs concerning the future of the countries in the region. Von Pott claimed that Glaise-Horstenau envisaged the resurrection of an independent Austria, perhaps as a part of some "Danubian Confederation" which would also include Czechoslovakia, Slovenia, Croatia, and possibly even Bavaria. In order to secure Allied support for his plan, he was willing to organize an anti-Nazi coup in the Balkans with the help of other high-ranking *Wehrmacht* officers of Austrian origin, including Colonel General Löhr, the Commander-in-Chief of Army Group E. The coup was supposed to be carried out by Croatian and Austrian units with the aim of seizing control over the Adriatic

---

was supposed to be the key witness in Hebrang's trial and give "false testimony" against him. KAW, B/67:145, Interview with Willibald Nemetschek conducted by Peter Broucek, 10 September 1981. Nemetschek told his interrogators after the war that one of the letters of safe conduct issued to the Partisan envoys in December 1943 bore the name of Ivan Jurišić, which was Hebrang's pseudonym. According to Nemetschek, the man who came with Stilinović to Zagreb in early 1944 was, in fact, Andrija Hebrang. HR HDA 1521, Box 31, File 24 Bakrač, Statement of Willibald Nemetschek. Othmar Unger said that the man in question "could have been Jurišić." Ibid., Box 31, File 546 Stilinović, Statement of Othmar Unger. Nemetschek also claimed that Hebrang was a member of the Partisan delegation that visited Glaise-Horstenau in his villa in the summer of 1944. Josef Halbwindl, the driver attached to the office of the plenipotentiary general, initially stated that Major von Pott ordered him to drive Hebrang back to Pisarovina, then refuted his statement, and then had it changed back to the original. Ibid., 1521, Box 9, File 327 von Pott, Statement of Josef Halbwindl. During his interrogation, Major von Pott did not mention Hebrang as a member of the Partisan delegation, nor did he mention any meetings between him and Glaise-Horstenau. Ibid., Box 9, File 123 Horstenau, Statement of Eugen von Pott. It should be noted that all the statements concerning Hebrang were extracted under pressure. Engelbert Teufelhardt, Glaise-Horstenau's liaison to the office of Archbishop Stepinac, stated that the general "negotiated with Hebrang" (KAW, B/67:145, Teufelhardt to Broucek, 13 August 1975), which some authors interpreted as confirmation of the claims found in the Yugoslav historiography. Kazimirović, *Nemački general,* p. 180. The vague wording used by Teufelhardt might also suggest that the negotiations were carried out through intermediaries, as is likely.

coastline and parts of Austria and Slovenia, and delivering them to the Allies.[234] The idea was compatible with the plans of the 20 July plotters which called for a separate peace with Great Britain and the United States. Glaise-Horstenau kept in frequent contact with Rudolf Graf von Marogna-Redwitz, a known Bavarian monarchist and head of the Austrian wing of the conspiracy, who was also the senior *Abwehr* official in Vienna. Their liaison was *Sonderführer* Karl Ludwig Freiherr von und zu Guttenberg, who was sent to Zagreb in early 1943 tasked with coordinating officers disaffected with the state of affairs in Germany.[235] The failed attempt on Hitler's life and von Guttenberg's subsequent arrest[236] did not put an end to Glaise-Horstenau's activities. The Allies' marked interest in the possibility of a separate arrangement with the Austrians in the Balkans was demonstrated by a leaflet dropped over Yugoslavia in mid-August that was addressed to six Austrian-born *Wehrmacht* generals, reminding them of their duty to help free their land of origin and to save the lives of Austrian-born soldiers under their command.[237] In more concrete terms, the Allies demonstrated a willingness to discuss the capitulation of German troops on both the local and regional level in the first days of September.[238]

---

[234] HR HDA 1521, Box 9, File 123 Horstenau, Statement of Eugen von Pott. Glaise-Horstenau's attitude toward an independent Austria is a subject of some controversy; he had actively supported the *Anschluss,* feeling that the Austrian Republic of 1918 could not survive. On the other hand, he had some connections to the Austrian resistance and allegedly felt betrayed by Hitler who would not honor Austria's "individuality." His biographer, Peter Broucek, concluded that the solution closest to Glaise-Horstenau's heart was a political change within the Third Reich which would also be acceptable to the Western Allies. Broucek, ed., *Ein General im Zwielicht,* Vol. III, pp. 42–43.

[235] Ibid., pp. 40–41.

[236] Several days after the assassination attempt, the head of the SD in Zagreb, SS Lieutenant Colonel Günther Hermann (another Austrian) informed Glaise-Horstenau that he had orders to arrest von Guttenberg. Upon hearing this, the general offered to smuggle von Guttenberg out to Partisan-held territory using the prisoner exchange contacts. Von Guttenberg refused, fearing reprisals against his family and the possibility that the Partisans would exchange him back at the first opportunity. Von Guttenberg had little to do with the Pisarovina cartel during his time in Zagreb; he traveled to the neutral zone only once. HR HDA 1521, Box 9, File 140 Guttenberg, Statement of Willibald Nemetschek; Maria Theodora von dem Bottlenberg-Landsberg, *Karl Ludwig Freiherr von und zu Guttenberg, 1902–1945: ein Lebensbild* (Berlin: Lukas Verlag, 2003), p. 253. His fears were not entirely unfounded; it seems that the Partisans had exchanged defectors on at least one occasion. NARA, T-311, Roll 188, 001000, Activity report of Chief Commissioner of Field Police with Army Group F and subordinated Secret Field Police Groups for September 1944 (12 October 1944).

[237] Broucek, ed., *Ein General im Zwielicht,* Vol. III, p. 43.

[238] In early September 1944, the head of the OSS mission to Mihailović, Lieutenant Colonel Robert McDowell, met with Rudi Stärker, the envoy of Minister Hermann Neubacher. Neubacher,

Glaise-Horstenau remained unscathed by the wave of retribution following the 20 July Plot, but his career did not survive the machinations of his adversaries, Ambassador Kasche and the *Ustashe* leader, Pavelić. The formal reason for the general's downfall was the accusation that he had made defeatist statements concerning the attempt of two *Ustashe* ministers (Ante Vokić and Mladen Lorković) to bring about a pro-Allied *putsch* in the NDH. In reality, Pavelić accused the general of being an accomplice, despite the fact that he was aware of the overtures made by the two ministers. Kasche was more than willing to join this scheme in the hope of eliminating his most serious political rival in the country. Glaise-Horstenau, disillusioned by the unwillingness of the top circles of the Third Reich to instigate internal reforms in the NDH, had already been seeking a different posting since the spring of that year. Consequently, he accepted the news of his removal from the post of the plenipotentiary general on 20 September with a calm heart; anticipating just such a decision on the part of his superiors, he had left Zagreb the previous week.[239]

The haste with which the general left the Croatian capital is probably related to one last attempt he had made to effect an arrangement with the Allies. On 27 September 1944, the chief of the Office of Strategic Services (OSS) station in Bern, Allen Dulles, informed his colleagues in Caserta, Italy, that Glaise-Horstenau was willing to go ahead with the plan of "freeing Austria" with the help of his fellow officers. As a further incentive, Dulles' source informed him that the Germans had already evacuated the coastal regions and that the Allies would not have any trouble landing there. Although the general had been relieved of his post just recently, he was willing to return to Zagreb and meet an American agent for detailed consultations. A preliminary meeting between Dulles' source and the agent could take place after 5 October in either the building of the Wiener Bankverein or at the seat of the Slavex Company.[240] Once contact was made, the agent would be taken to

---

an Austrian, offered to arrange a withdrawal of the German forces to the Sava–Danube line where they would be employed exclusively against the Red Army. McDowell replied that only unconditional surrender would be accepted. FRUS: *Diplomatic Papers, 1944,* Vol. 1, *General* (Washington, DC: GPO, 1966), pp. 549–50, Cables of Alexander C. Kirk, United States political adviser on the staff of the Allied Supreme Commander in the Mediterranean, to the Secretary of State, 7 September 1944. British liaison officers to the Macedonian Partisans demanded unconditional surrender from the German garrison in Prilep in the same period (see next chapter).

[239] Schmider, *Partisanenkrieg,* pp. 404–10; Broucek, ed., *Ein General im Zwielicht,* Vol. III, p. 453–54, Entry for October 1944.

[240] The choice of meeting place was not coincidental; Major von Pott had been an employee of this Viennese bank before the war. HR HDA 1521, Box 9, File 327 von Pott, Statement of Eugen von Pott. Whether the fact that he had also been a representative of the famous Warner Brothers studios contributed to this arrangement is not clear. *Nemačka obavještajna služba,* Vol. V, p. 119. The close ties between Slavex and the German intelligence and military authorities in Zagreb have already been discussed.

Glaise-Horstenau. If the Allies remained interested in his offers, the negotiations could be continued by an officer of appropriate rank. OSS HQ in Washington approved of the plan, despite misgivings about Glaise-Horstenau's personality.[241]

Frank Lindsay, who had hitherto been a liaison officer to the Slovene Partisans, was chosen for this mission and dispatched to Croatia. His superiors understood that it would be both wise and practical to inform the Partisans about Lindsay's mission and request their help. Tito had already been told of the possibility of a separate surrender of German forces and agreed to adhere to the guidelines issued by the Combined Chiefs of Staff on 18 August.[242] Lindsay therefore had no trouble obtaining the support of the Main HQ for Croatia. He gladly accepted their offer to send one of their men on a reconnaissance mission and report back whether or not Glaise-Horstenau was present in Zagreb. Much to Lindsay's disappointment, the Partisan agent returned with the news that the general had been arrested by the Gestapo two weeks earlier, and the mission was canceled.[243]

Glaise-Horstenau, as a strong advocate for contact with the Partisans, had managed to secure them a degree of legitimacy by his skillful maneuvering and personal engagement in the prisoner exchange process. It would be reasonable to assume that his successors would take an altogether different view in the wake of the failed 20 July Plot, but Glaise-Horstenau's departure actually had surprisingly little effect on the dealings in Zagreb and Pisarovina; prisoner exchanges continued on a regular basis, and contact with the NOVJ's Main HQ for Croatia was brokered via the same hands.[244] Glaise-Horstenau's successors[245] had no personal ambitions

---

[241] Franklin Lindsay, *Beacons in the Night: With the OSS and Tito's Partisans in Wartime Yugoslavia* (Stanford: Stanford University Press, 1993), pp. 220–21. According to Washington, Glaise-Horstenau was an "egotistical opportunist . . . almost completely without an ethical code. Give as little as you can and extract everything that you can."

[242] For the full text of the guidelines, see FRUS: *Diplomatic Papers, 1944*, Vol. 1, *General*, pp. 542–43, Combined Chiefs of Staff to Eisenhower and Wilson (18 August 1944); for Tito's acceptance of the guidelines and his intention to use the German POWs for road construction, see ibid., p. 554, Alexander Kirk to Secretary of State (21 September 1944). The Combined Chiefs of Staff was the supreme military staff for Great Britain and the United States tasked with conducting joint military operations.

[243] Lindsay, *Beacons in the Night*, pp. 222–24. Glaise-Horstenau was in fact not arrested, but rumors suggested that something happened to him. On 19 October 1944, Tito was informed that the general had "disappeared" from Zagreb one week previously. *Zbornik*/V/34/540, Main HQ for Croatia to Supreme HQ (19 October 1944).

[244] Of the principle German figures involved with the prisoner exchange, only Major von Pott left Zagreb with Glaise-Horstenau in October 1944. HR HDA 1521, Box 9, File 327 von Pott, Statement of Eugen von Pott.

[245] The inspector general of the NDH's armed forces, Hans Juppe, shouldered the running of the office of the plenipotentiary general after Glaise-Horstenau's departure. The post itself

and largely preferred things to remain *status quo*. Even if they had been desirous of a greater role, they would have found their freedom of action severely curtailed by the new power factor in the NDH, the office of the Commander-in-Chief Southeast (Army Group F). In light of the steadily deteriorating war situation, this command had great interest in keeping the back-channel open.

Despite the failure of the plan to contact Glaise-Horstenau, the Allies were still not ready to give up the idea of the capitulation of the German occupation forces in the Balkans. A new initiative to this effect came from the head of the American military mission to the Supreme HQ, Colonel Ellery Huntington, in November 1944. On the 26th, Tito ordered the Main HQ for Croatia to send one of its representatives to Zagreb and establish contact with the German high command there: "His mission is to discuss the terms of surrender of the German troops in our area of responsibility. . . . Our terms are: 1) They must surrender themselves and their weapons to us; 2) We guarantee their lives; officers may retain their decorations; and they shall all be repatriated to Germany after the war. Inform us immediately about the possible negotiations."[246] Tito insisted on these terms for two reasons. First, the surrender of two German Army groups to his forces, rather than to the Western Allies or even the Soviets, would cement the role of the new, Communist-controlled Yugoslavia in the anti-Nazi coalition and would greatly enhance her standing in the world. Second, there was fear that Yugoslav collaborationists would use the time needed for a staged withdrawal of the Germans to gain control of the western parts of the country and make peace with the Allies.[247]

Although no records of the German-Partisan talks from November and December have survived, it can be safely assumed that no progress was made. The terms proposed by the Supreme HQ were unacceptable to the German supreme command in the Balkans. The overriding concern was about not falling into Yugoslav captivity after three-and-a-half years of very brutal fighting. General Erich Schmidt-Richberg wrote that "both the command and the troops expected that the

---

remained empty until late November, when SS General Hans-Adolf Prützmann was appointed to it. Broucek, ed., *Ein General im Zwielicht*, Vol. III, p. 454, Entry for October 1944 and accompanying footnotes. Prützmann, however, remained in office for only six weeks and apparently visited Zagreb only once, in late December 1944. NARA, T-311, Roll 193, 000345, Telephone conversation between SS Colonel Constantin Canaris and Lieutenant General Heinz von Glydenfeldt, 23 December 1944, 10.15 hours. On 15 January 1945, Juppe returned to the post and stayed until the end of the war. In his post-war statement given to the U.S. military authorities, Juppe mentioned prisoner exchange only in the context of Glaise-Horstenau's activities in the NDH. Institut für Zeitgeschichte München (Institute for Contemporary History, Munich, hereinafter IfZ), ZS-0493, Interrogation of Hans Juppe (13 June 1947), retrieved from: http://www.ifz-muenchen.de/archiv/zs/zs-0493.pdf

[246] VA, 119/4, 1, 3–11, Supreme HQ to Main HQ for Croatia (26 November 1944); also reproduced in *Zbornik*/II/14/393.

[247] Schmider, "Der jugoslawische Kriegsschauplatz," p. 1066.

retreat [from Greece] would be continued to the German border, where we would link up with the German front facing the enemy from the East."[248] German commands in the field had already launched a propaganda campaign aimed at weakening their enemies' resolve to interfere with their withdrawal. The Partisans parried by attempting to draw local units to the negotiating table in the hope of effecting their surrender. Each side relied on the war-weariness of the other and claimed that humanitarian considerations were the main motive for their offers.[249]

Hans Ott remembered that around Christmas 1944, the German high command in Zagreb discussed the proposition that had allegedly been made by the Chief of the Croatian OZNA, General Ivan Krajačić. The idea was that the German occupation forces would be allowed to conduct a staged withdrawal if they would cease operations and refrain from leaving a path of destruction in their wake.[250] That this offer was, in fact, the cornerstone of the German negotiating position rather than the Partisan one, is confirmed by contemporary reports of Boris Bakrač from February 1945 onwards.[251] During his visit to Zagreb from 13–16 February, he was visited twice by Lieutenant Colonel von Stephani.[252] The latter wanted to know when the talks could be resumed and mentioned that the Yugoslavs could profit from them. He assured the Partisan envoy that the Germans had lost none of their earlier interest in the matter and that Colonel General Löhr was personally enthusiastic about it. Von Stephani emphasized the need for securing immediate communications between the two sides so that the envoys could meet within twenty-four hours if necessary. Bakrač repeated the demand for the separate, unconditional surrender of German forces in Yugoslavia. The lieutenant colonel replied that they "could not wage war on their own," implying that his superiors would not take

---

[248] Schmidt-Richberg, *Der Endkampf auf dem Balkan*, p. 147.

[249] German propaganda was designed to convince the Partisans that the German soldiers just wanted to return home in peace and that any attempt to stop them would only lead to unnecessary bloodletting. The Partisans retorted that Germany had already lost the war and to continue fighting would be senseless. For an example of German leaflets requesting free passage from the Partisans, see NARA, T-314, Roll 1630, 000774–5 (undated, probably the end of December 1944). The command of the 91st Army Corps had explicitly forbidden any local negotiations with the Partisans, fearing this would have a negative impact on the morale of the troops. Ibid., 000771, Instructions for Croatia (26 December 1944). For a German translation of a Partisan leaflet from the same period, see Kühnrich and Hitze, *Deutsche bei Titos Partisanen*, pp. 167–68.

[250] HR HDA 1521, Box 9, File 147 von Harling, Statement of Hans Ott.

[251] Bakrač's reports on meetings in Zagreb and Pisarovina during January do not mention the discussions on the German surrender/withdrawal.

[252] I have not been able to find anything on a German officer with this name. It is possible that "von Stephani" (alternative spelling: Stephany) was a pseudonym used by a staff member of Army Group E.

independent action on this question. As the Partisan plenipotentiary countered that now was the right moment to do exactly that, von Stephani said it was too early. "All right," Bakrač said, "if you really think it is still too early, go ahead and keep waiting." Despite Bakrač's uncompromising stand, von Stephani parted with the wish that the two of them should meet more often and expressed hope that by working together, they could persuade their superiors to "mitigate the horrors of war."[253]

The two envoys met again on 27 February during one of Bakrač's routine visits concerning a prisoner exchange. Upon being asked "how is our proposal going," the Partisan replied that he had nothing to add to what he had already said. By laying down their arms, the soldiers in Yugoslavia would not only secure themselves fair treatment in captivity, but would also render patriotic service to Germany—the country was in ruins and needed every man for the post-war reconstruction. Bakrač added that these talks only made sense if everyone involved recognized that the war was lost for Germany; otherwise, the whole matter was merely a waste of time. Von Stephani again had to use all his personal charm to convince Bakrač not to break off the contact. He said that any attempt to bring about an unconditional surrender would be doomed to failure. The Army was completely infiltrated by the SS and the Gestapo, and they could be expected to stage an internal coup the moment the surrender orders were issued by the high command. The lieutenant colonel said he would not inform his superiors of the deadlock, but would instead tell them that the Partisans were still considering the German proposals. He then implored Bakrač to try one more time to convince his leadership "to back down a little" and stop demanding the impossible. Just before the meeting concluded, von Stephani re-emphasized the need to meet as often as possible; only through continuous talks were they likely to achieve a solution that "would benefit all."[254]

It was obvious that Bakrač and his immediate superiors from the Main HQ for Croatia were not willing to depart from the original terms proposed in the late fall of 1944. The Germans therefore attempted to establish direct contact with Belgrade though someone who was thought to be more flexible. Vladimir Velebit, an old acquaintance of the engineer, Ott, and Tito's personal envoy during the talks in Livno in 1942 and the March Negotiations in 1943, was chosen. He had been known to the Germans as "Dr. Vladimir Petrović" until the summer of 1944 when the BBC inadvertently revealed his true identity.[255] The German police attaché immediately informed the RSHA about the consensus in Zagreb that Velebit was

---

[253] The German officer was trying hard to win over his Partisan counterpart. According to Bakrač, they parted "very amicably," with von Stephani asking him whether he personally needed anything or if "we on the outside [i.e. the Partisans]" needed medical supplies. HR HDA 1491, 2.41, 215, Bakrač's report on the visit to Zagreb from 13–16 February 1945 (undated).

[254] Ibid., 216, Bakrač's report on visit to Zagreb from 26 February–1 March 1945 (undated).

[255] Velebit, *Tajne i zamke*, p. 219. Velebit arrived in London in May 1944 as the chief of the NOVJ military mission.

not a Communist and that he was, in fact, sympathetic to the Western Allies.[256] In addition to these obvious "qualities," Velebit was likely to take interest in what was transpiring in Zagreb for personal reasons—his closest relatives were arrested and interned immediately after the fateful broadcast. The Germans did not blackmail him, knowing this would not produce any results, but offered their release as a token of goodwill. In exchange, both von Stephani and Ott (who in the interim had returned from hospital) requested Velebit's presence at the high-level meeting for which they were pressing Bakrač in mid-March 1945. The meeting was planned to take place in Pisarovina at the end of the month with von Weichs dispatching a personal representative to broker a deal. Bakrač told the German envoys that the choice of delegates rested exclusively in the hands of the Main HQ for Croatia. He added that since Velebit was entrusted with other tasks at the time, his presence might not be possible. The Germans replied that they had asked for Velebit "precisely because he had just returned from London."[257]

It would be safe to assume that the Germans thought that their propositions would be more acceptable to the Anglophile member of the new, British-sponsored coalition government than to the local military command which appeared firmly in Communist hands. It is not a coincidence that the "Austrian card" was re-played on this very occasion. Von Stephani expounded that the army was still fighting in Yugoslavia only owing to the "stupid whim" of the supreme command in Berlin. Although the Commander-in-Chief Southeast had some latitude in decision-making, the strong presence of the SS and the Gestapo made a separate surrender impossible at this juncture. The worsening military situation, however, meant that Hitler's hold over the Army could not last much longer. Colonel General Löhr, von Stephani continued, was an Austrian and understood the complexities of the region. He was more flexible than von Weichs (who was a German), and therefore more likely to seize the initiative once the right moment came. Löhr knew that Germany would be partitioned and Austria resurrected. Under these circumstances, his loyalties lay with his homeland and he would do everything to secure her future. To that effect, he would endeavor to appoint Austrians to the leading posts in the Army under his command. Bakrač commented in his report that "the conversation was, as always, permeated by the main question—why would we not take the territory when they were willing to give it to us without a fight?"[258]

<hr>

[256] HR HDA 1521, Box 9, File 327 von Pott, Archive of Hans Helm.

[257] HR HDA 1491, 2.41, 217, Bakrač's report on the visit to Zagreb from 12–16 March 1945 (undated). Velebit returned to Belgrade in early March 1945 after being appointed assistant to the Minister of Foreign Affairs. Velebit, *Tajne i zamke,* p. 340; See also "General Velebit extends his thanks," *Novosti,* 6 March 1945, p. 1, retrieved from: http://digicon.athabascau .ca/cdm/compoundobject/collection/ccan/id/156899/rec/1

[258] HR HDA 1491, 2.41, 217, Bakrač's report on the visit to Zagreb from 12–16 March 1945 (undated).

The high-level meeting the Germans were so keen to hold did not materialize. Von Stephani admitted on 27 March that he understood the reluctance of the Yugoslavs to compromise now that the war was practically over, but still expressed hope he would see Velebit in Pisarovina or Zagreb.[259] The Partisans should inform him by 11 April at the latest if they had an interest in such a meeting. Apart from the news that von Weichs was being relieved and that Löhr was taking over, the officer "said absolutely nothing new;" he merely repeated his old views and added that Löhr's new appointment could prove "very advantageous" for the Partisans. Bakrač gave no definitive answers and kept repeating that his superiors were reviewing the German proposals. Ott most likely sensed that the Partisans were, in fact, not interested in a deal, and pleaded with the Partisan envoy not to disclose this to von Stephani.[260]

During the envoys' next meeting in Zagreb, the German situation in Yugoslavia took a sharp turn for the worse; on 12 April 1945, the Yugoslav Army (official name of the Partisan forces as of 1 March) launched a major offensive aimed at breaking the stalemate on the Syrmian Front. The lines of Army Group E were pierced after two days of bitter fighting, and the Germans were compelled to begin a fighting withdrawal to the west.[261] As a consequence, they decided to raise the stakes on the negotiating table. In a conversation with Bakrač on 16 April, von Stephani alternated between threats and promises in another attempt to secure the right of free passage from the country for German troops. The continuation of fighting, he said, would mean further casualties for the Partisans and a complete devastation of the country. On the other hand, the Germans were prepared to leave all of their heavy equipment to the Yugoslavs if they were allowed to retreat to the Austrian border unobstructed. Von Stephani was surprised that the Main HQ for Croatia could not see the obvious advantages of such a deal and suggested the Yugoslavs bring forth a military expert who could recognize the value of the German offer. If the Croatian Partisans persisted in refusing these generous terms, the lieutenant colonel would gladly take the offer to their Slovene comrades. To this effect, he requested that the Main HQ for Slovenia be informed of the proceedings and that Ott be issued with a letter of safe conduct for a trip across the Croatian border.[262]

The "complete devastation of the country," von Stephani's threat, was the most likely reason why the Partisans agreed to host two high-level meetings in

---

[259] Velebit's relatives were released as promised on or about 1 April 1945. HR HDA 1491, 2.41, 44, To the 3rd Directorate of OZNA with the Ministry of People's Defense (17 April 1945).

[260] Ibid., 218, Bakrač's report on the visit to Zagreb from 26–29 March 1945 (undated).

[261] Karl Hnilicka, *Das Ende auf dem Balkan 1944/45: Die militärische Räumung Jugoslawiens durch die deutsche Wehrmacht* (Göttingen: Musterschmidt Verlag, 1970), pp. 130–33; *Oslobodilački rat*, Vol. II, pp. 576–81.

[262] HR HDA 1491, 2.41, 224, Bakrač's report on the visit to Zagreb from 16–19 April 1945 (undated).

Pisarovina in the last days of the war. The intention was to avoid the demolition of all strategically important objects in Zagreb, a move for which the Germans were already preparing.[263] The first meeting took place on 24 or 26 April 1945. The composition of the Partisan delegation bore witness to the importance they attached to the talks. Although Velebit was not amongst those present, General Krajačić, the Chief of the Croatian OZNA, was accompanied by Colonel Vicko Antić and Major Bakrač. The German delegation consisted of Glaise-Horstenau's old Chief of Staff, Colonel Hans-Harald von Selchow, Lieutenant Paul Manns, and the engineer, Hans Ott.[264] The details of the meeting are not known, but it can be assumed that the Germans offered to cancel the planned demolitions in exchange for safe passage from the country. The Yugoslavs almost certainly provided vague answers in the hope that the contact would not be broken off; they were stalling for time as their main forces stood only some eighty kilometers west of Zagreb.[265]

The final (and most dramatic) round of talks took place between 5 and 8 May 1945. On the 5th, Colonel von Selchow drove to Pisarovina and asked for terms of surrender. He was told that it would take another twenty-four hours until the terms were transmitted from Belgrade. By 6 May, Pisarovina was the frontline as the village and its surroundings were full of newly-arrived Yugoslav units preparing for an attack on Zagreb. As these troops knew nothing of the prisoner exchange arrangement, the arrival of Captain Albrecht von Brauchitsch in a car adorned with a white flag caused some sensation. Fortunately for the Germans, Bakrač was there to greet them and explain their presence. He was then asked to accompany them to Zagreb and discuss the terms with von Selchow. The idea of returning to the city amidst the chaos of the last days of the war was hardly appealing to the Partisan envoy. The way in which the Germans had treated him hitherto had been, in his own words, "beyond reproach," but the circumstances had changed—they were cornered and there was no way of telling what they might do next. Even if his immediate hosts remained correct, they had lost all control over the *Ustashe*. To make matters worse, Bakrač had no time to change and had to go to Zagreb for the first time wearing his Yugoslav major's uniform.[266]

---

[263] Schmidt-Richberg, *Der Endkampf auf dem Balkan,* p. 141. The Yugoslav leadership was very keen on taking the Croatian capital intact. At the beginning of 1945, Tito informed the Main HQ for Croatia that the British Royal Air Force may target the bridges outside of Zagreb, but that the city itself "must not be bombed." VA, 119/4, 2, 1–1, Supreme HQ to Main HQ for Croatia (2 January 1945).

[264] HR HDA 1521, Box 9, File 254 Manns, Statement of Hans Ott. Ott mentioned that Nemetschek was also present, but in fact he was still recuperating from his wounds in one of Zagreb's hospitals.

[265] *Oslobodilački rat,* Vol. II, pp. 624–26.

[266] HR HDA 1521, Box 9, File 368 von Selchow, Statement of Albrecht von Brauchitsch; Bakrač, "Razmjena ratnih zarobljenika," p. 857.

His apprehensions proved to be well-founded. As soon as the party left the Partisan-held territory, it encountered a *Ustashe* unit. Bakrač was dragged out of the car and his escort, a young intelligence officer from the 7th Serbian Brigade, was severely beaten. Von Brauchitsch's explanations fell on deaf ears as the *Ustashe* were equally mistrustful of the Germans—they were informed that a nearby German unit wanted to defect to the Yugoslavs. The situation was saved by a young *Ustashe* officer who decided it would be best to leave the matter to his superiors in Jastrebarsko. Along the way, they met a unit of the German Army, but the idea of placing themselves under the unit's protection apparently did not cross von Brauchitsch's mind ("I could have strangled him then and there with my own bare hands," an exasperated Bakrač later wrote). Fortunately, the *Ustashe* command in Jastrebarsko agreed to let them go about their business and they arrived at the office of the *Feldkommandantur* in Zagreb later that afternoon.[267]

The talks with von Selchow began immediately and the "wrangling," as the Yugoslav envoy called it, lasted until 02.00 the following day. The Germans offered to spare some military sites in Zagreb and its surroundings from demolition if the Yugoslavs would allow the remainder of Army Group E to withdraw to the Austrian border unobstructed.[268] Bakrač, in turn, informed him that the Yugoslavs could only accept the surrender of the Germans under the same conditions which Army Group C in Italy had agreed to before capitulating earlier that week. Von Selchow stated that the details surrounding the surrender in Italy were unknown to him and that he would have to request instructions from the high command which was already in Slovenia.[269] The talks were inconclusive, yet German sappers left the city untouched. Army Group E decided in the end not to carry out the demolitions. The reasons were twofold: first, the *Ustashe* leadership, supported by Ambassador Kasche, pleaded against such a move, hoping perhaps they would soon return to the country;[270] second, it seems probable that the German commanders had by then realized they would eventually have to surrender to the Yugoslavs. Under these circumstances, any demolitions in Zagreb would surely have adverse effect on the treatment of German prisoners.

Beginning on 7 May 1945, individual German units began surrendering to the Yugoslav Army. Others continued fighting, desperately trying to avoid a similar

---

[267] Ibid., p. 858.

[268] Ibid.

[269] HR HDA 1521, Box 9, File 368 von Selchow, Statement of Albrecht von Brauchitsch.

[270] Ibid., File 164 Ott, Statement of Siegfried Kasche; Schmidt-Richberg, *Der Endkampf auf dem Balkan,* pp. 140–41.

fate.[271] On that same day, von Brauchitsch picked up Bakrač and his escort, ostensibly in order to drive them back to the front line. The German captain, however, soon disclosed the true purpose of his visit—he wanted Bakrač to arrange an unobstructed withdrawal of a German unit that was fighting on the outskirts of the Croatian capital. Bakrač refused and was taken back to the city where he and the other Partisan officer had to spend two more days in hiding before being able to greet Yugoslav units on the streets of Zagreb on 9 May 1945.[272]

Intelligence Work in the Neutral Zone, 1943–1945

As the envoys of both sides were able to enter and exit enemy territory almost on a weekly basis, they were in a prime position to observe and report back to superiors everything of military interest.[273] All German representatives were in one way or another connected to the intelligence services. The engineer, Ott, was involved with various military, political, and police authorities in Zagreb, all of which he supplied with information. Although not involved directly in the prisoner exchange contacts, Ott's first superior from the Zagreb *Abwehr* station, Lieutenant Colonel Erich Klinkmüller, had a "lively interest" in these proceedings.[274] Ott was also called upon several times to provide briefings on the nature, strength, and disposition of the Partisans to high-ranking German officers, including Colonel Franz von Harling (chief intelligence officer of Army Group F) and SS Colonel Otto Kumm (Chief of Staff of the 5th SS Mountain Corps and later commander of the

---

[271] For more information on the German surrender in Yugoslavia, see Gaj Trifković, "The Forgotten Surrender: The End of the Second World War in Yugoslavia," *International Journal of Military History and Historiography* 37:2 (2017), pp. 147–72.

[272] Bakrač, "Razmjena ratnih zarobljenika," pp. 860–62. Ratko Anđelković, the young officer in Bakrač's company, undertook the trip to Zagreb on his own. As an intelligence officer, he hoped to gather useful information on enemy dispositions prior to the attack on the city itself. His enthusiasm almost cost him his life on several occasions. Apart from being beaten by the *Ustashe,* he was nearly lynched by a mob while hiding in the flat of a German soldier of Croatian origin who took care of him and Bakrač after the Germans left the city. Upon rejoining his unit on 9 May, he learned that he was suspected of desertion. He avoided capital punishment only after he had managed to convince his commander that he had acted in the best interest of the unit. Miladin Ivanović, *23. srpska divizija* (Belgrade: Republički odbor SUBNOR-a, 1994), pp. 404–09.

[273] One Partisan order from March 1944 read that a German car with a white flag occasionally comes to Pisarovina: "When this car appears, our units should take cover and not let themselves be seen by the passengers." *Zbornik*/V/25/53, Daily order of 2nd Brigade of 8th Division for 3 March 1944.

[274] HR HDA 1521, Box 9, File 206 Klinkmüller, Statement of Eugen von Pott.

7th SS Mountain Division *Prinz Eugen*).[275] He also shared information of military importance obtained through his various assets with Ambassador Kasche.[276] Willibald Nemetschek, although formally not an agent, was also active in procuring intelligence data on the Partisans. He gathered information from the exchange prisoners or from conversations he had with the people of Pisarovina and its surroundings during his frequent trips across the NDH and abroad.[277] The information was used by the intelligence section of the office of the plenipotentiary general for compiling situation reports. If the data seemed important enough, it was disseminated to various Army and security commands across occupied Yugoslavia. For instance, one report of the Higher SS and Police Leader in Serbia reads that the resistance movement tried to recruit both voluntary and involuntary workers headed for Germany for espionage tasks. This, the document states, had been learned "through prisoner exchange."[278]

The unsuccessful conclusion of Operation *Schwarz* and the growing Partisan strength in all parts of Yugoslavia was beginning to confirm that Tito, rather than Mihailović, was the most dangerous enemy of the Germans in the country.[279] As all attempts to quell the uprising through brute force alone proved to be futile, the Germans began considering a more refined approach aimed at striking at the enemy's head rather than his muscle. This strategy held that the uprising would be dealt a severe, if not fatal, blow if Tito could be eliminated through a surgical strike. The action was to be carried out by special units attached to various German divisions known as the *Trupps,* formed around a core of men from the Brandenburg

---

[275] Ibid., File 147 von Harling, Statement of Hans Ott; ibid., File 224 Kumm, Statement of Hans Ott.

[276] See the facsimile of the ambassador's memo from 27 November 1943 in Kazimirović, *NDH u svetlu nemackih dokumenata.*

[277] Major von Pott also said, without going into details, that Nemetschek probably carried out other "special intelligence tasks" for Glaise-Horstenau. HR HDA 1521, Box 9, File 289 Nemetschek, Statement of Eugen von Pott.

[278] *Nemačka obaveštajna služba,* Vol. VIII, p. 919, Higher SS and Police Leader in Serbia, Activity report for the period 1–31 August 1944 (1 September 1944).

[279] Whereas some German intelligence services tended to give precedence to Mihailović over Tito in terms of organization, strength, and discipline in the early months of 1943 (see the assessment made by Reinhard Gehlen's "Foreign Armies East" on 8 February 1943 in *Trials of War Criminals before the Nuernberg Military Tribunals under Control Council Law No. 10: Nuernberg, October 1946—April 1949,* Washington, DC: USGPO, Vol. XI, pp. 1016–20), there could be no doubt by the end of that year that Tito held the upper hand. *Zbornik/*XII/3/619–30, Commander-in-Chief Southeast, Situation estimate from the end of October 1943 (1 November 1943). For similar conclusions, see the report of the *Abwehr's* 3rd Section (intelligence on foreign armies) in NARA, T-77, Roll 883, 5632484, Enemy situation report (12 November 1943).

Division.[280] Approximately two weeks after the Armed Forces High Command approved the plan in mid-October 1943,[281] Marijan Stilinović was invited by Hans Ott and Captain Model to a lunch in the Esplanade Hotel in Zagreb. During the meal, they commented on the photographs published in a Berlin newspaper from the Gran Sasso raid conducted by German paratroopers which freed Mussolini. Ott jokingly remarked that Tito should be very careful lest the same thing happen to him. The Partisan envoy, however, took the remark very seriously and informed Supreme HQ about it in a radio message. The cable was intercepted and deciphered by the German listening service,[282] which had unpleasant consequences for Ott. He was first interrogated by SS Lieutenant Colonel Günther Hermann, the SD chief in Zagreb, and then later by his own *Abwehr* superiors in Army Group F in Belgrade. Fortunately for Ott, he managed to convince them that the whole thing was nothing but an accident and that he did not have any motive for passing on secrets to the Partisan envoy.[283]

Despite the incident, preparations for the assassination continued. On 28 October 1943, representatives of the 2nd Panzer Army and the Brandenburg Division discussed "Special Assignment Tito," which included an attack on the Bosnian town of Jajce where the Partisan leader was known to have his headquarters.[284] Two weeks later, the commander of the division submitted a detailed plan for the killing or capturing of the Partisan leader. The plan envisaged two possibilities: a) an airborne attack on Tito's stronghold, or b) assassination. The latter could be carried out either by an explosive package sent to Tito by two German agents posing as Allied officers, or by poison administered by "an agent infiltrated into Tito's circle."[285] Kidnapping was added to the list shortly thereafter, but this option would also require someone who could get close to the Supreme HQ. Ambassador

---

[280] Odić, *Neostvareni planovi*, pp. 175–79.

[281] NARA, T-311, Roll 285, 000790, Armed Forces High Command to Commander-in-Chief Southeast (15 October 1943).

[282] "Eng. Ott told Stilinović that about a month ago a plan was discussed which called for using paratroopers to kidnap Tito." NARA, T-313, Roll 196, 7456991, 2nd Panzer Army/ Intelligence section, Appendix to daily report for 9 November 1943.

[283] HR HDA 1521, Box 9, File Model, Statement of Hans Ott. Ott said after the war that he had intentionally disclosed the information to Stilinović. He probably did this to ingratiate himself with his Yugoslav captors. Major von Pott believed that the remark was made intentionally in the hope that Tito would move his headquarters to a location more suitable for a German attack. Ibid., File 164 Ott, Statement of Eugen von Pott. The incident also had a positive effect—thanks to the intercepted cable, the Germans learned Stilinović's real name. Ibid., Box 31, File 546 Stilinović, Statement of Willibald Nemetschek.

[284] NARA, T-313, Roll 192, 7452291–2, Memorandum on meeting with General von Pfuhl-stein and liaison officer to 2nd Regiment "Brandenburg" (28 October 1943).

[285] Ibid., 7452963–6, "Brandenburg" Division, Action against Tito (12 November 1943).

Kasche thought he had a solution to the problem. On 10 December, he informed the foreign ministry that he had introduced Lieutenant Boeckl, the leader of the mission against Tito, to Hans Ott. The latter was supposed to travel to Tito's HQ in a few days, and this opportunity could be exploited to bring one of Boeckl's men close to the target. Kasche added that he had not informed Ott about the plan.[286] There were two possible reasons for this: either the ambassador feared that the engineer would not agree, or there were concerns that Ott might repeat the mistake from October and let something slip during his talks with Partisan representatives.[287]

Even if Ott had been told of Boeckl's mission and had agreed to lead him to Tito, it is highly unlikely that he would have ever been brought anywhere near the target. On 9 November 1943, Tito received a cable from Dmitrov, warning him about a German agent posing as an officer with the Supreme HQ: "A link between this agent and the Germans is being maintained by the chief of the German intelligence service center, Ott, director of aluminum firm 'Hansa Leichtmetall' in Mostar. He works for General Glaise [Glaise-Horstenau] and uses the following codenames: 'Doctor Bauks' [*sic*], 'R,' '513.' This is for your information, so you can take appropriate measures."[288] One day later, Tito responded that the case of the German engineer-spy "was well-known" to the Supreme HQ. There were no enemy agents in the Supreme HQ, the cable continued, but there was a Partisan officer whose task was to extract information from Ott. "The issue is known to us and there is no reason to be worried."[289]

In his contacts with the Partisan envoys, Hans Ott had always tried to appear "as a German who was sympathetic and even friendly to the People's Liberation Movement."[290] According to his post-war statement, the Partisans tried to capitalize on this sentiment by attempting to recruit him as an agent. During a meeting in Pisarovina in the summer of 1944, Stilinović told Ott that the Yugoslavs considered him "one of their own," and asked him whether he was willing to supply information of military value. In exchange, the engineer was promised protection (presumably after the war) and was offered to be flown to Moscow to join the

---

[286] KAW, B/67:145, Kasche to Foreign Ministry (10 December 1943).

[287] Ott did not travel to the Supreme HQ, so the plan was canceled. Boeckl proved to be a poor choice for such a delicate mission because of his constant insobriety, and he was relieved of duty. His special detail, under the command of another officer, went into action with the paratroopers during the abortive attempt to capture Tito in Operation *Rösselsprung* on 25 May 1944. *Nemačka obaveštajna služba*, Vol. IX, p. 1489.

[288] *Sabrana djela*, Vol. XVII, p. 282, Dimitrov to Tito (9 November 1943).

[289] Ibid., p. 203, Tito to Dimitrov (10 November 1943).

[290] Ibid., p. 355.

"National Committee for a Free Germany"[291] if he so desired. Ott accepted and was questioned on the strength and dispositions of the German forces and of defense plans of various towns and cities under Axis control. He was also asked for details on the "new weapons," most likely the V-1 flying bombs the Germans had been using since mid-June 1944.[292]

The fact that Ott accepted the offer to disclose sensitive intelligence to the NOVJ's representatives did not mean that he had changed sides for good; one Partisan document from late October 1944 still calls him "the top German agent in our headquarters."[293] Ott almost certainly realized that the war was lost for the Third Reich and he sought to curry favor with the victors-to-be without actually defecting.[294] Whenever he was in Zagreb, Bakrač approached him with new requests for information. Ott was not forthcoming while in hospital after sustaining injuries in late January 1945, citing security fears as the reason for his silence.[295] After he had returned to duty in early March, he resumed his "spying" activities and supplied Bakrač with information on the strength and morale of German and NDH forces, as well as his personal impressions on the war situation in general. The intelligence he provided was of mixed value. For instance, he gave a reasonably accurate estimate of the overall German strength in the Balkans in late March, putting it at 170,000 men.[296] As their spring offensive in Syrmia got underway in mid-April, the Yugoslavs wanted to know more about the locations of various divisions and corps under Löhr's command. The partial list that Ott provided on 14 April (and which Bakrač related to his superiors immediately) was practically useless.[297] The engineer

---

[291] The committee (*Nationalkomitee Freies Deutschland*) was formed in mid-1943 in the Soviet Union around a cadre of German Communists and anti-fascists recruited from the ranks of German POWs.

[292] HR HDA 1521, Box 31, File 546 Stilinović, Statement of Hans Ott.

[293] HR HDA 1491, 2.41, 200, (untitled) (27 October 1944).

[294] Ott's colleagues, Nemetschek and Manns, followed suit and both were recorded providing confidential information to Bakrač in the early months of 1945. See HR HDA 1491, 2.41, 205 and 224, Bakrač's reports on visits to Zagreb on 15–18 January (undated) and 16 April 1945 (21 April 1945).

[295] Ibid., 206, Report on visit to Zagreb from 26 February–1 March 1945 (undated).

[296] Ibid., 207, Report on visit to Zagreb from 12–16 March 1945 (undated). Given that Army Group E totaled some 180,000 men in early May (NARA, T-77, Roll 780, 5507027, Strength of Eastern Front, 14 May 1945), it would be reasonable to assume that it had about 200,000 at the time Ott made his report.

[297] HR HDA 1491, 2.41, 221, (untitled) (14 April 1945). None of the three divisions Ott said were in Syrmia were actually there: the 118th *Jäger* was in Austria; the 114th *Jäger* was in Italy; and the 392nd Legionnaire was in the northern Croatian Littoral. The 181st Infantry was near Derventa, but it had not arrived from Bihać, as Ott claimed, but from Sarajevo. Of the three corps commands (the 34th, 69th, and 89th), Ott gave the correct location for only one (the 69th): the

also told the Yugoslav major that the Third Reich would use a new wonder weapon ("soporific gas") to influence the decisions at the San Francisco peace conference, and then sue for peace through President Harry Truman ("a newcomer, and therefore more understanding [than Roosevelt]"). These were, of course, nothing but rumors that illustrated the desperation of the Germans in the twilight of the war. Ott was no exception—in mid-April he asked Bakrač for advice on what course of action he personally should take in the following weeks. The latter answered him that he "could still be of great service" to the Yugoslavs, but only if he stayed where he was.[298] Ott stayed in Zagreb until early May, when he left for Slovenia and then to Austria. He returned again to the city in July 1945, a prisoner of the Partisans.[299]

In addition to the efforts of their envoys to Pisarovina, the Germans used the exchanged soldiers as a further source of intelligence on the Partisans. The returning men were required to give statements about general observations during their time spent in captivity. The interviews usually revolved around unit identification, movements, strength, armament, morale, and the supply situation of the guerrillas. The returnees were sometimes asked very specific questions. For instance, in November 1943, the 2nd Panzer Army was informed that the AVNOJ session was to take place in the Croatian town of Otočac. The Germans made a concerted intelligence effort to pinpoint the exact location of the building for the event in order to launch a precision air strike, but their efforts proved to be in vain; "the precise questioning of the German returnees, who had previously been kept in Otočac, produced no results."[300]

The mood of the local population within the neutral zone was also observed from within. In early December 1943, the returnees reported that the people of Pisarovina hoped for a German takeover, and that some were ready to provide active help to the troops.[301] German intelligence was also very interested in the level of cooperation between the Partisans and the Western Allies and their relations in general. One Croatian returnee reported in early January 1944 that although the British supply drops were becoming more frequent with each passing day, the

---

34th was not in Central Bosnia, but facing the Yugoslav Army in Syrmia; the 89th Corps was not in Yugoslavia at all, but in Germany. Retrieved from: http://www.axishistory.com/index.php/axis-nations/germany-a-austria/149-germany-heer/heer-korps/2800-lxxxix-armeekorps

[298] HR HDA 1491, 2.41, 224, Report on visit to Zagreb from 16–19 April 1945 (undated).

[299] HR HDA 1521, Box 9, File 164 Ott, Statement of Hans Ott.

[300] NARA, T-313, Roll 487, 000983, 3rd SS Panzer Corps to 2nd Panzer Army (14 November 1943).

[301] Ibid., Roll 488, 000439, Plenipotentiary General to 2nd Panzer Army (7 December 1943). The fact that the local population did not universally support the Partisans was confirmed during the German incursion into the neutral zone in May 1944 when some 100 people chose to leave the area with the German troops. *Zbornik*/V/27/201, Turopolje-Posavina Detachment to 34th Division (9 May 1944).

Partisans still "cursed" the "reactionary circles" in the West for supporting their greatest enemies, the Chetniks.[302] In late August 1944, one German traveling by wagon from Lika to Pisarovina for exchange used the opportunity to question the owner of the cart about Partisan airstrips in the area. The peasant told him that one such installation was currently under construction near Topusko; when completed, it would be used by the Allies for a large-scale airborne operation.[303] The soldiers returning from captivity in Western Bosnia and Northern Dalmatia during the summer of 1944 reported on renewed Partisan attempts to recruit their prisoners into the NOVJ's German units such as the Thälmann Company. According to the same reports, Poles drafted into the *Wehrmacht* were not eligible for exchange, but were kept with the guerrilla units. On one occasion, the returnees even saw a "real" German who had defected to the Partisans with his tank in anticipation of the Third Reich's imminent collapse. In addition to the usual observations on the strength and inner functioning of the enemy units which held them as prisoners, the returnees' statements also revealed the unpleasant truth that the Partisans had detailed knowledge of the organization and even names of individual officers in the German formations deployed in their sector. Consequently, the local commands saw themselves compelled to again issue orders concerning the handling of official documents in field conditions. As it was clear that soldiers were responding to interrogation even without the threat of physical harm (no such incidents were reported), the 264th Infantry Division distributed a German translation of a British leaflet on proper behavior of soldiers while in captivity.[304] In December 1944, the German military police reported that the intelligence provided by the exchanged soldiers had proven "essential" for clarifying the enemy situation.[305]

---

[302] NARA, T-311, Roll 286, 000173–4, Statement of Dr. Dušan Dragojlović (17 January 1944).

[303] Ibid., Roll 192, 000899, Intelligence section of Army Group F to various Luftwaffe commands (27 August 1944).

[304] BA-MA, RH-26/373/39, 373rd Infantry Division, Statements of Karl Müller, Ernst Gebauer, and Max Stade (1 and 17 July 1944); BA-MA, RH-26/264/19, 264th Infantry Division, Statement of Richard Wagner (8 September 1944); BA-MA, RH-26/264/20, 264th Infantry Division, Statements of Walter Weber and Karl Kauber (9 and 12 August 1944), Hans Ott (11 August 1944), and Peter Jensen (12 August 1944); ibid., 15th Mountain Corps to 2nd Panzer Army (25 August 1944); ibid., 264th Infantry Division, Evaluation of statements given by returnees from bandit captivity (1 September 1944); BA-MA, RH-26/264/21, 264th Infantry Division/Secret Field Police Group 9, Statements of Fritz Vanselow (16 and 22 September 1944), Walter Ruhm and Wilhelm Götzen (17 September 1944); BA-MA, RH-26/264/24, 264th Infantry Division to 15th Mountain Corps (10 September 1944). I wish to thank Sean Hansen for providing me with copies of these documents.

[305] NARA, T-311, Roll 188, 001039, Activity report of Chief Commissioner of Field Police with Army Group F and subordinated Secret Field Police Groups for December 1944 (5 January 1945).

The three men tasked with the handling of the prisoner exchange on the Partisan side were well versed in the spy trade thanks to long years of working underground as active Communists. With the exception of Marijan Stilinović, who remained first and foremost a politician, they all spent the last year and a half of the war working in the intelligence structures of the Croatian branch of the NOVJ. Josip Brnčić had been employed in the Main Intelligence Center of the Main HQ of Croatia and seemed suited for the job; after one of his last meetings with German envoys he reported that the enemy was in all probability deciphering the radio traffic between the Supreme HQ and the Croatian high command. He deduced this from the statements made by his opposite number that indicated the Germans knew exactly whom the Partisans wanted back, even before the formal request had been made.[306] Thanks in part to his performance at Pisarovina, he was made the 10th Corps' chief intelligence officer in March 1944. In early 1945, he was appointed Chief of the Third Directorate (military counter-intelligence) with the Croatian OZNA.[307] Bakrač had been a major serving with the same Directorate since the creation of the organization in the spring of 1944. In mid-July, the Party leadership in Northern Croatia suggested that he should officially join the Regional Intelligence Center (*Pokrajinski obavještajni centar,* or POC), ostensibly because of the great opportunities for information gathering he would have serving in his capacity as the main envoy to Zagreb.[308]

Bakrač's reports on his trips to Zagreb from 1944 and 1945 provide a useful overview of the intelligence activities the envoys performed while negotiating prisoner exchanges. The reports usually contained observations of Axis fortifications in and around the city, and the number and morale of the troops who manned them. For example, Bakrač once used a short stop in the village of Zdenčina (the last German outpost before the neutral zone) to scout its defenses and give an estimate of the garrison's strength.[309] In mid-January 1945, he wrote that the enemy positions along the road from Pisarovina to Zagreb remained unchanged since the last time he had described them. The "bunker-building frenzy" had subsided, the major said, and no new bunkers or trenches in the city itself could be observed. The streets were full of German military personnel, most of them in transit. Their morale was low, and an increasing number of desertions resulted in frequent checks by the military police.[310] The reports also contained details about the damage wrought by the Allied air raids. For instance, on 14 April 1944, the Main HQ

---

[306] *Jasenovac 1941–1945*, Vol. II, pp. 728, Report on prisoner exchange (15 March 1944).

[307] VA, 119/4, 2, 1–16/2, Supreme HQ to Main HQ for Croatia (30 January 1945).

[308] *Sjeverozapadna Hrvatska 1941–1945*, Vol. X, p. 477, KPH Commission for Northern Croatia to KPH Central committee (10 July 1944).

[309] HR HDA 1450, Roll D-1091, 142, Report on prisoner exchange (27 April 1944).

[310] HR HDA 1491, 2.41, 205, Report on visit to Zagreb on 15–18 January 1945 (undated).

for Croatia demanded more information on the effect of the bombing of Zagreb and the nearby airfield at Borongaj.[311] Two days later, Bakrač completed a list of installations damaged in the city and added that the "airfield was destroyed, but the hangers have largely remained intact."[312] The major also gave his impressions regarding the mood of the civilian population, details on everyday life, and the functionings of the NDH institutions.[313]

The visits to the Croatian capital also provided an opportunity to contact the resistance cells operating within the city. Bakrač wrote in mid-April 1944 that "since we have constantly been followed by [enemy] agents, we could only deliver the most important letters, but not much more."[314] One year later, the Partisan envoy met with a certain Major Gustin of the NDH's Home Guard, who provided him with the defense plan of Zagreb. This was a critically important piece of intelligence since the Yugoslav Army was expected to arrive at the city gates within several weeks. The information the major brought with him was encouraging: Zagreb would probably not be defended; the Home Guard were poorly armed and would not fight. "We can count 100% on the help of both the Home Guard and the civilian population," Bakrač concluded.[315]

One question which remains to be answered is whether the opposing sides used the prisoner exchange to infiltrate agents into enemy ranks. In order to provide an answer, one must examine the involvement of the SS and the SD in the prisoner exchange process. These organizations had been nominally prohibited from negotiating with the Partisans since November 1942, but in reality, the situation was quite different. Higher SS and Police Leader in Croatia, General Konstantin Kammerhofer, told his American interrogators that he, along with his subordinate, SS Lieutenant Colonel Günther Hermann of Action Group E in Zagreb, played an active role in the Pisarovina cartel "although we had no authorization to do so from the *Reichsführer-SS. . . .*"[316] The German envoy, Peternell, who died in May 1944, was Hermann's agent.[317] The camp at Jankomir, the main collection point for exchange prisoners, was

---

[311] *Zbornik*/V/26/692, Main HQ for Croatia to Žumberak area command (14 April 1944).

[312] HR HDA 1450, Roll D-1091, 139, Report on prisoner exchange (16 April 1944); the airfield was severely damaged in the raid, with a substantial loss of aircraft. Danijel Frka et al., *Zrakoplovstvo Nezavisne države Hrvatske 1941.–1945.* (Zagreb: P. C. Grafičke usluge, 1998), pp. 118–19.

[313] HR HDA 1491, 2.41, 205, 215 and 217, Reports on visits to Zagreb on 15–18 January, 13–16 February, and 12–16 March 1945 (all undated).

[314] HR HDA 1450, Roll D-1091, 139, Report on prisoner exchange (16 April 1944).

[315] HR HDA 1491, 2.41, 224, Report on visit to Zagreb on 16–19 April 1945 (undated).

[316] IfZ, ZS-0948, p. 39, Interrogation of Constantin [*sic*] Kammerhofer (31 March 1947), retrieved from: http://www.ifz-muenchen.de/archiv/zs/zs-0948.pdf

[317] HR HDA 1521, Box 9, File 196 Peternell, Archive of Hans Helm.

under the auspices of Action Commando 4 (Zagreb) of the SD. This same command often provided trucks for prisoner transports to Pisarovina, and its members went to the village on at least one occasion wearing *Wehrmacht* uniforms.[318]

According to several Yugoslav sources, Action Commando 4 concerned itself with the systematic infiltration of agents through prisoner exchange. The commando's chief, SS Major Rudolf Korndörfer, had personally led the operation and actively participated in the selection of the agents, some of whom were recruited in the Jankomir camp. The agents were mostly camouflaged as "replacement Partisans," i.e. the people who were offered for exchange instead of the individuals whom the Partisans demanded but purportedly could not be found. In one instance, two such agents were exchanged with a group of Partisans in mid-July 1944. This operation ended in failure as one of the agents was arrested only three days after she arrived in the Partisan-held territory and the other was forced into hiding. The Partisans became aware of the operation via their own agent, an Austrian deserter who had volunteered to return to spy for the Partisans and had been infiltrated through an exchange.[319]

This anecdote raises several points that warrant further discussion. Korndörfer's commando was directly subordinate to Hermann, who was very close to Glaise-Horstenau—so close, in fact, that he considered letting one of the 20 July conspirators (Guttenberg) escape because he was the general's close friend. Given that Glaise-Horstenau was very interested in keeping the back-channel to the Partisan commands open, it is unlikely that he would have supported any action which could compromise these contacts. Hans Helm, who was the police attaché to the German embassy and a man likely to possess knowledge of the SD's covert operations, said that he did not believe the contacts were used for the infiltration of agents for precisely the same reason.[320] The situation might have changed after both Glaise-Horstenau and Hermann left Zagreb between October and November 1944, but the available sources do not explicitly mention any further infiltrations akin to that of the early summer.[321]

---

[318] Ibid., File 289 Nemetschek, Statement of Erik Feldmann; ADAP/E/VII/209, Memo (28 November 1943).

[319] KAW, B/67:164, Živorad Mihailović-Šilja, *O razmeni zarobljenika*, pp. 13–16. The author allegedly quoted some German documents and the chief intelligence officer with the Main HQ for Croatia, Dalibor Jakša, but provided no footnotes. *Nemačka obaveštajna služba*, Vol. V, p. 588. As it is a textbook rather than an academic study, this work also does not include footnotes.

[320] HR HDA 1521, Box 9, File 164 Ott, Statement of Hans Helm. Helm was regularly informed of the contacts with the Partisans, but he preferred to avoid direct involvement. To avoid compromising the ongoing talks with the Partisans, he even forbid one of his top agents from trying to recruit Bakrač. Ibid., Box 31, File 24 Bakrač, Statement of Hans Helm.

[321] Although the "replacement Partisans" caused some apprehension, what really worried the NOVJ commands were the common defectors from the NDH's armed forces who came

Whether the Partisans exploited the prisoner exchange contacts for similar purposes is equally unclear. German deserters were known to have been used for counter-intelligence purposes on a local level, but the sources are silent on their possible involvement in more ambitious intelligence operations.[322] It is known that the Germans were prepared for this eventuality, at least since late 1944 when the Army's Secret Field Police became involved with the exchange cartel. On 25 November, it was decided that all returnees were to be isolated and subjected to questioning immediately after their release. The interrogators would then provide recommendations on the future deployment of the exchanged personnel.[323] This measure came none too soon, for the listening service had managed to intercept a cable from the Main HQ for Croatia which instructed the Partisan intelligence organizations to "recruit the captured German soldiers and send them across the lines as terrorists and propagandists." As the prisoner exchange arrangement offered an excellent opportunity for infiltrating these defectors back into German-held territory, the chief commissioner of the Field Police with Army Group F made the screening of returnees the main task of the Secret Field Police Group 171. The commissioner had personally briefed his subordinates on the interrogation guidelines and secured the full cooperation of the exchange commission under Nemetschek and Manns.[324]

---

over in droves nearly every month. HR HDA 1450, Roll D-1134, 605, Pisarovina command to 4th Corps HQ (27 March 1944); Ibid., Roll D-1082, 552–3, Instructions for military-intelligence service (8 December 1943).

[322] For one example, see Kühnrich and Hitze, *Deutsche bei Titos Partisanen,* p. 101. Milovan Dželebdžić's monograph on the Partisan intelligence service, *Obaveštajna služba u NOR-u* (Belgrade: Vojnoistorijski institut, 1987), does not mention the employment of German defectors and deserters as spies.

[323] NARA, T-311, Roll 195, 000634, Supplement to activity report of Abwehr officer with Army Group F for period 16–30 November 1944 (10 December 1944). As an appropriate location for accommodation of the returnees could not be found by early December, the debriefings had to take place in one of the military hospitals in the city. Ibid., 000526–7, Supplement to activity report of Abwehr officer with Army Group F for period 1–15 December 1944 (27 December 1944).

[324] Ibid., Roll 188, 001040–1, 111043, Activity report of Chief Commissioner of Field Police with Army Group F and subordinated Secret Field Police Groups for December 1944 (5 January 1945). Reports of this command for 1945 are not available. Until more evidence is found, it is impossible to say whether the suspicions concerning the infiltration of German defectors were proven or not.

The Prisoner Exchange Cartel and the Treatment of Prisoners, 1944–1945

As has been shown, the Germans began 1944 with an entirely new approach toward Partisan prisoners. The NOVJ was denied formal recognition, but its captured members were granted the coveted "prisoner of war" status which should have entitled them to the protection of international law. Whether the troops on the ground would be able to break with old habits was still questionable. Their commands therefore repeated the new regulations for weeks after they first become known. On 20 January 1944, the 15th Mountain Corps re-issued the leaflet from early December 1943 concerning the treatment of enemy captives and defectors which in part read "the enemy must be destroyed without thinking during the fighting itself," but that the Partisans who surrendered must be treated as prisoners of war.[325] Apart from special leaflets, troops were continually reminded of the new regulations in day-to-day orders: "It should be pointed out again, that captured bandits must be classified and treated as prisoners of war (they are not to be shot!)."[326] The documents from early 1944 also stressed the importance of prisoner exchange. For example, on 28 January, the intelligence officer of the aforementioned corps wrote that the office of the plenipotentiary general was "in constant need of exchange prisoners." These should be "active Partisans and not those forcibly mobilized," and Glaise-Horstenau's staff should be immediately informed of their number. In mid-February, the intelligence officer noted that the need for these people had become "very urgent!"[327] It seems that the new policy had the desired effect; for instance, the concerned KPJ district committee for Šibenik informed their superiors in February that "defectors and captured comrades are treated well [by the Germans], unless they are commanders. This dampens the fighting spirit and encourages surrender and defection." The 7th Division of the NOVJ reported in May that since some of its fighters were exchanged, the

---

[325] NARA, T-314, Roll 563, 001320, To German soldiers (20 January 1944).

[326] NARA, T-314, Roll 564, 000367, Transporting prisoners of war and defectors (15 February 1944). The 2nd Panzer Army issued similar guidelines in mid-March. Ibid., Roll 565, 000479–80, Treatment of bandit defectors (15 March 1944).

[327] NARA, T-314, Roll 563, 001327, Transporting prisoners of war and defectors (28 January 1944); NARA, T-314, Roll 564, 000366, Transporting prisoners of war and defectors (14 February 1944). The selection of suitable candidates for exchange was entrusted to divisional intelligence officers. *Nemačka obaveštajna služba*, Vol V, pp. 167, 170. For example, in late January 1944 in Western Bosnia, the 373rd Legionnaire Division arrested three women and one man suspected of harboring Partisans. Three of them were sent to Germany for forced labor, while the fourth, who was the oldest in the group, was added to the division's hostage pool. NARA, T-314, Roll 564, 000323, Activity report of Secret Field Police Group 9 for February 1944, 26 February 1944. As none of the four were "full-time" Partisans, they were not eligible for exchange.

"fence-sitters and ditherers" (*špekulanti i kolebljivci*) within the ranks ceased fearing capture.[328]

German primary sources for divisional and corps levels for the second half of 1944 are very sparse, but it seems that these orders were not changed until the end of the war. The much better preserved records of Army Groups E and F certainly do not offer any evidence to the contrary. Consequently, none of the eight high-ranking defendants (including Colonel General Löhr, six other generals, and one colonel) who were brought before the Yugoslav military tribunal in February 1947 were convicted on charges of ordering executions of captured Partisans after 1943.[329] This does not mean that the Germans relinquished the use of reprisals—now that the NOVJ had been essentially recognized as a regular army, it was expected to fight like one. However, as the Partisans continued alternating between open confrontation and asymmetrical warfare when it suited them, the Germans reacted by applying both spontaneous and premeditated reprisals. These were undertaken whenever there was a real or perceived instance of non-observance of the rules of war. Whereas a Partisan who was captured directly by the Germans while carrying his arms openly had a much better chance of survival than before, a civilian suspected of supporting a comrade engaged in underground activities or sabotage could expect little mercy if caught. The atrocities which took place in Dalmatia in the first six months of 1944 (see below) were to a large degree carried out by *Trupps*, special units made up of individuals of different nationalities under German command. One contemporary Chetnik report from Dalmatia illustrates the difference between the treatment of "regular" Partisans and that of their real or imagined supporters. Whereas 180 "active Partisans" were taken alive and then transported as laborers from Zadar to Germany, the *Trupps* immediately

---

[328] NARA, T-314, Roll 563, 001201, District committee for Šibenik to Regional committee for Dalmatia (16 February 1944); *Zbornik*/IX/6/55, 7th Division to 4th Corps (6 May 1944). During the fighting for the island of Šolta in May 1944, the Partisans evacuated their wounded by sea. One German unit noted that since the vessels being used were marked with a Red Cross, they were not fired upon. Ibid., 000078, Preliminary final report Šolta (12 May 1944). The restraint practiced by the German ground forces was unfortunately not practiced by the *Luftwaffe* or the *Kriegsmarine*. *Marin II* was a Partisan hospital ship used for ferrying the wounded from Šolta to Vis. The ship was strafed by German aircraft on 10 May 1944 with the result of two wounded. A day later, the ship was sunk by German attack boats at the entrance to the harbor of Vis; nearly all the wounded and the members of the crew perished. See *Zbornik*/VIII/2/320–27, 4th Naval Sector to NOVJ Navy Main HQ (12 May 1944) and ibid., pp. 330–32, NOVJ Navy Main HQ to all subordinated units (17 May 1944). The war diary of the *Kriegsmarine's* Admiral of the Adriatic merely reads that the attack boats sank "a larger passenger ship." NARA, T-1022, Roll 3956, War diary entry for 11 May 1944.

[329] For the verdict pertaining to Löhr and others, see Lopičić, ed., *Nemački ratni zločini*, pp. 21–51.

shot all Partisan sympathizers and suspicious civilians found wandering in the countryside.[330]

Despite the official policy, it had been observed that the troops were becoming increasingly undisciplined, even to the point of obeying the *Führerbefehle* only "conditionally." The frustration caused by three years of constant, grueling anti-guerrilla warfare began to have an effect on the front lines by way of widespread looting, arson, and massacres of civilians—even those supposedly friendly to the Axis cause.[331] The period from mid-1944 until the end of the war witnessed a resurgence of arbitrary violence against prisoners as well, as evidenced by a sampling of sixty verdicts handed down to German personnel who had served in Yugoslavia from 1941 to 1945 by Yugoslav military tribunals in the immediate post-war period. Out of sixty defendants, twenty were found guilty of shooting Partisan prisoners in the territory of the NDH in 1944 and 1945. Only three of these individuals were convicted of committing the crime during the first six months of 1944; the remaining seventeen were held responsible for the atrocities from July 1944 to May 1945. It is important to note that the majority of the accused were low- and mid-ranking officers below the rank of colonel. In one case, the Yugoslav tribunal had even indirectly exonerated the German high command from arbitrary shootings by stating that no general order stipulating the indiscriminate execution of all prisoners existed in 1943 and 1944.[332]

Captured Partisans were taken to NDH facilities and German camps in Croatia, or to German concentration camps in Belgrade and Zemun.[333] From there, they were shipped to POW camps or special camps inside Germany or in the

---

[330] *Zbornik*/XIV/3/657–60, HQ of Dinara Chetnik district to district commander (29 May 1944). Two additional examples include: the 264th Infantry Division shot two "suspects" after one of its vehicles hit a mine (NARA, T-314, Roll 563, 000741, Daily report for 9 June 1944); in July 1944, the 369th Infantry Division was ordered to burn two villages and hang all males capable of carrying arms as revenge for the killing of *Luftwaffe* Captain Kirschner and the suspected mutilation of his body (*Zbornik*/IV/27/638, Orders for Operation *Sonnenstich*, 11 July 1944). Civilians suspected of supporting hostile Chetniks were treated in the same way; the 7th SS Division burned three villages in Eastern Bosnia in late September 1944 after several of its members were killed by the Chetniks. NARA, T-311, Roll 193, 000804, Daily report for 20 September 1944.

[331] Schmider, "Der jugoslawische Kriegsschauplatz," pp. 1080–82. In April 1944, the 7th SS Mountain Division burned a number of Croatian villages in the Dalmatian hinterland and murdered some 2,000 inhabitants, many of whom had relatives serving in the NDH armed forces and various German formations.

[332] Lopičić, ed., *Nemački ratni zločini*, p. 235, Verdict to Anton Alimer (17 September 1949); for other verdicts, see ibid., parts II-VI.

[333] For instance, some 8,400 Partisans and Partisan suspects from the NDH were shipped to the Sajmište concentration camp in Belgrade from January 1943 to July 1944, retrieved from: http://www.open.ac.uk/socialsciences/semlin/sr/sajmiste-anhaltelager.php

occupied territories. According to the German Red Cross, the latter occupied a middle-ground between concentration camps and camps for "civilian internees." By the war's end, it appears as though all captured Partisans had been transferred to the POW camps which held the soldiers of the former Yugoslav royal army.[334] How many members of the NOVJ were sent to these camps in 1944 and 1945 is difficult to estimate. The Germans usually did not differentiate between those captured with arms and the civilians suspected of supporting them. In late July 1944, the quartermaster section of Army Group F reported that some 14,300 Italian prisoners "and bandits" were scheduled for transport to the Reich. A later report on the progress of the transport mentions only Italians, but not the Yugoslav prisoners. Indeed, it seems that the Italians continued to constitute the bulk of the prisoners in German custody. According to the post-war testimony of a German soldier serving with the 21st Army Prisoner Collection Point (*Armee-Gefangenensammelstelle 21*), the main task of his unit, formed in January 1945 in Sarajevo, was to handle "mostly" Italian POWs and deliver them to the *Wehrmacht's* transit camps in the region. Alfred Baumann, who served with Transit Camp 135 (*Dulag 135*) in Sarajevo during the same period, also remembered that the majority of inmates were Italian. In addition, he stated that "very few prisoners" were brought in during the first three months of 1945. When the camp was evacuated from Sarajevo to Zagreb in early April, it held close to 300 prisoners. In Zagreb, *Dulags* 135 and 185, which had been under the command of Army Group E, were disbanded. Their inmates were transferred to *Dulag* 161

---

[334] *Zur Geschichte der Kriegsgefangenen im Osten, Teil III—Lebensbedingungen und Sterblichkeit in Kriegsgefangenenlagern Jugoslawiens, Polens und der Tschechoslowakei (CSR)* (Bonn: Deutsches Rotes Kreuz Suchdienst, 1959), p. 27. There is no definitive number regarding the mortality rate of captured Partisans in these camps. According to the incomplete survey of war casualties from 1964, 3,747 members of the NOVJ from the territory of present-day Croatia died in captivity. Vladimir Geiger, "Ljudski gubici Hrvatske u Drugom svjetskom ratu koje su prouzročili 'okupatori i njihovi pomagači': brojidbeni pokazatelji (procjene, izračuni, popisi)," *ČSP* 3 (2011), p. 705. The *de facto* recognition of the NOVJ as a regular army brought an end to the suffering of the captured Partisans who had been sent to work camps in Norway in 1942–43. The camps were run by the SS, OT, and the *Wehrmacht*. More than 84% of the 1,373 prisoners who died in captivity and who are known by name died in the first two years. In January 1944, the prisoners received the first food parcels from the Red Cross and in April all camps came under the auspices of the *Wehrmacht*. These events signaled the beginning of a drop in the mortality rate. Dr. Barbara N. Wiesinger, "Iskustva i sećanja srpskih prinudnih radnika u nacional-socijalističkoj Nemačkoj 1941.–1945.," *Tokovi istorije* 3 (2006), p. 80; Dragan Cvetković, "Nemački logori u Norveškoj 1942.–1945. godine–numeričko određenje gubitaka jugoslavenskih zatvorenika," *Tokovi istorije* 2 (2012), pp. 96–97; http://logorcrvenikrst.wikidot .com/izlozba:internirci-jugoistocne-srbije-u-norveskoj By the end of the year, the prisoners were allowed to receive additional food parcels and clothing from the United States and Yugoslavia. *Zur Geschichte der Kriegsgefangenen,* p. 27.

of Army Group F, which was situated in the bricklaying district in the eastern part of the city.[335]

Details concerning the treatment of Partisans while in captivity are fragmentary and sometimes conflicting. Judging by the available information, conditions in German POW camps in the NDH were much better than those in occupied Serbia, where disease, torture, and executions claimed the lives of prisoners well into 1944.[336] Unlike in Serbia, the Partisans in Croatia were positioned to intervene on behalf of their men through the envoys in Pisarovina and Zagreb. In January, Brnčić protested the alleged maltreatment transpiring in the prisoner camps and demanded that the living conditions be improved. His German counterparts assured him "emphatically" of their commitment to the "principles of humanity."[337] In March, the Partisan plenipotentiary reported that although captives were no longer executed, the Germans refused to grant proper treatment to all of them without distinction. The conditions, Brnčić wrote, were made deliberately bad in order to encourage prisoners to volunteer for labor service in the Third Reich. Once a person complied, the treatment would improve immediately. As a result, even Partisan officers applied for this option in order to leave the camp and attempt to escape while en route to Germany.[338] The majority of the returnees in mid-April 1944 had no complaints regarding their stay in prisoner camps; only one man cited poor treatment in captivity, while another complained of unsatisfactory care in a Zagreb hospital.[339] It can be assumed that the steadily deteriorating situation

---

[335] VA, 70, 5, 7 and 9, Post-war interrogations of German camp personnel (circa 1947). *Dulags* were not meant to hold prisoners for a long period of time, but rather to facilitate their transit to camps in Germany. On 15 November 1944, Army Group F granted permission to use *Dulag* inmates for prisoner exchange. NARA, T-311, Roll 195, 000637, Contribution of Abwehr officer to the activity report of intelligence section for period 1–15 November 1944 (25 November 1944).

[336] For the description of the camps at Sajmište and Banjica, see Glišić, *Teror*, pp. 132–51. An outbreak of typhus in mid-1944 killed almost 10% of the prisoners in *Dulag* 172. NARA, T-311, Roll 195, 000745, Monthly report of the chief medical officer of Army Group F for July 1944 (7 August 1944).

[337] HR HDA 1450, Roll D-1090, 667–8, Report on the state of prisoner exchange (30 January 1944).

[338] *Jasenovac 1941–1945*, Vol. II, pp. 725–26, Report on prisoner exchange (15 March 1944).

[339] HR HDA 1450, Roll D-1091, 138, Report on prisoner exchange (16 April 1944). The promise made by the German negotiators in Zagreb and Pisarovina that the Partisan wounded would be treated in Axis hospitals was honored in late January 1944 when the 2nd Panzer Army issued the appropriate order. Odić, *Neostvareni planovi*, p. 194. The order seems to have remained in effect until the end of the war. References to the time spent in these institutions are often found in Yugoslav sources. See, for instance, VA, 119/1, 2, 1, 125, NOVJ Navy HQ to Main HQ for Croatia (27 February 1944); Milan Brunović and Tomo

and increasingly bitter fighting from mid-1944 onwards had an effect on the treatment of inmates—the Germans released almost 200 Partisans in November 1944 because they had no food for them. Likewise, the sorry state of the German returnees and their reports on the conditions in the Partisan camps from late 1944 and early 1945 (see below) certainly did not serve as an incentive to improve the lot of the captured Partisans.[340]

In February 1945, Bakrač protested against maltreatment in the camps, but even more so about the Germans occasionally handing over members of the NOVJ to the *Ustashe*.[341] However, being in German custody was still much more preferable than being a prisoner of the Croatian fascists. This was especially true for the inmates of NDH camps and prisons sought for exchange; sufficient evidence suggests that these individuals were often threatened with death or actually killed once it became clear they would be exchanged.[342] Apart from the capriciousness of individual *Ustashe* officers or police agents, the treatment of captured guerrillas was impacted by the inconsistent application of the official prisoner of war policies of Zagreb, which were often not aligned with German policies. The establishment of the neutral zone led the Ministry of Defense to order that all Partisans captured in the Zagreb area were to be brought to the provisional POW camp "Na Kanalu."[343] In late July 1944, the Ministry of Defense ordered that the prisoners should be treated according to the Geneva Convention and turned over to the Germans until a full-fledged POW camp could be established. Shortly thereafter, however, the ministry issued an order calling for the execution of between ten and fifty "insurgents or members of their families" for every slain member of the Home Guard or the *Ustashe*.[344] By the end of 1944, the NDH adopted a policy that was diametrically opposed to that of her senior partner. Captured "rebels" were not to be treated as lawful belligerents despite the fact that "German authorities acknowledged

---

Sović, *Bitka kod Obrova* (Zagreb: Udruženje boraca NOR općine Dugo Selo, 1965), pp. 124–26; interview with Viktor Malinarić, retrieved from: http://ipd-ssi.hr/?page_id=5296

[340] The Yugoslav Military Tribunal at Vršac sentenced to death Hans Götz, the commandant of the 21st Army Prisoner Collection Point, for allegedly having been responsible for the deaths of 280 prisoners between January and April 1945 (180 were executed; 100 died from typhus). Lopičić, ed., *Nemački ratni zločini*, pp. 466–69, Verdict to Hans Götz (7 October 1949).

[341] HR HDA 1491, 2.41, 215, Report on visit to Zagreb from 13–16 February 1945 (undated).

[342] *Sjeverozapadna Hrvatska 1941–1945*, Vol. IX, p. 814, Report of Dragan Carić to KPH Commission for Northern Croatia (22 May 1944); *Jasenovac 1941–1945*, Vol. III, p. 457, Statement of Lidija Zlatić about the time spent in Stara Gradiška concentration camp (13 January 1945).

[343] HR HDA 1450, Roll D-1090, 810, Military report for the period 17–24 February 1944.

[344] VA, CK KPH, Roll 42, 448, 469, Military report, 2 August 1944.

them as such," but were to be transferred to the custody of the Ministry of the Interior, i.e. sent to concentration camps. It was expressly forbidden to deliver these individuals to the Germans.[345]

Once a Partisan was in captivity, there were no rules to predict what may happen next. Hijaz Osmić was captured in central Bosnia as a member of the 17th Majevica Brigade during the German winter operations of 1943–1944. Until the group of prisoners he was with reached Zagreb, there was very little food and arbitrary beatings were commonplace—one Partisan commander was beaten more often than the others because he wore a bullet-riddled German officer's jacket. Once in Zagreb, all prisoners who could walk were called upon to volunteer for a prisoner exchange. Those who remained, some 150 including Osmić, were put on a train and shipped to a regular POW camp in Germany. The Partisans were quartered in a separate compound which was more strictly guarded than the rest of the facility. Osmić and his comrades spent fourteen seemingly uneventful months from February 1944 to mid-April 1945, when they were finally liberated by the advancing Americans.[346]

Franjo Liker, a platoon leader in the 3rd Demolition Battalion, was wounded and captured southeast of Zagreb in late March 1944. His captivity began with a curious incident when a guard made him remove his rank insignia: "This young German did him a favor, for Franjo would have been much worse off during the interrogation had he been [recognized as a commander]." Liker was then brought to Zagreb and interrogated for more than a month. As the investigation failed to produce any concrete evidence against him (i.e. that he was a Communist functionary), he was transferred to the camp "Na Kanalu." However, Liker was still not out of harm's way. Members of the *Ustashe* came to the camp and chose him and several others to be executed by firing squad. The Partisan commander had the good fortune that the camp commandant, Captain Maras, sympathized with the Partisans. In agreement with another German officer, Maras arranged for Liker's group to be sent to Germany as forced laborers. Liker was sent to a camp near the

---

[345] *Jasenovac 1941–1945*, Vol. II, pp. 787–88, Ministry of the Interior to the Prime Minister's office and the Ministry of Foreign Affairs (9 October 1944); HR HDA 1450, Roll D-1194, 401, Enemy situation report for the period 1–31 October 1944. This may have been a reaction to the amnesty proclaimed by the Partisan-controlled National Committee after the Tito-Šubašić agreement, but the amnesty was not valid for the *Ustashe*. Drago Karasijević, *Peti korpus NOVJ* (Belgrade: Vojnoizdavački zavod, 1985), pp. 274–75.

[346] Hijaz Osmić, "U neprijateljskim kandžama," in *Sedamnaesta majevička NOU brigada* (Tuzla: Univerzal, 1980), pp. 352–53. Osmić remembered that his camp, "IV.B Nuremberg," was liberated by the "7th American Division" on 14 April 1945. Camp "IV.B Nuremberg" did not exist; *Stalag* IV-b was located outside Mühlberg in Brandenburg and was liberated by Soviet troops. The U.S. 7th Armored Division entered *Stalag* IV-a, located at Hemer in Western Germany, on the above date and freed some 23,000 prisoners of various nationalities. Retrieved from: http://www.7tharmddiv.org/

Austrian capital of Vienna; he was employed in a shoemaker's shop in the city during the day and returned to the camp each evening. In early 1945, Liker used this arrangement to escape, and after an adventurous one-month journey, he managed to join first the Italian and then the Slovenian Partisans.[347]

Dobrivoje Krstić, who served in the 4th Sandžak Brigade, left a detailed account of his experiences in German captivity in early 1945. Wounded in his leg and unable to move, he and several of his comrades attempted to trick their way through the German lines in Eastern Bosnia. The ruse did not work and they were taken to a provisional prison already crowded with captured Partisans and civilians. After three days, Krstić received some food and basic medical treatment for the first time. Three weeks later, his group was shipped by train to Sarajevo. His injuries took a turn for the worse and he had to have an operation. In hospital, he was treated humanely and received three meals a day. When the hospital was transferred to Zagreb, Krstić went with them. There he continued recovering from his wounds in a room he shared with Germans and *Ustashe*. Once his identity was discovered by the latter, however, a Polish medical orderly had him moved to a room containing exclusively convalescing Partisans. After recuperating, the inmates were sent to *Dulag* 161 in Zagreb's brick factory. According to Krstić and several others[348] who were brought there in early 1945, the conditions were very harsh; it was damp and cold and the food was terrible—some recalled incessant interrogations and beatings. The prisoners were brought before a German commission and asked whether they preferred to go to Germany as laborers or to be exchanged in Pisarovina. Many opted for the first choice, fearing the second was merely a ruse to get them in front of a firing squad.[349]

It remains to be seen whether the establishment of the prisoner exchange cartel had any impact on the Partisan attitude toward German prisoners in the last sixteen months of the war. As previously detailed, the Main HQ for Croatia issued an order in mid-November 1943 that captured Germans were not to be executed "in principle" so that they could be used for exchange. As a result of the successful conclusion of the

---

[347] Vukašin Karanović, *Treći diverzantski odred 1941.–1945.* (Ivanić-grad: Municipality of Ivanić-grad, 1984), pp. 166–67.

[348] Nikola Božić, *Rovovi i mostobrani: Osma vojvođanska udarna brigada* (Novi Sad: Institut za istoriju, 1989), pp. 394, 497.

[349] Krstić was chosen to be exchanged by coincidence. While stating that Bela Palanka (approximately twenty kilometers from Niš) was his birthplace, he garnered the attention of a German officer: "I'll set you free if you carry a letter to my wife in Niš," the officer said. Krstić accepted and his name was added to the next group of prisoners to be exchanged in Pisarovina. After he rejoined the Partisans in April 1945, he kept his part of the bargain and traveled to Niš. By the time he arrived, the officer's wife had already left the town. Dobrivoje Krstić, "Moj drugi život," in *Četvrta sandžačka NOU brigada* (Belgrade: Vojnoizdavački i novinski centar, 1986), pp. 362–65.

negotiations regarding the neutral zone in mid-January 1944, these orders were changed. The vague clause was omitted and all subordinate units were now obliged, unequivocally, to take German prisoners (including wounded) alive, report their names, and prepare them for exchange: "We have reached an agreement with the German authorities on this issue." The same order was repeated on 20 January, with the addition that even captured *Ustashe* were to be spared for the same reason.[350]

These regulations applied only to the territory of Croatia; the Partisan units in Bosnia and Herzegovina did not receive similar instructions, although they had been under orders to spare and hold prisoners for some time already. Why Tito chose not to expand the application of this principle to other parts of Yugoslavia when, in fact, he was obliged to do so according to the preamble of the Zagreb agreement, is not clear. It would be safe to assume that this obligation was largely a nominal one and that it was included as a concession to the Partisans' recognition of the Supreme HQ's authority in the whole of Yugoslavia. In practical terms, the agreement was local in nature, and Tito most likely desired to first see if the Germans would honor the deal before taking any steps on a national level.[351] By the end of winter 1944, it appeared that their commitment to the prisoner exchange process and reduction of violence against captured Partisans was genuine. Almost certainly as a reciprocal measure to the order of the 2nd Panzer Army concerning the treatment of Partisan wounded in Axis hospitals, Tito released his own similar order in mid-March 1944. The order required that "the wounded soldiers of the German Army and other enemy formations" be treated humanely and provided with medical care by all units of the NOVJ.[352] These orders did manage to curb, but not eradicate, arbitrary executions of prisoners—the hatred toward the Germans was still prevalent among both Partisan leaders and common fighters; however, such incidents were investigated and not simply ignored, as had previously been the case, following German prodding or even independent of it.[353]

---

[350] VA, 119/1, 2, 4, 24, and 32–3, Main HQ for Croatia to all subordinated units (16 and 20 January 1944).

[351] In January 1944, the Supreme HQ signaled to the ICRC delegates its willingness to abide by the rules of the Geneva Convention on the condition that the Germans would do the same. The ICRC representatives discussed the issue in detail with the NOVJ's mission in Bari in May 1944, but no agreement was reached. *Zur Gechichte der Kriegsgefangenen,* pp. 24–27. The Yugoslav Red Cross received its first set of provisional rules in late September 1944. It would take another six months before the main council's request for the location, number, and personal data of all POWs in the custody of the Yugoslav Army would filter down the chain of command. VA, 15a, 6, 9, Provisional rules for the Organization of Red Cross for Yugoslavia (23 September 1944); Ibid., 119/4, 2–8/2, General Staff to Main HQ for Croatia (21 March 1945).

[352] *Zbornik/IV/23/320,* 3rd Corps to 16th Division (16 March 1944).

[353] Even Koča Popović, one of the more enlightened Partisan commanders, felt deep contempt, even disgust, toward the German prisoners he encountered. He likened Ilya Ehrenburg's

Beginning in the spring of 1944, the treatment of German prisoners was largely determined by the relations between the British and the Partisans. The Royal Navy and Royal Air Force began operating in the Adriatic in late 1943. In February 1944, the British landed two commando units on Vis and proceeded to launch amphibious operations against the German-held islands in cooperation with the Dalmatian Partisan units. The treatment of prisoners in these joint actions soon became a source of friction between the allies. In mid-April, General Henry Maitland Wilson, Allied Commander in the Mediterranean, informed the War Cabinet in London that the Partisans had shot some forty-five Germans who were accused of war crimes, and that the British should prepare to distance themselves publicly from the incident should the story break.[354] At the same time, Wilson dispatched a message to Tito in which he protested against this unlawful act and threatened that the good relations between the British and the Partisans might suffer because of it.[355]

The joint landing on Korčula in the final week of April was a resounding success—the local German garrison was all but destroyed and some 450 to 500 of its members were captured.[356] By 6 May, alarming news had reached London—the Partisans were apparently preparing for another round of executions. The War Cabinet decided that day that it would be best if Churchill intervened personally. Five days later, the Prime Minister dispatched a message to Tito in which he requested that all prisoners taken in the joint Anglo-Partisan actions be treated according to international law and all war crimes trials delayed until after the war. Although Churchill put an emphasis on humanitarian considerations, he also revealed the main source of British concern—as the island operations stood under

---

"Fritz" (representing an average German, completely loyal to Hitler) to a certain Fritz of the *Feldgendarmerie* who had been captured, and to Popović's "deep regret," released in exchange for some Partisans. The Partisan general also related the story of a German prisoner being shot by his Partisan escort in early March 1944: "We ordered an investigation." Vuksanović, ed., *Popović-Beleške,* pp. 202, 205, Entry for 7 March 1944. In January 1944, units of the 6th Corps executed several Germans they had captured aboard a train. The German envoys in Pisarovina demanded an explanation, and the Main HQ for Croatia inquired about the incident with the 6th Corps' command. HR HDA 1450, Roll D-1090, 515, Main intelligence center to Main HQ for Croatia, 8 January 1944; VA, 119/1, 2, 4, 14, Main HQ for Croatia to 6th Corps, 8 January 1944. I have not found any additional information on the findings of these inquiries or possible punishment of the perpetrators.

[354] TNA, CAB 79/74, 170, Minutes of War Cabinet meeting (6 May 1944); ibid., CAB 79/73, 98, Minutes of the War Cabinet meeting (13 April 1944).

[355] Dušan Biber, ed., *Tito-Churchill: strogo tajno* (Zagreb: Globus, 1981), p. 136, Wilson to Tito (13 April 1944).

[356] The Partisan navy reported shipping a total of 513 enemy prisoners from Korčula, but this figure might have included some civilians and collaborators. *Zbornik*/VIII/2/270, Daily report of 4th Naval Sector for 25 April 1944.

overall British command, the Germans might blame them for the executions and retaliate against some 100,000 British POWs held in Germany.[357]

Tito, fearful of harming his relations with the Allies, had already reacted to complaints made by British officers in the country. On 9 May, he ordered the 26th Dalmatian Division on Vis to refrain from any further executions and to send the suspected war criminals to his headquarters at Drvar, where they would face trial.[358] In his talks with the Deputy Chief of the British military mission, Lieutenant Colonel Vivian Street, Tito assured him that the shooting of the prisoners had taken place without his authorization and that such things would not happen in Dalmatia again. At the same time, he said that the severity of German atrocities would not allow the postponement of the trials until after the war. On 13 May, he repeated his message to the Dalmatian Partisans and the Navy command in a sharper tone: "You are not allowed to shoot anyone. You have already caused us a lot of trouble. I have made a commitment to the Allies in this respect."[359]

The assumption of Brigadier General Fitzroy Maclean that Tito would cling to the "Soviet precedent" of having war criminals[360] tried during the war proved to be incorrect. On 23 May, Tito dispatched a message to Churchill informing him of his decision to postpone the trials until after the war in accordance with the prime

---

[357] TNA, CAB 79/74, 170, Minutes of War Cabinet meeting (6 May 1944); ibid., FO 954/34, 94, Churchill to Tito (11 May 1944). This concern was not unfounded. In the last week of 1943, the 2nd Panzer Army instructed the 15th Mountain Corps to report any breaches of international law on the part of the Western Allies. NARA, T-313, Roll 488, 000086, 2nd Panzer Army to 15th Mountain Corps (27 December 1943).

[358] *Zbornik*/II/13/65, Tito to 26th Division (9 May 1944).

[359] Ibid., p. 95, Tito to 26th Division and NOVJ Navy HQ (13 May 1944).

[360] The Free Yugoslavia broadcasting station would occasionally publish the names of those individuals who were accused of being war criminals. Glaise-Horstenau's name was mentioned at least twice—in September 1943 and January 1944. He had probably been mistaken by Yugoslav propagandists for General Lüters because of their similar-sounding official titles. These broadcasts greatly irritated Glaise-Horstenau, as witnessed by the repeated entries in his diary ("If anyone had saved and not destroyed human lives in the Southeast, it was me." Broucek, ed., *Ein General im Zwielicht*, Vol. III, p. 255, Entry for September 1943; see also ibid., pp. 346–47, Entry for January 1944). What Glaise-Horstenau omitted from his diary is that he had taken steps to set the record straight. German envoys protested strongly on his behalf to Brnčić in January 1944, and even threatened to break off the contacts if the accusations were repeated. The matter was brought up again in March of the same year, although with less vigor. Brnčić reported to the Main HQ that he had given them an answer "according to [your] instructions." HR HDA 1450, Roll D-1090, 668, Report on state of prisoner exchange, 30 January 1944; *Jasenovac 1941–1945*, Vol. II, p. 727, Report on prisoner exchange, 15 March 1944. I could not find any information about these instructions, nor did I find evidence that the accusations were repeated for the remainder of Glaise-Horstenau's stay in Yugoslavia.

minister's wish. "I can assure you," the cable read, "that you will have no difficulties from our side in this matter."[361]

Maclean also reported on the Partisan attitude toward German prisoners in general. At the beginning of the war, the Germans were usually disarmed and released "or exchanged." Since the Germans failed to reciprocate and had instead continued shooting all captured Partisans as *francs-tireurs,* the latter responded in kind. As the result of the latest incident, however, Tito decided to hand over all prisoners captured in joint operations to the British.[362] Judging by the content of this message, the British military mission was unaware of the Pisarovina cartel and the effect it had on the Partisan prisoner policy. The Allies found out about the existence of some kind of exchange arrangement several days after Maclean had dispatched his report, as details of Tito's latest offer became known. He requested permission to transfer some 600 German prisoners from Vis to the Partisan base in Bari. This would presumably assuage British concerns over their safety and give them ample opportunity to question them. However, Tito wanted them back as soon as their exchange could be arranged. On 23 May, Allied Forces Headquarters turned down the request.[363] One captured British serviceman told his German captors that his side was against the exchange of captured Germans and that it was endeavoring to gain full control over the prisoners on Vis.[364] The deal was reached— the British could have all prisoners except the officers, ethnic Germans, and auxiliaries. On 13 June 1944, the majority of the prisoners from the island were loaded onto Allied vessels and shipped across the Adriatic to Italy.[365]

Tito had to back down owing to the situation he found himself in after the German attempt on his life in Drvar on 25 May 1944. After he barely escaped the SS paratroopers, he went to Vis, effectively placing himself under Allied protection.[366] The bitter taste remained, however, and from then on he sought every opportunity to deny the British the prisoners interned by the NOVJ.[367] When he

---

[361] Biber, ed., *Strogo tajno,* p. 149, Maclean to Orme Sargent (11 May 1944), and p. 162, Tito to Churchill (23 May 1943).

[362] Ibid., pp. 154–55, Partisan attitude to prisoners of war (18 May 1944). Up to this point, the Partisans jealously guarded their prisoners and only "loaned" them to the British for interrogation (see next chapter).

[363] Ibid., p. 162.

[364] NARA, T-314, Roll 563, 000016, Interrogation of Jack Holmes (8 June 1944).

[365] Statement of Hans Stemmer about time spent in captivity from 25 April to 28 December 1944 (17 February 1945); facsimile included in Weingartner, *Erinnerungen,* p. 201.

[366] In early June, there were 5,000 British troops on Vis, along with some 4,500 Partisans. TNA, CAB 79/75, 374, Suitability of the island of Vis as headquarters (7 June 1944).

[367] On at least one occasion, this decision stimulated prisoner exchanges on a local level. In early August, Tito prohibited the 2nd Assault Corps from delivering three Germans to the

did agree to turn them over, he made sure that the Allies received only the wounded soldiers and NCOs; officers and men fit to walk were retained for exchange.[368] The concern of the British for the welfare of captured Germans seemed excessive to the Partisans. It was a source of constant friction and led to a number of incidents.[369] Still, its effect cannot be denied. Most contemporary sources describe the treatment of German prisoners in the smaller camp on Vis and the larger one on the nearby island of Biševo during the spring and summer of 1944 as "good," "very good," or "beyond reproach." Thanks to Allied shipments, food was abundant and medical care was provided in the island's main hospital. The prisoners were used for road building and harvesting. Nazi Party members, ethnic Germans, and Croatian auxiliaries made up the penal platoon that was made to do the "hardest labor." Leisure time was usually spent playing cards and football, but also in taking short walks outside the camp (under escort, of course).[370]

The strong British presence in the Littoral, as well as the presence of the Supreme HQ in the same area (first at Drvar, then on Vis), had the desired effect. German returnees, captured guerrillas, and defectors all confirmed that the Partisans in the coastal region and the bordering parts of Bosnia were under orders to take prisoners and keep them (especially officers) for exchange.[371] Although the Partisans in the remainder of Croatia were under similar orders, they were more inclined to shoot their prisoners. One list of such incidents compiled by the

----

British mission and ordered them exchanged instead. *Zbornik*/II/13/640, Tito to 2nd Assault Corps (8 August 1944). For more on the exchanges in the area of this unit, see the next chapter. For another example of prisoners being denied to the British, see *Zbornik*/II/14/349, Tito to Main HQ for Macedonia (6 November 1944).

[368] Biber, ed., *Strogo tajno,* p. 385, Foreign Office to Minister-resident in the Mediterranean (3 December 1944).

[369] Koča Popović related an incident from Vis when the British attempted to arrest a high-level Partisan functionary for slapping a German soldier: "Captured German officers, when bathing, have their backs washed by English soldiers. They [the British] maintain the class distinction and class solidarity even in these circumstances. And they reproached us for intensifying the class struggle! . . . The English still want to fight this war in a gentlemanly fashion according to international regulations despite the fact that 195,000 people were murdered in Kiev alone by hanging, gas chambers, etc." Vuksanović, ed., *Popović-Beleške,* p. 202, Entry for 3 March 1944.

[370] NARA, T-314, Roll 566, 000206, Interrogation of Danilo Zlender (20 March 1944); Ibid., Roll 565, 001186–7, Interrogation of Milenko Sojić (10 June 1944); Statement of Hans Stemmer about time spent in captivity from 25 April to 28 December 1944 (17 February 1945); facsimile included in Weingartner, *Erinnerungen,* p. 201.

[371] NARA, T-314, Roll 566, 000204, Interrogation of Armi Kovacic (14 March 1944); ibid., 000027, Interrogation of Juray [*sic*] Skrlec (30 May 1944); NARA, T-314, Roll 565, 001181, Interrogation of Joso Mažar (19 June 1944).

German exchange commission in Zagreb in early August 1944, presumably intended for Boris Bakrač, contains no mention of the coastal sector.[372]

In the hinterland, where few liaison officers were present, the treatment could vary greatly, as attested by the soldiers released from the custody of the 4th Krajina, and the 19th and 20th Dalmatian Divisions during that summer. First of all, none of them witnessed any executions of prisoners. The captives of the 19th Dalmatian were, however, told to inform their command that a member of the Brandenburg Division had been hanged in reprisal for the hanging of an innocent civilian accused of sabotage in Biograd na Moru: "the real culprit," their captors informed them, "was in the vicinity [of the camp]." The second universally observed feature of guerrilla captivity was the wholesale plunder of uniforms, footwear, and private possessions—everything else was left to chance. In Ljubija (Western Bosnia), the prisoners were abused by both the Partisans and the civilian population. In Sanski Most, only twenty kilometers south of Ljubija, the town commandant treated them with conspicuous kindness. Of all three NOVJ formations, the 20th Dalmatian had the best record pertaining to the treatment of prisoners; they were neither tied up, nor beaten, nor forced to perform menial duties, and the wounded were "continually cared for" by Partisan doctors. Although the guerrillas in general were not above administering an occasional beating, six prisoners of the 19th Dalmatian suffered particularly cruel treatment at the hands of their captors. Volunteering for what they thought was an exchange, they were taken out of the camp and allegedly subjected to repeated physical assaults, water deprivation, and even electric shocks by a mustachioed "commissar in a red shirt" and his accomplices. Why the Partisans chose to single out these men, while treating the remaining twelve prisoners relatively correctly, is unclear. Upon their return to the camp, another "commissar" stepped in, forbade further mistreatment of the prisoners, and supplied them with water and medical aid. This part is left out of the original report, which, it should be noted, was written by a soldier who was a member of the Nazi Party, and co-signed by the remaining five men. In any case, captivity meant tremendous physical and psychological strain for all involved. Owing to the repeated warnings by the Partisans that there would be no mercy if they were captured again, the soldiers requested a transfer to the Italian or the Western Front, or at least to rear area services. Ultimately, their superiors granted them a transfer to other sectors of their division's zone of responsibility.[373]

---

[372] HR HDA 1451, 2.41, 156–7, (untitled) (4 August 1944).

[373] BA-MA, RH-26/373/39, 373rd Infantry Division, Statement of Karl Müller, Ernst Gebauer, and Max Stade (1 and 17 July 1944); BA-MA, RH-26/264/19, 264th Infantry Division, Statement of Richard Wagner (8 September 1944); BA-MA, RH-26/264/20, 264th Infantry Division, Statements of Walter Weber and Karl Kauber (9 and 12 August 1944), Hans Ott (11 August 1944), and Peter Jensen (12 August 1944); ibid., 15th Mountain Corps to 2nd Panzer Army (25 August 1944); BA-MA, RH-26/264/21, 264th Infantry Division/Secret

The treatment of German prisoners began to worsen during the last days of fall 1944. This coincided with the NOVJ's victories in Dalmatia and the rest of Yugoslavia and the steadily deteriorating relations with the Western Allies. The official policy remained nominally the same, but the OZNA reported that the treatment of captives was still not satisfactory and that the question of prisoners of war should be decided once and for all.[374] Some 600 Germans captured on the island of Brač in late September were the first to suffer the consequences of this change in attitude. According to eyewitnesses, some 150 of them were used to clear the German minefields on the island without specialized equipment, and those who survived were shot after they completed their work. Post-war accounts of survivors also mention executions of officers and the decimation of ordinary soldiers through hard labor and typhus on Vis and Biševo.[375] According to British reports, the situation in nearby Montenegro was hardly any better. Their liaison officers informed the Allied command that the 2nd Assault Corps executed some 200 Germans near the town of Grahovo in early December, allegedly as punishment for turning down a surrender ultimatum. The British filed an official protest with Tito, saying that such practices only served to reinforce the enemy's will to resist and needlessly endangered the lives of Allied POWs in Germany.[376] General Wilson was also concerned about the fate of the members of the so-called "Floydforce," the British ground unit

---

Field Police Group 9, Statements of Fritz Vanselow (16 and 22 September 1944), Walter Ruhm and Wilhelm Götzen (17 September 1944); BA-MA, RH-26/264/24, 264th Infantry Division to 15th Mountain Corps (10 September 1944).

[374] HR HDA 1491, 12.1.1, 12, Activity report of Croatian OZNA's 3rd Directorate for October 1944 (undated).

[375] See G. Minisini, "Die erschüternde Bilanz," and the accompanying essay by Matthias Roseanauer in Weingartner, *Erinnerungen,* pp. 238–39. Hans Stemmer remained on Vis until 2 December 1944. His contemporary report does not mention any atrocities. Statement of Hans Stemmer about time spent in captivity from 25 April to 28 December 1944 (17 February 1945), facsimile included in Weingartner, *Erinnerungen,* p. 201. According to one contemporary document, the 8th Corps still had eleven German officers and about 600 NCOs and men in POW camps on Vis in early October (*Zbornik*/V/34/520). The *Zbornik* volumes for the remaining months of 1944 do not include similar information, which may lead to the assumption that the editors sought to conceal the dwindling number of prisoners in this period. Paradoxically, the Partisan 6th Corps in Slavonia was under orders to capture as many Germans for exchange as possible. *Zbornik*/V/33/560, Main HQ for Croatia to 6th Corps (29 September 1944).

[376] Biber, ed., *Strogo tajno,* pp. 410–11, Draft of Wilson's message to Tito (22 December 1944). The message indicates 30 October–1 November as the date of the massacre, but the event probably took place in the aftermath of the battle of Ledenice one month later. For more details on this battle, see Michael McConville, *A Small War in the Balkans: British Military Involvement in Wartime Yugoslavia 1941–1945* (London: Macmillan, 1986), pp. 144, 273–95.

supporting Partisan operations in Southern Dalmatia and in the Montenegrin Littoral, should they become German captives. Consequently, regardless of the fact that the 2nd Corps' command categorically denied the accusations, Tito sought to assuage Wilson by issuing yet another order concerning the humane treatment of prisoners and threatening transgressors with "most severe punishment." The Marshal of Yugoslavia also informed Maclean that all captured enemy wounded would be handed over for treatment in Allied hospitals in Italy, but that all able-bodied prisoners would be retained for exchange.[377] According to a British eyewitness, some seventy German wounded were turned over to the British even before Tito's order had reached the units. The remaining Germans, some 200 in all, were marched off to Bileća and quartered in an outdoor fenced area outside of the town. Whether any of them were swapped in the November exchange in Eastern Herzegovina is unknown. Contrary to what the British had expected, these prisoners were not executed *en masse* after they left the country in early 1945. The remaining German officers were shot, but the NCOs and enlisted men were sentenced to manual labor. The survivors were repatriated to Germany after the war.[378]

Ironically, the drafting of Tito's order of 5 December 1944 coincided with mass atrocities against German prisoners committed by Dalmatian units during the autumn operations that culminated in the battle of Knin (25 November—9 December 1944).[379] Partisan troops, by then thoroughly brutalized, experienced victory on a grand scale which triggered a desire for revenge; their officers either could not or would not intervene. Contemporary Yugoslav reports are frighteningly reminiscent of similar German reports from the years when the German occupation forces had practiced unrestrained violence toward prisoners. One intelligence officer complained that not a single prisoner was brought in for questioning during two days of fighting around Knin; prisoners in his sector were taken several hundred meters behind the front line and shot without interrogation. He also said that "The enemy resistance would have been weaker had they not known what was going on. [As the enemy knew], he continued to fight tenaciously."[380] Croatian soldiers serving with the German legionnaire divisions

---

[377] See *Zbornik*/II/14/412, Tito to all regional and Corps commands (5 December 1944) and the accompanying footnotes; Biber, ed., *Strogo tajno,* p. 385, Bari to Minister-Resident, Central Mediterranean (3 December 1944).

[378] McConville, *A Small War,* pp. 292–93. Contemporary Yugoslav sources refer to some 355 German prisoners taken at Ledenice. *Zbornik*/III/8/507, 1st Boka Brigade, Operational report for the period 5 October–1 December 1944 (undated).

[379] For additional information on the NOVJ's campaign in the Adriatic Littoral, see Gaj Trifković, "The Long Way to Trieste: Operations in the Adriatic Littoral, 1944–1945," *Global War Studies* (Brécourt Academic, forthcoming).

[380] *Zločin i teror u Dalmaciji,* pp. 694–95, 3rd Directorate of OZNA for Croatia to Commissar of Main HQ for Croatia (13 April 1945). The Germans were terrified at the prospect of

were usually transferred into Partisan units if they defected or were captured. In Knin, their fate was uncertain even after they had become Partisans. The local branch of the OZNA wanted to shoot seventeen of them without collecting their particulars, let alone questioning them. A member of the judicial branch of the Main HQ for Croatia intervened and managed to save fourteen of them.[381] The captured Germans[382] were brought to the POW camp that was established in Knin after the battle. One OZNA officer reported on the conditions there in late February 1945:

> The prisoner camp under the auspices of [the Knin Area] Command is beneath all contempt. There is no order at all and it looks more like a torture chamber than a camp. The prisoners have no blankets, no heating, the rooms are terribly filthy and badly ventilated, the prisoners do not wash themselves, the sick are not being isolated from the healthy, etc. [The command] has done nothing to improve the situation. I am of the opinion that we should pay more attention to this, so that we could properly use the prisoners for the reconstruction of our country. If an Allied mission were to suddenly arrive [and find things as they are now], it would leave a very bad impression of us as barbarians.[383]

---

being taken captive by the Partisans. When a unit of the 118th *Jäger* Division was surrounded on the island of Hvar in September 1944, one lieutenant urged a breakthrough at all costs: "He had already been captured once and exchanged, and he did not want to experience it again," related Dr. Wilhelm Güther. Dr. Wilhelm Güther, "Wir und die Insel Hvar," in Weingartner, *Erinnerungen,* p. 254. Ott told Bakrač that the reason why the Germans were fighting so tenaciously was that they were afraid to surrender and that the sorry state of soldiers returning from captivity only served to reinforce this sentiment. HR HDA 1491, 2.41, 217, Report on visit to Zagreb from 12–16 March 1945 (undated).

[381] *Zločin i teror u Dalmaciji,* p. 86, Report of Drago Desput to Central committee of KPH (17 January 1945).

[382] The Germans reported 2,730 men killed or missing in the period from 1–5 December 1944 (NARA, T-311, Roll 184, 15th Mountain Corps to Army Group E, 8 December 1944), as well as some 700 wounded who had to be left behind in a railway tunnel outside of Knin. They all died when the ammunition that was stored in the tunnel ignited. Both sides accused the other of intentionally triggering the explosion. According to one German survivor, the explosion might have been caused by a stray bullet. Böhme, *Die deutschen Kriegsgefangenen,* Vol. I/1, p. 95.

[383] *Zločin i teror u Dalmaciji,* p. 688, OZNA of Knin area command to OZNA of 8th Corps (21 February 1945). The prisoners at the POW camp in Knin were also subjected to arbitrary executions. One such atrocity, involving eighty-one German and Italian prisoners, took place in mid-March 1945. "[The OZNA] is conducting an investigation and will report on the results." Ibid., p. 149, OZNA office in Knin to OZNA HQ for Dalmatia (18 March 1945).

In mid-April 1945, the Germans in Zagreb requested permission to evacuate the remaining German wounded from the northern Adriatic islands of Pag, Rab, and Krk, as well as the adjoining coastal area, by using a Red Cross ship. The Partisans were welcome to attach one of their delegates to ensure that the mission remained purely humanitarian in nature. Bakrač recommended that the request be granted as it "would spare us the trouble of having to care for the German wounded."[384] Apprehension regarding the fate of the German wounded proved to be correct—on 5 April 1945, the Partisans executed thirty German wounded on the island of Pag. When the German defectors protested, the Partisan commander replied that the shooting was vengeance for the death of the same number of his men. "Otherwise, I could not keep my men in line. This is like a rule [in our army]," he added.[385]

A German doctor captured near Knin later wrote that all the prisoners hoped to be exchanged.[386] This hope would materialize only for a comparatively small number of them. Unlike in previous years, the NOVJ now held a front line and had a well-defined rear area. POW camps were established in the coastal area and the inmates were used to remedy the chronic manpower shortage suffered by the Partisans. Common prisoners were put to menial tasks, such as unloading ships in Split and Zadar. Specialists were usually attached to the army rear services (workshops, etc.), but were also deployed to the front line; the engineer company of the 1st Dalmatian Brigade during the battle for Bihać in late March 1945 had in its ranks Austrians, Germans, Belgians, Dutch, and members of other nationalities.[387] Under these circumstances, massive prisoner exchanges did not seem as

---

[384] HR HDA 1491, 2.41, 224, Report on visit to Zagreb on 14 April 1945 (21 April 1945). The plan was probably scrapped due to heavy fighting in the area.

[385] Kühnrich and Hitze, *Deutsche bei Titos Partisanen*, pp. 195–96. According to the official historiography, the Yugoslav Army lost twenty-nine killed during the battle for the island. *Hronologija*, p. 1096.

[386] Böhme, *Die deutschen Kriegsgefangenen*, Vol. I/1, p. 96.

[387] Ante Kljaković, "Mineri na Bihaću," in *Naša Prva dalmatinska 1942.–1945.* (Split: Slobodna Dalmacija, 1982), Vol. II, p. 445. The author adds that one Austrian and one German were later awarded the Yugoslav "Order of Valor." Austrians were given preferential treatment in late October 1944 in order to entice them to join the newly-created "Austrian Battalions" of the NOVJ. *Zbornik*/II/14/355, Tito to Kardelj, 9 November 1944; *Zločin i teror u Dalmaciji*, p. 132, OZNA Dubrovnik to Mirko Glavina, 1 April 1945. The latter order stipulated that Germans should be used for "the hardest and most dangerous jobs." The recruitment drive was largely unsuccessful. The political commissar of the 31st Serbian Brigade separated Austrians from Germans on one occasion in October 1944 and gave them a speech calling for them to join the Partisans: "They listened attentively but none of them came forward; they were marched off to a POW camp together with the Germans." Isidor Đuković, *Trideset prva srpska NOU brigada* (Belgrade: Vojnoizdavački i novinski centar, 1987), pp. 31–32.

advantageous as before. Consequently, of all the Germans captured in Dalmatia in the last three months of 1944, it is known for certain that the Partisans only offered the exchange of a small number of soldiers from Brač and a group of about 120 prisoners from Knin. An estimated one-third of the latter did not survive the forced march to Pisarovina in mid-January 1945.[388] There was also one category of prisoners for whom the Partisans did not have much use in their rear area—German officers. In 1941, when the Communist-led guerrillas were still under the illusion that they were waging a class war, they executed all officers as representatives of the *bourgeoisie*. By 1945, self-interest had replaced ideology as the sole decisive factor in this matter since the Germans offered several Partisans in exchange for one officer (the exact ratio depended on rank). Consequently, an officer captured in the last phase of the war had a much greater chance of being sent to Pisarovina than a common soldier.[389]

Conclusion

The contact between the German military and political authorities in Zagreb and the Supreme HQ of the NOVJ was established in August 1942 and reached its zenith in March and April 1943. The talks that were held in this period helped achieve at least a partial de-escalation of violence toward the prisoners on both sides. The Axis spring offensive in May–June, carried out with intense brutality, cut these talks short and unraveled the progress made over the previous months. Both sides, however, were still very much interested in re-establishing contact and readily exploited the opportunity to do so when it was presented in July 1943 in Croatia.

Using the capture of a high-ranking German officer as a pretext, the Croatian Partisan leadership sent the veteran negotiator Marijan Stilinović to Zagreb. During his frequent visits to the Croatian capital in the summer and fall of 1943, he discussed the establishment of a permanent exchange cartel with Glaise-Horstenau

---

[388] Minisini, "Die erschüternde Bilanz," p. 239; Böhme, *Die deutschen Kriegsgefangenen*, Vol. I/1, pp. 85–87. In early February 1945, the Croatian OZNA instructed the 8th Corps to choose only healthy prisoners for future exchanges and secure their transport because "half of the last group died on the way [to Pisarovina]." *Partizanska i komunistička represija*, p. 196, Croatian OZNA to 8th NOVJ Corps (8 February 1945). It is possible that at least some of the Germans exchanged in March and April came from Dalmatia, but there is no conclusive evidence for this assumption.

[389] Eight officers were dispatched directly from Knin to Pisarovina in mid-December 1944. The 8th Dalmatian Corps added that one doctor chose to stay with the wounded rather than be exchanged. HR HDA 1491, 2.41, 160, Message from the 8th Corps (14 December 1944). Another group of officers who had been captured at Knin, including a colonel of the 373rd Legionnaire Division, were exchanged in Pisarovina in March 1945. Schraml, *Kriegsschauplatz*, p. 209.

and other members of his staff. Both sides had ulterior motives for these talks. The Partisans, for their part, still wanted to be acknowledged as a lawful belligerent and thereby gain political recognition. As for the Germans, Ambassador Kasche was convinced that the situation in the NDH could be stabilized through some kind of political arrangement with the Partisan movement. Glaise-Horstenau also wanted to explore this possibility, although he was much less optimistic than Kasche. On a more practical side, the German plenipotentiary general wanted to exploit the contacts for intelligence purposes.

The exchange agreement began to take shape in October 1943. The draft was ready by late November and it included provisions covering the humane treatment of prisoners and wounded soldiers, the establishment of POW camps, rights and obligations of captives, and burial procedures for the fallen. It was agreed to exchange prisoners as soon as possible on a one-to-one ratio. Despite the clause which called for the widening of the exchange agreement to other regions (most notably Serbia), the arrangement ultimately applied only to Croatia. The signing of the agreement was originally scheduled for mid-December, but was repeatedly postponed because the most senior German politician in the Balkans, Minister Plenipotentiary Hermann Neubacher, feared that signing any written agreements with the Partisan movement would be tantamount to recognizing Tito as a full member of the Allied camp. The German high command in Berlin had similar concerns and made it clear that it would give its blessing only if the arrangement remained as informal as possible. Although Tito had originally hoped for a written agreement for precisely this reason, the second session of the AVNOJ and the creation of a Communist-sponsored provisional government in late November 1943 may have induced him to change his mind. He probably feared that any written agreement involving the NDH would have adverse political consequences. Instead, both sides settled for an exchange of verbal pledges. The final text of the agreement was approved by the German military and political authorities in Belgrade, and the cartel became official in late January 1944.

The Partisan-held village of Pisarovina was designated as the main prisoner exchange point. Due to its favorable position and proximity to Zagreb, exchanges had been occurring there since late October 1943. In early 1944, the village and its environs were proclaimed a neutral zone; the Partisans pledged not to use it for offensive actions and the Germans would not occupy it. Despite several incidents (some of which were relatively serious), both sides were remarkably scrupulous about honoring the inviolability of this small patch of land. The "Special Commando for Prisoner Exchange" was responsible for the day-to-day operations on the German side. Likewise, the Partisans also had a special plenipotentiary who was entrusted with all matters pertaining to the cartel. Thanks to almost daily contact, the envoys developed close working relationships, and even personal relationships; the courtesies they granted to each other occasionally crossed the boundary of mere professional consideration—an important component for the efficient operation of the cartel. Apart from the pause in May and June 1944, prisoners were exchanged at least once a month until late April 1945.[390] The size and frequency of the swaps depended on the availability of suitable prisoners and on the sometimes intricate ratio system applied to prisoners of different ranks. For instance, the Germans had great difficulties in obtaining political prisoners from *Ustashe* concentration camps since the NDH authorities wanted to use them in exchange for their own men in Partisan captivity. Prisoners of similar rank were exchanged on a one-to-one ratio, but higher-ranking Axis captives could be worth as many as thirty Partisans (the case of General von Dewitz). On at least one occasion, the Germans retrieved some of their men by trading them for medical supplies.

The ongoing prisoner exchange offered both sides the opportunity to "take the pulse" of their enemy and engage in back-channel diplomacy. It has been documented that both Glaise-Horstenau and Kasche wanted to use the contacts in Zagreb and Pisarovina to further their own political aims. One option included spreading discord between the Communist command cadre and the majority of Partisans, who were not believed to be sympathetic to the idea of social revolution. It was thought that most of them could be induced to defect from the NOVJ via promises of fair treatment and some kind of political reform within the NDH. By the summer of 1944, Glaise-Horstenau had made contact with the representatives of the Croatian Peasant Party and some high-ranking *Ustashe* officials who contemplated a pro-Allied coup. At the same time, he convened a series of meetings with the moderate head of the Croatian Communists, Andrija Hebrang. The plenipotentiary general probably wanted to explore whether the Croatian Partisans would desert the Yugoslav cause in exchange for power-sharing in an independent Croatia backed by the Western Allies. Ambassador Kasche also had far-reaching political ideas, but unlike Glaise-Horstenau, he wanted to bolster rather than weaken the *Ustashe* regime. In order to do this, the ambassador hoped to split the Communist movement from within, but to also separate it from its allies abroad. The statements of Partisan envoys concerning the strained relations with Great Britain only served to strengthen Kasche's unshakable belief in the ultimate success of his endeavors. By late 1944, however, no one in the upper echelons of power in the Third Reich took him seriously.

The Partisans did not refrain from discussing political issues with the German representatives, although there is no evidence that they seriously contemplated even a local truce after the failure of the March Negotiations of 1943. The motives behind the similar offer they put forth in November of the same year are not entirely clear. Perhaps the offer was made in order to gauge the German reaction and keep them at the negotiating table. The contacts in Zagreb were put to good use one year later when Partisan representatives, acting in accordance with the Western Allies, broached the possibility of a separate, unconditional surrender of the German forces in Yugoslavia. The Germans, for their part, wanted to negotiate

---

[390] For a detailed overview of the prisoner exchanges in Pisarovina, see Appendix B.

their way out of the country in order to reinforce the Eastern Front. The Yugoslavs had no intention of allowing German forces to leave intact for reasons of prestige, but were careful not to appear inflexible before the German envoys in Zagreb; therefore, the talks lasted until the very last days of the war, but ended with no results apart from the fact that the city of Zagreb was spared from demolition.

Both the Partisans and the Germans sought to exploit the prisoner exchange contacts for intelligence purposes. The principle envoys on both sides were either full members of various intelligence services or were closely connected to them. They invariably used their frequent trips to enemy territory to report on all matters of interest such as enemy troop movements, troop strength and morale, and on the attitude and loyalty of the civilian population behind the lines. At one point, Kasche even wanted to use his envoy, Hans Ott, to infiltrate a German assassin close to Tito, but the plan never materialized. By early 1945, German negotiators like Nemetschek and Ott were increasingly prepared to supply the Partisans with sensitive information hoping that this would improve their standing with the future victors.

The soldiers returning from captivity were also a valuable source of information. Since most Partisan units did not have secure rear areas until late in the war, they had to take their prisoners with them. Consequently, captured German soldiers could observe more than their Partisan counterparts who were confined to camps and prisons as soon as they were transported from the battlefield. The question of whether the prisoner exchange cartel was used to infiltrate agents into enemy ranks remains unanswered. Some German sources claim that Glaise-Horstenau did not want to endanger the back-channel by cloak and dagger operations. It is possible that such actions were contemplated after Glaise-Horstenau left Zagreb in late 1944. At about the same time, the German counter-intelligence services were alerted to the possibility that the Partisans might attempt to infiltrate their own agents, recruited from amongst German prisoners and defectors.

Did the establishment of the prisoner exchange cartel help change the attitude of both sides toward prisoners? Theoretically, after mid-summer of 1943, the German armed forces were supposed to spare all prisoners as a result of Hitler's decision to augment the labor force available to the Third Reich with captured members of resistance movements. In reality, the troops found this departure from the previous policy of unrestrained violence difficult to comprehend. To make matters worse, the 2nd Panzer Army had effectively disregarded the order by widespread application of terror against real or imagined enemies in the territory of the NDH in the latter half of 1943. As a result, the officers and soldiers of the German occupation forces were even less inclined to obey the new regulations. The Partisans were finally granted POW status in December 1943 and German commands were determined to make troops treat them accordingly. The creation of the exchange system was repeatedly mentioned in orders from early 1944 and was meant as a further incentive for the troops to follow the guidelines issued on the proper treatment of prisoners. Although these orders never managed to completely eradicate brutality toward captured Partisans (especially toward those not fighting in a "reg-ular" manner) and their sympathizers, it seems that the troops obeyed them to a great degree in the last year and a half of the war.

Unlike the Germans, who considered the prisoner exchange merely an advantageous supplement to the existing policy of taking prisoners for the sake of augmenting the labor force, the Pisarovina agreement became the cornerstone of the NOVJ's prisoner policy in Croatia in 1944. Once the cartel became official, all units subordinated to the Main HQ for Croatia were explicitly instructed to spare their prisoners and keep them for exchange. As far as the Partisans were concerned, a live German was now worth more than a dead one. German prisoners also profited from the British presence in the region. Fearing reprisals against their own men in enemy captivity, the British exerted pressure on Tito to discipline his units and provide decent treatment to the German captives in Partisan custody. They also showed little understanding for the established system of prisoner exchange and sought to gain control of all prisoners captured in joint operations with the NOVJ in the Dalmatia region. As handing over the prisoners to the British without compensation represented a clear loss for the Partisans, Tito sought to have them exchanged before they could be handed over.

The period of fair treatment of prisoners had ended by September 1944. Rapidly deteriorating relations with the British meant that the Partisans did not pay as much attention to their complaints. Tito still intervened when prompted by the British, but the interventions were not backed by deeds. Late 1944 saw widespread killings and mistreatment of prisoners in Dalmatia and its hinterland. Comparatively few of them were exchanged since the Partisans now had for the first time a solid rear area where they could keep their prisoners and put them to work. Much like the Germans in 1941–1943, the Partisans now occupied a position of strength and saw no reason to comply with international law or the provisions of the exchange cartel.

Chapter 5

Local Prisoner Exchanges

1943–1945

Introduction

This chapter examines prisoner exchanges that various units negotiated independently of the Pisarovina cartel. To provide the proper context, the chapter will cover not only the exchanges from 1944 and 1945, but also those which took place in the year preceding the establishment of the neutral zone. This examination will illustrate the effects the centrally-negotiated agreement had on the conduct of the war in Yugoslavia, and demonstrate whether it improved the prisoners' lot and increased their chances of being exchanged. Furthermore, several non-violent contacts and negotiations pertaining to issues other than prisoner swapping will be discussed.

Treatment of Prisoners and Prisoner Exchanges, January–July 1943

Undoubtedly, the first successful large-scale prisoner exchange of September 1942 led both the Germans and the NOVJ to take steps, albeit small ones, to curb the indiscriminate killing of their captured foes by the end of that year. This was not the result of a concerted effort to move away from the abyss of barbarism, but rather both sides acting in their own self-interest—captives became bargaining chips for potential prisoner exchange. For the prisoners, this was a vastly more preferable situation than the hitherto practiced policy of giving no quarter.

It seems that the ramifications of this policy also impacted a region where local Partisans were not particularly keen on sparing German prisoners during 1942—northern Croatia. In mid-January 1943, the 13th NOVJ Brigade captured five ethnic Germans in the town of Samobor. The HQ of the 2nd Operational Zone sent the prisoners under escort to the Main HQ for Croatia with a note: "It would be good if you could get some of our comrades in return for them."[1] One month later, the 18th NOVJ Brigade tried to broker an exchange of ten ethnic Germans

---

[1] *Zbornik*/IX/3/113–14, 2nd Operational Zone to the Main HQ for Croatia (16 January 1943). I could not establish whether or not the Main HQ made the attempt to exchange the prisoners.

for some fifteen individuals held in Osijek by using the family connections of one of the captives. It is not known whether the exchange ever took place because some of the prisoners managed to escape. In any event, the increasing number of exchange proposals compelled the command of ethnic German armed formations (*Einsatzstaffel der deutschen Mannschaft,* or ES) to discuss the issue in official correspondence. "Order No. 2," dated 9 March 1943, expressly prohibited any talks with the Partisans who were "not a belligerent side in the sense of international law, but common criminals." Furthermore, such negotiations not only "strengthened their impudence" and provided them with propaganda dividends, but in fact helped prolong the war. The order also contained a grim warning that no captured ES member could hope for an exchange and that he should "save the last bullet for himself."[2]

The German 187th Reserve Division was deployed in the same region with the primary task of guarding the important communications contained therein. Throughout January and February 1943, the division had to fulfill that mission amidst increasing Partisan activity to the north of the Sava, as well as simultaneously provide a substantial force for Operation *Weiss.* On 18 February 1943, the Kalnik Partisan Detachment successfully raided a train between Križevci and Koprivnica and captured two members of the division. Two days later, a courier brought a letter from the Partisans in which they offered to exchange the two Germans for thirteen people imprisoned in Križevci, Koprivnica, Bjelovar, and Varaždin. Apart from the list of names, the letter also contained an invitation to a meeting on the 21st in the nearby village of Vrhovec: "We shall send one officer and twenty armed men. We guarantee a cease-fire for three hours before and three hours after the negotiations."[3]

The next day, the division's command ordered a search for the desired prisoners and requested their transfer to German custody. On the 23rd, the results of the inquiry concluded that of the thirteen individuals, NDH authorities could establish the whereabouts of only five. Four prisoners had already been transferred to concentration camps and one was in German custody in Zagreb. In addition, they reported having one other Partisan imprisoned in Koprivnica along with three Communists. Even before the inquiry was over, the division realized that the prospect of finding the prisoners and affecting their release from *Ustashe* police would be a difficult task. Therefore, all units were instructed to keep captured Partisans and other hostages with the division in the future, and "to not deliver them to

---

[2] *Zbornik*/V/12/277, 18th NOVJ Brigade to 3rd Operational Zone (28 February 1943); Central Archive of the Russian Ministry of Defense (TsAMO), Fond 500, Opis 12451, Document 621, p. 202, Statement of Emmerich Hefer and others (1 March 1943), and Document 622, p. 60, Order No. 2 (9 March 1943).

[3] *Hronologija*, p. 426; NARA, T-315, Roll 1553, 000543, Radio message from 462nd Reserve Regiment (20 February 1943).

Croatian authorities." The division was envisaging the creation of its own prisoner camp as well.[4]

The negotiations did not take place on the 21st, but were postponed until 25 February 1943—most likely because the Germans could not locate the required prisoners in time. On this day, representatives of the German 462nd Reserve Regiment met their Partisan counterparts from the Kalnik Detachment in the village of Subotica, outside of Koprivnica. Although the talks were held without the presence of NDH officials, no agreement could be reached.[5] Except for the fact that the Partisans tried to draw out the negotiations in an attempt to delay the impending German operation against the detachment, further details are unknown. This strategy was not successful and the offensive began two days later. The Partisan command, though hard-pressed, refused to release the two German prisoners, and they were forced to keep pace with the fast-moving guerrillas for the next several days. On 5 March, the war diary of the 187th Reserve Division noted that the captured soldiers exploited the confusion of battle to escape.[6] On the other hand, according to recent Croatian research, the prisoners did not escape but were released just before the Partisans attempted to break out of the encirclement. The detachment's historian concluded: "Who knows how these German officers felt about [this decision]? It has been rumored, and it is hard to tell whether it is true or not, that the officers sent a letter to the detachment, expressing their gratitude for the humane treatment [while in captivity]. Apparently the [two former prisoners] helped some Partisans captured around Bojana."[7]

The written statement of the two Germans about their time in captivity is interesting for several reasons. First, it shows that discipline in local detachments could be just as severe as in "regular" Partisan units, such as the Proletarian brigades—orders of superiors, especially commissars, were obeyed without question and drunkenness was punishable by death. Contrary to widespread rumors that the Partisans mutilated their prisoners, the Kalnik Detachment did not mistreat their prisoners in any way. "The greatest hatred" held by Partisans was directed at spies and the *Ustashe,* who were usually executed after a brief trial; Home Guards

---

[4] NARA, T-315, Roll 1553, 000137, 139, War diary entries for 21 and 22 February 1943; ibid., 000558, Radio message from 462nd Reserve Regiment (23 February 1943).

[5] The war diary of the 187th Reserve Division contains a reference to guidelines for negotiation issued by the division's HQ on the 24th. The entry for the 25th makes no mention of the talks despite the fact that General Glaise-Horstenau was informed of the proceedings on the 26th. Ibid., 000143, 145, Entries for 24 and 26 February 1943. The editor of the diary also did not include detailed reports on the matter as separate appendices to the division's war diary.

[6] NARA, T-315, Roll 1553, 000608, War diary entry for 5 March 1943; ibid., 000864, Experiences made in Communist bandits' captivity (undated).

[7] Žarko Miličević, *Kalnički partizanski odred* (Varaždin: TIVA, 2010), pp. 124, 128.

were first disarmed, stripped of their clothes, and then set free. The German prisoners were used for propaganda purposes by being led around villages while the population was told that "even German officers could become Communist bandits." The national and social composition of the detachment was especially interesting as the 600-strong group was comprised mostly of people from Zagreb. Their leaders were all intellectuals and ethnic Croats,[8] which must have attracted the attention of the Germans since the Communist uprising in Croatia was still viewed as fundamentally Serbian (at the time, the only sizable contingent of ethnic Croats in Partisan ranks came from Dalmatia). The statement also indicated that the influence of the *Ustashe* state was now beginning to wane, even in the capital itself.

The arrival of Vladimir Velebit to Slavonia during the March Negotiations in early spring of 1943 provided an additional impetus for prisoner exchange. On 14 April, the 3rd Operational Zone relayed the new instructions concerning the treatment of captured Germans to its subordinate units: "German prisoners, as well as members of the *Kulturbund* [i.e. ethnic Germans], are not to be executed, but disarmed and sent to the [rear] because they can be exchanged. Also, German soldiers can be stripped of their weapons but not of their uniforms."[9] The order produced immediate results. On 17 April, the Communist-led guerrillas captured an ethnic German on the outskirts of Daruvar and used him in the ongoing negotiations for the release of four of their comrades. According to one Partisan report, "the Kraut bandits" originally demanded eight rifles in return, but eventually agreed to accept their compatriot instead.[10] Approximately one month later, the German garrison in Okučani agreed to discuss an exchange of three soldiers captured from two supply trains ambushed at Lipovljani station.[11]

The proposed local exchange decribed above was the last one to occur before the launch of Operation *Schwarz* in mid-May 1943, along with its associated surge in brutality. The month-long fighting in northern Montenegro and Eastern

---

[8] NARA, T-315, Roll 1553, 000683–4, Experiences made in Communist bandits' captivity (undated).

[9] *Slavonija 1941–1945*, Vol. V, pp. 90–91, 3rd Operational Zone to 1st and 2nd Detachments (14 April 1943).

[10] Ibid., p. 117, Daruvar district to Ministry of the Interior, 18 April 1943 and p. 362, 3rd Operational Zone to Main HQ for Croatia, 23 May 1943. The above-mentioned story is the only example of Germans demanding weapons in exchange for Partisan prisoners that I have uncovered. This could imply that the negotiations were led by an ethnic German militia rather than the army.

[11] Ibid., p. 317, 3rd Operational Zone to Main HQ for Croatia, 20 May 1943. One Partisan document from late January 1944 reads in part: "Soldiers Joseph Haagen and Adalbert Doule captured on the Lipovljani station in June of this year [*sic*]. The 3rd Operational Zone led negotiations over their exchange, but the negotiations came to naught." HR HDA 1450, Roll D-1090, 667, Report on state of prisoner exchange (30 January 1944).

Bosnia and Herzegovina, marked by utter savagery, eradicated the limited improvements of the prisoners' lot which had emerged as a result of the March Negotiations. As a consequence, in the three-month period after the battle (roughly from mid-June to mid-September), both sides showed great reluctance to take prisoners and were even less willing to talk to each other directly. This especially applied to units outside of Slavonia, most notably those around the Supreme HQ and the 369th Legionnaire Division, which were still locked in a tenacious struggle in Eastern Bosnia.

The 369th, known as the Devil's Division, arrived in the NDH at the beginning of 1943 and quickly validated its moniker.[12] The great brutality with which this unit conducted itself in Operation *Weiss* and subsequent fighting is attributable to several factors. One determinant was the personality of its commander, Fritz Neidholdt, whose formative experience as a professional soldier was made amidst the carnage of the Eastern Front in the First World War.[13] Another aspect was that its German officers and NCOs were inexperienced in guerrilla warfare and had no knowledge of the political complexities in the country; therefore, they often opted for what appeared to be the easiest solution—the application of brute force. The third element was the Partisans' policy of applying different standards of treatment to prisoners according to their nationality, aimed at undermining the morale of the Croatians who constituted the majority of the division's personnel. Whereas the Croatians were often released after being stripped of their clothes, their German NCOs and officers were shot.[14] The Partisans apparently did not spare the common soldiers of the Devil's Division during the turmoil of Operation *Schwarz*. The division reported the largest number of missing of all German units engaged in the battle—a total of 233.[15] Even if one assumes that a large number of missing were killed in battle and remained where they fell during the Partisan breakthrough, there is no evidence that the Main Operational Group had any prisoners

---

[12] The unit's nickname was adopted from the Austro-Hungarian 42nd Infantry Division, formed in Croatia, which earned it for valor during the Great War. Ivan Košutić, *Hrvatsko domobranstvo u Drugom svjetskom ratu* (Zagreb: Matica Hrvatska, 1992), pp. 7–8.

[13] According to historian Ben Shepherd, those German officers who fought in the East during the First World War showed a greater propensity for brutality in anti-guerrilla operations in the Second World War than their colleagues who served on the Western Front. The difference can be attributed to the fact that the war in the East was conducted with less regard for international law than in the West, as well as to the strong influence of Social Darwinism and anti-Slav sentiment in the Wilhelmine army. Neidholdt fought on the Eastern Front for the duration of the war. Ben Shepherd, *Terror in the Balkans: German Armies and Partisan Warfare* (Cambridge, MA: Harvard University Press, 2012), pp. 28–56, 215–35.

[14] NARA, T-315, Roll 2154, 000120, War diary entry for 15 January 1943 (19.45 hours).

[15] NARA, T-314, Roll 560, 000750, After-action report for Operation Schwarz (20 June 1943).

with it when it reached the relative safety of Jahorina Mountain. This fact alone ensured that the division would carry out the orders on the treatment of captured guerrillas with special vigor.[16]

The breakthrough from the encirclement along the Sutjeska did not bring an end to the fighting in the region; throughout June, July, and August, the battered Partisan divisions made their way through Eastern Bosnia, scattering NDH units and storming a string of smaller garrisons in the process. The 7th SS Mountain and 369th Division hounded the Partisans, attempting to lure them into a pitched battle. This campaign was every bit as savage as the one preceding it. In mid-July 1943, the headquarters of the 2nd Proletarian Division reported that it had captured several soldiers of the Devil's Division. The prisoners belonged to various nationalities, including Slovenes and Poles. The Partisans reported that "All were killed except for a Croat, a member of the SKOJ, who was taken into our ranks."[17] The 369th reported no less than 861 enemy dead and only twelve prisoners in the first three weeks of July. Reminiscent of the closing days of Operation *Schwarz*, the Germans monitored intelligence on the whereabouts of Partisan hospitals and dispatched patrols to locate and capture them. Once located, the patients and medical personnel faced a grim fate. On 17 July, in the vicinity of Šekovići, the 1st Battalion of the 370th Grenadier Regiment reported forty-three enemy dead with no friendly casualties. The booty included one defunct heavy machine gun and "thirty stretchers and medical supplies . . . ; the stretchers were destroyed as they were lice-ridden." One day later in the same area, the division reported twenty-nine "severely wounded enemy" and two captured members of the medical staff. The division continued to report executions of seriously wounded Partisans into early August despite the official change in attitude toward guerrilla prisoners which was taking shape at this time.[18]

---

[16] These orders remained the same for Operation *Schwarz*. During a conference with Neidholdt on 17 June, Lüters merely pointed out that prisoners should be interrogated before being shot. NARA, T-315, Roll 2154, 001530, Conference with Commander of German Troops in Croatia in Sarajevo on 17 June 1943 at 11.00 (20 June 1943).

[17] *Zbornik*/IV/35/546–47, 2nd Proletarian Division to Supreme HQ (14 July 1943).

[18] NARA, T-315, Roll 2155, 000416, 385, 394, 400, 517, War diary entries for 20 July 1943 (10.00 hours), 17 July 1943 (13.45 hours), 18 July 1943 (03.00 and 19.00 hours), 3 August 1943 (22.00 hours); for more details on the massacre, see also Žarko Cvetković, "Lečenje i evakuacija ranjenika i bolesnika u NOR-u," in *Sanitetska služba u Narodnooslobodilačkom ratu Jugoslavije 1941–1945: iskustva sanitetske službe NOV i POJ (JA) iz četverogodišnjeg narodnooslobodilačkog rata 1941–1945* (Belgrade: Vojnoizdavački i novinski centar, 1989), Vol. IV, p. 58; Alfred Nick, "Zaštita ranjenika i bolesnika u narodnooslobodilačkom ratu," in ibid., p. 281.

Limited De-escalation and Surge in Exchange Activities, September–December 1943

As mentioned in the previous chapter, the treatment of guerrilla prisoners began to change once Hitler issued his order of 19 July 1943 stipulating that captured "bandits" should be treated as prisoners of war in order to weaken the Partisans' resolve to fight and to secure a steady supply of forced labor for the German war industry. The *de facto* recognition of POW rights for captured Partisans facilitated a wave of prisoner exchanges throughout Yugoslavia. German units on the ground now accepted Partisan exchange proposals more readily, and were even willing to initiate talks. The first such case took place in the vicinity of Ruma in Syrmia in late August 1943. On the 23rd, a company of the 173rd Reserve Division's engineer battalion was conducting drills when it was suddenly attacked by the 3rd Vojvodina Brigade of the NOVJ. The company was practically destroyed: sixty-three Germans were killed; three were wounded; and twenty-three captured. The number of prisoners would have been higher had the Partisans not executed some of the wounded Germans (according to a German witness), while the Yugoslav historiography claims that, following a brief tribunal, those killed were sentenced to death for crimes committed in Yugoslavia.[19]

Immediately after the battle, the local German command decided to sound out the Partisans on the possibility of an exchange.[20] Contact with the Partisans was established through the efforts of the German police and one of its local ethnic German associates, a man named Felinger. Once he delivered the exchange offer to the Partisans, they informed the Main HQ for Vojvodina, which consented to the negotiations. Vukašin Bivolarević (known to his comrades as "Volf"), a former sergeant in the former royal army and now a high-ranking guerrilla commander, was chosen to be the NOVJ's envoy. He was to travel to a crossroads just outside of Ruma where German negotiators would be waiting for him. Due to technical

---

[19] NARA, T-311, Roll 285, 000774, 173rd Reserve Division for Army Group F (2 September 1943); Labović and Basta, *Partizani za pregovaračkim stolom 1941–1945*, p. 185. It is worth mentioning that the Vojvodina Partisans released three captured German soldiers in mid-June 1943 after "their innocence had been proven." *Zbornik*/I/VI/350, Operational report of the Main HQ for Vojvodina, Entry for 13 June 1943. The release of prisoners so late in the war in Syrmia can be attributed to the efforts to popularize the NOVJ amongst the ethnic Germans who constituted a sizable percentage of the local population.

[20] Heinrich Scheuering from Nuremberg lost his 17-year-old son in the Ruma ambush and wrote a letter to the Armed Forces High Command in which he blamed the officers' negligence for the disaster. In support of his argument, Scheuering wrote that it was the "bandits," rather than the German command, who offered to exchange the survivors. NARA, T-77, Roll 1421, Investigation of an incident in Croatia (9 October 1943). This letter also shows that the German public was aware of the fact that the army was occasionally swapping prisoners with the guerrillas in the Balkans.

difficulties, Bivolarević arrived late and failed to locate his counterparts. Aware of the possible consequences that his failure to appear might have for the captured Partisans, Bivolarević proceeded to Ruma alone. His decision was not without risk since he was armed and wore the uniform of a Partisan commander. Fortunately, he was able to enter the town without difficulty and meet with Felinger, whom he already knew. They drove to the German headquarters where the local commander awaited them. Bystanders witnessed an odd scene when he and Bivolarević exchanged salutes and even shook hands. The negotiations were held in the presence of representatives of the German police and security service. Bivolarević presented two lists of people the Partisans wanted in exchange for the captured soldiers: one contained the names of Partisans who had been captured; the other, the names of individuals who had defected to the Germans. After checking the names, the Germans told Bivolarević that none of the requested individuals remained in Ruma, but the German commander instead offered all Partisans and Communist sympathizers held in the local prison—a total of sixty-three men and women. Realizing that demanding specific individuals was unlikely to produce any results, Bivolarević agreed to the terms.[21]

Once the deal was struck, the German commander made a very unusual gesture—he invited the Partisan envoy for a drink in the nearby tavern. They were accompanied by Gestapo officials, although Bivolarević remembered that his counterpart was not pleased with their presence. The details of the conversation were not recorded, yet one can assume that the German officer had no other agenda than to satisfy his curiosity regarding his adversary. When they finished their drinks, Bivolarević insisted on paying, saying it was the host's obligation to treat his guests. "Host?," inquired the German. "Well, I was born here," replied the Partisan, "whereas you are here only temporarily; tomorrow you will be gone." Unlike the police officials, the officer seemed to be amused by the answer. Emboldened, Bivolarević decided to ask for a favor—he wanted to buy some cooking utensils for his unit. The German officer agreed and, as it was a Sunday, arranged for a store to be opened so that Bivolarević could purchase what he needed.[22]

---

[21] Labović and Basta, *Partizani za pregovaračkim stolom 1941–1945*, pp. 185–89.

[22] Ibid., p. 189; According to other sources, the chief German negotiator was the notorious local Gestapo official, Anton Bauer: http://www.subnor.org.rs/spomen-ploca-volfu#more -541 This episode illustrates the fact that the German police and the SD were not averse to negotiating with the Partisans directly, despite the fact that the higher commands took an unfavorable view of these activities. The handbook on the German intelligence service, prepared by the Yugoslav State Security in the 1950s, states that the German police command in Osijek negotiated several times with the Partisans regarding prisoner exchange. "The contacts were established through ethnic German village elders, while the talks themselves were conducted by the [Osijek Police] command members," *Nemačka obaveštajna služba*, Vol. V, p. 521.

The sources cataloging the exact number of prisoners exchanged as the result of the negotiations in Ruma differ. One contemporary German report states that twenty-three soldiers of the engineer company were released by 2 September 1943. In a post-war testimony, an intelligence officer of the 173rd Reserve Division mentioned some thirty Germans being exchanged in the period between 15 August and 30 September 1943.[23] It is possible that the negotiators agreed that an additional number of Germans would be delivered as soon as they were in Partisan custody. For instance, on 11 September, the 3rd Vojvodina Brigade ambushed a train several kilometers east of Ruma and captured twenty-five railway men and two German soldiers. The former were freed, but the latter were kept for exchange "at the earliest opportunity."[24] As no further exchanges between the 173rd Reserve Division and the Vojvodina Partisans have been recorded, it is possible that these two prisoners were subsequently freed as part of the Ruma agreement. Given that the exchange was successful, it is surprising that the two sides did not continue swapping prisoners in Syrmia. Judging by the testimony of the intelligence officer, the Germans had little incentive to take prisoners after observing the sorry state their men were in when they returned from captivity.[25]

The 173rd Reserve Division's sister unit, the 187th, also began receiving renewed exchange proposals from the Croatian Partisans at this time. The divisional war diary noted that on 6 September, the guerrillas were offering seven German soldiers in exchange for ten of their own, including six women. In keeping with the usual practice, the diarist did not include any additional details about the event, and it is not known if the exchange occurred. The same goes for the outcome of the negotiations from late October, when the Partisans offered two NCOs for one civilian and the wife of a Home Guard officer who had defected. The division refused to let the woman go, but had no objections to releasing the civilian in exchange for the two Germans.[26]

The late summer of 1943 also saw the first attempt to conduct a local exchange in Bosnia since April 1942, when the Ozren Partisan Detachment swapped prisoners with the Axis garrison in Tuzla. Due to the fragmentary nature of primary

---

[23] NARA, T-311, Roll 285, 000774, 173rd Reserve Division to Army Group F (2 September 1943); Böhme, *Die deutschen Kriegsgefangenen in Jugoslawien*, Vol. I/1, p. 85.

[24] Radovan Panić, *Treća vojvođanska NOU brigada* (Belgrade: Vojnoizdavački zavod, 1980), p. 108.

[25] The exchange at Ruma still has enormous symbolic significance for surviving Partisan veterans. On 2 September 2011, the 68th anniversary of the event, a plaque dedicated to Vukašin Bivolarević was erected on the spot where the exchange took place: http://www .subnor.org.rs/spomen-ploca-volfu#more-541 The veterans gathered there again in September 2012: http://www.sremskenovine.co.rs/2012/09/godiswica-razmene-zarobqenika/

[26] NARA, T-314, Roll 1544, 000025 and 000077, War diary entries for 6 September and 24 October 1943.

documents from this period, it is difficult to establish the prisoners' origins or the outcome of the event; it is only known that the 373rd Legionnaire Division was offered an exchange of thirteen German prisoners on or about 17 September 1943. It is impossible to tell[27] whether these prisoners belonged to a group of Germans (probably the division's own men) whom the 11th Kozara Brigade had been guarding since late August while waiting for permission from the 2nd Bosnian Corps to arrange a swap, or whether they came from a group of fourteen men from the 114th *Jäger* Division who had been captured east of Bihać and then taken to Mrkonjić Grad.

As previously indicated, the Partisans applied violence selectively when dealing with ethnic German prisoners, provided they were not members of the 7th SS *Prinz Eugen* Division. In the summer of 1943, while a glimmer of hope remained that they could be induced to participate in the People's Liberation Movement, the decision to collectively punish the German minority for collaborating with the Nazi regime had not yet been imposed. These efforts culminated in the creation of the "German Company 'Ernst Thälmann'" on 15 August 1943 in Slavonia as an element of the Podravina Detachment. The command language was German and the company's members were allowed to wear the German national tricolor on their caps. The detachment was ordered to mobilize as many Germans as possible in the shortest possible time in order to upgrade the company to a full battalion.[28]

In early October 1943, the company accepted into its ranks two German deserters from the Knin garrison in Dalmatia—Klaus Löwe and Adam König. In late September, they staged a skirmish with the Partisans in order to mask their escape. Their families, however, were still in Germany and could face retribution if details of their desertion were ever disclosed. In order to dispel any doubt concerning the incident, the Partisan unit which accepted the deserters sent a letter to the German command requesting to "exchange" Löwe and König. The offer was framed in such a way that it would be unacceptable to the Germans. The offer was turned down, and the deserters were free to go to Slavonia for service with the German company.[29]

By the beginning of October 1943, the Partisans in Montenegro, under the command of the recently formed 2nd Assault Corps, had made substantial gains due to the Italian capitulation. They disarmed a large number of smaller Italian

---

[27] NARA, T-313, Roll 483, 000396, 15th Mountain Corps to 2nd Panzer Army (17 September 1943); Đuro Milinović and Dragan Karasijević, *Jedanaesta krajiška NOU brigada* (Bosanska Gradiška: SUBNOR, 1982), p. 58; NARA, T-313, Roll 488, 001276, Statement of Joachim Javorski (27 September 1943).

[28] *Zbornik*/V/18/170–72, 2nd Croatian NOVJ Corps to all subordinated units (15 August 1943).

[29] Nail Redžić, *Telmanovci: Zapisi o njemačkoj partizanskoj četi Ernst Telman* (Belgrade: Narodna armija, 1984), pp. 25–26.

units and managed to persuade the Italian *Taurinense* Division to join their cause. As a result of these successes, spirits were high amongst the Communist-led guerrillas. Vukašin Nenezić, a youngster belonging to the Lovćen Partisan Detachment, was especially impressed by the stories of how Italians were surrendering across the country without even a shot being fired. Nenezić and his brother, Stevan, were posted as lookouts for traffic on the Danilovgrad–Cetinje road when a motorized column suddenly appeared; Vukašin was certain it was Italian, his brother thought it was German. Not heeding Stevan's advice, Vukašin sprang from his cover and ran to the road, hoping to bluff the column into surrendering. "I do not know how I could have been so reckless," recalled Nenezić decades after the events, "... stories about the Italian soldiers and their [quick] disarmament carried me down to the road. I thought I, too, would be able to perform such a feat, to do something I could brag about my whole life." As soon as the column stopped, he realized he had made a huge mistake as he was promptly surrounded by an officer and several soldiers in German uniforms. "The officer ... listened to what I had to say, said something to me in perfect Serbo-Croatian, and ordered the soldiers to disarm me. I was in no position to resist."[30]

The Lovćen Detachment was informed soon thereafter that Nenezić was still alive and in Podgorica prison. He would have been left to his fate had his relatives not intervened with the detachment's command. Jovana Stanojević, Nenezić's aunt, proposed exchanging him for a German sergeant who had recently been captured; she also volunteered to personally take the letter of offer to the garrison in Podgorica. The commissar agreed, saying that he would do everything to effect the young man's release, whereas "the Kraut NCO was not worth a bean" to him. Consequently, the detachment requested a one-to-one exchange which should take place "immediately, if possible, according to all military regulations and at the designated location." Furthermore, the Partisans would "guarantee the safety of your delegation as this is not the first time that we have exchanged prisoners.[31] Members of your delegation should come with a white flag; caution them not to leave the road, especially once they enter our territory. . . . We expect your answer through the bearer of this letter." Stanojević went straight to Podgorica and delivered the message. After a short deliberation, the Germans drafted a written response in which they agreed to the terms. One day later, a car with its horn blaring and a white flag waving entered the Partisan territory outside of Danilovgrad. The Germans and the Partisans exchanged salutes and, without further formalities, made the exchange.[32]

---

[30] Labović and Basta, *Partizani za pregovaračkim stolom 1941–1945,* pp. 217–18.

[31] This section most likely refers to the prisoner exchanges with the Italians.

[32] Labović and Basta, *Partizani za pregovaračkim stolom 1941–1945,* pp. 219–21; *Zbornik/* III/5/202, Main HQ for Montenegro and Bay of Kotor to 2nd Assault Corps (12 October 1943).

The fact that the Lovćen Detachment originally had no intention of proposing an exchange, as well as the scornful comment about the captured German NCO, implies that the exchange at Danilovgrad was an exception, rather than the rule, in Montenegro during the final months of 1943. Indeed, judging by the available sources, the Montenegrin Partisans took a hard line toward German prisoners. It is important to note that such an attitude was officially sanctioned by the 2nd Assault Corps, the highest Partisan command in the area. On 23 September, the corps instructed its 3rd Division that it was not to release a single German captured around Kotor, irrespective of the manner in which he surrendered. That this was, in fact, a thinly veiled execution order is corroborated by other documents from this period. On 11 October 1943, 800 Italians of the former *Taurinense* Division who volunteered to fight against the Germans were formed into the *Aosta* Brigade and attached to the 3rd Division. The division used the captured Germans on at least one occasion to strengthen the bonds with its new allies. On 20 October, the division's intelligence section reported that the Italians' morale was "pretty high. The hatred toward the Germans is obvious. Two days ago, we handed over several captured Germans for execution, which they carried out with conspicuous pleasure."[33] On 9 November, the HQ of the 2nd Corps prepared a document for the Main HQ for Macedonia containing advice on the formation and functioning of brigade-sized units. Amongst other topics, the corps' commander and political commissar wrote the following: "The brigades must be especially imbued with great hatred toward the Chetniks and the Germans. . . . We, for instance, are destroying all enemies in combat without mercy. We will not recognize the Germans as prisoners [of war] until they recognize our army and with it [the rights of] our prisoners."[34]

A similar situation was also witnessed in neighboring Eastern Herzegovina which was within the area of operations of the 2nd Assault Corps. The "take-no-prisoners" policy practiced by the newly-formed 29th Herzegovinian Division of the NOVJ in the closing months of 1943 was responsible for the death of one important German prisoner who could have been used to affect the release of Partisan fighters captured in the area. The incident took place in late November 1943 as the 29th came to grips with the 7th SS Division *Prinz Eugen* around the town of

---

[33] This was an act of vengeance for the brutal treatment of the division's members who had fallen into German hands. Exactly how many were shot by the Germans is unknown. One report to the 2nd Panzer Army dated 7 October 1943 mentioned the execution of eighteen officers of the *Taurinense*. Gerhard Schreiber, *Die italienischen Militärinternierten im deutschen Machtbereich 1943–1945: Verraten-Verachtet-Vergessen* (Munich: Oldenbourg Verlag, 1990), pp. 198–99.

[34] *Zbornik*/II/5/95, 289–90, 2nd Assault Corps to 3rd Division (23 September 1943) and 3rd Division to 2nd Assault Corps (20 October 1943); *Zbornik*/II/6/131, 2nd Assault Corps to Main HQ for Macedonia (9 November 1943).

Gacko. On 26 November, a Partisan brigade ambushed a battalion of the SS mountain troops, inflicting heavy casualties in the process, and captured the unit's commander, Major Horst Strathmann.[35] Four days later, the 5th SS Mountain Corps informed the 2nd Panzer Army that negotiations for his exchange had begun and requested information on the number of prisoners that could be used for this purpose. The army relegated the matter to the SD which agreed to help and inquired about the timeline for the completion of the swap.[36] The local commands knew that the chance for a successful exchange grew slimmer with each passing day, so to buy more time, the Germans requested in writing on 2 December that the captured major be spared. Otto Kumm, who took command of the *Prinz Eugen* Division in 1944, wrote that the division's offer to exchange Strathmann "for any required number of captured Partisans was turned down with the cynical answer that he had already been shot for the crimes of the fascists."[37] Whether knowledge of Strathmann's service in the Buchenwald concentration camp contributed to his demise is difficult to ascertain; the Partisans would have found the temptation to shoot a high-ranking officer of the notorious SS division hard to resist even without knowing his background.[38]

Local Prisoner Exchanges, 1944–1945

By the beginning of 1944, the impact of the high-level negotiations in Zagreb was increasingly felt on the ground. Due to the fact that prisoner exchange was now officially approved and given legal framing, units began using this tool to retrieve their missing men. In order to regulate exchanges at the local level, the commanding general of the 2nd Panzer Army issued instructions to this effect on 18 February 1944. The purpose of the document was to enable the divisions to get their men out of captivity as quickly as possible, thereby saving time and reducing internal paperwork. From that point forward, the units did not need permission each time they sought to conduct a swap. They were also encouraged to exchange not only their own members, but all Germans and foreigners serving in the German occupation forces whom the Partisans were willing to exchange. All returnees were to be interrogated and the results submitted to a military judge in order to

---

[35] *Zbornik*/IV/20/287, Activity report of 2nd Brigade for the period 1–15 December 1943 (Entry for 2 December 1943).

[36] NARA, T-313, Roll 485, 001049–51, 5th SS Mountain Corps to 2nd Panzer Army (30 November) and Notification for 5th SS Mountain Corps (undated; probably sent the same day or shortly thereafter).

[37] Otto Kumm, *Vorwärts, Prinz Eugen! Die Geschichte der 7. SS-Freiwilligen-Division "Prinz Eugen"* (Dresden: Winkelried Verlag, 2007), p. 138.

[38] Steffen Grimm, *Die SS-Totenkopfverbände im Konzentrationslager Buchenwald* (Hamburg: Diplomica Verlag, 2011), p. 64.

establish whether the circumstances of their capture included any offense that warranted a court martial. In addition, all units, including the police and other subordinated formations, were reminded that Hitler's instruction of 18 August 1943 concerning the treatment of captives was to be obeyed at all times. General Rendulic also voiced his concerns about the possibility of foul play on the part of the Partisans, who could use the system to first plant spies posing as POWs and then extract them through prisoner exchange. Special emphasis was put on the manner in which the negotiations were to be conducted, always making it clear to the enemy that "a prisoner exchange in no way represents an agreement or a treaty which could be interpreted as a recognition of Tito's bands as [a legitimate] belligerent force in any form."[39]

On the Partisan side, the only attempt to regulate local exchanges came from the Main HQ for Croatia. As previously described, this command had prohibited its subordinate units from conducting local swaps without its permission. This posed a serious problem as an exchange had to be made quickly if it was to be successful. The KPJ's district committee for Šibenik devoted one part of its activity report for January 1944 to this issue: "Can we make a direct exchange when the life of a comrade is at stake? The Germans have captured a good Party member, and we have taken some of them prisoner. Our people say that a direct exchange is prohibited and that prisoners must be sent to the Main HQ. By the time they arrive there, our comrade could be long dead."[40] Despite this example, and possibly other requests for freedom of action, a unit in Dalmatia was prohibited from conducting exchanges without first consulting the Main HQ for Croatia.

It seems that this order was not matched by similar instructions from regional Partisan commands outside of present-day Croatia. By the end of 1943 and the beginning of 1944, units merely instructed their men to take German prisoners and either bring them to brigade or divisional headquarters, or send them to provisional POW camps. It was up to officers on the spot to decide what to do with their captives; they could be kept with the unit, offered for local exchange, or sent to the corps' command which would then send them to Pisarovina.[41]

---

[39] German Federal Archives–Military Archives (hereinafter BA-MA), RS 3-7/14, Order of commander of 2nd Panzer Army (18 February 1944). I wish to thank Dr. Klaus Schmider for providing me with a copy of this document.

[40] NARA, T-311, Roll 563, 001210, District committee for Šibenik, activity report for January 1944 (16 February 1944). In late February, the HQ of the Partisan Navy requested permission from Main HQ for Croatia to exchange three members of the People's Liberation Movement who were hospitalized in Šibenik. VA, 119/1, 2, 1, 125, NOVJ Navy HQ to Main HQ for Croatia (27 February 1944). It is not known whether permission was granted.

[41] *Zbornik*/IV/20/515, Order of 3rd Herzegovina Brigade (28 December 1943); *Zbornik*/I/7/17, Order of 2nd Proletarian Division (8 January 1944); *Zbornik*/IV/22/221, Order of 27th East Bosnian Division (12 February 1944).

As early as 7 January 1944, the Germans learned from prisoner interrogations that "Tito had forbidden the shooting of prisoners," news important enough to be included into the normally terse daily reports.[42] Five weeks later, the Brandenburg Division[43] decided to try its luck in the exchange business. On 14 February, one of its companies had a clash with Partisans outside of Pljevlja. It lost several men, including one severely wounded soldier who had to be left behind. The Main Partisan HQ for Sandžak reported: "On the 16th, the Germans requested an exchange of this man for one Partisan, but he had already succumbed to his wounds. The exchange was offered in writing."[44]

In late March 1944, the command of the 7th SS Mountain Division *Prinz Eugen* decided to try its luck again, this time with the 3rd Corps of the NOVJ in Eastern Bosnia: "Consistent with the talks on prisoner exchange which were held between the German military authorities and your Main HQ for Croatia, we request the exchange of Dr. Lunzer [captured in early February in the same area] and all other members of the *Wehrmacht* who might be in your custody. In pursuit of this goal, I invite you to send one or more envoys to Rogatica in order to discuss this and possible future exchanges." The remarkable thing about this letter is the format in which it was written. It was addressed to "Major General Sir Kosta Nadj, Commander of the 3rd Corps," a rare, if not singular, instance of Germans addressing one of the guerrilla commanders in the field with his self-chosen title along with the honorary "sir." Furthermore, the letter emphasized that the Partisan delegation would be treated "in accordance with internationally accepted norms" and would "naturally" be provided with safe conduct, and was signed by a first lieutenant on behalf of the divisional commander. Judging by the salutation and style of the offer, the Germans were very interested in the safe return of Dr. Lunzer; otherwise, it would be hard to understand why the 7th SS Division would address the Partisans as their equals, especially in light of the ongoing "blood feud" between this unit and the guerrillas.[45]

The spring of 1944 saw further attempts at prisoner exchange in Bosnia with varying degrees of success. The 12th Slavonian Brigade reported in early April that a plane had crashed on Motajica Mountain and that the pilot, Dietrich Perkuhn,

---

[42] NARA, T-78, Roll 331, 6288126, Daily report of Commander-in-Chief Southeast (7 January 1944).

[43] The Brandenburg Division was a special unit formed under the auspices of the *Abwehr* on the eve of the Second World War. It was comprised of highly-trained individuals fluent in foreign languages. The unit's mission was to carry out raids and sabotage deep in the enemy's rear areas. By 1943, the majority of the division was deployed in Yugoslavia, where it served in a purely infantry role.

[44] *Zbornik*/I/16/360–61, Main HQ for Sandžak to 2nd Assault Corps (17 February 1944).

[45] BA-MA, RS 3-7/11, 7th SS Mountain Division, To the commander of 3rd Corps Major General Sir Kosta Nadj (22 March 1944).

was captured: "The Krauts offered to exchange him and we will try to make this happen." According to German intelligence, the pilot had a broken arm and was treated in a guerrilla hospital. However, when the local German command refused to exchange him on Partisan terms (demanding fifteen individuals for Perkuhn), he was shot.[46] By contrast, four German NCOs were successfully exchanged for an unknown number of Partisans near Bosanski Novi around 12 June 1944. Although the returnees' statements do not explicitly name the NOVJ units involved, closer analysis combined with that of other sources point to the 4th Krajina Division and its 8th Brigade. This brigade was reported moving north to Bosanski Novi in mid-June by the intelligence section of the 15th Mountain Corps. Moreover, both the brigade's official monograph and one of the German prisoners mention a theatrical performance about the 6th Army's demise at Stalingrad which defamed Field Marshal Friedrich Paulus and the army, which the Germans unsurprisingly found "offensive and in poor taste."[47]

The coastal region of Croatia became contested ground beginning with the German occupation in the aftermath of the Italian capitulation. The irregular warfare on land was supplemented by a "small war" at sea. The nascent Partisan navy, sometimes in cooperation with British vessels, attacked coastal shipping, conducted reconnaissance raids, and generally sought to make life as miserable as possible for the enemy. All the while, it played a deadly cat-and-mouse game with its German counterpart which resulted in numerous small-scale naval engagements.[48] On one such occasion on 9 February 1944, the Germans captured the Partisan armed boat NB-10 *Sloga,* along with her thirteen crew members. One of the captives was Ivan Morđin (nicknamed "Crni"), a member of the regional committee of the KPJ for Dalmatia. Eight days later, a boat aptly named *Neutralni* ("The Neutral One") was dispatched to the German garrison in Korčula with a written offer

---

[46] *Zbornik*/IV/24/35, Activity report of 12th Slavonian Brigade for the period 20–31 March 1944 (1 April 1944); HR HDA 1491, 5.13.10, 111, (untitled) (4 August 1944).

[47] BA-MA, RH-26/373/39, 373rd Infantry Division, Statements of Karl Müller, Ernst Gebauer, and Max Stade (1 and 17 July 1944); Izudin Čaušević, *Osma krajiška NOU brigada* (Belgrade: Vojnoizdavački zavod, 1981), p. 273; NARA, T-314, Roll 565, 001116, 15th Mountain Corps, Enemy Situation (23 June 1944). The monograph on legionnaire divisions reads that several members of the 373rd were exchanged in late summer 1944 after ". . . a few weeks [in captivity]. They were treated relatively well, although they were dirty, lice-ridden, and extremely emaciated." Schraml, *Kriegsschauplatz,* p. 198. It is not known whether they were exchanged locally or as a part of the Pisarovina cartel.

[48] The war was conducted in true privateering style. One Partisan order read that all captured "side arms, watches, pocket knives, wallets, and similar items are to be divided amongst the fighters for their own needs. The rest is to be delivered to the Navy HQ. The sector's chief of staff will be responsible for the fair division of spoils." VA, 2023, 2, 4/1, NOVJ Navy HQ to 1st Naval Sector (5 May 1944). Needless to say, this order was not compatible with the provisions of international law.

signed by the commander of the 4th Operational Zone of the NOVJ Navy, Srećko Manola.[49] *Neutralni,* however, failed to fulfill her mission for unknown reasons and a second courier boat had to be dispatched on 1 March. The boat arrived safely to Vela Luka where the letter was delivered to the Germans. Shortly before noon, a major arrived with an answer—the exchange was set for 10 March at the same place, weather permitting. He guaranteed that the *Luftwaffe* would not interfere, but he also demanded that the Allied planes do the same. The German interpreter also informed the Partisans that Crni escaped shortly after he had been captured, but was killed by a patrol two days later.[50]

Undeterred by Crni's death, the Partisans decided to proceed with the exchange until problems arose with securing the chosen German prisoners. The prisoners were supposed to come from the POW camp at Vis, the main NOVJ base in the Adriatic, but forty of them, including those who had been selected by the German command, had been "loaned" to the British in mid-February and transferred to Bari for interrogation. The British now refused to return the prisoners, saying that they had not been "loaned" to them but, in fact, surrendered permanently.[51] On 9 March, the NOVJ mission in Bari filed a protest and demanded the immediate return of the Germans. The mission's head was none other than Vladimir Velebit, no stranger to the exchange business. Aware of the intelligence value of returnees in general, he advised against the exchange of the Germans from Vis, saying it would compromise the island's defenses.[52] This suggestion was overruled by the NOVJ Navy HQ which now had permission from the Main HQ for Croatia to conduct the exchange as scheduled.[53]

One day later than agreed, on 11 March shortly after 11.00, a motorboat carrying both a white flag and the flag of the Yugoslav Partisans entered the harbor of Vela Luka on Korčula. There were five Partisans escorting the thirteen Germans aboard, five of whom were seriously wounded. An hour later, they were joined by Lieutenant Gschweitl who was head of the proceedings on behalf of the 118th *Jäger* Division. A cursory check of the manifest revealed that the Partisans did not bring the soldiers who were on the Germans' original list. The lieutenant informed

---

[49] *Zbornik*/VIII/2/26–27, 32, Reports of 4th Operational Zone of NOVJ Navy to NOVJ Navy HQ on 17 and 20 February 1944; Manola's letter, dated 17 February 1944, is reproduced in Weingartner, *Erinnerungen,* p. 202a.

[50] HR HDA 1896, NOV-43/5907, 4th Naval Sector to NOVJ Navy HQ (2 March 1944).

[51] One British order from late February unequivocally stipulated that "German prisoners received from the Partisans will not be handed back." *Dalmacija 1941–1945,* Vol. X, p. 1232, Allied Forces in Dalmatia, Urgent operation No. 1 (25 February 1944).

[52] *Zbornik*/II/12/194, 228, Cables of NOVJ mission in Bari to NOVJ Navy HQ on 2 and 9 March 1944.

[53] VA, 119/1, 2, 1, 147, NOVJ Navy HQ to Main HQ for Croatia (8 March 1944) and VA, 119/1, 2, 4, 118, Main HQ for Croatia to NOVJ Navy HQ (9 March 1944).

his counterpart that he would have to wait until his superiors decided on whether or not to accept the exchange on new terms. At 20.00, the message finally arrived and was an unpleasant surprise for all—the Germans refused to accept the eight healthy "replacement" prisoners that the Partisans had brought with them and demanded that the seriously wounded stay behind, but without compensation. The guerrilla envoy protested, saying he would be shot if he returned to Vis with five fewer German prisoners and no exchanged Partisans; he gave up only after Gschweitl threatened to use force. The lieutenant had even more difficulty convincing the eight Germans to reboard the vessel and return to captivity. One of them, a naval administration official, was particularly adamant about not leaving Korčula, saying he would rather face a German court-martial than be a prisoner of the guerrillas again. Gschweitl repeatedly sent cables to his superiors, arguing the case on behalf of the eight men, but to no avail. At 23.00, the German command lost patience and ordered the lieutenant to force the German prisoners back on board and they finally complied, but with great reluctance. Before the vessel departed, Gschweitl informed the Partisan envoy that his side was still willing to conduct the exchange under the original terms in two weeks' time—on 25 March 1944.[54]

It was more than four months before the Partisans decided to contact the island's garrison again. On 21 August 1944, a raiding party of the 118th *Jäger* Division's 750th Regiment made a night landing on the small island of Vrnik and captured six Partisans, including a local Party leader and two German deserters. The district committee in Dubrovnik immediately requested permission to send parliamentarians to Korčula to broker an exchange. The request was granted and a three-man delegation, including "a comrade who had already been to Vela Luka" (presumably in March), was dispatched to the island on the 23rd. The Partisans proposed to exchange the men from Vrnik for some twelve *Kriegsmarine* sailors recently captured on the Pelješac peninsula. The Germans agreed on the 24th, and also suggested the possibility of including the men from NB-10 *Sloga* into the deal.[55] The war diary of the 750th Regiment mentions that the planned continuation of talks scheduled for the 25th or 26th of August had to be canceled due to "tactical measures." On the 29th and 31st, Partisan envoys visited Korčula again,

---

[54] Gschweitl's four-page report on the event, dated 12 March 1944, can be found in Weingartner, *Erinnerungen,* pp. 202a-202d. The card index of the Military Archive in Belgrade states that Box 2086 contains Partisan-German correspondence pertaining to this exchange (items numbered 1–10). During my visit to the archive in March 2013, I was told that these documents could not be found in the aforementioned box. From the brief summaries available in the card index, it is evident that the Partisan command dispatched another letter to the garrison of Korčula on 20 March and that the courier boat brought back the German answer on the same day (document Nos. 8 and 9). Six days later, the Partisans delivered a new list of German prisoners available for exchange (document No. 10). I could not find any evidence that the correspondence continued after this date.

[55] HR HDA 1896, NOV-43/5913, 5th Naval Sector to NOVJ Navy HQ (24 August 1944).

but no further details are known. The exchange probably did not materialize because of the mercurial situation in southern Dalmatia which compelled the Germans to begin evacuating the island on 9 September.[56]

The 118th *Jäger* Division did not remain out of the exchange proceedings for long, however. In mid-October 1944, its reconnaissance battalion was engaged in heavy fighting around the town of Imotski. On one occasion, Partisan units of the 8th Dalmatian Corps exploited the gap in the German lines and attacked an isolated outpost at the village of Zagvozd. The small garrison was overrun after several hours of fighting, losing all fifty-seven men in the process—forty-five as prisoners. On 23 October 1944, twenty-three of these soldiers were exchanged for the same number of Partisans outside Imotski; the rest were sent off to the rear.[57]

At approximately the same period of time, the division's 750th Regiment was negotiating a prisoner exchange around Ljubuški in neighboring Western Herzegovina. The Partisans were represented by an eighteen-year old girl, who arrived at the German HQ dressed in her best uniform and fully armed. She crossed the lines on more than one occasion acting as a courier between the two sides. The exchange was made on a bridge over the Trebižat River outside Ljubuški, where eleven guerrillas were swapped for twelve soldiers. Originally, both sides had agreed to exchange twelve men each at a 1:1 ratio, but the Germans failed to find the twelfth person. Just as it seemed that the Partisans would insist on the terms and return to the hills with the remaining German, he started crying and begged them to let him go with the others. A senior Partisan officer pushed the terrified soldier across the bridge exclaiming, "Damn you, you can go as well, just stop whining! We can easily find another one like you; do not think you are something special!"[58] This anecdote once again illustrates the decisive influence of an individual commander's whim on the course of a prisoner exchange.

We have seen how the Anglo-Partisan alliance in Dalmatia in late winter of 1944 suffered over the question of prisoners and their exchange. This issue proved equally problematic for intra-Axis relations in that same region during the same time frame. In mid-February 1944, all three sides (Partisans, Germans, and the

---

[56] BA-MA, RH-37/4835, War Diary of 750th Jäger Regiment, Entries for the 23rd, 24th, 28th, 31st August and 9th September 1944.

[57] Max Frey, "Der Kampf bei Zagvozd und meine Gefangennahme," in Weingartner, *Erinnerungen*, pp. 274–75.

[58] Jure Galić, *Vrijeme i ljudi: svjedočenje* (Sarajevo: Svjetlostkomerc d.d., 2005), pp. 351–52. According to the book *Nemačka obaveštajna služba* (Vol. V, pp. 387–88), the branch office of the German Secret Field Police in Western Herzegovina arranged a meeting between an intelligence officer of the 118th Division and the local Partisans on an unspecified date. As a result of the talks, some 150 prisoners were exchanged. This would have been the largest local exchange of the war by far, but I could not find any additional evidence that it actually took place.

Ustashe) lost valuable members in skirmishes around Sinj and were eager for their return. In addition to the three German soldiers (presumably of the 264th Infantry Division), the Communist-led guerrillas had in their custody one *Ustasha*, two Home Guard officers, and two civil servants. The 27th *Ustashe* Battalion in Sinj had nineteen prisoners, including two female members of the KPJ who were functionaries of the local branch of the Women's Anti-fascist Front (*Antifašističko vijeće žena*, or AFŽ). At first it seemed that the Partisans would be willing to trade with the *Ustashe* directly, but then changed their minds and offered the exchange to the Germans instead, demanding the two women in return for the three soldiers. The local *Ustashe* commander described this move as a "cunning ploy" to steal his two most important prisoners, leaving him no one to bargain with in exchange for the lives of NDH officials.

The Germans reacted just as the *Ustashe* commander feared (and the Partisans hoped) when one of their officers arrived at *Ustashe* HQ on 18 February and demanded they hand over the two women. A heated discussion ensued as the *Ustashe* commander refused to obey, whereupon the German officer "slammed his fist on the table and shouted, 'I am in charge here!'" As the *Ustashe* still would not comply, the 15th Home Guard Regiment was called upon to help mediate a solution. At a meeting in the regiment's HQ, it was agreed to present a united front and demand that all eight Axis prisoners be swapped for the same number of Partisans.[59] This incident accentuates the fact that prisoner exchange was a thorny issue not only locally, but also in dealings between NDH and German authorities at the highest levels in Zagreb. "The German officer's attitude . . . and the tone he used made a very bad impression and made cooperation difficult," the *Ustashe* commander from Sinj wrote in his report. He also requested detailed instructions concerning the rules of conduct, inquiring if German prisoners have priority over Croatian prisoners in an exchange, and whether the NDH authorities were obliged to deliver their Partisan prisoners to the Germans even if they were needed for the exchange of Home Guard and *Ustashe* officers.[60]

The 264th Infantry Division and the NOVJ units in its area of responsibility pursued exchange activities well into the summer of 1944. In late May, a Partisan defector told the Germans that the 19th Dalmatian Division held two of their

---

[59] *Dalmacija 1941–1945*, Vol. X, p. 587 (20th Division to 8th Corps, 14 February 1944), p. 693 (KPH District committee for Middle Dalmatia to KPH Regional committee for Dalmatia, 26 February 1944), and pp. 1578–79 (27th Ustashe Battalion to Main Ustashe HQ, 26 February 1944). The exchange is mentioned in the monograph on the Mosor Partisan Detachment, but without further details. Miroslav Velić, Ante V. Petrić, and Mate Vuletić, *Mosorski partizanski odred* (Split: IHRPD, 1985), p. 257. A local party organization document from late March 1944 references "two female comrades who have recently been exchanged." *Dalmacija 1941–1945*, Vol. X, p. 1129, KPH County committee for Split to KPH Regional committee for Dalmatia (31 March 1944).

[60] Ibid., p. 1579, 27th Ustashe Battalion to Main Ustashe HQ (26 February 1944).

officers and three privates and intended to swap them, but it was uncertain whether the offer had yet been made. The five-week period between early August and mid-September saw no fewer than four successful exchanges, with each side releasing a total of thirty-two prisoners.

It should be noted that all of these deals were negotiated on a case-by-case basis rather than as the result of a wider, regional arrangement as was the standard in Herzegovina (see below). As always, happenstance played a major role in the lot of prisoners. *Sonderführer* Richard Wagner, a South Tyrolean working as a military interpreter, earned the nickname "Professor" while in captivity. Because of his nickname, the Partisans believed he was a professor, and thus an officer, and repeatedly postponed his release, bringing Wagner to the verge of a nervous breakdown. Despite this misconception, and the rumor that Wagner had mistreated captured Partisans in Zadar, he was exchanged in mid-August. Senior Corporal Fritz Vanselow had the rare distinction of being freed only five days after his capture. His good luck was another man's misfortune; Peter Krög had been waiting almost two months for an exchange only to be suddenly told that Vanselow would take his place. Then, on the evening before the swap (15 September 1944), a Partisan officer assured Krög that he would be released as well and tasked him with conveying an ultimatum to the HQ of the 264th Infantry. As part of a country-wide effort to induce *Wehrmacht* garrisons to surrender—a strategy launched with the blessing of the Western Allies—the division was being promised correct treatment and the release of its personnel within eight weeks after the cessation of hostilities. The threat of reprisals in the case of non-compliance would become a reality three months later in the aftermath of the Battle of Knin.[61]

After it was occupied in October 1943, Montenegro was placed under direct German rule. *Feldkommandantur* 1040, established in Podgorica, was subordinated to the Military Commander in the Southeast located in Belgrade, rather than to the 2nd Panzer Army. Since they were effectively a part of the occupation system in Serbia, the authorities in the Montenegrin capital were not keen on negotiating with the guerrillas. In late July 1944, the 7th Montenegrin Assault Brigade made an attempt to exchange some German soldiers it had captured in recent fighting. The brigade addressed its offer to the German command in Podgorica and requested an answer, along with a date and place for the exchange. The Germans chose not to respond to the letter, possibly due to the timing of the Partisan offer—it coincided with von Stauffenberg's failed attempt on Hitler's life on 20 July.

---

[61] NARA, T-314, Roll 565, 001178, 15th Mountain Corps, Interrogation of Juray [*sic*] Skrlec (30 May 1944); BA-MA, RH-26/264/19, 264th Infantry Division, Statement of Richard Wagner (8 September 1944); BA-MA, RH-26/264/20, 264th Infantry Division, Intelligence section to personnel section (10 August 1944); ibid., Statement of Walter Weber (12 August 1944); BA-MA, RH-26/264/21, Secret Field Police Group 9, Statement of Fritz Vanselow (16 and 22 September 1944); BA-MA, RH-26/264/24, 264th Infantry Division to 15th Mountain Corps (10 September 1944).

Fearing that any kind of negotiations with the guerrillas might be mistaken for treason, General Wilhelm Keiper, the head of the military administration in the country, decided not to accept the exchange. Indeed, the shooting of ten Partisan suspects on 20 July in Cetinje seemingly confirmed that the German command in Montenegro opted to maintain a hard line with respect to the treatment of captured guerrillas.[62]

The late summer of 1944 saw heavy fighting in northern Bosnia as the 13th SS Mountain Division *Handschar* tried to stem the rising Partisan tide. In early September, during the fighting north of Tuzla, the 18th Croatian Brigade of the NOVJ ambushed a German staff car and killed three of its occupants.[63] The sole survivor, SS Lieutenant Lünen, a communications officer in the *Handschar's* HQ, was captured. According to one *Handschar* veteran, the Partisans dragged the lieutenant along with them "for weeks" before killing him.[64] Lünen's presence in the Partisan camp was witnessed by the Canadian surgeon, Colin Dafoe, who was attached to the NOVJ's 3rd Corps operating in the area. Dafoe spoke to this "fine-looking, well-nourished, young blond German officer" in English and even offered him a cigarette—an act which did not please the Partisans. The next time Dafoe met the prisoner, he was being led away by two Partisans. He never saw him again, but he did see the lieutenant's "beautiful jackboots on a Partisan officer later."[65] The reason why the guerrillas did not immediately shoot Lünen ("a member of the Nazi Party and an officer of the hated *Handschar* Division," as Dafoe recollected) was because he was needed for exchange for some activists held in *Ustashe* prisons. The swap was proposed by the Germans and discussed with the envoys of the NOVJ's 38th Division. As the Germans could not provide the individuals the Partisans wanted, the negotiations were broken off and the unfortunate SS officer was executed.[66]

---

[62] Labović and Basta, *Partizani za pregovaračkim stolom 1941–1945*, p. 221; *Hronologija*, p. 817.

[63] Blagoje Pop Pejanović, "Borba za Srnice," in *18. hrvatska istočnobosanska narodnooslobodilačka udarna brigada* (Tuzla: IGTRO "Univerzal," 1988), pp. 479–80.

[64] George Lepre, *Himmler's Bosnian Division: The Waffen-SS Handschar Division 1943–1945* (Atlglen, PA: Schiffer, 1997), p. 223.

[65] Brian Jeffrey Street, *The Parachute Ward: A Canadian Surgeon's Wartime Adventures in Yugoslavia* (Toronto: Lester & Orpen Dennys, 1987), Chapter 17, retrieved from: http://www.collectionscanada.gc.ca/eppp-archive/100/200/300/editio/parachute/html/chap-17.html

[66] Esad Tihić, *Posavsko-trebavski NOP odred* (Belgrade: Vojnoizdavački zavod, 1983), p. 223. One veteran of the *Handschar's* 28th Regiment remembered there was an attempt to swap prisoners with Tito's men. As this unit operated north of Tuzla at the time of Lünen's capture, it is possible that he was referring to the above-mentioned episode. Television documentary *Bosnier in der Waffen-SS* (Mainz: 3Sat, 12 July 1998). I wish to thank Mr. George Lepre for providing me with this information; Lünen's name found its way into Bakrač's

One of the most interesting cases of prisoner exchange occurred around Derventa in northern Bosnia in September 1944. There were no German units in the town, but there was a *Soldatenheim* (literally "Soldiers' Home," a place where soldiers could spend leisure time) staffed by twenty-six nurses of the German Red Cross. After the Home Guard garrison defected on 8 September, Derventa fell to units of the NOVJ's 5th Corps and the nurses were captured. The news caused a flurry of activity in the office of the plenipotentiary general in Zagreb. On 16 September, Colonel von Selchow placed a telephone call to the operations officer of Army Group F, requesting permission to fly to Brod to try to exchange the nurses.[67] Von Selchow's request was granted, but it is unknown whether or not he made the trip. We do know, however, that the head of the German exchange commission, Willibald Nemetschek, traveled to the area for the same reason. Nemetschek's job was made considerably easier by Colonel von Funck, Glaise-Horstenau's old chief of staff who had hosted Marijan Stilinović during his first visit to Zagreb in August 1942. In his new function as the *Feldkommandant* in Brod, von Funck was able to give Nemetschek information on the whereabouts of the headquarters of the 5th Partisan Corps where the negotiations were to take place. Furthermore, he provided the vehicles which transported the exchanged nurses back to the German lines.[68]

The last recorded attempt at prisoner exchange in Bosnia happened in March 1945. This was precipitated by the capture of Colonel August Ritter von Eberlein, the commander of the 639th Security Regiment. On 26 February, an armored train in which the colonel was riding was ambushed near Busovača. The Partisans managed to immobilize the train, chase off a portion of its crew, and pummel the rest into submission by artillery fire. Twenty-eight Germans, including von Eberlein and his son, were captured by the 6th Krajina Brigade that day. The conditions experienced immediately after his capture were especially unpleasant for the elderly colonel who was forced to wade through the freezing Lašva River with the rest of the column—his request to be allowed to cross the river without wetting his feet went unheeded. Von Eberlein's subsequent protest and invocation of international law provoked a stern rebuke that Germans only thought of conventions when they were losing.[69]

---

notes, most probably as a result of Nemetschek's inquiries. HR HDA 1491, 5.13.10, 193, Exchanges (undated).

[67] NARA, T-311, Roll 193, 000633, Telephone conversations on 16 September 1944 (17.00 hours).

[68] HR HDA 1521, Box 9, File 123 Glaise-Horstenau, Nemetschek's statement on Colonel Freiherr von Funck.

[69] *Zbornik*/IV/34/225–26, Activity report of 6th Krajina Brigade, Entry for 26 February 1945; Nikola Japundža, "Kako je zarobljen štab njemačke borbene grupe 'Eberlajn,'" in *Šesta krajiška NOU brigada: ratna sjećanja* (Bečej: GRO "Proleter," 1985), pp. 686–87.

The colonel was brought to the HQ of the 4th Krajina Division and interrogated. During the questioning, he suggested the idea of exchange and the division forwarded the request on to the 5th Corps. By coincidence, the necessity for a local exchange had recently arisen. Elements of the 7th SS Mountain Division suddenly arrived in the 4th Krajina Division's sector on 1 March. One day later, a vigorous attack forced two Partisan brigades to retreat and leave the division's rear elements in Vitez defenseless. The Germans entered the town and captured a number of Partisans from the 11th Krajina Brigade, as well as thirty-seven horses, sixty-two rifles, fourteen machine guns, two submachine guns, one mortar, and various other supplies.[70]

After the battle, news reached the Partisans that the Germans would be willing to discuss the exchange of Colonel von Eberlein; his capture did not go unnoticed as he was also a colonel in the *Sturmabteilung* (SA) and a known nationalist figure from the days of revolutionary upheaval in Germany in the aftermath of the First World War.[71] The 1st Battalion of the 11th Krajina Brigade was therefore tasked with taking a letter from the corps across the lines to the German command. The courier who volunteered for the job was blind-folded when he reached the German pickets, and then taken to a command post where he delivered the offer. Labović and Basta claim that von Eberlein was exchanged for a number of Partisans plus the weapons and equipment the Germans had captured in Vitez; however, a number of sources claim otherwise. Dragomir Radišić, the political commissar of the 1st Battalion at that time, claims that the exchange failed to materialize since the 7th SS withdrew from Vitez on 12 March 1945.[72] The activity report of the 4th Krajina Division for March (compiled in the first week of April) still shows the division short of its ten missing and one captured men, as well as all the equipment lost in Vitez. This should come as no surprise as there is no conclusive evidence that the Germans ever traded weapons and military equipment for prisoners.[73] Furthermore, there is at least one document which confirms that von

---

[70] Drago Karasijević, *Četvrta krajiška NOU divizija* (Belgrade: Vojnoizdavački i novinski centar, 1988), p. 397.

[71] Ernst Percy Schramm, *Kriegstagebuch des Oberkommandos der Wehrmacht 1940–1945* (Herrsching: Manfred Pawlak Verlag, 1982), Vol. VIII, p. 1131, War diary entry for 27 February 1945; Ellen Latzin, "Bayern und die Pfalz: eine historische Beziehung voller Höhen und Tiefen," *Einsichten und Perspektiven* 2 (Special Issue, 2006).

[72] Labović and Basta, *Partizani za pregovaračkim stolom 1941–1945*, pp. 267–68; Dragomir-Radiša Radišić, "U 1. bataljonu 11. krajiške NOU kozarske brigade, od Prijedora do slobode," in *Kozara u Narodnooslobodilačkom ratu: zapisi i sjećanja* (Belgrade: Vojnoizdavački zavod, 1978), Vol. VI, pp. 397–98.

[73] *Zbornik*/IV/34/613, Activity report of 4th Krajina Division for March 1945 (9 April 1945). According to the statements of several Dalmatian Partisans, the Germans used a local prisoner exchange on the outskirts of Sinj in 1944 to offer ten light machine guns of various

Eberlein could not have been exchanged in the field and that he remained in captivity. On 31 March 1945, the OZNA for Bosnia and Herzegovina dispatched one of its officers to the Main HQ for Croatia with a letter which read, in part, that the Bosnian units had a large number of German prisoners whose exchange could not be completed locally due to the military situation: "It should be mentioned that one of them is Colonel Eberlein-Ritter [*sic*]. . . ." Another document shows that the Partisans prepared a list of thirty individuals who should be requested from the Germans for von Eberlein's release. Boris Bakrač's records of the proceedings in Pisarovina during the last weeks of the war, however, do not mention von Eberlein's exchange.[74]

Mini-Cartel in Eastern Herzegovina, 1944

Eastern Herzegovina, or more precisely the area around Stolac, was the scene of a series of contacts between the Partisans and the Germans between June and September 1944. These contacts led to an unwritten agreement on prisoner exchange which was, in essence, a scaled-down version of what took place in Pisarovina. The delegates also discussed and corresponded on issues beyond those related to prisoner swap. The most extraordinary aspect of these talks was that they were led by two units which previously had abysmal records regarding the treatment of enemy captives—the 369th Infantry and 29th Herzegovina Divisions.

It all began when the South Herzegovina Partisan Detachment captured two German NCOs from the Devil's Division on 20 June 1944. One day later, the Partisan command dispatched a letter to the German command in Stolac offering to exchange the NCOs for two captured Partisans, including one "political worker."[75] The garrison replied affirmatively and invited Partisan delegates to Stolac, where the exchange could be made. The answer also requested that the Partisans send one of their brigade officers as "there is much to be discussed on the issue of military law [and its application] between the warring sides."[76] The Partisan HQ responded on the 26th, declining the invitation and proposing instead that the meeting be held on the "neutral" territory of Hill 286, near the hamlet of Poplat just south of the town. Both delegations were to arrive at the meeting location waving white flags, bearing no arms, and escorted by no more than one platoon which

---

types in return for a single German-made MG 42. Velić, Petrić, and Vuletić, *Mosorski partizanski odred,* p. 310.

[74] HR HDA 1491, 5.13.10, 38, OZNA for Bosnia and Herzegovina for the Main HQ for Croatia (31 March 1945); ibid., 189, Eberlein (undated). Von Eberlein died in captivity in Sarajevo in 1949.

[75] VA, 1627, 2, 15, South Herzegovina Partisan Detachment to Stolac garrison (21 June 1944).

[76] Ibid., Document No. 17, Stolac garrison to South Herzegovina Partisan Detachment (23 June 1944).

would remain some distance away.[77] The Germans agreed to these terms, and the political worker was exchanged for a German soldier on 27 June 1944.[78]

The second exchange was scheduled to take place in two days' time at the same location. Zora Kruševac-Roganović, chosen for the exchange, remembered the treatment she received in Stolac:

> The town commander . . . took my coat like a true gentleman and handed my bag over to his orderly. I was walking between him and the captain, who was our interpreter; behind us came soldiers. It looked like a wedding procession with people [watching us] from the streets. Once we arrived at Poplat, the commander and the captain took off their pistol belts, selected a bottle of cognac, and went to a hill some 500 meters away. The negotiations lasted for quite some time. About one o'clock in the afternoon, a flare was fired [from a signal pistol]. I walked to the hill escorted by a soldier of the Devil's Division. From the opposite side came our man [leading] one uniformed Kraut. . . . [The envoys then] ended their meeting with the exchanges "Death to fascism!" and "Heil Hitler!" [and parted].[79]

The negotiations lasted for four hours and were conducted in a "very correct" manner by both sides. The Partisans were represented by Danko Kundačina and Miloš Stamatović, the commander and the political commissar of the South Herzegovina Partisan Detachment, respectively. The German commandant of Stolac, although fluent in Serbo-Croatian, did not talk much. The chief German negotiator was 1st Lieutenant Kurz, the intelligence officer of the 369th Infantry Division. The Partisan delegation opened the talks by protesting against the atrocities that followed the German operations in the area and the subsequent harsh treatment of captured Partisans and their sympathizers. In short, the German Army was not obeying the provisions of international law, a fact for which it would be "criminally prosecuted in the near future." Stamatović then moved on to political questions and stated that the Partisan movement would never accept the breakup of Yugoslavia as orchestrated by the Axis powers. Their army was an independent force, comprised of all Yugoslav nationalities, including ethnic Germans who had their own company in Slavonia. Behind the tightly organized NOVJ stood a political body, the AVNOJ, which was tasked with administering the liberated areas through a

---

[77] Ibid., Document Nos. 16 and 19, South Herzegovina Partisan Detachment to Stolac garrison (23 and 26 June 1944).

[78] Mensur Seferović, *Trinaesta hercegovačka NOU brigada* (Belgrade: Vojnoizdavački i novinski centar, 1988), p. 44. The exchange could not be made under the original terms because the Germans failed to produce the two people demanded by the Partisans.

[79] Ibid., pp. 44–45. "Death to Fascism—Freedom to the People!" was the official slogan of the NOP.

network of People's Liberation Councils. Since the movement had been recognized by all of the members of the anti-fascist coalition, it could lay claim to being the sole legitimate representative of Yugoslavia in this conflict.[80]

Kurz responded that the NDH was a sovereign state and an ally of the Third Reich; it had the right to defend itself against Communist subversion and to apply coercive measures against civilians who supported the guerrillas. He added that the Germans had already taken the necessary steps to ensure that all Partisan prisoners and suspicious civilians were treated correctly by the Gestapo and NDH authorities; the *Ustashe* and the Chetniks were also under orders to deliver captured Partisans alive or face the death penalty. However, it was the 29th Division which was killing prisoners and thus breaking "an earlier agreement" negotiated between Hans Ott and the Supreme HQ of the NOVJ in November 1942. The Germans were opposed to such actions and proposed that the prisoners should be exchanged in the future. Kurz therefore requested that the negotiations be continued at a higher level, preferably with the commander of the 2nd Assault Corps, Peko Dapčević. He then inquired as to the location of the final resting place of the *Luftwaffe* Ace, Captain Joachim Kirschner, and about the possibility of a transfer of his remains to Mostar. The Partisan delegation replied that it was not authorized to accept or refuse these requests, but could only relate them to their superiors. The Germans also proposed a truce along the lines of communication in Eastern Herzegovina; in exchange, they would refrain from incursions into the surrounding countryside. This request was refused on the spot.[81]

In a letter dated 30 June 1944, the commander and the political commissar of the South Herzegovina Partisan Detachment informed the 29th Herzegovina Division of the proceedings, requested instructions, and suggested that Kirschner's body be offered in exchange for Partisan prisoners.[82] After consulting with the command of the 2nd Assault Corps, the division instructed the detachment to convey the following message to the garrison at Stolac: German prisoners would be treated according to international law; both sides should strive to exchange prisoners as soon as they were available; legionnaries of Slavic origin would not be exchanged as they were mostly deserters who were coming over because of the "unbearable conditions" in the German Army; Captain Kirschner's body would not be exhumed; and the 2nd Assault Corps was considering the offer for direct negotiations and would inform the garrison about its decision in due time.[83]

---

[80] Labović and Basta, *Partizani za pregovaračkim stolom 1941–1945*, pp. 256–57; VA, 1627, 2, 23, South Herzegovina Partisan Detachment to 29th Herzegovina Division (30 June 1944).

[81] Ibid.

[82] Ibid. This detail was not mentioned in any of the Yugoslav works dealing with the prisoner exchange in Herzegovina in 1944.

[83] Ibid., Document No. 27, South Herzegovina Partisan Detachment to Stolac garrison (1 July 1944).

The planned exchange of Lieutenant Stojan Vukčević, a Yugoslav-Canadian member of the British military mission to the 2nd Assault Corps, was the main topic of the German-Partisan correspondence in July and August 1944. The Partisan envoys requested his release at the meeting on 29 June and offered one soldier of the Devil's Division in return. The Germans refused to exchange him for a common soldier as the "customs of war" required that he be exchanged for one NCO and at least two soldiers. They added that Vukčević was currently in Mostar and that he would be brought to Stolac as soon as the Partisans agreed to their terms. The correspondence continued throughout the next two weeks, but no agreement could be reached as the Partisans kept insisting that one private was all they could offer. The German summer offensive in Eastern Herzegovina (codenamed *Sonnenstich*) began on 13 July and lasted for two weeks, during which the negotiations were on hold.[84]

Although the results of the exchanges up to this point were relatively meager (both sides received only two prisoners each), the command of the 29th Herzegovina Division recognized the potential value of these contacts. As a result, the division issued an order on 16 July 1944 to all subordinated units that "all Krauts, but especially officers and NCOs who surrender of their own free will during the fighting, are not to be killed but brought to this command instead."[85] The impact of the exchange arrangement on Hill 286 could be felt even beyond the immediate confines of Eastern Herzegovina. In July 1944, the 5th SS Mountain Corps hosted a conference for representatives from all intelligence services active in its operational area. There were twenty-five people present, including intelligence officers from operational units, the *Abwehr's* "Front Reconnaissance Troops," Secret Field Police, and the SD. Lieutenant Walter Kurz of the 369th Infantry gave a report on the question of prisoners and the successful exchange agreement with the Partisans in Eastern Herzegovina. Based on his lecture, it was concluded that all units should strive to capture as many guerrillas as possible in order to exchange them for German soldiers in captivity.[86]

On 31 July, the 29th Herzegovina Division sent five Germans and one Croatian legionnaire ("infected with syphilis and therefore impossible to treat in Partisan hospitals") to the detachment, along with the names of six individuals the corps wanted released in return. One day later, the division dispatched another two

---

[84] See the letters from Stolac garrison to the South Herzegovina Partisan Detachment in ibid., Document Nos. 26 (30 June 1944), 28 (1 July 1944), 30 (3 July 1944), 32 (6 July 1944), and 34 (9 July 1944); Partisan letters can be found in ibid., Document Nos. 27 (1 July), 31 (5 July 1944), and 35 (10 July 1944). In his letter to the Partisans dated 30 June 1944, Lieutenant Kurz also wrote that he was sorry that his camera did not function properly, and expressed his wish to take more photographs with the Partisans the next time they met.

[85] VA, 1145/2, 2, 14, 29th Herzegovina Division to all subordinated units (16–17 July 1944).

[86] *Nemačka obaveštajna služba,* Vol. V, p. 158.

prisoners (one member of the OT and one wounded Croatian soldier) for the same purpose. The detachment was authorized to do whatever was necessary to affect Vukčević's release; captured civilian sympathizers and some Home Guards arrested for supporting the Partisans were to come second. As it was planned to expand the exchange, the envoys were instructed to demand a list of prisoners from Mostar. Last but not least, the division cautioned the detachment not to use a depreciatory tone in its correspondence with the opposite side; letters to the garrison should forthwith be addressed to the "temporary occupation command at Stolac."[87]

Despite the sharpening of the tone, the two commands continued working on a solution to Vukčević's case during the first two weeks of August. On the 3rd, the Partisans requested the list of prisoners held in Mostar and Dubrovnik, and offered a number of "full-blooded" Germans in exchange. The letter continued with a claim that soldiers of other nationalities who were caught in the recent fighting did not want to be returned and the Partisans would not force them. As for Vukčević,

---

[87] VA, 1145/1, 1, 9–1, 29th Herzegovina Division to South Herzegovina Partisan Detachment (31 July 1944); ibid., 1627, 2, 36/1–2, 29th Herzegovina Division to South Herzegovina Partisan Detachment (1 August 1944). The Germans replied in kind by changing the header of their messages "to the still-existent headquarters of the Partisan bands in southern Herzegovina." As the Partisans attached great importance to the formal aspect of negotiations with the Germans, the response of the town command did not go unanswered: "The way in which you addressed this command in your last letter shows that you intentionally deny the fact that we are an army recognized by our allies, an army [whose fighting prowess] you have felt on your own skin . . . during the past three years of fighting. On the other hand, you are occupiers and your command in Stolac is temporary." Ibid., Document No. 36/3–2, South Herzegovina Partisan Detachment to Stolac garrison, 11 August 1944. The Devil's Division was no stranger to written duels with Partisan units. On one such occasion in early 1944, a German captain from the garrison at Jajce sent an envelope full of propaganda leaflets, letters of safe conduct for deserters, and tobacco rationing stamps to a battalion of the 1st Proletarian Brigade. In a letter addressed to the Partisan commander personally, the captain advised him to think the situation over and inform the garrison of when and where he wanted to surrender his unit. Both amused and angry, the Partisan commander prepared an answer, written in German, which contained "a torrent of taunts, loathful remarks, and insults." The letter, along with a single cigarette made of Herzegovinian tobacco, was sent through the same peasant who had brought the envelope. The courier soon returned with the reply from the garrison's command. The answer consisted of the Partisan commander's original letter with all grammatical errors underlined with green pencil. Underneath the original text the German officer added in Serbian: "Next time, please respond in Serbo-Croatian; altogether, thirty-six errors; grade—F." The Partisans later concluded that the German officer ("a known Gestapo official") wanted to test their nerves and throw them off balance just before the garrison made a sally against the Partisan positions on the outskirts of the town. Ljubiša Veselinović, "Neobična prepiska," in *Prva proleterska brigada: sećanja boraca* (Belgrade: Vojno delo, 1963), Vol. II, pp. 579–81.

the guerrillas were ready to offer one medical NCO for him, but other prisoners had to be exchanged no later than 13 August or they would be returned to the 29th Division.[88] As the Germans failed to deliver the individuals wanted by the Partisans, the exchange appeared to be doomed; the South Herzegovina Partisan Detachment was already complaining that the prisoners were becoming a burden.[89] The garrison in Stolac therefore proposed to swap Vukčević immediately for the NCO at hand, while the difference could be settled in future exchanges.[90]

The exchange took place in the last week of August; some Yugoslav sources claim that seven Germans were released on this occasion for Vukčević alone.[91] In all probability, the Partisans gave one NCO for the British officer while the remaining six were swapped for the same number of Partisan sympathizers from the lists provided by the 29th Herzegovina Division in late July and early August. This assumption is confirmed in a letter to the German command dated 30 August in which the Partisans promised to include one private they owed for Vukčević in the exchange that was set for 2 September 1944. On this occasion, the Partisans received one of their fighters and five civilian sympathizers for three German soldiers.[92]

---

[88] VA, 1627, 2, 36/2–2 and 26/3–2, South Herzegovina Partisan Detachment to Stolac garrison (3 and 8 August 1944).

[89] VA, 1144/2, 1, 28, South Herzegovina Partisan Detachment to 29th Herzegovina Division (12 August 1944).

[90] VA, 1627, 2, 40, Stolac garrison to South Herzegovina Partisan Detachment (12 August 1944).

[91] Danilo Komnenović and Muharem Kreso, *Dvadeset deveta hercegovačka divizija* (Belgrade: Vojnoizdavački zavod, 1979), p. 296. The exchange of Stojan Vukčević illustrates how German units in the NDH learned to disregard orders from above if they ran contrary to their immediate needs. On 18 August 1944, just several days before the British officer was exchanged, Hitler issued secret instructions according to which the members of Allied and Soviet military missions were not to be treated as prisoners of war, but executed. NARA, T-311, Roll 192, 000601, Commander-in-Chief Southeast to Army Group F and 2nd Panzer Army, 18 August 1944. The order was not to be passed on to commands below the corps level. It is known that Vukčević had been brought to Mostar, the seat of the 5th SS Mountain Corps, in July; therefore, Hitler's instructions could have easily been carried out. However, they elected not to kill the Bristish officer as it would have condemned several German soldiers in Partisan captivity to a very uncertain fate. Incidentally, I have not encountered any instances of commands in the field actually obeying these instructions.

[92] Komnenović and Kreso, *Dvadeset deveta hercegovačka divizija*, p. 506; VA, 1627, 2, 45, South Herzegovina Partisan Detachment to Stolac garrison (30 August 1944). The correspondence was interrupted several times in late August by the Chetniks. The Partisans demanded that the Germans protect the courier link between the two commands from their unruly auxiliaries. Ibid., Document Nos. 43 and 45, South Herzegovina Partisan

By this time, the frequent correspondence between the two sides and the occasional prisoner exchange on Hill 286 had evolved into a small cartel defined by verbally agreed upon rules. The negotiations were conducted by the South Herzegovina Partisan Detachment on behalf of the 29th Herzegovina Division on the one side, and by the 369th Anti-tank Battalion on behalf of the 369th Infantry Division on the other. It is noteworthy that this battalion had convened a special commission headed by Sergeant Swoboda and tasked it with overseeing all aspects of prisoner exchange.[93] One letter written by Lieutenant Kurz in early September 1944 provides insight into the inner mechanisms of the agreement. The prisoners were swapped according to their rank: a German officer was worth one Partisan officer, seven fighters, or ten civilians; an NCO was worth one NCO, three fighters, or seven civilians; an ordinary soldier was worth one soldier or five civilians. The Partisans were understandably very interested in the release of their civilian supporters. They were also very eager to settle scores with those who had defected to the Axis. In reply to one such request, Kurz wrote that the individuals "who returned to civilian life in order to support Europe's struggle against foreign enemies" were under German protection and, consequently, could not be exchanged. The Partisans also wanted to include members of the NDH's armed forces in the deal, but this idea was rejected by the Germans with the explanation that these people were exchanged under a separate agreement between the NDH and the Supreme HQ of the NOVJ, so the Partisans "should talk directly to Zagreb." The real reason was, of course, that the Germans did not want to "waste" their prisoners on the soldiers of unreliable NDH formations. The main allies of the 369th Legionnaire Division in Eastern Herzegovina were the Chetniks, and the Germans duly took their needs into consideration. For instance, the Partisans were informed that all Muslims and Croats who were captured as members of the NOVJ were eligible for exchange; the Serbs, on the contrary, were recruited into Chetnik ranks. Lieutenant Kurz also mentioned that according to the same international law the Partisans so often invoked in their letters, it was permitted to relieve prisoners only of their weapons. This was a reminder that the guerrillas were continuously breaking their promise not to strip (and plunder) their German captives.[94] The refusal to exchange the body and decorations of Captain Kirschner for prisoners was met with indignation: "According to our opinion and to the

---

Detachment to Stolac garrison, 23 and 30 August 1944. Consequently, the Germans began marking the envelopes destined for the Partisans with a note: "Prisoner exchange—free passage allowed." Seferović, *Trinaesta hercegovačka,* p. 119.

[93] Schraml, *Kriegsschauplatz,* p. 72.

[94] On 30 August 1944, the South Herzegovina Partisan Detachment informed the garrison in Stolac that the German prisoners would be returned in the same uniforms they were wearing at the time of their capture. The detachment also promised to pass along the German complaints over this issue to their superiors. VA, 1627, 2, 45.

traditions of Western culture, [the return of a body] is a purely humane and chivalrous act."[95]

The first week of September was spent in preparations for another exchange. The Partisans offered two medical NCOs (one from the OT and another from the Devil's Division) in exchange for eight individuals, including one councilman of the Communist-sponsored regional parliament for Bosnia and Herzegovina, the *Zemaljsko antifašističko vijeće narodnog oslobođenja Bosne i Hercegovine* (State Anti-fascist Council of People's Liberation of Bosnia and Herzegovina, or ZAVNOBiH).[96] The Germans replied that the exchange could not take place on 10 September as proposed because some of the requested prisoners had not yet arrived from Sarajevo and elsewhere. The letter also contained a threat: "At the same time, we wish to inform you that this will be the last exchange if you persist in refusing to exchange the Croats [who are in your custody]. We know for certain that they want to be exchanged [with the others]. We consider it our duty to show solidarity with our allies."[97] The South Herzegovina Partisan Detachment attempted to calm the situation by offering "the only Croat" they had for one of their fighters who was believed to be in a hospital in Dubrovnik. At the same time, the guerrilla command reaffirmed its position that the prisoners of Slav origin would not be exchanged unless they wanted to be, and "at this moment, there are no such people."[98]

The Partisan response also read that circumstances demanded the exchange be completed "in a most urgent manner." This sense of urgency was a result of the newly-arrived 13th Herzegovina Brigade issuing an ultimatum to the garrison in Stolac on 7 September 1944 without consulting the South Herzegovina Partisan Detachment beforehand. The ultimatum recounted the state of Germany's desperate military and diplomatic situation in general, and especially pointed out that all escape routes from the Balkans were severed. In order to avoid unnecessary bloodshed, the garrison was summoned to surrender and disarm all collaborationist units under their command. If they agreed, they would be treated according to the rules of the Geneva Convention; if not, they would be "considered criminals and

---

[95] Ibid., Document No. 46, Stolac garrison to South Herzegovina Partisan Detachment (2 September 1944).

[96] Ibid., Document No. 49, South Herzegovina Partisan Detachment to Stolac garrison (7 September 1944); Komnenović and Kreso, *Dvadeset deveta hercegovačka divizija*, p. 105.

[97] VA, 1627, 2, 51, Stolac garrison to South Herzegovina Partisan Detachment (9 September 1944).

[98] Ibid., Document No. 50, South Herzegovina Partisan Detachment to Stolac garrison (9 September 1944). In the same letter, the detachment informed the Germans that none of the five members of the OT for whom they were searching (ibid., Document No. 51) were in the custody of the 29th Herzegovina Division.

treated accordingly." The Germans did not respond and the garrison remained in the town until late October.[99]

The ultimatum signaled an end to the prisoner exchange on Hill 286. The South Herzegovina Partisan Detachment was disbanded and its personnel were transferred to the newly-created 14th Herzegovina Brigade. The brigade's HQ delivered all documentation pertaining to the prisoner exchange to higher commands so that they could "continue to work on this matter." The 29th Division did not see fit to continue contact with the Germans in Stolac in light of the growing strength of the Partisan movement and the steadily deteriorating position of the enemy. The 14th Brigade, on the contrary, still desired to exchange prisoners even after the collapse of the Stolac arrangement. By mid-November, the brigade was deployed around Nevesinje, still facing elements of the 369th Infantry Division. When fourteen of its members (including one Italian) were captured, the unit contacted the German garrison and requested an exchange. The letter of offer included the threat that the Partisans would exact reprisals on German prisoners should anything happen to the captive Partisans. This was, in fact, a hollow threat because the brigade did not have any prisoners; the true purpose of the ultimatum was to buy time for collecting a sufficient number of Germans for the exchange. The brigade ordered its battalions to go on a prisoner hunt while requesting help from the 29th Division. Eventually, the prisoners needed for exchange arrived from the POW camp in Bileća. In the interim, the Germans had agreed to the offer and the fourteen Partisans were swapped for an equal number of Germans between 23 and 25 November 1944.[100]

Ultimately, the spirit of the mini-cartel forged at Hill 286 failed to have a lasting impact on the conduct of the 29th Herzegovina Division as a whole. The

---

[99] Komnenović and Kreso, *Dvadeset deveta hercegovačka divizija*, p. 506; Seferović, *Trinaesta hercegovačka*, pp. 118–19. There is no evidence to suggest that the ultimatum to Stolac was linked to the similar call for surrender of German forces in Western Macedonia issued at approximately the same time. The concept was probably devised by local Partisan commands who hoped to exploit the crisis caused by the defection of Germany's Balkan allies and the arrival of the Red Army on the Yugoslav borders.

[100] Ilija Perišić, "Prva omladinska brigada NOVJ u Hercegovini i aktivnosti skojevske organizacije," in *Četrnaesta hercegovačka NOU brigada* (Belgrade: Vojnoizdavački i novinski centar, 1988), p. 21; Vukašin Senić, Mile Vukalović, et al., "Borbena dejstva brigade," in ibid., pp. 70–71. This book provides 25 November as the date of exchange, whereas German primary sources suggest that the exchange took place at least two days earlier. One intelligence report reads that according to the statements of "exchanged prisoners," the Partisans in the "Bileća–Gacko area" were commanded by British officers. NARA, T-311, Roll 184, Supplement to the daily report of Army Group E for 23 November 1944. The monograph on the 14th Herzegovina Brigade claims that one of its battalions went on a hunt for exchange prisoners near Sarajevo as late as January 1945. Mirko Ignjatić, "Političko-vaspitni rad u brigadi," in *Četrnaesta hercegovačka*, pp. 172–73.

pattern from nearby Dalmatia repeated itself—once victory was near, some of the officers and men saw no reason to abide by the rules of warfare. This attitude caused a great loss of life amongst German prisoners taken in the early months of 1945. One of the worst atrocities occurred in the area of Nevesinje in mid-February, where the 10th and 13th Brigades decimated the 369th Regiment of the 369th Legionnaire Division. Ferid Buturović, a 19-year-old political officer with the 10th, remembers seeing prisoners destined for the "Thirteenth Battalion" (in Partisan parlance, those earmarked for execution) being led to the rear, followed by the sound of gunfire, and his failed attempt to prevent the shooting of a young, slightly wounded German soldier by a fellow commissar.[101] Just how many prisoners perished is unknown, but the affair was bloody enough to upset the division's command: "It must be clear from the start that we must not kill prisoners. . . . It was incorrect to kill so many prisoners at Bišina [outside Nevesinje]. It was also wrong from a practical standpoint. Imagine the dividends of having so many Germans put to work, some of whom were experts indispensable for the reconstruction and redevelopment of our country. One must take care that not a single prisoner is killed in the future. Never forget that we are a state and that we therefore must govern ourselves accordingly and act like a regular army of a modern state."[102]

Prisoner Exchanges on the "Regular" Fronts, 1944–1945

All of the previously described prisoner exchanges occurred under the conditions of the guerrilla warfare raging in Yugoslavia—with some exceptions—since the beginning of the war. The fighting was characterized by asymmetric tactics, lack of secure rear areas, as well as the selective application of international law on the part of the Communist-led guerrillas. Although the Partisans were increasingly able to fight in a "regular" fashion when it suited them, this style of combat was practiced only when necessary (e.g. covering a retreat). Losses in manpower and matériel incurred by superior enemy firepower were difficult to replace and were usually disproportionate to the number of casualties inflicted on the enemy. The arrival of the Red Army and the liberation of Serbia in October–November 1944 alleviated the problems of manpower and supply to a great degree. Serbia represented a large, almost untouched, manpower pool which could now be exploited to the fullest. The quick establishment of a civilian authority enabled the NOVJ

---

[101] Ferid Buturović, *Kuća mostarskog kadije: sjećanja mostarskog skojevca, ilegalca i partizana* (Sarajevo: Ferid Buturović-SUBNOR Sarajevo, 2015), pp. 162–64.

[102] *Zbornik*/IX/9/19, Political commissar of NOVJ 29th Division to all brigade commissars (1 March 1945). At least one captured German witnessed the executions and lived to tell the story. Schraml, *Kriegsschauplatz*, p. 122. According to the same source, the Partisans spared only those strong enough to be used as porters.

to launch a massive conscription drive which soon augmented the strength of the divisions in Serbia to approximately 8–10,000 men apiece.[103] With the Red Army controlling a safe ground link to the territory, these large units could now be equipped with Soviet arms, which included T-34 tanks and Ilyushin IL-2 ground-attack aircraft. Thus equipped, the NOVJ units were sent to engage the Germans along a fixed front which had been created in the province of Syrmia in the aftermath of the battle for Belgrade. However, the regular warfare fought in the trenches in Syrmia was far different than the fighting to which the Partisan units were accustomed, although it was precisely the type of combat at which German units excelled. Consequently, the NOVJ suffered a series of bloody reversals while trying to achieve a breakthrough in the winter and early spring of 1945. They would succeed finally in mid-April, less than a month before the capitulation of Germany.[104]

Both sides now facing each other in Syrmia were regular armies, at least as far as appearance and fighting techniques were concerned; however, their practices remained largely unchanged. For instance, one German police battalion commander complained in December 1944 that a prisoner captured by his men "could have contributed to our knowledge of enemy intentions . . . had he not been shot while trying to escape."[105] About the same time, Ruža Dević, an 18-year-old nurse attached to the 8th Vojvodina Brigade, was not far from Osijek when her unit was overrun by the Germans and *Ustashe*. She was taken captive, along with other prisoners (the slightly wounded) who could be transported to the rear; the seriously wounded were summarily executed.[106] The situation was hardly any better on the opposite side of the front. Despite repeated orders regarding the fair treatment of prisoners, the Partisan units on the ground often reverted to their old methods. On 3 February 1945, the 25th Division of the NOVJ, deployed on the flank of the Syrmian Front to the south of the Sava, was ordered to send a captured German officer "most urgently" (repeated twice in the message) to the 14th Corps' HQ. One day later, the corps sent the following message to the division: "It is impossible to understand why you have failed to send us the German prisoners [*sic*]. Your treatment of prisoners not only goes against our orders, but prevents us from gaining a

---

[103] Petranović, *Istorija Jugoslavije*, Vol. II, pp. 414, 439; Ljubivoje Pajović, Dušan Uzelac, and Milovan Dželebdžić, *Sremski front 1944–45* (Belgrade: BIGZ, 1979), p. 153.

[104] Schmidt-Richberg, *Der Endkampf auf dem Balkan*, pp. 76–89, 91–96, 111–13, 116–27. See also Gaj Trifković, "Carnage in the Land of Three Rivers: The Syrmian Front 1944–1945," *Militärgeschichtliche Zeitschrift* 75:1 (2016), pp. 94–122.

[105] NARA, T-315, Roll 1300, 001008, 2nd Battalion of 1st Volunteers' Police Regiment "Croatia," Comment of battalion commander (2 December 1944).

[106] Nikola Božić, *Rovovi i mostobrani: Osma vojvođanska udarna brigada* (Novi Sad: Institut za istoriju, 1989), pp. 393–94.

clearer picture of the situation; on top of that, it is a direct violation of the Supreme HQ's order concerning the treatment of prisoners."[107]

There is no evidence that the regular NOVJ units on the Syrmian Front ever attempted to exchange prisoners at the local level. The Yugoslavs also did not attempt to use the German prisoners from camps in Serbia for exchange in neighboring Croatia.[108] This was largely due to the technical difficulties and challenges of transferring prisoners over a long, roundabout route halfway across the country to Pisarovina. To create a separate cartel for the Syrmian Front would have required a political will which was no longer present amongst the high-level Yugoslav leaders. Indeed, for political reasons as well as for prestige, the decision was made not to exchange the inmates of prisoner camps in Serbia and to encourage units in the field to follow suit. First of all, it would have been impossible to engage in exchanges without drawing the attention of the numerous Soviet representatives in the country, and Tito had been striving to stay out of the limelight ever since the heated exchange with the Comintern in the first half of 1943. Second, gaining control over Serbia made Tito the undisputed ruler of the new Yugoslavia. The Communist-controlled government was now in charge of the most populous province of the country. Its rule had all the trappings of a sovereign state, including civilian administration, control over its own economic resources, internal security, and a regular army. Possessing prisoners was a symbolic sign of the new state's military power. Prestige now carried more weight with the Partisans than practical considerations; the German prisoners were worth more clearing rubble off the streets of Belgrade in full view of the populace than for prisoner exchange. Third, it is likely that the Yugoslavs were now suffering from the same arrogance which had plagued the Germans in the first phase of the war. With their strength continually increasing, and the outcome of the war certain, they were less likely to make concessions of any kind to their enemy.

Negotiations in Macedonia, 1943–1944

In September 1943, occupied Yugoslavia was in turmoil as a result of the capitulation of Fascist Italy. All warring factions now directed their efforts to reaching the former Italian occupation zone as fast as possible. The prize was the occupation of the Adriatic coast and the capture of the 300,000-strong Italian contingent,

---

[107] *Zbornik*/IV/33/101, 129, 14th Corps to 25th Division (3 and 4 February 1945). Gojko Nikoliš, a veteran Partisan doctor, witnessed a long column of German prisoners being led to the rear on 12 April 1945 in Syrmia and commented that "their fate was not enviable." Nikoliš, *Korijen,* p. 654.

[108] One of the rare exceptions to the rule is the previously-mentioned case involving five Germans who were captured at Batina in December 1944 and released on receipt at Kutina in early April 1945 (see Chapter 4).

together with its vast stock of arms and supplies. The 2nd Army was increasingly losing cohesion amidst the confusion caused by the recent developments. As central command dissipated, each Italian commander had to now determine his own course of action: some surrendered their units to the Germans or to one of the competing guerrilla movements; some volunteered to join one of the factions; and others attempted to take a neutral course and move to the coast hoping they could be ferried across the Adriatic back to Italy.[109]

The capitulation of Italy provided a much-needed boost to the NOP in the western part of (present-day) Macedonia. Just as in the parts of Yugoslavia formerly occupied by the Italians, the Partisans and the Germans—along with their Bulgarian allies—were competing against one another in the attempt to secure territory and to disarm as many Italian units as possible. This led to the first skirmishes between the guerrillas and the German occupation forces in Macedonia. During the fighting around the town of Kičevo on the first day of November 1943, the Partisans managed to capture several German soldiers and officers, including one lieutenant colonel. Two days later, the HQ of the Macedonian 2nd Operational Zone dispatched a letter to the German garrisons in Struga and Gostivar proposing a meeting to discuss the exchange of these men for leading Macedonian Communists held in Bulgarian prisons. At the end of the letter came a threat specifying that unless the exchange was made within the next five days, the Partisans would have the captives tried by their military court "for crimes committed against our people." This, they added, would be done "in agreement with and the approval of our mighty allies, the Soviet Union, England, and America." In order to appear as "regular" as possible, the Macedonian Partisans signed their letter "2nd Brigade of the Macedonian People's Liberation Army," although no such unit existed as of then.[110]

The letter was couriered to Struga by a peasant and arrived there on 4 November. The German *Feldkommandant* replied the following day with a letter in which he addressed his adversaries with their self-chosen title. He wrote that they agreed to the exchange taking place as soon as the number of Macedonian prisoners in Struga could be established. In addition, the Germans requested that one seriously wounded soldier be released from Partisan captivity for medical treatment. That same day, the Partisans replied: "You have not fully understood our letter. We want to exchange the prisoners we have for our national fighters who are in prisons and

---

[109] For a brief overview of the operations following the Italian surrender in Yugoslavia, see Schmider, *Partisanenkrieg*, pp. 301–03.

[110] Koce Solunski, *Apostolski: od raganje do general* (Skopje: MM, 1983), p. 234. The sources differ as to the number of prisoners in Kičevo: Solunski mentions thirteen; the official historiography, eighteen (*Hronologija*, p. 602); German sources refer to three officers and fourteen missing men. NARA, T-501, Roll 266, 000386, Daily report of Armed Forces Commander Southeast (5 November 1943).

concentration camps in Bulgaria. We will inform you of their names when our del-egations meet on the road between Mešeišta and Botun. You have to clear the issue with Bulgarian occupation authorities in Macedonia beforehand so you can inform us whether you can agree to the exchange in principle. . . . We remind you that we agree to a one-to-one exchange only if we get those people in whom we are interested." The Partisans concluded the letter by saying that a doctor was sent to the wounded soldier. The Germans replied on the 7th, thanking the guerrilla com-mand for the humane treatment of their injured comrade. As for the exchange, the reply read that the Bulgarian government would have to be informed of the names of the prisoners in question before granting approval for their release. Further-more, the Germans agreed to the one-to-one ratio and requested that the Partisan envoys bring the list of names to the meeting scheduled for 8 November. On that day, the Partisan command provided a list containing the names of fourteen peo-ple. The accompanying letter reemphasized the request that the exchange take place as soon as possible, but also warned that the arrangement would be null and void if even one of the people from the list failed to appear for exchange.[111]

The meeting was held as planned, but the specifics are unknown except that it failed to produce any results. A Partisan report dated 18 November summed up the situation: "We are conducting written and verbal negotiations with the Ger-man commands in Struga and Bitola for the exchange of the Germans captured in Kičevo. We requested the release of the following comrades from Bulgarian pris-ons and camps. . . . [They should be exchanged on a ratio of] one-to-one. The Ger-mans tried to get these comrades from the Bulgarians, but there is still no news."[112] Ever since the negotiations had begun, the Germans had difficulties procuring the prisoners for the exchange. On 5 November, the German plenipotentiary general in Albania requested twenty-five Macedonian prisoners for the exchange, stating he needed them by the evening of 6 November. On the 6th, the 2nd Panzer Army informed the local *Abwehr* command that the prisoners would not reach their des-tination until the 7th, and that the command should buy more time by protracting the talks.[113] However, once the Partisans made it clear that they wanted specific prisoners, the Germans were compelled to seek Bulgarian help. The German embassy in Sofia was therefore tasked with obtaining the release of the particular Macedonian Communists wanted by the Partisans. On 13 November, the Bulgar-ian Ministry of War turned down the request. The Bulgarian government was, in

---

[111] V. A. Ivanovski, "Prilog kon proučuvanjeto na prašanjeto na razmena na zarobenici za vreme na narodnoosloboditelnata vojna na Makedonija 1941–1944," *Istorija: Spisanie na sojuzot na istoriskite društva na SR Makedonija* 9:1 (1973), pp. 63–65.

[112] Solunski, *Apostolski,* pp. 234–35.

[113] NARA, T-313, Roll 488, 000444, 2nd Panzer Army to Army Group E (5 November 1943); NARA, T-313, Roll 487, 000817, 2nd Panzer Army to Abwehr Troop 214 (6 November 1943).

principle, opposed to exchanging military personnel for political prisoners; furthermore, it feared that these particular Communists would resume their anti-Axis activites if they were freed.[114]

The Partisans were apparently not informed of this news and the two commands continued with their correspondence, exchanging letters again between 19 and 21 November. On the 26th, the Germans requested another meeting to be held on the 27th.[115] The probable reason for these protracted negotiations was that the Germans had widened the agenda by including a request of a different kind. Even before these contacts, the Bulgarians had attempted to approach the Partisans through civilian intermediaries with the proposal that they cease attacking Axis traffic on the vitally important Struga–Kičevo road in exchange for supplies. The Partisans responded to the idea by shooting two of the envoys and threatening the rest. According to the monograph on the Partisan Battalion *Slavej,* which provided security for the Partisan delegations and also played an active role in the proceedings, the topic resurfaced during the November negotiations. The Germans probably tried to condition the release of the high-ranking members of the Communist Party on obtaining rights of free passage for their convoys on the Struga–Kičevo road. The Germans professed they had no interest in the territory surrounding this supply route; they even went so far as to say that the Partisans were welcome to shoot anything that strayed to the left or right of the road. The request was turned down on orders from the Main Partisan HQ for Macedonia. In early December, the talks were cut short by an Axis offensive launched against the guerrilla-held territory in Western Macedonia, and were not continued thereafter.[116]

As has been shown in most of the examples cited above, the side that initiated an offer of prisoner exchange usually did it with some degree of haste. This was understandable given the uncertain fate which awaited prisoners, even if they survived immediate capture. The best chance to get one's prisoners returned was to swap them before the captors changed their minds. There is, however, something extraordinary about the haste with which the Macedonian Partisans wanted to exchange their captured comrades. The important political decisions made at the

---

[114] Dančo Zografski, "Pregovorite so bugarskiot i germanskiot garnizon vo Prilep 1944 godina," in *Prilep i prilepsko vo NOV 1944–15 maj 1945 godina. Materijali od Naučniot sobir održan na 14, 15 i 16 mart 1983 godina* (Skopje: SUBNOR Prilep, 1985), Vol. I/1, pp. 331–32.

[115] Ivanovski, "Prilog kon proučuvanjeto," pp. 65–66.

[116] Stojan Risteski, *Partizanskot odred "Slavej": Prilog kon proučavanjeto na Debrca vo NOB, 1941–1944* (Skopje: NIO Studentski zbor, 1990), pp. 79–82. I have been unable to find German documentation to confirm the claim (Solunski, *Apostolski,* p. 232) that the Germans extended the negotiations in order to lull the Partisans into a false sense of security. Under the new circumstances, the German prisoners became a liability and were executed after the offensive commenced. Marjan Dimitrijevski, *Politikata na Tretiot Rajh kon Makedonija 1933–1945* (Skopje: Institut za nacionalna istorija, 2001), pp. 81–82.

highest levels in early November may have been the cause. On 5 November 1943, Tito informed the Croatian Communists that the second session of the AVNOJ would take place in Jajce as soon as it could be organized; six days later, Croatian and Slovenian delegates were ordered to prepare for the trip.[117] A similar invitation to the Macedonian branch of the KPJ has not been found and it remains uncertain whether one was ever sent. Nevertheless, the Macedonians still had to nominate their delegates for the session in order to give it an all-Yugoslav composition. The region was entitled to forty-two councilmen, but due to technical difficulties, the names of only seven could be confirmed by the opening of the session on 29 November.[118] Of these seven people, two were with the Main HQ for Macedonia, two were in Moscow, and three (Mara Naceva, Bane Andreev, and Lazar Koliševski) were in Bulgarian captivity—their names were on the top of the list of the fourteen prisoners the Macedonian Partisans wanted in exchange for the Germans captured at Kičevo.[119] All three were high-level Communist officials and it was natural that their comrades would have wanted them back even had they not been nominated for membership in the AVNOJ. However, the proximity of the date of the announcement of the session to that of the exchange offer suggests that the Macedonian Partisans wanted the trio freed so that they could either act in the full capacity as absentee members, or even make the trip to distant Jajce. The other possible reason for the sense of urgency is that the Macedonian Communists formed the so-called "Initiative Committee" in mid-November 1943, a body which would serve as the basis for the creation of the Macedonian provincial government.[120] In either case, the presence of the captive Party veterans was required. The fact that they were nominated as councilmen for the AVNOJ while the talks with the Germans in Struga were being conducted suggests that the local Partisan leadership believed they would successfully be exchanged. However, once the

---

[117] *Zbornik*/II/11/30, Tito to Main HQ for Croatia (5 November 1943); ibid., p. 49, Kardelj to Central committee of KPH (11 November 1943).

[118] Ibid., p. 164, Vukmanović to Tito (30 November 1943).

[119] Novica Veljanovski, *"AVNOJ i Makedonija,"* in *Glavniot štab na narodnoosloboditelnata vojska i partizanskite odredi na Makedonija, 1941–1945: po povod devedeset godini od ragnjeto na Mihailo Apostolski* (Skopje: Institut za nacionalna istorija, 1996), p. 238; Solunski, *Apostolski,* pp. 234–35. Amongst the Macedonian Partisans, choosing the candidates for the exchange was overshadowed by the fear that if the negotiations failed, the Germans and Bulgarians could exact reprisals on these important members of the KPJ. These fears proved to be unfounded and all three survived captivity. On a side note, one of them, Lazar Koliševski, would become the first head of the collective Yugoslav leadership after Tito's death in 1980.

[120] Vanče Stojčev, "Macedonia during the Second World War, 1941–1945," in Todor Čepreganov, ed., *History of the Macedonian People* (Skopje: Institut za nacionalna istorija, 2008), p. 266.

negotiations were broken off in early December, the Macedonian branch of the KPJ saw no alternative but to compile another list of nominees for the AVNOJ on 11 December which did not contain these three original names.[121]

Unlike in other parts of Yugoslavia, the Partisan presence in Macedonia was hardly noticeable prior to the spring of 1943; the first "regular" unit was not formed until mid-November 1943. The talks held near Struga in November 1943 therefore played an important role in strengthening the self-confidence of the nascent Partisan movement in Macedonia. The fact that the representatives of the German occupation forces came to their territory in order to negotiate on an equal footing was understood to be a sign of recognition from their powerful enemy. For their part, they did everything to look and act like a regular army; thus, the 2nd Operational Zone became the 2nd Macedonian Brigade in order to lend additional credence to their letters to the local German command. The members of the delegation and the fighters chosen to provide security were specially dressed for the occasion in order to appear as soldier-like as possible. The Macedonian Partisans also did not fail to remind the Germans in the original letter that their army was a member of the wider anti-fascist coalition. Allied help, provided by airdrops, was put to good propaganda use. During a pause at one of the meetings outside Struga, the Germans had the opportunity to talk with common Partisan fighters. One of them had a lunch consisting of British-made tinned food and fresh white bread. When asked by a German how he had acquired such food, the Partisan replied, "Well, we have ovens, barracks, you name it."[122]

Macedonia gained strategic importance in the late summer of 1944. In light of the developments on the Eastern Front, it was only a matter of time before Army Group E would have to begin its withdrawal from Greece in order to avoid being cut off from its supply lines, and the shortest route to the northwest was through the Vardar valley. However, the Germans had only a limited presence in Macedonia as the country was occupied by their Bulgarian allies. The loyalty of Bulgarian units was becoming increasingly questionable in view of the Red Army's rapid advance toward Yugoslavia's eastern borders. German fears materialized when Bulgaria declared its neutrality on 26 August and began pulling its forces out of Serbia and Greece. It was now just a matter of days before the country would change sides for good. The Macedonian Partisans were under twin orders to attack major communications in order to stall German troop movements from

---

[121] *Zbornik*/II/11/164, Vukmanović to Tito (30 November 1943).

[122] Risteski, *Slavej*, p. 82. The talks at Struga served to increase the national self-awareness of Macedonians in the early 1990s after the breakup of Yugoslavia. The manner in which the German command had conducted the negotiations, and the way in which it addressed its Partisan adversary, were taken as proof in the 1990s that the newly-created Macedonian Army traced its roots back to 1943. "Od tajnite arhivi: makedonskata vojska priznata 1943 godina," *Delo* (10 September 1993), pp. 16–17.

Greece and to attempt to win over Bulgarian units for a joint struggle against the Germans.[123]

The town of Prilep in Western Macedonia was situated on an important road linking Florina with Veles in the Vardar valley. In order to gain control of the town, the 41st Partisan Division began negotiations with the Bulgarian garrison, demanding that they either lay down their arms or join the fight against the Germans. The Bulgarian commander acquiesced to the second option only after his country declared war on Germany on 9 September. Prilep was the scene of heavy fighting in the following days as the arriving German reinforcements attempted to wrestle control of the area from the joint Partisan-Bulgarian forces. By 20 September, the town was firmly under German control.[124]

Even before the fighting began in earnest, Partisan commands in the region toyed with the idea of demanding the surrender of the German garrison in Struga, promising in return that the prisoners would be treated in accordance with the Hague Convention. The surrender was demanded in the joint name of the Main HQ for Macedonia and the British military mission in the country. On 10 September, Mihajlo Apostolski, the chief of the Main HQ, gave the green light for issuing the ultimatum. Whether this was ever done is not clear, but judging by the German sources, there had been some "diplomatic" activity in the region at that time. In a memorandum on enemy dispositions in Macedonia, compiled on or about 10 September, the intelligence section of Army Group F noted that several Partisan brigades were combined into a Macedonian Division in the south of the country—this information was obtained from a "bandit parliamentary."[125]

By the end of September, the Allies decided to widen the demand to include all major garrisons in Western Macedonia. Consequently, Captain Miller, an officer of the SOE and the British representative to the Macedonian Partisans, invited the German commander in Prilep, Major Gresser, for a round of negoitations on the 25th. Gresser replied that he would accept only if British representatives were present as well. The Partisans agreed, and the talks between Gresser and two representatives of the 41st Division of the NOVJ were held in the first days of October, with Miller acting as an observer. The conference was largely inconclusive, at least as far as the issue of surrender was concerned; the delegations merely agreed to meet

---

[123] *Oslobodilački rat,* Vol. II, pp. 346–48. For a detailed description of operations in Macedonia from September to November 1944, see Robert Trajkovski, *Vermahtot i Makedonija* (*1943–1944 godina*) (Bitola: SBM, 2018), pp. 203–372.

[124] Ibid., p. 349; Zografski, "Pregovorite," p. 335.

[125] Zografski, "Pregovorite," p. 335; NARA, T-311, Roll 193, 000394, Memorandum on bandit activity in Macedonia as of 10 September 1944; the document is undated, but judging from the time period it covers, it was prepared on 10 September at the earliest, or shortly thereafter. The 41st Division, created on 25 August in a village some twenty kilometers east of Prilep, was the first large Partisan formation from Macedonia. *Oslobodilački rat,* Vol. II, p. 344.

again after having "additionally considered the matters involved." The British captain used the opportunity to deliver a written demand for the unconditional surrender of the German garrisons in Prilep, Bitola, Veles, and Skopje. The ultimatum stated that the war would soon be over; that Allied armies were advancing from both the east and the west; that any further resistance would only result in more bloodshed; and that "In the event of surrender, all prisoners would receive fair treatment according to the Geneva Convention."[126]

No further meetings between the delegations took place, most likely due to the arrival of new German reinforcements in Macedonia. "The call for surrender to [our] commander of Prilep made by an English liaison officer is refused," noted the intelligence section of Army Group F on 3 October.[127] However, the possible surrender of the garrisons was not the only issue discussed during the talks, for the delegations also agreed on a prisoner exchange, the details of which were to be finalized at a later date. On 15 October, the HQ of the NOVJ's 41st Division sent a letter to Major Gresser, along with a list of 145 Germans in Partisan captivity. The major was asked to provide a similar list of captured Partisans who could be exchanged for these soldiers. At the same time, the 41st Division repeated the call for unconditional surrender to garrisons in Prilep and Bitola. It was the combination of the offer to exchange prisoners and an ultimatum to capitulate that most likely brought the talks to an end, as the Germans were not likely to give concessions under pressure.[128]

By early November 1944, the rear guard of Army Group E had reached the area around the Macedonian capital, Skopje. The fact that the city would soon be abandoned did not cause the Germans to lower their guard. Acting on information obtained through one of their agents, two German counter-intelligence units, the 375th Front Reconnaissance Troop and the 621st Secret Field Police Group, conducted a raid on a shop located in the old Turkish Quarter of Skopje on 3 November. They arrested not only the six people they found there, but another six who tried to enter the shop shortly thereafter because investigations proved they had been actively supporting the "bandits" by working as couriers, propagandists, or liaisons. The search of the shop yielded a sizable quantity of various items, including weapons, leaflets, food, and a wireless set. All suspects were brought to the German prison in the city.[129]

The arrest of these people coincided with the negotiations led by the quartermaster section of the German 22nd Mountain Corps over the exchange of

---

[126] Zografski, "Pregovorite," pp. 335–36.

[127] NARA, T-311, Roll 194, 000178, Evening report of intelligence section (3 October 1944).

[128] NARA, T-311, Roll 183, 000071, War diary entry for 15 October 1944; Bora Mitrovski, *Petnaesti (makedonski) udarni korpus NOVJ* (Belgrade: Vojnoizdavački zavod, 1983), pp. 118–19.

[129] NARA, T-311, Roll 188, 001068, Activity report of Group of Secret Field Police 510 for October, November, and December 1944 (25 December 1944).

some ninety German prisoners for a similar number of Partisans. The negotiations dragged on for some time, mostly because the local collaborationists did everything possible to sabotage any arrangement between the Germans and the NOVJ. As the date of German departure from the area was nearing, there was fear that they would execute their Partisan prisoners. The Germans, for their part, knew that if they did not secure the release of their own men while they still had contact with their Partisan captors, they would not be able to do so once they left Skopje. They therefore agreed to the Partisan condition that the twelve people arrested in the raid be included in the exchange.[130] The deal was finally struck with the help of a collaborationist official of the city administration who had actually been a Partisan agent since 1941. On 10 November 1944, a column of about 100 prisoners, escorted by German soldiers and some citizens, left Skopje and headed to the nearby village of Sopište. The Partisans were waiting for them along with their German prisoners. The swap was done in groups of ten until all captives were exchanged. The Partisan delegation included natives of Skopje who could verify the identity of the exchanged prisoners. This extra caution was taken out of fear that the Germans might attempt to infiltrate agents posing as captured Partisans, but the concern proved to be unfounded. Ninety-three released Germans were too weak and malnourished to join the units based in Skopje in the forthcoming retreat; they were instead sent first to Kraljevo and then to Sarajevo by train.[131] In the end, because the reprisal rules were still in place, these Partisan sympathizers were exchanged at the very last moment. On 13 November 1944, one day before they left Skopje, the Germans shot nine residents suspected of sabotage.[132]

Negotiations and Prisoner Exchange in Slovenia, 1943–1945

After the demise of the Kingdom of Yugoslavia, Slovenia was divided between the Axis powers: the Italians occupied the area known as the Ljubljana Province (southwestern Slovenia) and the Germans took the rest. The Germans informally annexed the Slovene regions, placing them under civilian rule of the provincial *Gauleiter* (Nazi regional leaders/provincial governors) of Carinthia and Styria. Their harsh rule included forced Germanization and the expulsion of some 80,000 Slovenes to Serbia and Croatia, making the Communist cause more appealing to a considerable part of the population. The guerrilla war which followed the occupation was perhaps smaller in scope when compared to Bosnia or Croatia, but was nonetheless extremely bloody; Slovenia lost an estimated 6% of its population,

---

[130] Ibid.

[131] Hans Em, "Razmena na zarobenici: migovi što se pametat," in *Dokumenti i materijali za osloboduvanjeto na Skopje, oktomvri–19 noemvri 1944* (Skopje: Istoriski arhiv, 1968), pp. 255–56; NARA, T-314, Roll 1630, 000283, War diary entry for 16 November 1944.

[132] Dimitrijevski, *Politikata na Tretiot Rajh,* pp. 118–19.

proportionally more than Serbia.[133] The Germans took over the former Italian occupation zone in Slovenia in September 1943 and made it a part of the so-called "Operational Zone Adriatic Littoral" (*Operationszone Adriatisches Küstenland,* or OZAK). Apart from the Slovene regions, it also included Istria and the Italian provinces of Trieste, Udine, and Gorizia. Whereas in the Ljubljana Province the Germans organized a collaborationist government, they retained the Italian administrative apparatus in the remainder of the zone. Although the OZAK was technically a part of Mussolini's Republic of Salò, the Nazi governor of Carinthia, Friedrich Rainer, held the highest political authority; militarily, the zone was under the auspices of the *Wehrmacht's* Army Group C based in Italy as of November 1943.

Due to the fact that the fighting took place on what was effectively the territory of the Third Reich, the Germans consistently refused to grant privileged status to captured Partisans. For most of the war, the latter were usually shot immediately after capture, used as reprisal hostages, or sent to extermination camps like Buchenwald, Dachau, or Auschwitz.[134] The difference in approach to counterinsurgency between the 2nd Panzer Army in Bosnia and Croatia and the German units in occupied Slovenia is best illustrated by the order issued in late February 1944 by the military commander in the OZAK, General Ludwig Kübler. Echoing the grim orders released by various German generals in Serbia and the NDH in the bleak years of 1941–1943, Kübler proclaimed that the war against the Partisans must be fought in the manner in which it was fought in the occupied territories in the East.[135] Not until August of 1944 did it occur to some units under his command that those people forcibly recruited into Partisan ranks could be sent to Germany as laborers instead of being killed on the spot; for comparison, occupation authorities in Serbia had introduced this option as early as March of 1942.[136] SS General

---

[133] Tomasevich, *Occupation and Collaboration,* pp. 83–94, 121–23; *Zbornik žrtve vojne in revolucije: Referati in razprava s posveta v Državnem svetu 11. in 12. novembra 2004, ki sta ga pripravila Državni svet Republike Slovenije in Institut za novejšo zgodovino v Ljubljani* (Ljubljana: Republika Slovenija, Državni svet, 2005), pp. 17–18.

[134] Interviews with survivors from Istria can be found at: http://ipd-ssi.hr/?page_id=211

[135] Gerhard Schreiber, "Die Wehrmacht und der Partisanenkrieg in Italien: '. . . auch gegen Frauen und Kinder,'" in Ernst Willi Hansen, Gerhard Schreiber, and Bernd Wegner, eds., *Politischer Wandel, organisierte Gewalt und nationale Sicherheit: Beiträge* (Munich: Oldenbourg Verlag, 1995), pp. 253–54. The full text of Kübler's order can be found in NARA, T-77, Roll 787, 5516517–20, Corps' order No. 9 (22 February 1944). In light of subsequent events in the OZAK, it is important to note that Governor Rainer managed to have this order rescinded. Ibid, 5516453, Conversation with General Kübler (undated, probably either 14 or 15 March 1944).

[136] *Zbornik*/VI/15/867–68, After-action report of 137th Mountain Regiment (12 August 1944).

Erwin Rösener, the head of German counter-insurgency efforts in Slovenia, had issued the order to treat the captured guerrillas as prisoners of war in the autumn of 1943 and again in 1944,[137] but the order was only haphazardly followed.

The decision on how to treat prisoners was the responsibility of the units on the ground, but fair treatment of Partisan prinsoners was the exception rather than the rule. For instance, northwest of Udine in late October 1944, the Germans liberated seventy-nine servicemen: four members of the *Luftwaffe,* two border guards, and the rest officers and men of the Order Police. All of them claimed that they were treated decently by the guerrillas and the local population. The Commander of Order Police in the OZAK, SS Colonel Hermann Kintrup, forbade incorrect treatment and "unnecessary harshness toward captured bandits from this area" (underlined in the original).[138] One other German commander who operated in late 1944 in what constitutes present-day Štajerska/Lower Styria was noted for his clemency toward captured guerrillas.[139] At the same time, the collaborationist propaganda apparatus in Ljubljana Province, acting with the consent of, if not on direct orders from, German authorities, maintained that the Partisans could not count on the protection of international law.[140]

The Slovenian Partisans, much like their comrades in the rest of the country, treated their prisoners according to the military formation to which they belonged.[141] Ethnic Slovenes who were forcibly recruited into various German units were usually taken into the guerrilla ranks or set free. Such treatment was sometimes applied to ethnic German *gendarmes* as well if they showed no enthusiasm for the Nazi cause and were not involved in war crimes. Knowing that the humane treatment of prisoners could have an adverse effect on the enemy's morale, the Partisans continued to release German *gendarmes* periodically well into 1944.[142] Foreign nationals serving in the German Army (for instance, Soviet citizens) were usually welcome to join the guerrilla ranks; however, "pure Germans" from the frontline SS police formations and *Wehrmacht* were not extended the

---

[137] *Zbornik*/VI/8/434, Daily order No. 4 (6 November 1943); Tone Kregar, *Vigred se povrne: Druga svetovna vojna na Celjskem* (Celje: Muzej novejše zgodovine, 2009), p. 112.

[138] Commander of Order Police in the OZAK, Ic 1612 J./Ne. [No subject], 24 October 1944. I wish to thank Darko Cafuta for providing me with a copy of this document from Arhiv Slovenije (Archives of the Republic of Slovenia).

[139] Milan Ževart, "Elaborat štaba Treeckove bojne skupine o narodnoosvoboditelnem boju na Štajerskem," *Časopis za zgodovino i narodopisje* 153:2 (1990), p. 160.

[140] Š.J., "Zakaj so komunistične izgube tako visoke?," in *Slovensko domobranstvo,* 28 December 1944, p. 14, retrieved from: http://www.dlib.si/stream/URN:NBN:SI:DOC-IZGYWCAU /6e2b81b8-9ccf-4e93-a282-7f54637b6012/PDF

[141] *Zbornik*/VI/13/43, 4th Operational Zone to Main HQ for Slovenia (18 April 1944).

[142] *Zbornik*/VI/15/609, 4th Operational Zone to Main HQ for Slovenia (20 August 1944).

same courtesy and were usually executed after capture. There were many exceptions to this, depending on the circumstances on the ground. In Slovenia, just as in other parts of Yugoslavia, local Partisan commanders had the last word on the fate of prisoners.[143]

Despite the brutal occupation policy, Slovene Partisans and the German authorities were not averse to negotiating with each other. In July 1943, the command of the Gorenjska/Upper Carniola Operations Zone held negotiations with some Gestapo representatives from Bled. The Germans stated that they were members of the anti-Nazi resistance and that they would allow free passage for the Partisan Prešern Brigade through their territory, as well as provide the guerrillas with weapons and supplies. The offer turned out to be a ploy; the German forces surrounded and destroyed a considerable part of this unit on 1 August 1943 while it waited for the promised arms delivery.[144]

Mid-September 1943 saw contacts between the Partisans and the Germans in the Soča/Isonzo River Valley. In exchange for a local cease-fire and the right of free passage on the road from Kobarid to Udine and Gorica/Gorizia, the commander of the SS Battalion *Karstwehr* offered to release a number of inmates from the prison in Udine and recognize the rights of Slovenes living in the region. The Partisans replied that they had no authority to make such decisions, but that they would pass the offer on to their superiors, and added that the release of prisoners would be a good starting point for further negotiations. On 16 September 1943, fifty-six prisoners were released from Udine. A German officer who escorted them to Partisan territory had the chance to meet several captured German soldiers and make sure they were treated correctly.[145] One day later, at a meeting held on the Partisan territory around Trnovo, German envoys announced their intention to publish a leaflet informing the population about the event as well as the imminent cessation of hostilities. Despite the fact that the Partisans disapproved, the Germans followed through with the plan the next day. The guerrillas reacted by capturing the two motorcyclists who were distributing the leaflets. The prisoners (one of whom was slightly wounded) were returned to the German garrison in Bovec/Flitsch with a letter calling for another round of talks. The SS battalion commander was furious that there was still no word from higher Partisan commands, and he

---

[143] Ževart, "Elaborat," pp. 167, 176–77, 183; Kregar, *Vigred se povrne,* pp. 112–14; Thomas Barker, *Social Revolutionaries and Secret Agents: The Carinthian Slovene Partisans and Britain's Special Operations Executive* (New York: Columbia University Press, 1990), p. 107.

[144] Stanko Petelin, *Prešernova NOU brigada* (Belgrade: Vojnoizdavački zavod, 1975), pp. 18–27.

[145] In late September, the Germans found a draft of a letter in which the Partisans demanded that they be recognized as a regular army and that their captured members be treated as prisoners of war; in the case of non-compliance, they threatened to shoot seven German prisoners. NARA, T-354, Roll 606, 001079, Interrogations of prisoners and captured enemy documents (29 September 1943).

broke off the meeting. The next day, the Partisans sent another two letters to Bovec. In the first, they apologized for the attack on the motorcyclists and expressed their gratitude for the release of prison inmates. In the second, they informed the German command that their proposals had been turned down.[146] Several days later, the Germans launched a massive effort to secure the border region between Slovenia and Italy.[147]

The Germans made similar overtures to the Partisan 7th Corps in Dolenjska/ Lower Carniola in mid-December 1943. The Gestapo office in Sevnica sent a letter, via a woman who had connections to the guerrillas, requesting a meeting with the local Partisan command. The letter was passed from the HQ of the 15th Partisan Division to the Main HQ for Slovenia. The supreme leadership of the Slovene Partisans decided to accept the German offer and Boris Kidrič, the political commissar of the Main HQ, was tasked with working out the guidelines for the Partisan delegation. Both sides agreed to hold the talks in the village of Mokronog on 18 December 1943 while under a 24-hour truce in the area. In the early morning, an "honor guard" consisting of twenty-eight Partisans smartly dressed and polished for the occasion, entered the village where their German counterparts were already waiting, lined up in front of the local tavern which would host the talks. The envoys followed soon thereafter. On the Partisan side were Pero Popivoda and Jože Jurančič, the commander and the head of the Party organization of the 15th Division, respectively, and Milan Vidmar, a university professor from Ljubljana; the Germans were represented by a *Wehrmacht* major, a major from the SD, and one interpreter. After exchanging formalities, which included inspecting the honor guard, the delegations entered the tavern and commenced the talks.[148]

---

[146] Tone Kebe, "Zgodbe iz NOB na Kobariškem," *Borec* 1 (1979), pp. 29–44 and *Borec* 3 (1979), pp. 167–80; Franjo Bavec-Branko, *Bazoviška brigada* (Ljubljana: Odbor Bazoviške brigade, 1970), pp. 40–43. This episode was briefly mentioned in a document published in the *Zbornik* in the late 1950s. Judging by the ellipses, the editors chose to omit some parts. *Zbornik*/VI/7/92, Operational HQ for Western Slovenia to Main HQ for Slovenia (24 September 1943).

[147] On 23 September 1943, the 2nd SS Panzer Corps issued an order stating that Partisan commanders were to be shot, but common Partisans were to be treated as prisoners of war. NARA, T-354, Roll 606, 000977, Special orders of intelligence officer, 23 September 1943. However, only a day later, Hitler explicitly ordered the troops to crush the uprising "with ruthless severity" and to execute anyone captured with arms. "After the operation," the order continued, "the Slovenian people must not represent a threat to us." Ibid., 001007, Führer's order, 24 September 1943.

[148] Zdenko Zavadlav, *Partizani, obveščevalci, jetniki: iz dosjeja Zavadlav 1944–1994* (Ljubljana: Horvat M&M, 1996), p. 99; Ivo Pirkovič, "Pozabljena diplomacija v gozdu," *Delo* (3 July 1980), p. 21. Pirkovič based the description of the negotiations in Mokronog on an unpublished interview with Jurančič. I would like to thank Dr. Boris Mlakar of the Institute for

The Germans came to the point immediately—they wanted a truce along the lines of communication leading from Ljubljana over Novo Mesto to Karlovac in Croatia. In return, they would not attack the Partisan-held territory and would even supply it with goods. As the Partisans refused to discuss this proposition, the Germans moved on to the second point of discussion, the exchange of prisoners. The Partisan delegation readily acceded to swapping captives in the future and appointed Jurančič as the liaison officer for these matters. Political questions never lagged far behind the issue of prisoner exchange; the guerrilla envoys demanded recognition of the Slovene Partisans as a legitimate belligerent force, while the Germans refused to discuss the issue, stating they were not authorized to do so. The NOVJ plenipotentiaries then asked for their counterparts' opinion on the Slovene collaborationists. The Germans did not seem to be much concerned over the fate of their auxiliaries. According to some sources, they called them "traitors of the worst sort" and even mentioned their transfer to the Eastern Front; other sources say the Germans showed no interest in the civil war between the Partisans and the Slovene Home Guards and would not intervene on behalf of their charges.[149]

With the official part of the talks concluded, the Germans treated their negotiating partners to a lunch. At the table, they discussed the war situation in general, each side expressing a firm belief in final victory. The atmosphere gradually became more cordial and pleasantries were exchanged—smiling delegates were even photographed in front of the tavern. The Gestapo officer asked Jurančič about his background, offering to arrange a safe trip for him to Štajerska/Styria, where his next of kin lived. When the latter declined, saying that his brother and sister were executed there in German reprisals, the major offered to at least deliver a letter to his parents to inform them that he was alive and well. Jurančič accepted and scribbled a few words on a piece of paper. Five days after the talks, he received an

---

Contemporary History in Ljubljana who kindly provided me with a copy of this article, as well as other material, pertaining to Partisan-German contacts in Slovenia.

[149] Pirkovič, "Pozabljena diplomacija," p. 21; Interview with Dr. Boris Mlakar, *Mladina* 48 (1 December 2003), retrieved from: http://www.mladina.si/93264/slo-intervju—bernard _nezmah/?utm_source=tednik%2F200348%2Fclanek%2Fslo%2Dintervju%2D%2Dbernard %5Fnezmah%2F&utm_medium=web&utm_campaign=oldLink Arhiv Slovenije, AS 1877, 32/I, Report of the Slovenian Home Guard intelligence service of 31 December 1943; In a letter dated 7 January 1944, the British ambassador to the Yugoslav government-in-exile, Ralph Stevenson, informed his superior, Anthony Eden, about the details of the proceedings provided by his source, the British liaison officer with the Slovenian Main HQ. According to him, the Partisans did not provide an unambiguous answer to the German truce proposal. Stevenson's letter can be found in TNA, FO 536/11/59 106027 (synopsis of both documents courtesy of Dr. Mlakar). Lieutenant Colonel Peter A. Wilkinson of the SOE, who was at the Slovenian Main HQ at the time, wrote in his "Memorandum on the Revolt in Slovenia" (27 April 1944) that the Partisans rejected the offer "with scorn." Barker, *Social Revolutionaries*, p. 111.

answer from his parents through the Gestapo office in Sevnica. What was even more remarkable is that Jurančič's parents were no longer harassed by the occupation authorities for the duration of the war.[150]

At first glance, the negotiations at Mokronog appear to be a failure; the Partisans would not accept the cease-fire and the Germans would not consider legitimizing a guerrilla army on their own soil. The available evidence, however, shows that the lot of at least some prisoners was improved in the months immediately following the talks. On 21 December 1943, the Main HQ for Slovenia informed the HQ of the 3rd Operational Zone that there was an opportunity to swap prisoners with the Germans. Consequently, the units should strive to capture as many officers as possible and report the results to the high command.[151] On 13 January 1944, the 7th Corps' 18th Division (which had crossed over into Croatia in the meantime) captured two German NCOs and one Russian in German service near Ogulin. The prisoners were not killed, but offered in exchange for seven Partisans who had been wounded in Slovenia and one female fighter. The Germans agreed to swap prisoners, but had only eight Croatian Partisans on hand. The 18th Division declined to accept them and insisted on exchanging only those Partisans who were members of the division; the German command could only promise to do everything in its power to secure their release.[152]

The fact that the 18th Division decided to contact its nearest German counterpart over a prisoner exchange was not in itself problematic; the fact that it failed to keep higher commands abreast of the proceedings caused some discontent, however. The division informed the 7th Corps about the deal only after it had been struck; consequently, the corps "could not include the names of those comrades who deserved to be exchanged more than others." For the same reason, the matter could not be relegated to the Main HQ for Slovenia "so that you [Main HQ] could make the exchange yourselves." The last line shows that prisoner exchange ceased to be a matter of local importance only. The highest Partisan commands in the country were not only taking a keen interest in the developments, but were also willing to take an active part in the proceedings.[153] As in Croatia, the leading Partisan circles

---

[150] Pirkovič, "Pozabljena diplomacija," p. 21.

[151] *Zbornik*/VI/9/244, Main HQ for Slovenia to 3rd Operational Zone (21 December 1943).

[152] *Zbornik*/VI/10/171, 18th Division for 7th Corps (15 January 1944) and p. 281, 18th Division for 7th Corps (20 January 1944). I have been unable to determine whether or not the exchange took place. According to one document, the *Ustashe* released six male and six female inmates from Stara Gradiška concentration camp on 16 January 1944 so that they could be "exchanged in Slovenia." VA, CK KPH, Roll 42, 340, Letter from the Party organization in Stara Gradiška (April 1944).

[153] *Zbornik*/VI/10/276, 7th Corps to Main HQ for Slovenia (20 January 1944). Lieutenant Colonel Wilkinson was told by the Partisans that two German attempts to contact the Main HQ for prisoner exchange were "scornfully rejected in principle." Nevertheless, Wilkinson

in Slovenia sought to curb "independent" negotiating activities by individual units, fearing that these could only be interpreted as a sign of weakness.[154]

Two documents from late March 1944 offer additional proof that both sides had taken further steps aimed at reducing the levels of violence toward prisoners. On 29 March, the 18th Division reported that a German surprise attack cost the division nine dead and sixty-three captured. The latter were taken to nearby Kočevje and interrogated. According to the Partisan intelligence service, the Germans would not let the Slovenian collaborators beat the captured guerrillas, saying "they considered them prisoners of war." That same day, the division issued an order for an attack on a German outpost in the vicinity of Kočevje which read in part: "Prisoners are not to be killed, but brought to the division's HQ and interrogated. . . . This especially applies to Germans and their officers who can be exchanged." It is safe to assume that the quoted provision came as a direct result of the news from Kočevje and the experiences of the 18th Division around Ogulin earlier that year.[155]

The spring of 1944 also saw two cases of attempted exchange in the vicinity of Celje (outside of the 7th Corps' area of responsibility). On 12 March, the 6th Partisan Brigade ambushed a car belonging to the head of the municipality of Gornji Grad and captured two of his daughters. The Partisans offered to exchange them for ten of their own, including two functionaries. The local German police chief reported to his superiors at the end of April that "our uncompromising stand" on the issue compelled the Partisans to release their female hostages without compensation.[156] Notwithstanding this refusal to trade political prisoners for civilians, the local police in Celje were not completely opposed to exchanging prisoners, especially if it enabled them to settle scores with deserters. In early June, one *gendarmerie* station was successfully stormed by the guerrillas largely due to the information provided by two *gendarmes* of Slovenian origin from Celje who had defected to the Partisans. The German after-action report claims that the two were supposed to be exchanged, presumably so they could be punished.[157]

---

added, "important prisoners are undoubtedly exchanged from time to time." Barker, *Social Revolutionaries,* p. 94.

[154] The 4th Operational Zone issued a special order on an unspecified date prohibiting units from negotiating prisoner exchanges on their own. The same command repeated the order in the early summer of 1944. *Zbornik*/IX/6/493, 4th Operational Zone to all subordinated units (29 June 1944).

[155] *Zbornik*/VI/12/291, 18th Division to 7th Corps (29 March 1944) and p. 298, 18th Division to Main HQ for Slovenia (29 March 1944).

[156] *Zbornik*/VI/12/146, 4th Operational Zone to Main HQ for Slovenia (14 March 1944); *Zbornik*/VI/13/695, Monthly report of police and SD chief in Lower Styria to SS General Rösener (27 April 1944).

[157] *Zbornik*/VI/14/544, 4th Operational Zone to Main HQ for Slovenia (1 July 1944) and p. 726, District gendarmerie command at Trbovlje to gendarmerie command at Celje (7 June 1944).

The last recorded attempt at local prisoner exchange in Yugoslavia also occurred in the vicinity of Celje during the very last days of the war. The Partisans belonging to the 14th NOVJ Division captured Konrad Heidenreich, *Einsatzleiter* (Major General) of the OT (and the designer of the famous *Waldbühne* built for the Berlin Olympics in 1936) outside the village of Preloge in mid-April 1945. Frank Lindsay, an OSS operative with the Slovenian Partisans, wrote in his memoirs that his aide's request to interrogate Heidenreich was refused and the major general was shot. Lindsay added that the incident made Dušan Kveder, the commander of the Main HQ for Slovenia, "irate because he wanted to echange the [major] general for Partisan prisoners, including his cousin."[158]

The exact circumstances of Heidenreich's death are still shrouded in mystery. What is known is that he was hit in the shoulder while trying to escape after his car was ambushed on the morning of 16 April 1945. He spent a couple of days with the 13th Slovenian Brigade and received medical attention before being sent to the HQ of the 4th Operational Zone. On or about 19 April, the HQ reported that Heidenreich was refusing to divulge any information of military importance, claiming he knew nothing about the organization and functioning of the three German armies he had been working with since mid-1944. Requests for instructions concerning the major general's fate apparently went unanswered. There are two versions regarding what happened next. According to the official version, Heidenreich made another attempt to escape and was shot near the Sava River, presumably while en route to the Main HQ for Slovenia. According to the other version, several local witnesses claimed the major general was brought to the village of Gornja Ponikva (present-day Ponikva pri Žalcu), where he was tried and executed.[159]

To compound matters further, there is evidence that the Partisans were willing to discuss Heidenreich's exchange weeks after the presumed date of his death. On 20 April 1945, the Partisans released some German prisoners (allegedly including the major general's driver) who testified several days later that Heidenreich was alive and eligible for exchange. Furthermore, it was known that the Partisans were, in general, willing to trade their captives, sometimes even just for salt.[160] Upon receiving this information, Alfred Kofler (the major general's adjutant) and an OT official named Aust (the major general's deputy) set off for Slovenia and established contact with the Partisans around Preloge. According to Kofler, the

---

[158] *Zbornik*/VI/19/730, 14th NOVJ Division, Activity report for April 1945 (undated); Lindsay, *Beacons in the Night*, p. 326.

[159] Mirko Fajdiga, *Bračičeva brigada na Štajerskem, Koroškem, in Gorenjskem* (Maribor: Založba Obzorja, 1994), Vol. II, pp. 588–92.

[160] Heidenreich Family Archives, Draft of the letter from Cynthia Heidenreich to ICRC office Hamburg, October 1945; private communication from Dr. Conrad E. Heidenreich (22 November 2014).

negotiations relating to Heidenreich's exchange took place on 7 and 8 May 1945 and nearly ended in his release. However, news of the unconditional surrender of the Third Reich made the talks redundant and they were cancelled, after which Kofler and Aust embarked on an "adventurous journey" back to Austria.[161]

The question remains why the Slovenian Partisans kept the Germans in the dark about Heidenreich's death. One possible explanation is that it may have been done out of fear of reprisals against high-ranking members of the People's Liberation Movement. Likewise, the Partisan leadership may have thought that the Germans would be more cooperative on their exchange if the prospect of Heidenreich's release appeared to be a real possibility. The major general's capture (and his demise) came at the same time that the Slovenes were offering all their important prisoners in return for Vito Kraigher and other high-ranking Slovene functionaries. In these circumstances, it also appears highly unlikely that the HQ of the 4th Operational Zone would have dared to execute Heidenreich on its own. Furthermore, the major general was obviously fit enough to walk, and had already tried to escape once. Faced with a choice of either losing a high-value prisoner or killing him, the Partisans usually opted for the latter.

Negotiations and Truce in the Operational Zone Adriatic Littoral, March–November 1944

As early as March 1944, the Italian prefect of Gorizia, Count Marino Pace, attempted to establish contact with the local Partisans. According to information obtained through their contact in the provincial administration, Major Leonardo Muzzolini, the Partisans knew that the prefect wanted to discuss matters pertaining to the welfare of the civilian population. On 18 May 1944, Pace sent a letter to the Partisans officially requesting a meeting; transportation, accommodation, and security for the Partisan envoys were guaranteed. After having consulted with higher authorities, the intelligence section of the Partisan 9th Corps deployed in the Slovene Littoral (Primorska) decided to provide Pace with an audience. Initially, the Partisan delegation consisted of two members instructed to only listen and not make any offers or commitments. On 15 June 1944, Pace and Muzzolini picked up the Partisan envoys in guerrilla-held territory. They first drove to Gorizia where they were joined by Pace's deputy, Pirro Locatelli, and a Partisan intelligence operative of Italian origin, Marcello Tausig (referred to as Marcello Kralj in several documents). They traveled together to a villa near the village of Tapogliano where the negotiations were scheduled to take place.[162]

---

[161] Heidenreich Family Archives, Alfred Kofler to Cynthia Heidenreich (23 October 1945). Kofler did not include additional details about these talks in his letter.

[162] Zavadlav, *Partizani*, pp. 92–93.

Pace opened the talks by expressing his disappointment that the Partisan delegation was not empowered to make decisions on the proposals he was about to put forth. The prefect added that he was speaking in his name only, and not for the Germans. He proposed the creation of a neutral zone, the boundaries of which could be established later, where the Germans and the Partisans would refrain from fighting one another. Pace said that he would also speak to Rainer about the matter. Locatelli pointed to the difficulties in supplying the civilian population around Gorizia with food due to the Partisan attacks on the convoys, and backed Pace's proposal as a means of alleviating the suffering of the civilians. The only thing that the Partisans would agree to was to relay the details of the talks to their superiors and to hold another meeting with the prefect. The envoys parted at about 12.30 after a "lunch worthy of counts."[163]

The Partisans immediately informed their commands about the content of the first round of negotiations. Miro Perc, the head of the local branch of OZNA, approved of the continuation of contacts and suggested that the next meeting be held on Partisan territory near Gorizia, and that he was willing to take part as one of the NOVJ representatives. His attendance, however, was canceled when the regional Partisan authorities reaffirmed their opposition to upgrading the delegation in a letter dated 24 June 1944. Instead, the negotiating team would be expanded by the addition of two members of the so-called Economic Commission who would discuss the possible exchange of goods and other supply matters with Pace. The Partisans would also propose an exchange of prisoners and request the recognition of the Primorska Partisans as legitimate belligerents. The site chosen for the negotiations was a villa in Bilje belonging to a local aristocrat. Prestige and honor were the catalysts for the choice of location, as confirmed by one of the Partisan delegates, Zdenko Zavadlav: "We wanted to treat Pace to the same feast he had provided for us in Tapogliano, and thus show him that the Partisans were civilized people capable of organizing [such a meeting] despite the war and occupation."[164]

On 26 June 1944, the two delegations met at the arranged place and began the second round of talks. Count Pace was disappointed that no high-ranking Partisan officials were present, for this time he had brought definite propositions with him. Acting now with German consent, Pace delivered a list of rail and road communications the Germans wanted spared of demolition. Zavadlav and the others insisted on discussing prisoner treatment and exchange instead. The count responded that he would take the matter up with the Germans and added that he could arrange a meeting with someone from the HQ of Army Group C if the Partisans so desired. Pace continued that the main issue for him was that the guerrillas accept a hands-off agreement along the lines of communication; all other issues could then be settled to mutual benefit. The economic questions were tackled

---

[163] Ibid., p. 93.

[164] Ibid., pp. 93–94.

by Locatelli and Peter Srebrnič, the official from the Economic Commission. Amongst other topics, they discussed the possibility of harvesting grain without the presence of Germans, the supply of foodstuffs to the population of Gorizia in exchange for civilian clothing, as well as the sharing of the cisterns which had been captured by the Partisans. According to Srebrnič's report, all these issues were resolved in an amicable manner, and after the luncheon, the Axis envoys left the villa, escorted by Kralj.[165]

During the negotiations, Pace promised to send a written document detailing the German demands through Muzzolini within the next two days. When the document failed to arrive as promised, the Partisans instructed Muzzolini to inform Pace that the talks would be discontinued. The story was far from over, however. In the last days of June, Kralj returned from the 9th Corps' intelligence section, where he had been transferred after the second round of talks, bearing the corps' permission to continue the negotiations with the prefect. On 2 July, the count, accompanied by Muzzolini, appeared at the Partisan base at Renča where he was informed of the news. The delegates then proceeded to establish a date for the next round of talks. After Kralj suggested 5 July, he was asked whether he would be willing to cease hostilities so that the negotiations could take place in peace. Kralj agreed, provided the higher Partisan commands approved of the arrangement.[166]

Two days after the meeting, the entire Slovene Littoral was in an uproar as rumors of the alleged Partisan-German truce spread like wildfire. The courier who arrived from Gorizia to the Partisan HQ reported on the profound sense of disbelief with which both the Slovenian and Italian populations greeted the news. He also informed Zavadlav that the local German command had already announced the truce in a circular order issued to the collaborationist forces. At first, Zavadlav was just as confused as everyone else, but eventually he ordered Kralj to contact Muzzolini to cancel the truce and any further negotiations. The latter appeared at Renča on 5 July 1944 bringing a message from the German command: they would refrain from all hostile actions on that day if the Partisans would do the same; those officers responsible for prematurely disclosing information would be punished; the leading fascist in the town was already under arrest; and the fascist organization at Gorizia would be abolished. The courier also added that the Germans were ready for further negotiations.[167]

On 15 July 1944, the Germans' willingness to continue negotiations was evident when four German envoys entered Partisan territory outside of Opatija in the Croatian part of Istria, as reported by the Main HQ for Croatia to the Supreme

---

[165] Ibid., pp. 94–95.

[166] Ibid. Zavadlav wrote that the meeting took place on 3 July, but it is evident from contemporary German documents that the German command had been informed of the terms by mid-afternoon of 2 July at the latest (see below).

[167] Ibid., p. 95.

HQ.[168] Two Germans were left behind as hostages while the remaining two and one Partisan representative headed for the town in order to negotiate "the peaceful retreat of the German army from Istria."[169] Three days later, the Croatian command received a sharply-worded cable from Tito: "The actions of the Istrian comrades are highly reprehensible. They were not supposed to negotiate anything with the Germans, especially not without our express permission. We think that the whole matter was devised to compromise our relations with the Allies. All contacts with the Germans in Istria are to be severed. . . ."[170]

On the 23rd, the Main HQ attempted to clarify the situation. They explained that the previous communication had not been relayed properly as the negotiations were not led by military units, but by a member of the Opatija Party committee without prior knowledge of the higher Party forums: "No deal was made . . . fighting against the Germans never ceased."[171] This was not the only attempt by the Axis forces in the region to initiate negotiations with the NOVJ. In the same cable in which the Main HQ for Croatia first informed Tito of the Opatija episode, it was reported that the Croatian Home Guards attempted to establish contact outside of Sušak. The commander of the local garrison, Colonel Hinko Resch,[172] was seeking a written deal "on all military questions" with the Partisans. He expressed his desire to come to the guerrilla territory for talks if his personal safety would be guaranteed: "He had informed the German military authorities of his initiative and they approved his action," recorded the Partisans. Despite the willingness of the local Partisan commands to receive Resch and hear him out, the meeting never materialized. According to the telegram from Main HQ for Croatia to Tito on 1 August 1944, the Germans insisted on escorting the colonel with two armored cars, which he refused.[173] What precisely Resch or the German commands in that

---

[168] German units around Opatija were informed of the cease-fire on 5 July and apparently obeyed it until the 13th, when Battle Group Rijeka (*Kampfgruppe Fiume*) broke it due to continued Partisan attacks in the area. NARA, T-1022, Roll 2552, War Diary of the Naval Defense Command Istria, Entries for 5 and 13 July 1944. The appearance of the German envoys in Opatija only two days later illustrates the confusion which reigned during these days.

[169] VA, 119/4, 1, 1–16, Main HQ for Croatia to Supreme HQ (15 July 1944).

[170] VA, 119/2, 3, 6–7, Supreme HQ to Main HQ for Croatia (18 July 1944).

[171] Ibid., Main HQ for Croatia to Supreme HQ (23 July 1944).

[172] Colonel Hinko Resch (1893–1945) is sometimes credited with saving thousands of people (including Jews) from German and *Ustashe* camps and prisons in Rijeka after the Italian capitulation, according to the only detailed biography available in either printed or electronic form: http://www.lokalpatrioti-rijeka.com/forum/viewtopic.php?p=50279 Resch, although not a Partisan sympathizer, knew several people with ties to the People's Liberation Movement. He was killed by the *Ustashe* in late April 1945.

[173] Unlike the incident involving the Germans from Opatija, Tito allowed the Partisans in the vicinity of Sušak to communicate with the colonel. VA, 119/4, 1, 1–16, Supreme HQ to

part of Istria hoped to achieve by negotiations remains a mystery. The intelligence branch of the Main HQ for Croatia concluded that the whole episode was nothing but a German propaganda ploy aimed at "spreading confusion and reaping the benefits from it."[174]

The Reasons Behind the Germans' Request to Obtain a Cease-fire in the Littoral

Rainer told his Yugoslav captors after the war that he approved of the truce based on the directive Hitler gave him upon his appointment as the High Commissioner for the OZAK. The directive stated that Rainer's main task was to maintain peace and order: "If the Partisans remained calm, the mission would be fulfilled." Furthermore, the former governor of Carinthia claimed the arrangement would have eased the suffering of the civilian population around Gorizia who were facing constant food shortages because the Partisans controlled the surrounding territory.[175] Wartime documents confirm that Rainer's statements, given in a Yugoslav prison, were not designed to simply portray him in the best possible light. Like Ambassador Kasche, this ardent Nazi was convinced that the insurgency could not be defeated by military means alone. His approach, which included increasing reliance upon native administrations, granting amnesty to guerrillas, and curbing the prerogatives of military tribunals, brought him in conflict with Army commanders, most notably Kübler.[176] It is therefore more than likely that Rainer welcomed the truce as a means to "passify the bandits to a certain degree," and thus facilitate the functioning of administration and undisrupted economic activity in the Littoral.[177] It is also possible that he hoped the talks would pave the way for further negotiations for a more permanent political arrangement between the Partisans and local occupation authorities.

Still unsure as to precisely how Hitler would react to such imaginative interpretations of his orders, Rainer decided to consult SS General Odilo Globocnik, the chief of police and security forces in the Littoral, and General Kübler, his

---

Main HQ for Croatia (17 July 1944); VA, 119/2, 3, 6–8 and 6–9, Cables from Main HQ for Croatia to Supreme HQ (1 and 4 August 1944).

[174] HR HDA 1450, D-1091, 483, 626, OZNA to Main HQ for Croatia (1 August 1944).

[175] Facsimile of Rainer's statement given to Yugoslav authorities in 1947, reproduced in Zavadlav, *Partizani,* Part III, Document No. 9 (unpaginated).

[176] NARA, T-312, Roll 1638, 001040–1, Memorandum from a meeting between Gustav von Zangen and Walter Warlimont (16 May 1944); ibid., 001063–4, Memorandum from a meeting between Gustav von Zangen and Ludwig Kübler (28 May 1944).

[177] NARA, T-312, Roll 1640, 000825, Telephone conversation between Gustav von Zangen and Ludwig Kübler at 17.50 hours (2 July 1944).

Wehrmacht counterpart.[178] Globocnik apparently agreed immediately, but Kübler decided to first seek permission from his superiors, General Gustav von Zangen, commander of the Army Detachment Zangen, and Field Marshal Albert Kesselring, Commander-in-Chief of Army Group C. These three high-ranking officers weighed the pros and cons of a temporary truce (*Verhandlungsruhe*) in a series of telephone conversations in the afternoon hours of 2 July 1944. Unlike Rainer, they took the Partisans' warning not to mistake their readiness to negotiate for a sign of weakness or a desire for a permanent settlement at face value. Even so, it seemed that the Germans did not have much to lose if the truce were to be accepted; the guerrillas would refrain from moving their units during the talks, whereas the Axis forces could move theirs without fear of sabotage or ambush. The generals reasoned that even if "the action" failed in the end, it would gain them several precious days to repair transport facilities which had suffered heavily during the past month.[179] Consequently, Kübler's superiors, not averse to negotiating with the guerrillas in Italy, gave the green light for the truce.[180]

The second possible explanation is that the SS Propaganda Regiment Kurt Eggers, elements of which were deployed in the OZAK, was the real authority behind Count Pace. The objective of the operation would be to discredit the Partisans and sow confusion within their ranks; the premature announcement of the cease-fire on the 4th may have been this regiment's doing. Rainer was questioned about this possibility and said that to his knowledge, Pace had no connection to the SS unit. He added that it was possible that the regiment simply seized the opportunity when it presented itself in early July and attempted to exploit it propagandistically.[181] There is, however, circumstantial evidence that the regiment

---

[178] Facsimile of Rainer's statement given to Yugoslav authorities in 1947, reproduced in Zavadlav, *Partizani,* Part III, Document No. 9 (unpaginated).

[179] German intelligence noted in June that the guerrillas were conducting an orchestrated campaign against railway lines in the OZAK with the aim of completely closing down these vital communications, probably at the behest of the Western Allies. NARA, T-312, Roll 1640, 001038, 001029, Bandit activity reports for the first and second half of June 1944 (14 and 29 June 1944).

[180] Ibid., 000817, Telephone conversation between Gustav von Zangen and Ludwig Kübler at 18.25 hours (2 July 1944). Only two weeks earlier, von Zangen's men successfully exchanged some prisoners with Italian Partisans at Bardi, southwest of Parma. Ibid., 001045–8, Report of staff surgeon Dr. Rüll (21 June 1944). Army Group C negotiated "live-and-let-live" agreements with Italian Partisans at Breno and Edolo, north of Brescia, in August and September 1944. Roberto Spazzali, "La missione del conte Marino Pace, prefetto di Gorizia, tra i partigiani di Circhina (11 settembre–12 ottobre 1944)," *Studi goriziani* 85 (January–June 1997), p. 49.

[181] Zavadlav, *Partizani,* p. 96; Facsimile of Rainer's statement given to Yugoslav authorities in 1947, reproduced in ibid., Part III, Document No. 9 (unpaginated).

may not have acted on its own. According to the previously quoted stenographs of telephone conferences between the German military commanders, they thought that the only real value of the negotiations lay in their propaganda potential. The talks would have a "psychological effect on the bandits and their leadership" and open the possibility of a "major propaganda action aimed at bandits and the civilian population," which would lead to the "weakening of [their] fighting spirit" and "encourage desertion."[182] It is therefore possible that the Kurt Eggers Regiment had been instructed on 2 July to prepare accordingly, and that it took action two days later. Additional proof that the rumors about the rapprochement between the Partisans and the occupation authorities in the Littoral were not groundless can be found in Globocnik's activity report from early February 1945. The report reads in part that the focal points of the German propaganda effort "were still" revolving around encouraging defection and "subversive slogans like 'Tito negotiates with the Germans.'"[183]

Confusion was widespread on both sides and at all levels. German signals intelligence intercepted a radio message from the 7th Corps of the NOVJ which in part read that the local German commander in the town of Postojna offered to defect to the Partisans. In another intercepted message, local Chetniks reported that the truce purportedly included arms deliveries by the Germans to the Partisans, and also speculated that the agreement was made with the consent of Moscow and Berlin.[184] The collaborationist forces were, understandably, terrified at the prospect of a German-Partisan rapprochement. General Leo Rupnik, the head of the Slovene collaborationist government, protested to SS General Rösener, emphatically stating that his Home Guards would never accept this cease-fire. Rösener was compelled to publicly renounce the truce in the daily newspaper, *Slovenec:* "It is rumored that an agreement with the bandits has been made in the Littoral. These allegations remain but a rumor for us in the Ljubljana Province. . . . The struggle will continue until the victorious end!"[185]

In order to clarify the matter, the SS general traveled to Trieste over the following days for a meeting with Governor Rainer. According to the latter's post-war

---

[182] NARA, T-312, Roll 1640, 000819, Telephone conversation between Gustav von Zangen and Ludwig Kübler at 17.50 hours (2 July 1944).

[183] The Chief of Security Police and Security Service in the OZAK, Report No. 6 for the period 25 January–4 February 1945 (5 February 1945), p. 3 in *Nationalsozialismus, Holocaust, Widerstand und Exil 1933–1945*, retrieved from: https://www.degruyter.com/view/db/dghfo

[184] NARA, T-311, Roll 195, 000720, Army Group F to Army Group C and OZAK (12 July 1944). Later, both rumors turned out to be false. NARA, T-311, Roll 195, 000717, Army Group F to 2nd Panzer Army (22 July 1944).

[185] *Slovenec* (7 July 1944), p. 1, retrieved from: http://www.dlib.si/details/URN:NBN:SI:DOC-GOXPDXCR/?pageSize=20&frelation=Slovenec+(1873)&query=%27keywords%3dslovenec++1944.%40AND%40keywords%3d07.07.1944%27

interrogation, Rösener told him he feared he would lose control over the Slovene Home Guard if the truce remained in force. He therefore had to make a public proclamation against it in order to dispel the fears of the collaborators. The general continued that the lack of a unified German policy, as overtly demonstrated by recent events, was detrimental to the Third Reich's authority and prestige in the region. In Rainer's opinion, the real reason for Rösener's opposition to the negotiations was his injured pride from being excluded from the matter. In light of these facts, Rainer could not hope to persuade him to widen the truce to his area of responsibility around the Slovene capital. Fearing that any pressure on Rösener to change his mind would cause him to report the whole matter to Himmler and Hitler, Rainer did not press the matter any further. He accepted the general's word that the troops in the Ljubljana province would not undertake any activities over the following days, and would closely monitor the effects of the truce. "I did not believe the cease-fire would last for much longer," concluded Rainer.[186]

Available sources are contradictory about whether the truce actually become effective on 5 July, as well as how long it lasted. Rainer remembered that General Kübler told him that the truce had been "mostly observed" by both sides for about two weeks.[187] On the other hand, Kesselring's HQ informed Army Group F on or about 11 July about the negotiations and that the "bandits" repudiated the truce and made it clear they would continue with armed actions. The report added that Pace would try again, but that the outcome was not predictable.[188] On 16 July 1944, the daily report of the Main HQ of the NDH Home Guard read: "The truce in Istria, which commenced on 5 July between the Partisans and the Germans, has been canceled."[189]

An examination of the NOVJ's 9th Corps activity reports for the first three weeks of July lends support to a truce being enacted for at least a few days. The corps' two divisions and four detachments carried out twenty-two armed actions in the period between 25 June and 4 July, and a further thirty-six from 6–18 July 1944. None of the units reported any activity for 5 July, and only one was active on the 6th. These two days of quiet could safely be ascribed to the rumors of a truce. Faced with conflicting reports, the units most likely held off operations until clarification came from higher commands. Once this arrived, there was a noted increase in sabotage and attacks on Axis positions in the area which culminated in the storming of the garrison in Hotavlje (30km NE of Gorizia) on 18 July. One day

---

[186] Facsimile of Rainer's statement given to Yugoslav authorities in 1947, reproduced in Zavadlav, *Partizani*, Part III, Document No. 9 (unpaginated).

[187] Ibid.

[188] NARA, T-311, Roll 195, 000792, Army Group F to 2nd Panzer Army (11 July 1944).

[189] *Zbornik*/V/30/732, Daily report of Main HQ of Home Guard for 16 July 1944.

later, the Germans launched their own offensive against the 9th Corps.[190] Judging by these facts, it seems that Kesselring's message was closest to the truth—the two-week "truce" Kübler was referring to was actually a period which saw no major activities on either side. By the beginning of the last week of the month, all illusions regarding the truce had vanished. On 22 July 1944, Army Group F informed the 2nd Panzer Army about the situation in the Slovenian Littoral: "Truce with the bandits did not materialize. . . . The bandit leadership apparently ordered a truce for the duration of the talks, but later canceled this order."[191]

The previously-quoted intelligence report of Army Group F dated 11 July mulled the reasons behind the initial readiness of the Partisan leadership to negotiate: "In particular, it is unclear if it had been a decision of a local bandit command, or if Tito had something to do with it." This was important because the negotiations in Primorska coincided with rumors regarding an impending Allied landing in Istria. Some suspected that the true aim of the Partisans was to lull the Germans into a false sense of security prior to the invasion.[192] On the other hand, others thought that the British themselves engineered the truce through Pace, who was rumored to have ties with the remaining Anglophiles in Mussolini's Italian Social Republic. According to this theory, the British were not desirous of the Communist Partisans gaining the upper hand in the Littoral. The truce was devised to provide time for the Germans to reinforce their presence before conducting an all-out offensive to destroy the guerrillas before the Allies landed.[193]

There is no factual evidence to support this theory. What is certain is that Churchill and Tito were wary of each other's intentions concerning the Littoral, but neither would go so far as to work with the Germans in order to thwart the other. During their meeting in Naples on 12–13 August 1944, they agreed to cooperate in the event of a landing in Istria. Behind the scenes, Churchill hoped that the operation would not only shorten the war, but also deny this important region to the Soviets and their Yugoslav proxies. Tito, for his part, was already publicly laying

---

[190] *Zbornik*/VI/15/38–59, Activity report of 9th Corps for the period 5–20 July 1944 (20 July 1944); *Hronologija*, p. 825.

[191] NARA, T-311, Roll 195, 000717, Army Group F to 2nd Panzer Army (22 July 1944).

[192] NARA, T-311, Roll 195, 000736–7, Overview of enemy situation in Southeast (11 July 1944); ibid., Roll 190, 000799, War diary of Army Group F, Entry for 10 July 1944. The possibilities of a landing in Istria and a subsequent advance to Vienna (known as the "Ljubljana Gap Strategy") were discussed in British military circles beginning in March 1944 as one of the possible operations against "Fortress Europe." Thomas M. Barker, "The Ljubljana Gap Strategy: Alternative to Anvil/Dragoon or Fantasy?," *The Journal of Military History* 56 (1992), pp. 61–62.

[193] This version of events came from an ex-Gestapo official, Paul Dusch, during his interrogation in an OZNA prison in 1948; a facsimile of his statement was reproduced in Zavadlav, *Partizani,* Part III, Document No. 5 (unpaginated).

claim to the region for Yugoslavia (it had been a part of Italy since the Treaty of Rapallo in 1920). In a letter to Stalin in the beginning of September, he stated that the People's Liberation Movement "would not be pleased" by the prospects of an Allied landing on the eastern coast of the Adriatic, but if it did occur, the Partisans would prefer that it take place in Istria[194] which was far from Serbia and where there were no Chetniks to rally to the Allies.

The Germans continued monitoring the news concerning possible operations in Istria throughout that year. On the first day of September, a "reliable double agent" informed them that the Allies were planning to land at Trieste in five days with full knowledge of the Partisans.[195] Although the landing did not take place, the Germans continued to be on the lookout for any signs of renewed diplomatic activity on the part of the Partisans in the Littoral. On 25 November, General Kübler informed his superiors that the "bandits" in Istria were not showing any "readiness to negotiate."[196]

Judging by the available sources, the contacts with Count Pace were maintained exclusively by the local Partisan commands and without any interference from the Supreme HQ. Zavadlav, who was arrested in 1948 for being a supporter of Stalin (and, conveniently, a Gestapo agent during the war), was questioned regarding his decision to maintain negotiations despite knowing that Pace's efforts were aimed at brokering a cease-fire with the hated German invader. Zavadlav replied that he had done so as an attempt to recruit the count for the Partisan cause.[197] The whole operation, from the Partisan point of view, was meant to serve intelligence purposes; the negotiations were seen as an opportunity to take the pulse of the enemy and an attempt to discern the real motives behind his proposals. A lasting truce with the Axis forces in the area was not contemplated, as

---

[194] Churchill, *Second World War,* Vol. VI, pp. 80, 133–34; Petranović, *Istorija Jugoslavije,* Vol. II, p. 330.

[195] NARA, T-311, Roll 286, Intelligence section of Army Group F to Army Group F HQ (1 September 1944).

[196] NARA, T-311, Roll 197, 000151, Intelligence summary No. 6 of the 97th Army Corps (25 November 1944).

[197] The count was not known for Nazi leanings but held strong sympathies for the former Austro-Hungarian Monarchy, which had once reigned over the Littoral and adjacent Italian regions. His moderate policies and knowledge of the Slovene language made him an ideal choice for prefect of ethnically-mixed Gorizia. Zavadlav, *Partizani,* p. 96. When asked by the interrogator why he had not arrested Pace in Renče, Zavadlav answered that the prefect was not considered "a hostile element." Interrogation of Zdenko Zavadlav (16 November 1948), facsimile reproduced in ibid., Part III, Document No. 11 (unpaginated). Interestingly, Pace effected the release of Zavadlav from the German prison in Trieste in November 1943 after an intervention from the Partisan's father. Interrogation of Zdenko Zavadlav (26 October 1948), facsimile reproduced in ibid., Part III, Document No. 11 (unpaginated).

evidenced by Perc's instructions to Zavadlav in late June and the hasty canceling of the truce by the latter on 4 July, as well as by the attacks conducted on rail communications and collaborator strongpoints in the days following the announcement of the truce. Kralj's clumsy acceptance of the Axis envoys' proposal of a cease-fire for the duration of the talks was probably blown out of proportion due to widespread rumors and by the German propaganda apparatus. Nonetheless, the misunderstanding proved to be his undoing—he was ordered back to the HQ of the 9th Corps, where a public prosecutor opened an investigation against him which led to his execution for "negotiating with the Germans."[198]

Despite the unwanted fallout resulting from the talks with the prefect of Gorizia, the highest leadership of the Slovene Partisans was still very much interested in utilizing contacts with the enemy for propaganda purposes. In a letter dated 23 July 1944, the Main HQ advised the 4th Operational Zone to establish contacts with both Home Guard and German garrisons and use the current international situation to undermine their morale. "Needless to say, none of these contacts may be used for achieving some kind of truce with the Germans or the Slovene collaborators," the letter stated. One day later, the Main HQ commander specifically mentioned the Gorizia episode in his letter to the 9th Corps: "Inform us in particular about the possibilities of renewing the contacts which were established between Kralj and Rainer's representatives; we hereby warn you that the renewal of these contacts may under no circumstances be accompanied by any talk of a cease-fire. The contacts should be used to accelerate the disintegration which has set into the ranks of the Germans and the White Guards. Any attempt to treat this matter as Kralj did will be considered a provocation."[199]

The final act of the Gorizia episode began in early September when Count Pace was invited to a new round of talks. On this occasion, the Partisans promised to send envoys from the very top ranks. On 11 September, Pace, Locatelli, and Muzzolini appeared on guerrilla-held territory as agreed and met Zavadlav, who was to act as their liaison. After a long, arduous journey they arrived in the village of Trebuša, where they were received by Miro Perc. The fact that no higher-ranking delegates from the Slovenian leadership arrived for the talks that day raised Pace's suspicion. His suggestion to postpone the meeting was, however, courteously declined and the Axis delegates were essentially forced to spend the night in the village. The next day, Perc informed the trio that they were under arrest. Pace's protests, made both verbally and in writing, had no effect. The prisoners were kept in an attic of the local tavern under constant supervision until 7 October when the order came for them to march south with a group of Partisans. After three days of

---

[198] Military tribunal of the 9th Corps to provincial branch of OZNA for Primorska (15 August 1944), facsimile reproduced in Zavadlav, *Partizani,* Part III, Document No. 4 (unpaginated).

[199] *Zbornik*/VI/15/94, 129, messages of the Main HQ to 4th Operational Zone (23 July 1944) and to 9th Corps (24 July 1944).

marching in bad weather, Locatelli could not continue any farther because of his heart condition and he had to be left behind. Fearing for his life, the prefect decided to attempt an escape; the party was in the vicinity of a rail line and he was sure he would meet Axis troops nearby. On the night of the 12th, Pace quietly slipped out of the cabin he shared with his escort and stumbled upon a German patrol shortly thereafter.[200]

It is not entirely clear what prompted the Partisans to initiate the talks or what caused Pace's delegation to be arrested. The count was sure they were destined for execution by firing squad, "just as they had done with the two [*sic*] of their own envoys from the July talks." In fact, the local chief of the OZNA did want to execute them, but the service's main center overruled the decision and demanded the prisoners be brought to the headquarters in Bela Krajina. Regardless, the prefect of Gorizia narrowly escaped death. His only satisfaction came after the German 188th Mountain Division launched an incursion into Partisan territory around Postojna and inflicted considerable damage—a success largely due to the detailed information provided by the prefect after his miraculous escape.[201]

Although the truce talks did not have any long-lasting impact, they seem to have paved the way for "ordinary" talks on prisoner exchange in the Primorska region. In August 1944, a Partisan brigade commander was captured north of Gorizia. The Germans apparently wanted to exchange him for one of their own officers, but the negotiations failed for unknown reasons. The commander was kept in prisons in Gorizia and Trieste, only to be executed in the last days of the war. A similar fate befell a certain woman (known as "Nesnes") held captive by Italian Partisans fighting under the command of the 9th Corps. Since the Germans "refused to exchange" her, she was still with the Antonio Gramsci Brigade when the unit came under attack on the morning of 19 November 1944 northeast of Trieste. As the Partisans started to withdraw, Nesnes refused to go with them. "After it became clear that all attempts to motivate her to move were in vain, and as the enemy was rapidly approaching, she had to be killed," the Partisans reported.[202]

---

[200] Spazzali, "La missione," pp. 62–68. Locatelli also managed to escape in the following days; Muzzolini's health suffered severely during captivity (heart and intestinal problems) and he probably died during the march. Ibid., p. 55.

[201] Facsimile of Rainer's statement given to Yugoslav authorities in 1947, reproduced in Zavadlav, *Partizani*, Part III, Document No. 9 (unpaginated); Facsimile of letters from provincial branch of OZNA to OZNA center for Slovenia (12, 16, and 19 September 1944), reproduced in ibid., Document No. 13 (unpaginated); Spazzali, "La missione," p. 54.

[202] *Zbornik*/VI/17/767, Garibaldi Natisone Division, activity report for November 1944 (4 December 1944). It appears that the only successful prisoner exchange in Primorska occurred in early October 1944 when three Partisans were exchanged for one German officer. Dr. Boris Mlakar's letter to the author (19 November 2012).

Conclusion

The years 1943–1945 saw numerous prisoner exchange activities on a local level between the Partisans and various German formations. The frequency of these contacts was largely determined by the scale and ferocity of the fighting. The willingness of a unit commander to offer or accept an exchange was thus dependent on the manner in which the high commands on both sides decided to wage the war. The year 1943 provides the best example of this situation. Under the influence of the successful negotiations in the final months of 1942, both sides recognized the benefits of exchange and took the first steps in departing from a "no-prisoner" policy which had hitherto been the rule. Although negotiating with the enemy still lay in the exclusive domain of the high commands, individual units were encouraged, or in the case of the units around the Partisan Supreme HQ, ordered to take prisoners. The knowledge that the exchange of prisoners was now either tacitly or openly approved by higher authorities made units on the ground more comfortable with the idea of contacting the enemy directly.

The limited progress made in the final months of 1942 was undone by the series of large-scale anti-partisan operations in the first half of 1943. Operations *Weiss* and *Schwarz* were designed to destroy the core of the NOVJ by a maximum application of force and violence. The fighting in the first eight or so months of 1943 was therefore marked by the widespread shooting of prisoners on both sides. This renewed escalation of the fighting affected the willingness of local commands to exchange prisoners. Whereas there were two recorded exchange attempts in the period from January to August 1942, there was only one in the same period in 1943 (Moslavina). One important factor contributed to the revival of exchange activities in the late summer of 1943 and that was Hitler's order from 19 July regarding the treatment of captured guerrillas. This instruction granted Partisans privileged status and signaled the beginning of a departure from the way the German counter-insurgency had previously been conducted. Not only was there a steady supply of prisoners who could be exchanged, but the units were more likely to enter into negotiations with the Partisans now that they were *de facto,* if not *de jure,* recognized as lawful belligerents. The result was that the last four months of 1943 saw twice as many exchange attempts as in the previous twenty months combined. The fact that prisoner exchange was officially recognized in early 1944 by the highest authorities on both sides as a legitimate tool gave a decisive boost to local swaps. The 2nd Panzer Army issued an order which encouraged subordinate units to seek out their guerrilla counterparts and exchange as many German prisoners as possible in their respective zones of responsibility. The Partisan units not commanded by the Main HQ for Croatia apparently did not receive a similar order, but even if they had, it would not have made much of a difference. Prisoner exchange was accepted as a necessity and had been practiced since the beginning of the war. The Partisans offered the last recorded local exchange as late as March 1945, less than two months before the conflict in Europe finally ended.

In pursuit of this policy, the Partisans made attempts to exchange captives in all parts of Yugoslavia, with the notable exception of Serbia proper and, to a lesser extent, Montenegro. They were most numerous in Bosnia and Herzegovina, the regions where the lion's share of the fighting took place until the late summer of 1944, but instances were also recorded in Sandžak, Syrmia, Dalmatia, parts of Slovenia, and in Macedonia. The guerrillas' negotiating partners came from all types of German formations deployed in the region irrespective of their composition or experience in the Balkans: all-German *Jägers;* legionnaire units with Croatian personnel; newly-arrived reserve divisions; special forces (the Brandenburg Division); and others. Especially interesting is the relatively frequent involvement of the *Waffen-SS* units, security services, and police in the local negotiations with the Partisans. They took part in roughly one-fourth of all recorded exchange attempts, a remarkably high figure considering the ideological background of these formations. The nominal prohibition of any contact with the Communists, issued in November 1942 by the highest circles in the SS hierarchy, should have excluded any involvement in such activities, but it did not. The troops on the ground had to adjust to the realities of war in the Balkans just as their army counterparts did.

It must be noted that the exchange talks these units were involved in usually concerned either German civilians (the laborers at Osijek in 1943 and two women at Celje in 1944); non-combatants (the case of Dr. Lunzer); or members of formations other than the SS (the exchange at Ruma, or the von Eberlein episode). The generous terms offered by the SS Division *Prinz Eugen* for one of its officers in late November 1943 in Eastern Herzegovina may have been an attempt to induce the Partisans to spare members of the SS in the future. Unfortunately, the Partisans' insistence on maintaining their "no-prisoner" policy meant that very few SS soldiers survived immediate capture, let alone were available for exchange.

Concerns over the prisoners' well-being and ultimate fate remained the prime motivation for swapping them. Despite the fact that both sides took steps to curb the levels of violence directed at their captives from late 1943 through early 1944, the brutality inherent to irregular warfare could not be eradicated. If a prisoner could not be exchanged soon after his (or her) capture, s/he could be regarded as lost, either to a labor camp or a firing squad. Whether an exchange was requested or accepted was still very much the prerogative of a unit's commander just as it was in the early days of the war. Ideology or arrogance, however, carried significantly less weight compared to 1941; only one of the unsuccessful exchange attempts discussed in this chapter (Podgorica, July 1944) failed on the grounds of the unwillingness to negotiate with "bandits" or with "fascists." The majority of local attempts often failed for more practical reasons, such as prisoner escape (Moslavina) or premature death of the wounded (Sandžak). The mercurial tactical situation, a hallmark of irregular warfare, also accounted for at least two unsuccessful swaps: one at Korčula in late 1944 and the other in central Bosnia in 1945.

A local exchange was typically a matter of the two units immediately facing one another coming to an agreement; once contact was broken off due to tactical necessities, it was very difficult to re-establish. Furthermore, in the event that one of the parties had to move on, there was no assurance that the unit replacing it would be able to conclude the deal. Neither was there any guarantee that the new commander in the area would be willing to go through all the trouble required to exchange people whom he did not know. Unlike Pisarovina, local deals were all about swapping particular prisoners, not just prisoners in general. The failure of one side to produce the requested captives, whether they were common soldiers (Korčula in early 1944) or high-ranking Party members (Struga, November 1943), would invariably lead to the cancellation of talks. This often had dire consequences for the prisoners in Partisan custody as they were no longer a valuable asset, but a logistical and security burden (the cases of Lünen and Perkuhn from March and September 1944, respectively); necessity and practicality would then take precedence over orders issued from late 1943 onwards concerning the humane treatment of German captives.

An examination of facts and figures reveals that there were a total of forty-five cases of local exchange in the years 1943 through 1945. The influence of the Pisarovina cartel is clearly visible. Whereas 1943 saw thirteen exchange attempts, 1944 and 1945 saw more than twice as many (thirty-two): of these, nineteen attempts ended in failure owing to some of the above-mentioned reasons; no information is available on the outcome of six swaps; nineteen attempts were concluded successfully; and one was a special case (Kobarid). Due to the fragmentary nature of sources, it is difficult to provide a precise number of soldiers on both sides who were rescued from captivity in this manner. The prisoners were usually exchanged on a 1:1 ratio, but exceptions were made depending on the rank or importance of a particular individual. Under the assumption that the 1:1 ratio applied to those cases of exchange attempts for which no definitive data exists, it can be determined that the total number of exchangees in the years 1943–1945 was approximately 650. Out of these, about 270 were Germans while 370 were Partisans and their sympathizers,[203] representing approximately one-third of the total number of people exchanged in Pisarovina. The difference can be attributed to several factors. Unlike the neutral zone, where the negotiators got to know and learned to trust each other through repeated dealings, two units rarely had the chance to negotiate more than one exchange. Before a second opportunity could present itself, the unit might have already been transferred to another sector where it faced totally different conditions, such as an increased intensity in the level of fighting or enemy units with unknown attitudes or policies toward prisoners.

Just what was possible to achieve when two sides contacted each other regularly is best illustrated in the example of the 369th Infantry and 29th Herzegovina

---

[203] Not included in this figure are some 150 Germans who were allegedly exchanged by the 118th *Jäger* Division in Herzegovina. This would have been the largest local exchange on record; however, the author could not find a second source to confirm that this event actually occurred.

Divisions. These formations were waging their own little war in a clearly defined geographical region (Eastern Herzegovina) over a long period of time (from February 1944 onwards) with practically no interference from the outside. Although it took several months before the idea of prisoner exchange developed between these two units, the concept was quickly embraced as it brought obvious advantages to both sides. In order to ensure that future exchanges could be easily arranged as well, both sides agreed to institutionalize the process into a more formal system. As in Pisarovina, this included relegating all responsibility for prisoner exchange to specially chosen commands: the 369th Anti-tank Battalion and the South Herzegovina Partisan Detachment. These bodies, in turn, appointed delegates who worked out the details on a case-by-case basis through correspondence and meetings. The swaps were always made at the same place (Hill 286), which both sides agreed to keep demilitarized. The system worked well—at least four exchanges took place there in the period from late June to early September 1944, with a fifth agreed upon but canceled. Despite the fact that the collapse of the German positions around Stolac in the early autumn also spelled the end of the arrangement, the South Herzegovina Partisan Detachment (recently absorbed into the 14th Brigade) and the 369th traded prisoners once more in November, a feat which can clearly be attributed to the positive experiences at Hill 286. All in all, some sixty prisoners on both sides were exchanged in Eastern Herzegovina; this modest number would have increased had the system been expanded to include a wider area and other units as well.

Negotiations at the local level were usually led without ulterior motives, but that was not always the case. Using contacts pertaining to prisoner exchange in order to discuss other issues was practiced by both sides in the last two years of the war. The idea of trading prisoners for security, although not new (the talks at Veliko Gradište on the Danube in 1941 serve as one example), only became attractive in the second half of 1943. The capitulation of Italy in September of that year provided a major impetus for the Partisan movement, and the Germans faced an increasingly aggressive enemy who grew stronger by the day. Securing vital lines of communication remained the primary task of the German occupation forces. The overstretched and undermanned German units often found it an impossible task to accomplish through brute force alone, so some commanders sought to complete their mission by using less conventional methods. Thus, the SS *Karstwehr* Battalion offered some sixty hostages to the Slovene Partisans if they would agree to evacuate the strategic Predil Pass in northwestern Slovenia in October 1943. The guerrillas accepted the offer at first and accepted the prisoners, but conveniently changed their minds just before they had to fulfill their part of the bargain. Such a turn of events did not spell the end to German-Partisan contact in Slovenia. In mid-December 1943, their delegations met in the village of Mokronog, not far from the Croatian border, to discuss several issues. The main objective of the German delegation was to obtain a cessation of sabotage on the all-important ground communications linking the Slovenian capital Ljubljana with Karlovac in Croatia.

The Partisans, for their part, wanted to be officially recognized as a legitimate belligerent force by their enemy. As neither side was willing to give way on these main issues, a compromise was reached only on the question of prisoner exchange.

The Germans attempted to reach a similar arrangement in the Slovene Littoral in the late spring and early summer of 1944. Acting through civilian intermediaries, they proposed a cease-fire on rail communications between Trieste and Gorizia, offering in exchange economic cooperation with the local guerrillas. The Partisans pushed for a prisoner exchange and demanded to be treated as a regular army. As it was customary to proclaim a local truce for the duration of talks (e.g. Moslavina, Mokronog), the Partisans did the same on the eve of the fourth round of negotiations scheduled to take place on 5 July 1944. Owing either to a misunderstanding or, more likely, a deliberate ploy by a German propaganda unit stationed in the area, the news leaked out that the Partisans had agreed to a permanent cease-fire. There was widespread confusion over the following days as units on all sides attempted to discover what had or had not transpired. In fact, sabotage and small-scale attacks against Axis installations never let up and large-scale fighting resumed within two weeks after the incident. Despite this episode, the guerrillas were interested in continuing the contacts, now with the intention of undermining the morale of the Germans and their native collaborators. Their decision to take the Axis envoys captive in September 1944, however, spelled the end for further negotiations in the Littoral.

In early November 1943, the Germans noticed the great interest shown by the Macedonian Partisans in obtaining the release of some of their comrades from Bulgarian camps. Although the government in Sofia quickly refused to turn them over to their allies for exchange, the Germans decided to hide this fact from the Partisans and protract the negotiations. By holding out the prospect that the captured Communists might yet be exchanged, the Germans sounded out the Partisans about the possibility of granting the right of free passage to Axis convoys along the important Struga–Kičevo road. The Partisans declined and the region became embroiled in heavy fighting as the Germans reverted to force of arms in order to secure the aforementioned supply artery. In September and October of 1944, prisoner exchange negotiations were used by the Partisans and British liaison officers as a pretext for contacting the German garrison in Prilep. What the Partisans really wanted was to discuss the capitulation of German forces in Western Macedonia. In September, the Germans deliberately protracted the talks until reinforcements could reach them. By October 1944, Macedonia was flooded by the retreating units of Army Group E withdrawing from Greece, and the contact was severed for good.

It is noteworthy that the majority of the German proposals involving the exchange of prisoners for promises of security along their supply arteries occurred in the peripheral regions of Yugoslavia. Whereas there were four attempts to obtain these agreements in Slovenia and Macedonia, only two such instances were recorded in the nexus of the fighting—the territory of the NDH—and even these two episodes (at Stolac and Sušak in the summer of 1944) took place on the country's borders. One possible explanation for the discrepancy could lay in the perceptions held by the Germans about how their Partisan enemy functioned. Due to immense communication and geographic difficulties, the NOVJ's branches in Slovenia and Macedonia received general guidelines from Tito and the Supreme HQ, but they had great latitude in executing those orders. In addition, both of these formations claimed to be the national armies of the Slovene and Macedonian peoples who had chosen of their own free will to be part of a wider, all-Yugoslav People's Liberation Movement. It would therefore be reasonable to assume that the Germans on the ground thought that the local, "national" Partisans would somehow be more agreeable to offers of a local truce than the "regular" units close to the Supreme HQ.

Chapter 6

Closing Thoughts

As each chapter in this work contains extensive conclusions, as well as numerous explanatory footnotes throughout, a few general observations herein should be sufficient.

Frequent exchanges of able-bodied prisoners between the occupation forces and a resistance movement, partly through a cartel negotiated directly between their high commands, were a distinctive feature of the Second World War in Yugoslavia. At first glance, it seems surprising that this topic remained on the historiographical sidelines for almost seventy years. During the forty-five years of socialism, Yugoslav historians devoted themselves almost exclusively to the research of war-related topics; exploits of nearly every Partisan unit, no matter how trivial, were dutifully recorded and published. The vast majority of these works, however, were laden with ideological overtones to varying degrees. Historians avoided all topics which might blemish the lionized image of Partisans as uncompromising, yet noble, freedom-fighters—the mortal enemies of Nazism. The subject of enemy prisoners was one of the sensitive areas researchers preferred to avoid because any objective, in-depth analysis of the topic would produce results in sharp contrast to the official version of events. The truth was that the Partisans followed the rules and customs of war only when it suited them and they had no qualms about negotiating with the hated "fascist invaders." The demise of socialism in the early 1990s did not remove ideology and day-to-day politics from the historiography—the communist political agenda was merely replaced with that of the nationalists. The result was that the Partisans' diplomatic dealings with the occupation forces were commonly presented as proof that the Communists collaborated with the Nazis. As Western authors were themselves not completely immune from taking sides (especially during the Cold War), this controversial topic remained shrouded in misconceptions and over-simplifications. For instance, the notion that the guerrillas indiscriminately slaughtered all their captives according to "Balkan tradition" is still present in some quarters. In reality, the Partisans' approach was much more nuanced, with practical considerations far outweighing unmitigated bloodlust in determining the fate of their prisoners.

The conflict in Yugoslavia was a brutal affair, combining elements of liberation war, civil war, and ideological war. It was to a great extent a conflict of unrestrained violence that did not discriminate between combatant and non-combatant. In these circumstances, captives on all sides could not expect to receive fair treatment.

Since the prisoners' lot could not be improved by invoking international law or principles of humanity, the only remaining option was to appeal to the enemy's self-interest. The Yugoslav Partisans were the first to act upon this realization primarily because prisoner exchange had been practiced in the Balkans for centuries, regardless of the intensity of the conflict in question. Decisions to spare enemy prisoners for exchange originated first with local commanders who wanted to rescue a relative or fellow unit member, not from orders handed down from higher authorities. In general, the willingness to offer an exchange, as well as the treatment of German prisoners, depended on three factors: ideological considerations, policies on enemy prisoners, and external influences.

The first factor dominated the Partisans' attitude on this matter in the period from July until December 1941. The illusion that class struggle was the root cause of the war caused the Partisans to treat common German soldiers well because they were thought to be peasants and workers manipulated by their reactionary officers into fighting for Hitler. Initially, the Germans' increasing brutality was not countered with officially sanctioned mass reprisals against the prisoners. As it became clear that the occupying forces would not reciprocate this clemency, the Partisans then adopted a no-prisoner policy which was more or less pursued for the first eight months of 1942. The third phase began in early September after the first successful prisoner exchange between the Partisan Supreme HQ and German authorities in the NDH, and lasted, with periodic interruptions, until the end of the war. Pragmatism, rather than ideology or respect for international law, or a desire for revenge, was at the heart of the new policy—a German prisoner was only worth sparing because he could now be traded for incarcerated Partisans or valuable Party members. These considerations led to the creation of the permanent exchange cartel with the German command in Zagreb in late 1943. The success of the Pisarovina arrangement influenced Partisan commands across Yugoslavia to also spare their prisoners for exchange.

External influences gained prominence in early 1944. The British were concerned that any atrocity perpetrated by the Partisans would result in reprisals against their own countrymen held as prisoners in Germany. Tito, anxious to keep his alliance with the British afloat, agreed to issue unequivocal orders for the proper treatment of German captives and to ensure they were obeyed. Beginning in late summer of 1944, however, Tito's concern about British attitudes and the prisoners' lot began to wane for two reasons: the Red Army's presence in Yugoslavia meant he was no longer dependent on British goodwill for much-needed materials and supplies; and the Partisan movement was now operating from a position of strength, giving him no particular reason to offer the Germans concessions of any kind. Hence, Tito showed little interest in curbing the increasingly violent behavior of Partisan/Yugoslav units on the ground or in punishing those responsible for atrocities against German prisoners.

The Germans were the last of the Axis powers to recognize the potential benefits of prisoner-taking and exchange. Unlike the Italian Army, which had led protracted counter-insurgency campaigns in Africa in the decades leading up to the Second World War, the Germans had only limited experience with this type of conflict and had no opportunity (or inclination) to change their ways. Consequently, Italian commanders were much more flexible on the issue of prisoners and were ready to negotiate with guerrillas for the release of their men vitually from the first day of the uprising. The same position applied to the civil and military authorities of the NDH. They shared a common history with their enemy, and knew well that the only way to save the lives of their compatriots was to trade them for those of their enemy. General Glaise-Horstenau once observed that German foreign policy knew only of "either bombs or embraces."[1] The same can be said about the German Army. Unlike their Italian counterparts, German officers were, for the most part, politically aloof, showing little to no understanding of the immensely complicated political landscape of the Balkans. They were the product of a doctrine which revolved around the idea of total and utter annihilation of the enemy on the battlefield. It was long maintained that this approach was valid for both regular and irregular warfare. As time passed, however, and as the Germans sank ever deeper into the Balkans quagmire, units on the ground began to show more flexibility in dealing with their guerrilla opponents.

The German occupation authorities in Yugoslavia did not possess a unified policy regarding prisoners; hence, the treatment of captured Partisans varied from region to region and depended on several factors. Serbia was considered the main bastion of the occupation system in the entire region, and the Germans believed they could hold the country through brute force alone. Under these circumstances, negotiating with the guerrillas over a local prisoner exchange was deemed counter-productive and was therefore discouraged. As a consequence, the struggle between the Serbian Partisans and the occupying forces remained almost as bloody in 1944 as it was in 1941. The Germans faced an altogether different situation in the NDH compared to Serbia. Their troop contingent there was too weak to keep the insurgency in check, and widespread reprisals failed to achieve similar results because the fear of *Ustashe* terror kept a large part of the population under arms regardless of their application. Faced with a resolute enemy of steadily increasing strength, the German military, diplomatic, and police authorities were more willing to negotiate than their counterparts in Serbia. The first successful prisoner exchange in September 1942 paved the way for further talks with the Partisans, but it did not result in the modification of old guidelines in which captured guerrillas were to be promptly executed. This approach began to change only after the realities of the war forced Hitler to alter the policy toward members of guerrilla movements across Europe in July–August 1943. More conscientious German commanders in the NDH, such as General Glaise-Horstenau, used this semi-formal recognition of the Partisans' rights as legitimate belligerents to push for a

---

[1] Broucek, ed., *Ein General im Zwielicht*, Vol. III, p. 369 (Entry for January 1944).

lasting exchange agreement. The cartel, sanctioned by the *Wehrmacht's* Supreme Command, went into effect in January 1944. Unlike the Partisans, who adopted prisoner exchange as the mainstay of their prisoner policy, the Germans saw the cartel merely as a useful addition to the existing regulations concerning the treatment of captured Partisans. This allowed for most of the ordinary prisoners to be shipped off to Germany for forced labor, as per Hitler's instructions, and for the more prominent Partisans to be kept for exchange. Due to the paucity of sources and lack of scholarly research on the subject, it is difficult to ascertain to what extent German troops on the ground followed the new policies. It seems that the reprisals in 1944 and 1945 were directed primarily against those Partisans who did not fight as regular soldiers and those civilians perceived to be their supporters. On the other hand, any Partisan openly carrying arms when captured had a much better chance of survival in the last seventeen months of the war than they had in the early years.

Whereas the negotiations on prisoner exchange brought at least a partial de-escalation of violence towards enemy captives, the political talks between the Partisan representatives and the envoys of German military and political authorities in Zagreb produced no results whatsoever. This should come as no surprise given the irreconcilable differences between the disparate ideologies that the envoys represented. The talks became almost an end unto themselves—a channel of communication both sides wanted to keep open. Paradoxically, it was Ambassador Kasche, a committed Nazi, who was probably the only person on either side who believed in the possibility of a lasting arrangement. There is no conclusive evidence that the Partisan leadership ever sincerely hoped for a rapprochement with the Germans. Tito's offer of a truce in March, and the subsequent pause in sabotage along the Zagreb-Belgrade railway in April of 1943, were the result of a desperate operational situation rather than a change in his convictions. According to some authors, this diplomatic initiative showed that Tito was not averse to entering into tactical collaboration with the occupation authorities in order to gain the upper hand against his civil war opponents—the same circumstances that led to the trial and execution of Draža Mihailović after the war. Unlike the Serb nationalist movement, whose talks with the Germans usually resulted in concrete joint actions against the common enemy, neither primary sources nor the vast secondary literature offer any evidence that the diplomatic contacts on political or prisoner issues led to collaboration between the NOVJ and the German occupation forces. In fact, there is evidence to the contrary. The establishment of the neutral zone and the intensification of local exchange contacts went hand in hand with the ever-increasing intensity of operations in the last twenty months of the war.

Much ink has been spilled over the anti-British sentiments of the Partisans and their self-professed readiness to forcefully oppose the Allied landings in Dalmatia. There can be no doubt that the Communist leadership was wary of British intentions in the Balkans, especially in the period prior to May 1943. Although the arrival of the first British military mission to the Supreme HQ signaled the beginning of

Anglo-Partisan cooperation, Tito remained convinced that Whitehall was attempting some sort of scheme aimed at undermining the Partisans' position in the country. His envoys did not hide their sentiment from the Germans during their meetings, and even accentuated it in order to keep them interested in continuing the contacts, especially during the crisis of March 1943. Several high-ranking Partisan officers mentioned during the March Negotiations that they were actively considering the possibility of armed conflict with the British should they intervene openly in favor of the Chetniks. Fortunately for the Yugoslav Communists, the course of events never put them in a position to follow through on their statements. Regardless of what they said or felt, the fact remains that the alliance between the Partisan Movement and the British survived throughout the war despite its troubled nature.

This book is the first attempt at a comprehensive analysis of non-violent contacts between the Partisans and the German occupation authorities in Yugoslavia in the Second World War. Far from being the final word on the subject, it should serve as a starting point for further research on various aspects of the history of POWs in the conflict.[2] As with much of the history of the Western Balkans, the phenomenon of prisoner exchange has an element of paradox. Yugoslavia was probably the only place in war-torn Europe where representatives of two irreconcilable ideologies, Communism and Nazism, met regularly at the negotiating table. Both were primarily motivated by the desire to save the lives of their own men, but the talks did mitigate, however marginally, the horrors of the war.

---

[2] Other areas that require additional research include prisoner exchanges with other Axis powers, such as the Italians or Bulgarians, or the general history of POWs in the region in the 20th century.

Acknowledgments

I would like to thank the people without whose help this book could not have been written: my brother, Dr. Mak Trifković of the University of Victoria in Victoria, British Columbia, who was instrumental in obtaining digital copies of German documents; Dr. Alwin Fill of the *Apsolvent/-innen-Stipendien-Gesellschaft* in Graz for securing a financial grant for my archival research abroad; Dr. Klaus Schmider of the Royal Military Academy Sandhurst for copies of rare German documents and many useful suggestions concerning the text; Dr. Boris Mlakar of the Institute for Contemporary History in Ljubljana, Slovenia, for providing me with document summaries, book excerpts, and valuable comments on wartime events in Slovenia; Dr. Peter Broucek for detailed advice concerning research in the Military Archive in Vienna; Dr. Roberto Trajkovski for information on events in Macedonia; Ms. Marlisa Fašaić for information on and photographs of her grandfather, Eduard Peternell; Dr. Conrad E. Heidenreich for documents and information on his father; the Museum of Pančevo, Serbia, and the Institute for International Sociology in Gorizia, Italy, for sending me copies of their publications; Dr. Siegfried Beer of the University of Graz for his useful suggestions and corrections and for providing me with additional literature on the involvement of British and U. S. intelligence agencies in Yugoslavia; Sean Hansen, Duncan Bare, and Darko Cafuta for providing me with documents from the German Federal Archives, U. S. National Archives, and Archives of Slovenia, respectively; Dr. Carl Bethke, Patricia Hoover, Rhea Ivanuš, Dr. Dino Mujadžević, Dr. Milan Ristović, Mladen Stilinović, Mario Šimunković, Dr. Aleksej Timofejev, Dr. Geoffrey Swain, and Dr. Maurice Williams for helping in various ways; the same goes for my many colleagues from "Axis History Forum" and "Forum-der-Wehrmacht;" employees of the Museum of Bosnia and Herzegovina in Sarajevo, the Croatian State Archives in Zagreb, the Serbian Military Archive in Belgrade, and the Military Archives in Vienna for their kind assistance during my research in their institutions.

I also wish to express my gratitude to Sharon and Robert von Maier, who spent almost as many hours editing the manuscript as I spent writing it. Special thanks go to Goran Despotović from Belgrade who has graciously provided me and many other researchers with a wealth of primary and secondary sources pertaining to the Second World War in Yugoslavia. Last but not least, I wish to thank my wife, Lejla, for her support and for always patiently bearing with me.

Appendix A

Prisoner Exchanges in Yugoslavia

1. Local exchanges

1941

Date and Place	No. of captured Partisans involved	No. of captured Germans involved	Success	Comments
1. Late July–Early August, Valjevo	1	1	No	German prisoner escaped
2. Mid-August, Gornji Milanovac	6	1	Yes	One source claims that altogether 40 hostages (including civilians) were released by the Germans
3. Late August, Valjevo	1	1	No	Partisans offered the Serbian mayor of Valjevo
4. Late August, Kikinda	1	1	Yes	
5. August–September, Knin	?	2	No	Germans shot as spies
6. Early September, Niš	?	7	No	No response from the Germans; prisoners executed
7. Late September, Veliko Gradište	20–30 civilian hostages	12	No	
8. Late September, Čačak	A number of hostages from local prison	3	No	
9. Early October, Zvornik	?	3	?	Not known if the exchange took place
10. Mid-November, Leskovac	3	1	No	Germans refused the exchange offer

1942

Date and Place	No. of captured Partisans involved	No. of captured Germans involved	Success	Comments
11. Early April, Doboj	5	3	Yes	
12. March–April, Stolac	131	43	No	2 to 7 German wounded exchanged for medical supplies
13. Early September, Posušje	38–49	10	Yes	Exchange conducted by the Supreme HQ; 22 Home Guards released with Germans

1943

Date and Place	No. of captured Partisans involved	No. of captured Germans involved	Success	Comments
14. Late February, Bjelovar	13	2	No	German prisoners escaped
15. Late March, Konjic	17	27	Yes	Exchange conducted by the Supreme HQ
16. Mid-April, Daruvar	4	1	Yes	
17. Mid-May, Foča	3	3	No	Partisans released; German prisoners refused to go back
18. Mid-May, Okučani	?	3	No	
19. Late August–early September, Ruma	63	23–30	Yes	
20. Early September, Northern Croatia	10	7	?	
21. Mid-September, Kobarid	56	?		Hostages released in exchange for the cessation of Partisan attacks on lines of communication
22. Late September, Western Bosnia	?	13	?	
23. Late October, Northern Croatia	2	2	?	

Date and Place	No. of captured Partisans involved	No. of captured Germans involved	Success	Comments
24. Mid-October, Danilovgrad	1	1	Yes	
25. November, Struga	25	13–18	No	
26. Late November–early December, Eastern Herzegovina	?	1	No	German prisoner shot

1944

Date and Place	No. of captured Partisans involved	No. of captured Germans involved	Success	Comments
27. January, Ogulin	8–16	3	?	Not known if the exchange took place
28. January–February, Šibenik	3	?	?	Not known if the exchange took place
29. Mid-February, Pljevlja	?	1	No	German soldier died of wounds before the exchange could be arranged
30. February–March, Korčula	13	13	No	5 German prisoners retrieved by force
31. February–March, Sinj	2	3	Yes	
32. Mid-March, Celje	10	2	No	Partisans offered 2 civilians; Germans refused to trade them for fighters
33. Late March, Eastern Bosnia	?	1	?	Not known if the exchange took place
34. Late March, Northern Bosnia	15	1	No	Partisan offer refused; German prisoner shot
35. Early June, Celje	?	2	No	2 *gendarmes* were defectors and Germans wanted to exchange them back
36. Mid-June, Bosanski Novi	?	4	Yes	
37. June–September, Stolac	15	10	Yes	Altogether 4 successful exchanges; another exchange planned for early September (2 Germans for 8 Partisans), but failed

Date and Place	No. of captured Partisans involved	No. of captured Germans involved	Success	Comments
38. Late July, Podgorica	?	?	No	Unknown number of prisoners involved
39. Early August, Dalmatia	17	17	Yes	
40. Mid-August, Vodice	1	1	Yes	
41. August, Trieste-Gorizia	1	1	No	Captured Partisan executed in 1945
42. Late August, Korčula	6–19	13	No	
43. Late August, Vrlika	?	11	Yes	
44. Mid-September, Drniš	3	3	Yes	
45. Early September, Tuzla	?	1	No	Negotiations failed; German prisoner shot
46. September, Derventa	?	26	Yes	26 Red Cross nurses for an unknown number of Partisans
47. Mid-October, Prilep	?	145	No	Exchange offered, but not completed
48. Late October, Imotski	23	23	Yes	
49. October–November, Ljubuški	11	12	Yes	
50. Early November, Skopje	100	93	Yes	
51. Mid-November, Trieste	?	1	No	Captured collaborator shot
52. Late November, Nevesinje	14	14	Yes	

1945

Date and Place	No. of captured Partisans involved	No. of captured Germans involved	Success	Comments
53. March, Vitez	?	?	No	German Colonel Eberlein and some other prisoners offered in exchange for an unknown number of Partisans; exchange did not take place
54. Early May, Dolenjska	?	1	No	OT-General Konrad von Heidenreich died before the exchange could be made

Altogether 58 attempted prisoner exchanges: 23 successful, 27 unsuccessful, outcome of
7 unknown, 1 special case (Kobarid).
Approximate number of captured Yugoslavs involved: 900
Approximate number of captured Germans involved: 600
Approximate number of exchanged Yugoslavs: 400
Approximate number of exchanged Germans: 300
Note: Lower estimate; where precise figures are not known, it is assumed that the prisoners
were exchanged one-for-one; the list contains data only on cases of prisoner exchange
mentioned in the present work and it is almost certainly not complete.

Appendix B

Prisoner Exchanges in Pisarovina

1943

Date	No. of Partisan prisoners exchanged	No. of German prisoners exchanged	Comments
1. 30 October	60	16	11 Home Guards
2. Late November	47	?	
3. 12 December	32	?	

1944

Date	No. of Partisan prisoners exchanged	No. of German prisoners exchanged	Comments
4. 18 January	60	44	16 *Ustashe*
5. 21 January	30	147 ethnic German laborers	Delivered on receipt:
6. 10 March	57		8 German soldiers in late January;
7. 15 March	15		
8. 25 March	21		27 German soldiers in late March
9. 7 April	5	20	41 Home Guards
10. 15 April	32		
11. 25 April	32		
12. 27 April	23	?	

Date	No. of Partisan prisoners exchanged	No. of German prisoners exchanged	Comments
13. 6 July 14. 14 August 15. 30 September 16. 12 October	37 10 82 24	164 German soldiers[1] (probably including two deliveries on receipt around Ogulin and by Moslavina Detachment)	24 Home Guards 2 *Ustashe*
17. 15 November	184	?	30 German soldiers delivered on receipt around Ogulin
18. 20 November	79	?	26–36 Axis soldiers delivered on receipt in Moslavina (late 1944; precise date unknown)
19. 4 December	32	?	
20. 20 December	39	?	8 German officers from Knin probably included

1945[2]

Date	No. of Partisan prisoners exchanged	No. of German prisoners exchanged Comments
21. 17 January	36	78
22. 26 January	?	16
23. 25 February	?	41
24. 1 March	87–90	?
25. 12 March	40	26
26. 26 March	40	35
27. 29 March	30	7

---

[1] According to Ambassador Kasche (NARA, T-311, Roll 194, 000440, Memorandum on duty travel to Zagreb on 13 October 1944, 14 October 1944), who stated that 164 soldiers had been exchanged "in the recent time." One assumes this refers to the period from the resumption of exchange in early July until mid-October.

[2] According to Boris Bakrač (Bakrač, *Razmjena zarobljenika*, p. 849), there were altogether eleven prisoner exchanges in Pisarovina from 15 January to 29 March 1945. I was able to trace only seven.

| 28. | 11 April | ? | 53 | Additional 5 German soldiers delivered on receipt by Moslavina Detachment |
| 29. | 28 April | 16–18 | 54 | |

Number of prisoners exchanged: Partisans = 1,150–1,155; Germans = 779.[3]

For comparison: The 2nd Panzer Army had between 4,674 and 6,677 MIA from January to November 1944.[4] The overall number of MIAs in the Balkans (including Greece and Albania) for the period 22 June 1941 to 20 April 1945 is estimated at 23,976.[5]

---

[3] Sum of the figures provided in the table; the actual number is certainly higher, given that we have only incomplete information for nine exchanges. Willibald Nemetschek estimated that the grand total of exchangees, both sides included, was 2,000. KAW, B/67:145, Interview with Willibald Nemetschek conducted by Peter Broucek (10 September 1981).

[4] NARA, T-311, Roll 195, 001029, Summary of losses in area of responsibility of Commander-in-Chief Southeast (14 January 1945); the higher figure represents the sum of ten-day casualty returns of the Chief Army Surgeon (*Heeresarzt*), originally retrieved from: http://ww2stats.com (Note: Although this website is no longer available, the author has the relevant pages archived on a storage device.)

[5] NARA, T-78, Roll 414, 6383191, Losses of Field Army incurred through enemy action from 22 June 1941 to 20 April 1945 (25 April 1945). Yugoslav historiography was conspicuously silent on the overall number of missing the NOVJ had during the four years of war. Authors usually cited the official figures for killed (305,000) and wounded (425,000), but failed (or chose not) to mention the number of missing persons. The probable reason is that the Partisans did not always prefer to fight to the death, and that the NOVJ was plagued by desertion and defection, especially from early 1944 onward. Vlado Strugar mentioned in his one-volume history of the war that, in addition to members of the Yugoslav royal army and civilian laborers, some 34,000 "Patriots" (presumably Partisans and their sympathizers) waited for repatriation from Germany in mid-1945. Vlado Strugar, *Der jugoslawische Volksbefreiungskrieg 1941 bis 1945* (Berlin: Deutscher Militärverlag, 1969), p. 300.

Appendix C
Dramatis Personae

Bakrač, Boris (25 March 1912, Slavonska Požega – 29 November 1989, Zagreb)

Bakrač became an engineer in 1936 and a full-fledged member of the KPJ in 1942. In March 1944, he was made the chief NOVJ envoy to Pisarovina and remained in this post until May 1945. He made twenty-five visits to Zagreb and had fifteen additional meetings with German representatives elsewhere. He developed very close, even friendly, relations with his counterparts, which were essential for the smooth running of the prisoner exchange cartel. In the immediate post-war period, Bakrač joined the ministry of construction and after 1960 had a successful career as a member of the International Olympic Committee.

Brnčić, Josip (1914, Fužine – ?)

Brnčić was a KPJ veteran, taking part in illegal activities since 1932. In late 1943, he was serving as an intelligence officer with the Main HQ of Croatia, and in January 1944 he was chosen to be Stilinović's successor as the NOVJ plenipotentiary in Zagreb and Pisarovina. He oversaw the functioning of the neutral zone in its first three months. Brnčić took a personal interest in prisoner exchange since his brother was held in *Ustashe* custody. His exchange in March 1944 coincided approximately with the appointment of Brnčić to the post of chief intelligence officer with the 10th NOVJ Corps, which led many to believe that the release of his brother was the main reason behind his involvement with the exchange cartel. After the war, he had a career in the judiciary, serving as the public prosecutor, president of the Croatian Supreme Court, and as Yugoslav minister of justice.

Broz, Josip (7 May 1892, Kumrovec – 4 May 1980, Belgrade)

Tito was born a peasant in the Croatian province of Zagorje. He traveled widely for a person of his social background. He had a variety of jobs before settling on being a full-time revolutionary in the mid-1920s. In 1940, after a long period of intra-party struggle, he was made Secretary-General of the KPJ. He took a keen interest in the contacts with the Germans, which he saw as an opportunity for gaining political recognition of the Partisan movement. He made a serious error of judgment by offering a cease-fire to the Germans in March and April 1943. Although he later denied responsibility for the statements made by his envoys, there is no doubt that he was the main architect of the March Negotiations. After Moscow reprimanded him sternly for making overtures to the Germans, Tito deemed it prudent to stay out of the limelight; from mid-1943, the Main HQ for Croatia would be solely responsible for maintaining contact with the German authorities in Zagreb. The dominant features of Tito's attitude to the whole question of POWs were pragmatism and self-interest—if sparing German prisoners would help release worthy Party members or improve relations with Western Allies, he would see that his orders on humane treatment of captives were followed. After he had secured the KPJ's hold on power and Soviet backing in late 1944, his interest in the fate of prisoners faded. He was the undisputed ruler of socialist Yugoslavia until his death in 1980.

Glaise-Horstenau, Edmund (27 February 1882, Braunau am Inn – 20 July 1946, Langwasser)

Glaise-Horstenau was an Austrian officer, politician, and member of the Nazi Party. He welcomed the first contacts with the Partisans in the summer of 1942 for both political and military reasons. As an opponent of the *Ustashe* regime, he was keen on exploring the possibility of change in the political landscape of the country: non-Communist Partisans would be allowed to join the process if they repudiated the Yugoslav idea and ceased their struggle against the Axis. In the end, neither he nor any other high-ranking German officer in Yugoslavia found the courage to press for the removal of Pavelić with sufficient vigor. In more practical terms, Glaise-Horstenau viewed the prisoner exchange contacts as a useful tool for intelligence gathering and "feeling the pulse" of Partisan leadership. He used his considerable charm and numerous connections to "legalize" prisoner exchange and make it acceptable to Berlin even before it became officially sanctioned in early 1944. His successors as Plenipotentiary German General in Croatia did not take any deeper interest in prisoner exchange or back-channel diplomacy, fearing perhaps that they would not be able to master the intricacies as well as Glaise-Horstenau. He committed suicide while in American custody in 1946.

Kasche, Siegfried (18 June 1903, Strausberg/Berlin – 19 June 1947, Zagreb)

Kasche joined the Nazi Party in 1926 and barely escaped being executed along with other SA leaders during the "Night of the Long Knives." He was appointed ambassador to the NDH in mid-April 1941 and soon turned into a vociferous supporter of the *Ustashe* regime. By mid-1942, however, not even Kasche could deny that some sort of internal reform was necessary if the state was to survive. Kasche therefore welcomed the establishment of first contacts with the Supreme HQ in August 1942, and lobbied for the continuation of talks with Đilas and Velebit in early spring of 1943. He sincerely believed that the Partisans were on the verge of changing sides and that their movement could be split from within and thus neutralized through a sustained diplomatic effort. Undeterred by the deteriorating situation in the country and the fact that Tito had obviously no intention of leaving the anti-fascist alliance, Kasche remained committed to his agenda until the end of the war. The ambassador tried to portray his activities in the best possible light during his trial in Zagreb in 1947. He claimed that his efforts were aimed at easing the suffering of civilians and soldiers on both sides. He often repeated that he aided the Partisan movement through medical shipments. Kasche even requested that Velebit, Stilinović, and Koča Popović appear as defense witnesses, which they declined. Kasche was found guilty and hanged after the trial.

Nemetschek (alternatively Nemecek or Nemeček), Willibald (26 August 1916, Zagreb – ?)

Nemetschek was born to an ethnic German family from Zagreb. He was called up for service with the *Wehrmacht* in 1940, returning to Croatia in May 1941 to serve as an interpreter with Glaise-Horstenau's staff. In the summer of 1943, he began playing an active part in prisoner exchange negotiations and by 1944 he had become the chief "technical" envoy tasked with overseeing the day-to-day exchange operations. In this capacity, he did many favors for the Partisans, such as affecting the release of their relatives and friends, carrying post and various other items from Zagreb to Pisarovina, etc. In exchange, Bakrač provided him with a letter of protection that enabled Nemetschek to stay in the country after the German capitulation. The Partisan envoy also managed to secure a job for him in a state-owned construction firm. Nemetschek's ordeal began in 1948 after the fall of Andrija Hebrang. He was arrested and interrogated by the Yugoslav secret police who planned to use him as a witness against Hebrang. Nemetschek's wife was told that he had gone to Germany with another woman, when in fact he had been sentenced to eight years in prison. He was released on parole in 1954, but was not allowed to emigrate. As the authorities wanted to force him into accepting Yugoslav citizenship, he escaped to Austria in 1972.

Ott, Hans (8 November 1892, Brühl/Rhein – ?)

A decorated veteran of the First World War, Hans Ott had a degree in mining engineering. His job took him on numerous field trips during the 1930s, including the

Dutch East Indies and Brazil. As an employee of the Hansa Leichtmetall company, he arrived in Yugoslavia in September 1941. The idea of a direct prisoner exchange between the Supreme HQ and the German authorities in Zagreb originated with him in the aftermath of his capture in Livno in August 1942. A man of undeniable charisma, he soon won the confidence not only of Glaise-Horstenau and Kasche, but also, to a certain extent, of the Partisans. From then until late 1943, he served as the main German negotiator in the talks with the Partisans. At the same time, he was an agent of the *Abwehr* and a source of reliable intelligence on the Partisan movement. He returned to Pisarovina in July 1944 as Ambassador Kasche's envoy, and had talks with Andrija Hebrang on various political issues. He was wounded in January 1945 while making a trip to the neutral zone, and remained in hospital for several weeks. Seeing that the war was lost, he tried to curry favor with the victors by supplying them with intelligence on German troop movements and other information of interest. On 9 May 1945, he contacted some Partisan units near Dravograd/Unterdrauburg by using the letter of safe conduct which had been previously issued to him. He remained there until 13 July; on 17 July he was transferred to a prison in Zagreb. The exact date and place of his death are not known; Willibald Nemetschek last saw him in 1948 during the investigation of the Hebrang case. Milovan Đilas wrote in his memoirs that Ott was "hauled back" to Yugoslavia by the secret police, and that he stayed in prison "until his sad end," answering questions about the existence of a German mole in the Supreme HQ during the war.

Peternell, Eduard (23 October 1901, Otočac – 2 May 1944, south of Zagreb)

Eduard Peternell was the only envoy on either side who died while on duty in the neutral zone. He was born to Austrian parents in Otočac, Croatia, where his father served as an officer in the army of the Dual Monarchy. Peternell spent the interwar period in Zagreb working as an electrician. According to Willibald Nemetschek, he served as a guard in the concentration camp for Jewish women and children in Loborgrad north of Zagreb (the camp existed from September 1941 to October 1942 and was run by members of the ethnic German organization in the NDH). According to Peternell's family, he did not serve as a guard but as a supply official; troubled by what he saw, he helped the inmates by providing them with food and water whenever he could. The details on his service in the Organization Todt or on his connections to the SD are unknown. The transfer to Glaise-Horstenau's negotiating detail apparently brought relief to Peternell, but not to his wife. His frequent absences from home were a constant source of friction caused by the fear that their six children would be left without support in case something happened to him. Unfortunately for historians, his wife gave all of Peternell's documents, letters, and photographs to an unknown person after his death.

Pott, Eugen von (17 October 1893 – ?)

Eugen von Pott was a junior Austro-Hungarian officer and the son of Glaise-Horstenau's fellow officer and friend, Emil von Pott. For several years he was a clerk with the Zagreb subsidiary of the Wiener Bankverein. When the office of the plenipotentiary general was established in Zagreb in April 1941, he was transferred to Glaise-Horstenau's staff. In his capacity as the chief intelligence officer, von Pott was involved with the negotiations from the very beginning. By late 1943, he was in overall charge of the prisoner exchange. He did not travel much to Pisarovina, preferring to work from his office in Zagreb. Von Pott was on good terms with Stilinović, but kept Bakrač at arm's length. He left the city with Glaise-Horstenau in October 1944 and moved to Linz. In February 1949, the Yugoslav secret police kidnapped him and brought him to Yugoslavia with the intent of using him as a witness against Hebrang. His fate is still unknown.

Stilinović, Marijan (27 November 1904, Sveta Nedelja by Samobor – 6 December 1959, Zadar)

Stilinović joined the Communist Youth in 1920. He spent the years 1929 to 1932 and 1933 to 1941 in prison. After he and a large group of Communists escaped from prison in Sremska Mitrovica in the summer of 1941, he was assigned to the Supreme HQ's Agitprop (agitation and propaganda) section. One year later he was chosen to accompany Ott to Zagreb, to arrange the exchange of the Germans captured at Livno. According to his superiors, "he sometimes lacks the necessary severity . . . he works independently, but hesitates when it comes to making decisions on his own." However, Stilinović was flexible enough to be employed as a negotiator, and he could be relied upon to consult his superiors before making commitments. A German official commented that Stilinović knew just enough German so that one could converse with him and, "although a dedicated follower of Tito, he is forthcoming, deals with matters one at a time, and is never too rigid in defending his own point of view." He spent the second half of 1943 in Zagreb, negotiating the prisoner exchange cartel with Glaise-Horstenau and his staff. Once the agreement was reached, he was transferred to other duties. Like his colleague Hans Ott, Stilinović was a troubleshooter who kept coming back to the negotiating table whenever needed. His war diary is an important source of information on the first exchange in 1942. His plan to broaden his memoirs to include the contacts from 1943 onwards was thwarted by his premature death in 1959.

Velebit, Vladimir (19 August 1907, Zadar – 29 August 2004, Zagreb)

Vladimir Velebit, a lawyer by profession, was from an esteemed Zagreb military family. In 1939, he was accepted into the Communist Party after having successfully performed a number of clandestine, high-risk missions. In the summer of 1942, he was involved in the exchange proceedings due to his knowledge of German, but it soon became clear that he had diplomatic skills as well. In November of 1942, he led a Partisan delegation during the inconclusive negotiations in Livno. During the March Negotiations he replaced Đilas as the chief Partisan envoy, and helped free his pre-war acquaintance, Tito's wife, Herta Haas. From mid-1943 until the end of the war, Velebit served as Tito's liaison officer to various Allied commands, both at home and abroad. Although he did not take part in the negotiations with the German authorities after May 1943, they requested his mediation on at least two occasions in 1944 and 1945. In the early 1950s, he served as the ambassador to Rome and London, and from 1960 to 1967 he worked for the United Nations.

Selected Bibliography

A Treatise on the Juridical Basis of the Distinction Between Lawful Combatant and Unprivileged Belligerent (Charlottesville, VA: Judge Advocate General's School, 1959).

Aitken, Robert, and Marilyn Aitken, *Law Makers, Law Breakers and Uncommon Trials* (Chicago: American Bar Association, 2007).

Anić, Nikola, "Operacija 'Weiss': Četvrta neprijateljska ofenziva," in A. H. Pape and Nikola Anić (eds.), *Drugi svjetski rat* (Belgrade: Narodna knjiga, 1980), Vol. II, pp. 243–46.

Antonić, Zdravko (ed.), *Zapisi Pere Đukanovića: Ustanak na Drini* (Belgrade: SANU, 1994).

Arsenić, Borko, "Bitka završena u virovima Sane," in *Prva krajiška udarna proleterska brigada: sjećanja boraca* (Prijedor: Skupština opštine, 1981), pp. 393–401.

Atkinson, Rick, *An Army at Dawn: The War in North Africa, 1942–1943*, Volume One of the Liberation Trilogy (New York: Henry Holt, 2002).

Avakumović, Ivan, *Mihailović prema nemačkim dokumentima* (London: Oslobodjenje, 1969).

Bajt, Aleksandar, *Bermanov dosije* (Belgrade: Srpska reč, 2006).

Bakrač, Boris, "Razmjena ratnih zarobljenika i uhapšenika na području Pisarovine," in *Treća godina narodno-oslobodilačkog rata na području Karlovca, Korduna, Like, Pokuplja i Žumberka* (Karlovac: Historijski arhiv u Karlovcu, 1977), pp. 845–63.

Bank, Jan, "Finale u sjevernoj Africi: kraj rata u pustinji," in A. H. Pape and Nikola Anić (eds.), *Drugi svjetski rat* (Belgrade: Narodna knjiga, 1980), Vol. II, pp. 218–27.

Barker, Thomas, *Social Revolutionaries and Secret Agents: The Carinthian Slovene Partisans and Britain's Special Operations Executive* (New York: Columbia University Press, 1990).

Bavec-Branko, Franjo, *Bazoviška brigada* (Ljubljana: Odbor bazoviške brigade, 1970).

Biber, Dušan, "The Yugoslav Partisans and the British in 1944," in William Deakin, Elisabeth Barker, and Jonathan Chadwick (eds.), *British Political and Military Strategy in Central, Eastern and Southern Europe in 1944* (London: Macmillan, 1988), pp. 111–27.

Blagojević, Andrija, "Borbe 4. bataljona od formiranja do početka Pete neprijateljske ofanzive," in *Petnaesta majevička brigada: sjećanja i članci* (Belgrade: Vojnoizdavački zavod, 1979), pp. 170–74.

Blečić, Vujadin, "Oko Leskovca 1941. godine," in *Ustanak naroda Jugoslavije 1941: Zbornik sjećanja* (Belgrade: Vojno delo, 1964), Vol. V, pp. 815–21.

Böhme, Karl W., *Die deutschen Kriegsgefangenen in Jugoslawien* (Munich: Verlag Ernst und Werner Gieseking, 1962), Vol. I/1.

Bojić, Milosav, *Posavski partizanski odred: Posavina i Tamnava u oružanom ustanku* (Belgrade: Vojnoizdavački i novinski centar, 1987).

Borković, Milan, *Kvislinška uprava u Srbiji 1941–1944* (Belgrade: Sloboda, 1979), Vol. I.

Bošnjak, Ljubomir, *Diverzantska dejstva u narodnooslobodilačkom ratu 1941.–1945.* (Belgrade: Vojnoistorijski institut, 1983).

Bottlenberg-Landsberg, Maria Theodora von dem, *Karl Ludwig Freiherr von und zu Guttenberg: 1902–1945: ein Lebensbild* (Berlin: Lukas Verlag, 2003).

Božović, Luka, "Omladinci na Balinovcu," in *Treći kragujevački bataljon Prve proleterske brigade: sećanja boraca* (Kragujevac: Svetlost, 1974), Vol. II, pp. 153–61.

Božić, Nikola, *Rovovi i mostobrani: Osma vojvođanska udarna brigada* (Novi Sad: Institut za istoriju, 1989).

Božović, Srđan, *Nemački zločin u Alibunaru 1941.* (Pančevo: Zavičajni muzej Pančevo, 2004).

Brašanac, Vojin, "Kroz Užičku republiku od Kragujevca do Prijepolja," in *Užička republika: Zbornik sećanja* (Užice: Narodni muzej-Muzej ustanka 1941, 1981), Vol. I, pp. 398–402.

Brunović, Milan, and Tomo Sović, *Bitka kod Oborova* (Zagreb: Udruženje boraca NOR općine Dugo Selo, 1965).

Bryden, John, *Fighting to Lose: How the German Secret Intelligence Service Helped the Allies Win the Second World War* (Toronto: Dundurn, 2014).

Buturović, Ferid, *Kuća mostarskog kadije: sjećanja mostarskog skojevca, ilegalca i partizana* (Sarajevo: Ferid Buturović-SUBNOR Sarajevo, 2015).

Casagrande, Thomas, *Die Volksdeutsche SS-Division "Prinz Eugen": die Banater Schwaben und die nazionalsozialistichen Kriegsverbrechen* (Frankfurt: Campus Verlag, 2003).

Churchill, Winston S., *The Second World War* (Boston: Houghton Mifflin, 1985), Vols. IV and VI.

Čaušević, Izudin, *Osma krajiška NOU brigada* (Belgrade: Vojnoizdavački zavod, 1981).

Čolaković, Rodoljub, *Zapisi iz oslobodilačkog rata* (Sarajevo: Oslobođenje, 1985–86), Vol. II.

Ćurguz, Dragutin, and Milorad Vignjević, *Drugi krajiški narodnooslobodilački (Kozarski) partizanski odred "Mladen Stojanović": izdano povodom 40-godišnjice kozarske epopeje* (Prijedor: Nacionalni park Kozara, 1982).

Cvetković, Žarko, "Evakuacija i lečenje ranjenika i bolesnika u NOR-u," in *Sanitetska služba u Narodnooslobodilačkom ratu Jugoslavije 1941–1945: iskustva sanitetske službe NOV i POJ (JA) iz četverogodišnjeg narodnooslobodilačkog rata 1941–1945* (Belgrade: Vojnoizdavački i novinski centar, 1989), Vol. IV, pp. 9–93.

Deakin, F. W. D., *Bojovna planina* (Belgrade: Nolit, 1973).

Dedijer, Vladimir, *Novi prilozi za biografiju Josipa Broza Tita* (Rijeka: Liburnija, 1981), Vols. I and II.

Demić-Pihler, Borka, "Poslednji čaj za ranjenike," in *Užička republika: Zbornik sećanja* (Užice: Narodni muzej-Muzej ustanka 1941, 1981), Vol. I, pp. 612–14.

Dimitrijevski, Marjan, *Politikata na Tretiot Rajh kon Makedonija 1933–1945* (Skopje: Institut za nacionalna istorija, 2001).

Djilas, Milovan, *Wartime* (New York: Harcourt Brace Jovanovich, 1977).

Druga dalmatinska proleterska brigada (Split: Institut za historiju radničkog pokreta Dalmacije, 1982).

Đuković, Isidor, *Trideset prva srpska NOU brigada* (Belgrade: Vojnoizdavački i novinski centar, 1987).

Đuković, Isidor, *Austro-ugarski ratni zarobljenici u Srbiji 1914–1915* (Belgrade: IP Signature, 2008).

Đurašinović, Vojin Kostja, "Partizanska država," in *Užička republika: Zbornik sećanja* (Užice: Narodni muzej-Muzej ustanka 1941, 1981), Vol. I, pp. 214–27.

Đuretić, Veselin, *Saveznici i jugoslovenska ratna drama* (Belgrade: Veselin Đuretić, 1988).

Đurić, Živka, "Takovski bataljon u borbama oko Gornjeg Milanovca," in *Užička republika: Zbornik sećanja* (Užice: Narodni muzej-Muzej ustanka 1941, 1981), Vol. I, pp. 433–36.

Dželebdžić, Milovan, *Obaveštajna služba u NOR-u* (Belgrade: Vojnoistorijski institut, 1987).

Em, Hans, "Razmena na zarobenici: migovi što se pametat," in *Dokumenti i materijali za osloboduvanjeto na Skopje, oktomvri-19 noemvri 1944* (Skopje: Istoriski arhiv, 1968), pp. 25–26.

Fajdiga, Mirko, *Bračičeva brigada na Štajerskem, Koroškem, in Gorenjskem* (Maribor: Založba Obzorja, 1994), Vol. II.

Faroqhi, Suraiya, *The Ottoman Empire and the World Around It* (London: I. B. Tauris, 2006).

Ford, Kirk, Jr., *OSS and the Yugoslav Resistance, 1943–1945* (College Station: Texas A&M University Press, 1992).

Freudiger, Kerstin, *Die juristische Aufarbeitung von NS-Verbrechen* (Tübingen: Mohr Siebeck, 2002).

Frey, Max, "Der Kampf bei Zagvozd und meine Gefangennahme," in Otto Weingartner (ed.), *Erinnerungen an die 118. Jäger-Division (frühere 718. Inf.Div.)* (Klagenfurt: self-published, 1982), pp. 274–75.

Frka, Danijel, Josip Novak, and Siniša Pogačić, *Zrakoplovstvo Nezavisne države Hrvatske 1941.–1945.* (Zagreb: P. C. Grafičke usluge, 1998).

Galić, Jure, *Vrijeme i ljudi: svjedočenje* (Sarajevo: Svjetlostkomerc d.d., 2005).

Glišić, Venceslav, *Teror i zločini nacističke Nemačke u Srbiji 1941.–1944.* (Belgrade: Izdavačko preduzeće "Rad," 1970).

Glišić, Venceslav, *Užička republika* (Belgrade: Nolit, 1989).

Gordić, Miloš, "Čuvao sam nemačke zarobljenike," in *Užička republika: Zbornik sećanja* (Užice: Narodni muzej-Muzej ustanka 1941, 1981), Vol. II, pp. 486–89.

Grimm, Steffen, *Die SS-Totenkopfverbände im Konzentrationslager Buchenwald* (Hamburg: Diplomica Verlag, 2011).

Gumz, Jonathan E., *The Resurrection and Collapse of Empire in Habsburg Serbia, 1914–1918* (Cambridge: Cambridge University Press, 2009).

Güther, Willhelm, "Wir und die Insel Hvar," in Otto Weingartner (ed.), *Erinnerungen an die 118. Jäger-Division (frühere 718. Inf.Div.)* (Klagenfurt: self-published, 1982), pp. 242–51.

Haberl, Othmar Nikola, *Die Emanzipation der KP Jugoslawiens von der Kontrolle der Komintern/KPdSU, 1941–1945* (Munich: Oldenbourg Verlag, 1974).

Hall, Richard C., *The Balkan Wars, 1912–1913: Prelude to the First World War* (New York: Routledge, 2002).

Hnilicka, Karl, *Das Ende auf dem Balkan 1944/5: Die militärische Räumung Jugoslawiens durch die deutsche Wehrmacht* (Göttingen: Musterschmidt Verlag, 1970).

Hoptner, Jacob B., *Yugoslavia in Crisis, 1934–1941* (New York: Columbia University Press, 1962).

Hronologija Narodnooslobodilačkog rata 1941.–1945. (Belgrade: Vojno istorijski institut, 1964).

Hurem, Rasim, *Kriza NOP-a u Bosni i Hercegovini krajem 1941. i početkom 1942.* (Sarajevo: Svjetlost, 1972).

Ignjatić, Mirko, "Političko-vaspitni rad u brigadi," in *Četrnaesta hercegovačka omladinska NOU brigada* (Belgrade: Vojno izdavački zavod, 1988), pp. 165–81.

Ivanović, Miladin, *23. srpska divizija* (Belgrade: Republički odbor SUBNOR, 1994).

Karanović, Vukašin, *Moslavački partizanski odred 1941.-1945.* (Kutina: Skupština općine Kutina i Općinski odbor SUBNOR-a Kutina, 1981).

Karanović, Vukašin, *Treći diverzantski odred 1941.-1945.* (Ivanić-grad: Municipality of Ivanić-grad, 1984).

Karasijević, Drago, *Peti korpus NOVJ* (Belgrade: Vojnoizdavački zavod, 1985).

Karasijević, Drago, *Četvrta krajiška NOU divizija* (Belgrade: Vojnoizdavački i novinski centar, 1988).

Kazimirović, Vasa, *NDH u svetlu nemačkih dokumenata i dnevnika Gleza fon Horstenau 1941.-1944.* (Belgrade: Nova knjiga, 1987).

Kazimirović, Vasa, *Nemački general u Zagrebu* (Kragujevac: Prizma, 1996).

Klajn, Lajco, *The Past in Present Times: The Yugoslav Saga* (Lanham, MD: University Press of America, 2007).

Komnenović, Danilo, and Muharem Kreso, *Dvadeset deveta hercegovačka divizija* (Belgrade: Vojnoizdavački zavod, 1979).

Koprivnica, Momir, "Prva akcija u Mokrom i borba sa Nijemcima na Romaniji," in *Sarajevo u revoluciji* (Sarajevo: Svjetlost, 1977), Vol. II, pp. 409–12.

Korać, Dušan, *Kordun i Banija u Narodnooslobodilačkoj borbi i socijalističkoj revoluciji* (Zagreb: Školska knjiga, 1986).

Košutić, Ivan, *Hrvatsko domobranstvo u Drugom svjetskom ratu* (Zagreb: Matica Hrvatska, 1992).

Kovačević, Radivoje, *Sjeveroistočna Bosna 1944–1945: prilog istoriografiji* (Brčko: Savez udruženja boraca NOR-a Brčko Distrikta BiH, 2002).

Kovačević, Veljko, *Ratna sjećanja* (Belgrade: Vojnoizdavački i novinski centar, 1989).

Krabbe, Oluf, *Danske soldater i kamp på Østfronten 1941–1945* (Odense: Odense Universitetsforlag, 1976).

Kregar, Tone, *Vigred se povrne: Druga svetovna vojna na Celjskem* (Celje: Muzej novejše zgodovine, 2009).

Krstić, Dobrivoje, "Moj drugi život," in *Četvrta sandžačka NOU brigada* (Belgrade: Vojnoizdavački i novinski centar, 1986), pp. 362–65.

Kučan,Viktor, *Borci Sutjeske* (Belgrade: Zavod za udžbenike i nastavna sredstva, 1996).

Kumm, Otto, *Vorwärts, Prinz Eugen! Geschichte der 7. SS-Freiwilligen-Division "Prinz Eugen"* (Dresden: Winkelried Verlag, 2007).

Kušec, Vjera, "Razmjenom do slobode," in *Sarajevo u revoluciji* (Sarajevo: Svjetlost, 1979), Vol. III, pp. 305–10.

Kübler, Friedrich, *Kosaken mit uns im Kampf gegen Stalin und dem Bolschewismus. Überlebende berichten* (Bad Herrenalb: self-pub., 1982).

Kühnrich, Heinz, and Franz-Karl Hitze, *Deutsche bei Titos Partisanen: Kriegsschicksale auf dem Balkan in Augenzeugenberichten und Dokumenten* (Schkeuditz: GNN Verlag, 1997).

Labović, Đurica, and Milan Basta, *Partizani za pregovaračkim stolom 1941.-1945.* (Zagreb: Naprijed, 1986).

László Rajk and His Accomplices Before the People's Court (Budapest: Budapest Printing Press, 1949).

Latifić, Safet, "Bilo nas je petorica," in *Sutjeska: Zbornik radova* (Belgrade: Vojnoizdavački zavod "Vojno delo," 1959), Vol. III, pp. 259–67.

Leković, Mišo, *Ofanziva proleterskih brigada u leto 1942* (Belgrade: Vojnoistorijski institut, 1965).

Leković, Mišo, *Martovski pregovori 1943.* (Belgrade: Narodna knjiga, 1985).

Lepre, George, *Himmler's Bosnian Division: The Waffen-SS Handschar Division, 1943–1945* (Atlglen, PA: Schiffer, 1997).

Lieb, Peter, *Konventioneller Krieg oder NS-Weltanschauungskrieg? Kriegführung und Partisanenbekämpfung in Frankreich 1943/44* (Munich: Oldenbourg Wissenschaftsverlag, 2007).

Lindsay, Franklin, *Beacons in the Night: With the OSS and Tito's Partisans in Wartime Yugoslavia* (Stanford: Stanford University Press, 1993).

McConville, Michael, *A Small War in the Balkans: British Military Involvement in Wartime Yugoslavia, 1941–1945* (London: Macmillan, 1986).

Maclean, Fitzroy, *Eastern Approaches* (London: Jonathan Cape, 1949).

Manoschek, Walter, *Serbien ist Judenfrei: Militärische Besatzungspolitik und Vernichtung der Juden in Serbien* (Munich: Oldenbourg Verlag, 1995).

Marjanović, Jovan, *Draža Mihailović između Nemaca i Britanaca* (Zagreb: Globus, 1979).

Marjanović, Miladin-Ujko, "Nemci su ranjenike streljali dum-dum mecima," in *Užička republika: Zbornik sećanja* (Užice: Narodni muzej-Muzej ustanka 1941, 1981), Vol. II, pp. 654–58.

Martinović, Ratko, *Od Ravne Gore do Vrhovnog Štaba* (Belgrade: Rad, 1979).

Meyer, Hermann Frank, *Von Wien nach Kalavryta: die blutige Spur der 117. Jäger-Division durch Serbien und Griechenland* (Möhnesee: Bibliopolis, 2002).

Milidragović, Petar, "Pobjeda na Badrljačama," in *Hercegovina u NOB-u* (Mostar: Istorijski arhiv Hercegovine, 1986), Vol. IV, pp. 124–39.

Miličević, Žarko, *Kalnički partizanski odred* (Varaždin: TIVA, 2010).

Milinović, Đuro, and Dragan Karasijević, *Jedanaesta krajiška NOU brigada* (Bosanska Gradiška: SUBNOR, 1982).

Minisini, G., "Die erschüternde Bilanz," in Otto Weingartner (ed.), *Erinnerungen an die 118. Jäger-Division (frühere 718. Inf.Div.)* (Klagenfurt: self-published, 1982), pp. 238–39.

Mitrović, Dojčilo, *Srbija u Narodnooslobodilačkoj borbi: Zapadna Srbija* (Belgrade: Nolit, 1975).

Mitrović, Mitra, "Crno-Belo," in *Užička republika: Zbornik sećanja* (Užice: Narodni muzej-Muzej ustanka 1941, 1981), Vol. I, pp. 352–58.

Mitrovski, Bora, *Petnaesti (makedonski) udarni korpus NOVJ* (Belgrade: Vojno izdavački zavod, 1983).

Momčilović, Đorđe, *Kako do brigade: Trinaesta vojvođanska udarna brigada* (Kikinda: Odbor za negovanje tradicija Trinaeste vojvođanske udarne brigade, 1979).

Müller, Rolf-Dieter, and Gerd R. Ueberschär, *Hitler's War in the East, 1941–1945: A Critical Assessment* (New York: Berghahn Books, 2008).

Narodni heroji Jugoslavije (Belgrade: Mladost, 1975).

Naša Prva dalmatinska 1942.–1945. (Split: Slobodna Dalmacija, 1982), Vol. II.

Neff, Stephen C., "Prisoners of War in International Law: The Nineteenth Century," in Sibylle Scheipers (ed.), *Prisoners in War* (Oxford: Oxford University Press, 2010), pp. 57–73.

Nemačka obaveštajna služba (Belgrade: Savezni sekretarijat unutrašnjih poslova, 1959), Vols. V, VI, VIII, IX.

Nenadović, Aleksandar, *Razgovori s Kočom* (Globus: Zagreb, 1989).

Neretva: proleterske i udarne divizije u bici na Neretvi (Belgrade: Vojnoizdavački zavod, 1965), Vol. III.

Neubacher, Hermann, *Sonderauftrag Südost 1940–1945: Bericht eines fliegenden Diplomaten* (Göttingen: Musterschmidt Verlag, 1956).

Nađ, Kosta, and Jovo Popović, *Bihaćka republika: Ratne uspomene Koste Nađa* (Zagreb: Spektar, 1982).

Nick, Alfred, "Zaštita ranjenika i bolesnika u narodnooslobodilačkom ratu," in *Sanitetska služba u Narodnooslobodilačkom ratu Jugoslavije 1941–1945: iskustva sanitetske službe NOV i POJ (JA) iz četverogodišnjeg narodnooslobodilačkog rata 1941–1945* (Belgrade: Vojnoizdavački i novinski centar, 1989), Vol. IV, pp. 271–300.

Nikičević, Tamara, *Goli Otoci Jova Kapičića* (Podgorica: n.p., 2010).

Nikoliš, Gojko, *Korijen, stablo, pavetina* (Zagreb: Liber, 1981).

Odić, Slavko, *Neostvareni planovi* (Zagreb: Naprijed, 1961).

Odić, Slavko, and Slavko Komarica, *Noć i magla: Gestapo u Jugoslaviji* (Zagreb: Centar za informacije i publicitet, 1977).

Odić, Slavko, and Slavko Komarica, *Partizanska obavještajna služba 1941–1942: šta se stvarno događalo* (Zagreb: Centar za informacije i publicitet, 1988), Vol. III.

Opća enciklopedija Jugoslovenskog leksikografskog zavoda (Zagreb: JLZ, 1977–82), Vol. I.

Oslobodilački rat naroda Jugoslavije (Belgrade: Vojnoistorijski institut JNA, 1957), Vols. I and II.

Osmić, Hijaz, "U neprijateljskim kandžama," in *Sedamnaesta majevička NOU brigada* (Tuzla: Univerzal, 1980), pp. 352–53.

Pajović, Ljubivoje, Dušan Uzelac, and Milovan Dželebdžić, *Sremski front 1944.–45.* (Belgrade: BIGZ, 1979).

Panić, Radovan, *Treća vojvođanska NOU brigada* (Belgrade: Vojnoizdavački zavod, 1980).

Pantelić, Milojica, Radovan M. Marinković, and Vladimir Nikšić, *Čačanski narodnooslobodilački partizanski odred "Dr. Dragiša Mišović"* (Čačak: Čačanski glas, 1982).

Parmaković, Dragoslav, *Mačvanski partizanski odred* (Šabac: Fond narodnooslobodilačke borbe Podrinja, 1973).

Pavone, Claudio, *A Civil War: A History of the Italian Resistance* (London: Verso Books, 2013).

Pejanović Blagoje, Pop, "Borba za Srnice," in *18. hrvatska istočnobosanska narodnooslobodilačka udarna brigada* (Tuzla: IGTRO "Univerzal," 1988), pp. 478–80.

Penezić, Milan, "Puštanje na slobodu nemačkih zarobljenika u Jablanici," in *Užička republika: Zbornik sećanja* (Užice: Narodni muzej-Muzej ustanka 1941, 1981), Vol. II, pp. 632–33.

Perišić, Ilija, "Prva omladinska brigada NOVJ u Hercegovini i aktivnosti skojevske organizacije," in *Četrnaesta hercegovačka omladinska NOU brigada* (Belgrade: Vojnoizdavački zavod, 1988), pp. 15–36.

Perović, Milivoje, *Srbija u Narodnooslobodilačkoj borbi: Južna Srbija* (Belgrade: Nolit, 1961).

Petelin, Stanko, *Prešernova NOU brigada* (Belgrade: Vojnoizdavački zavod, 1975).

Petersen, Neal H., *From Hitler's Doorstep: The Wartime Intelligence Reports of Allen Dulles, 1942–1945* (University Park: Pennsylvania State University Press, 1996).

Petranović, Branko, *Istorija Jugoslavije 1918.–1988.* (Belgrade: Nolit, 1989), Vol. II.

Petranović, Branko, *Srbija u Drugom svetskom ratu* (Belgrade: Vojnoizdavački i novinski centar, 1992).

Poznanović, Rade, Milun Raonić, and Milorad Radojčić, *Tragom izdaje: svedočenja o izdaji četnika i streljanju na Krušiku, u Valjevu 1941* (Valjevo: Lazar Ninković, 1987).

Primorac, Rudolf, *Operativno-taktička iskustva iz prve polovine narodnooslobodilačkog rata* (Belgrade: Vojnoizdavački i novinski centar, 1986).

Radanović, Milan, *Oslobođenje. Beograd, 20. oktobar 1944.* (Belgrade: Rosa Luxemburg Stiftung, 2014).

Radić, Simo A., "Neprijatelj o porazu na Badrljačama," in *Hercegovina u NOB-u* (Mostar: Istorijski arhiv Hercegovine, 1986), Vol. IV, pp. 140–46.

Radišić Radiša, Dragomir, "U 1. bataljonu 11. krajiške NOU kozarske brigade, od Prijedora do slobode," in *Kozara u Narodnooslobodilačkom ratu: zapisi i sjećanja* (Belgrade: Vojnoizdavački zavod, 1978), Vol. VI, pp. 393–401.

Redžić, Nail, *Telmanovci: Zapisi o njemačkoj partizanskoj četi Ernst Telman* (Belgrade: Narodna armija, 1984).

Rendulic, Lothar, *Gekämpft, gesiegt, geschlagen* (Wels-Heidelberg: Welsermühl, 1952).

Risteski, Stojan, *Partizanskot odred "Slavej": Prilog kon proučavanjeto na Debrca vo NOB, 1941–1944* (Skopje: NIO Studentski zbor, 1990).

Sanitetska služba u Narodnooslobodilačkom ratu Jugoslavije 1941–1945: iskustva sanitetske službe NOV i POJ (JA) iz četverogodišnjeg narodnooslobodilačkog rata 1941–1945 (Belgrade: Vojnoizdavački i novinski centar, 1989), Vol. IV.

Savičević, Lazar, "Pokošeno polje," in *Treći kragujevački bataljon Prve proleterske brigade: sećanja boraca* (Kragujevac: Svetlost, 1974), Vol. II, pp. 139–46.

Savić, Branka, "Sa radio stanicom," in *Užička republika: Zbornik sećanja* (Užice: Narodni muzej-Muzej ustanka 1941, 1981), Vol. II, pp. 494–509.

Senić, Vukašin, Mile Vukalović, Veljko Gerun, and Milosav Kundačina, "Borbena dejstva brigade," in *Četrnaesta hercegovačka omladinska NOU brigada* (Belgrade: Vojnoizdavački zavod, 1988), pp. 37–158.

Schmider, Klaus, *Partisanenkrieg in Jugoslawien 1941–1944* (Hamburg: Mittler, 2002).

Schmider, Klaus, "Auf Umwegen zum Vernichtungskrieg? Der Partisanenkrieg in Jugoslawien, 1941–1944," in Rolf-Dieter Müller and Hans-Erich Volkmann (eds.), *Die Wehrmacht: Mythos und Realität* (Munich: Oldenbourg Verlag, 1999), pp. 910–22.

Schmider, Klaus, "Der jugoslawische Kriegsschauplatz (Januar 1943 bis Mai 1945)," in Karl-Heinz Frieser, *Das Deutsche Reich und der Zweite Weltkrieg* (Munich: Deutsche Verlags-Anstalt, 2007), Vol. VIII, pp. 1009–88.

Schmidt-Richberg, Erich, *Der Endkampf auf dem Balkan: Die Operationen der Heeresgruppe E von Griechenland bis zu den Alpen* (Heidelberg: Kurt Vowinckel Verlag, 1955).

Schraml, Franz, *Kriegsschauplatz Kroatien: die deutsch-kroatischen Legions-Divisionen: 369., 373., 392. Inf.-Div. (kroat.) ihre Ausbildungs- und Ersatzformationen* (Neckargemünd: Kurt Vowinckel Verlag, 1962).

Schreiber, Gerhard, *Die italienischen Militärinternierten im deutschen Machtbereich 1943–1945: Verraten-Verachtet-Vergessen* (Munich: Oldenbourg Verlag, 1990).

Schreiber, Gerhard, "Die Wehrmacht und der Partisanenkrieg in Italien: '. . . auch gegen Frauen und Kinder,'" in Ernst Willi Hansen, Gerhard Schreiber, and Bernd Wegner (eds.), *Politischer Wandel, organisierte Gewalt und nationale Sicherheit: Beiträge* (Munich: Oldenbourg Verlag, 1995), pp. 251–68.

Seferović, Mensur, *Trinaesta hercegovačka NOU brigada* (Belgrade: Vojnoizdavački i novinski centar, 1988).

Shepherd, Ben, *War in the Wild East: The German Army and Soviet Partisans* (Cambridge, MA: Harvard University Press, 2004).

Shepherd, Ben, *Terror in the Balkans: German Armies and Partisan Warfare* (Cambridge, MA: Harvard University Press, 2012).

Sjećanja boraca stolačkog kraja (Stolac: Opštinski odbor SUBNOR-a, 1984).

Škoro, Gojko, "Izbeglice u Kremnima," in *Užička republika: Zbornik sećanja* (Užice: Narodni muzej-Muzej ustanka 1941, 1981), Vol. II, pp. 667–69.

Škoro, Gojko, *Istina je u imenima: Stradali u užičkom okrugu u Drugom svetskom ratu* (Užice: Spomen-obeležje Kadinjača, 2002).

Solunski, Koce, *Apostolski: od raganje do general* (Skopje: MM, 1983).

Special Operations: AAF Aid to European Resistance Movements, 1943–1945 (n.p.: AAF Historical Office, 1947).

Stankova, Marietta, *Georgi Dimitrov: A Biography* (London; New York: I. B. Taubis, 2010).

Springer, Paul Joseph, "American Prisoner of War Policy and Practice from the Revolutionary War to the War on Terror," Ph.D. dissertation, Texas A&M University, 2006.

Stanković, Milivoje, *Prvi šumadijski partizanski odred* (Belgrade: Narodna Knjiga, 1983).

Stojčev, Vanče, "Macedonia during the Second World War, 1941–1945," in Todor Čepreganov (ed.), *History of the Macedonian People* (Skopje: Institut za nacionalna istorija, 2008), pp. 249–86.

Strecker, A., "An der Drina," in Otto Weingartner (ed.), *Erinnerungen an die 118. Jäger-Division (frühere 718. Inf.Div.)* (Klagenfurt: self-published, 1982), pp. 14–23.

Street, Brian Jeffrey, *The Parachute Ward: A Canadian Surgeon's Wartime Adventures in Yugoslavia* (Toronto: Lester & Orpen Dennys, 1987).

Strugar, Vlado, *Der jugoslawische Volksbefreiungskrieg 1941 bis 1945* (Berlin: Deutscher Militärverlag, 1969).

Sutjeska: Zbornik radova (Belgrade: Vojnoizdavački zavod "Vojno delo," 1959), Vol. III.

Swain, Geoffrey, *Tito: A Biography* (London: I. B. Tauris, 2011).

Terzić, Velimir, *Slom Kraljevine Jugoslavije 1941* (Belgrade: Partizanska knjiga, 1984), Vol. II.

Tessin, Georg, *Verbände und Truppen der deutschen Wehrmacht und der Waffen-SS im Zweiten Weltkrieg, 1939–1945* (Osnabrück: Biblio Verlag, 1978), Vol. I.

Thayer, Charles, *Hands Across the Caviar* (London: Michael Joseph, 1953).

Tihić, Esad, *Posavsko-trebavski NOP odred* (Belgrade: Vojnoizdavački zavod, 1983).

Timofejev, Aleksej J., *Rusi i Drugi svetski rat u Jugoslaviji: uticaj SSSR-a i ruskih emigranata na događaje u Jugoslaviji 1941–1945.* (Belgrade: Institut za noviju istoriju Srbije, 2010).

Tito, Josip Broz, *Autobiografska kazivanja* (Belgrade: IRO Narodna knjiga, 1983), Vol. I.

Tko je tko u NDH: Hrvatska 1941.–1945. (Zagreb: Minerva, 1997).

Tomasevich, Jozo, *War and Revolution in Yugoslavia, 1941–1945: The Chetniks* (Stanford: Stanford University Press, 1975).

Tomasevich, Jozo, *War and Revolution in Yugoslavia, 1941–1945: Occupation and Collaboration* (Stanford: Stanford University Press, 2001).

Tomić, Branimir, "Kako smo uhvatili Hansa Tilera," in *Sedma srpska udarna brigada: zbornik sećanja* (Belgrade: Stručna knjiga, 1988), Vol. I, pp. 208–09.

Trajkovski, Robert, *Vermahtot i Makedonija (1943–1944 godina)* (Bitola: SBM, 2018).

Trifković, Gaj, "Schwarz auf Weiss: 1943-Das Jahr der deutschen Großoperationen in Jugoslawien," Master's thesis, Karl-Franzens University Graz, 2010.

Velebit, Vladimir, *Tajne i zamke drugog svjetskog rata* (Zagreb: Prometej, 2002).

Velić, Miroslav, Ante V. Petrić, and Mate Vuletić, *Mosorski partizanski odred* (Split: IHRPD, 1985).

Veljanovski, Novica, "AVNOJ i Makedonija," in *Glavniot štab na narodnoosloboditelnata vojska i partizanskite odredi na Makedonija, 1941–1945: po povod devedeset godini od ragnjeto na Mihailo Apostolski* (Skopje: Institut za nacionalna istorija, 1996), pp. 227–43.

Veselinović, Ljubiša, "Neobična prepiska," in *Prva proleterska brigada: sećanja boraca* (Belgrade: Vojno delo, 1963), Vol. II, pp. 579–81.

Vidović, Žarko, *Treća proleterska sandžačka brigada* (Belgrade: Vojnoizdavački zavod, 1972).

Višnjić, Petar, *Prodor II. i V. divizije NOVJ u Srbiju 1944* (Belgrade: Vojnoizdavački zavod, 1968).

Vitorović, Aleksandar, *Srbija u Narodnooslobodilačkoj borbi: Centralna Srbija* (Belgrade: Nolit, 1967).

Voinović, Stevo, *Na službi kod Dangića* (Kragujevac: Pogledi, 2001).

Vojna enciklopedija (Belgrade: Vojnoizdavački zavod, 1973), Vols. V, VIII.

Vojvodić, Gajo, *Priča jednog proletera* (Cetinje: Obod, 1987).

Vujasinović, Todor, *Ozrenski partizanski odred* (Sarajevo: Svjetlost, 1978).

Vujošević, Jovan, "1941—Prve oružane akcije protiv okupatora," in A. H. Pape and Nikola Anić (eds.), *Drugi svjetski rat* (Belgrade: Narodna knjiga, 1980), Vol. I, pp. 266–70.

Vujošević, Jovan, "Od Stolica do Rudog: Prva neprijateljska ofanziva," in A. H. Pape and Nikola Anić (eds.), *Drugi svjetski rat* (Belgrade: Narodna knjiga, 1980), Vol. I, pp. 273–78.

Vujošević, Jovan, "Fočanski period: rezultati okupatorsko-kvislinške ofenzive u Istočnoj Bosni," in A. H. Pape and Nikola Anić (eds.), *Drugi svjetski rat* (Belgrade: Narodna knjiga, 1980), Vol. II, pp. 100–03.

Vukić, Pero, "Kako je zarobljen štab njemačke borbene grupe 'Eberlajn,'" in *Šesta krajiška NOU brigada: ratna sjećanja* (Bečej: GRO "Proleter," 1985), pp. 685–87.

Weinberg, Gerhard L., *A World at Arms: A Global History of World War II* (Cambridge: Cambridge University Press, 1994).

Wheeler, Mark C., *Britain and the War for Yugoslavia* (New York: Columbia University Press, 1980).

Wilson, Peter H., "Prisoners in Early Modern European Warfare," in Sibylle Scheipers (ed.), *Prisoners in War* (Oxford: Oxford University Press, 2010), pp. 39–56.

Williams, Heather, *Parchutes, Patriots, and Partisans: The Special Operations Executive and Yugoslavia, 1941–1945* (London: C. Hurst, 2003).

Wylie, Neville, "Ungentlemanly Warriors or Unreliable Diplomats? Special Operations Executive and 'Irregular Political Activities' in Europe," in Neville Wylie (ed.), *The Politics and Strategy of Clandestine War: Special Operations Executive, 1940–1946* (London: Routledge, 2007), pp. 109–30.

Wylie, Neville, *Barbed Wire Diplomacy: Britain, Germany, and the Politics of Prisoners of War, 1939–1945* (Oxford: Oxford University Press, 2010).

Yugoslav Authors, "Parlament nove Jugoslavije: formiranje Narodnooslobodilačke vojske u Jugoslaviji i prvo zasjedanje AVNOJ-a," in A. H. Pape and Nikola Anić (eds.), *Drugi svjetski rat* (Belgrade: Narodna knjiga, 1980), Vol. II, pp. 119–22.

Zastavniković, Ljubomir, "Mrtvački sanduci ostali su na obali Sane," in *Prva krajiška udarna proleterska brigada: sjećanja boraca* (Prijedor: Skupština opštine, 1981), pp. 402–05.

Zavadlav, Zdenko, *Partizani, obveščevalci, jetniki: iz dosjeja Zavadlav 1944–1994* (Ljubljana: Horvat M&M, 1996).

Zbornik žrtve vojne in revolucije: Referati in razprava s posveta v Državnem svetu 11. in 12. novembra 2004, ki sta ga pripravila Državni svet Republike Slovenije in Institut za novejšo zgodovino v Ljubljani (Ljubljana: Republika Slovenija, Državni svet, 2005).

Živanović, Boško, Miodrag Jovanović, and Damnjan Popović, *Pomoravlje u Narodnooslobodilačkoj borbi 1941–1945* (Svetozarevo: Sreski odbor saveza boraca NOR-a, 1961).

Zografski, Dančo, "Pregovorite so bugarskiot i germanskiot garnizon vo Prilep 1944 godina," in *Prilep i prilepsko vo NOV 1944–15 maj 1945 godina. Materijali od Naučniot sobir održan na 14, 15 i 16 mart 1983 godina* (Skopje: SUBNOR Prilep, 1985), Vol. I/1, pp. 329–38.

Zorić, Milan N., *XIII krajiška brigada* (Belgrade: Vojnoizdavački zavod, 1968).

Zur Geschichte der Kriegsgefangenen im Osten, Teil III, Lebensbedingungen und Sterblichkeit in Kriegsgefangenenlagern Jugoslawiens, Polens und der Tschechoslowakei (CSR) (Bonn: Deutsches Rotes Kreuz Suchdienst, 1959).

Index

Macedonian Division, 348
Maček, Vladko, 72, 146
Maclean, Fitzroy, 63n190, 252, 294, 295
Mačva, 37, 39
Main Headquarters of the People's
    Liberation Partisan Detachments of
    Yugoslavia, 19, 30
Main Operational Group: Operation
    Schwarz and, 180–85; Operation *Weiss*
    and, 137–40, 151, 187, 188
Main Partisan HQ for Croatia: atrocities by
    Dalmatian units against German
    prisoners, 300; Banja Luka massacre
    and, 217; ban on railway sabotage in
    1943, 174–75; Bosnia, Herzegovina, and
    the Pisarovina exchange cartel and,
    223–24; drafting of the exchange cartel
    at Pisarovina and, 214, 216, 220, 222,
    223–25; "exchange on receipt" policy
    and, 218–19; German reprisal killings
    in 1945 and, 244; key figures in the
    Pisarovina exchange cartel, 225–26;
    local prisoner exchanges in 1943–1945
    and, 307, 320; murder of Eduard
    Partenell and, 236–37; NOVJ-German
    economic cooperation and, 254–55;
    NOVJ-German political talks in 1943
    and, 250–51, 254–55; NOVJ-German
    talks on the terms of German surrender,
    266, 268–69, 270; OSS mission to
    Croatia and, 265; Partisan-German
    negotiations in Istria and, 361–62, 363;
    prisoner exchanges at Pisarovina and,
    237, 241, 247; prisoner exchanges prior
    to the Pisarovina neutral zone, 199,
    206–09, 217–18; relationship with the
    Allies in late 1943, 253; request for
    intelligence on the effects of Allied
    bombing in Zagreb, 280–81; Marijan
    Stilinović and, 102; treatment of
    German prisoners, 215, 291–92;
    treatment of Italian prisoners, 210;
    treatment of Russian emigrants in
    German service, 210–11n51
Main Partisan HQ for Macedonia, 318,
    345, 346, 348

Main Partisan HQ for Sandžak, 321
Main Partisan HQ for Slovenia, 270, 354,
    356, 358, 369
Main Partisan HQ for Vojvodina, 313
Majevica Brigade, 171–72, 182
Majevica Detachment, 158
Manns, Paul, 246, 271, 277n294, 283
Manola, Srećko, 323
March Negotiations (1943): Berlin's
    response to halt the talks, 159–63;
    effects on German operations in
    Herzegovina and Eastern Bosnia,
    185–91; first round of talks in Sarajevo,
    149–51; German intelligence gathering
    and, 154–55; German-Partisan truce
    and, 140, 142, 145, 151, 157–59,
    171–73, 174–75, 191, 192; growing
    confidence of Tito and the KPJ, 169–70;
    introduction to, 135–40; March 11–14
    negotiations in Gornji Vakuf, 140–48;
    Operation *Schwarz* and, 179–85, 194;
    Partisan request for recognition from
    Germany, 144, 191; Partisan resistance
    to British involvement in the Balkans,
    381; Partisan-Soviet relations and,
    163–70, 193; summary and conclusions,
    191–95; Tito's difficulties with Moscow
    over, 163–70; Tito's motives for
    entering, 192–93; Vladimir Velebit and
    Milovan Đilas visit Zagreb, 156–59;
    Vladimir Velebit's trip to Slavonia,
    174–75, 310; Vladimir Velebit's trip to
    Zagreb and release of the German
    prisoners, 151–56
Mareth Line, 164n78
Maria José, Princess of Italy, 164n78
Marin II (Partisan hospital ship), 285n328
Marinković, Ivo, 144, 145, 146, 157n60,
    199, 200–01, 202n16, 215–16
Marković, Miloš. *See* Đilas, Milovan
Marković, Momčilo-Moma, 34–35
Marogna-Redwitz, Rudolf Graf von, 263
Martinović, Ratko, 16, 17, 26–27
Marxist ideology: changing Partisan view
    of German prisoners and, 46–47,
    65–67, 302, 378

New Perspectives on the Second World War

Series Editor: Robert von Maier

New Perspectives on the Second World War is a series that focuses on the period 1919–1945. With contributions from many of the most distinguished World War II scholars and researchers, the series encourages an international and inter-disciplinary approach to a wide variety of subject areas and explores numerous aspects of the war that are often neglected. The Second World War was a truly global conflict with myriad contemporary ramifications and this series provides a wealth of exemplary scholarship to further the study of this important event.

Series Editor Robert von Maier is Publisher and Editor-in-Chief at Brécourt Academic.

Email Inquiries: Robert von Maier at globalwarstudies@gmail.com

Books in the Series

Decision in the Atlantic: The Allies and the Longest Campaign of the Second World War
Edited by Marcus Faulkner and Christopher M. Bell

The Sea and the Second World War: Maritime Aspects of a Global Conflict
Edited by Marcus Faulkner and Alessio Patalano

Parleying with the Devil: Prisoner Exchange in Yugoslavia, 1941–1945
Gaj Trifković